Beginning Programming
ALL-IN-ONE DESK REFERENCE
FOR
DUMMIES®

by Wallace Wang

WILEY

Wiley Publishing, Inc.

Beginning Programming All-In-One Desk Reference For Dummies®

Published by
Wiley Publishing, Inc.
111 River Street
Hoboken, NJ 07030-5774
www.wiley.com

Copyright © 2008 by Wiley Publishing, Inc., Indianapolis, Indiana

Published by Wiley Publishing, Inc., Indianapolis, Indiana

Published simultaneously in Canada

For general information on our other products and services, please contact our Customer Care Department within the U.S. at 800-762-2974, outside the U.S. at 317-572-3993, or fax 317-572-4002.

For technical support, please visit www.wiley.com/techsupport.

Wiley also publishes its books in a variety of electronic formats. Some content that appears in print may not be available in electronic books.

Library of Congress Control Number: 2008927908

ISBN: 978-0-470-10854-3

Manufactured in the United States of America

10 9 8 7 6 5 4 3 2 1

WILEY

About the Author

I started off as a writer and wound up becoming a computer programmer. Then I wound up circling around again to become a writer about computers. I've spent most of my life writing about and programming a variety of personal computers ranging from an ancient PC running MS-DOS 1.25 to Windows XP PC to the latest Macintosh computer running Mac OS X Leopard. My only preference for any computer is to use one that works.

I first learned about programming from my high school's ancient teletype terminal that connected to a mainframe computer through a 300 baud acoustic modem that often disconnected me in the middle of my BASIC programming sessions. At the time, I didn't know much about programming. I just taught myself BASIC from a book and illegally gained access to the teletype terminal by using somebody else's password. Later in the year, I actually signed up for a computer class and finally gained legitimate access to the teletype terminal to do everything I had been doing illegally long before.

The first time I wrote a BASIC program on my own, it was a game that simulated flying a nuclear-armed bomber through a variety of anti-aircraft defenses including surface-to-air missiles and jet fighters trying to shoot you down. When this program worked for the first time, I felt like Dr. Frankenstein watching his creation twitch and come to life. To this day, I still experience that same feeling of exhilaration in creating something from an idea and turning it into an actual working program. Only other programmers can understand this strange sense of power and elation that comes from a working program, and it's this same sense of wonder and exploration that I hope you'll experience as you use this book to explore the world of programming on your own computer.

I may be considered a computer veteran after all these years, but that doesn't mean that I can't still experience that same feeling of satisfaction in typing that final command and watching an entire program work exactly as I wanted. Although I've written plenty of other books both on computers *(Microsoft Office 2007 For Dummies)* and far away from computers altogether *(Breaking Into Acting For Dummies)*, I find that programming still fascinates me to this day.

As an author, I hope to help you discover your own path to learning programming, and as a programmer, I hope to provide an overview of computer programming in general. You may not become an expert programmer after reading this book, but if you come away with a greater appreciation for programming, then I'll know I'll have fulfilled my duty as both an author and programmer for this.

Dedication

This book is dedicated to anyone who wants to learn how to program a computer. Computer programming can be one of the most creative ways to express your ideas so if you have your heart set on writing programs for fun or profit, you've just joined a select group of fellow renegades, entrepreneurs, and hobbyists who find programming an enjoyable intellectual exercise. When lost in the world of programming, you can often elevate your spirit to lofty heights of pleasure and wind up crashing right back down to Earth again when a single syntax error causes your program to crash an entire computer. Welcome to the wonderful world of programming. You deserve to achieve whatever your mind can envision and your programming skills can create.

Acknowledgments

This is the part of the book that most people skip over since it usually lists a bunch of names that most people have never heard before, so before you can skip over this page, I'd like to thank you for buying (or at least reading) this book. If you're interested in learning to program a computer, you've already separated yourself from the masses who are ecstatic when they can just get their computer to work in the first place. As a programmer, you have the power to control how people may use computers in the future, and this power can give you the chance to help others or make someone completely helpless in their agony when trying to use a computer, so use your programming skills wisely.

On another note, this book owes part of its existence to Bill Gladstone and Margot Hutchison at Waterside Productions and another part of its existence to Katie Feltman at Wiley Publishing for turning this project into reality. Some other people who helped shape this project include Pat O'Brien and Vince McCune.

I also want to acknowledge all the stand-up comedians I've worked with over the years including Darrell Joyce (http://darrelljoyce.com), Leo "the Man, the Myth, the Legend" Fontaine, Chris Clobber, Bob Zany (www.bobzany.com), Russ Rivas (http://russrivas.com), Don Learned, Dante, and Dobie "The Uranus King" Maxwell. Another round of thanks goes to Steve Schirripa (who appeared in HBO's hit show "The Sopranos") for giving me my break in performing at the Riviera Hotel and Casino in Las Vegas, one of the few old-time casinos that hasn't been blown up to make way for yet another luxury hotel and casino targeting rich people who want to lose their money faster.

Additional acknowledgements also go to my fellow radio co-hosts: Rick Gene, Drizz, Justin Davis, and Dane Henderson, who shared the airwaves with me during our year at 103.7 FreeFM in San Diego. Having our own radio show gave us all an excuse to go places and do things that we wouldn't normally get to do such as visiting a UFO cult that built a landing strip for a flying saucer, exploring a museum that promotes creationism, and visiting Comic-Con where people dress up as their favorite comic book super heroes. (I tried to give ten bucks to anyone who would let me pour gasoline on them and light a match so they could attend Comic-Con dressed up as the Human Torch, but nobody was willing to take me up on that offer.)

I'd also like to acknowledge Cassandra (my wife) and Jordan (my son) for putting up with my long hours and my insistence that everyone dump their Windows XP PCs right away (an easy decision since they never worked right anyway) and migrate completely to the Macintosh. Final thanks go to Bo, Scraps, and Nuit (my cats) along with a final farewell to Tasha, who was a special breed called a Korat. R.I.P.

Publisher's Acknowledgments

We're proud of this book; please send us your comments through our online registration form located at www.dummies.com/register/.

Some of the people who helped bring this book to market include the following:

Acquisitions, Editorial, and Media Development

Project Editor: Pat O'Brien

Acquisition Editor: Katie Feltman

Copy Editor: Jen Riggs

Technical Editor: Vince McCune

Editorial Manager: Kevin Kirschner

Media Project Supervisor: Laura Moss-Hollister

Media Development Specialist: Angela Denny

Editorial Assistant: Amanda Foxworth

Sr. Editorial Assistant: Cherie Case

Cartoons: Rich Tennant (www.the5thwave.com)

Composition Services

Project Coordinator: Patrick Redmond

Layout and Graphics: Claudia Bell, Reuben W. Davis, Melissa K. Jester

Proofreaders: Laura Albert, John Greenough, Jessica Kramer, Christine Sabooni

Indexer: Ty Koontz

Publishing and Editorial for Technology Dummies

    Richard Swadley, Vice President and Executive Group Publisher

    Andy Cummings, Vice President and Publisher

    Mary Bednarek, Executive Acquisitions Director

    Mary C. Corder, Editorial Director

Publishing for Consumer Dummies

    Diane Graves Steele, Vice President and Publisher

    Joyce Pepple, Acquisitions Director

Composition Services

    Gerry Fahey, Vice President of Production Services

    Debbie Stailey, Director of Composition Services

Contents at a Glance

Table of Contents

Introduction

*I*f you enjoy using a computer, you may have even more fun learning to control a computer by writing your own programs. To learn how to program a computer, you need to understand three different subjects.

First, you have to understand that computer programming is nothing more than problem solving. Before you even think about writing a program, you need to know what problem you want your program to solve and how it will solve it.

Second, you need to learn the basic ideas behind computer programming in general. Although programming a Windows computer is different from programming a Macintosh or a super computer, the general principles are the same. By learning what these common programming principles are and why they exist, you can learn different ways to tell a computer what to do, step-by-step.

Finally, you also need to learn a specific programming language. A programming language represents just one way to express your ideas in a language that the computer can understand. By combining your knowledge of a programming language with programming principles and the type of problem you want the computer to solve, you can create your own computer programs for fun or profit.

Who Should Buy This Book

If you have any interest in programming but don't know where to start, this book can give you a nudge in the right direction. You won't learn how to write programs in a specific programming language, but you'll learn the basics about computer programming so you'll have no trouble learning more on your own.

If you already know something about programming, this book can still help you learn more by introducing you to the variety of programming languages available and make it easy for you to learn different programming languages quickly. The more you understand the advantages and disadvantages of different programming languages, the better you'll be able to choose the language that's best suited for a particular task.

Whether you're a novice or an intermediate programmer, you'll find this book can work as a tutorial to teach you more and as a reference to help refresh your memory on programming topics you may not normally use everyday. This book won't turn you into an expert overnight, but it will open the doors to more information about programming than you might have ever known even existed.

How This Book Is Organized

To help you learn about computer programming, this book is divided into several minibooks where each minibook is self-contained so you can read them in any order you wish.

Book I: Getting Started

This first book provides a general overview of computer programming. This is where you'll learn how programming evolved, the latest techniques to make programming faster and easier, how different programming languages work, what type of tools programmers use, and how programmers create large projects. This book gives you a broad understanding of programming so you'll understand how programming solves different types of problems.

Book II: Programming Basics

No matter what type of computer you want to program or which programming language you use, programming follows the same basic principles and this book explains how they work. This is where you'll learn the parts of a typical program and how they work to create a working program. This book also explains the purpose of a user interface and the elements that make up a user interface.

Book III: Data Structures

All programs manipulate data, which means they need a way to store that data temporarily in something called a data structure. Data structures form the heart of any program. Think of data structures as closets or drawers for holding information. Depending on the type of information you need to store and how you need to use it, you may need to use different types of data structures. By understanding the different data structures available and the pros and cons of each, you'll learn the best type of data structure to use for your particular program.

Book IV: Algorithms

An algorithm is just a specific method for solving a problem. There are literally an infinite number of ways to solve any problem, but computer programmers generally run into the same type of problems over and over, which means they've also discovered the most efficient algorithms to solve for specific tasks. This book introduces different types of algorithms and explains how they work and when you might want to use them.

Book V: Web Programming

Traditional programs run on a computer, but the advent of the Internet has created a new field of programming known was Web programming. Instead of running on a single computer, Web programs are stored on one computer (called a server) but run and displayed on a second computer (called a client). If you've ever ordered anything off the Internet, you've used a program designed to run on Web pages. Learning Web programming isn't hard, but it often requires using different types of languages and techniques, which is what you'll learn about in this book.

Book VI: Programming Language Syntax

This book explains the basic features of programming languages and then shows how different programming languages implement those features, which is known as the language syntax. Knowing the syntax of different languages can show you the flaws and benefits of each language so you'll know when to use a particular language over another. If you regularly need to program in different languages, this book makes a handy reference to show you how to accomplish a specific task in different languages along with showing you unusual features that appear in one programming language but not in another one.

Book VII: Applications

Knowing how to program a computer is nice, but ultimately useless if you don't know how to apply your programming skills to doing something productive, so this book explains several fields of computer programming. By reading this book, you can learn what types of programming appeals to you. By combining your knowledge of programming with a particular field of interest, you can carve a niche for yourself in any field you choose.

How to Use This Book

You can use this book as a tutorial or a reference. Although you can just flip through this book to find the information you need, programming novices should start with Book I before tackling any other books. After you understand the basics of programming from Book I, then you can freely jump around to read only the information that interests you.

Icons Used in This Book

Icons highlight important or useful information that you might want to know about.

This highlights information that can save you time or make it easier for you to do something.

This icon emphasizes information that can be helpful, though not crucial, when writing a program.

Look out! This icon highlights something dangerous that you need to avoid before making an irreversible mistake that could make you curse your computer forever.

This icon highlights interesting technical information that you can safely ignore, but which might provide additional background about programming a computer.

Getting Started

The best way to learn anything is to jump right in and not be afraid to make mistakes. To learn programming, you'll need access to a computer and a way to write programs in a particular programming language. You won't learn specific programming techniques in this book. Instead, you'll learn a lot about a wide variety of programming topics so you'll be in a better position to decide what you need to learn next.

Programming is more than learning a particular programming language or even knowing how to program a particular type of computer. Basically, programming is about tackling difficult problems and breaking them down into smaller problems until you solve one big problem. If you like the idea of solving problems, then you'll find this may be the perfect book to introduce you to the wonderful world of computer programming.

Book I

Getting Started

The 5th Wave   By Rich Tennant

"Why, of course. I'd be very interested in seeing this new milestone in the project."

Contents at a Glance

Chapter 1: Getting Started Programming a Computer

In This Chapter

✔ Understanding how computer programming works

✔ History of computer programming

✔ Discovering programming

✔ Getting started

*B*elieve it or not, if you can write a recipe on an index card, you can program a computer. At the simplest level, computer programming is nothing more than writing instructions for a computer to follow, step by step. The most important part of programming isn't in knowing how to write a program or how to use a particular programming language, but in knowing what to create in the first place.

Some of the most popular and useful computer programs were created by people who didn't have any formal training in math or computer science. Dan Bricklin invented the spreadsheet while studying for his MBA at Harvard Business School. Scott Cook, who worked in marketing and product development at Proctor & Gamble, created the popular money-management program *Quicken* after hearing his wife complain about the tedium of paying bills. Nineteen-year old Shawn Fanning created *Napster,* the first peer-to-peer file-sharing network, after hearing a friend complain about the difficulty of finding his favorite songs on the Internet.

The point is that anyone can figure out how to program a computer. What's more important than knowing how to program a computer is knowing what to do with your programming skills. As Albert Einstein said, "Imagination is more important than knowledge." After you have an idea for a program, you can use programming to turn your idea into reality.

How Computer Programming Works

Computer programming is nothing more than problem solving. Every program is designed to solve a specific problem. The more universal the problem (calculating formulas in a spreadsheet, managing your money, or searching for music files over the Internet), the more useful and popular the program will be.

Identifying the problem

Before you even touch a computer, identify the specific problem you want the computer to solve. For example, spreadsheets eliminate the tedium of writing and calculating formulas manually. Word processors make editing and formatting text fast and easy. Even video games solve the problem of keeping people amused.

Although the most popular programs solve universal problems, literally thousands of programs are designed to solve specific problems in niche markets, such as hotel reservation software, construction billing and invoice management programs, and dental office management programs. If you can identify a problem that a computer can solve or simplify, you have an idea for a computer program.

You must know exactly what you want your program to do before you start designing and writing it. One of the most common reasons why programs fail is because the program doesn't solve the right problem that people really need.

The FBI's $170 million dollar flop

The FBI had a problem. They had so much information, stored on paper, scattered among so many agents around the country that finding and using this information was nearly impossible. One agent might have vital information that could help a second agent crack a case, but unless those two agents knew what each other had, that information might as well never have existed in the first place.

So the FBI had a bright idea. Create a computer program that would allow agents to store and share information through the computer. Several years and a $170 million dollars later, the FBI had its program, dubbed *Virtual Case File*, which consisted of over 700,000 lines of error-prone commands that never even worked. Rather than try to salvage the project,

the FBI decided it was easier just to cancel the whole thing and basically flush $170 million taxpayer dollars down the drain.

What went wrong? Although many factors contributed to the project's failure, one reason stands out in particular. According to an audit of the program conducted by the U.S. Department of Justice, a prime cause for failure was "poorly defined and slowly evolving design requirements." In other words, the FBI never knew exactly what they wanted the program to do.

How can you aim at a target if you don't know what it is? You can't. Or you can try, just as long as you spend $170 million dollars to discover that if you don't know what you want, you're probably never going to get it.

Defining the steps

After you know what you want your program to do, the second step is defining all the steps that tell the computer how to solve that particular problem. The exact steps that define how the program should work is called an *algorithm*. An algorithm simply defines one of many possible ways to solve a problem.

There's no single "best" algorithm for writing a program. The same program can be written literally in a million different ways, so the "best" way to write a program is any way that creates a useful, working, and reliable program as quickly as possible. Anything else is irrelevant.

Knowing what you want the computer to do is the first step. The second step is telling the computer how to do it, which is what makes programming so difficult. The more you want the computer to do, the more instructions you need to give the computer.

Think of a computer program as a recipe. It's easy to write a recipe for making spaghetti. Just boil water, throw in the noodles until they're soft, drain, and serve. Now consider a recipe for making butternut squash and potato pie with tomato, mint, and sheep's milk cheese from Crete. Not as simple as boiling water to make spaghetti, is it?

The same principle holds true for computer programming. The simpler the task, the simpler the program. The harder the task, the bigger and more complicated the program:

✦ If you just want a program that displays today's date on the screen, you won't need to write many instructions.

✦ If you want to write a program that simulates flying a space shuttle in orbit around the Earth, you'll need to write a lot more instructions.

The more instructions you need to write, the longer it takes and the more likely you'll make a mistake somewhere along the way.

Ultimately, programming boils down to two tasks:

✦ **Identifying exactly what you want the computer to do**

✦ **Writing step-by-step instructions that tell the computer how to do what you want**

The History of Computer Programming

Although computer programming may seem like a recent invention, the idea behind writing instructions for a machine to follow has been around for over a century. One of the earliest designs for a programmable machine (computer) came from a man named Charles Babbage way back in 1834.

That was the year Charles Babbage proposed building a mechanical, steam-driven machine dubbed the Analytical Engine. Unlike the simple calculating machines of that time that could perform only a single function, Charles Babbage's Analytical Engine could perform a variety of tasks, depending on the instructions fed into the machine through a series of punched cards. By changing the number and type of instructions (punch cards) fed into the machine, anyone could reprogram the Analytical Engine to make it solve different problems.

The idea of a programmable machine caught the attention of Ada Lovelace, a mathematician and daughter of the poet Lord Byron. Sensing the potential of a programmable machine, Ada wrote a program to make the Analytical Engine calculate and print a sequence of numbers known as *Bernoulli numbers*.

Because of her work with the Analytical Engine, Ada Lovelace is considered to be the world's first computer programmer. In her honor, the Department of Defense named the Ada programming language after Ada Lovelace.

Although Charles Babbage never finished building his Analytical Engine, his steam-driven mechanical machine bears a striking similarity to today's computers. To make the Analytical Engine solve a different problem, you just needed to feed it different instructions. To make a modern computer solve a different problem, you just need to run a different program.

Over a hundred years later, the first true computer would appear in 1943 when the U.S. Army funded a computer to calculate artillery trajectories. This computer, dubbed ENIAC (Electronic Numerical Integrator and Computer), consisted of vacuum tubes, switches, and cables. To give ENIAC instructions, you had to physically flip its different switches and rearrange its cables.

The first ENIAC programmers were all women.

Physically rearranging cables and switches to reprogram a computer would work, but it was tedious and clumsy. Rather than physically rearranging the computer's wiring, computer scientists decided it'd be easier if you could leave the computer physically the same but just rearrange the type of instructions you give it. By giving the computer different instructions, you could make the computer behave in different ways.

In the old days, computers filled entire rooms and cost millions of dollars. Today, computers have shrunk so far in size that they're essentially nothing more than a little silicon wafer, about the size of a potato chip. These silicon wafers are called the central processing unit (CPU), a microprocessor, or just a processor.

A *processor* is essentially an entire computer. To tell the processor what to do, you have to give it instructions written in *machine language* — a language that the processor can understand.

To make faster computers, engineers smash two or more processors together and make them work as a team. So instead of having a single processor in your computer, the latest computers have two, four, six, or more processors working side by side.

Talking to a processor in machine language

To understand how machine language works, you have to understand how processors work. Basically, a processor consists of nothing more than millions of tiny switches that can turn on or off. By turning certain switches on or off, you can make the processor do something useful.

Instead of physically turning switches on or off, machine language lets you turn a processor's switches on or off by using two numbers: 1 (one) and 0 (zero) where the number 1 can mean "turn a switch on" and the number 0 can mean "turn a switch off." So a typical machine language instruction might look like this:

```
1011 0000 0110 0001
```

If the preceding instruction doesn't make any sense, don't worry. The point is that machine language is a just way to tell a processor what to do.

Using 1's and 0's is *binary arithmetic.* Because binary arithmetic can be so hard to read, programmers also represent binary numbers in hexadecimal. Where binary arithmetic uses only two numbers, *hexadecimal* uses sixteen numbers (0–9 and A–F). So the binary number 1011 0000 0110 0001 could be represented as the hexadecimal number: B061.

Machine language is considered the *native* language of CPUs, but almost no one writes a program in machine language because it's so tedious and confusing. Mistype a single 1 or 0 and you can accidentally give the wrong instruction to the CPU. Because writing instructions in machine language can be so difficult and error-prone, computer scientists have created a somewhat simpler language — *assembly language.*

Using assembly language as a shortcut to machine language

The whole purpose of assembly language is to make programming easier than machine language. Basically, one assembly language command can replace a dozen or more machine language commands. So rather than write ten machine language commands (and risk making a mistake in all ten of those commands), assembly language lets you write one command that does the work of ten (or more) machine language commands.

Not only does this reduce the chance of mistakes, but it also makes writing a program in assembly language much faster and easier.

The goal of every programming language is to make programming simpler and easier. Unfortunately, because no one can define exactly what "simpler" and "easier" really means, computer scientists keep creating new and improved programming languages that promise to make programming simpler and easier, at least until someone else invents another new and improved programming language.

To understand how assembly language works, you must first understand how processors store and manipulate data. The *processor* is the "brain" of the computer that does all the work. By itself, the processor is fairly useless. (Think of Einstein's brain floating in a jar of formaldehyde. It may be one of the smartest brains in the world, but if it can't communicate with the outside world, it's completely useless as anything other than a very unusual paperweight.)

Like Einstein's brain in a jar, your computer's processor is useful only if it can communicate with the outside world. The processor communicates with the other parts of the computer through a series of wires called a *bus*.

When a processor needs to work with data, it retrieves it from another part of the computer (such as the hard disk or memory) and temporarily stores that data in a storage area called a *register*, as shown in Figure 1-1.

The processor then edits the data in its registers and sends the changed data back to another part of the computer, such as its memory or hard disk.

So computer programming progressed from physically rearranging wires and switches (with ENIAC), to flipping switches using 1's and 0's (with machine language), to telling the computer which data to store in which registers and how to manipulate that data (with assembly language).

A typical assembly language command might look like this:

```
mov al, 061h
```

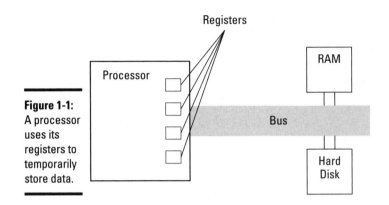

Figure 1-1:
A processor
uses its
registers to
temporarily
store data.

This command tells the processor to move (mov) the hexadecimal number 061h into the specific register named al. Other assembly language commands might tell the processor to add (add) or subtract (sub) a value from the number stored in a specific register.

When you use assembly language, you have to tell the processor what data to store in which registers, how to manipulate the data in its registers, and when to remove data out of its registers.

Sound tedious? It is. Although assembly language is far easier to understand and write than machine language, it's still too complicated to use for creating really big computer programs, like word processors or video games.

In the old days, most programs were written in assembly language, but as programs grew larger and more complicated, assembly language proved too cumbersome to write, edit, and modify.

The biggest problem with assembly language is that you need to manipulate the processor's registers just to do the simplest tasks. If you wanted to add two numbers together, you'd have to tell the processor to store a number into a register, add a second number to the number in the register, and then yank the result out of the register.

Forcing people to know how to manipulate the processor's registers before they can program a computer is like forcing people to know how their carburetor works before they can drive a car. Ideally, you don't want to tell the processor how to manipulate data in its registers; you just want the processor to add two numbers without worrying about specific registers. So to make computer programming even easier, computer scientists have hidden the technical details of manipulating registers by creating *high-level languages.*

Every processor understands only its own particular assembly language. So an Intel Core 2 processor won't understand the assembly language of a PowerPC processor and vice versa. However, some companies make processors that work identically to other processors. For example, a company called Advanced Micro Devices (AMD) makes processors that work just like Intel processors, so an assembly language program written for an Intel processor also works on an AMD processor.

Hiding the details of a computer with a high-level language

The whole purpose of high-level languages is to make programming more intuitive. So rather than tell the computer to store the number 2 in register al, add the number 3 to the number stored in register al, and then yank out the result from register al, high-level languages let you tell the computer what to do and not worry about how the computer does it. So a typical high-level language command might look like this:

```
Total = 2 + 3
```

As you can see, high-level languages are much easier to read and understand, even if you know nothing about programming. Where assembly language forces you to tell the processor what to do and how to do it, high-level languages just let you tell the processor what to do.

Some popular high-level languages include FORTRAN (FORmula TRANslator), BASIC (Beginner's All-purpose Symbolic Instruction Code), COBOL (COmmon Business Oriented Language), and Pascal (named after the French philosopher Blaise Pascal).

Besides making programming more intuitive, high-level languages also make programming easier because a single high-level language command can do the work of a dozen (or more) assembly language commands.

A thousand lines of assembly language commands might do nothing more than multiply two numbers together. A thousand lines of high-level language commands might create a video game, a music player, or a stock market analysis program. By using high-level languages, programmers can spend more time being productive and less time worrying about the technical details of the computer.

Combining the best of both worlds with the C programming language

High-level languages isolate you from the technical details of programming, but by isolating you from these details, high-level languages also limit what you can do. So as a compromise between assembly language (which can manipulate the processor) and high-level languages (which isolate you from the details of manipulating the processor), computer scientists created an intermediate language dubbed *C*.

The idea behind the C programming language is to give programmers the ability to manipulate the processor directly like assembly language, but also give you the chance to ignore these technical details, if you want, like a high-level language.

As a result, a C program doesn't look as cryptic as assembly language, but also isn't as easy to read as a high-level language, as the following C program demonstrates:

```c
#include <stdio.h>
int main(void)
{
  printf("Hello World!\n");
  exit(0);
}
```

Just by looking at this C program, you can probably figure out that it prints Hello World! on the screen. However, you might see a bunch of cryptic curly brackets, back slashes, and other odd symbols and characters that may make no sense whatsoever. Don't worry. Just notice how confusing C programs can look while at the same time being somewhat understandable.

Because C lets you directly control the processor like assembly language, but still write programs that look somewhat understandable and easy to read and write, most major programs, such as operating systems like Microsoft Windows, Linux, and Mac OS X, are written in C.

Pros and cons of programming languages

The whole purpose of machine language, assembly language, high-level language, and the C language is to give you different ways to give instructions to the processor (computer). Ultimately, it doesn't matter which type of programming language you use because it's possible to write the exact same program in machine language, assembly language, a high-level language (like BASIC or FORTRAN), and C.

The only difference is that writing a program in machine language takes a really long time and is very difficult to write, fix, and understand. A similar program written in assembly language is smaller and simpler than an equivalent machine language program.

Writing the same program in the C language makes the program even smaller and much easier to write and understand. If you use a high-level language, the program would most likely be the smallest and easiest to understand out of them all.

So given these advantages of C or high-level languages, why would anyone ever use machine language or assembly language? The answer is simple: speed and efficiency.

If you want to write the smallest, fastest program possible, use machine language because machine language is the native language of all computers. Unfortunately, machine language is so hard to understand, write, and modify that writing anything but small programs in machine language is nearly impossible.

Rather than use machine language, most programmers use assembly language when they need speed and efficiency. Assembly language creates small and fast programs, but they'll never be as small or fast as machine language programs. That's because processors understand only machine language, so when you write an assembly language program, you have to translate that assembly language program into machine language.

Translating assembly language into machine language by hand would be slow and error-prone, so computer scientists have created special programs that can do this automatically. These programs are *assemblers*.

An assembler takes an assembly language program and converts it into machine language, but this conversion process isn't perfect. That's why assembly language tends to create bigger and slower programs than equivalent hand-crafted machine language programs. However, assembly language programs are much easier to write and modify later than machine language, so assembly language is used much more often than machine language.

High-level languages are much easier to write and understand than machine or assembly language. The problem is that processors don't understand high-level languages either, so you have to translate a high-level language program into equivalent machine language commands.

Doing this by hand is nearly impossible, so computer scientists have created special programs — *compilers* — to do this for them. A compiler does nothing more than take a program written in a high-level language and translates it into equivalent commands written in machine language.

This translation process isn't perfect so that's why programs written in high-level languages tend to be much bigger and slower than equivalent programs written in machine or assembly language. So when programmers want to create large, complicated programs that still run fast and take up as little space as possible, they tend to rely on the C programming language. That's why so many programs are written in C because C creates programs *nearly* as small and fast as assembly language programs, while also being *nearly* as easy to write and understand as high-level languages. (Note the emphasis on the word "nearly.")

As a general rule, if you want to make programming easy where speed and efficiency aren't that crucial, use a high-level programming language. If you want to make a small and fast program and don't care how inconvenient it may be to write it, use machine or assembly language.

What if you want to write a big and fast program (like an operating system or word processor) and also make it convenient for you to write? You'd use the C programming language.

Ultimately, no one cares what language you use just as long as your program works. A program that works is far better than a small, fast, and efficient program that doesn't work. Think of a programming language as a tool. A good programmer can use any tool well, but a bad programmer can screw up using the best tool in the world.

The programmer's skill always determines the quality of any program; the type of programming language used is always secondary. So the goal isn't to become a "C programmer" or a "FORTRAN programmer." The goal is to become a *good* programmer, regardless of the language you ultimately use.

Figuring Out Programming

After you understand that programming is nothing more than telling a computer how to solve a problem, you may wonder how you can get started figuring out programming on your own. If you want to figure out how to program a computer, this is what you need:

✦ Desire

✦ A computer

✦ An editor

✦ An assembler or a compiler

✦ A lot of time on your hands

Discover more about programming tools, like an editor and a compiler, in Book I, Chapter 4.

Desire beats technical training every time

Desire is probably the biggest factor in studying how to program a computer. Many people think that you need a college degree or a mathematical background to know computer programming. Although a college degree and a mathematical background can definitely help, it's not necessary. Saying you need to know math before figuring out computer programming is like saying you need a college degree in biology before you can reproduce.

Some of the most influential and popular programs in the world were created by people who had no formal training in computer programming or computer science. (Conversely, that also means that some of the most intelligent PhD candidates in computer science have done nothing to make this world a better place using their programming skills.)

So if you have an idea for a program, you can create it. After you have the desire to understand computer programming, you have (almost) everything you need to program a computer.

Picking a computer and an operating system

If you want to know how to program a computer, you need a computer to practice on. You can actually discover programming on any computer from a top-of-the-line machine, to an obsolete relic (that was once a top-of-the-line machine), to a simple handheld computer. As long as you have a computer, you can find out how to program it.

Although it's possible to figure out programming by using an ancient Commodore-64 or an antique Radio Shack TRS-80, it's probably best to figure out programming on a computer that's going to be around in the future. That way you can directly apply your programming skills to a computer used in the real world, which boils down to a computer that runs one of the following operating systems: Windows, Linux, or Mac OS X.

An *operating system* is a special program that makes all the hardware of your computer work together. The operating system tells the processor how to work with the hard disk, read keystrokes typed on a keyboard, and display information on the monitor. Without an operating system, your computer is nothing more than separate chunks of hardware that does absolutely nothing.

One of the most popular operating systems in the world is UNIX, commonly run on big, expensive computers. Linux is based on UNIX, so if you understand how to program a Linux computer, you can also program a UNIX computer and vice versa.

Because so many businesses use computers that run Windows, many computer programmers focus their efforts on discovering how to write Windows programs. If you want to make money, write programs for the computers that most people use. At the time of this writing, that's *any computer that runs Windows.*

Although the Windows market is the largest, don't ignore these markets:

✦ *Mac OS X* is the operating system that runs the Macintosh computer.

Apple Macintosh computers are growing steadily in popularity, so the Mac OS X market will be lucrative for the future.

✦ *Linux* is a *free* operating system for almost every computer (including PCs).

   Linux is becoming more popular with big companies (as opposed to individual users), so there's a growing market for talented Linux programmers.

If you want to prepare yourself for the future, it's probably best to begin programming on any computer that runs Windows, Linux, or Mac OS X.

With the right software (`www.parallels.com`), it's possible to run both Windows and Linux on a Macintosh computer that's also running Mac OS X. That way you can practice writing programs for three different operating systems on a single Macintosh computer.

Writing programs with an editor

After you have a computer that runs Windows, Linux, or Mac OS X, the next step is to get an editor. An *editor* acts like a simple word processor that lets you type, change, and save program commands in a file.

In the world of computer programming, a single program command is a *line of code*. Most programs consist of thousands of lines of code, although a large program (like Microsoft Windows) consists of millions of lines of code. When you write a program, you don't tell people, "I'm writing a program." You say, "I'm writing code." It sounds cooler — at least to other programmers.

Almost every operating system comes with a free editor:

✦ In **Windows,** the free editor is Notepad.

✦ In **Linux,** hundreds of free editors — like Vi and Emacs — are available.

✦ **Mac OS X** comes with a free word processor called TextEdit, which can work as a text editor.

If you're using Mac OS X, you may find it easier to use a dedicated text editor such as TextWrangler (`www.barebones.com`) or jEdit (`www.jedit.org`). Both TextWrangler and jEdit are free.

Unlike a word processor, which offers commands for formatting text to make it look pretty or appear in different colors, a text editor is just designed for typing commands in a particular programming language, such as assembly language or C:

✦ The simplest editor just lets you type commands in a file.

✦ More sophisticated editors can help you write a program by

   • Color-coding program commands (to help you identify them easily)

   • Indenting your code automatically (to make it easier to read)

   • Typing in commonly used commands for you

Figure 1-2 shows a simple editor used to write a BASIC program that creates a lunar lander video game.

Without an editor, you can't write a program. With an editor, you can write a program, and with a really good editor, you can write a program quickly and easily.

Professional programmers often get passionate (to the point of fanaticism) about their favorite editors. The quickest way to get into an argument with programmers is to either insult their favorite programming language or insult their favorite editor. If you insult a programmer's mother, the programmer will probably just shrug and not care one bit.

A file full of program commands is called the program's *source code.* Think of a program's source code as the recipe that makes the program work. If someone can steal or copy your source code, he's effectively stolen your program. That's why companies like Microsoft jealously guard the source code to all their programs, such as Microsoft Windows or Excel.

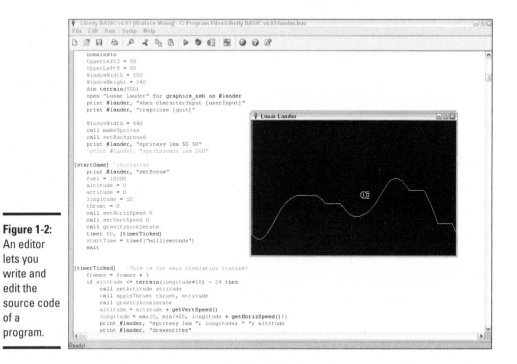

Figure 1-2:
An editor
lets you
write and
edit the
source code
of a
program.

Converting source code with an assembler or compiler

An editor lets you type and save program commands *(source code)* in a file. Unless you've written a program completely in machine language, your source code might as well have been written in Swahili because processors don't understand any language other than machine language.

So to convert your source code into machine language commands, you have to use an assembler (if you wrote your program commands in assembly language) or a compiler (if you wrote your program commands in the C language or a high-level language, like BASIC).

After converting your source code into equivalent machine language commands, an assembler or compiler saves these machine language commands in a separate file, often called an *executable file,* or just an *EXE file.* When you buy a program, such as a video game or an antivirus program, you're really buying an executable file. Without an assembler or a compiler, you can't create your program.

Compilers translate source code into *machine language,* which is the native language of a specific processor. But what if you want your program to run on different processors? To do this, you have to compile your program into machine language for each different processor. You wind up with one executable file for each processor, such as an executable file for an Intel Core Duo 2 processor and a separate executable file for a PowerPC processor.

Many Macintosh programs advertise themselves as a *Universal Binary* — the program actually consists of two executable files smashed into a single file:

✦ One executable file contains machine language code for the *PowerPC processor* (used in older Macintosh computers).

✦ The second executable file contains machine language code for the *Intel processor* (used in new Macintosh computers).

Most compilers work only on one specific operating system and processor. So a Windows compiler can only create programs that run under the Windows operating system. Likewise, a Linux compiler can only create programs that run under the Linux operating system.

If you write a program that runs under Windows, you can re-compile it to run under Linux. Unfortunately, you may have to modify your program slightly (or a lot) to make it run under Linux.

Big companies, like Microsoft and Adobe, can afford to pay programmers to write and modify programs to run under different operating systems, such as Windows and Mac OS X. Most smaller companies and individuals don't have the time to rewrite a program to run under multiple operating systems. That's why most small companies write programs for Windows because it's the largest market. If the program proves popular, they can later justify the time and expense to rewrite that program and compile it to run under Mac OS X.

Choose your compiler carefully. If you use a compiler that can create only Windows programs, you may never be able to re-compile that program to run on a different operating system, such as Linux or Mac OS X. One reason Microsoft gives away their compilers for free is to trap people into writing programs that can run only under Windows. For example, if you write a program with Microsoft Visual Basic, you can't run that program on Mac OS X without major modifications, which most people will probably never do.

Translating source code with an interpreter

In the old days, compilers were notoriously slow. You could feed source code to a compiler and literally come back the next morning to see if the compiler was done. If you made a single mistake in your program, you had to correct it and re-compile your program all over again — with another overnight wait to see if it even worked.

Trying to write a program with such slow compilers proved maddening, so computer scientists created something faster called an *interpreter*. Just like a foreign language interpreter who listens to each sentence you speak and then translates that sentence into another language, a computer interpreter does the same thing.

Type a program command into an interpreter, and the interpreter immediately translates that command into its equivalent machine language command. Type in another command, and the interpreter translates that second command right away.

The problem with interpreters is that they only store the equivalent machine language commands in memory instead of in a separate file like a compiler does. If you want to sell or distribute your program, you have to give people your source code, along with an interpreter that can convert your source code into machine language commands. Because giving away your source code essentially means giving away your program, everyone who wants to sell their programs uses a compiler instead of an interpreter.

The original reason why computer scientists developed interpreters was because compilers were so slow. But after computer scientists started creating faster compilers, most people stopped using interpreters and just used compilers. Nowadays, computer scientists use interpreters for running certain types of programming languages known as *scripting languages.* (Find out more about scripting languages in Book I, Chapter 3.)

Combining a compiler with an interpreter to create p-code

Creating separate executable files for each processor can get clumsy and giving away your source code with an interpreter may be unreasonable, so a third approach is to compile your program into an intermediate format called *byte-code* or *pseudocode* (often abbreviated as *p-code*). Unlike compiling source code directly into machine language, you compile your program into a p-code file instead.

You can take this p-code file and copy it on any computer. To run a p-code file, you need a special p-code interpreter, or a *virtual machine.* The virtual machine acts like an interpreter and runs the instructions compiled into the p-code file.

✦ The advantage of p-code is that you can distribute a single p-code version of your program, which can run on multiple computers.

✦ P-code has a couple disadvantages:

  • P-code programs don't run as fast as programs compiled into machine language.

  • If a computer doesn't have the right virtual machine installed, it can't run your program.

The most popular programming language that uses p-code is Java. After you write a Java program, you can compile it into a p-code file, which can run on any computer that has a copy of the Java virtual machine (VM), such as Windows, Mac OS X, and Linux.

The theory behind p-code is that you write a program once and you can run it anywhere. The reality is that every operating system has its quirks, so it's more common to write a program and be forced to test it on multiple operating systems. More often than not, a p-code program runs perfectly fine on one operating system (like Windows) but suffers mysterious problems when running on another operating system (such as Linux). Languages, such as Java, are getting better at letting you run the same program on multiple operating systems without major modifications, but be careful because p-code doesn't always work as well as you might think.

Taking the time to understand

Programming is a skill that anyone can acquire. Like any skill, the best way to understand is to take the time to experiment, make mistakes, and learn from your failures. Some programmers prefer to spend their time mastering a single programming language. Others prefer to master the intricacies of writing programs for a specific operating system, such as Windows. Still others spend their time discovering a variety of programming languages and writing programs for different operating systems.

There is no right or wrong way to figure out programming. The only "right" way is the way that works for you. That's why self-taught programmers can often write programs that are just as good (or even better) than programs written by PhD computer scientists.

Like any skill, the more time you spend programming a computer, the better you get. This book is designed to help you get started, but ultimately, it's up to you to take what you know and start programming your own computer.

Believe it or not, programming a computer is actually fairly straightforward. The hard part is trying to write a program that actually works.

Getting Started with Programming

You can read about computer programming from a book, but the best way to understand computer programming is to actually write some programs on a real computer. If you don't have a computer, borrow a friend's computer or find some other way to get access to a computer. Trying to become skilled at computer programming without a computer is like trying to become skilled at swimming without any water.

To find out about programming, you need an editor and a compiler that works on your computer. Although you could buy an editor and a compiler, why bother when you can find so many editors and compilers for free?

You can figure out programming by using a free editor and a compiler; if you later decide you don't like programming or the particular editor and compiler you're using, you haven't lost any money, so just erase it off your computer.

Starting with Windows

To encourage as many people as possible to write programs for Windows, Microsoft gives away free compilers called Visual Basic Express, Visual C++ Express, Visual C# Express, and Visual J++, which you can download from the Internet at `http://msdn.microsoft.com/vstudio/express`.

Most professional programmers use Microsoft compilers, so if you're interested in knowing how to write programs for Windows, you might as well discover programming through one of Microsoft's compilers as well.

If you don't want to use one of Microsoft's free compilers, plenty of free alternatives are just as good (or better). One popular compiler company is Borland, which offers three free compilers called Turbo C++, Turbo C#, and Turbo Delphi. You can download these at `www.turboexplorer.com`.

By giving away free compilers, companies like Microsoft and Borland hope to get you "hooked" on using their tools so you'll eventually buy the more advanced, professional versions that offer additional features. If you need to write programs professionally, you'll probably want to buy these professional versions, but when you're just starting to program, these free compilers are great ways to discover programming without having to spend any money.

Some other free Windows compilers include Dev-C++ and Dev-Pascal (`www.bloodshed.net`) and Just BASIC (`www.justbasic.com`).

Starting with Mac OS X

The most popular compiler for writing Mac OS X programs is *Xcode,* which comes with every Macintosh, although you can download the latest version for free at `http://developer.apple.com/tools`. Xcode is the same compiler that Microsoft, Adobe, and even Apple use to create programs like Microsoft Excel, Adobe PhotoShop, and iTunes.

Although most Mac OS X programmers use the free Xcode program to help them write programs, you can always buy other compilers for the Macintosh. The main reason to buy a compiler, rather than use the free Xcode tool, is if you want to use a programming language that Xcode doesn't offer, such as BASIC. (Xcode lets you write programs in C, C++, Objective-C, and Java.)

Starting with Linux

The most popular free compiler for Linux is GCC, which stands for GNU Compiler Collection (`http://gcc.gnu.org`). Unlike other compilers that can compile only a single programming language, the GCC compiler can compile programs written in a variety of different programming languages.

The GCC compiler can compile programs written in C, C++, Objective-C, FORTRAN, Java, and Ada. If these names of programming languages mean nothing to you, don't worry. The ability to compile different programming languages just means that you can use the GCC compiler when writing a program in one of the more popular programming languages.

The GCC compiler is the same compiler used in Apple's Xcode program.

I discuss in Book I, Chapter 3 that BASIC is one of the most popular beginner's programming languages. If you want to write and compile a BASIC program for Linux, you can't use the GCC compiler. Instead, you can grab a free copy of REALbasic (www.realbasic.com).

REALbasic gives away the Linux version of their compiler because they hope you'll pay for the professional version, which lets you compile your programs for Linux, Windows, and the Mac OS X operating systems. If you just want to write BASIC programs in Linux, you can use the free version of REALbasic for as long as you want.

Starting with Java

No matter which operating system you use, you can always get started programming with the Java language. If you want to write and run Java programs, you need

✦ **A Java compiler and virtual machine,** which you can download for free from Sun Microsystems (http://java.sun.com)

✦ **An editor** because the Java compiler doesn't include one. If you want an editor to help you write Java programs, you can get a free one called NetBeans (www.netbeans.org), BlueJ (www.bluej.org), or Eclipse (www.eclipse.org).

Knowing Programming versus Knowing Programming Language

There's a big difference between knowing how to program compared to knowing a specific programming language. This book describes how programming works, which means you'll understand the principles behind programming no matter what programming language you decide to use.

When you understand a specific programming language, you'll figure out how to write a program using that language. Don't confuse knowing how to program with knowing a programming language!

When people learn to speak their native language, they often think their particular spoken language is the only way to talk. So when they learn a foreign language, they try to speak the foreign language just like they speak their native language, but using different words. That's why literal translations of foreign languages can sound so funny and awkward to a native speaker.

That's exactly the same problem with understanding programming. To understand programming, you have to use a specific programming language, but each programming language works a certain way. So if you know how to write programs in the C programming language, you might mistakenly think that the way the C language works is the way computer programming also works, but that's not true.

Like human languages, programming languages differ wildly. Someone who knows how to write programs in the C language thinks differently about programming than someone who knows how to write programs in assembly language.

So to describe how programming works, this book uses a variety of examples from different programming languages. You don't have to understand how each program example in this book works. Just understand that programming languages can look and solve identical problems in wildly different ways.

First, try to understand general programming principles without worrying about the way a particular programming language works. Then try to understand how a particular programming language works. As long as you know how to keep these two topics separate, you can figure out how to program a computer without the distraction of knowing a particular programming language.

Programming languages rise and fall in popularity all the time, so if you know only one programming language, your skills may become obsolete within a few years.

At one time, most programmers used assembly language. Then they used Pascal. When Pascal fell out of favor, programmers gravitated toward C. Because C was so hard to understand, many people started using BASIC. At the time of this writing, programmers have been flocking toward C++, C#, and Java. Tomorrow, who knows which programming language will be popular?

Focus on understanding programming and then worry about understanding a particular programming language. After you understand how programming works, you can adapt to the next popular programming language of tomorrow, whatever that might be.

Chapter 2: Different Methods for Writing Programs

In This Chapter

✔ Spaghetti programming

✔ Structured programming

✔ Event-driven programming

✔ Object-oriented programming

*T*he goal of computer science is to find the best ways to write a program. The reality of computer science is that nobody really knows what they're doing, so they're making up stuff as they go along and pretending that there's a scientific basis for everything they do. The fact that multimillion dollar programming projects routinely fall behind schedule and sometimes never work at all pretty much shows that computer programming is still less a science than an art.

Despite these problems, computer scientists are always searching for ways to make programming easier, faster, and more reliable by constantly developing

✦ **Better tools**

✦ **Better programming languages**

✦ **Better techniques for writing programs**

Just as a carpenter doesn't build a house with rusty saws and a broken hammer, computer scientists are always developing better tools to help them write, fix, and create programs. One of the first improvements computer scientists made was in developing faster compilers. Instead of waiting overnight to see if a program worked, programmers could use a fast compiler that could show them the results in seconds. Other tool improvements included editors that would show programmers the specific line where an error occurred and special programs (known as *debuggers*) for making sure that every part of a program worked correctly.

Another way to improve programmer efficiency involves creating better programming languages. Assembly language was easier to write and modify than machine language, and high-level languages are easier to write and modify than assembly language.

Computer scientists are constantly inventing new programming languages or improving existing ones. These improvements or new languages typically offer some feature that existing languages don't offer or solve certain types of problems that existing languages do poorly. For example, the C++ language improves upon the C language, whereas the Java language improves upon the C++ language.

Perhaps two of the biggest problems with programming involve writing a program from scratch and modifying an existing program. When you write a program from scratch, you want to write a working program quickly with as few problems as possible.

That's why programming languages include so many built-in commands. The idea is that the more built-in commands available, the fewer commands you'll need to use to write a program and the shorter and easier your program will be to write in the first place.

In addition, many programming languages include built-in error-checking features to keep you from writing a program that doesn't work. With some languages, it's possible to write commands that work perfectly, but can also crash the computer if you give those commands the wrong type of data.

In Book I, Chapter 3, you find out more about the features of different programming languages.

Half the battle of programming is writing a program that works. The second half is modifying that program later. When you need to modify an existing program, you must first understand how that existing program works and then you need to modify it without messing up the existing program commands.

To help you understand how a program works, many programming languages let you divide a large program into separate parts. The theory is that if one part of a program isn't working or needs to be modified, you can yank out part of the program, rewrite it, and then plug it back into the existing program, much like snapping Lego building blocks together.

Finally, all the best tools and the latest programming languages aren't going to help you unless you know how to use them correctly. That's why computer scientists are constantly developing new programming techniques that work no matter what tools or language you use.

In Book I, Chapter 4, you find out more about the different programming tools computer scientists have created to make programming easier, faster, and more reliable.

The rest of this chapter discusses programming techniques based on problems encountered by programmers working in the real world. Basically, computer scientists keep developing and refining programming techniques after they see what really works and what doesn't.

Spaghetti Programming without a Plan

In the early days of programming, most programs were fairly short and simple. A typical program might just calculate a mathematical equation, which to a computer, is just a little more challenging than adding two numbers together.

To write such small, single-task programs, programmers would typically start typing commands in their favorite programming language with little planning, just to write a program quickly.

Unfortunately, many programs aren't just written once and then used forever. If a program isn't working exactly right, or if the program needs to do something new that the original programmer didn't include, you must take an existing program and modify it.

Modifying an existing program sounds simple, but it's not. First, you must understand how the program works so you'll know exactly how to modify that program. If you try modifying a program without understanding how it works, there's a good chance you could wreck the program and keep it from working, much like ripping out cables from your car engine without knowing what you're really doing.

After you understand how a program works, the second step involves writing new commands into the existing program. Now, here's where the problem occurs. Take an existing program and modify it once. Now take that same program and modify it again. Now take that same program and modify it 20 more times, and what do you get? Most likely, you'll have a mish-mash collection of code that works, but isn't organized logically, as shown in Figure 2-1.

Modifying a program several times by yourself might not be so bad because you probably remember what you changed and why. But what happens if seven other programmers modify the same program seven different times and then none of them are around to help you understand what changes they made? If you guessed you'll wind up with a bigger mess than before, you're right.

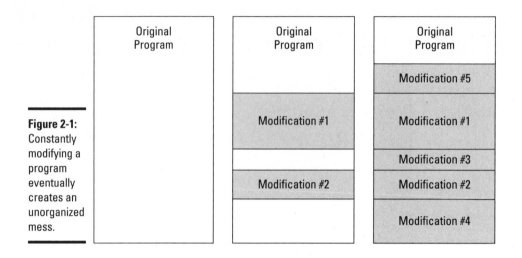

Figure 2-1:
Constantly
modifying a
program
eventually
creates an
unorganized
mess.

With constant modifications, a small, simple program can grow into a convoluted monstrosity that may work, but nobody quite understands how or why. Because the program consists of so many changes scattered throughout the code, trying to figure out how the program even works can get harder with each new modification.

With a simple program, the computer follows each command from start to finish, so it's easy to see how the program works. After a program gets modified multiple times, trying to follow the order of commands the computer follows can be like untangling spaghetti, hence the term *spaghetti programming*.

As programs kept getting bigger and more complicated, computer scientists realized that just letting programmers rush out to write or modify a program wasn't going to work any more. So that's when computer scientists created the first programming techniques to help programmers write programs that'd be easy to understand and modify later.

Planning Ahead with Structured Programming

The problem with programs created without any planning is that it inevitably leads to a mess. So the first step involves keeping a program organized right from the start.

Spaghetti programming with the GOTO Command

Although you can write spaghetti programs in any language, the BASIC programming language is most closely associated with spaghetti programming. Early versions of BASIC used a *GOTO* command, which essentially told the computer to "go to" another part of the program.

The problem with the GOTO command was that it could tell the computer to "go to" any part of the program. If you had a large program that consisted of several hundred (or several thousand) lines of code, the GOTO command could tell the computer to jump from one part of the program to another in any order, as the following BASIC program shows:

```
10 GOTO 50
20 PRINT "This line prints
   second."
30 END
40 GOTO 20
50 PRINT "This prints first."
60 GOTO 40
```

Line 10 (the first line) tells the computer to "go to" line 50.

Line 50 tells the computer to print, This prints first. on-screen. After the computer follows this command, it automatically runs the next command below it, which is line 60.

Line 60 tells the computer to "go to" line 40.

Line 40 tells the computer to "go to" line 20.

Line 20 tells the computer to print, This line prints second. After the computer follows this command, it automatically follows the command on the next line, which is line 30.

Line 30 tells the computer this is the end of the program.

Even though this program consists of six lines, you can already see how the GOTO command makes the computer jump around, so it's hard to understand how this program works. Now imagine this program multiplied by over several hundred lines of code, and you can see how spaghetti programming can make reading, understanding, and modifying even the simplest program much harder.

The three parts of structured programming

To keep programs organized, structured programming teaches programmers that any program can be divided into three distinct parts:

+ **Sequences**
+ **Branches**
+ **Loops**

Sequences

Sequences are simply groups of commands that the computer follows one after another. Most simple programs just consist of a list of commands that the computer follows from start to finish, as shown in Figure 2-2.

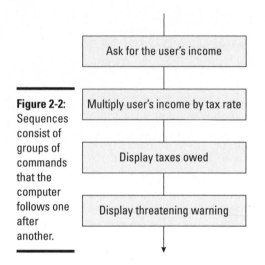

Figure 2-2:
Sequences
consist of
groups of
commands
that the
computer
follows one
after
another.

Branches

Branches consist of two or more groups of commands. At any given time, the computer may choose to follow one group of commands or another. Branches allow a program to make a decision based on a certain condition.

For example, at the end of most video games, the program asks you, "Do you want to play again (Yes or No)?" If you choose Yes, the program lets you play the video game again. If you choose No, the program stops running, as shown in Figure 2-3.

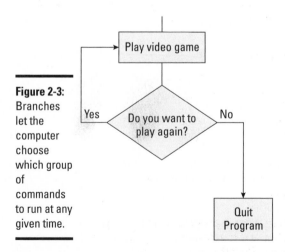

Figure 2-3:
Branches
let the
computer
choose
which group
of
commands
to run at any
given time.

A branch starts with a command that evaluates a condition (such as determining whether the user chose Yes or No) and then based on this answer, chooses which group of commands to follow next.

Loops

Sometimes you may want the computer to run the same commands over and over again. For example, a program might ask the user for a password. If the user types an invalid password, the program displays an error message and asks the user to type the password again.

If you wanted your program to ask the user for a password three times, you could write the same group of commands to ask for the password three times, but that'd be wasteful. Not only would this force you to type the same commands multiple times, but if you wanted to modify these commands, you'd have to modify them in three different locations as well. Loops are basically a shortcut to writing one or more commands multiple times.

A loop consists of two parts:

✦ **The group of commands that the loop repeats**

✦ **A command that defines how many times the loop should run**

By combining sequences, branches, and loops, you can design any program and understand how the program works at each step.

Dividing a program into sequences, branches, and loops can help you isolate and organize groups of related commands into discrete "chunks" of code. That way, you can yank out a chunk of code, modify it, and plug it back in without affecting the rest of the program.

Top-down programming

For small programs, organizing a program into sequences, branches, and loops works well. But the larger your program gets, the harder it can be to view and understand the whole thing. So a second feature of structured programming involves breaking a large program into smaller parts where each part performs one specific task. This is also known as *top-down* programming.

The idea behind top-down programming (as opposed to bottom-up programming) is that you design your program by identifying the main *(top)* task that you want your program to solve.

For example, if you wanted to write a program that could predict the next winning lottery numbers, that is a *top* design of your program. Of course, you can't just tell a computer, "Pick the next winning lottery numbers." You must divide this single (top) task into two or more smaller tasks.

One of these smaller tasks might be, "Identify the lottery numbers that tend to appear often." A second task might be, "Pick the six numbers that have appeared most often and display those as the potential future winning numbers."

The idea is that writing a large program may be tough, but writing a small program is easy. So if you keep dividing the tasks of your program into smaller and smaller parts, eventually you can write a small, simple program that can solve that task. Then you can paste these small programs together like building blocks, and you'll have a well-organized big program — theoretically.

Now if you need to modify part of the large program, just find the small program that needs changing, modify it, and plug it back into the larger program, and you've just updated the larger program.

Ideally, each small program should be small enough to fit on a single sheet of paper. This makes each small program easy to read, understand, and modify. When you divide a large program into smaller programs, each small program is a *subprogram*.

If you divide a program into multiple subprograms, you have two options for where to store your subprograms:

✦ **Store all of your subprograms in a single file.**

This option is fine for small programs, but after you start dividing a program into multiple subprograms, trying to cram all of your subprograms into a single file is like trying to cram your entire wardrobe of shirts, pants, and underwear into your sock drawer. It's possible, but it makes finding anything later that much more difficult.

✦ **Store subprograms in separate files, as shown in Figure 2-4.**

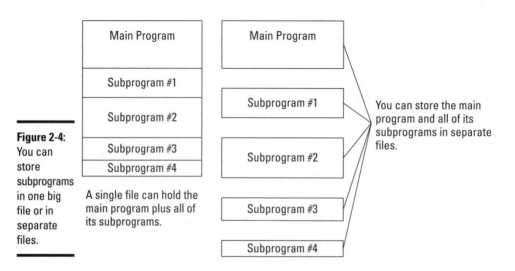

Figure 2-4:
You can store subprograms in one big file or in separate files.

Structured Programming and Pascal

You can use structured programming techniques with any programming language, including machine or assembly language. However, the one language most closely associated with structured programming is Pascal.

Unlike other languages that later adopted structured programming, Pascal was designed to encourage (force) programmers to use structured programming from the start. A typical Pascal program might look like this:

```
Program Print2Lines;
Begin
   Writeln ('This prints
     first.');
   Writeln ('This line prints
     second.');
End.
```

Without knowing anything about the Pascal language, you can immediately make sense out of what it does.

- First, it prints the line, This prints first.

- Next, it prints the second line, This line prints second.

Unlike the preceding BASIC example that allows spaghetti programming, Pascal forces programmers to structure programs using sequences, branches, and loops. As a result, Pascal helps programmers create well-organized programs that can be much easier to read and understand.

Storing subprograms in separate files offers three huge advantages.

- The fewer subprograms crammed into a single file, the easier it can be to find and modify any of them.

- If you store subprograms in a separate file, you can copy that file (and any subprograms stored in that file) and then plug it into another program. In that way, you can create a library of useful subprograms and reuse them later.

- By reusing subprograms that you've tested already to make sure they work properly, you can write more complicated programs in less time, simply because you're reusing subprograms and not writing everything from scratch.

Making User Interfaces with Event-Driven Programming

In the early days, using a program was fairly simple. After typing the command to run a particular program, that program might ask a question such as

```
What is your name?
```

At this point, you had no choice but to type a name, such as **Joe Smith**. After you typed in your name, the program might respond with

```
Hello, Joe Smith. What month were you born?
```

The moment you typed in a month, such as **April**, the program might respond:

```
What day were you born?
```

And so on. If you wanted to type your day of birth before your month of birth, you couldn't because the program controlled your options.

Not surprisingly, using a computer like this was frustrating to most people, so computer scientists soon invented something called a *graphical user interface* (abbreviated as GUI).

A GUI displays multiple options to the user in the form of pull-down menus, windows, buttons, and check boxes. Suddenly, instead of the computer dictating what the user could do at any given time, the user could tell the computer what to do at any given time, just by choosing one of many available commands.

Forcing each program to display menus and windows had two advantages for users:

✦ **It made using a computer much easier.** Instead of having to type in commands, users could just click the command they wanted to use.

✦ **It's fairly easy to figure out how to use different types of programs.** After you understand that you can choose the Print command in the File menu, you know how to print in any program whether it's a word processor, a database, or an image editing program.

Unfortunately, although pull-down menus made programs easy for users, they made writing programs much harder for the programmers:

✦ Programmers had to write extra commands just to display all these fancy pull-down menus and windows. (Even worse, programmers had to make sure all those extra commands used to create pull-down menus and windows actually worked correctly.)

✦ Programmers now had to write programs that could react to whatever command the user chose. Rather than present the user with options in a specific, predictable order, programs had to handle the unpredictable choices of the user.

To solve this dual problem of creating pull-down menus and knowing how to handle the different commands the user might choose at any given time, computer scientists developed *event-driven programming*.

In event-driven programming, an *event* is something that the user does, like clicking a pull-down menu or clicking a button displayed in a window. Event-driven programming simply focuses on displaying different commands on-screen and then handling these different events when they occur.

Event-driven programming divides programming into three distinct parts:

✦ **The user interface:** The commands the user sees on-screen

✦ **The event handler:** The part of your program that reacts to the commands the user chooses from the user interface

✦ **The actual program:** The part of your program that actually does something useful, such as drawing pictures or predicting the winners of horse races

In the old days, creating a user interface essentially tripled your work:

1. Write your program.

2. Write commands to create a user interface.

3. Write commands to make your user interface actually work.

Event-driven programming eliminates this problem. Instead of forcing you to write commands to display pull-down menus and windows on-screen, event-driven programming lets you visually design your user interface, such as the number, placement, and size of buttons.

After you've designed your user interface (without having to write a single command to do it), you can write short programs that respond to everything the user could possibly do, which is called an *event.* If the user clicks a pull-down menu, that's an event. If the user clicks a button in a window, that's a different event. When you write a small program to handle an event, the program is called an *event handler.*

Without event-driven programming, you'd be forced to write commands to create a user interface and more commands to make the user interface work. With event-driven programming, you just have to write commands to make your user interface work. The fewer commands you must write, the faster you can create a program and the easier the program will be to read, understand, and modify later.

The most popular event-driven programming language is Visual Basic, although Microsoft has adopted event-driven programming for their Visual C#, Visual C++, and Visual J++ compilers as well. Other popular event-driven programming languages include REALbasic (www.realbasic.com) and Delphi (www. turboexplorer.com).

Event-driven programming doesn't replace structured programming; it supplements it. Structured programming techniques are useful for helping you write your program. Event-driven programming is useful for helping you design a user interface for your program.

Basically, event-driven programming divides programming into three distinct steps: designing the user interface, writing event handlers to make the user interface work, and writing the actual program.

Designing a user interface

The main advantage of event-driven programming is how quickly it allows you to design a user interface without writing a single command whatsoever. Instead of writing commands, you create a user interface using a two-step process:

1. **Visually draw your user interface on a window by choosing which user interface parts you want, such as buttons, check boxes, or menus, as shown in Figure 2-5.**

    After you've drawn your user interface, you wind up with a *generic* user interface.

2. **Customize each part of your user interface by defining its appearance and behavior.**

To customize part of a user interface, you must modify that user interface's properties. Each part of your user interface contains properties that define its appearance and behavior. For example, if you wanted a button to appear in color, you'd change that button's `Color` property. If you wanted to change the size of a button, you'd modify that button's `Width` or `Height` property, as shown in Figure 2-6.

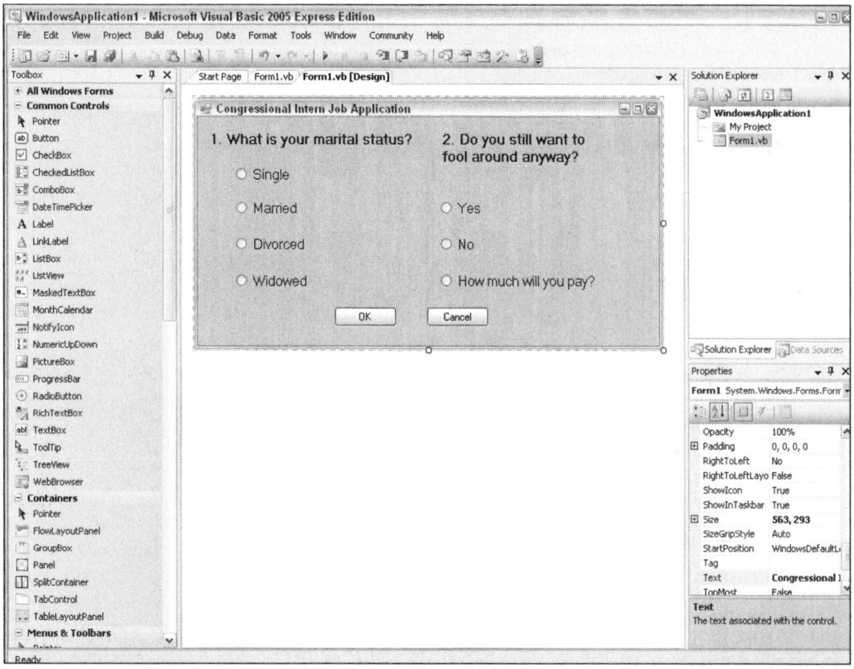

Figure 2-5:
Designing a user interface involves drawing what you want to appear on your program's user interface.

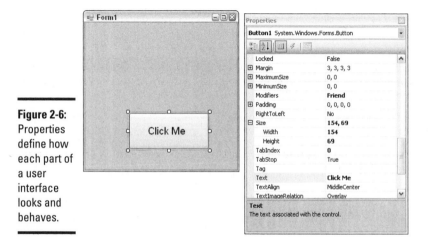

Figure 2-6:
Properties define how each part of a user interface looks and behaves.

With event-driven programming, designing a user interface involves drawing your user interface and then customizing it by changing its properties. After you've designed your user interface, it will appear to work but it won't actually do anything until you write an event handler.

Writing event handlers

The whole purpose of an event handler is to work as a middleman between your actual program and your program's user interface. To create an event handler, you need to identify the following:

✦ **A user interface item,** such as a button or a check box

✦ **The event,** such as a click of the mouse

The combination of a user interface item and a specific event uniquely defines an event handler, as shown in Figure 2-7.

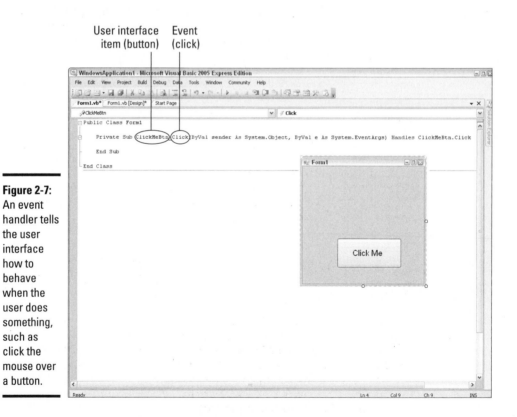

Figure 2-7:
An event handler tells the user interface how to behave when the user does something, such as click the mouse over a button.

The user can do dozens of different possible events, but the most common events are clicking the mouse or moving the mouse pointer over an item. Event handlers typically do one of three things:

+ **Identify what the user did,** such as click a button
+ **Retrieve information from the user interface,** such as when the user types something in a text box
+ **Display information to the user,** such as displaying an error message

After you've written one or more event handlers for your user interface, you have a complete working user interface. Now you just have to attach this user interface to a working program.

Writing your program

Some people write their program first and then design a user interface around it. Other people design their user interface first and then write their program to work with it. The whole point of event-driven programming is to separate your program from your user interface so you can focus on making each part work individually.

Event-driven programming focuses mostly on designing a user interface and making it work, but does little to help you write your actual program. To write your program, you can use structured programming or object-oriented programming (or both, or neither).

After you've written your program, you "attach" the program to your user interface by writing event handlers. Event handlers "glue" your user interface to your actual program. With event-driven programming, you can be pretty sure that your user interface will always work perfectly. You just have to worry about errors in your main program.

Organizing a Program with Object-Oriented Programming

Structured programming helps you organize and divide your program into smaller, more manageable pieces. For small- to medium-sized programs, dividing a program into smaller programs is fine, but the larger your program gets, the more smaller programs you'll have to worry about. Eventually, computer scientists discovered that they needed another technique for dividing large programs into parts, so they called this new technique *object-oriented programming* (often abbreviated as OOP).

Object-oriented programming solves two glaring problems with structured programming: reusability and modeling.

Reusability means that you can collect smaller programs that work together, store them in a larger group called an object, and then plug those objects into different programs like Lego building blocks. Where structured programming encourages reusability by letting you reuse subprograms, object-oriented programming encourages reusability on a larger scale by letting you reuse objects (which contain multiple smaller programs). Reusing individual subprograms is like using bricks to build a house. Reusing objects is more like using pre-manufactured walls to build a house.

Modeling means that programming is more intuitive. One of the reasons why assembly language is so hard to understand is because manipulating data in the processor's registers has nothing to do with solving problems like adding two numbers together. Likewise, dividing a large program into smaller tasks, using structured programming, does nothing to help you understand the actual problem the program is trying to solve.

For example, suppose you had to write a program to land a rocket on the moon. This is how you might write this program using structured programming:

```
Land a rocket on the moon
    Launch rocket
    Guide rocket through space
    Find a landing area on the moon
    Put rocket down on landing area
```

So far, structured programming seems logical, but what happens when you keep dividing tasks into smaller tasks? Just focusing on the `Guide rocket through space` task, we might wind up with the following:

```
Guide rocket through space
    Get current coordinates
        Compare current coordinates with moon coordinates
    Adjust direction
```

Dividing the `Adjust direction` task into smaller tasks, we might get this:

```
Adjust direction
    Identify current speed and direction
        Determine angle needed to steer towards the moon
        Fire thrusters to change the angle of the rocket
```

Notice that the deeper you keep dividing tasks, the more removed you get from knowing what the main purpose of the program may be. Just by looking at the task `Identify current speed and direction`, you have no idea whether this task involves flying a rocket to the moon, driving a car down a road, or controlling a walking robot to an electric outlet to recharge its batteries.

The more you divide a larger task into smaller tasks, the harder it can be to understand what problem you're even trying to solve. This gets even worse when you start writing actual program commands.

The two parts of most programs are the commands that tell the computer what to do and the data that the program manipulates. So if you wrote a program to identify the current speed and direction of a rocket, the commands would tell the computer how to retrieve this information and the speed and direction would be the actual data the program uses.

Essentially, program commands are separate from the data that they manipulate. If one part of a program manipulates data incorrectly, the rest of the program winds up using that contaminated data and you, as the programmer, won't know which part of the program screwed up the data. This is like sitting in a baseball game, ordering a hot dog from a vendor, and having six people pass your hot dog down to you. When you see fingerprints all over your hot dog, can you tell which person touched your food?

Objects isolate data

Object-oriented programming avoids this problem by combining data and the commands that manipulate them into a single entity called (surprise!) an *object*. With object-oriented programming in the hot dog vendor analogy, instead of passing your hot dog to half a dozen other people, the hot dog vendor comes directly to your seat and hands you your hot dog. Now if you saw fingerprints all over your hot dog, you'd know that the fingerprints could only have come from the hot dog vendor.

Besides keeping data isolated from other parts of your program, object-oriented programming also helps you divide a large program into smaller ones. Although structured programming divides a large program into the tasks that need to be performed, object-oriented programming divides a large program into real-life objects.

So if you were designing a program to launch a rocket to the moon, object-oriented programming would let you divide the program into objects. One object might be the `rocket`, a second object might be the `moon`, and a third object might be the `Earth`.

You can also divide a large object into smaller ones. So the `rocket` object might be divided into an `engine` object and a `guidance` object. The `engine` object could be further divided into a `fuel pump` object, a `nozzle` object, and a `fuel tank` object.

Suppose you wrote a program to calculate a rocket's trajectory to the moon, and the engineers suddenly designed the rocket with a more powerful engine? With object-oriented programming, you could just yank the `engine` object out of your program, rewrite or replace it, and plug it back into the program again.

In structured programming, modifying the program to reflect a new rocket engine would mean finding the program commands that manipulate the data that represents the engine's thrust, and then making sure that new data gets fed into the program at the proper location and still works with any other program commands that also handle that same data. (If the explanation in this paragraph sounded confusing and convoluted to you, that just shows you the less-than-intuitive problem of modifying a structured program versus an object-oriented program.)

Objects simplify modifications

Besides organizing a large program into logical pieces, objects have another purpose — *code reusability.* Just as in high school, it was always easier to copy someone else's homework rather than do it yourself, so programmers find that it's easier to copy and reuse somebody else's program rather than write their own from scratch.

In structured programming, you could divide a large program into subprograms and then store those subprograms in a separate file. Now you could copy that file to reuse those subprograms in another program.

Copying subprograms makes programming easier, but here are two problems:

✦ **What if you copy a subprogram and then later find an error in that subprogram?** Now you'll have to fix that subprogram in every copy. If you made 17 copies of a subprogram, you'll have to fix the same error 17 times in 17 different copies of the same subprogram.

✦ **What if you want to modify and improve a subprogram?** Suppose you find a subprogram that asks the user to type in a password of no more than 10 characters, but you want your program to allow users to type in passwords up to 25 characters. At this point, you could either

  • **Write your own password-verifying subprogram from scratch (which would take time).**

  • **Copy the existing subprogram and modify it (which would take much less time).** It's easier to make a copy of an existing subprogram and then modify this copy. Now you'll have two copies of (almost) the same subprogram, but uh oh! Suddenly, you discover an error in the original subprogram. Once again, you have to correct this error in the original subprogram and also in the modified subprogram. If you made 20 different modifications to a subprogram, you now have the problem of not only correcting the error in every copy of the original subprogram, but also fixing that same error in all your modified versions of that original subprogram.

But after you modify a subprogram, will you remember which subprogram you copied and modified originally? Even worse, you could copy a subprogram and modify it, and then copy your modified subprogram and modify that copy. Do this several times and you'll wind up with several slightly different versions of the same subprogram, but now you may not have any idea which subprogram you copied originally.

So now if you find an error in the original subprogram, how can you find and fix that same error in any modified copies of that subprogram? Most likely, you can't because you won't know for sure which modified versions of the subprogram you (or another programmer) might have created.

Because programmers are always going to copy an existing program that works, object-oriented programming helps manage the copying process by using *inheritance*. The whole idea behind inheritance is that rather than making physical copies of a subprogram, you have only one copy of a subprogram at all times.

Instead of physically copying a subprogram, objects *inherit* a subprogram by essentially pointing to the subprogram that they want to copy. Not only does this save physical space by eliminating the need to make copies of a subprogram, but this also makes it easy to modify subprograms.

If you find an error in a subprogram, just correct the error in the original subprogram and that's it. Any objects that have inherited commands from that subprogram now point automatically to the modified version of the original subprogram, as shown in Figure 2-8.

By isolating commands in objects and using inheritance, objects can get the advantages of copying subprograms without the disadvantages of having multiple physical copies scattered all over the place.

Object-oriented programming makes programs easier to write (by dividing a large program into parts), easier to understand (by organizing subprograms into objects that mimic the actual problem the program is trying to solve), and easier to modify (by automatically updating any copies of subprograms). All these advantages allow you, as the programmer, to focus more on solving problems and less on keeping track of trivial details.

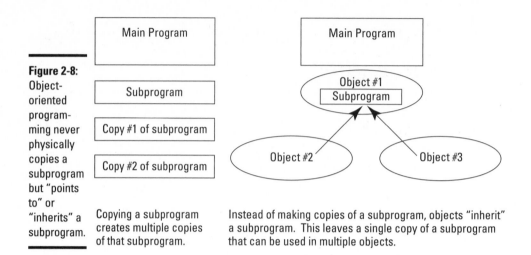

Figure 2-8:
Object-
oriented
program-
ming never
physically
copies a
subprogram
but "points
to" or
"inherits" a
subprogram.

Copying a subprogram creates multiple copies of that subprogram.

Instead of making copies of a subprogram, objects "inherit" a subprogram. This leaves a single copy of a subprogram that can be used in multiple objects.

Discover more about the details of object-oriented programming in Book II, Chapter 7. For now, it's just important that you understand why programmers use object-oriented programming. Then you can worry about figuring out how to use object-oriented programming.

Designing Programs with Today's Methodology

Each step, from spaghetti programming, to structured programming, to event-driven programming, to object-oriented programming, is meant to guide programmers into writing better-organized programs that can be modified quickly and easily. Today, object-oriented programming is popular, but tomorrow, another programming methodology will likely arrive to deal with the shortcomings of object-oriented programming.

With the exception of spaghetti programming (which you want to avoid), structured programming, event-driven programming, and object-oriented programming can be used by themselves or together. You might use object-oriented programming to divide a program into objects, and then use structured programming to organize the commands you write and store inside each object. Finally, you can use event-driven programming to design a fancy user interface so people know how to use your program.

By using each programming methodology's strengths, you can create a well-designed program, on time, that actually works. Given the track record of government agencies and Fortune 500 corporations, creating working software on time is the closest thing to a miracle that most people will ever experience in a lifetime.

Chapter 3: Types of Programming Languages

In This Chapter

- ✔ Deciding on your first language
- ✔ Discovering teaching languages
- ✔ Understanding curly bracket languages
- ✔ Determining artificial intelligence languages
- ✔ Figuring out scripting languages
- ✔ Understanding database query languages
- ✔ Comparing different programming languages

*A*fter you understand how to plan, organize, and create a program through one or more methodologies (such as structured programming, event-driven programming, or object-oriented programming), you're ready to start utilizing a particular programming language.

Just as your native spoken language can shape the way you think and speak, so can your first computer programming language influence the way you think, design, and write a computer program.

You can choose from literally thousands of different programming languages with obscure names, like Icon, Algol 60, APL, Forth, and Scheme. Although you can understand programming by using any programming language, it's probably best to know at least one of the more popular programming languages, such as BASIC or C.

Knowing a popular programming language, like BASIC or C, simply gives you more opportunities to work. More people use BASIC and C, which means more jobs are available for programmers who know BASIC or C. Just as knowing English, Chinese, Spanish, or Arabic allows you to travel and speak with more people around the world (compared to knowing Swahili, Mayan, or Eskimo), so can knowing BASIC or C give you more opportunities to work and write programs anywhere you go.

Sometimes there's a good reason to know an obscure programming language. One of the oldest programming languages, COBOL, was heavily used by businesses back when computers filled entire rooms and cost tens of thousands of dollars. Because many COBOL programs are still running today, COBOL programmers can actually make a nice living because so few programmers know COBOL. So knowing an obscure language might limit your opportunities, but at the same time, if someone needs a programmer who knows a particular programming language, you could be the only one they could hire (and have to pay big bucks as a result).

Choosing Your First Language

So should you start studying BASIC or C as your first programming language? Yes and no, depending on who you ask.

C the BASIC choices

Here's why you might consider studying either BASIC or C as your first programming language.

✦ Because BASIC and C are two of the most popular languages used, you need to know one (or both) of them eventually, so you might as well start understanding them right from the beginning.

✦ BASIC was originally designed to teach programming, so understanding BASIC can be easy, fun, and fast.

✦ By studying BASIC, you can focus on understanding programming principles without getting lost in the technical details of how a computer or operating system works, or learn confusing commands or cryptic syntax that can make programming harder than necessary.

Understanding C can be important because so many programming languages (such as Java, C++, C#, and Perl) are based on the C language. So after you know C, you'll have no trouble understanding Java, C++, or practically any other programming language based on C.

With so many people using C (or languages like Java or C++, which are derived from C), any C programmer can find plenty of work, so knowing C is practically a necessity for anyone who wants to make a living as a programmer. Because you'll probably need to know C eventually, you might as well start with C from the beginning.

Having second thoughts

Ultimately, there's no "perfect" programming language to know and use because every programming language is designed to solve one problem extremely well (and hopefully prove useful enough to solve other problems, too). BASIC was designed to be easy to understand. C was designed to create efficient and powerful programs.

BASICally disrespected

From a financial point of view, BASIC programmers usually earn less than C programmers, even if they're doing the exact same job. Part of the reason for this is that BASIC suffers from the perception that it's a *toy language* — unsuitable for commercial use. Although that was true at one time, the BASIC language has evolved to the point where it can do practically anything C or other languages can do.

Although you can use BASIC to create anything from satellite navigation systems to Wall Street financial trading programs, BASIC programmers will probably always get paid less, so you'll need to know another language like C anyway, just to get paid more. Because BASIC programmers tend to get paid less than other programmers, many programmers feel that they might as well skip BASIC and just figure out C instead.

C, it's kinda hard

There's nothing wrong with studying C as your first programming language. The biggest problem with C is that it's not an intuitive language for beginners to learn and understand. With its cryptic syntax and odd use of symbols in place of actual words, understanding C means trying to figure out how to program while also wrestling with trying to figure out C, which essentially doubles the effort needed to know how to program a computer.

As a result, many beginners get frustrated with C as their first programming language and wind up more confused than ever. Imagine how many people would want to drive a car if it meant knowing how to refine their own gasoline and build their own engine. Understanding C isn't quite as difficult as refining gasoline or building a combustion engine, but it can seem that way, especially when you're programming for the first time and you start with the C language.

So if you're going to begin programming, you should definitely understand C eventually, but not necessarily as a first language. You don't need to know BASIC, but BASIC can definitely help you understand how programming works. If you figure out BASIC first and then figure out C, you'll know two of the most popular languages on the planet.

The more programming languages you know, the better you can understand the benefits and drawbacks of all programming languages, including favorites like BASIC and C. Ultimately, the best programming language to discover first is the language that makes programming easiest and fun for you, whether that language is as simple as BASIC, as arcane as assembly language, or as obscure as SNOBOL.

To help you understand the goals of different programming languages and the methods they use to achieve these goals, consider the different categories of programming languages.

Teaching Languages

The goal of *teaching languages* is to teach novices how to program for the first time, so teaching languages tend to be simple to learn and easy to understand. (Common sense might tell you that all programming languages should be simple to learn and easy to understand, but they're not. Languages, like C and C++, are designed for maximum computer efficiency whereas programmer efficiency is secondary. That's why C and C++ programs can be so hard to read and understand.)

Three popular teaching languages include BASIC, Logo, and Pascal. Besides making programming easy and fun, teaching languages also try to help you understand general programming principles that you can apply no matter what programming language you might later wish to know.

Getting back to BASIC

Back in 1963, programming was difficult because you had to know how the computer worked before you could write a program. As a result, only scientists, engineers, and mathematicians tended to program a computer.

Programming back in the early days of computers meant typing commands on a series of punch cards and feeding the punch cards into the computer. Then you had to return an hour later (or sometimes even overnight) to see the results of your program. If you made just one mistake, your program wouldn't run. Then you'd have to correct that one mistake and try to run your program again. If the computer found a second mistake, it wouldn't run the program either, and you'd have to try again. Needless to say, programming like this was tedious, slow, and frustrating.

At Dartmouth University, two professors, John Kemeny and Thomas Kurtz, decided that non-scientists could also benefit from computer programming by writing programs for themselves. (Scientists, engineers, and mathematicians tended only to write programs for themselves too, but how many ordinary people could use a program that would calculate a quadratic equation?)

Both John Kemeny and Thomas Kurtz have created an "official" version of BASIC called True BASIC (www.truebasic.com). Despite this official version of BASIC, many other companies, such as Microsoft, have created variations, or *dialects,* of BASIC. These BASIC dialects — like Visual Basic and REALbasic — are actually more commonly used than the official True BASIC version.

Principles

Because programming was so difficult, both John Kemeny and Thomas Kurtz decided to create a new programming language specifically designed to teach novices how to program. The goals of their new programming language, dubbed *BASIC* (Beginner's All-purpose Symbolic Instruction Code), consists of several principles:

+ **Be easy for beginners to understand and use.**

+ **Be a general-purpose programming language.**

+ **Be interactive.**

+ **Shield the user from understanding the computer hardware and operating system.**

Descriptive commands

To make the language easy to understand, BASIC uses descriptive commands, which is something most programming languages don't use. For example, this assembly language program prints the words Hello, world! on-screen:

```
title   Hello World Program
dosseg
.model small
.stack 100h

.data
hello_message db 'Hello, world!',0dh,0ah,'$'

.code
main   proc
       mov    ax,@data
       mov    ds,ax

       mov    ah,9
       mov    dx,offset hello_message
       int    21h

       mov    ax,4C00h
       int    21h
main   endp
end    main
```

Looking at the preceding assembly language program, isn't what the preceding commands are telling the computer simple and intuitive? (If you answered, "Yes," you're either a computer genius or completely delusional.)

Now look at the command you need to use to print `Hello, world!` in BASIC:

```
PRINT "Hello, world!"
```

That's it — a single line. To print `Hello, world!` on-screen, you can either write a 17-line assembly language program (and risk making a mistake on all 17 different lines), or you can write a one-line BASIC program that's immediately obvious and intuitive.

Versatility

Both professors Kemeny and Kurtz didn't just want to create a programming language that was easy to understand, but they also wanted to create a programming language that could be put to practical use as well. That way, novices could understand BASIC and then use BASIC to write actual programs. After all, there's no point in using BASIC to teach programming only to force programmers to later use a completely different language if they wanted to write a useful program.

So BASIC not only provides descriptive commands like `PRINT`, but it also provides enough commands so you can write practically any type of program. The only type of program you can't create easily in BASIC are programs that require you to understand and access the actual hardware of the computer or operating systems.

One reason C programmers look down on BASIC as a toy language is because BASIC doesn't let you access the hardware or operating system like C does. But one reason why C programs fail is precisely because programmers incorrectly manipulate the computer hardware or operating system. By shielding you from the details of the computer or operating system, BASIC reduces the chance that your program accidentally crashes the computer.

Shielding you from having to know the technical details of the computer hardware or operating system is actually another goal of BASIC. By using BASIC, you can focus on solving a problem and not get distracted by the technical details of the computer.

Another goal of BASIC is to provide the programmer with instant feedback. Most programming languages force you to write an entire program before you can run it. BASIC, on the other hand, was originally designed to let you type in a single BASIC command at a time, and the computer tells you right away whether the command works.

Such instant feedback made BASIC programming much easier and faster than traditional programming languages. In addition, such rapid feedback helped novices quickly figure out what they were doing wrong so they could correct their mistakes right away.

The Interactivity of BASIC Interpreters

One reason why programming in the old days was so time-consuming was because you could never run a program until you compiled *(translated)* it into machine language. So if you wrote a program in a language like COBOL, you had to compile it into machine language first. Not only were early compilers notoriously slow (taking hours to compile even the simplest programs), but compilers also required that you write a complete program, even if you just wanted to write a single command.

BASIC avoided this problem by using an interpreter instead. Unlike a compiler that would convert an entire program into machine language, an interpreter would convert each command into machine language and show you the results of your command right away.

Because an interpreter could show you what each command would do, you could see right away if you typed a correct command or not. Such instant feedback could help you catch on to programming faster. Think how fast you can understand a foreign language if you can practice on someone sitting right in front of you. Now think how fast you could understand a foreign language if you had to write a letter to a pen pal overseas and then wait three weeks for a reply. That's the difference between a *compiler* in the old days (like writing and waiting for a letter from overseas) and an *interpreter* (like talking to someone face to face).

Nowadays, compilers are so fast that you can get near-instant feedback with most programming languages, so this initial advantage of BASIC is no longer relevant. Almost all of today's versions of BASIC use a compiler instead of an interpreter.

Turtle graphics with Logo

BASIC introduced the idea of giving programmers instant feedback every time they typed in another BASIC command. If you typed in the following BASIC command:

```
PRINT 2+4
```

The BASIC interpreter would display the following on-screen:

```
6
```

Although giving programmers instant feedback made figuring out programming easier, a computer scientist named Seymour Papert felt that programming should be accessible to everyone, including children. Because few children are excited about adding 2+4 together and seeing the number 6 appear, Seymour Papert thought that a better form of instant feedback for children would involve seeing the results of your program visually.

So in 1967, Seymour invented a new programming language — *Logo* — which was designed especially for teaching children. The main idea behind Logo is that rather than create a program to solve abstract problems, like mathematical equations, Logo shows children how to draw pictures on-screen.

With Logo, you give commands to an imaginary robot commonly called a *turtle*. To write a program (and draw pictures), you have to give the "turtle" commands that tell it which way to move, when to start drawing pictures (known as *turtle graphics*), and when to move without drawing pictures. The following Logo program tells the turtle to draw a square, as shown in Figure 3-1.

```
PENDOWN
FORWARD 100
LEFT 90
FORWARD 100
LEFT 90
FORWARD 100
LEFT 90
FORWARD 100
LEFT 90
```

Figure 3-1: Programming in Logo means giving commands to a "turtle" and telling it where to move to draw pictures.

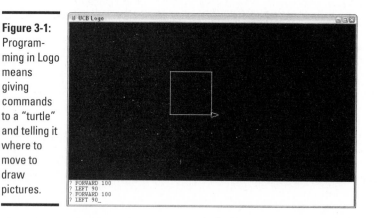

By drawing pictures in Logo, even novice programmers could pick up the principles of programming without even realizing it. Logo has succeeded as an educational tool for both teaching programming and teaching students how to think logically and solve problems. Logo has proven popular for graphics, animation, music, mathematics, and even robotics.

Unlike BASIC though, Logo has remained primarily an educational tool with few programmers using Logo to develop commercial applications. As a result, you're hard pressed to find jobs available for Logo programmers; so Logo is a great language to find out a different way to program a computer, but it's not likely to translate into marketable programming skills any time in the near future. If you study Logo just to explore new ways of thinking, you won't be disappointed.

Logo relies primarily on an interpreter instead of a compiler because an interpreter can give you instant feedback for each command you type into the computer.

The philosophy of Pascal

Unlike BASIC or Logo, which was designed to make programming interactive and fun, Pascal was designed to force programmers to design and organize a program using structured programming techniques (see Book I, Chapter 2).

Early versions of BASIC made it easy to write spaghetti programs because a BASIC program consisted essentially of one glob of commands lumped together inside a single file. The larger your BASIC program got, the more confusing it became to read and understand.

Pascal tackled this problem by encouraging programmers to divide a large program into smaller subprograms. Each subprogram would solve a single problem and act like a Lego building block. Slap enough subprograms together and you could create a much larger and more complicated program.

Although Pascal was initially designed to teach good programming habits, Pascal eventually became popular for writing many commercial programs. Early versions of the Macintosh operating system were even written in Pascal. Computer scientists eventually added so many features to Pascal that Pascal's power could nearly rival that of the C language.

For a brief period of time during the 1980s, Pascal was arguably more popular than BASIC. One of the most popular Pascal compilers of all time was Borland Software's Turbo Pascal, which later morphed into the event-driven, object-oriented programming language that's now known as Delphi (www.turbo explorer.com).

Pascal's greatest strength was that it was almost as easy to understand as BASIC and almost as fast, efficient, and powerful as C. Reading a Pascal program was much easier than reading a similar C program, as the following programs demonstrate.

```
Program Hello_World;

Begin
  Writeln ('Hello World!');
End.
```

Without even knowing much about programming, you can figure out what the preceding Pascal program does, just because Pascal commands consist of descriptive words. Now take a look at the equivalent C program, which is fairly easy to understand, but littered with cryptic characters and symbols:

```
#include <stdio.h>

main()
{
  printf ("Hello World!\n");
}
```

Although Pascal combined the best features from BASIC and C, Pascal's popularity also plummeted because of these similarities, too.

BASIC started adopting structured programming techniques, which made BASIC easier to understand than Pascal but just as easy to write organized programs like Pascal. On the other extreme, C started adopting similar structured programming techniques as well, so you had the power of C with nearly all the advantages of structured programming emphasized by Pascal. Given a choice between using Pascal, which was almost as easy to use as BASIC and almost as powerful as C, or using BASIC (which was easier to figure out than Pascal) or C (which was more powerful than Pascal), programmers found few reasons to use Pascal any more.

Despite Pascal's fading popularity, you can still understand Pascal as a first language and then find a job writing and modifying Pascal programs. However, Pascal programmers aren't in as much demand as C programmers, so study Pascal to better understand good programming principles and then apply those skills to writing programs in other languages.

The inventor of Pascal, Niklaus Wirth, eventually created an improved version of Pascal dubbed Modula-2. The U.S. Department of Defense created a similar programming language, called Ada, which was also based on Pascal. Like Modula-2, Ada was designed to encourage structured programming and allow programmers to create and manage large programs by storing subprograms in separate files called modules (in Modula-2) and packages (in Ada).

Other teaching languages

Although BASIC, Logo, and Pascal may be the more popular teaching languages available, plenty of other people have created their own languages to teach people how to program a computer. Because these languages are developed by individuals or companies, they're *proprietary* languages — a single company or individual controls the language. (In comparison, languages like BASIC, Logo, and Pascal all have official "standards," although most companies that offer BASIC, Logo, or Pascal compilers often deviate from the official "standard" anyway.)

The main disadvantage of proprietary languages is that you probably won't find much work writing programs in any little-known, proprietary language. The advantage of proprietary languages is that they can often be much better at solving specific types of problems. In this case, proprietary teaching languages can make understanding programming much easier and more exciting than BASIC, Logo, or Pascal.

KPL (Kid's Programming Language)

One of the newest proprietary teaching languages is *KPL* (Kid's Programming Language), which you can download for free from www.kidsprogramming language.com. The idea behind KPL is that kids like playing video games, so why not create a programming language that can teach kids how to program their own video games?

Creating video games in languages like BASIC, Logo, or Pascal is difficult, but creating video games in KPL is easy, as shown in Figure 3-2. In the process of creating real video games that they can play, kids also learn to read, type, do math, and understand the principles of computer programming.

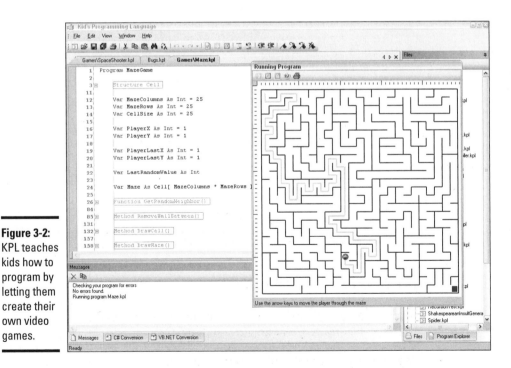

Figure 3-2: KPL teaches kids how to program by letting them create their own video games.

If the idea of using a "kid's" programming language to figure out programming bothers you, grab a copy of KPL's more sophisticated version, *Phrogram* (www.phrogram.com). Like KPL, Phrogram is free. (If you want to compile your video games into programs that you can give or sell to others, buy the commercial version of Phrogram.)

Both KPL and Phrogram use a proprietary language that combines the readability of Pascal with the object-oriented features of more advanced languages, as shown in the following example:

```
Program HelloWorld
    Method Main()
        PrintLine ("Hello, World!")
    End Method
End Program
```

The goal of KPL and Phrogram is to make programming simple, easy, and fun by focusing on graphics, sound, and animation so you can create video games. After you know how to program with KPL or Phrogram, you can migrate to more popular languages later.

Alice

The latest programming technique for creating, organizing, and maintaining large programs is object-oriented programming. Unfortunately, figuring out object-oriented programming can be difficult, especially for beginners who already have enough trouble just figuring out how to program a computer.

So to help beginners understand object-oriented programming, Carnegie Mellon University has created a free programming language dubbed Alice (www.alice.org). To make programming fun and teach object-oriented principles at the same time, Alice lets beginners write simple programs to animate characters on the screen, as shown in Figure 3-3.

When you write an Alice program, your commands create an animated character on-screen. Then you need to write additional commands to tell that animated character how to move to create a simple story. In the process of telling the animated character how to move, you wind up discovering both how to program and how to use object-oriented principles while having fun in the process.

Like most teaching programming languages, Alice programming uses plain English commands, like move forward or play sound. By using simple commands, Alice lets you focus on understanding the principles of object-oriented programming without getting bogged down in understanding the peculiar syntax of a specific programming language.

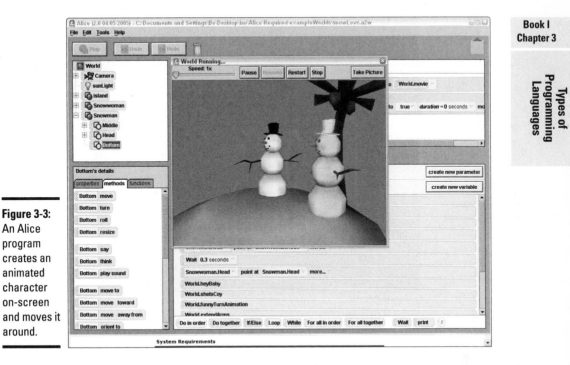

Figure 3-3:
An Alice
program
creates an
animated
character
on-screen
and moves it
around.

Lego Mindstorms

Kids love building things with Lego building bricks, so to encourage kids to
build actual working robots, Lego has released their Lego robot-building kit,
Mindstorms NXT. Not only can you build a working robot with Lego bricks, but
you can also program it using the Lego NXT-G programming language.

To write a program in NXT-G, you don't have to type a thing. Instead, you
create a program by arranging icons that represent different type of actions
your robot can do, such as `move forward` or `respond to a light`. After
writing your program on your computer, you load that program into your
Lego robot and watch it go.

By using Lego Mindstorms NXT, anyone can figure out both programming
skills and robot-making skills. Unlike KPL, Logo, or Alice, Lego Mindstorms
NXT lets you see your working program in action as a walking, rolling, or
crawling Lego robot.

Programming a killer robot

Studying how to program by controlling a Lego robot can be fun, but to combine the thrill of controlling a robot with the joy of playing a video game,
computer scientists have also created games that let you write a simple
program for controlling a battling robot, as shown in Figure 3-4.

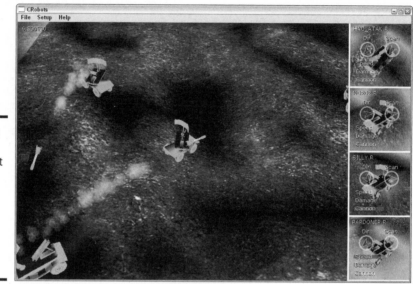

Figure 3-4:
Using a battle robot to study programming can make programming more exciting.

Instead of writing a program just to control a robot, these games force you to write a program to move a robot on-screen, search for other robots nearby, and then attack those other robots with a cannon.

After you finish your program, you can see the results by watching your robot battle another robot in a gladiator-style battle. Write a "good" program, and your robot can defeat another robot. Write a "bad" program, and your robot gets blasted into chunks of (virtual) charred metal.

To program a "battling robot," use a simplified version of a popular programming language, such as Java or C++. That way you not only figure out the basics of a popular programming language, but you can also start writing "real" programs that actually do something interesting right from the start. Table 3-1 lists some popular "battling robot" programming games.

Table 3-1	Popular "Battling Robot" Programming Games	
Program Name	*Language Used*	*Where to Find It*
Robocode	Java	`http://robocode.source-forge.net`
C++ Robots	C++	`http://www.gamerz.net/c++robots`
CRobots-3D	C	`http://antru.ru/crobots3d`

"Curly Bracket" Languages

If you know BASIC or Pascal, you can rush out and start writing programs without ever needing to know another programming language again for the rest of your life. However, it's far more common for programmers to know two or more programming languages. Typically, the one language that most programmers know is one that belongs to a family of related languages known as the "curly bracket" family.

The "curly bracket" language family gets its name because they use curly brackets to define the start and ending of a block of commands, such as

```
#include <stdio.h>

void main()
{
    printf("Notice how the curly brackets\n");
    printf("identify the beginning and end\n");
    printf("of your commands?\n");
}
```

Rather than use curly brackets, many other programming languages use descriptive words, like Begin or End, to identify the start and end of a block of code.

The most popular "curly bracket" language is C. The C language is popular for several reasons:

✦ **Power**

✦ **Efficiency**

✦ **Portability**

The power of C

The C language is a curious combination of assembly language and high-level languages, like BASIC. Like assembly language, C provides commands for directly manipulating every part of the computer, including memory, hard disks, and printers. Like a high-level language, C lets you focus on the logic of your program without worrying about the technical details of the computer so you get the best of both assembly language and high-level languages.

Because C programs are *nearly* (note the emphasis on the word "nearly") as easy to write and understand as high-level languages but still give you the power of accessing the computer's hardware like assembly language, C is often used for creating large, complicated programs (such as operating systems and word processors) along with more exotic programs (like antivirus utilities or disk diagnostic programs).

With great power comes great responsibility, and C is no exception. Because C programs can access every part of the computer's hardware, C programs can fail dramatically by crashing other programs, including the entire operating system.

The efficiency of C

A C compiler tends to create smaller, faster, more efficient programs than compilers for other programming languages. The reason is that the C language is much simpler and thus easier to translate into equivalent machine language commands.

What makes the C language simpler is its small number of commands or keywords. *Keywords* are special commands used in every programming language. The more keywords a programming language uses, the fewer commands you need to make the computer do something. The fewer keywords a programming language offers, the more commands you need to make the computer do something.

Think of keywords like words in a human language. The fewer words you know, the more limited your communication is. If a little kid only knows the word *hot,* he can only express himself in a limited manner, such as describing something as very hot, a little hot, or not so hot. However, if a kid knows a lot of different words, he can express himself much better. Rather than use two or more words to describe something as very hot, a little hot, or not so hot, a kid with a richer vocabulary could describe the same items as scalding, warm, or cool.

A programming language with a lot of keywords means you can write a program with fewer commands. That's great from the programmer's point of view, but inefficient from the computer's point of view.

The more keywords used in a language, the more work the compiler needs to do to translate all these keywords into machine language. As a result, programs written in languages that use a lot of keywords tend to run much slower than programs written in C.

A C program compiles to smaller, more efficient machine language commands because instead of offering a large number of keywords, the C language offers just a handful of keywords. This makes it easy for a compiler to translate the limited number of keywords into machine language.

However, as a programmer, you need to use C's limited number of keywords to create subprograms that mimic the built-in commands of other programming languages. Because this can be impractical, the C language often includes libraries of subprograms that mimic the built-in commands of other programming languages.

The bottom line is that C programs tend to run faster and more efficiently than equivalent programs written in other programming languages. So if you need speed, efficiency, and access to the computer hardware, the C language is the most popular choice.

The portability of C

By using much fewer commands than most programming languages, the C language makes it easy to create compilers that can translate a C program into machine language. Because it's so easy to create C compilers, compared to creating compilers for other programming languages, you can find a C compiler for nearly every computer and operating system.

Theoretically, this means it's possible to take a C program, written on Windows, copy it to another computer and operating system, and run that program on a different operating system, like Linux or Mac OS X, with little or no modifications. When you can copy and run a program on multiple computers and operating systems, the program (and the language it's written in) is portable.

So not only does C create small, fast, and efficient programs, but C also allows you to copy and run your program on different operating systems and computers. Given all these advantages, the C language has few equivalent rivals.

Adding object-oriented programming with C++

Although the C programming language is popular, it's not perfect. When object-oriented programming became popular for designing and maintaining large programs, computer scientists created an object-oriented version of C called C++.

Because more people are writing and organizing large programs with object-oriented programming, more programs are being written in C++. Some people study C so they can understand the peculiarities of the C language. When they feel comfortable with C, they start studying C++ and object-oriented programming.

Other people just skip C and start studying C++ right away. The theory is that as a professional programmer, you'll probably wind up writing and modifying C++ programs anyway, so you might as well study C++ from the start. After you know C++, you pretty much know enough to teach yourself how to write and modify C programs, too.

True portability with Java

Although C and C++ programs are supposed to be *portable* — you can copy and run them on other computers — they're not really. Sometimes, you have to make minor changes to get a C/C++ program to run on another computer, but more often, you have to make major changes.

So that's why Sun Microsystems created the Java programming language. Like C++, Java is also based on the C language, but includes several features to make Java programs safer than C or C++ programs. Specifically, Java isolates the programmer from directly accessing the computer's memory. This reduces the power of Java somewhat, but translates into safer programs that (hopefully) won't crash as often as C/C++ programs do.

Perhaps the most important feature of Java is its portability. Rather than attempt to compile a Java program into machine language for different types of processors, Java compiles Java programs into an intermediate file format called *bytecode* or *pseudocode* (also called *p-code*).

To run a Java program that's compiled into bytecode, you need a free program, or a Java virtual machine (VM). As long as a computer has a Java VM, it can run a Java compiled bytecode program.

Like most promises made by computer scientists, Java programs aren't always portable. It's perfectly possible to write a Java program correctly, compile it to bytecode format, and make the program run perfectly on a specific computer and operating system. But copy that same bytecode program to another computer, and suddenly, the Java program doesn't run correctly. The problem can occur when the Java VM, on the other computer, has errors in it. So although Java programs are more portable than C/C++ programs, they still aren't 100 percent portable.

Besides creating full-fledged programs, like word processors or spreadsheets, Java can also create smaller programs, or *applets,* which can be used to create interactive Web pages.

So if you're looking for a programming language that makes programming safer and more portable, consider Java. Java programmers are in demand almost as much as C/C++ programmers, and the similarities between Java and C/C++ make it relatively easy to understand after you know C. (Or you can study Java first and then study C/C++ later.)

Safer programming with C#

Microsoft took one look at C/C++ and decided they could create an improved language, which they dubbed C# (pronounced *C-sharp*).

C# advantages

C# has a couple advantages over languages such as C, C++, and even Java.

Object oriented

One main advantage of C# over C++ is that C# is a true object-oriented programming language, so you have to use object-oriented programming to write a program in C#.

Forcing you to use only object-oriented programming techniques might seem like a drawback until you realize that C++ is a hybrid language that lets you choose whether to use object-oriented programming. Although C++ gives you, the programmer, more flexibility, C++ programs can also be a mish-mash of structured programming mingled in with object-oriented programming.

Trying to decipher such a mix of programming techniques can be confusing. By forcing all programmers to use object-oriented programming (and isolate their structured programming techniques only inside objects), C# programs can be much easier to understand and modify.

The pros and cons of type-safe languages

So why isn't every programming language type-safe? Good question; here are two reasons:

- ✔ **Creating a type-safe language means more work to create a compiler that can examine an entire program and check to make sure data types (such as `numbers` and `text`) aren't getting changed around unexpectedly.** This translates into a slower and more complicated compiler, which is more work for the programmers who have to create the compiler in the first place.

- ✔ **Type-safe languages can be restrictive,** like trying to ride a motorcycle in a padded suit. The padded suit may protect you, but it also restricts your movement. Similarly, by not checking that data types remain consistent throughout a program, other languages give the programmer more freedom.

Use this freedom wisely and you can create programs without the nuisance of type-safe checking, which can feel like having your mom staring over your shoulder every time you browse the Internet. Use this freedom poorly and you'll wind up writing a program that crashes the computer.

Although non-type-safe languages are popular, the growing trend is to use type-safe languages that protect the programmer from writing programs that can mess up its data and crash the entire computer. Java, C#, and other languages, such as Pascal, are considered type-safe languages.

Type safe

A second advantage of C# is *type-safe* language. Basically, if a C# program stores data, such as a whole number (such as 3 or 49, but not 5.48), the C# compiler checks to make sure no other part of the program accidentally changes that whole number into a decimal.

With languages that aren't type-safe, the compiler lets a program change data types, such as storing a decimal or negative number where the program expects a whole number. Obviously, if your program is expecting a whole number but instead receives a decimal number, the program may get confused and crash.

.NET compatibility

Because Microsoft invented C#, they also invented a special program — the .NET framework. The idea behind the *.NET framework* is that instead of compiling a C# program into machine language, you compile a C# program into *p-code,* which is similar to the bytecode intermediate file format of Java.

Theoretically, you can run a C# program on any computer that has the .NET framework on it. Realistically, the only computers that have the .NET framework are computers running the Windows operating system. So if you write a C# program, you're essentially locked into writing programs that run only under Windows. A band of hardy programmers are trying to rewrite the .NET framework to run under the Linux operating system, but this doesn't have the official blessing of Microsoft, so C# programs are guaranteed to work only on Windows.

The .NET framework allows you to both

✦ **Run C# programs on any computer with the .NET framework.**

✦ **Write programs in multiple languages that all link together through the .NET framework, as shown in Figure 3-5.**

By letting you write a program with different languages, the .NET framework lets you use each language's strengths without being forced to put up with that language's weaknesses.

The only programming languages you can use with the .NET framework are languages specifically designed to work with the .NET framework. So if you want to write a program using a combination of C# and BASIC, you have to find a BASIC compiler that works with the .NET framework, such as Microsoft's own Visual Basic language.

A final advantage of the .NET framework is that it lets you use event-driven programming to create your user interface and then write event handlers in any .NET language, such as C#.

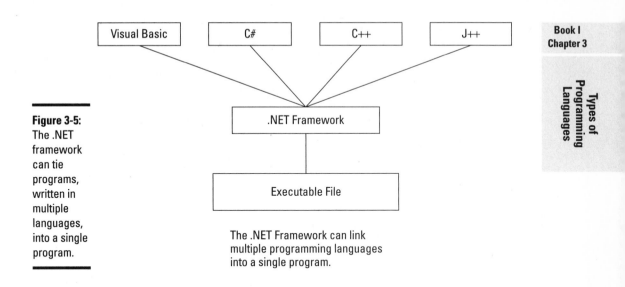

Figure 3-5:
The .NET
framework
can tie
programs,
written in
multiple
languages,
into a single
program.

The .NET Framework can link
multiple programming languages
into a single program.

Because C# is similar to C, C++, and Java, you can study C# first and then study
the other languages (or vice versa). The main drawback with C# is that you can
only use C# to write Windows programs. If you want to write programs for
Linux, Mac OS X, or other operating systems, you can't use C#.

For that reason, many programmers prefer to first understand C or C++, and
then understand C#. If you don't mind being limited to writing only Windows
programs, go ahead and study C#.

Choosing a curly bracket language

If you plan to write programs professionally, you'll probably need to know a
curly bracket language. If you know C, C++, Java, or C#, you can pick up any
of the other curly bracket languages fairly easily:

✦ Knowing C can be great because it's the basis for all the other languages.

   While figuring out C, you can get used to its cryptic syntax without
   having to worry about understanding object-oriented programming at
   the same time.

✦ Begin with C++ if you want to get started using the (currently) most
   popular programming language in the world.

   While figuring out C++, you can ignore its object-oriented features. After
   you feel comfortable with writing C++ programs, you can gradually start
   developing object-oriented programming techniques as well.

If you want to write programs that can run on different computers, use Java:

✦ Java forces you to know object-oriented programming right from the start (like C#), so knowing Java means you can figure out object-oriented programming at the same time. Because Java isn't as confusing as C or C++, understanding Java first is likely much easier than understanding C or C++.

✦ If you're using only a Windows computer, consider trying C#.

The C# language is quickly becoming the standard language for writing Windows programs, so if that's what you want to do, figuring out C# is your best bet. As long as you know at least one curly bracket language, you know one of the most popular programming languages in the world.

Artificial Intelligence Languages

Programming languages, such as C and BASIC, are often considered procedural or functional languages because they divide a large program into separate procedures or functions that tell the computer how to solve a problem step by step.

Although telling the computer what to do step by step might seem like the most logical way to program a computer, another way to program a computer is by using a declarative language. Instead of describing how to solve a problem, declarative programming languages describe

✦ **Facts:** Information about the problem

✦ **Rules:** Relationships between this information

By using facts and rules, programs written in declarative languages can literally figure out an answer on their own without being told explicitly how to do it.

Ultimately, every program, including those written in declarative languages, must get translated into machine language. That means every program must eventually tell the computer how to solve a problem step by step. Declarative languages simply free you from having to describe these steps to the computer.

The most popular declarative programming language is *Prolog* (short for Programming in Logic). A typical Prolog fact might look like this:

```
father("Sally", "Jesse").
```

The preceding fact tells the computer that Jesse is the father of Sally. Now if you want to know who the father of Sally might be, you could ask the following:

```
?- father("Sally", X).
```

Using the fact that earlier stated that the father of Sally was Jesse, the preceding Prolog command would simply return:

```
X = "Jesse".
```

At this point, Prolog simply uses a pre-defined fact to come up with an answer. Notice that even in this simple example, no instructions told the Prolog program how to use the fact that Jesse is the father of Sally.

A list of facts by themselves can be made more useful by including rules that define relationships between facts. Consider the following Prolog program that defines two facts and one rule:

```
father("Jesse", "Frank").
father("Sally", "Jesse").

grandFather(Person, GrandFather) :-
    father(Person, Father),
    father(Father, GrandFather).
```

The two facts tell the computer that Frank is the father of Jesse, and Jesse is the father of Sally. The grandfather rule tells the computer that someone is a grandfather if they're the father of someone's father.

Suppose you typed the following Prolog command:

```
?- grandFather("Sally", Y).
```

The Prolog program tells the computer to use its known facts and rules to deduce an answer, which is:

```
Y = "Frank".
```

In other words, Frank is the grandfather of Sally. (Frank is the father of Jesse, and Jesse is the father of Sally.)

Just from this simple example, you can see how different a Prolog program works compared to a program written in BASIC or C. Instead of telling the computer how to solve a problem, declarative programming languages let you state the facts and the rules for manipulating those facts so the computer can figure out how to solve the problem.

A Prolog program can actually create additional facts (and delete old facts) while it's running, so it can appear to think. That's why Prolog is commonly used in the field of artificial intelligence. The whole idea behind artificial intelligence is to make computers smarter and literally think for themselves. (That's because computer scientists have pretty much given up hope that people will ever get smarter or begin to think for themselves.)

Just as knowing two or more human languages can help you better understand how people communicate, so can knowing two or more different programming languages help you better understand how programming can work. The key is to figure out two different programming languages, like C++ and Prolog. Knowing two similar programming languages, like C++ and C#, doesn't show you much of a difference.

One of the most popular programming languages favored by the artificial intelligence community is LISP (which stands for *LISt Processing*). The basic idea behind LISP is that everything is a list that can be manipulated by the computer. For example, a typical LISP command might look like this:

```
(print "Hello world")
```

This LISP command is a list that displays the following on-screen:

```
"Hello world"
```

The enclosing parentheses define the start and end of a list. A different way to print `"Hello world"` on-screen would be to use this LISP command:

```
(list "Hello world")
```

The preceding command would print the following:

```
("Hello world")
```

In this case, the list command tells the computer to treat `"Hello world"` as a list, so it encloses it in parentheses. Now consider what happens if you insert a command (list) inside another command (list):

```
(list (print "Hello world"))
```

This is how the preceding LISP command works:

1. **The innermost command (list) runs first, which is the (print "Hello world") list. This displays the following on-screen:**

```
"Hello world"
```

2. From the computer's point of view, the original `LISP` command now looks like this:

```
(list "Hello world")
```

This command now displays the following on-screen:

```
("Hello world")
```

So the command

```
(list (print "Hello world"))
```

prints the following:

```
"Hello world"
("Hello world")
```

In the previous example, LISP treats the `(print "Hello world")` list first as a command (to print `"Hello world"` on-screen) and then as data to feed into the list command to display the list `("Hello world")` on-screen.

With traditional programming languages, like C or BASIC, commands and data are separate where data may change but commands never change. With LISP, a list can be both a command and data. That makes it possible for a program to change its lists (treated either as *data* or as a *command*), essentially allowing a program to modify itself while running, which can mimic the learning and thinking process of a human being.

As you can see, both LISP and Prolog offer radically different ways to program a computer compared to C or BASIC. Just as languages, like C and BASIC, free you from the tedium of manipulating registers and memory addresses to program a computer, so do LISP and Prolog free you from the tedium of writing explicit step-by-step instructions to program a computer.

Although the idea that a LISP program can modify its own commands might seem like science fiction, LISP is actually the second oldest programming language still in use today. (FORTRAN is the oldest programming language still in popular use.) LISP was invented in 1958, and although it's been used primarily as a research tool, people have created commercial programs using LISP.

Scripting Languages

Languages, such as C and C++, are often dubbed *system programming languages* because they can create programs that access and manipulate the hardware of a computer, such as an operating system (Linux and Windows) or a utility program (an antivirus or anti-spyware program). However, using systems programming languages, like C++, for everything can get clumsy.

Rather than write an entirely new program from scratch using a systems programming language, more people are likely to use an existing program and customize it in some way. Programming languages that customize existing programs are typically called *scripting languages*.

Scripting languages work with one or more existing programs and act as "glue" that connects different parts of an existing program together. For example, the Microsoft Office suite consists of a word processor (Microsoft Word), a spreadsheet (Microsoft Excel), and a database (Microsoft Access). By using the scripting language that comes with Microsoft Office, you can write a program that can automatically yank information from an Access database, create a chart from that information in an Excel spreadsheet, and then copy both the data and its accompanying chart into a Word document for printing.

Trying to yank information from a database, create a chart with it, and print the data and chart using a systems programming language, like C++ or Pascal, would mean creating everything from scratch including a database, a spreadsheet, and a word processor. By using a scripting language, you use existing components and simply "glue" them together. The existing components do all the work while the scripting language just passes the data from one component to another.

Because scripting languages work with existing programs, they differ from traditional programming languages (like C++ or BASIC) in two important ways.

First, because scripting languages work with one or more existing programs, scripting languages are usually interpreted rather than compiled. Therefore, if someone else wants to run your program, written in a scripting language, they need the source code to your program along with all the programs your scripting program needs, such as Microsoft Word and Microsoft Access. As a result, scripting languages are used less to create commercial applications and more to create custom solutions.

Second, to make scripting languages easy to understand and use, even for non-programmers, most scripting languages are *typeless* languages. (Systems programming languages, like C++ and Pascal, are *strongly-typed* or *type-safe* languages.)

Strongly-typed languages force you to define the type of data your program can use at any given time. So if your program asks the user to type a name, a strongly-typed language makes sure that the user doesn't type in a number by mistake. This protects a program from accidentally trying to manipulate the wrong type of data, which could crash the program as a result.

In comparison, typeless languages don't care what type of data the program stores at any given time. This makes writing programs much easier because your program assumes if it's going to yank data from a particular program, such as Microsoft Excel, the data is probably going to be the right "type" anyway, so type-checking would just be restrictive and tedious.

Scripting languages are typically used in four different ways:

+ **To automate repetitive tasks**

+ **To customize the behavior of one or more programs**

+ **To transfer data between two or more programs**

+ **To create standalone programs**

Automating a program

At the simplest level, scripting languages (also called *macro languages*) can automate repetitive tasks that essentially record your keystrokes so you can play them back at a later time. For example, if you regularly type the term *Campylobacteriosis* (a disease caused by the Campylobacter bacteria), you have two choices:

+ **Type that phrase manually and hope that you spell it correctly each time.**

+ **Type this phrase just once (the easier solution), record your keystrokes, and use those captured keystrokes to create a scripting language program that you can save and run in the future.**

Figure 3-6 shows a scripting language, VBA (Visual Basic for Applications), that's captured keystrokes and saved them in a VBA scripting language program.

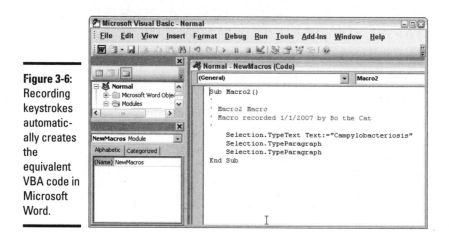

Figure 3-6: Recording keystrokes automatically creates the equivalent VBA code in Microsoft Word.

Customizing a program

Besides letting you automate a program, scripting languages also let you customize a program, which can make the program easier. For example, you might have a spreadsheet that calculates your company's invoices. However, to use this spreadsheet, you need to know the specific place in the spreadsheet to type new invoice information. Type this information in the wrong place, and the spreadsheet doesn't work right.

To avoid this problem, you can write a program in a scripting language that can display a window with boxes to type in new invoice information. Then the scripting language program automatically plugs that new information in the correct place in the spreadsheet every time.

For even more power, a scripting language can combine automation with customization to make programs perform tasks on their own. If you use the Mac OS X operating system, you can use its built-in scripting language — *AppleScript* — to control your Macintosh.

For example, you can write an AppleScript program that tells your computer to download files over the Internet at a specific time each day, move files from one folder to another while renaming those files in the process, or retrieve waiting e-mail messages and sort them into categories. Figure 3-7 shows an AppleScript program that can retrieve stock quotes off the Internet.

Figure 3-7:
AppleScript lets you customize and automate the Mac OS X operating system.

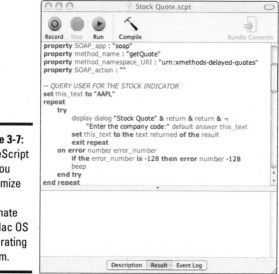

Transferring data among multiple programs

Built-in scripting languages can help you automate or customize a program, but what if you use a program that doesn't include a scripting language? Or what if you need to transfer data between two or more programs, but neither program uses the same scripting language? In these cases, you'll need to use a scripting language that isn't tied to any particular program, such as Perl, Python, Ruby, or JavaScript.

When scripting languages link two or more programs together, the scripting language programs are often referred to as *glue*. So if you have a Web page that lets users type in their names, addresses, and credit card numbers, and a database program that stores customer information, you could use a scripting program to glue the Web page to the database. The user would type information into the Web page, and the scripting language would then yank this data off the Web page and shove it into the database.

By gluing programs together, scripting languages let you combine existing programs to create custom applications. Because scripting languages are interpreted rather than compiled, they can run on any computer with the proper language interpreter. So whether you use Windows, Linux, or Mac OS X, you can still use the same scripting language (and programs) on different computers.

Creating separate applications

Because scripting languages are so easy to understand and use, some scripting languages can create standalone programs. One of the most popular scripting languages used for developing standalone programs is Visual Basic.

Unlike scripting languages, like Perl or Python, which link separate programs together, Visual Basic links program components together. To create a Visual Basic program, you design the program's user interface consisting of pull-down menus, buttons, and check boxes. Then you write Visual Basic commands to link all these separate user interface components together to create a working program.

Like most scripting languages, Visual Basic isn't compiled to machine code like traditional programming languages, such as C++. Instead, Visual Basic programs get stored in an intermediate (p-code) file. To run a Visual Basic program, include a special run-time file, which interprets the p-code file and actually runs the program.

Another popular scripting language used to create standalone applications is *Revolution,* which uses a scripting language similar to AppleScript. Like Visual Basic, Revolution doesn't compile your programs into machine code. Instead, Revolution creates an intermediate file *(p-code)* that attaches directly to a run-time interpreter. Because the Revolution run-time interpreter can run on different operating systems, you can create a Revolution program that can run on different operating systems (such as Windows, Linux, and Mac OS X).

Database Programming Languages

Programming languages, such as C++, are general-purpose languages because they can literally be used to create any type of program from operating systems and word processors to antivirus utilities and video games. However, in the business world, the most common type of custom programs needed are those that store and retrieve data, such as invoices, inventory, customer information, and so on.

Although it's possible to write a database program in C++, that essentially doubles the amount of work you need to do.

+ **Write your program's user interface and commands for manipulating data.**

+ **Write commands to store and retrieve data, essentially creating a database program from scratch.**

Rather than rewrite (and test) your own database program, it's much easier just to customize an existing database program instead. Many database programs include their own programming language. By using a database programming language, you just have to customize the appearance of the database program by designing a user interface along with commands for manipulating data. The database program does all the work of storing, retrieving, and rearranging the actual data so you can focus on what your program should do with data and not with the technical details for how it should store data.

The dBASE programming language

One of the earliest database programming languages for personal computers was dBASE. By using the dBASE language, you could create a user interface, write commands for storing data, and write additional commands for retrieving and manipulating that data.

The following dBASE code creates a simple menu and waits for the user to type in a choice by choosing a number from 1–6.

```
SET TALK OFF
USE CUSTOMER.DAT

STORE 0 TO choice
STORE " No. Name    Title    Address" TO head
DO WHILE choice <> 6
ERASE
```

```
@ 3,1 SAY "
   =====================================================""
@ 4,26 SAY "Main Menu"

@ 5,1 SAY "
   =====================================================""
@ 8,26 SAY "1) Display Customer File"
@ 10,26 SAY "2) Display Record"
@ 12,26 SAY "3) Input Record"
@ 14,26 SAY "4) Delete Record"
@ 16,26 SAY "5) Print Customer File"
@ 18,26 SAY "6) Exit"
STORE 0 TO choice
```

Although the dBASE code may initially look cryptic, you can see how the dBASE language works like traditional programming languages. The SAY command simply prints information on-screen much like the BASIC PRINT command or the C printf command.

At one time, dBASE was so popular that competing companies released similar dBASE-like languages with names like *FoxPro, dBXL,* and *Clipper.* The original dBASE language and all of its various dialects are referred to under the generic name of *xBASE.*

Early versions of the dBASE language were interpreted but later versions were compiled, allowing programmers to write complete database programs and sell them to others. The main difference between dBASE and languages such as C++ is that traditional programming languages can be used to create anything whereas dBASE is meant just for creating programs that need to store and retrieve data.

Three popular database programming languages are

- ✦ **Clarion** (www.softvelocity.com)
- ✦ **4th Dimension** (www.4d.com)
- ✦ **Alpha Five** (www.alphasoftware.com)

One major drawback of database programming languages is that not as many programmers know them compared to traditional languages, like C++ and BASIC. Therefore, if someone writes a custom database application with dBASE, Clarion, 4th Dimension, or Alpha Five, nobody else can modify that program unless they also know dBASE, Clarion, 4th Dimension, or Alpha Five.

Adding database access to traditional languages

Because so many businesses needed programs that manipulated data (hotel reservations, hospital patient tracking, inventory management, and so on), programmers often had to teach themselves a database programming language, such as dBASE, rather than use their favorite programming languages, like C++ or BASIC.

To let programmers continue using their favorite (and familiar) programming languages, many companies started adding database access to their language compilers. Two popular languages that offer database access features include Microsoft's Visual Basic and Borland's Delphi (based on the Pascal programming language).

By adding database features to a familiar language, programmers could continue using their favorite programming language without having to know a completely different database programming language. In addition, programmers could use their favorite language to add more sophisticated features that might be impossible for a database programming language to create, such as the ability to display animation.

Customizing database programs

Perhaps the simplest way to create database applications is to use a database program that includes its own scripting language. By writing simple programs *(scripts),* you can glue the different parts of your database together, such as a script that transfers data from a database file to a user interface.

One of the most popular Windows database programs, Microsoft Access, offers the VBA (Visual Basic for Applications) scripting language. Of course, Microsoft Access runs only on the Windows operating system, so if you need to create database applications that run on both Windows and Mac OS X, you can choose FileMaker (www.filemaker.com).

Like Microsoft Access, FileMaker offers a scripting language: *ScriptMaker.* Best of all, you can create standalone versions of your FileMaker databases and sell them to anyone who uses Windows or Mac OS X.

Many specialized database programs, such as medical office management programs or multilevel marketing programs, have been created using FileMaker.

Comparing Programming Languages

With so many different programming languages available, the real question isn't "Which programming language should I study and use?" Instead, the real question you should ask is "How can I become a better programmer and choose the best language for solving a particular problem?"

Programming languages just offer different ways to express your ideas, and depending on what you need to accomplish, sometimes a language like C++ is best and sometimes another language like LISP might be better. The goal is to choose the best language for the job.

Unfortunately, it's impossible to know and master every programming language, so it's usually best to focus on mastering two or three languages instead. The more you know about using a particular language, the faster and more efficient you can write programs in that language.

A mediocre programmer using a programming language designed for a particular job is likely more efficient than an expert programmer using an inappropriate language for that same job. Assembly language might create the fastest and most efficient programs, but if you need to write a program quickly and you don't care about efficiency, a scripting language like Perl might be much easier and faster. Sometimes, a program that gets the job done now is preferable to a program that works ten times as fast but takes a million times longer to write.

Chapter 4: Programming Tools

In This Chapter

✔ Choosing a compiler and interpreter

✔ Using a virtual machine

✔ Editors, debuggers, toolkits, and profilers

✔ Help file creators

✔ Installers and disassemblers

*T*he two most important tools a programmer needs are an editor and a compiler. An *editor* lets you type and save language commands (called the *source code*) in a plain text file. (Unlike a word processor file, a text file doesn't contain any formatting, like italics or fonts.) A *compiler* converts your source code into machine code and stores those machine code commands in a separate file (often called an *executable file*). After you store your program in an executable file, you can sell and distribute that executable file to others.

An editor and a compiler are absolutely necessary to write and distribute programs. However, most programmers also use a variety of other tools to make programming easier. To help them track down problems *(bugs)* in a program, programmers use a special tool, a *debugger.* To help them identify which parts of a program may be making the entire program run too slow, programmers can use another tool, a *profiler.*

For distributing programs, programmers often use a help file creator and an installer program. The *help file creator* makes it easy for the programmer to create, organize, and display help that the user can read while using the program. The *installer program* makes it easy for users to copy all the necessary files on to their computer so the program runs correctly.

Finally, programmers may also use a special tool — a *disassembler* — which can pry open another program to reveal how it works. Disassemblers are often used by security professionals to analyze how viruses, worms, and spyware programs work. For less honorable uses, programmers can also use a disassembler to dissect a rival program and study how it works.

Programmers often get so attached to their favorite programming tools that they'll argue the merits of their favorite editor or compiler with all the passion of a religious fanatic. Just as there is no single programming language that's the best language to use at all times, so there is no single programming tool that's the best tool to use all the time.

Choosing a Compiler

No two compilers work exactly alike, even compilers designed for the same language, such as two competing C++ compilers. It's perfectly possible (and quite common) to write a program that works perfectly with one compiler but doesn't run at all under another compiler without minor (or massive) changes.

When Microsoft wrote the Macintosh version of their Microsoft Office suite, they used *CodeWarrior,* which is a C++ compiler. Unfortunately, the Code Warrior compiler ran only on the PowerPC processors, which were used in the older Macintosh computers. When Apple switched to Intel processors, Microsoft had to dump the CodeWarrior compiler and use a different compiler, *Xcode.*

Because CodeWarrior and Xcode are both C++ compilers, Microsoft could theoretically compile the same C++ program under both CodeWarrior and Xcode with no problems. Realistically, Microsoft had to rewrite major portions of their C++ programs just to get them to run under the Xcode compiler. So the moral of the story is that switching compilers is rarely an easy decision, so it's important to choose the "right" compiler from the start.

At one time, the CodeWarrior compiler was considered the "right" compiler to use for creating Macintosh programs. What made CodeWarrior suddenly turn into the "wrong" compiler was when Apple switched from PowerPC processors to Intel processors. Everyone who had used the CodeWarrior compiler had to switch to the Xcode compiler. So what may seem like the "right" compiler at the time could later turn out to be the "wrong" compiler later through no fault of your own or the compiler company.

When choosing a compiler, you have to consider your needs, the compiler company's reputation, and the compiler's technical features.

Defining your needs for a compiler

The most important choice for a compiler centers solely on what you need. Follow these steps:

1. **Decide which programming language you want to use.**

If you want to write C++ programs, you need a C++ compiler. If you want to write BASIC programs, you need a BASIC compiler.

2. **Decide which operating system you want to use.**

If you want to write C++ programs for the Mac OS X operating system, your choices immediately narrow down to the small list of C++ compilers that run under the Mac OS X operating system.

3. Choose a compiler that has the best chance of being around years from now.

- Most companies prefer using compilers from brand-name companies, like Intel or Microsoft.

Even compilers from big-name companies are no guarantee against obsolescence. Microsoft has stopped supporting their compilers over the years, such as Microsoft Pascal and Visual Basic 6. So if you used either of these compilers to write a program, you had to change compilers when Microsoft stopped developing them.

- Many people are choosing "open source" compilers.

Open source simply means that the source code to the compiler is available freely to anyone. Not only does this mean that open source compilers are free (compared to the hundreds of dollars you can pay for a brand-name compiler from Intel or Microsoft), but open source also guarantees that the compiler can't become obsolete due to lack of support.

If you use a compiler from a company that goes out of business, you're forced to transfer (or *port*) your program to another compiler, which means having to rewrite the program to run under a different compiler.

Because anyone can examine and modify the source code to an open source compiler, anyone can make changes to the compiler to improve it. One of the most popular open source compilers is GCC (http://gcc.gnu.org), which stands for *GNU Compiler Collection.*

Xcode, the free compiler that Apple distributes with every Macintosh computer, is actually the GCC compiler.

Originally, GCC only compiled C source code, but later versions of GCC now compile several different languages, including C, C++, Java, Ada, and Objective-C, with more programming languages being supported every day. Even better, the GCC compiler also runs on a variety of operating systems, such as Windows and Linux, so if you write a program using the GCC compiler, you can recompile your program to run under another operating system with minimal (hopefully) changes.

The GCC compiler actually consists of two parts:

✦ The **front-end** of the compiler translates source code into an intermediate format.

- To write C++ programs, you must use the C++ front-end of the GCC compiler.

- To write Ada programs, use the Ada front-end of the GCC compiler.

- By creating front-ends for different languages, programmers can make the GCC compiler compile more programming languages.

✦ The **back-end** of the compiler finishes translating the intermediate code into actual machine code.

Evaluating the technical features of a compiler

After you choose a particular programming language and pick which operating systems you want your programs to run on, your list of compiler choices is likely narrowed down to one or two choices. Given two compilers that both meet your needs, you can pick the "best" compiler by examining their technical features.

The technical features of a compiler are meaningless if

✦ The compiler stops being developed and supported.

✦ The compiler can't run under the operating system or processor you need in the future.

✦ A particular technical feature is something you don't need or care about.

Supported language standards

No two compilers are alike, even those that compile the same programming language, such as C++. The problem is that every programming language has an official "standard," but the standard for most programming languages is usually far behind what people in the real world are actually using. (By the time an official standards committee agrees on the features of a given programming language, programmers have already created new features that eventually become standards in future versions of that language.)

As a result, most compilers support a given language standard plus additional features that programmers have developed. Therefore, every compiler actually works with a different dialect of a programming language. So C++ programs that run under the Microsoft Visual C++ compiler may or may not run the same when compiled under the GCC compiler, even though both compilers claim to support the "standard" C++ programming language.

Language standards are nice but generally useless when comparing compilers. What's more important is whether a particular compiler offers the specific features you need or want, regardless of whatever particular standard it may follow.

Code generation and optimization

Every compiler converts source code into machine language, but some compilers can translate source code into more efficient machine language commands than other compilers. As a result, it's possible to compile the same C++ program under two different C++ compilers and create identically working programs that consist of different machine language instructions.

The goal of every compiler is to create a program that takes up as little memory and disk space as possible while running as fast as possible. Usually, compilers make a trade off. To make a program run faster, the executable file may take up a large amount of disk space or require a lot of memory. If the compiler can reduce the size of your program and the amount of memory it needs to run, it may create a slow program.

To help you tweak your program for the best balance of speed, size, and memory requirements, many compilers offer optimization settings. By fiddling with these optimization settings, you can tell the compiler how to speed up or shrink your program, as shown in Figure 4-1.

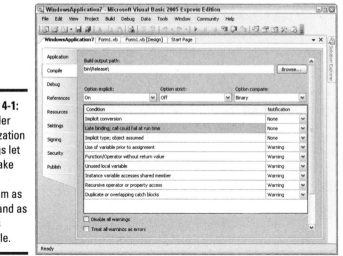

Figure 4-1:
Compiler optimization settings let you make your program as small and as fast as possible.

One major feature of a compiler's code generation capabilities involves speed, which can measure two different features:

✦ **Speed can refer to how quickly the compiler works in translating your source code to machine code.**

In the old days, compilers could take hours or days to compile a simple program. Nowadays, compilers often work in minutes or even seconds. Shove in a program that consists of 800,000 lines of code, and in less than a minute, the compiler can create an executable file for you. The faster the compiler works, the less time you waste running and testing your program.

✦ **The speed of a compiler can refer to the performance of the machine language code that the compiler creates.**

Given the same program, one compiler may create a program that runs quickly whereas a second compiler may create that same program that runs much slower.

Ideally, you want a compiler that both *compiles* fast and creates programs that *run* fast.

Target platforms

Most compilers can compile programs only for a specific operating system, such as Windows or Linux. However, what happens if you need to write a program that runs on two or more operating systems?

You could write the program twice with two different compilers — one for each operating system. So if you wanted to write a C++ program that runs under Windows and Mac OS X, you could compile that program by using Microsoft Visual C++ (for Windows) and then write a similar program to compile by using Xcode (for Mac OS X).

Of course, writing the same program two times for two different compilers on separate operating systems is a tremendous waste of time. As an alternative, some compilers are known as *cross-compilers* — they can create programs that work on multiple operating systems, such as Windows, Linux, and Mac OS X. Figure 4-2 shows the REALbasic cross-compiler, which lets you choose whether to compile a program for Windows, Linux, or Mac OS X.

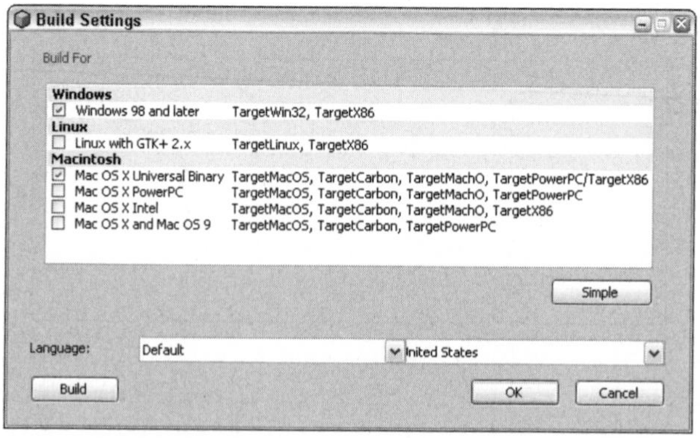

Figure 4-2:
A cross-compiler lets you write a program and compile it for multiple operating systems at the click of a mouse.

Build Settings
Build For
Windows
☑ Windows 98 and later TargetWin32, TargetX86
Linux
☐ Linux with GTK+ 2.x TargetLinux, TargetX86
Macintosh
☑ Mac OS X Universal Binary TargetMacOS, TargetCarbon, TargetMachO, TargetPowerPC/TargetX86
☐ Mac OS X PowerPC TargetMacOS, TargetCarbon, TargetMachO, TargetPowerPC
☐ Mac OS X Intel TargetMacOS, TargetCarbon, TargetMachO, TargetX86
☐ Mac OS X and Mac OS 9 TargetMacOS, TargetCarbon, TargetPowerPC
Simple
Language: Default United States
Build OK Cancel

With a cross-compiler, you can write a program once and compile it to run on multiple operating systems, effectively doubling or tripling your potential market. Without a cross-compiler, you need to write a program for each compiler, under a different operating system, essentially doubling or tripling your work.

Although the idea of writing a program once and having it run on multiple operating systems might seem appealing, cross-compilers aren't perfect. Chances are good you'll have to tweak your program to run under each operating system, but those minor tweaks can be much easier than rewriting huge chunks of your program if you had to use two separate compilers.

Cost

Paying more for a compiler doesn't necessarily mean you're getting a better compiler. The GCC compiler is free and is one of the best compilers available. Generally, if you want to use a popular programming language, such as C++, you can find a free compiler, but if you want to use a more obscure programming language, such as LISP or Modula-2, you'll probably have to pay for a compiler.

Because Windows is the most common operating system in the world, you can find plenty of free compilers. Some of these compilers are free only for personal use, but if you want to create programs to sell commercially, you have to pay for the compiler. Table 4-1 lists some popular free Windows compilers.

Table 4-1	Free Windows Compilers	
Compiler Name	*Programming Language*	*Where to Find It*
GCC	C, C++, Objective-C, Java, FORTRAN, and Ada	http://gcc.gnu.org
Visual Basic Express 2005	BASIC	http://msdn.microsoft.com/vstudio/express
Visual C# Express 2005	C#	http://msdn.microsoft.com/vstudio/express
Visual C++ Express 2005	C++	http://msdn.microsoft.com/vstudio/express
Turbo C++	C++	www.turboexplorer.com
Turbo C#	C#	www.turboexplorer.com
Turbo Delphi	Pascal	www.turboexplorer.com
Dev-C++	C++	www.bloodshed.net
Dev-Pascal	Pascal	www.bloodshed.net
Free Pascal	Pascal	www.freepascal.org
Visual Prolog	Prolog	www.visual-prolog.com
GNU Prolog	Prolog	http://gprolog.inria.fr

The Mac OS X operating system is much less common than Windows, so you can choose from far fewer free compilers. However, Table 4-2 lists some Mac OS X compilers that you can use for free.

Table 4-2	Free Mac OS X Compilers	
Compiler Name	*Programming Language*	*Where to Find It*
Xcode	C, C++, Objective-C	`http://developer. apple.com/tools/xcode`
GNU Pascal	Pascal	`www.gnu-pascal.de`
Free Pascal	Pascal	`www.freepascal.org`

The original Macintosh operating system was written in Pascal, but the newer Mac OS X operating system is written in Objective-C.

Because Linux is free, most Linux compilers are free as well. Table 4-3 lists some popular free Linux compilers. The REALbasic Linux compiler is free, but if you want REALbasic's cross-compilation feature to develop programs for Windows and Mac OS X, you have to pay for the professional edition. Likewise, the Intel C++ and FORTRAN compilers are free only for non-commercial use. If you plan to develop commercial applications, you have to pay for the compiler.

Table 4-3	Free Linux Compilers	
Compiler Name	*Programming Language*	*Where to Find It*
GCC	C, C++, Objective-C, Java, FORTRAN, and Ada	`http://gcc.gnu.org`
GNU Prolog	Prolog	`http://gprolog. inria.fr`
GNU Pascal	Pascal	`www.gnu-pascal.de`
Free Pascal	Pascal	`www.freepascal.org`
REALbasic	BASIC	`www.realbasic.com`
Intel C++	C++	`www.intel.com`
Intel FORTRAN	FORTRAN	`www.intel.com`

Finding an Interpreter

Interpreters are commonly used for scripting languages, such as Perl or Python, but rarely used for systems programming languages, such as C++. That's because if you write a program and use an interpreter, you must distribute a copy of your source code with the interpreter. Giving away your source code essentially gives away your program, so most commercial programs use a compiler instead.

In the old days, many companies sold language interpreters (the most popular were interpreters for running BASIC programs), but nowadays, most interpreters are given away for free as part of an operating system (such as Mac OS X) or another program (such as Microsoft Word). Interpreters for open source programming languages, such as Perl, Python, and Ruby, are also given away for free.

Operating system interpreters

One of the most common uses for an interpreter is for creating short programs to automate another program, such as an operating system. The Mac OS X operating system includes an interpreter, dubbed *Script Editor,* for running programs with the AppleScript language. After you write a program *(script)* that's particularly useful, you can even compile it into a standalone program, too.

The Script Editor program is usually buried inside the Applications folder on your Macintosh's hard disk.

Although Windows doesn't include a similar macro language interpreter, you can visit Microsoft's web site (`www.microsoft.com/downloads`) and download *Microsoft PowerShell,* a free interpreter.

PowerShell is designed for *system administrators* (people who need to control multiple computers, such as those connected to a network) to control and automate Windows. By writing simple programs in PowerShell, administrators can automate their routine tasks, such as starting or stopping a program, or moving files from one location to another.

PowerShell consists of simple commands (called `command-lets` or `cmdlet`) that perform a single task. By combining multiple `cmdlets` together where one `cmdlet` feeds data into another `cmdlet`, you can create more complicated programs.

Web page interpreters

Nearly every Web browser comes with a JavaScript interpreter. Web page designers use JavaScript for creating interactive Web pages, verifying information typed on a Web page (such as a username and password), or opening pop-up windows that display advertisements.

JavaScript is the programming language used to create DashBoard *widgets,* which are mini-programs that can pop up on the screen of a Mac OS X computer.

Most Web browsers include a free JavaScript interpreter, but to avoid trademark problems, Microsoft calls their JavaScript interpreter *JScript,* which they include with their Internet Explorer browser.

The advantages of interpreted languages

A program run by an interpreter is almost always slower than the same program compiled into machine language, so why not compile every language rather than run them under an interpreter?

One of the reasons is that creating a compiler for multiple operating systems is much more difficult than creating an interpreter for multiple operating systems. To create a compiler, you need to know how to translate a programming language into machine code, but because operating systems can run under different processors (such as the PowerPC or Intel processors), you have to translate language commands into completely different machine language commands. Creating a compiler that works correctly for one processor is hard enough, but creating that same compiler to work under multiple processors identically and error-free is much more difficult.

Compiling a program into machine language is great when you want to distribute a program to others. However, languages like Ruby or Perl are often used to create short programs that run on a Web server. Using an interpreter may run a program slower, but you can write a program and run it right away without compiling it first. Also, by running the source code directly, interpreters let you see the source code of each program that's running, so you can edit that source code and run it right away to see how your changes affect the program. You can still do this with a compiler, but having to compile a program and then store a separate executable version of that program is a minor annoyance that you can avoid completely just by using an interpreter.

✔ Compilers are great for distributing programs.

✔ Interpreters are much better for writing and running shorter programs when you don't care whether anyone can see or copy the source code.

Although JavaScript interpreters can be found in any Web browser, you may have to download and install interpreters for other programming languages. Some popular programming languages for running programs on Web *servers* (those computers responsible for displaying and retrieving information from Web pages, such as shopping data) include

✦ **PHP** (www.php.net)

✦ **Perl** (www.perl.com)

✦ **Python** (www.python.org)

✦ **Ruby** (www.ruby-lang.org)

The preceding four languages not only have free interpreters that you can copy, but their interpreters also run on different operating systems. That means a Ruby or Perl program written on a Windows computer should run identically if copied and run on a Linux or Mac OS X computer.

Compiling to a Virtual Machine

The problem with compilers is that they're difficult to make for multiple operating systems and processors. The problem with interpreters is that they need the source code of a program to run, making interpreters unsuitable for distributing software. To solve both these problems, computer scientists created a third alternative — a virtual machine.

To protect the source code of a program, a *virtual machine* lets you compile your program into an intermediate file called *bytecode* or *pseudocode* (also known as *p-code*). To make a program run on multiple operating systems, you need a virtual machine that runs on each operating system, as shown in Figure 4-3.

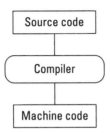

A compiler normally converts source code directly into machine code for a specific type of processor.

Figure 4-3:
A virtual machine acts like a combination of an interpreter and a compiler.

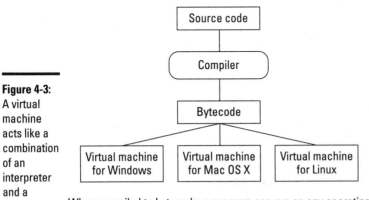

When compiled to bytecode, a program can run on any operating system that has the bytecode virtual machine installed.

When you compile a program into bytecode, it's still possible to reverse engineer, or *disassemble,* that bytecode file and view the original source code.

The most popular programming language that uses a virtual machine is Java (http://java.sun.com), which was created by Sun Microsystems. The idea behind Java is to let you write a single program in Java, compile it into a bytecode file, and then distribute that bytecode file to any computer that has a Java virtual machine installed.

IBM has created and released its own Java compiler dubbed *Jikes* (http://jikes.sourceforge.net), which is supposedly faster than the official Java compiler from Sun Microsystems. Another Java compiler, GCJ (http://gcc.gnu.org/java), can compile Java programs into either bytecode or machine code.

Theoretically, you can write a program once and make it run on Windows, Linux, and Mac OS X with no modifications whatsoever. Realistically, you may still need to tweak the program a bit to get it to run flawlessly on different operating systems, but that's still much easier than writing a program from scratch for another operating system.

Although Java can run the same program on multiple operating systems, the virtual machine will never be as fast as a similar compiled program. As a result, Java programs can run sluggishly, especially on older computers.

Despite these drawbacks, Java has grown in popularity. Many companies write and sell programs entirely written in Java. As computers get faster and Sun Microsystems improves the performance of its virtual machine, programs written in Java probably will run fast enough for most uses.

Writing a Program with an Editor

To write programs, you need an editor, which acts like a special word processor just for helping you write commands in your favorite programming language. After you type your program commands in an editor, you can save this file (known as the *source code*). Then, you can feed this source code file into a compiler to turn it into a working program.

Editors

You can choose from two types of editors. Your best bet probably depends on whether you write programs in more than one programming language.

Standalone

A *standalone editor* is nothing more than a separate program that you run when you want to edit your program. You run the *compiler* separately.

If you regularly write programs in different programming languages, you might want to use a standalone editor. That way you can get familiar with all the features of a single editor.

You can buy standalone editors, but here are two popular free ones. Both of these editors run on multiple operating systems (such as Windows and Linux):

✦ **GNU Emacs (www.gnu.org/software/emacs/emacs.html)**

✦ **VIM (www.vim.org)**

The sidebar, "Common editor features," lists features you find in most editors, including standalone editors.

Integrated development environment (IDE)

An *integrated development environment (IDE)* combines an editor with a compiler in a single program so you can easily edit a program and compile it right away. An IDE gives you access to these features within a consistent user interface, as shown in Figure 4-4.

If you mostly write programs in a single programming language, using an IDE can be more convenient than a standalone editor.

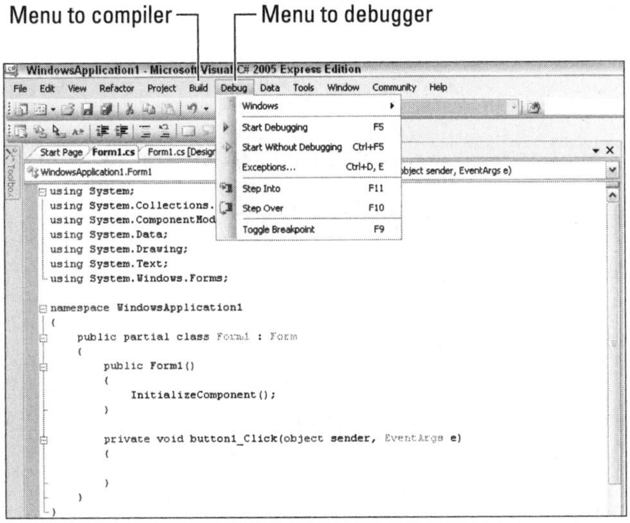

Menu to compiler ⌐ ⌐ Menu to debugger

Figure 4-4:
An IDE
provides
access to
multiple
program-
ming tools
within a
single user
interface.

Common editor features

Whether you prefer a standalone editor or an integrated development environment (IDE), most editors offer the following features:

✔ **Multiple undo/redo commands** let you experiment with making changes to your source code. If they don't work out, you can "undo" your changes.

Typically, editors let you undo a large number of changes you made, such as the last 100 changes.

✔ **Multiple file editing** comes in handy so you can view different files in separate windows and copy code from one window to another, or just study how one part of your program will interact with another part of that same program.

✔ **Syntax completion and highlighting** is when the editor recognizes certain programming languages, such as C++ and Java. The moment you type a valid language command, the editor can finish typing that command for you at the touch of a button, thereby, saving you time. So if you type a typical IF-THEN statement, the editor automatically types in a generic IF-THEN statement (complete with necessary parentheses), so you just type in the actual data to use.

✔ **Syntax highlighting** occurs after you write a program; the editor highlights valid language commands to help you separate language commands from any data and commands you create. Without syntax highlighting, source code can look like a mass of text. With syntax highlighting, source code can be easier to read and understand.

✔ **Macros** let you customize the editor and essentially program the editor to repeat commonly needed tasks, such as always displaying program commands in uppercase letters.

✔ If the editor doesn't offer a feature you want or need, its macro language lets you add that feature in. Without a macro language, an editor won't give you the flexibility to work the way you want.

✔ **Project management** helps you keep your source code files organized. Most programs no longer consist of a single file, but of multiple files. Trying to keep track of which files belong to which project can be confusing, so an editor can help you store and organize your files so you won't lose track of them.

Features

In addition to a compiler and all the usual features of standalone editors (as listed in the sidebar, "Common editor features"), many IDEs include other features in a convenient user interface:

✦ **Debugger** helps identify problems in your program.

✦ **File management** helps organize the source code for your various projects.

✦ **Profiler** helps identify which parts of your program may be slowing down the performance of your entire program.

✦ **GUI designer** helps you design the appearance of your program's windows, pull-down menus, and buttons.

Free software

Many compilers come with their own IDE, but you can always use another IDE or a standalone editor instead. These IDEs are popular (and free):

✦ **NetBeans:** `www.netbeans.org`

   Designed for writing Java programs but can also be used for writing C/C++ programs as well. Available for multiple operating systems.

✦ **Eclipse:** `www.eclipse.org`

   Designed for writing Java programs, but can also be used for writing C/C++, PHP, and even COBOL programs as well. Available for multiple operating systems.

✦ **SharpDevelop:** `www.icsharpcode.net`

   A Windows-only IDE designed for writing C# and Visual Basic.NET programs.

Fixing a Program with a Debugger

Eventually, everyone makes a mistake writing a program. That mistake could be as simple as typing a command wrong or forgetting a closing parenthesis, or it can be as complicated as an algorithm that works perfectly except when receiving certain data. Because writing error-free programs is nearly impossible, most programmers use a special tool — a debugger.

Program errors are dubbed *bugs,* so a *debugger* helps you find and eliminate bugs in your program.

Two common debugger features include

✦ **Tracing or stepping**

✦ **Variable watching**

Not all bugs are equal:

✦ Some bugs are just **annoying,** such as the wrong color on a pull-down menu.

✦ Some bugs are **critical,** such as a bug that adds two numbers wrong in an accounting program.

✦ Any bug that keeps a program from running correctly is a **show stopper.**

Stepping line by line

Stepping (or *tracing*) lets you run your program, line by line, so you can see exactly what the program is doing at any given time. The second you see your program doing something wrong, you also see the exact command in your program that caused that problem. Then you can fix the problem, as shown in Figure 4-5.

Sometimes when programmers find one error and fix it, their fix accidentally creates another error in the program.

Here are the two types of debuggers:

+ **Source-level:** Lets you examine your source code line by line. So if you write a program in BASIC, a source-level debugger shows you each line of your entire BASIC program.

+ **Machine-language:** Lets you examine the machine language code, line by line, that your compiler created from your source code. Programmers often use machine-language debuggers to examine programs when they don't have access to the source code, such as a computer virus or a rival's program.

Stepping line by line through a small program may be feasible, but in a large program that consists of a million lines of code, stepping line by line would take far too long. So to make stepping easier, most debuggers include break-points and stepping over/stepping out commands.

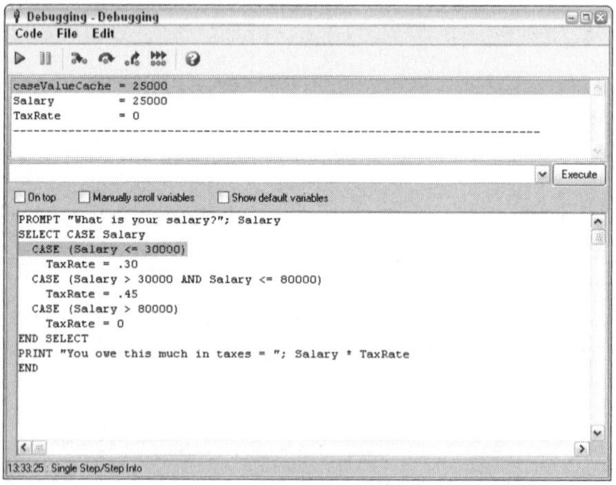

Figure 4-5:
Stepping
through a
program,
line by line,
can help
you find
errors or
bugs in your
program.

```
 Debugging - Debugging
Code  File  Edit

 ▷  II   ⅔  ⟳  ⸖  ≫   ?

caseValueCache = 25000
Salary         = 25000
TaxRate        = 0
-----------------------------------------------------------------

                                              ▾   Execute
□ On top    □ Manually scroll variables   □ Show default variables
PROMPT "What is your salary?"; Salary
SELECT CASE Salary
    CASE (Salary <= 30000)
        TaxRate = .30
    CASE (Salary > 30000 AND Salary <= 80000)
        TaxRate = .45
    CASE (Salary > 80000)
        TaxRate = 0
END SELECT
PRINT "You owe this much in taxes = "; Salary * TaxRate
END

13:33:25 : Single Step/Step Into
```

Breakpoints

A *breakpoint* lets you skip over the parts of your program that you already know work. So if you have a program that's 10,000 lines long and you know the problem is somewhere in the last 1,000 lines of code, there's no point stepping through those first 9,000 lines of code.

A breakpoint lets you tell the computer, "Skip from the beginning of the program to the breakpoint and then step through the rest of the program line by line." Figure 4-6 shows how you can highlight a line with a breakpoint. That way your program runs from the beginning to the first breakpoint. After your program stops at a breakpoint, you can step through the rest of your program line by line.

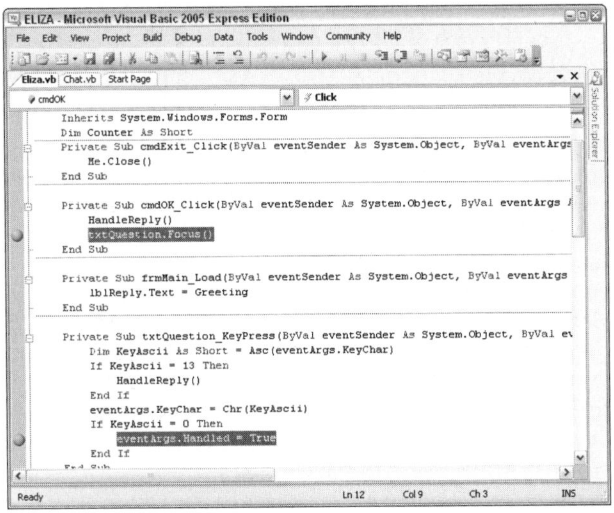

Figure 4-6:
Breakpoints let you skip over parts of your program that you don't want to examine line by line.

Over and out

The stepping over and stepping out commands are used to debug a large program that consists of multiple subprograms. Normally, stepping would force you to examine every subprogram, line by line. However, what if you know the problem isn't in a specific subprogram?

By using the step over and step out commands, you can avoid stepping through lines of code stored in a subprogram.

Step over

To avoid stepping through every subprogram, debuggers let you use the step over command. This tells the computer, "See that entire subprogram? Treat it as a single command and don't bother stepping through it line by line." Figure 4-7 shows how the step over command works.

The step over command lets you completely skip over any lines of code stored inside of a subprogram.

Step out

Suppose you start examining a subprogram line by line and suddenly want to stop. As an alternative to stepping through the rest of the subprogram, you can use the `step out` command, which tells the computer, "Stop stepping through the subprogram line by line right now!"

Watching variables

When you step or trace through a program, line by line, you can see how the program works. For more insight into your program's behavior, you can *watch your variables.*

You can read more about variables in Book II, Chapter 2. For now, just think of a *variable* as a temporary place to store data, such as a number or a word.

Watching a variable lets you see what data your program is storing and using at any given time. That way if your program is supposed to print a name but actually prints that person's phone number, you can step through your program line by line, and watch to see which line stores the wrong data for the program to print.

Not only can you "watch" how your program stores data, but a debugger also lets you change data while your program is running. By changing data, you can see how your program responds.

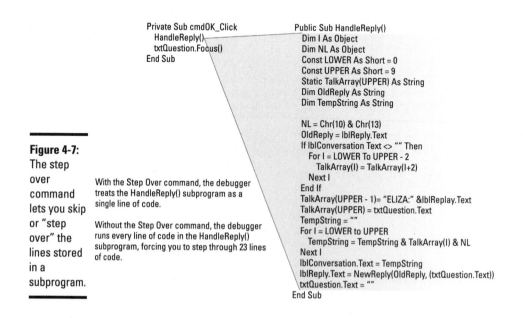

Figure 4-7:
The step over command lets you skip or "step over" the lines stored in a subprogram.

With the Step Over command, the debugger treats the HandleReply() subprogram as a single line of code.

Without the Step Over command, the debugger runs every line of code in the HandleReply() subprogram, forcing you to step through 23 lines of code.

```
Private Sub cmdOK_Click
    HandleReply()
    txtQuestion.Focus()
End Sub
```

```
Public Sub HandleReply()
    Dim I As Object
    Dim NL As Object
    Const LOWER As Short = 0
    Const UPPER As Short = 9
    Static TalkArray(UPPER) As String
    Dim OldReply As String
    Dim TempString As String

    NL = Chr(10) & Chr(13)
    OldReply = lblReply.Text
    If lblConversation.Text <> "" Then
        For I = LOWER To UPPER - 2
            TalkArray(I) = TalkArray(I+2)
        Next I
    End If
    TalkArray(UPPER - 1)= "ELIZA:" &lblReplay.Text
    TalkArray(UPPER) = txtQuestion.Text
    TempString = ""
    For I = LOWER to UPPER
        TempString = TempString & TalkArray(I) & NL
    Next I
    lblConversation.Text = TempString
    lblReply.Text = NewReply(OldReply, (txtQuestion.Text))
    txtQuestion.Text = ""
End Sub
```

For example, suppose a program asks the user to type in his age. If you run your program and type in a valid age, such as **15**, you can see how your program handles the number 15. But what happens if the user types in an invalid number, such as **0** or **-17**?

A good programmer always makes sure the program doesn't accept invalid data, but suppose part of your program changes the age data by mistake. Depending on the age, sometimes the program changes the age to 0, sometimes it changes it to a negative number (-12), sometimes it changes it to an outrageously large number (486).

To find out how and why your program seems to randomly change the age, you can step through your program and watch the number stored as the age. By changing your variable while the program is running, you can type in different age values to see how your program responds.

By doing this, you can suddenly see that any time the age is less than 5, your program turns the age into 0; any time the age is greater than 5 but less than 45, the program turns the age into a negative number; and any time the age is greater than 45, the program turns the age into a huge number, like 486.

Without the ability to change the value of the age variable while the program is running, debugging a program is much slower and more tedious. By changing the value of the age variable while the program is running, you can test different values without having to trace through the program multiple times using different values. Just run the program once and change the value of the age variable as many times as you want, as shown in Figure 4-8.

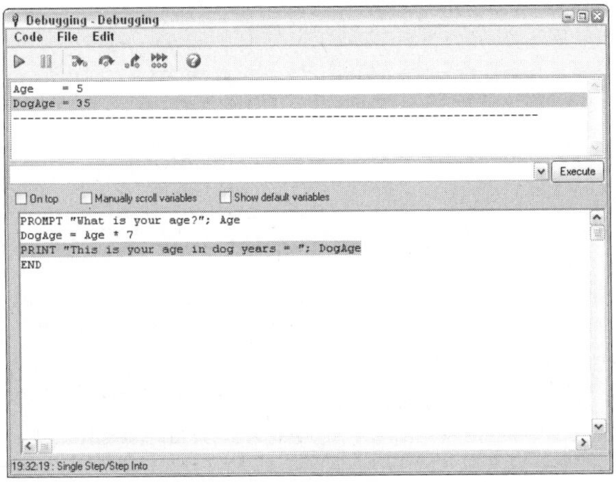

Figure 4-8:
Watching and changing variables can show you how a program reacts to different data.

Saving Time with Third-Party Components

Programmers are naturally lazy and often look for the simplest way to solve any problem. So when faced with creating a program, programmers prefer to cheat by using *third-party components,* which are programs that somebody else has created already (and hopefully tested).

Third-party components usually offer commonly needed features, such as a word processor, a spreadsheet, or a database, that you can plug into your own program. So instead of having to write your own word processor, you can buy a word processor component and plug it into your own program; now your program has word processing capabilities with little additional programming on your part.

Third-party components can give your program instant features, but they can also give you instant problems, too. If the third-party component doesn't work right, your program won't work right either and you can't fix the problem until the company that sells the third-party component fixes the problem. Basically, third-party components put you at the mercy of another company. If that other company stops updating and improving their component, you're stuck with an outdated and possibly buggy component.

Depending on the features, third-party components can range in cost from a few hundred dollars to a few thousand dollars or more. Most third-party components aren't cheap, but because they can save you a lot of time, they may be worth the price.

Optimizing a Program with a Profiler

Not all parts of a program are equal. Some parts of a program may only run once or twice, whereas other parts of a program may run hundreds or even thousands of times. For example, suppose you have a program that stores names and addresses. To use this program, you must first type in your name and password before you can sort and search through the program's list of names and addresses.

In this example, the part of the program that asks for a username and password runs only once, but the part of the program that searches and sorts through your list of names and addresses may run multiple times. So which part of your program determines its speed? The part that runs once (asking for a username and password) or the part that runs multiple times (searching and sorting names and addresses)?

Obviously, if you want to speed up your program, you'd focus on the part that runs most often, and that's what a profiler does. A *profiler* examines your program and identifies the most frequently used parts of that program. After you know which parts of your program run most often, you can work on making that part of the program run faster, a process known as *optimizing*.

Profilers typically use two methods for examining a program:

✦ **Sampling:** This examines your entire program at fixed time intervals. Through sampling, a profiler can get a rough estimate on which parts of your program (often referred to as *hot spots*) are being run most often.

✦ **Instrumentation mode:** After you use sampling to identify hot spots, you can use this mode to examine the program in more detail to determine exactly what each program line does.

By identifying the hot spots, you can speed up your entire program by rewriting or optimizing those frequently run parts of the program.

By optimizing a small part of your program, such as ten percent of that program, you can often improve the entire program's performance dramatically.

Creating a Help File

Hardly anyone reads software manuals, so when people need help, they typically turn to the program's help file for answers. This *help file* is essentially the software manual organized as miniature Web pages that you can view and click to see similar (linked) information, as shown in Figure 4-9.

Almost every program has a help file, but creating a help file can be tedious and time-consuming. So to simplify this process, many programmers use special help file creation programs.

Just as a word processor makes it easy to write, edit, and format text, help file creators make it easy to write, edit, organize, and link text together to create a help file.

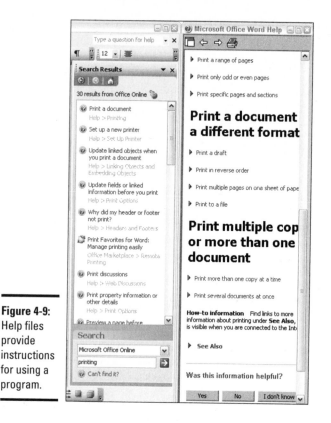

Figure 4-9:
Help files
provide
instructions
for using a
program.

Installing a Program

Before anyone can use your program, they need to install it. Because programs can consist of dozens of separate files, most programs use a special installation program that makes sure all necessary files are copied on to a user's computer.

To use an installation program, identify all the files that make up your program and where to store them — either in a single location (folder) or scattered in multiple locations (folders).

Although the main purpose of an installer is to make sure all program files get copied to the user's hard disk, installers often give you the option of displaying graphics or playing music while your program installs on the user's computer. You can specify which graphic and audio files to display and play as well as how long to display and play them, as shown in Figure 4-10.

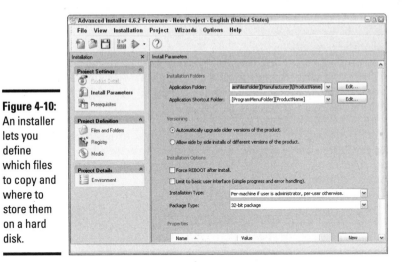

Figure 4-10:
An installer
lets you
define
which files
to copy and
where to
store them
on a hard
disk.

Dissecting Programs with a Disassembler

A disassembler acts like a reverse compiler. A compiler converts your program (written in any programming language, such as C++ or Pascal) into machine language, a disassembler takes an executable file (which contains machine language code) and converts it into assembly language.

Disassemblers can't convert machine language back into its original source code language (such as C++) because disassemblers can't tell which programming language was originally used. An executable file created from a C++ program looks no different than an executable file created from a Pascal or BASIC program. Therefore, disassemblers simply convert machine language into assembly language.

Disassemblers have both honorable and shady uses. On the honorable side, antivirus companies use disassemblers to dissect how the latest viruses, worms, and Trojan Horses work. After they know how these nasty programs work, they can figure out how to detect, stop, and remove these malicious programs.

On the shady side, many companies use disassemblers to tear apart their rival's products and see how they work. After you know how a competitor's program works, you can copy those features and use them in your own program.

Programming languages, such as Java, C#, and Visual Basic.NET, get compiled into bytecode format; therefore, a disassembler can reverse compile a bytecode file into its original source code. So, if you compile a Java program into bytecode format, a Java disassembler can convert the bytecode file into Java source code. Likewise, if you compile a C# or Visual Basic.NET program, you can disassemble that bytecode file into its original C# or Visual Basic.NET source code.

To protect their bytecode files from disassemblers, programmers use another program — an obfuscator. An *obfuscator* essentially scrambles a bytecode file. The bytecode file can still run, but if others try to disassemble an obfuscated bytecode file, they can't retrieve the original source code.

If you use a programming language that compiles into bytecode (such as Java, C#, or Visual Basic.NET), consider using an obfuscator to protect your source code from prying eyes.

At the bare minimum, all you need is an editor (to write programs) and a compiler (to convert your programs into executable files). However, most programmers use a debugger, a help file creation program, and an installer. Although most programmers are happy when they can get their program to work, some programmers use a profiler to help them speed up and optimize their program.

Finally, some programmers use disassemblers to peek inside the inner workings of other programs, such as viruses or rival software. Disassemblers are never necessary for creating a program, but they can prove useful for legal and not so legal purposes.

The tools of a programmer are highly subjective. Some programmers swear by certain tools, such as their favorite editor or compiler, whereas others are happily with whatever tool is available. Just remember that programmer tools can help you write faster and more reliable programs, but the best tool in the world can never substitute for decent programming skill in the first place.

Chapter 5: Managing Large Projects with Software Engineering

In This Chapter

✔ Choosing your software engineering method

✔ Using CASE to automate software engineering

✔ The pluses and minuses of software engineering

*W*riting a small program is easy. You just type your program in an editor and shove your source code through a compiler. If you find any problems, dig through the source code, fix the problem, and recompile the whole thing all over again. No matter how many bugs pop up in your program, chances are good your program is small enough so you can hunt any bugs and wipe them out without much trouble.

What happens if you need to write a massive program to control the flight of a satellite in orbit or an automatic safety system for monitoring a nuclear plant? Unlike simple programs that can consist of a few hundred lines of code, massive programming projects can contain millions of lines of code. How can you create such a large program, let alone debug, test, and maintain it?

That's where software engineering comes into play. Just as it's much easier to pitch a pup tent by yourself than it is to construct a skyscraper on your own, it's also easier to write a simple program by yourself, but nearly impossible to write a million-line program all by yourself.

When you have to write a huge program, you probably can't do it alone, so you need to work with a team of programmers and coordinate your efforts. Even before you write a single line of code, you need a plan for creating the program from the start. Just as no one starts welding I-beams together to build a skyscraper without making plans first, no one tackles a massive software project without a lot of planning ahead of time.

Software engineering is about creating guidelines to help people consistently write reliable programs within a reasonable amount of time. The fact that governments and Fortune 500 companies routinely start massive software projects with no plans (and often abandon them after never getting them to work despite spending millions of dollars) is proof that software engineering is a nice term that often gets completely ignored in the real world.

Software Engineering Methods

In the early days of computer programming, a single programming genius might create a program. However, relying on the inspiration and creativity of a single genius isn't a way to run a business. If the programming genius dies or quits, the company selling that program won't know how to fix or update the program later.

So the idea behind software engineering is to remove a company's dependence on a single programming genius and establish a systematic method for creating software that can be done with an army of competent programmers rather than a single inspired programming wizard.

Over the years, computer scientists have created a variety of software engineering methods, which all have advantages and disadvantages. No matter which software engineering method is popular today or tomorrow, the goals are always the same:

+ Make it easy to write large computer programs within a reasonable period of time.

+ Create software that works reliably.

Writing large programs is hard enough. Being able to create large programs within a strict deadline is much harder and making sure the software can be trusted to work reliably is even tougher. Software engineering methods try to solve these problems in various ways with different results, ranging from complete success (rare) to abysmal failures (more common than you might like to think).

Designing a program with the waterfall model

The *waterfall model* of software engineering divides the task of creating a large software project into distinct parts with each part being fully completed before the other part can even begin.

Typically, the waterfall method divides a software project into four parts, as shown in Figure 5-1:

+ Analysis

+ Design

+ Implementation

+ Testing

The idea behind the waterfall method is to complete tasks one at a time so that you're always focusing on a single task.

Book I
Chapter 5

Managing Large
Projects with
Software
Engineering

Figure 5-1:
The
waterfall
method
divides a
project into
four distinct
and
mutually
exclusive
steps.

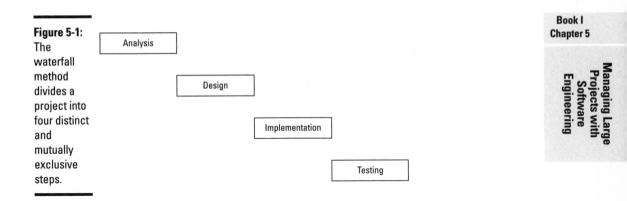

Analysis

The first step is to analyze the project to determine exactly what the program's supposed to do. (Surprisingly, many people, companies, and government agencies skip this first step all the time.)

During this analysis step, the *customer* (the person or group that wants the program) defines exactly what they want the program to do, which are the *requirements*. The programmers read these requirements and ask the customer for clarification until they "think" they understand exactly what the customer wants. At this point, the analysis step is done, and the customer can no longer ask for any more changes.

When a customer's requirements are written down, they're often called the program specifications or just the *specifications*.

One common problem is that the customer may ask for a new feature that he didn't ask for initially. By shutting down the analysis step, the waterfall method prevents the customer from coming back two days before the project is done and asking, "Can't you add just one more feature? It'll only set the project back another 3 months and require rewriting 90 percent of the program from scratch. And by the way, we aren't going to pay you for the delay either."

The most common problem during the analysis phase is that the programmers never clearly understand what the customer wants:

✦ Sometimes the customer clearly defines what he wants, and the programmers misinterpret it.

✦ Sometimes the customer doesn't really know what he wants, so he keeps changing his mind, making it impossible for the programmers to define everything the program's supposed to do.

After the programmers complete the analysis step, they should know exactly what the program is supposed to do. Then they can start the design phase and decide how they'll create this program.

Design

The design phase is when the programmers write a plan for creating a program that meets all the customer's requirements. This can involve deciding how to break the overall program into smaller parts and then assigning each part to a different programming team.

At the design phase, the programmers also need to decide on

+ The programming language to use

+ A specific compiler and other tools to use

+ Procedures for keeping all programmers in constant contact with each other so one programmer doesn't accidentally duplicate the efforts of another programmer

The biggest problem with the waterfall model is that if one step isn't completed correctly, the rest of the steps won't work correctly either. For example, if the analysis part of the waterfall model is done poorly, then it will be impossible for the design part to be accurate.

+ Many times the design doesn't accurately reflect what the customer wants. Because the programmers talk only to the customer during the analysis phase, they may cheerfully design a program that almost does what the customer wants, but not quite. That means the programmers often create a program that the customer can't even use without moderate-to-extensive modifications.

+ During the design phase, every programmer is supposed to know what the customer wants, but sometimes programmers leave and new programmers get added. These new programmers may not have participated in the analysis phase, so now they have to take time to understand what the customer wants, which delays the design phase for the entire project.

When everyone finishes deciding how to create the project within a specific deadline, the design phase is considered over. By forcing programmers to design a program on paper and create a plan for writing that program, the waterfall method makes sure that nobody starts writing the program until they first have a clear idea what they're doing.

Implementation

After the design phase is done, the implementation phase begins with programmers actually writing their portion of the program. If the programmers developed a clear plan during the design phase, they can monitor their progress during the implementation phase and see, at any given time, what needs to be done next.

If the programmers don't fully understand the design, the program that they write reflects this misinterpretation. Sometimes after writing part of the program, the programmers suddenly realize that their initial design was flawed, but now it's too late to change, so the project winds up being harder to create than expected.

After everyone finishes writing their part of the program, they put it all together, like a giant jigsaw puzzle. At this point, all further programming stops, and the testing phase begins.

Testing

The testing phase insures that the entire program works. If the programmers find any problems, they fix the bugs and then test to make sure their fixes don't accidentally wreck another part of the program.

When the program finally works, the testing phase is over and the program's ready for delivery.

In theory, the waterfall method makes sense because everyone has a clear idea what needs to be done at any given time. Unfortunately in the real world, life rarely works according to theory.

After the testing phase, the program should be complete, but if the customer's idea of what he wanted and the programmers' analysis, design, and implementation of those ideas aren't completely accurate, the customer may wind up with a program that *almost* does what it's supposed to do. To add new features or features that should've been in the program to begin with, the waterfall method starts with a new analysis phase all over again, with the possibility that the revised program could wind up just as flawed as before.

Although the waterfall method makes sense and can work, it assumes that

✦ A project can progress through a series of distinct steps that are done once and are never needed again for the remainder of the project.

✦ The time needed to complete each step can be *predicted.*

✦ Each step can accurately translate the customer's needs from the preceding step.

Despite the rationale behind the waterfall method, it hasn't consistently produced large, reliable programs on schedule. The biggest flaw with the waterfall method is its rigidity. If one phase gets stalled for any reason, the entire project grinds to a halt. If programmers misinterpret the customer's requirements between two different steps (such as the analysis and design phase), the error can continue down through each succeeding phase, resulting in a final program that's flawed (at best) or completely unusable (at worst).

Evolving a program with extreme programming

In response to the over-structured waterfall method, programmers have gone to the opposite side with *extreme programming* (often abbreviated as *XP*).

The whole idea behind extreme programming (or *agile programming*) is to recognize that all four phases (analysis, design, implementation, and testing) are not distinct, isolated steps but integrated steps that flow back and forth throughout the life of a project.

Phases

Instead of the analysis, design, implementation, and testing phases defined by the waterfall method, extreme programming defines four different, mutually overlapping phases:

+ Coding

+ Testing

+ Listening

+ Designing

Extreme or waterfall?

Which approach is better? The answer: Both and neither:

🖝 Although you may not want to be as regimented and rigid as the waterfall model, you may appreciate its structure and emphasis on defining every phase before moving on to the next step.

🖝 If you're the type of person who needs more structure, extreme programming may be too chaotic.

Whichever method — or combination of methods — you choose, the ultimate goal of any software engineering method is to provide a systematic way to create large, reliable programs on a consistent basis and as quickly as possible.

Book I
Chapter 5

Managing Large
Projects with
Software
Engineering

Advocates of extreme programming argue that the only truly important product of the system development process is *code*. Without a working program, you have nothing.

Coding is more than just typing in program commands — it also includes figuring out the best way to write that program in the first place. For instance, in extreme programming, when faced with several alternatives for a programming problem, one should simply code all solutions and determine with automated tests (which I discuss in the following section) which solution is most suitable.

Coding also means communicating on a consistent basis with

+ **The customer.** Constant communication with the customer means that the customer can always see the program's progress and offer feedback on what the program's doing right and what it's doing wrong. By doing this, extreme programming lets the customer play an active role in shaping the final program.

   Under the waterfall method, the customer can give feedback to the programming team only during the analysis phase. After the analysis phase is complete, the customer never sees the program until it's completed the testing phase. By that time, the program may not look or act anything like the customer wanted.

+ **Other programmers.** Constant communication with other programmers on the project means not only talking with them, but writing clear, concise program designs that can't be misinterpreted. By constantly communicating with other programmers, extreme programming encourages programmers to know exactly what other programmers are doing so putting together the various parts of the program can be much simpler.

   Under the waterfall method, it's perfectly possible for teams of programmers to work independently only to find later that their different program parts don't work together like they're supposed to.

Sequence

Unlike the waterfall method, which is predictive and process-oriented, extreme programming is adaptive and people-oriented. Extreme programming adapts to the customer's needs (rather than shutting the customer out after the analysis phase is complete). By keeping the customer involved, the program's directed by the customer's needs rather than a fixed time schedule.

Extreme programming follows this general sequence:

1. **The customer defines the program requirements.**

   The customer may need more features later, but initially, the customer knows the main features he needs in a program.

2. **A small team of programmers designs a simple program (a *prototype*) that acts like a model for the customer to study and approve.**

   Because this prototype is a simple program, it's easy to make and even easier to modify based on the customer's feedback and desire.

3. **The programmers implement their idea as an actual program, with the customer giving them feedback along the way.**

   By keeping the customer in close contact with the programmers, extreme programming makes sure the customer can make changes to the program while the changes are still easy to make, rather than when the program's finally done.

4. **After the programmers create a simple program that the customer likes, the programmers can slowly start adding additional features that the customer may suddenly want.**

In this way, a program evolves slowly with the customer guiding its development at all times.

Extreme programming isn't without its critics, who argue the following points:

✦ The chaotic nature of extreme programming means that it's nearly impossible to determine when a project gets done.

✦ The close relationship between the customer and the programmers can be crucial.

✦ If a programmer suddenly leaves, the entire project can slow down while the customer gets used to working with a new programmer (and vice versa).

✦ Close communication is essential between

  • The programmers and the customers

  • The programmers themselves

Without constant communication, an extreme programming project can fall apart.

Automating Software Engineering with CASE

**Book I
Chapter 5**

Managing Large
Projects with
Software
Engineering

Software engineering consists of generally accepted practices for writing reliable software on time. Avoiding spaghetti programming (see Book 1, Chapter 2) is one example of an accepted software engineering practice.

To make software engineering practices easier to follow, computer scientists have developed Computer-Aided Software Engineering(CASE) tools. CASE tools are meant to simplify the practices of software engineering. The easier it is for programmers to follow software engineering practices, the more likely they'll do it and create reliable software. Some common CASE tools include

+ Project modelers

+ Code generators

+ Source code formatters

+ Revision control

+ Project management

Modeling a large project

Before programmers rush off to write a program, they need to design it first. The problem with designing a program is making sure everyone understands the design, and part of understanding a program design is using a consistent method.

For example, one programmer might design a program by scribbling a few notes on a napkin, whereas a second programmer might design a program by typing a description of that program in a word processor document.

Neither approach is good or bad, but the problem lies in understanding everyone's design. The programmer who scribbles notes on a napkin may understand the design of his program perfectly, but nobody else may understand the design of that program.

To make sure everyone can understand the design of a program, everyone needs to use the same design method.

Flowcharts

One of the earliest modeling methods are flowcharts, as shown in Figure 5-2. Flowcharts must specify every action and decision that the program goes through.

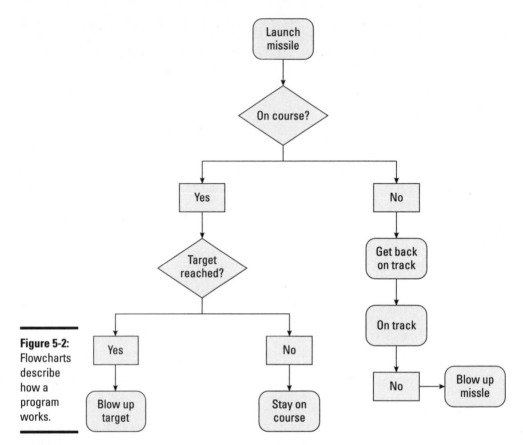

Figure 5-2:
Flowcharts
describe
how a
program
works.

Flowcharts work for designing small programs, but when designing a large program, flowcharts have a couple of problems:

✦ The flowchart can soon become so large and confusing that creating it can take way too much time to complete.

✦ A large flowchart can be so complicated that nobody bothers using it, which makes creating the flowchart a waste of time in the first place.

Unified Modeling Language (UML)

Rather than describe every possible action that the program might do, other modeling methods just describe the parts of the program. One of the more popular methods for describing a program is the Unified Modeling Language (UML).

Book I
Chapter 5

Managing Large
Projects with
Software
Engineering

Like flowcharts, UML provides a way to visually design a program with universally understood symbols and diagrams. Unlike flowcharts, which model only a program's actions, UML offers different types of models for defining a program:

✦ Functional models

✦ Object models

✦ Dynamic models

You don't have to use every type of diagram to define your program; use as many as you need.

Of course, UML and other modeling methods are never perfect:

✦ Just because you model a program perfectly doesn't always mean that design is actually feasible. Many designs may look perfect on paper but fail dramatically when put into actual use. (Think of the watertight doors on the *Titanic*.)

✦ Modeling methods, such as UML, offer so many different diagrams that it's possible that two diagrams of the same program can describe mutually exclusive features. Because each type of a diagram focuses on a different view of the program, you could create conflicting designs.

Despite these problems, design methods like UML are still an improvement over no design plans whatsoever. Just remember that UML diagrams are meant to offer a standard way to model programs so other people can see and understand your design before you start writing any actual code in a specific programming language.

Functional model

A *UML functional model* (or a Use Case diagram) describes how a user interacts with the program, as shown in Figure 5-3. By displaying users as stick figures and program functions as an oval, Use Case diagrams make it easy to see what the program is supposed to do without confusing you with how the program will do it.

Object model

A *UML object model* (or a Class diagram) defines how to divide a program into parts or objects. Each Class diagram defines an object's name, data (properties), and operations (methods), as shown in Figure 5-4.

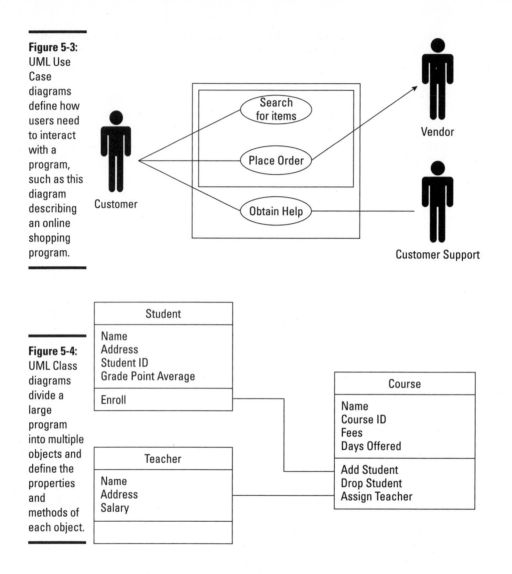

Figure 5-3:
UML Use Case diagrams define how users need to interact with a program, such as this diagram describing an online shopping program.

Figure 5-4:
UML Class diagrams divide a large program into multiple objects and define the properties and methods of each object.

An object's properties define the type of data it can hold whereas an object's methods define what type of actions the object can perform. In Figure 5-4, the three classes are Students, Teachers, and Courses. Students have properties, such as their names and student ID numbers; Teachers have properties, such as their names and salaries; and Courses have properties, such as its name and days offered.

The Student class also has an Enroll method to model a student's actions in choosing a course to take. The Course class has three methods — Add Student, Drop Student, and Assign Teacher. By using UML Class diagrams, programmers can define objects and how they interact with each other without worrying about the specifics of any object-oriented programming language.

Dynamic model

A *UML dynamic model* (or a Sequence diagram) describes the sequences a program follows, as shown in Figure 5-5. Sequence diagrams are similar to flowcharts because they describe what a program does at any given time, but not necessarily how a program works, which is unlike a flowchart.

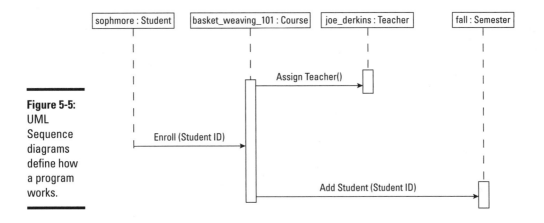

Figure 5-5: UML Sequence diagrams define how a program works.

Sequence diagrams show you the order that events occur, the messages passed from one object to another, and the actual names of all interacting objects.

The boxes at the top of the Sequence diagram in Figure 5-5 shows object names and the classes they're based on (such as a `sophomore` object based on the `Student` class). The vertical dotted lines *(lifelines)* show how long an object exists. The arrows show the messages objects send to each other. A Sequence diagram helps explain the interaction between different objects.

Generating code automatically

Designing a program by using UML or some other modeling method can be great, but there's a big gap between designing a program and actually writing code that follows that design. To eliminate this problem of transferring a program design into working code, computer scientists have created special programs dubbed *code generators*. The basic steps for using a code generator are as follows:

1. **Design a program in a specific format, such as a UML diagram.**

2. **Feed that model (UML diagram) in to the code generator.**

   The code generator cranks out working code in a specific programming language.

3. **Modify or compile this source code and have a working program that accurately reflects your original design.**

If you change your design, the code generator can crank out new code based on your revised design. Code generators keep your design and code synchronized.

In the early days of computers when people had to write programs in assembly language, compilers were considered code generators because you could give them source code written in a language, like FORTRAN or COBOL, and the compilers would generate the proper machine language commands from that source code.

Formatting source code automatically

If you write a program by yourself, the source code for your entire program likely looks consistent. However, if you're working on a large program with multiple programmers, every programmer has his or her own unique style. Ultimately, the program may work, but it resembles a patchwork collection of code where each chunk of code can look completely different even if the entire program is written in the same programming language, as shown in Figure 5-6.

To solve this problem, computer scientists have created source code formatters. These programs rearrange the appearance of source code so that it appears uniform. Now instead of looking at a patchwork collection of code written by different programmers, an entire large program can look like it was written in a single style.

By looking at source code that's formatted the same, programmers can easily read and understand the entire program.

Book I
Chapter 5

Managing Large
Projects with
Software
Engineering

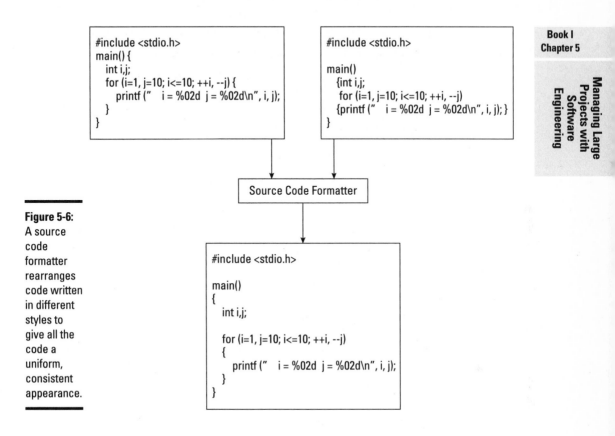

Figure 5-6:
A source
code
formatter
rearranges
code written
in different
styles to
give all the
code a
uniform,
consistent
appearance.

Tracking revisions in code

Modifying a program by yourself is easy, but what happens if you're working with a team of multiple programmers? It's possible that one programmer modifies the program while a second programmer modifies a copy of the program. Now you wind up with two slightly different versions of the same program. Which one should you use?

The answer is to avoid this problem in the first place by using a revision control program.

A *revision control program* acts like a librarian and stores a program's source code in a single location — a *repository.* If a programmer needs to modify the source code, he or she needs to check out that source code, much like checking out a book from a library.

If another programmer wants to modify that same source code, the version control program may offer four choices:

✦ It may simply lock anyone else from modifying any source code that's been checked out. This prevents multiple programmers from working on different copies of the same source code.

✦ It may let another programmer check out a second copy of the source code and make any changes to it. At this point, you wind up with two modified copies of the same source code.

✦ When both programmers return their modified versions of the same source code back to the repository, the version control program merges all changes back into a single copy. This has the advantage of letting multiple programmers work on the same source code but also has the disadvantage that merging changes might wind up scrambling the original source code beyond recognition.

✦ For additional protection, version control programs also archive old versions of source code so if someone totally messes up the program, he or she can always retrieve an earlier version of the program and start all over again.

Version control programs are essential to coordinate the activities of multiple programmers, although they can also be handy for individual programmers. The main points are to

✦ Always keep a copy of your old source code (so you can retrieve it again if necessary).

✦ Always keep your changes to the source code organized.

The Pros and Cons of Software Engineering

Programming is more than just writing code and seeing if it works. The larger the program, the more complicated it gets, and the more tools you likely need to keep everything organized. Can software engineering guarantee that you'll write better and more reliable programs? Nope.

All that software engineering techniques and practices can do is encourage you to write programs by using proven techniques. However, it's still possible to follow every software engineering principle and wind up writing a confusing program that doesn't work.

Software engineering has improved from the early days of letting programmers loose and hoping they wrote something useful, to today's programming projects with software engineering tools available to guide a project at every step of the way.

Think of software engineering as a way to funnel your thinking and actions toward writing well-designed and easy-to-understand programs. Programming geniuses will likely find software engineering practices too restrictive and confining, but they exist for your own protection, like seat belts in a car.

Book I
Chapter 5

Managing Large
Projects with
Software
Engineering

Without software engineering, only a handful of programming geniuses could ever write a large program successfully. With software engineering, teams of average programmers can write that same large program. The program may lack the elegance of one written by a programming genius, but it will likely work well enough to be useful.

In the computer industry, being good enough is all that most people want and need.

Book II

Programming Basics

The 5th Wave   By Rich Tennant

Oh come on — how fatal can it be?

FATAL ERROR

Contents at a Glance

Chapter 1: How Programs Work

In This Chapter

✔ Using keywords

✔ Arranging a Program

✔ Dividing programs into subprograms and objects

✔ Building a user interface

*P*rogramming is nothing more than problem-solving. Every program is designed to solve a specific problem, such as taking the trouble out of editing text (a word processor), calculating rows and columns of numbers (spreadsheets), or searching and sorting information (a database).

Before you write any program, you must first know what problem you want the computer to solve. Computers are best at solving repetitive tasks, such as calculating rows and columns of numbers in a spreadsheet. Anyone can do similar calculations by hand, but computers make the task much faster and accurate.

After you know what problem to solve, the next step is figuring out how to solve that problem. Many problems may have multiple solutions. For example, how can someone get from the airport to your house? One way might be to take the highway, which may be the simplest route although not necessarily the fastest. Another way may take you through winding roads that can be harder to navigate.

In general, every problem has multiple solutions with each solution having its pros and cons. Should you tell someone to take the shortest way to your house (which might be harder to follow) or the easiest way to your house (which might take longer to get there)?

Computer programs face this same dilemma in choosing the "best" solution. One solution might be slow, but require less memory to run. Another solution might be fast, but require gobs of memory. When deciding on a solution, you always have to consider additional factors, such as what type of computer the program runs on, what type of environment the program is used in, and what type of people are using it.

After you choose a solution, the next step involves dissecting how your chosen solution works so that you can translate those steps into instructions for the computer to follow.

Every program consists of step-by-step instructions. Just as you can write the same instructions for a person in English, French, Spanish, Arabic, or Japanese, so can you write the same program for a computer in different programming languages.

You can literally write a program with thousands of possible programming languages. Every programming language is designed to solve one problem exceptionally well, but may solve other types of problems poorly.

For example, the BASIC programming language is meant to teach programming, but it's not very good for controlling the hardware of a computer, such as for writing an operating system or antivirus program. On the other hand, the C programming language is meant to give you absolute control over every part of the computer so that's why most operating systems and antivirus programs are written in C. However, the C language can be much more frustrating and confusing for novices to understand compared to BASIC.

Ideally, you want to pick the programming language best suited for solving your particular problem. Realistically, you probably know only a handful of programming languages, so out of all the languages you know, you have to pick the one language that's best suited for solving your problem.

You can write any program in any programming language. The only difference is that some programming languages can make writing certain programs easier than others. The "best" programming language to use is always the language that makes writing a program easy for you.

Using Keywords as Building Blocks

Every program consists of one or more commands *(instructions),* and each command is a *line of code* or a *statement.* The more lines of code, the more complicated the program.

The goal of programming is to write the fewest lines of code that do the maximum amount of work.

Each command tells the computer to do one thing. Put enough commands together and you can create a simple program, as shown in Figure 1-1.

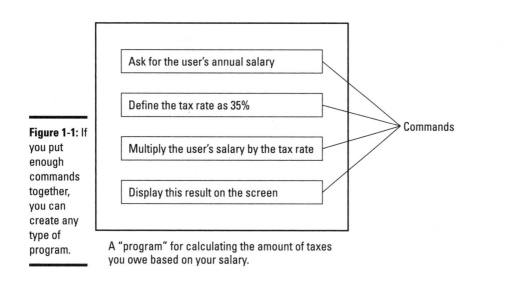

Figure 1-1: If you put enough commands together, you can create any type of program.

A "program" for calculating the amount of taxes you owe based on your salary.

Every programming language provides a list of commands dubbed *keywords* or *reserved words*. By typing keywords one after another, you can tell the computer what to do.

A programming language's *keywords* act like the letters of the alphabet. Type letters in different combinations and you can create different words. Type keywords in different combinations and you can create different commands, as shown in Figure 1-2.

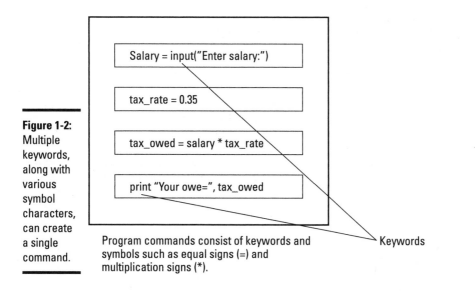

Figure 1-2: Multiple keywords, along with various symbol characters, can create a single command.

Program commands consist of keywords and symbols such as equal signs (=) and multiplication signs (*).

More versus fewer keywords

Computer scientists are divided on whether it's better for a programming language to offer a lot of keywords:

✔ By offering a lot of keywords, a programming language can let programmers write fewer keywords that do more work.

✔ By offering fewer keywords, a programming language makes programmers write a lot of simple keywords just to do something that another language might be able to do with one keyword.

Given these choices, having a lot of keywords in a programming language seems to make more sense. The problem is that the more keywords used, the harder it is to write a compiler for that programming language. The harder it is to write a compiler, the less efficient that compiler is in converting source code into machine language, just as it's much harder to translate a Russian scientific paper into English than it is to translate a Russian children's story into English.

That's one problem with the Ada programming language. Ada uses lots of keywords, which makes programming easier but creating compilers for Ada much harder. This is one of the reasons why Ada compilers are much less widespread than compilers for the C programming language.

Unlike Ada, C offers a bare minimum of keywords. This makes programming in C harder because you need to write a lot of keywords to do something as seemingly simple as storing a text string. However, C's handful of keywords makes it much easier to write a C compiler.

To compensate for the lack of keywords, most C compilers include libraries of commonly used subprograms that can make C programming easier and more useful.

As a result, you can find C compilers for practically every computer because it's much easier to write a C compiler than it is to write an Ada compiler. The more C compilers available, the easier it is to transfer (*port*) a C program to another computer. The C programming language is popular partly because you can run C programs on almost every computer.

With a lot of keywords, Ada makes programming easier for humans but harder for computers. In contrast, a handful of keywords in C makes programming harder for humans but much easier for computers. Given a choice between Ada or C, more people choose C, so having a programming language with fewer keywords seems to be more efficient (at least for the computer).

Organizing a Program

Every program consists of one or more commands, but there are different types of commands. Some commands tell the computer how to manipulate data, such as adding two numbers together. Other commands might tell the computer how to print data, display it on-screen, or save it on a disk.

Although you could jumble all your commands together and still have a working program (see Book 1, Chapter 2 for more on programs), make your program easier to read and modify by organizing similar commands in different parts of your program.

So if your program isn't printing correctly, you don't have to search through your entire program to find the faulty commands. Instead, you can just look at the part of your program where you grouped all your printing commands, as shown in Figure 1-3.

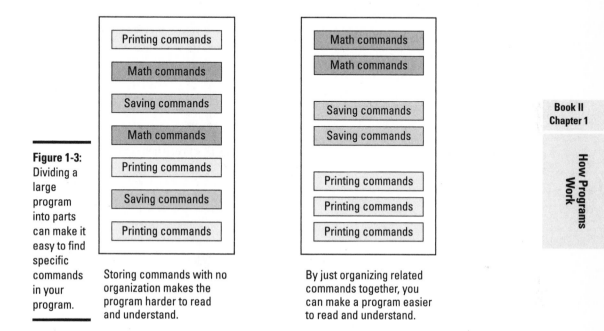

Figure 1-3: Dividing a large program into parts can make it easy to find specific commands in your program.

Storing commands with no organization makes the program harder to read and understand.

By just organizing related commands together, you can make a program easier to read and understand.

When you write a simple program that consists of a handful of commands, organizing related commands in groups isn't too important, but when you start writing bigger programs that consist of hundreds or thousands of commands, organizing commands can mean the difference between writing a program that nobody can understand or a program that's easy for anyone to understand and modify.

When you save your program, you save it as a single file on the computer. However, the more commands you write, the bigger your program gets, and the bigger the file you need to store the whole program.

No matter how carefully you organize your commands, eventually your program will get too big and cumbersome as a single massive file to read and modify easily. That's when you need to break your program into smaller parts.

Dividing a Program into Subprograms

The smaller the program, the easier it is to write, read, and modify later. So rather than create a massive program, with related commands organized into groups, you can divide a large program into smaller pieces, or *subprograms*.

Subprograms essentially break up a large program into multiple miniature programs with each miniature program acting like a building block to create a much larger program, as shown in Figure 1-4. So rather than build a large program entirely out of keywords, you can build a program out of keywords and subprograms (which are themselves made up of keywords).

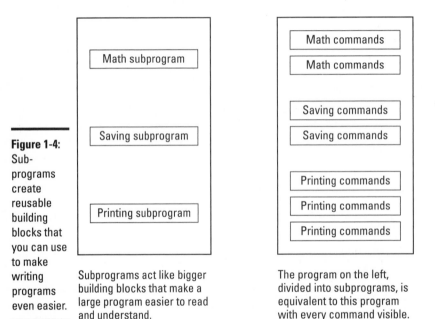

Figure 1-4: Sub-programs create reusable building blocks that you can use to make writing programs even easier.

Subprograms act like bigger building blocks that make a large program easier to read and understand.

The program on the left, divided into subprograms, is equivalent to this program with every command visible.

Think of subprograms as a way to create keywords that aren't built into the programming language. For example, the C programming language doesn't have any keywords for working with text strings, so programmers have used C's existing keywords to create subprograms that can work with text strings. By using these existing subprograms, other C programmers can manipulate text strings without writing their own commands.

Using keywords alone to create a program is like trying to build a skyscraper out of bricks. It's possible, but it takes a long time to layer enough bricks to reach the height of a typical 50-story skyscraper.

Using subprograms to create a larger program is like using I-beams to build a skyscraper. Essentially, I-beams act like bigger bricks the same way that subprograms act like bigger building blocks than keywords by themselves.

You can store subprograms in two places:

+ **In one file**

+ **In separate files**

Storing subprograms in the same file is no different than grouping related commands together in one file. This is like storing your socks, underwear, and shirts in the same drawer but pushing them into separate corners. The drawer may be organized, but such an arrangement is suitable only if you don't have many clothes to worry about. The moment you get more clothes, you need a bigger drawer to hold it all.

Book II
Chapter 1

How Programs Work

The same holds true with storing subprograms in a single file. Eventually, if you group enough commands into subprograms, a single file crammed full of subprograms can still be cumbersome to read and modify.

To keep files down to a reasonable size, programmers store subprograms in separate files, as shown in Figure 1-5. Not only does this avoid cramming everything into a single file, but separate files also give you the option of creating reusable libraries of subprograms that you can copy and reuse in another program.

Libraries of subprograms, stored as separate files, are discussed in Book 1, Chapter 4.

Programmers often sell their libraries of subprograms to others, although each library of subprograms is usually designed to work only with a specific programming language and operating system, such as C++ running on Windows. Many Windows libraries of subprograms are stored as dynamic link libraries (DLL) although you may see some libraries sold as something called *ActiveX* controls or *.NET components.*

The name simply tells you what type of programming languages and computers you can use the programming library on. So if you're using a programming language that can use ActiveX controls, you can buy third-party libraries of subprograms stored as ActiveX controls. If you're using a programming language that can use .NET components, you can use subprogram libraries stored as .NET components.

When you get a library of subprograms (for free or for a price), you may also get the source code to those subprograms. With the source code, you can modify the subprograms. However, most subprogram libraries don't include the source code so that you have to pay for an updated version of the subprogram library.

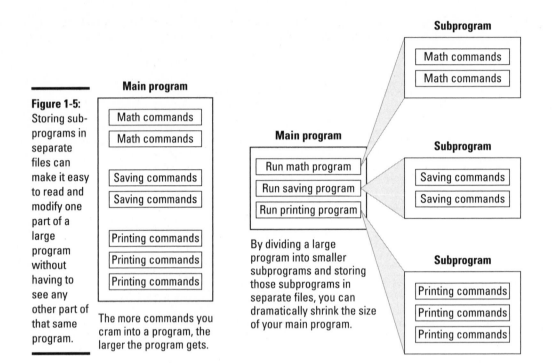

Figure 1-5:
Storing subprograms in separate files can make it easy to read and modify one part of a large program without having to see any other part of that same program.

The more commands you cram into a program, the larger the program gets.

By dividing a large program into smaller subprograms and storing those subprograms in separate files, you can dramatically shrink the size of your main program.

By storing subprograms in separate files, you can write a program with multiple programming languages. That way you can write your main program in BASIC and then write subprograms in C or Java. By doing this, you don't have to limit yourself to the strengths and weaknesses of a single programming language. Instead, you can take advantage of the strengths of each programming language.

If you're writing a hard disk diagnostic program, you could write the whole thing in C because C is great for accessing the hardware of a computer. However, you may find that C is too clumsy for printing reports or displaying information on-screen. In that case, what are your choices? You can

✦ **Use C to write the whole program.** This is great for accessing computer hardware but hard for writing the rest of the program, like the user interface.

✦ **Use an easier language, like BASIC, to write the whole program.** This is great for writing every part of the program except the part needed to access the computer hardware.

✦ **Use a mix of two or more programming languages.** Use BASIC to write most of the program and then use C to write a subprogram to access the computer hardware.

By giving you the option to choose the best programming language for a specific task, subprograms help make it easier for you to write larger programs, as shown in Figure 1-6.

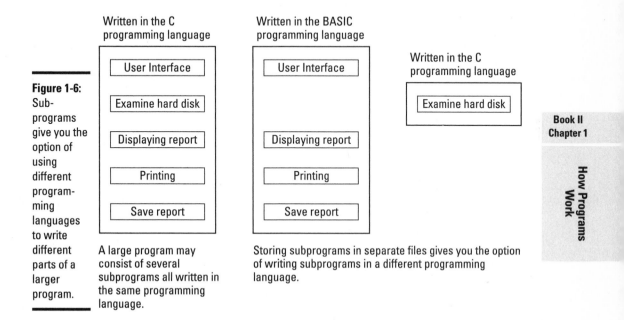

Figure 1-6: Sub-programs give you the option of using different program-ming languages to write different parts of a larger program.

Written in the C programming language

Written in the BASIC programming language

Written in the C programming language

A large program may consist of several subprograms all written in the same programming language.

Storing subprograms in separate files gives you the option of writing subprograms in a different programming language.

Dividing a Program into Objects

The more complicated programs get, the larger they get. If programs get too big, they get harder to write, understand, and modify. This is why dividing a large program into multiple smaller subprograms can make programming much easier. Just write a bunch of little programs and then paste them together to create a bigger program.

Unfortunately, dividing a large program into subprograms isn't without its problems:

✦ In theory, if you want to update a program, you can modify a subprogram and plug that modified subprogram back into the main program to create an updated version.

✦ In reality, that almost never works. The problem comes from the fact that subprograms aren't always independent entities that you can yank out and replace without affecting the rest of the program. Sometimes one subprogram relies on data manipulated by a second subprogram. Change that first subprogram, and those changes could affect that first subprogram in a domino-like effect, as shown in Figure 1-7.

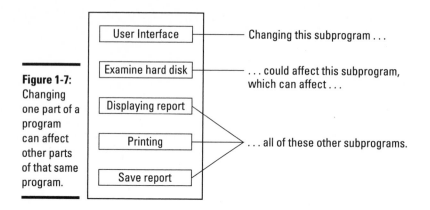

Figure 1-7:
Changing
one part of a
program
can affect
other parts
of that same
program.

When subprograms are highly dependent on each other, they're *high, strong,* or *tight coupling.* When subprograms aren't dependent on each other, they're *low, weak,* or *loose coupling.* You want your subprograms to have *low, weak,* or *loose coupling.* That way, changing one part of your program doesn't accidentally affect another part of your program.

To enforce weak coupling, computer scientists have created *object-oriented programming (OOP).* The main idea behind OOP is to divide a large program into objects.

Objects act like "super" subprograms. Whereas subprograms give programmers the choice of making a tightly or loosely coupled subprogram, objects force programmers to create loosely coupled subprograms.

By forcing programmers to create loosely coupled subprograms, objects make it easy to modify a program without worrying about any unintended side effects. OOP lets you yank out an object, modify it, and plug it back in without worrying if your changes might affect the rest of the program.

Objects offer another advantage over subprograms. Whereas subprograms typically represent a specific action, objects represent specific physical items in the real world.

For example, if you're writing a program to control a robot, you could divide the program into the following subprograms that make the robot:

✦ Move

✦ Sense obstacles (through sight and touch) in its way

✦ Navigate

If you're using OOP, you could divide that same program into objects that represent the robot's

✦ Legs

✦ Eyes (video camera)

✦ Brain

The way you divide a large program into parts isn't important. What's important is how easy it is to modify those separate parts later. Suppose you rip the legs off your robot and replace them with treads. In an OOP, you can yank out the Legs object and replace it with a Treads object, as shown in Figure 1-8.

First use of "Sub programs" needs to be one word in the first paragraph of the artwork. Also, shouldn't "real world components" be hyphenated to be "real-world components"?

Figure 1-8:
Object-oriented program-ming divides your program into logical parts that correspond to the real world.

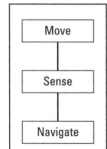

Subprograms are often tightly coupled with each other, so making changes in one subprogram can affect other subprograms.

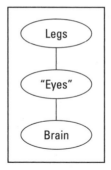

Objects divide a program into logical, real world components that are loosely coupled to each other. Changing one object almost never affects any other objects.

Although the robot now uses treads instead of legs to move, the Brain object can still give the same type of commands to make the robot move, such as Move Forward, Move Backward, and Stop.

How do you change the equivalent program divided into subprograms? First, you have to change the Move subprogram to reflect the change in movement from legs to treads. Then you may need to change the Navigate subprogram so it knows how to navigate in different directions with treads instead of legs. Finally, make sure the changes you make in the Navigate and Move subprograms don't accidentally affect the Sense subprogram.

Sounds like a lot of work just to make a simple change? It is, and that's why loose coupling between subprograms is so important. Because programmers can't always be trusted to make sure their subprograms are loosely coupling, OOP forces them to do it whether they like it or not.

Creating a User Interface

The three actions of most programs are

✦ **Get data.**

✦ **Manipulate that data.**

✦ **Create a result.**

A football-picking program takes in data about both teams, uses a formula to predict a winner, and prints or displays its answer on-screen. A hotel reservation program gets a request for a room from the user (hotel clerk), scans its list of rooms for one that's available and that matches the user's criteria (no smoking, two beds, and so on), and displays that result on-screen.

Basically, every program takes in data, calculates a result, and displays that result. To accept data from the user and display a result back to the user again, every program needs a user interface, as shown in Figure 1-9.

Figure 1-9:
The user interface accepts data and displays the results of its calculations back to the user.

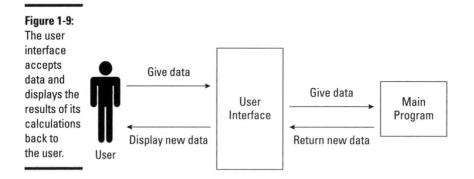

The user interface of most computer programs includes drop-down lists, buttons, and dialog boxes. If a program doesn't get data from a person, its user interface may be just a physical cable connection because its user could be another computer feeding it information like stock quotes.

To create a program, you have to create both your program and your user interface. The user interface acts like a middleman between the user and the program. Here are three common ways to create a user interface:

+ **Create it from scratch.**
+ **Use a subprogram library.**
+ **Use a rapid application development (RAD) tool.**

Creating your own user interface takes time to write and even more time to test. Although nothing's wrong with creating your own user interface, the time spent creating a user interface could be better spent writing your actual program. For that reason, few programmers create their own user interfaces unless they have special needs, such as designing a user interface to be used by blind or disabled users.

Because creating a user interface can be so troublesome and most user interfaces look alike anyway, some programmers create libraries of subprograms that do nothing but create a user interface. That way you can create your program, slap on the user interface by adding the library of subprograms, and have a finished program.

Because nearly every program needs a user interface, and most user interfaces look the same anyway (at least on the same operating systems, such as Windows or Mac OS X), programmers have created RAD tools that simplify creating user interfaces, as shown in Figure 1-10.

The RAD tool creates your user interface so that all you need to do is write commands to make your program work with that user interface.

In general, the more complicated the problem you want the computer to solve, the larger and more complicated your program is. To manage a large program, programmers divide a large program into subprograms or objects.

Of course, it's entirely possible to write a great program crammed into a single file with commands scattered all over the place, but such a program is difficult to modify later. You can also divide a program into subprograms and objects and still wind up with a program that doesn't work.

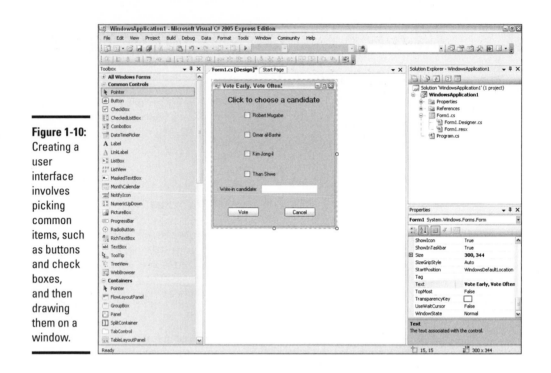

Figure 1-10:
Creating a user interface involves picking common items, such as buttons and check boxes, and then drawing them on a window.

In the end, the only result that matters is whether the program does what it's supposed to do. If you can create programs that work on a consistent basis, you're not only a successful programmer but probably a highly paid one as well.

Chapter 2: Variables, Data Types, and Constants

In This Chapter

✔ **Declaring your variables**

✔ **Defining data types**

✔ **Storing and retrieving data in a variable**

✔ **Using constant values in variables**

✔ **Defining a variable's scope**

*E*very program consists of a list of instructions that tell the computer what to do. The simplest program consists of a single instruction, such as one that tells the computer to display the words, `Hello, world!` on-screen.

Of course, any program that does the same thing over and over again isn't very useful or interesting. What makes a program useful is when it can accept information from the outside world and then respond to that information.

So instead of just displaying `Hello, world!` on-screen, a more useful program might ask for the user to type his name in so the program could display `Hello, Bob!`

Programs don't always have to get information from a person. Sometimes, programs can retrieve data that's stored somewhere else, such as a list of employees stored on another computer.

That program could access this database over a network and determine which person has been assigned to which computer in the building. Then the program can retrieve each person's name so when he turns on the computer, the program displays his name on his screen.

An even more sophisticated program could work with a Web cam hooked up to the computer along with a database that includes employee names and their photographs. So every time any computer's Web cam spots someone sitting at the computer, the program could examine the person's image through the Web cam, compare that image to the photographs of all employees stored in the database, and then find the name that matches the person. Then the program could display that person's name on-screen.

To be useful, every program needs to retrieve and respond to data from an outside source whether it comes from a person, a device such as a Web cam, or even another computer program. Where the data comes from is less important than what the program does with the data after the program receives it.

Declaring Variables

If somebody handed you a $20 bill, you could put it in your pocket. When someone hands a program some data, the program also needs a place to put that data. Programs don't have pockets to store stuff, so they store stuff in *variables*.

Just as your pockets can hold money, rocks, or dead frogs, so can a variable hold different types of data, such as numbers or words. The contents of a variable can vary, which is why they're dubbed *variables*.

The whole purpose of variables is to make a program more flexible. Rather than behave the same way using identical data, programs can retrieve, store, and respond to data from the outside world.

Creating a variable

You can't shove anything in your pockets until you have a pocket. Likewise, you can't shove any data in a variable until you first create that variable. To create a variable, you must first *declare* that variable.

Declaring a variable tells the computer, "I need a pocket to store data." When you declare a variable, the computer carves up a chunk of its memory for your program to use for storing data.

Of course, you can't just dump data in a variable without knowing how to find it again. In the real world, you can find something by remembering whether you stored it in the left or right pocket. In a program, you can remember where you stored data by giving a variable a unique name. When you create a variable, you declare that variable's name at the same time as the following BASIC code demonstrates:

```
X = 9
```

This BASIC code tells the computer the following:

1. **Create a variable.**

2. **Give that variable the name X.**

3. **Store the number 9 in the variable named X.**

Variable naming conventions

Variable names are for your convenience only; the computer doesn't care what names you choose for your variables. Computers are perfectly happy using generic variable names, like X or Y, but the more descriptive the name, the easier it is for you (or another programmer) to understand what type of data the variable holds.

For example, looking at the earlier BASIC code of X = 9, can you tell what the X or the number 9 represents? Now look at the same code, but using a descriptive variable name:

```
BaseballPlayers = 9
```

By just changing the variable X to a more descriptive BaseballPlayers name, you can guess that the number 9 refers to the number of players on a baseball team.

Variable names can be as simple as a single word, such as Age, Name, or Salary. However, a single word may not adequately describe the contents of some variables, so programmers often use two or more words for their variable names.

This is where different programmers use different styles. Some programmers like to cram multiple words into one long variable name like this:

```
salestax
```

For two words, this can be acceptable, but when creating variable names out of three or more words, this can start getting messy, such as

```
salestaxfor2008
```

To help identify the separate words that make up a long variable name, some programmers use the underscore character, such as

```
sales_tax_for_2008
```

Other programmers prefer to use uppercase letters at the beginning of each new word, such as

```
SalesTaxFor2008;
```

You can always mix and match both conventions if you want, such as

```
SalesTaxFor_2008;
```

No matter which naming style you prefer, it's best to stick with one style to prevent your program from looking too confusing with so many different variable naming styles all over the place.

Every variable needs a unique name. If you try to give two variables identical names, the computer gets confused and refuses to run your program.

In some languages, such as the curly bracket family, which includes C, C++, and Java, variable names are case-sensitive. Therefore, a variable named salestax is considered completely different than a SalesTax variable.

Creating variables in a command

The simplest way to create a variable is when you need it in a command. Suppose you have a program that asks the user for his annual salary, such as the following command (written in the Python programming language):

```
salary = input("What is your annual salary?")
```

This command displays, `"What is your annual salary?"` on-screen and waits for the user to type in a number.

As soon as the user types in a number, such as **20000**, the program needs a variable to store this number. In this example, the program creates a `salary` variable and stores the number 20000 in that variable.

Creating variables whenever you need them in a command is simple and convenient — and potentially troublesome if you aren't careful. The biggest problem is that when you create a variable within a command, that variable can store any type of data.

Variables can hold two types of data:

- ✦ **Numbers,** which are typically used to represent quantities or measurements.
- ✦ **Text** (sometimes called *strings,* as in "text strings") is used to represent non-numeric data, such as names or mailing addresses.

You can always perform mathematical calculations on numbers, but never on text. So if a program expects to store a number in a variable, it gets confused if it receives text instead. The following Python program works perfectly just as long as the user types in a number.

```
salary = input("What is your annual salary?")
taxrate = 0.30
print "This is how much you owe in taxes = ", salary * taxrate
```

This program works as follows:

Line 1: The program displays, `"What is your annual salary?"` Then it waits for the user to type in a number. If the user types in **20000**, the program stores the number 20000 in the `salary` variable.

Line 2: Store the number 0.30 in the `taxrate` variable.

Line 3: Multiply the number in the `salary` variable by the number in the `taxrate` variable and print out the result. If the `salary` variable holds the number 20000, the program prints, `"This is how much you owe in taxes = 6000.0"`.

Instead of typing the number 20000, what if the user types in **20,000**? Because the program doesn't recognize 20,000 as a valid number (because of the comma), the program treats 20,000 as text that's no different than twenty thousand. Trying to multiply the number 0.30 by the text 20,000 doesn't make sense, so the program stops running, as shown in Figure 2-1.

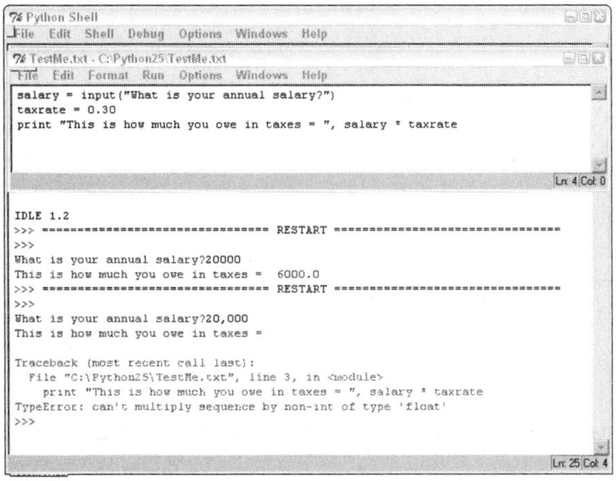

Book II Chapter 2

Variables, Data Types, and Constants

Figure 2-1: If a program tries to store the wrong type of data in a variable, the program stops running.

Declaring the data type of a variable

You can never stop users from typing in the wrong type of data, such as typing in the words **twenty thousand** instead of the number 20000. However, you can protect yourself from trying to do something wrong, like multiplying a number by text. In the Python programming language, the following program actually runs:

```
salary = input("What is your annual salary?")
taxrate = "Thirty percent"
print "This is how much you owe in taxes = ", salary *
    taxrate
```

In this program, the third line tries to multiple the `salary` variable by the `taxrate` variable. If the program asks the user, `"What is your annual salary?"`, and the user types **20000**, the third line of the program tries to multiply 20000 (stored in the `salary` variable) by `Thirty percent`. Obviously, you can't multiply a number by a word, so this program would appear to work but prints only:

```
This is how much you owe in taxes =
```

The problem occurs because the program multiplies the `salary` variable by the text `Thirty percent`. Even though the program appears to run, it doesn't run correctly.

If you're writing a small program, you could examine your program, line-by-line, to see where the problem might be, but in a large program that might consist of thousands of lines, trying to track down this simple problem could be time-consuming and frustrating.

To avoid this problem, many programming languages force you to define *(declare)* your variable names plus the type of data they can hold. By doing this, you can have the compiler check your program to make sure you aren't mixing data types accidentally, such as trying to multiply a number by text.

If your program does try to mix data types by multiplying a number by text, the compiler refuses to run your program, displays an error message, and highlights the problem so you can fix it right away, as shown in Figure 2-2.

Declaring variables

Every programming language has its own way of declaring variables and defining a data type:

- In the C programming language, you declare the data type followed by the variable name:

  ```
  int salary;
  ```

- In the Pascal programming language, you first define a variable declaration heading (Var) and then declare the variable name followed by the data type:

  ```
  Var salary : integer;
  ```

- In the Visual Basic programming language, you declare the variable name by using a `Dim` keyword, followed by the variable name, the `as` keyword, and then the data type of that variable: `Dim salary as Integer`.

All three programming language examples create the same `salary` variable and define that variable to hold only integer data types, which are any whole number, such as 45, 1093, or -39.

In many programming languages, you must always declare a variable before you can use it (otherwise, the computer doesn't know what type of data you want to store in that variable). Most of the time, you declare your variables at the top of a program. This makes it easy for anyone to see both how many variables the program uses, and all their names and data types at a glance.

Although it's possible to bury a variable declaration in the middle of a program, doing so makes it harder for other programmers to find. Putting your variable declarations at the top of your program is considered good programming practice for the same reason that books put their table of contents in the front of the book rather than burying it in the middle. Everyone expects to open a book and be able to browse the book's contents just by looking at the table of contents. Likewise, programmers expect to find all the variable names and data types just by looking at the top of a program.

Book II
Chapter 2

Variables,
Data Types,
and Constants

Figure 2-2:
You can't compile your program until the compiler is certain that you aren't mixing different data types.

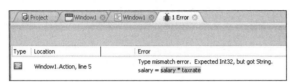

Using Different Data Types

Defining a specific data type makes it easy to

✦ **Know the type of data a variable can hold (either numbers or text).**

✦ **Restrict the range of data the variable can hold.**

✦ **Identify whether a variable can hold a number or text can keep your program from trying to add or multiply a number by a word, which doesn't work.** Figure 2-3 shows the different categories of data types within most programming languages.

Common Programming Data Types

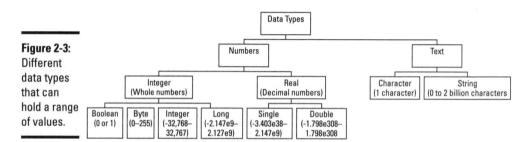

Figure 2-3:
Different data types that can hold a range of values.

Defining the range of data can prevent a variable from storing incorrect data. For example, if your program asks the user to type in his age, invalid data would include negative numbers, zero, and extremely large numbers, such as 259.

The range of numbers listed for `Long`, `Single`, and `Double` data types are listed as exponential numbers (that's the little *e*). So the `Long` data type can store a number as large as 2.147 with the decimal place moved nine places to the right or approximately 2,147,000,000.

Every programming language offers different data types, so use Figure 2-3 as a guideline rather than a strict reference.

For example, if you want to store a person's age in a variable, you probably want to store it as a whole number (such as 45) rather than a real number (such as 45.029).

Next, you want to choose a data type that contains the range of values a person's age might be. From Figure 2-3, you can see that a `Boolean` data type can only hold a 0 or 1. An `Integer` data type can hold negative numbers as small as -32,768 or positive numbers as large as 32,767. However, the range of an `Integer` data type is too large for a person's age. Nobody has a negative age and nobody has an age anywhere close to 32,767.

So the best data type to choose for storing a person's age is the `Byte` data type, which can store numbers from 0 to 255. If your program tries to store a number less than 0 or greater than 255 as a person's age, the `Byte` data type screams in protest and refuses to do it, a process known as *type-checking*.

Type-checking only makes sure that your program doesn't try to store incorrect data in a variable, but it can't protect against a clumsy user typing in his age as a negative number or a massively unrealistic number. To prevent user input error, programs must validate that the data is correct. If a person types **0** for his age, your program must refuse to accept the incorrect data and ask the user to try again. That means you must always write extra commands in your program to check for valid data that's received from the outside world.

Another reason to use different data types is to reduce the amount of memory your program needs. It's possible to declare an `Age` variable as either a `Byte` or `Integer` data type, as shown in the following Visual Basic code:

```
Dim Age as Byte
```

Or

```
Dim Age as Integer
```

Although both `Age` variables can store whole numbers, such as `39`, the `Byte` data type uses less memory (1 byte) than the `Integer` data type (4 bytes).

A *byte* is just a measurement unit where 1 byte represents the space needed to store a single character (such as `B` or `8`). In comparison, a typical sentence requires 100 bytes of storage, a page in a book might require 10,000 bytes, and a novel might require 1 million bytes.

Bytes measure both storage space and memory so a `Byte` data type (storing the number 48) needs only 1 byte of space whereas an `Integer` data type (storing the same number 48) would need four times as much space. If you choose the wrong data type, your program still works, but it uses up more hard disk space or memory than necessary. Table 2-1 lists common storage requirements for different data types.

Table 2-1	Typical Storage Requirements for Different Data Types
Data Type	*Storage Size*
Byte	1 byte
Boolean	2 bytes
Character	2 bytes
Integer	4 bytes
Single	4 bytes
Long	8 bytes
Double	8 bytes
String	10 bytes + (2 * string length)

(If you had a string consisting of three letters, that string would take up 10 bytes of storage space plus (2 multiplied by three letters or 10 + (2 * 3), which is 16 bytes.)

So when declaring variables as specific data types, you want to choose the data type that can

✦ **Hold a range of valid values.**

✦ **Uses the least amount of space as possible.**

Storing Data in a Variable

After you declare a variable, store data in that variable as the following C program demonstrates:

```
int age;
age = 15;
```

Line 1: Declares the age variable as an integer data type.

Line 2: Stuffs the number 15 into the age variable.

You can assign a fixed value (like 15) to a variable or any equation that creates a value, such as

```
taxes_owed = salary * 0.30;
```

If the value of the salary variable is 1000, this command multiplies 1000 (the salary variable's value) by 0.30, which is 300. The number 300 then gets stored in the taxes_owed variable.

When storing data in variables, make sure the variable is either empty or contains data you can afford to lose. Variables can hold only one item at a time, so storing a new value in a variable wipes out the old value, as shown in Figure 2-4 and in the following BASIC code:

```
Salary = 25000
Salary = 17000 + 500
PRINT "This is the value of the Salary variable = ", Salary
```

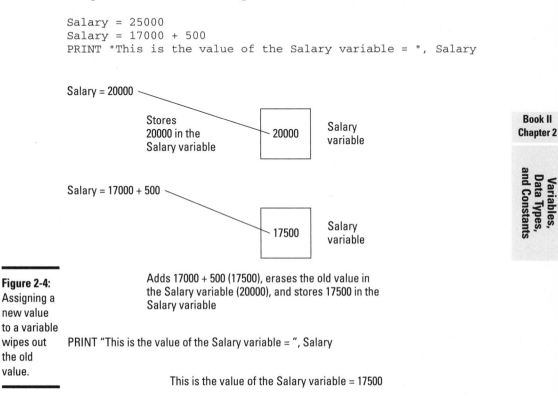

Figure 2-4:
Assigning a new value to a variable wipes out the old value.

If you store a value in a variable and then immediately store a second value in that same value, you wipe out the first value in that variable. Obviously, there's no point in storing data in a variable only to wipe it out later, so when you store a value in a variable, you'll eventually want to use that value again. (Otherwise, there's no point in storing that data in the first place.)

Retrieving Data from a Variable

After you store data in a variable, you can treat that variable exactly like a fixed value. In this first Python language example, the print command just prints, "This is when I plan on retiring = 65".

```
print "This is when I plan on retiring = ", 65
```

Replacing the fixed value (65) with a variable and assigning the value of 65 to that variable creates the following:

```
age = 65
print "This is when I plan on retiring = ", age
```

Line 1: Stores the value 65 into the `age` variable.

Line 2: Prints, `"This is when I plan on retiring = "`, takes the last value stored in the `age` variable (which is 65), and prints that value out so the entire message that appears on the screen is:

```
This is when I plan on retiring = 65
```

Besides using variables as if they're a fixed value, you can also assign the value of one variable to another, such as

```
first_number - 39
second_number = first_number + 6
```

Line 1: Stores the number 39 into the `first_number` variable.

Line 2: Adds the number 6 to the value in the `first_number` variable (39) and assigns this sum (45) into the `second_number` variable.

You can also modify a variable by itself, as shown in this example:

```
people = 5
people = people + 12
```

Line 1: Stores the value of 5 into the `people` variable.

Line 2: Tells the computer to do the following:

1. **Find the value stored in the `people` variable (5) and add it to the number 12 for a total of 17.**

2. **Store the value of 17 into the `people` variable, wiping out the last value stored there (which was 5).**

Essentially, variables are nothing more than values that can change while the program runs. In the preceding example, one moment the value of the `people` variable was 5, and the next moment the value of that same `people` variable was 17.

Using Constant Values

As a general rule, never use fixed values directly in your program. The reason for this is simple. Suppose you need to calculate the sales tax in three different places in your program. Near the top of your program, you might have a command like this:

```
Material_cost = Item_cost + (Item_Cost * 0.075)
```

Buried in the middle of your program, you might have another command like this:

```
Product_cost = Part_cost + (Part_Cost * 0.075)
```

Near the bottom of your program, you might have a third command like this:

```
Project_cost = Material_cost + Product_cost + (Material_cost
    + Product_cost) * 0.075
```

In all three commands, the number 0.075 represents the current sales tax (7.5 percent). What happens if the sales tax suddenly jumps to 8 percent? Now you have to go through your entire program, find the number 0.075, and replace it with the number 0.080.

Searching and replacing one value with another can be tedious, especially in a large program. As an alternative to using fixed values directly in your commands, you can use constants instead.

As the name implies, constants are like variables that hold only a single value that never changes. So you could define the value of your sales tax just once, as the following Visual Basic code shows:

```
Const sales_tax as Single = 0.075
```

This command tells the computer:

✦ Use the `Const` keyword to create a `sales_tax` constant.

✦ Define the `sales_tax` variable as a `Single` data type.

✦ Store the value `0.075` into the `sales_tax` variable.

By using constants, you can eliminate fixed values in your commands and replace them with a constant instead, such as

```
Const sales_tax as Single = 0.075
Material_cost = Item_cost + (Item_Cost * sales_tax)
Product_cost = Part_cost + (Part_Cost * sales_tax)
Project_cost = Material_cost + Product_cost + (Material_cost
    + Product_cost) * sales_tax
```

Now if the sales tax changes from 0.075 to 0.080, you just need to change this value in one constant declaration, such as

```
Const sales_tax as Single = 0.080
```

This one change effectively plugs in the value of 0.080 everywhere your program uses the `sales_tax` constant. So constants offer two advantages:

+ **They let you replace fixed values with descriptive constant names.**

+ **They let you change the value of a constant once and have those changes occur automatically in the rest of your program.**

  So use constants to replace fixed values and use variables to store different types of data retrieved from the outside world. Every program needs to use variables, but not every program needs to use constants.

After you understand how to store data temporarily in variables, your program can start manipulating that data to do something useful.

Defining the Scope of a Variable

The scope of a variable defines which part of your program can store and retrieve data in a variable. Because variables store data that your program needs to work correctly, your program must make sure that no other part of the program accidentally modifies that data.

If your program stores a person's credit card number in a variable, you don't want another part of your program to accidentally retrieve that data and change the numbers around or send a hundred copies of each credit card number to customers outside the company.

So when creating variables, limit the variables' scope. The *scope* simply defines which parts of your program can access a variable. When you declare a variable, you also define one of three possible scope levels for that variable:

+ **Global**

+ **Module**

+ **Subprogram**

Handling global variables with care

In a global variable, any part of your program can access that variable, including storing new data in that variable (and wiping out any existing data already stored in that variable), changing the data in a variable, or wiping out the data in a variable altogether, as shown in Figure 2-5.

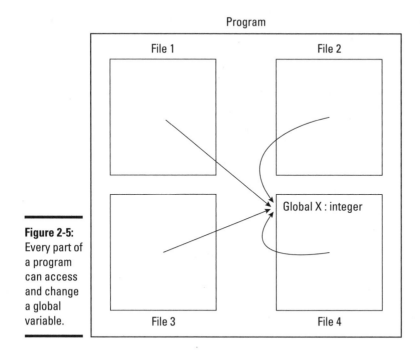

Program

File 1

File 2

Global X : integer

File 3

File 4

Figure 2-5:
Every part of
a program
can access
and change
a global
variable.

Use global variables sparingly. If you create a global variable and some part of your program keeps modifying that variable's data by mistake, you have to search through your entire program to find which command is messing up that variable. If you have a million-line program, guess what? You have to examine a million lines of code to find the one line that's changing that variable by mistake. If that's your idea of fun, go ahead and use global variables.

In the old days, all programming languages let you create global variables, and it was up to the programmer to make sure no commands accidentally modified that variable in unintended ways. When writing small programs, programmers can do this easily, but when working on massive programs created by teams of programmers, the odds of abusing global variables increases dramatically.

Think of a shelf where you can store your books, wallet, and laptop computer. If you're the only person who has access to that shelf, you can be sure anything you put on that shelf is there when you look for it again.

Now imagine putting your shelf of personal belongings (books, wallet, and laptop computer) on a shelf located in Grand Central Station where thousands of people can grab anything they want off that shelf or put something else on there instead. Would you feel safe leaving your wallet and laptop on such a shelf? If not, you probably wouldn't feel safe putting your data in a global variable either.

Because global variables can be so dangerous, most programming languages don't let you create a global variable unless you specifically tell the computer to create one. To create a global variable, you often have to use a special keyword, such as `global` or `public`, such as

```
Global X : Integer
```

The preceding command tells the computer to create a global variable, called X, that can hold an integer data type. You type a global variable declaration in any file that contains your main program or a library of subprograms.

Restricting scope to a module

A *module* is another term for a separate file. If you divide a large program into subprograms and store those subprograms in a separate file, each file is a module. A *module variable* lets you create a variable that can be accessed only by code stored in that particular module, as shown in Figure 2-6.

The advantage of module variables is that they give you the convenience of a global variable but without the danger of letting every part of a program access that variable. Instead, module scope limits access only to code in that file.

Although an improvement over global variables, module variables also have some of the disadvantages of global variables. If a file contains a lot of subprograms, trying to find which line of code is messing up your module variable can still be troublesome.

To create a module variable, you generally just declare a variable at the top of any file except you don't use the `Global` or `Public` keyword. In some programming languages, you declare a module variable with the `Private` keyword, such as

```
Private X : integer;
```

The preceding code would declare a module variable called X, which can hold an integer data type.

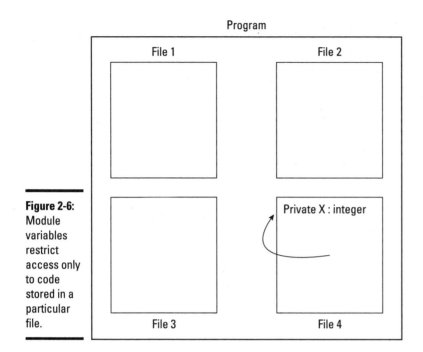

Figure 2-6:
Module variables restrict access only to code stored in a particular file.

Program

File 1

File 2

Private X : integer

File 3

File 4

Isolating variables in a subprogram

Because global and module variables can be dangerous to use because any part of a program can change them, most programmers use global and module variables sparingly. Most of the time, programmers declare variables within a subprogram. Therefore, the only code that can access that variable is inside the subprogram itself, as shown in Figure 2-7.

To create a variable with subprogram scope, you have to declare your variable at the top of that particular subprogram. The subprogram effectively isolates that variable from any other part of your program.

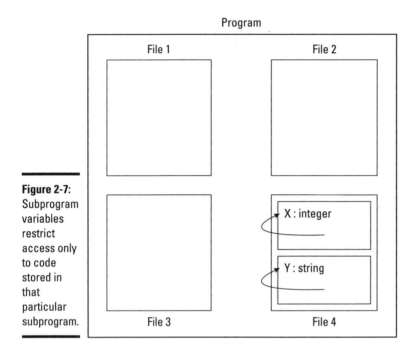

Figure 2-7: Subprogram variables restrict access only to code stored in that particular subprogram.

Passing data among subprograms

If one subprogram needs to use data stored in another subprogram, what's the solution? The easiest (and most dangerous) solution is to let multiple subprograms access that variable as a global or module variable.

The better solution is to isolate that variable as a subprogram variable and then share or *pass* that data to another subprogram. This means you have to declare two subprograms variables, one in each subprogram. Although cumbersome (now you know why programs create global or module variables instead), passing data from one variable to another, dubbed *parameter passing,* helps keeps the data isolated in only the subprograms that actually need to use that data, as shown in Figure 2-8.

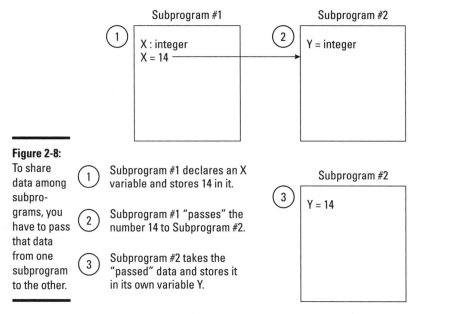

Figure 2-8:
To share data among subprograms, you have to pass that data from one subprogram to the other.

(1) Subprogram #1 declares an X variable and stores 14 in it.

(2) Subprogram #1 "passes" the number 14 to Subprogram #2.

(3) Subprogram #2 takes the "passed" data and stores it in its own variable Y.

TIP

As a general rule, restrict the scope of your variables as small as possible. This makes sure that as few lines of code can access that variable and mess up your program.

Chapter 3: Manipulating Data

In This Chapter

✔ **Using assignment and math operators**

✔ **Understanding string manipulation**

✔ **Using comparison and Boolean operators**

✔ **Performing data type conversions**

*E*very program accepts data from the outside world, manipulates that data in some way, and then calculates a useful result. Data can be

✦ **Numbers**

✦ **Text**

✦ **Input from a keyboard, controller, or joystick (for a video game)**

To manipulate numbers, computers can perform a variety of mathematical operations, which is just a fancy way of saying a computer can add, subtract, multiply, and divide. To manipulate text (or *strings*, as in "text strings"), computers can perform a variety of string manipulation operations, which can chop out a letter of a word or rearrange the letters that make up a word.

Every programming language provides built-in commands *(operators)* for manipulating numbers and strings, but some programming languages are better at manipulating numbers (or *strings*) than others.

For example, FORTRAN is specifically designed to make scientific calculations easy, so FORTRAN has more operators for mathematical operations than a language such as SNOBOL, which was designed primarily for manipulating text strings. You can still manipulate strings in FORTRAN or calculate mathematical equations in SNOBOL; however, you need to write a lot more commands to do so.

Programming languages typically provide two types of data manipulation commands:

✦ **Operators** are usually symbols that represent simple calculations, such as addition (+) or multiplication (*).

✦ **Functions** are commands that perform more sophisticated calculations, such as calculating the square root of a number.

Unlike operators, which are usually symbols, functions are usually short commands, such as SQRT (square root).

By combining both operators and functions, you can create your own commands for manipulating data in different ways.

Storing Data with the Assignment Operator

The simplest operator that almost every programming language has is the *assignment operator,* which is nothing more than the equal sign (=) symbol, such as

```
VariableName = Value
```

The assignment operator simply stores or *assigns* a value to a variable. That value can be a fixed number, a specific string, or a mathematical equation that calculates a single value. Some examples of the assignment operator are shown in Table 3-1.

Table 3-1	Examples of Using the Assignment (=) Operator
Example	*What It Does*
Age = 35	Stores the number 35 into the Age variable
Name = "Cat"	Stores the string "Cat" into a Name variable
A = B + 64.26	Adds the value stored in the B variable to the number 64.26 and stores the sum in the A variable
Answer = "Why"	Stores the string "Why" in the Answer variable

Using Math to Manipulate Numbers

Because manipulating numbers (or *number crunching*) is such a common task for computers, every programming language provides commands for addition, subtraction, multiplication, and division. Table 3-2 lists common mathematical operations and the symbols to use.

Table 3-2	Common Mathematical Operators		
Operation	*Symbol*	*Example*	*Result*
Addition	+	3 + 10.27	13.27
Subtraction	−	89.4 − 9.2	80.2
Multiplication	*	5 * 9	45
Division	/	120 / 5	24
Integer division	\	6 \ 4	1
Modulus	% or mod	6 % 4 or 6 mod 4	2
Exponentiation	^	2^4	16

Integer division always calculates a whole number, which represents how many times one number can divide into another one. In Table 3-2, the 6 \ 4 operation asks the computer, "How many times can you divide 6 by 4?" You can only do it once, so the calculation of 6 \ 4 = 1.

Some other examples of integer division are

23 \ 5 = 4

39 \ 7 = 5

13 \ 3 = 3

The modulus operator divides two numbers and returns the remainder. Most of the curly bracket languages, such as C++, use the percentage sign (%) as the modulus operator whereas other languages, such as BASIC, use the mod command. Some examples of modulus calculation are

23 % 5 = 3

39 % 7 = 4

13 % 3 = 1

The exponentiation operator multiplies one number by itself a fixed number of times. So the 2^4 command tells the computer to multiply 2 by itself four times or 2 * 2 * 2 * 2 = 16. Some other examples of exponentiation are

2^3 = (2 * 2 * 2) = 8

4^2 = (4 * 4) = 16

9^1 = (9 * 1) = 9

Organizing equations with operator precedence

To do multiple calculations, you can type one mathematical calculation after another, such as

```
X = 34 + 7
Y = X * 89
```

Although this works, it can get clumsy, especially if you need to write more than a handful of equations. As a simple solution, you can cram multiple equations into a single, big equation, such as

```
Y = 34 + 7 * 89
```

The problem is, how does the computer calculate this equation? Does it first add 34 + 7 and then use this result (41) to multiple with 89? Or does it first multiply 7 by 89 and then add this result (623) to 34?

Depending on the order it calculates its mathematical operators, the result is either 3649 or 657, two obviously different answers.

To calculate any equation with multiple mathematical operators, computers follow rules that define which mathematical operators get calculated first (known as *operator precedence*). Table 3-3 lists common operator precedence for most programming languages where the top operators have the highest precedence, and the lowest operators at the bottom of the table have the lowest precedence.

Table 3-3	Operator Precedence
Operator	*Symbol*
Exponentiation	^
Multiplication	*
Division	/
Integer division	\
Modulus arithmetic	% or mod
Addition	+
Subtraction	–

If an equation contains operators that have equal precedence, the computer calculates the result from left to right, such as

```
X = 8 – 3 + 7
```

First, the computer calculates 8 – 3, which is 5 Then it calculates 5 + 7, which is 12.

If an equation contains operators with different precedence, the computer calculates the highest precedence operator first. Looking at this equation, you can see that the multiplication (*) operator has higher precedence than the addition (+) operator.

```
Y = 34 + 7 * 89
```

So the computer first calculates 7 * 89, which is 623 and then adds 34 to get 657.

What if you really wanted the computer to first calculate 34 + 7 and then multiply this result by 89? To do this, you have to enclose that part of the equation in parentheses, such as

```
Y = (34 + 7) * 89
```

The parentheses tell the computer to calculate that result first. So first this is how the computer calculates the preceding equation:

```
Y = (34 + 7) * 89
Y = 41 * 89
Y = 3649
```

You should always use parentheses to make sure the computer calculates your equation exactly the way you want.

Using built-in math functions

Using basic mathematical operators, you can create any type of complicated formulas, such as calculating a quadratic equation or a generating random numbers. However, writing equations to calculate something as common (to scientists and mathematicians, anyway) as logarithms, might seem troublesome. Not only do you have to waste time writing such an equation, but you have to spend even more time testing to make sure it works correctly as well.

So to prevent people from rewriting commonly needed equations, most programming languages include built-in math functions that are either

+ **Part of the language itself** (such as in many versions of BASIC)

+ **Available as separate libraries** (such as math libraries included with most C compilers)

The advantage of using built-in math functions is that you can use them without having to write any extra command that you may not want to do or may not know how to do. For example, how do you calculate the square root of a number?

Most likely, you won't have any idea, but you don't have to because you can calculate the square root of a number just by using that language's built-in square root math function. So if you wanted to know the square root of 34 and store it in an `Answer` variable, you could just use the `sqrt` math function, such as

```
Answer = sqrt(34)
```

In some languages, such as BASIC, it doesn't matter if you type a math function in either uppercase or lowercase. In other languages, such as C, commands like `SQRT` and `sqrt` are considered two completely different functions, so you must know if your language requires you to type a math function in all uppercase or all lowercase.

Table 3-4 lists some common built-in math functions found in many programming languages.

Table 3-4	Common Built-In Math Functions	
Math Function	*What It Does*	*Example*
abs (x)	Finds the absolute value of x	abs (–45) = 45
cos (x)	Finds the cosine of x	cos (2) = – 0.41614684
exp (x)	Returns a number raised to the power of x	exp (3) = 20.0855369
log (x)	Finds the logarithm of x	log (4) = 1.38629436
sqrt (x)	Finds the square root of x	sqrt (5) = 2.23606798

By using math operators and math functions, you can create complex equations, such as

```
x = 67 * cos (5) + sqrt (7)
```

Rather than plug fixed values into a math function, it's more flexible just to plug in variables instead, such as

```
Angle = 5
Height = 7
X = 67 * cos (Angle) + sqrt (Height)
```

Manipulating Strings

Just as math operators can manipulate numbers, so can string operators manipulate strings. The simplest and most common string operator is the *concatenation operator,* which smashes two strings together to make a single string.

Most programming languages use either the plus sign (+) or the ampersand (&) symbol as the concatenation operator, such as

```
Name = "Joe " + "Smith"
```

or

```
Name = "Joe " & "Smith"
```

In the Perl language, the concatenation symbol is the dot (.) character, such as

```
$Name = "Joe " . "Smith";
```

In the preceding examples, the concatenation operator takes the string `"Joe "` and combines it with the second string `"Smith"` to create a single string that contains `"Joe Smith"`.

When concatenating strings, you may need to insert a space between the two strings. Otherwise, the concatenation operator smashes both strings together like `"JoeSmith"`, which you may not want.

For more flexibility in manipulating strings, many programming languages include built-in string functions. These functions can help you manipulate strings in different ways, such as counting the number of characters in a string or removing characters from a string. Table 3-5 lists some common built-in string functions found in many programming languages.

Not all programming languages include these string functions, and if they do, they'll likely use different names for the same functions. For example, Visual Basic has a `Trim` function for removing characters from a string, but Perl uses a `substr` function that performs the same task.

Table 3-5	Common Built-In String Functions	
String Function	*What It Does*	*Example*
length (*x*)	Counts the number of characters in a string (x), including spaces	length (Hi there!) = 9
trim (*x, y*)	Removes characters from a string	trim (Mary, 1) = ary
index (*x, y*)	Returns the position of a string within another string	index (korat, ra) = 3
compare (*x, y*)	Compares two strings to see if they're identical	compare (A, a) = False
replace (*x, y, z*)	Replaces one string from within another	replace (Batter, att, ik) = Biker

Finding Strings with Regular Expressions

Before you can manipulate a string, you first must *find it.* Although some programming languages include string searching functions, most of them are fairly limited to finding exact matches of strings.

To remedy this problem, many programming languages (such as Perl and Tcl) use regular expressions. (A *regular expression* is just a series of symbols that tell the computer how to find a specific pattern in a string.)

If a programming language doesn't offer built-in support for regular expressions, many programmers have written subprogram libraries that let you add regular expressions to your program. By using regular expressions, your programs can perform more sophisticated text searching than any built-in string functions could ever do.

Pattern matching with the single character (.) wildcard

The simplest way to search for a pattern is to look for a single character. For example, you might want to know if a certain string begins with the letter *b,* ends with the letter *t,* and contains exactly one character between. Although you could repetitively check every three-character string that begins with *b* and ends with *t,* like *bat* or *but,* it's much easier to use a single-character wildcard instead, which is a dot or period character (.).

So if you want to find every three-letter string that begins with a *b* and ends with a *t,* you'd use this regular expression:

```
b.t
```

To search for multiple characters, use the (.) wildcard multiple times to match multiple characters. So the pattern `b..t` matches the strings *boot* and *boat* with the two (..) wildcards representing the two characters between the *b* and the *t.*

Of course, the `b..t` pattern doesn't match *bat* because *bat* has only one character between the *b* and the *t.* Nor does it match *boost* because *boost* has more than two characters between the *b* and the *t.*

When using the (.) wildcard, you must know the exact number of characters to match.

Pattern matching for specific characters

The (.) wildcard can find any character whether it's a letter, number, or symbol. Rather than search for any character, you can also search for a list of specific characters by using the square bracket [ ] symbols.

Enclose the characters you want to find inside the square brackets. So if you want to find all strings that begin with *b,* end with *t,* and have an *a, o,* or *u* between, you could use this regular expression:

```
b[aou]t
```

The preceding example finds words, like *bat* or *bot,* but doesn't find *boat* or *boot* because the regular expression looks only for a single character sandwiched between the *b* and the *t* characters.

As an alternative to listing the specific characters you want to find, you can also use the not (^) character to tell the computer which characters you don't want to find, such as

```
b[^ao]t
```

This tells the computer to find any string that doesn't have an *a* or an *o* between the *b* and the *t,* such as *but.* If you have the string *bat,* the b[^ao]t regular expression ignores it.

Pattern matching with the multiple character (*) and (+) wildcards

Sometimes you may want to find a string that has a specific character, but you don't care how many copies of that character you may find. That's when you can use the (*) wildcard to search for zero or more specific characters in a string.

So if you want to find a string that begins with *bu* and contains zero or more *z* characters at the end, you could use this regular expression:

```
buz*
```

This finds strings like *bu, buz, buzz,* and *buzzzzzz.* Because you want to find zero or more copies of the *z* character, you place the (*) wildcard after the *z* character.

The (*) finds zero or more characters, but what if you want to find at least one character? That's when you use the (+) wildcard instead. To search for a character, you place the (+) wildcard after that character, such as

```
buz+
```

This finds *buz* and *buzzzz* but not *bu* because the (+) wildcard needs to find at least a *z* character.

Pattern matching with ranges

Wildcards can match zero or more characters, but sometimes you may want to know whether a particular character falls within a range or characters. To do this, you can use ranges. For example, if you want to know whether a character is any letter, you could use the pattern [a-z] as follows:

```
bu[a-z]
```

This finds strings, such as *but, bug,* or *bus,* but not *bu* (not a three-character string). Of course, you don't need to search for letters from *a* to *z.* You can just as well search for the following:

```
bu[d-s]
```

This regular expression finds *bud* and *bus* but not *but* (because the *t* lies outside the range of letters from *d* to *s*).

You can also use ranges to check whether a character falls within a numeric range, such as

```
21[0-9]
```

This finds the strings *212* and *210.* If you only wanted to find strings with numbers between 4 and 7, you'd use this regular expression:

```
21[4-7]
```

This finds the strings *215* but not the strings *210* or *218* because both 0 and 8 lie outside the defined range of 4–7. Table 3-6 shows examples of different regular expressions and the strings that they find.

This section shows a handful of regular expression symbols you can use to search for string patterns. A lot more regular expressions can perform all sorts of weird and wonderful pattern searching, so you can always find out more about these other options by browsing www.regular-expressions.info.

By stringing multiple regular expression wildcards together, you can search for a variety of different string patterns, as shown in Table 3-6.

Table 3-6   Examples of Pattern Matching with Different Regular Expressions

Pattern	Matches These Strings
t..k	talk
	tusk
f[aeiou]t	fat
	fit
	fet
d[^ou]g	dig
	dmg
zo*	zo
	zoo
	z
zo+	zo
	zoo
sp[a–f]	spa
	spe
	spf
key[0–9]	key4
p[aei].[0–9]	pey8
	pit6
	pa21

You can always combine regular expressions to create complicated search patterns, such as the last regular expression in Table 3-6:

```
p[aei].[0-9]
```

This regular expression might look like a mess, but you can dissect it one part at a time. First, it searches for this four-character pattern:

✦ The first character must start with *p*.

✦ The second character must only be an *a, e,* or *i:* `[aei]`.

✦ The third character defines the (`.`) wildcard, so it can be anything from a letter, number, or symbol.

✦ The fourth character must be a number: `[0-9]`.

As you can see, regular expressions give you a powerful and simple way to search for various string patterns. After you find a particular string, you can manipulate it with the built-in string manipulation functions and operators in a specific programming language.

Using Comparison Operators

Unlike math and string operators that can change data, comparison operators compare two chunks of data to determine which one is bigger than the other. Table 3-7 lists common comparison operators. When comparison operators compare two items, the comparison operator returns one of two values: `True` or `False`.

A single comparison operation is also called a *conditional expression*.

The values `True` and `False` are known as Boolean values or Boolean arithmetic. (The mathematician who invented Boolean arithmetic is named George Boole.) Computers are essentially built on Boolean arithmetic because you program them by flipping switches either on (`True`) or off (`False`). All programming ultimately boils down to a series of on-off commands, which is why machine language consists of nothing but 0's and 1's.

Table 3-7	Common Comparison Operators		
Comparison Operator	*What It Means*	*Example*	*Result*
= or ==	Equal	45 = 37 A = A	False True
<	Less than	563 < 904 a"< A	True False
<=	Less than or equal to	23 < – 58 b < – B	True False
>	Greater than	51 > 4 A > a	True False
>=	Greater than or equal to	76 >= 76 a > – z	True False
< > or !=	Not equal to	46 < > 9 a < > a	True False

Many curly bracket languages, such as C, use ! = as their not equal comparison operator instead of < >.

Curly bracket languages, such as C and C++, use the double equal sign (==) as the equal comparison operator whereas other languages just use the single equal sign (=). If you use a single equal sign in C/C++, you'll assign a value rather than compare two values. In other words, your C/C++ program will work, but it won't work correctly.

Knowing whether two values are equal, greater than, less than, or not equal to one another is useful to make your program make decisions, which you read about in Chapter 4 of this mini-book.

Comparing two numbers is straightforward, such as

5 > 2

Comparing two numbers always calculates the same result. In this case, 5 > 2 always returns a `True` value. What gives comparison operators more flexibility is when they compare variables, such as

Age > 2

Depending on what the value of the `Age` variable may be, the value of this comparison can be either `True` or `False`.

Comparing numbers may be straightforward, but comparing strings can be more confusing. Remember, computers only understand numbers, so they use numbers to represent characters, such as symbols and letters.

Computers use the number 65 to represent *A*, the number 66 to represent *B*, all the way to the number 90 to represent *Z*. To represent lowercase letters, computers use the number 97 to represent *a*, 98 to represent *b*, all the way up to 122 to represent *z*.

The specific numbers used to represent every character on the keyboard can be found on the ASCII table, which you can view at `www.asciitable.com`.

That's why in Table 3-7 the comparison between A > a is `False` because the computer replaces each character with its equivalent code. So the comparison of characters

"A" > "a"

actually looks like this to the computer:

65 > 97

The number 65 isn't greater than 97, so this comparison returns a `False` value.

Comparing a string of characters works the same way as comparing single characters. The computer examines each string, character by character, and translates them into their numeric equivalent. So if you had the comparison

"aA" > "aa"

The computer converts all the characters into their equivalent values, such as

97 65 > 97 97

The computer examines the first character of each string. If they're equal, it continues with the second character, a third, and so on.

In the preceding example, the computer sees that the numbers 97 (which represent the character *a*) are equal, so it checks the second character. The number 65 *(A)* isn't greater than the number 97 *(a),* so this comparison returns a `False` value.

What happens if you compare unequal strings, such as

```
"aA" > "a"
```

The computer compares each character as numbers as follows:

```
97 65 > 97
```

The first numbers of each string (97) are equal, so the computer checks the second number. Because the second string *(a)* doesn't have a second character, its value is `0`. Because 65 > 0, the preceding comparison returns a `True` value.

Now look at this comparison:

```
"Aa" > "a"
```

The computer translates these characters into their equivalent numbers, as follows:

```
65 97 > 97
```

Comparing the first numbers *(characters),* the computer sees that 65 > 97, so this comparison returns a `False` value. Notice that as soon as the computer can decide whether one character is greater than another, it doesn't bother checking the second character in the first string.

Using Boolean Operators

Comparison operators always return a `True` or `False` value, which are Boolean values. Just as you can manipulate numbers (addition, subtraction, and so on) and strings (trimming or searching for characters), so can you also manipulate Boolean values.

When you manipulate a Boolean value, you get another Boolean value. Because there are only two Boolean values (`True` or `False`), every Boolean operator returns a value of either `True` or `False`.

Most programming languages offer four Boolean operators:

✦ Not

✦ And

✦ Or

✦ Xor

Like comparison operators, Boolean operators are most useful for making a program evaluate external data and react to that data. For example, every time you play a video game and get a score, the video game uses a comparison operator to compare your current score with the highest score. If your current score is greater than the highest score, your score now becomes the highest score. If your score isn't higher than the highest score, your score isn't displayed as the highest score.

Using the Not operator

The Not operator takes a Boolean value and converts it to its opposite. So if you have a True value, the Not operator converts it to False and vice versa. At the simplest example, you can use the Not operator like this:

```
Not(True) = False
```

Like using fixed values in comparison operators (5 > 2), using fixed values with Boolean operators is rather pointless. Instead, you can use variables and comparison operators with Boolean operators, such as

```
Not(Age > 2)
```

If the value of the Age variable is 3, this Boolean operation evaluates to

```
Not(Age > 2)
Not(3 > 2)
Not(True)
False
```

Using the And operator

The And operator takes two Boolean values and converts them into a single Boolean value. If both Boolean values are True, the And operator returns a True value. Otherwise, the And operator always returns a False value, as shown in Table 3-8, or the *Truth table*.

Table 3-8		The And Truth Table
First Value	*Second Value*	*Result*
True	True	True
True	False	False
False	True	False
False	False	False

So if the value of the Age variable is 3, this is how the following And operator evaluates an answer:

```
(Age > 2) AND (Age >= 18)
(3 > 2) AND (3 >= 18)
True AND False
False
```

If the value of the Age variable is 25, this is how the And operator evaluates an answer:

```
(Age > 2) AND (Age >= 18)
(25 > 2) AND (25 >= 18)
True AND True
True
```

The And operator only returns a True value if both values are True.

Rather than use the word *and* to represent the And operator, curly bracket languages, such as C/C++, use the ampersand (&) symbol instead.

Using the Or operator

Like the And operator, the Or operator takes two Boolean values and converts them into a single Boolean value. If both Boolean values are False, the Or operator returns a False value. Otherwise, the Or operator always returns a True value, as shown in Table 3-9.

Table 3-9		The Or Truth Table
First Value	*Second Value*	*Result*
True	True	True
True	False	True
False	True	True
False	False	False

So if the value of the Age variable is 3, this is how the following Or operator evaluates an answer:

```
(Age > 2) OR (Age >= 18)
(3 > 2) OR (3 >= 18)
True OR False
True
```

If the value of the Age variable is 1, this is how the Or operator evaluates an answer:

```
(Age > 2) OR (Age >= 18)
(1 > 2) OR (1 >= 18)
False OR False
False
```

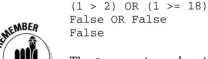

The Or operator only returns a False value if both values are False.

Rather than use the word *or* to represent the Or operator, curly bracket languages, such as C/C++, use the vertical line (|) symbol instead.

Using the Xor operator

The Xor operator is an exclusive Or. The Xor operator takes two Boolean values and converts them into a single Boolean value:

✦ If both Boolean values are True or both Boolean values are False, the Xor operator returns a False value.

✦ If one value is True and the other is False, the Xor operator returns a True value, as shown in Table 3-10.

Table 3-10	The Xor Truth Table	
First Value	*Second Value*	*Result*
True	True	False
True	False	True
False	True	True
False	False	False

So if the value of the Age variable is 3, this is how the following Xor operator evaluates an answer:

```
(Age > 2) XOR (Age >= 18)
(3 > 2) XOR (3 >= 18)
True XOR False
True
```

If the value of the Age variable is 1, this is how the Xor operator evaluates an answer:

```
(Age > 2) XOR (Age >= 18)
(1 > 2) XOR (1 >= 18)
False XOR False
False
```

The Xor operator returns a False value if both values are False or if both values are True.

Rather than use the word *xor* to represent the Xor operator, curly bracket languages, such as C/C++, use the caret (^) symbol instead.

Boolean operators are used most often to make decisions in a program, such as a video game asking, "Do you want to play again?" When you choose either Yes or No, the program uses a comparison operator, such as

```
Answer = "Yes"
```

The result depends on your answer:

✦ If your answer is Yes, the preceding comparison operation returns a True value.

   If this comparison operation is True, the video game plays again.

✦ If your answer is No, the preceding comparison operation returns a False value.

✦ If this comparison operation is False, the video game doesn't play again.

Converting Data Types

Programming languages are often divided into two categories, depending on their variables:

✦ A **type-safe** language forces you to declare your variables, and their data types, before you can use them.

   See Chapter 2 in this mini-book for more information about declaring variables types.

✦ A **typeless** language lets you store any type of data in a variable.

One moment a variable can hold a string, another moment it can hold an integer, and then another moment it might hold a decimal number.

Both type-safe and typeless languages have their pros and cons, but one problem with type-safe languages is that they prevent you from mixing data types. For example, suppose you need to store someone's age in a variable. You might declare your `Age` variable as a `Byte` data type, like this in Visual Basic:

```
Dim Age as Byte
```

As a `Byte` data type, the `Age` variable can hold only numbers from 0–255, which is exactly what you want. However, what if you declare an `AverageAge` variable as a `Single` (decimal) data, and a `People` variable as an `Integer` data type, such as

```
Dim People as Integer
Dim AverageAge as Single
```

**Book II
Chapter 3**

At this point, you have three different data types: `Byte`, `Integer`, and `Single`. Now what would happen if you try mixing these data types in a command, such as

```
AverageAge = Age / People
```

The `AverageAge` variable is a `Single` data type, the `Age` variable is a `Byte` data type, and the `People` data type is an `Integer` data type. Type-safe languages, such as C or Pascal, scream and refuse to compile and run this program simply because you're mixing data types together.

So to get around this problem, you must use special data conversion functions that are built-in to the programming language. Data conversion functions simply convert one data type into another so that all variables use the same data type.

Most programming languages have built-in data conversion functions, although their exact names vary from one language to another.

In the preceding example, the `AverageAge` variable is a `Single` data type, so you must convert every variable to a `Single` data type before you can store its contents into the `AverageAge` variable, such as

```
Dim People as Integer
Dim AverageAge as Single
Dim Age as Byte
AverageAge = CSng(Age) / CSng(People)
```

The `CSng` function converts the `Age` variable from a `Byte` to a `Single` data type. Then the second `CSng` function converts the `People` variable from an `Integer` to a `Single` data type. Only after all values have been converted

Manipulating Data

to a `Single` data type can you store the value into the `AverageAge` variable, which can hold only a `Single` data type.

When you convert data types, you may lose some precision in your numbers. For example, converting an `Integer` data type (such as 67) to a `Single` data type means converting the number 67 to 67.0. But what if you convert a `Single` data type (such as 3.14) to an `Integer` data type? Then the computer rounds the value to the nearest whole number, so the number 3.14 gets converted into 3. What happened to the 0.14? The computer throws it away. So when converting between data types, make sure you can afford to lose any precision in your numbers or else your program may wind up using inexact values, which could wreck the accuracy of your calculations.

No matter what type of data you have, every programming language allows multiple ways to manipulate that data. The way you combine operators and functions determines what your program actually does.

Chapter 4: Making Decisions by Branching

In This Chapter

✔ Using the IF-THEN, IF-THEN-ELSE, and IF-THEN-ELSEIF **statements**

✔ **Using multiple Boolean operators**

✔ Using the SELECT CASE **statement**

The simplest program lists commands one after another in a sequence, much like following the steps of a recipe. Follow a recipe step by step and you always create the same dish. If a program lists commands step by step, the computer always produces the same result.

In some cases, you may want a program to do the exact same thing over and over again, such as a simple program to display traffic signals. However for most programs, you want the computer to react to outside data. To make a computer respond in different ways, a program needs to offer two or more choices for the computer to follow.

When you quit a program, the program may ask, "Do you really want to exit?" At this point, the program is giving the computer a choice of two possible actions to take based on your answer.

If you answer Yes, the computer quits the program. If you answer No, the computer keeps running the program.

When a program gives the computer a choice of two or more commands to follow, that's called a *branching* or *decision* statement.

All branching statements work the same way:

✦ A comparison operator (or a *conditional expression*) compares an expression (such as A > 45) to determine a True or False value.

✦ The branching statement offers at least two groups of commands for the computer to follow based on whether its comparison is True or False.

Picking One Choice with the IF-THEN Statement

The simplest branching statement is an IF-THEN statement, which looks like this:

```
IF (Something is True or False) THEN Command
```

The IF-THEN checks if something is True or False:

+ If something is True, the IF-THEN command tells the computer to run exactly one command.

+ If something is False, the computer doesn't run this command.

An example of a simple IF-THEN statement might occur while playing a video game, such as

```
IF (Player hit the Pause button) THEN Pause game
```

If the player hit the pause button (True), you want the computer to pause the game. If the player doesn't hit the pause button (False), you don't want to pause the game, as shown in Figure 4-1.

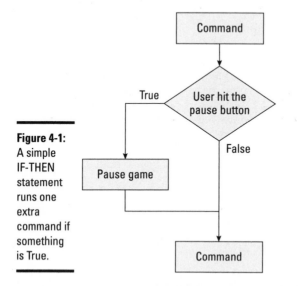

Figure 4-1:
A simple
IF-THEN
statement
runs one
extra
command if
something
is True.

The simple IF-THEN statement runs only one command if a certain condition is True. What if you want to run two or more commands? In that case, you must define a list of commands to run. A group of commands is sometimes called a *block of commands* or just a *block*.

So if you want to run more than one command in an IF-THEN statement, you must define a block of commands. In the curly bracket language family, such as C, you use curly brackets to define the beginning and end of a block of commands, such as

```
if (True or False)
   {
   command #1
   command #2
   .

   .
   command #3
   )
```

In C/C++, there is no "then" keyword used to create the IF statement.

The curly brackets tell the IF-THEN statement to run the entire block of commands enclosed within the curly brackets.

In other languages, the IF-THEN statement itself defines the start of a block and then you use an END IF command to define the end of a block, such as this BASIC language example:

```
IF (True or False) THEN
   Command #1
   Command #2
   .

   .
   Command #3
END IF
```

Finally, some languages, such as Pascal, force you to explicitly declare the beginning and end of a block of commands with the begin and end keywords, such as

```
If (True or False) then
   Begin
      Command #1
      Command #2
      .

      .
      Command #3
   End;
```

No matter what language you use, the idea is the same; you must define the beginning and end of all the commands you want the IF-THEN statement to run.

Picking Two Choices with the IF-THEN-ELSE Statement

The simple IF-THEN statement either runs a command (or block of commands) or it doesn't. But what if you want the computer to take one action if
something is True and a completely different action if something is False?
In that case, you must use a variation — an IF-THEN-ELSE statement.

The IF-THEN-ELSE statement gives the computer a choice of two mutually
exclusive choices, as shown in Figure 4-2.

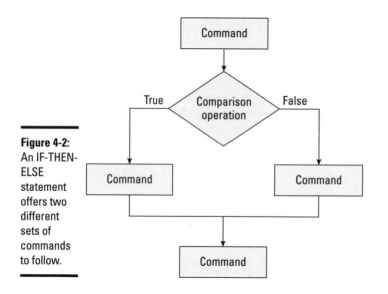

Figure 4-2:
An IF-THEN-
ELSE
statement
offers two
different
sets of
commands
to follow.

Like the simple IF-THEN statement, the IF-THEN-ELSE statement can run a
single command or a block of commands, such as

```
if (True or False) then
  {
  command #1
  command #2
  .
  .
  command #3
  }
else
  {
  command #1
```

```
command #2
  .
  .
command #3
)
```

The `IF-THEN-ELSE` statement tells the computer, "Check if something is `True`. If so, follow this set of commands. Otherwise, follow this second set of commands."

One problem with the `IF-THEN-ELSE` statement is that it only checks a single condition. If that single condition is `False`, it always runs its second set of commands, such as

```
IF (Salary > 100000) THEN
  TaxRate = 0.45
ELSE
  TaxRate = 0.30
END IF
```

In this BASIC language example, if the value of the `Salary` variable is greater than 100000, the `TaxRate` variable is always set to 0.45.

However, if the `Salary` variable isn't greater than 100000 (it's less than or equal to 100000), the `ELSE` portion of the `IF-THEN-ELSE` statement always sets the `TaxRate` variable to 0.30.

The `IF-THEN-ELSE` always gives the computer a choice of exactly two, mutually exclusive choices. What if you want to give the computer three or more possible choices? Then you must use the `IF-THEN-ELSEIF` statement.

Picking Three or More Choices with the IF-THEN-ELSEIF Statement

The `IF-THEN-ELSEIF` statement offers two advantages over the `IF-THEN-ELSE` statement:

✦ **You can check a condition for each set of commands.**

✦ **You can define three or more separate sets of commands for the computer to follow.**

Not all programming languages, such as C/C++, offer the `IF-THEN-ELSEIF` statement.

Checking a condition for each set of commands

The IF-THEN-ELSEIF statement only runs a command (or block of commands) if some condition is True, as shown in Figure 4-3.

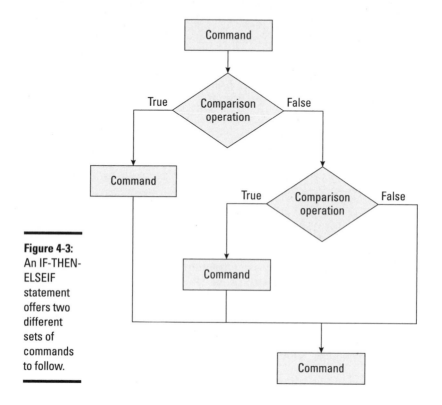

Figure 4-3:
An IF-THEN-ELSEIF statement offers two different sets of commands to follow.

If every conditional expression is False, the IF-THEN-ELSE statement doesn't run any commands. Only if one of its conditional expressions is True does the IF-THEN-ELSE statement run exactly one set of commands, such as

```
IF (Salary > 100000) THEN
  TaxRate = 0.45
ELSEIF (Salary > 50000) THEN
  TaxRate = 0.30
END IF
```

In this example, the computer has three possible choices:

- ✦ If Salary > 100000, set TaxRate = 0.45.

- ✦ If Salary > 50000 (but less than 100000), set TaxRate = 0.30.

- ✦ If Salary <= 50000, do nothing.

The first choice checks if the value of the `Salary` variable is greater than 100000, such as 250000. If so, it tells the computer to set the `TaxRate` variable to 0.45 and immediately exit out of the entire `IF-THEN-ELSEIF` statement.

The second choice only checks if the value of the `Salary` variable is greater than 50000. What happens if the `Salary` value is 150000? In that case, the first choice runs (Salary > 100000), so this second choice would've never been checked at all.

So although the second choice might seem to run if the `Salary` variable is greater than 50000, it really won't run unless Salary > 50000 and the first choice did not run, which means that the `Salary` variable must be less than or equal to 100000.

If the value of the `Salary` variable is equal or less than 50000, the third choice isn't to run any additional commands at all. Unlike the `IF-THEN-ELSE` statement, which always runs at least one set of commands, it's possible for an `IF-THEN-ELSEIF` statement to run zero commands.

Offering three or more choices

The advantage of the `IF-THEN-ELSEIF` statement is that you can check for multiple conditions and give the computer three or more possible commands (or block of commands) to follow.

To give the computer additional choices, you can just keep tacking on additional `ELSEIF` statements, such as

```
IF (True or False) THEN
   Command
ELSEIF (True or False) THEN
   Command
ELSEIF (True or False) THEN
   Command
END IF
```

This example now gives the computer three possible sets of commands to follow. If none of these conditions is `True`, the `IF-THEN-ELSEIF` statement may do nothing.

To keep checking for additional conditions, you have to add additional `ELSEIF` statements, such as

```
IF (True or False) THEN
   Command
ELSEIF (True or False) THEN
   Command
ELSEIF (True or False) THEN
   Command
```

Book II
Chapter 4

Making Decisions
by Branching

```
ELSEIF (True or False) THEN
   Command
ELSEIF (True or False) THEN
   Command
END IF
```

This example gives the computer five possible commands (or blocks of commands) for the computer to follow, although it's possible that the computer still follows zero commands.

The IF-THEN-ELSEIF statement makes the computer run exactly zero or one command (or block of commands), no matter how many additional ELSEIF statements you add on.

If you want to make sure the IF-THEN-ELSEIF statement always runs one command (or block of commands), you can tack on the ELSE statement at the very end, such as

```
IF (True or False) THEN
   Command
ELSEIF (True or False) THEN
   Command
ELSEIF (True or False) THEN
   Command
ELSEIF (True or False) THEN
   Command
ELSE
   Command
END IF
```

The ELSE statement at the end insures that the entire IF-THEN-ELSEIF statement always runs at least one command. Notice that the ELSE statement doesn't check a condition because it runs only if all preceding conditions are False, such as in the following example:

```
IF (Age > 65) THEN
   Status = Retired
ELSEIF (Age > 20) THEN
   Status = Working
ELSE
   Status = Bum
END IF
```

In this example, the IF-THEN-ELSEIF statement gives the computer three possible choices:

+ Set Status = Retired only if Age > 65

+ Set Status = Working only if Age > 20 (and less than or equal to 65)

+ Set Status = Bum only if Age is less than or equal to 20 (which means the other two conditions are False)

Playing with Multiple Boolean Operators

To make a decision in an `IF-THEN` statement, the computer must use a conditional expression that's either `True` or `False`. Simple conditional expressions might be

```
Age = 55
Salary <= 55000
Name <> "John Smith"
```

You can also use Boolean operators (`AND`, `OR`, `NOT`, and `XOR`) to calculate multiple conditions. Suppose you want to check if a variable falls within a range of values, such as being greater than 20 but less than 65:

In most programming languages, you can type a Boolean operator in lowercase (and), uppercase (AND), or a mix of both upper and lowercase (And). Whichever style you like best, use it consistently throughout your program.

```
(Age > 20) AND (Age <= 65)
```

Chapter 3 of this mini-book contains more information about how Boolean operators work.

Table 4-1 shows how different values for the `Age` variable determine the value of the preceding Boolean expression.

Table 4-1	Multiple Boolean Expressions Ultimately Evaluate to a Single True or False Value		
Value of the Age Variable	*Value of (Age > 20) Expression*	*Value of (Age <= 65) Expression*	*Value of Complete Boolean Expression*
15	False	True	False
35	True	True	True
78	True	False	False

Because multiple Boolean expressions ultimately evaluate to a single `True` or `False` value, you can use multiple Boolean expressions in any `IF-THEN` statements, such as

```
IF (Age > 20) AND (Age <= 65) THEN
   Status = Working
ELSE
   Status = Bum
END IF
```

There's no limit to the number of Boolean expressions you can combine with Boolean operators. The following is a perfect valid Boolean expression that ultimately evaluates to a single `True` or `False` value:

```
(Age > 20) AND (Age <= 65) OR (Age = 72) OR (Name = "John")
```

 The more Boolean expressions you string together with Boolean operators, the more confusing everything gets so it's generally best to use no more than two Boolean expressions and a single Boolean operator (AND, OR, NOT, or XOR) at a time.

Making Multiple Choices with the SELECT CASE statement

The `IF-THEN-ELSEIF` statement can check multiple conditions and offer two or more choices for the computer to follow. However, the more choices available, the harder the `IF-THEN-ELSEIF` statement can be to understand, as shown in the following example:

```
IF (Age = 65) THEN
   Status = Retired
ELSEIF (Age = 21) THEN
   Status = Working
ELSEIF (Age = 15) THEN
   Status = Student
ELSE
   Status = Baby
END IF
```

For two or three choices, the `IF-THEN-ELSE` statement may be easy to understand, but after you need to offer four or more choices, the `IF-THEN-ELSEIF` statement can start getting clumsy. As an alternative, most programming languages offer a `SELECT CASE` statement:

```
SELECT CASE Variable
CASE X
   Command #1
CASE Y
   Command #2
END SELECT
```

The SELECT CASE statement examines a variable and if it's equal to a specific value, the computer follows a command (or block of commands). The preceding SELECT CASE statement is equivalent to the following IF-THEN-ELSEIF statement:

```
If Variable = X THEN
   Command #1
ELSEIF Variable = Y THEN
   Command #2
END IF
```

The basic idea behind the SELECT CASE statement is to make it easier to list multiple choices. Both an IF-THEN-ELSEIF statement and a SELECT CASE or switch statement perform the same function; it's just that the SELECT CASE statement is easier to read and understand.

Consider the following IF-THEN-ELSEIF statement:

```
IF (Age = 65) THEN
   Status = Retired
ELSEIF (Age = 21) THEN
   Status = Working
ELSEIF (Age = 15) THEN
   Status = Student
END IF
```

Rewriting this as a SELECT CASE statement might look like this:

```
SELECT CASE Age
CASE 65
   Status = Retired
CASE 21
   Status - Working
CASE 15
   Status = Student
END SELECT
```

As you can see, the SELECT CASE statement is much less cluttered and easier to read and understand than the IF-THEN-ELSEIF statement.

The switch statement in C (and similar languages)

Instead of using a SELECT CASE statement, curly bracket languages, like C, use a switch statement. The equivalent SELECT CASE statement written as a switch statement in C looks like this:

Book II
Chapter 4

**Making Decisions
by Branching**

```
switch (Variable)
   {
   case X: Command #1;
           break;
   case Y: Command #2;
   }
```

A SELECT CASE statement in BASIC might look like this:

```
SELECT CASE Age
CASE 65
   Status = Retired
CASE 21
   Status - Working
CASE 15
   Status = Student
END SELECT
```

The equivalent switch statement in C might look like this:

```
switch (age)
   {
   case 65: status = retired;
            break;
   case 21: status = working;
            break;
   case 15: status - student;
   }
```

The most crucial difference between the SELECT CASE statement in other languages and the switch statement in the curly bracket languages is the use of the break command. If you omit the break command, the switch statement doesn't know when to stop running commands.

In the preceding example, the break command stops the computer from running the other commands stored in the rest of the switch statement. So if the value of the age variable is 65, the preceding C program does the following:

1. **Set the status variable to retired.**

2. **Stop running the switch statement.**

Suppose you didn't include the break command, as follows:

```
switch (age)
   {
   case 65: status = retired;
   case 21: status = working;
   case 15: status - student;
   }
```

If the value of the age variable is 65, this is how this C program works:

1. **Set the status variable to retired.**

2. **Set the status variable to working.**

3. **Set the status variable to student.**

Without the break command, the curly bracket languages, like C, simply run every command all the way through the switch statement until it reaches the bottom, which probably isn't what you want.

When using the switch statement in C (and other curly bracket languages), always use the break command unless you specifically don't need it, as I explain in the following section.

Matching multiple values in a SELECT CASE statement

One major limitation of the SELECT CASE statement is that it only checks if a variable matches a single value, such as

```
SELECT CASE Age
CASE 65
   Status = Retired
CASE 21
   Status - Working
CASE 15
   Status = Student
END SELECT
```

This SELECT CASE statement doesn't do anything unless the value of the Age variable is exactly 65, 21, or 15. If the value of the Age variable is 66, 23, or 17, the preceding SELECT CASE statement does nothing.

Matching exact values may be useful, but sometimes you may want to run the same command (or block of commands) if a variable matches one or more values. For example, rather than match the number 65 exactly, you might want the SELECT CASE statement to match 65, 66, or 67. In that case, you can write the SELECT CASE statement like this:

```
SELECT CASE Age
CASE 65, 66, 67
  Status = Retired
CASE 21
  Status - Working
CASE 15
  Status = Student
END SELECT
```

With a `switch` statement in a curly bracket language, like C, you can do the following:

```
switch (age)
  {
  case 67:
  case 66:
  case 65: status = retired;
           break;
  case 21: status = working;
           break;
  case 15: status - student;
  }
```

By not using the `break` command if the value of the `age` variable is 67 or 66, the computer just continues down, line by line, until it runs the command if the `age` variable was 65. Then it hits the `break` command directly under the `status = retired` command and stops.

The `switch` command can be easier to read because all the matching values (67, 66, 65, 21, and 15) appear in a vertical column. The equivalent SELECT CASE statement can be slightly harder to read because all the values don't line up in a single vertical column.

Checking a range of values

The problem with the SELECT CASE statement is that it needs to match a value exactly. Although you could type in all possible values to match, that can get clumsy, as in the following that sets `Status = retired` if the `Age` variable is between 65 and 75:

```
SELECT CASE Age
CASE 65, 67, 68, 69, 70, 71, 72, 73, 74, 75
  Status = Retired
CASE 21
  Status - Working
CASE 15
  Status = Student
END SELECT
```

To avoid this problem, many languages let you check for a range of values. So if you want to check if a variable is equal or greater than 65 and less than or equal to 75, you could define the range of 65 TO 75 like this:

```
SELECT CASE Age
CASE 65 TO 75
  Status = Retired
CASE 21
  Status - Working
```

```
CASE 15
   Status = Student
END SELECT
```

The curly bracket languages, like C and C++, don't let you check for a range of values in a switch statement.

Comparing values

Listing a range of values can be useful, but what if there's no upper (or lower) limit? For example, anyone over the age of 65 might be considered retired, so you need to use a comparison operator to check a variable with a value, such as Age >= 65.

To use a comparison operator in a SELECT CASE statement, languages such as BASIC use the following syntax:

```
SELECT CASE Age
CASE IS >= 65
   Status = Retired
CASE 21 TO 64
   Status - Working
CASE 15
   Status = Student
END SELECT
```

In this example, the first part of the SELECT CASE statement tells the computer to check if the value in the Age variable is (note the IS keyword) >= 65.

The second part of the SELECT CASE statement checks if the Age variable falls within the range of 21 to 64.

The third part of the SELECT CASE statement checks if the Age variable is exactly equal to 15.

As you can see, each part of a SELECT CASE statement can check a value by matching it exactly, checking a range of values, or using a comparison operator.

The curly bracket languages, like C and C++, don't let you use comparison operators in a switch statement.

Running at least one command with the ELSE statement

It's possible for a SELECT CASE statement to run zero commands if the CASE statement can't match a variable to any specific value, such as

```
SELECT CASE Age
CASE 65
   Status = Retired
CASE 21
   Status - Working
CASE 15
   Status = Student
END SELECT
```

The preceding SELECT CASE statement doesn't do anything if the Age variable is 13, 25, or 81. To make sure the SELECT CASE statement always runs at least one command, you must add the ELSE statement, such as

```
 SELECT CASE Age
CASE 65
   Status = Retired
CASE 21
   Status - Working
CASE 15
   Status = Student
ELSE
   Status = Bum
END SELECT
```

In this example, if the value of the Age variable is 24 or 5, it doesn't match any of the specific values, so the command under the ELSE statement runs instead (Status = Bum).

Instead of using the ELSE statement, the curly bracket languages use a default statement, such as

```
switch (age)
   {
   case 65: status = retired;
            break;
   case 21: status = working;
            break;
   case 15: status - student;
            break;
   default: status = bum;
   }
```

Both the ELSE and default statements force the SELECT CASE (or switch) statement to always do something.

As a general rule, use the IF-THEN statements for making the computer choose one or more commands (or blocks of commands). If you need the computer to choose from three or more commands (or blocks of com-mands), the SELECT CASE (switch) statement may be easier to read and write instead.

Branching simply gives the computer multiple options to use when running. By accepting outside information and comparing its value, a branching statement can help the computer choose an appropriate response out of many possible responses.

**Book II
Chapter 4**

**Making Decisions
by Branching**

Chapter 5: Repeating Commands by Looping

In This Chapter

✔ Looping a fixed number of times with a FOR-NEXT loop

✔ Looping zero or more times with a WHILE loop

✔ Looping at least once with a DO loop

✔ Playing around with nested loops

✔ Exiting prematurely from a loop

✔ Examining your loops

To write any program, you must specify what the computer needs to do at any given time. Sometimes, you may need to write the same command multiple times. For example, suppose you want to print your name five times. You could just write the same command five times like this:

```
PRINT "John Smith"
PRINT "John Smith"
PRINT "John Smith"
PRINT "John Smith"
PRINT "John Smith"
```

Writing the same five commands is cumbersome. Even worse, what if you suddenly decide you want to print your name not just five times, but five thousand times? Do you really want to write the same command five thousand times?

Probably not, which is why computer scientists invented loops. A *loop* is just a shortcut for making the computer run one or more commands without writing those commands multiple times. So rather than type the same command five times as in the preceding example, you could use a loop like this:

```
FOR I = 1 TO 5
  PRINT "John Smith"
NEXT I
```

This tells the computer to run the `PRINT "John Smith"` command five times. If you want to print John Smith five thousand times, you just have to change the number of times you want the loop to run by replacing the 5 with 5000, such as

```
FOR I = 1 TO 5000
   PRINT "John Smith"
NEXT I
```

Loops basically make one or more commands run more than once, as shown in Figure 5-1.

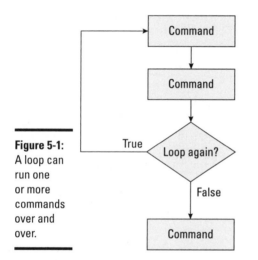

Figure 5-1:
A loop can
run one
or more
commands
over and
over.

Looping a Fixed Number of Times with the FOR-NEXT Loop

The simplest loop runs one or more commands a fixed number of times, such as five or ten times. Such loops that run a fixed number of times are FOR-NEXT loops and look like this:

```
FOR Variable = InitialValue TO EndValue
   Command
NEXT Variable
```

The first line serves two purposes. The first time the FOR-NEXT loop runs, this line sets the value of the variable to an initial value, such as 1. The second and all additional times the FOR-NEXT loop runs, it checks if its variable is still within a range of values, such as between 1 and 10. If so, the FOR-NEXT loop runs again.

The second line consists of one or more commands that you want to run multiple times.

The third line tells the FOR-NEXT loop to increase the value of its variable by 1 and run the FOR-NEXT loop again.

The FOR-NEXT loop defines four items:

✦ **A variable**

✦ **The initial value of the variable (usually 1)**

✦ **The ending value of the variable**

✦ **One or more commands that run multiple times**

Using a FOR-NEXT loop variable

Like all variables, the name of a FOR-NEXT loop variable can be anything, although it's best to use a descriptive name if possible. So if you want to print the names of all the employees of a company by using a FOR-NEXT loop, you could use EmployeeID as a descriptive variable name, such as

```
FOR EmployeeID = 1 TO 150
   PRINT EmployeeName
NEXT EmployeeID
```

This example would print out each name (EmployeeName) starting with the employee who has the EmployeeID of 1 and continuing until it prints the employee with the EmployeeID of 150.

If your FOR-NEXT loop variable is meant only for counting and doesn't represent anything, like employee numbers, you can just use a generic variable name, such as I or J, such as

```
FOR I = 1 TO 15
   PRINT "John Smith"
NEXT I
```

This FOR-NEXT loop just prints the name "John Smith" on-screen 15 times.

Never change the value of a FOR-NEXT loop's variable within the loop or else you risk creating an *endless loop* — the computer keeps running the same commands over and over again without stopping. This makes your program appear to *freeze* or *hang,* essentially stopping your program from working altogether. The following example creates an endless loop:

```
FOR I = 1 TO 5
  PRINT "John Smith"
  I = 3
NEXT I
```

This FOR-NEXT loop runs five times. The first time the FOR-NEXT loop runs, the value of the I variable is set to 1. But within the FOR-NEXT loop, the value of the I variable is then set to 3. So each time the FOR-NEXT loop runs again, it checks to see if the I variable's value is between 1 and 5.

Because the FOR-NEXT loop always resets the value of the I variable to 3, the I variable never falls outside the range of 1 to 5, so this FOR-NEXT loop runs indefinitely.

The curly bracket language family creates a FOR-NEXT loop that looks slightly different than the way other languages do. For example, this is how BASIC creates a FOR-NEXT loop:

```
FOR I = 1 TO 15
  PRINT "John Smith"
NEXT I
```

This is the equivalent FOR-NEXT loop in C:

```
for (i = 1, i <= 15, i++)
  {
  printf("John Smith");
  }
```

The first line consists of three parts:

+ **i = 1:** Sets the value of the i variable to 1

+ **i <= 15:** Makes the FOR-NEXT loop keep repeating as long as the value of the i variable is less than or equal to 15

+ **i++ --:** Increases the value of the i variable by 1

In any programming language, you can add 1 to any variable by doing this:

```
I = I + 1
```

The curly bracket language family gives you a shortcut for adding 1 to any variable, which is known as the *increment operator,* such as

```
i++
```

This is equivalent to

```
i = i + 1
```

The increment operator is used more often than writing out the entire $i = i + 1$ command because it's much shorter. There's also a similar decrement operator that looks like

```
i--
```

This is equivalent to

```
i = i - 1
```

Counting by a different range

Normally, the FOR-NEXT loop counts from 1 to another number, such as 15. However, you can also count from any number range, such as 23 to 41, 102 to 105, or 2 to 8. The main reason to use a different range of numbers is if those numbers represent something in your program.

For example, suppose employees are assigned an employee number starting with 120 and there are four employees, as shown in Table 5-1.

Table 5-1	A Database of Employee Names Assigned with Specific Employee ID Numbers
Employee Name	*Employee ID Number*
John Smith	120
Maggie Jones	121
Susan Wilson	122
Emir Kelly	123

You could use a FOR-NEXT loop like this:

```
FOR EmployeeID = 120 TO 123
   PRINT EmployeeName (EmployeeID)
NEXT EmployeeID
```

Each time this FOR-NEXT loop runs, it prints the employee name associated with a particular employee number, so it prints out the following:

```
John Smith
Maggie Jones
Susan Wilson
Emir Kelly
```

Counting by different number ranges is useful only if those numbers mean something to your program. If you just need to count a fixed number of times, it's much clearer to count from 1 to a specific value instead. The following FOR-NEXT loop actually runs four times (120, 121, 122, and 123):

```
FOR EmployeeID = 120 TO 123
   PRINT EmployeeName
NEXT EmployeeID
```

Notice that counting from 120 to 123 doesn't make it clear exactly how many times the FOR-NEXT loop runs. At first glance, it appears that the FOR-NEXT loop may repeat only three times.

To clarify exactly how many times the FOR-NEXT loop runs, it's always much clearer to count from 1, such as

```
FOR EmployeeID = 1 TO 4
   PRINT EmployeeName
NEXT EmployeeID
```

Counting by different increments

Normally, the FOR-NEXT loop counts by 1. So consider the following FOR-NEXT loop:

```
FOR I = 1 TO 4
   PRINT "The value of I = ",I
NEXT I
```

This FOR-NEXT loop would print

```
The value of I = 1
The value of I = 2
The value of I = 3
The value of I = 4
```

If you want to count by a number other than 1, you must define an increment. So if you want to count by 2, you'd have to define an increment of 2, such as

```
FOR I = 1 TO 4 STEP 2
   PRINT "The value of I = ",I
NEXT I
```

This modified FOR-NEXT loop would only print

```
The value of I = 1
The value of I = 3
```

Although many languages, such as BASIC, assume the FOR-NEXT loop always increments by 1 unless you specifically tell it otherwise, the curly bracket languages always force you to define an increment value. To define a FOR-NEXT loop in C to increment by 2, you can define i = i + 2, as follows

```
for (i = 1, i <= 4, i = i + 2)
  {
  printf("The value of i = %d", i);
  }
```

Counting backward

Rather than count forward from 1 to 4, you can also make a FOR-NEXT loop count backward, such as

```
FOR I = 4 DOWNTO 1
  PRINT "The value of I = ",I
NEXT I
```

Much like using different number ranges, such as 34 to 87, counting backward makes sense only if those numbers have a specific meaning to your program, such as

```
FOR I = 10 DOWNTO 1
  PRINT I
NEXT I
PRINT "BLASTOFF!"
```

This example would print

```
10
9
8
7
6
5
4
3
2
1
BLASTOFF!
```

Although languages, such as BASIC, use a specific keyword (DOWNTO) to make a FOR-NEXT loop count backward, curly bracket languages let you count backward by changing both the initial and ending value of the `for-next` variable and then defining an increment that subtracts instead of adds, such as

```
for (i = 10, i >= 1, i = i - 1)
  {
  printf("%d\n", i);
  }
printf("Blastoff!");
```

Looping Zero or More Times with the WHILE Loop

The FOR-NEXT loop is great when you know exactly how many times you want to run one or more commands. However, what if the number of times you want to run a loop can vary?

For example, you might have a loop that asks the user for a password, as shown in Figure 5-2. How many times should this loop run?

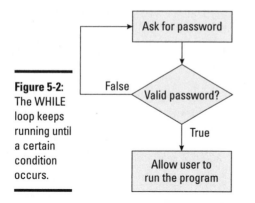

Figure 5-2: The WHILE loop keeps running until a certain condition occurs.

The answer is that the loop should keep running until the user types in a valid password. Because you don't know how many times the loop needs to run, you need to use a WHILE loop to check a True or False (Boolean) expression. In this case, the Boolean expression is, "Did the user type in a valid password?" If the answer is yes (True), the user can run the program. If the answer is no (False), the loop asks the user to try typing in a password again.

The WHILE loop typically looks like this:

```
WHILE (True or False Boolean expression)
   Command
   Command to change Boolean expression
WEND
```

With the curly bracket languages, the `WHILE` loop looks like this:

```
while (True or False Boolean expression)
  {
  command
  command to change Boolean expression
  }
```

The `WHILE` loops consists of four parts:

✦ The beginning of the `WHILE` loop, which checks a Boolean expression for a `True` or `False` value

✦ One or more commands to run

✦ One or more commands that can change the Boolean expression in the beginning of the `WHILE` loop

✦ The end of the `WHILE` loop

Book II
Chapter 5

Repeating
Commands
by Looping

Before the `WHILE` loop runs even once, it checks a Boolean expression for a `True` or `False` value. If this value is `True`, the `WHILE` loop runs. If this value is `False`, the `WHILE` loop doesn't run.

Within the `WHILE` loop there must be one or more commands that can change the Boolean expression of the `WHILE` loop to `False`.

If a `WHILE` loop doesn't include at least one command that can change its Boolean expression, the `WHILE` loop runs indefinitely, creating an endless loop that hangs or freezes your program.

The following `WHILE` loop keeps asking for a password until the user types **SECRET**:

```
DIM Answer as String
PROMPT "Enter password: ", Answer
WHILE (Answer <> "SECRET")
  PRINT "Invalid password!"
  PROMPT "Enter password: ", Answer
WEND
```

Right before most `WHILE` loops is usually a line that sets an initial value to a variable used in the loop's Boolean expression. In the preceding example, the value of the `Answer` variable is set *(initialized)* to `Answer`, which is whatever the user types in response to the `Enter password:` prompt. Then the `WHILE` loop checks if the value of the `Answer` variable is `SECRET`.

The first line defines the `Answer` variable as a `string` data type. The second line asks the user for a password and stores that answer in the `Answer` variable.

The `WHILE` loop first checks if the `Answer` variable is `SECRET`. If not, the loop runs the two commands that print `Invalid password` and then asks `Enter password:` on-screen once more.

Whatever reply the user types gets stored in the `Answer` variable. Then the `WHILE` loop checks this `Answer` variable again before running.

You can make a `WHILE` loop count like a `FOR-NEXT` loop. Suppose you had the following `FOR-NEXT` loop:

```
FOR I = 10 DOWNTO 1
  PRINT I
NEXT I
PRINT "BLASTOFF!"
```

The equivalent `WHILE` loop might look like this:

```
I = 10
WHILE (I >= 1)
   PRINT I
   I = I - 1
WEND
PRINT "BLASTOFF!"
```

Although the `WHILE` loop can count, notice that it takes more lines of code to do so, and the `WHILE` loop isn't as easy to understand as the `FOR-NEXT` loop. If you need a loop to run a fixed number of times, use the `FOR-NEXT` loop. If you aren't sure how many times you need a loop to run, use the `WHILE` loop.

Looping at Least Once with the DO Loop

Before a `WHILE` loop runs, it checks a Boolean expression to see if it's `True` or `False`. If this Boolean expression is `False`, the `WHILE` loop never runs at all. What if you want to insure that the loop runs at least once? In that case, you must use a `DO` loop.

A `DO` loop acts like an upside-down `WHILE` loop. First the `DO` loop runs once and then it checks a Boolean expression. A typical `DO` loop looks like this:

```
DO
   Command
   Command to change the Boolean expression
LOOP WHILE (True or False Boolean expression)
```

This DO loop keeps repeating while a Boolean expression remains False. As long as this Boolean expression stays False, the DO loop keeps running.

You could use a DO loop to ask the user to type in a password like this:

```
DIM Password as String
Password = ""
DO
  PROMPT "Enter password: ", Password
LOOP WHILE (Password <> "SECRET")
```

This DO loop always prints Enter your password: at least once before checking its Boolean expression Password = "SECRET". If this Boolean expression is False, the DO loop stops running. If this Boolean expression is True, the DO loop repeats again.

Like the WHILE loop, you often need to initialize a variable right before the DO loop. This variable is usually part of the loop's Boolean expression to determine when the loop can stop running.

In the curly bracket language family, the DO loop looks like this:

```
do
   {
   command
   command to change Boolean expression
   }
 while (True or False Boolean expression);
```

This DO loop keeps repeating while a Boolean expression is True. The moment this Boolean expression becomes False, the DO loop stops running.

Playing with Nested Loops

Every loop (FOR-NEXT, WHILE, and DO) can run one or more commands multiple times. Therefore, it's possible for a loop to run another loop (which in turn can run a third loop, and so on).

When loops appear inside one another, they're *nested loops*.

The following shows a FOR–NEXT loop nested inside another FOR–NEXT loop, as shown in Figure 5-3:

```
FOR I = 1 TO 4
  PRINT "Outer loop run #"; I
  FOR J = 1 TO 3
    PRINT "   Nested loop run #"; J
  NEXT J
NEXT I
```

Figure 5-3:
A nested loop appears inside another loop.

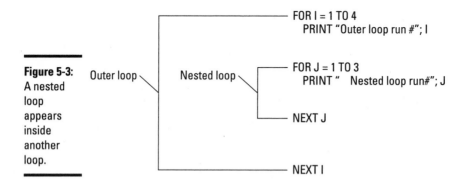

When one loop is nested inside another loop, the inner *(nested)* loop runs first. Then the outer loop runs once. Then the outer loop repeats running the nested loop again.

With nested loops, the nested *(inner)* loop runs more often than the outer loop.

In the preceding example, the outer loop runs 4 times and the nested loop runs 3 times, so the nested loop ultimately runs 12 times (3 * 4), as shown here:

```
Outer loop run #1
    Nested loop run #1
    Nested loop run #2
    Nested loop run #3
Outer loop run #2
    Nested loop run #1
    Nested loop run #2
    Nested loop run #3
Outer loop run #3
    Nested loop run #1
    Nested loop run #2
    Nested loop run #3
```

```
Outer loop run #4
   Nested loop run #1
   Nested loop run #2
   Nested loop run #3
```

The more nested loops you have, the harder it can be to tell exactly what your program actually does. As a general rule, it's best to nest only one loop inside another.

Prematurely Exiting from a Loop

Loops normally run a fixed number of times (with a FOR-NEXT loop) or until a Boolean expression changes (with a WHILE or DO loop). However, it's possible to exit prematurely out of a loop by using a special EXIT command.

Prematurely exiting a loop means not waiting for the loop to stop on its own, such as

```
DO
   Play video game
   IF Player wants to quit THEN EXIT
LOOP UNTIL (Game over)
```

In this case, the loop ends in one of two ways: when the game ends or when the user specifically quits the game.

To prematurely exit a loop, you always need to check if another Boolean expression is True or False. Generally, it's not a good idea to prematurely exit out of a loop because it can make your program harder to understand.

The curly bracket languages don't have an EXIT command but a break command, which works the same way, such as

```
do
   {
   Play video game;
   if (Player wants to quit) break;
   }
while (Game over <> True);
```

Checking Your Loops

Although loops eliminate the need to write the same command multiple times, loops also introduce the risk of making your program harder to understand as a result (and also harder to fix and update). So when using loops, keep these points in mind:

+ To loop a fixed number of times, use a FOR-NEXT loop.

+ To loop zero or more times, use a WHILE loop.

+ To loop at least once, use a DO loop.

+ Both WHILE and DO loops usually need a variable that's used to check a Boolean expression to determine when the loop ends.

+ A WHILE or DO loop always needs a command that changes its Boolean expression that determines when the loop will eventually stop.

+ A loop that never stops running is an *endless loop.*

+ Some programming languages let you use an EXIT (or break command) to stop a loop prematurely. Use this with caution because it can make your program harder to understand.

When using a loop, always make sure you know how that loop will eventually stop.

Almost every program needs to use loops, so make sure you understand the differences between all the different loop variations you can use. Ultimately, loops let you run multiple commands without explicitly writing them all out, so think of loops as a programming shortcut.

Chapter 6: Breaking a Large Program into Subprograms

*T*he bigger the program, the harder that program is to read, fix, and modify. Just as it's easier to spot a spelling mistake in a recipe printed on a single page compared to trying to find that same spelling mistake buried inside a 350-page cookbook, so is it easier to fix problems in a small program than a big one.

Because small programs can perform only simple tasks, the idea behind programming is to write a lot of little programs and paste them together, like building blocks, creating one massive program. Because each little program is part of a much bigger program, those little programs are *subprograms,* as shown in Figure 6-1.

The biggest problem with dividing a large program into multiple subprograms is to make each subprogram as independent, or *loosely coupled,* as possible. That means if one subprogram fails, it doesn't wreck the entire program along with it, like yanking out a single playing card from a house of cards.

One major advantage of subprograms is that you can isolate common program features in a subprogram that you can copy and reuse in another program. For example, suppose you wrote a word processor. Although you could write it as one massive, interconnected tangle of code, a better approach might be dividing the program functions into separate parts. By doing this, you could create a separate subprogram for

✦ **Displaying pull-down menus**

✦ **Editing text**

✦ **Spell checking**

✦ **Printing a file**

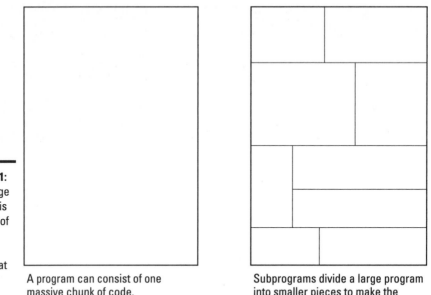

Figure 6-1:
Every large
program is
made up of
smaller
subpro-
grams that
act as
building
blocks.

A program can consist of one
massive chunk of code.

Subprograms divide a large program
into smaller pieces to make the
large program easier to create and
modify.

If you wanted to write a horse race prediction program, you wouldn't have
to write the whole thing from scratch. You could copy the subprograms from
another program and reuse them in your new project, as shown in Figure 6-2.

By reusing subprograms, you can create more complicated programs faster
than before. After programmers create enough useful subprograms, they can
store these subprograms in a "library" that they and other programmers can
use in the future.

Creating and Using Subprograms

A subprogram essentially yanks out two or more commands from your main
program and stores them in another part of your main program or in a separate file, as shown in Figure 6-3.

The reasons for isolating commands in a subprogram (and out of your main
program) are to

✦ **Keep your main program smaller and thus easier to read and modify.**

✦ **Isolate related commands in a subprogram that can be reused.**

✦ **Make programming simpler and faster by just reusing subprograms
from other projects.**

Display pull-down menus	
Spell checking	Printing files
Editing text	

A word processor can consist of four separate subprograms that work together.

Display pull-down menus	
Calculate the winning race horse	Printing files
Analyze race horse statistics	

A completely different program, such as a horse race prediction program, can reuse subprograms to make programming faster and easier.

Figure 6-2: Reusing subprograms can make writing new programs easier and faster.

Figure 6-3: Subprograms let you remove and isolate commands out of your main program.

Main program

Display pull-down menus

Ask user for a temperature in Celsius

Store temperature in the X variable

Calculate Fahrenheit by using this formula
(9/5 C * X) + 32

Store formula result in the Y variable

Display Fahrenheit value on the screen

Without subprograms, you must list every step, which can make your main program bigger and harder to read.

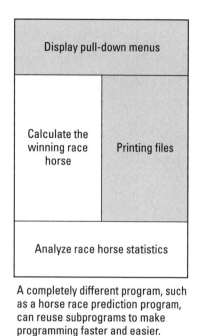

Main program

Display pull-down menus

Convert to Fahrenheit

Display Fahrenheit value on the screen

Subprogram

Ask user for a temperature in Celsius

Store temperature in the X variable

Calculate Fahrenheit by using this formula
(9/5 * X) + 32

Store formula result in the Y variable

By removing a group of commands and storing them in a subprogram, your main program can be smaller and easier to read.

Creating a subprogram

Every subprogram consists of a unique name and one or more commands. You can name a subprogram anything although it's usually best to give a subprogram a descriptive name. So if you create a subprogram to convert yards into meters, you might name your subprogram `Yards2Meters` or `MetricConverter`.

A descriptive name for a subprogram can help you identify the purpose of that subprogram.

After you define a name for your subprogram, you can fill it up with one or more commands that tell that subprogram what to do. So if you wanted to write a subprogram that prints your name on-screen, your main subprogram might look like this:

```
SUB PrintMyName
  FOR I = 1 TO 5
    PRINT "John Smith"
  NEXT I
END SUB
```

The preceding BASIC language example defines the beginning of a sub-program by using the `SUB` keyword followed by the subprogram's name, `PrintMyName`. The end of the subprogram is defined by the `END SUB` keywords.

Not every language defines subprograms with keywords. In the curly bracket language family, the main program is called `main` and every subprogram is just given its own name, such as

```
print_my_name ()
  {
  for i = 1; i < 5; i++)
    {
    printf ("John Smith");
    }
  }
```

Instead of using the term *subprogram,* the curly bracket languages use the term *function.*

You can store subprograms in the same file as the main program or in a separate file. If you store a subprogram in the same file as the main program, you can place the subprogram at the beginning or end of the file, as shown in Figure 6-4.

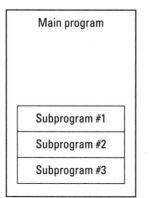

Main program

Subprogram #1

Subprogram #2

Subprogram #3

Subprogram #1

Subprogram #2

Subprogram #3

Main program

Figure 6-4: Subprograms usually appear at the beginning or end of a file.

Some programming languages make you store subprograms at the end of a file, after the main program.

Other programming languages make you store subprograms at the beginning of a file, before the main program.

BASIC and curly bracket languages, such as C, usually put subprograms at the end of the main program. Other languages, such as Pascal, put subprograms at the beginning of the main program.

"Calling" a subprogram

After you isolate commands inside a subprogram, your program can't run those commands until it "calls" the subprogram. Calling a subprogram basically tells the computer, "See those commands stored in that subprogram over there? Run those commands now!"

To call a subprogram, you must use the subprogram's name as a command. So if you had the following subprogram:

```
SUB PrintMyName
  FOR I = 1 TO 5
    PRINT "John Smith"
  NEXT I
END SUB
```

To run this subprogram, you use its name as a command in any part of your program like this:

```
PRINT "The subprogram is going to run now."
PrintMyName
END
```

The preceding BASIC program would print the following:

```
The subprogram is going to run now.
John Smith
John Smith
John Smith
John Smith
John Smith
```

Every subprogram needs a unique name so when you call that subprogram to run, the computer knows exactly which subprogram to use. You can call a subprogram from any part of a program, even from within another subprogram.

In the curly bracket language family, calling a subprogram *(function)* is the same. Use the subprogram's name as a command. So if you had the following subprogram:

```
print_my_name ()
  {
  for i = 1; i < 5; i++)
    {
    printf ("John Smith");
    }
  }
```

You could call that subprogram *(function),* as follows:

```
main ()
  {
  print_my_name ();
  }
```

If you've stored a subprogram in a separate file, you may need to go through two steps to call a subprogram. First, you may need to specify the filename that contains the subprogram you want to use. Second, you need to call the subprogram you want by name.

In the curly bracket languages, like C, you specify a filename where your subprogram is stored like this:

```
#include <filename>
main()
  {
  subprogram name ();
  }
```

In this C example, the `#include<filename>` command tells the computer that if it can't find a subprogram in the main program file, look in the file dubbed *filename.*

The #include command tells the computer to pretend that every subprogram stored in a separate file is actually *included* in the main program file.

Passing Parameters

Each time you call a subprogram, that subprogram runs its commands. So if you had a subprogram like this:

```
SUB PrintJohnSmith
  FOR I = 1 TO 5
    PRINT "John Smith"
  NEXT I
END SUB
```

Calling that subprogram from another part of your program would always print the name *John Smith* exactly five times. If you wanted a subprogram that could print the name *Mary Jones* 16 times, you'd have to write another similar subprogram, such as

```
SUB PrintMaryJones
  FOR I = 1 TO 16
    PRINT "Mary Jones"
  NEXT I
END SUB
```

Obviously, writing similar subprograms that do nearly identical tasks is wasteful and time-consuming to write. So as a better alternative, you can write a generic subprogram that accepts additional data, called *parameters*.

These parameters let you change the way a subprogram works. So rather than write one subprogram to print the name *John Smith* 5 times and a second subprogram to print the name *Mary Jones* 16 times, you could write a single subprogram that accepts 2 parameters that define

+ **The name to print**

+ **The number of times to print that name**

```
SUB PrintMyName (PrintTimes as Integer, Name as String)
  FOR I = 1 TO PrintTimes
    PRINT Name
  NEXT I
END SUB
```

The list of parameters, enclosed in parentheses, is a *parameter list*.

This BASIC language example defines a subprogram named `PrintMyName`, which accepts two parameters. The first parameter is an integer variable — `PrintTimes` — which defines how many times to print a name.

The second parameter is a string variable — `Name` — which defines the name to print multiple times.

Every programming language offers slightly different ways of creating a subprogram. Here's what an equivalent Python subprogram might look like:

```
def print_my_name(printtimes, name):
    for i in range(printtimes):
        print name
```

By writing a generic subprogram that accepts parameters, you can create a single subprogram that can behave differently, depending on the parameters it receives.

To give or *pass* parameters to a subprogram, you need to call the subprogram by name along with the parameters you want to give that subprogram. So if a subprogram accepted two parameters (an integer and a string), you could call that subprogram by doing the following:

```
PrintMyName (5, "John Smith")
PrintMyName (16, "Mary Jones")
```

The first command tells the `PrintMyName` subprogram to use the number 5 and the string *John Smith* as its parameters. Because the number defines how many times to print and the string defines what to print, this first command tells the `PrintMyName` subprogram to print *John Smith* five times.

The second command tells the `PrintMyName` subprogram to use the number 16 and the string *Mary Jones* as its parameters, which prints *Mary Jones* 16 times, as shown in Figure 6-5.

Calling a subprogram works the same way in other programming languages. So if you want to call the following Python subprogram:

```
def print_my_name(printtimes, name):
    for i in range(printtimes):
        print name
```

You could print the name *John Smith* four times with this command:

```
print_my_name(4, "John Smith")
```

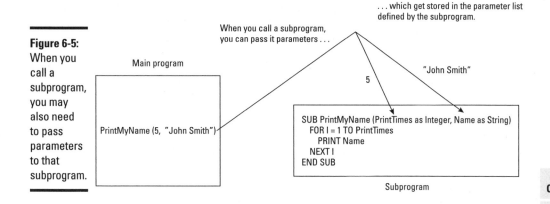

Figure 6-5:
When you
call a
subprogram,
you may
also need
to pass
parameters
to that
subprogram.

When you call a subprogram, you must give it the exact number and type of parameters it expects to receive. So the PrintMyName subprogram accepts two parameters whereas the first parameter must be an integer and the second parameter must be a string, such as

```
PrintMyName (4, "Hal Berton")
PrintMyName (53, "Billie Buttons")
```

If you don't give a subprogram the right number of parameters, your program doesn't work. So if a subprogram is expecting two parameters, the following doesn't work because they don't give the subprogram exactly two parameters:

```
PrintMyName (4)
PrintMyName (4, 90, "Roberta Clarence")
```

The first command doesn't work because the PrintMyName subprogram expects two parameters, but this command passes only one parameter.

The second command doesn't work because this command passes three parameters, but the PrintMyName subprogram expects only two parameters.

Another problem is that you give the subprogram the exact number of parameters, but not the right type of parameters. So this subprogram expects to receive an integer and a string, so the following subprogram calls don't work because they give it the wrong data:

```
PrintMyName (98, 23)
PrintMyName ("Victor Harris", 7)
```

The first command doesn't work because the PrintMyName subprogram expects an integer and a string, but this command tries to give it two numbers.

The second command doesn't work because the `PrintMyName` subprogram expects an integer first and a string second, but this command gives it the data in the wrong order.

If a subprogram doesn't need any parameters, you can just call that subprogram by using its name, such as

```
PrintMyName
```

If you aren't passing any parameters in some programming languages, you must leave the *parameter list* (the stuff between the parentheses) blank, such as

```
printMyName ();
```

Passing parameters by reference

When a program calls and passes parameters to a subprogram, the computer makes duplicate copies of those parameters. One copy of those parameters stays with the main program and the second copy gets passed to the subprogram.

Now if the subprogram changes those parameters, the values of those parameters stay trapped within the subprogram, as shown in Figure 6-6.

Figure 6-6: Normally when you pass parameters to a subprogram, the computer makes a second copy for the subprogram to use.

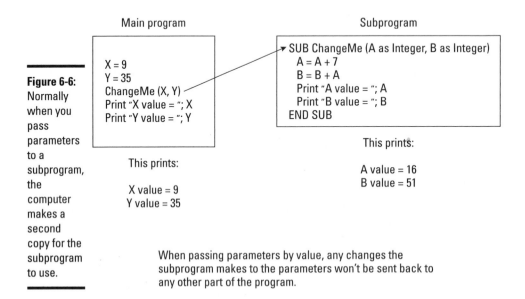

When you pass parameters to a subprogram and make duplicate copies of those parameters, that's called *passing by value.*

Most of the time when you call a subprogram and pass it parameters, you don't want that subprogram to change the value of its parameters; you just want the subprogram to modify its behavior based on the parameters it receives, such as the subprogram that prints a name a fixed number of times.

Rather than give a subprogram parameters that modify its behavior, you can also give a subprogram parameters that the subprogram can modify and send back to the rest of the program.

To make a subprogram modify its parameters, you must use an *x* called *pass by reference.* Essentially, instead of letting a subprogram use a copy of data, passing by reference gives the subprogram the actual data to manipulate, as shown in Figure 6-7.

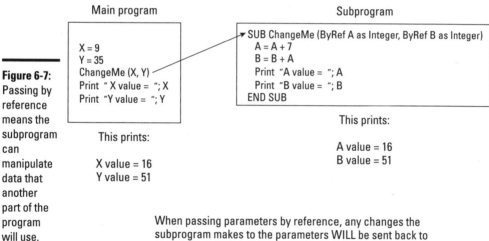

Figure 6-7: Passing by reference means the subprogram can manipulate data that another part of the program will use.

Suppose you have a subprogram that converts temperatures from Celsius to Fahrenheit with this formula:

```
Tf = ((9/5)*Tc)+32
```

Your subprogram could look like this:

```
SUB ConvertC2F (ByRef Temperature as Single)
  Temperature = ((9/5) * Temperature) + 32
END SUB
```

This is how the preceding subprogram works:

+ The first line defines the subprogram name — ConvertC2F — and its parameter list as accepting one Single variable called Temperature. To specify that this parameter will be passed by reference, this BASIC language example uses the ByRef keyword.

+ The second line plugs the value of the Temperature variable into the conversion equation and stores the result back in the Temperature variable, erasing the preceding value that was stored there.

+ The third line ends the subprogram. At this point, the modified value of the Temperature variable is sent back to the main program to use.

Every programming language uses different ways to identify when a parameter will be passed by reference. The BASIC language uses the ByRef keyword whereas the C language uses the ampersand symbol (&) to identify parameters passed by reference. In the following C example, the *a* parameter is passed by value but the *x* parameter is passed by reference:

```
subprogram_example (int a, float &x);
```

If you had the following BASIC subprogram:

```
SUB ConvertC2F (ByRef Temperature as Single)
  Temperature = ((9/5) * Temperature) + 32
END SUB
```

You could call that subprogram like this:

```
DIM Temp AS SINGLE
Temp = 12
PRINT "This is the temperature in Celsius = "; Temp
ConvertC2F (Temp)
PRINT "This is the temperature in Fahrenheit = "; Temp
END
```

Running this program would produce the following:

```
This is the temperature in Celsius = 12
This is the temperature in Fahrenheit = 53.6
```

Notice that right before calling the ConvertC2F subprogram, the value of the Temperature variable is 12, but the ConvertC2F subprogram changes that value because the subprogram was passed the Temperature value by reference. What happens if you run the same program except change the subprogram to accept parameters passed by value instead, such as

```
DIM Temp AS SINGLE
Temp = 12
PRINT "This is the temperature in Celsius = "; Temp
ConvertC2F (Temp)
PRINT "This is the temperature in Fahrenheit = "; Temp
END

SUB ConvertC2F (Temperature as Single)
   Temperature = ((9/5) * Temperature) + 32
END SUB
```

This program would print the following:

```
This is the temperature in Celsius = 12
This is the temperature in Fahrenheit = 12
```

Although the `ConvertC2F` subprogram changed the value of the `Temperature` variable, it never passes the changed value back to the main program. So the main program blissfully uses the current value of the `Temperature` variable, which is always `12`.

Passing data by reference means that the subprogram can change any data used by another part of a program. This can increase the chance of problems because the more ways data can be changed, the harder it can be to track down errors.

Storing values in a subprogram name

One problem with passing parameters by reference is that you may not always know when a subprogram will change its parameter values. To make it clear when a subprogram returns modified data, you can create a special type of subprogram called a *function*.

A function is nothing more than a subprogram with the subprogram name representing a value. So a typical function might look like this:

```
FUNCTION Name (parameter list) AS DataType
   Commands
   RETURN value
END FUNCTION
```

In BASIC, you identify a function with the `FUNCTION` keyword to define a subprogram as a function. After listing a parameter list, the first line also defines the data type that the function name can hold, such as an `integer`, a `string`, or a `single` (decimal) number.

Defining a function in the C language looks like this:

```
datatype function_name (parameter list)
  {
  commands
  return value
  }
```

Inside the function, one or more commands must calculate a new result. Then you use the RETURN keyword to define what value to store in the function name. Whatever value this is, it must be the same data type that you defined for the function name in the first line. So if you defined a function as a String data type, you can't return an integer value from that function.

A typical function in BASIC might look like this:

```
FUNCTION ConvertC2F (Temperature AS SINGLE) AS SINGLE
  Temperature = ((9/5) * Temperature) + 32
  RETURN Temperature
END FUNCTION
```

The function name ConvertC2F can hold a Single data type.

Unlike a subprogram that may or may not return a modified value, functions always return a value. To call a function, you must assign the function name to a variable or use the function name itself as a variable, such as

```
PRINT "Temperature in Fahrenheit = "; ConvertC2F (12)
```

Because functions always return a value, they (almost always) have a parameter list. So you can identify functions in a program by looking for the parameter list in parentheses.

```
DIM Temp AS SINGLE
Temp = 12
PRINT "Temperature in Celsius = "; Temp
PRINT "Temperature in Fahrenheit = "; ConvertC2F (Temp)
END

FUNCTION ConvertC2F (Temperature AS SINGLE) AS SINGLE
  Temperature = ((9/5) * Temperature) + 32
  RETURN Temperature
END FUNCTION
```

Unlike a subprogram that you can call just by typing its name on a line by itself, you can call a function only by using that function name as if it's a variable.

This same function as seen in the Python language might look like this:

```
def convertc2f(temperature):
    new = ((9.0/5.0) * temperature) + 32
    return new
```

To run this function, you could use the following program:

```
temp = 12
print "Temperature in Celsius = ", temp
print "Temperature in Fahrenheit = ", convertc2f(temp)
```

Repeating a Subprogram with Recursion

In Chapter 5 of this mini-book, you can read about loops that can repeat one or more commands multiple times. If you want to repeat the commands stored in a subprogram, you can just call that subprogram from within a loop, such as

```
FOR I = 1 TO 4
   Subprogram name
NEXT I
```

This example would run all the commands in a subprogram four times. However, here's another way to run a subprogram multiple times: *recursion.* The idea behind recursion is that instead of defining how many times to run a subprogram, you let the subprogram call itself multiple times, such as

```
SUB MySubprogram
   MySubprogram
END SUB
```

When this subprogram runs, it calls itself, essentially making a second copy of itself, which then makes a third copy of itself, and so on. A common problem used to demonstrate recursion is calculating a *factorial* (which multiples a number by a gradually decreasing series of numbers).

Not every programming language supports recursion, such as some versions of BASIC.

A factorial is often written like this:

```
4!
```

To calculate a factorial, you multiply a number (4, in this case) by a number that's one less (3) and keep repeating this until you get the value of 1, such as

```
4! = 4 * 3 * 2 * 1
   = 24
```

To calculate a factorial, you could use a BASIC program like this:

```
FUNCTION Factorial (N as INTEGER) as REAL
  IF N > 1 THEN
    Factorial = N * Factorial (N- 1)
  ELSE
    Factorial = 1
END FUNCTION
```

This function uses recursion to run another copy of itself, as shown in Figure 6-8.

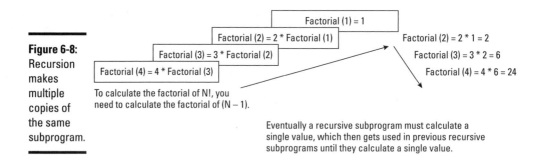

Figure 6-8: Recursion makes multiple copies of the same subprogram.

Ultimately, every subprogram that calls itself needs to end. (Otherwise, it can get trapped in an endless loop, which hangs or freezes your computer.) When a subprogram finally ends, it returns a value to the preceding subprogram, which returns its value to the preceding subprogram, and so on until a value is finally calculated by the first copy of the subprogram that initially ran.

The advantage of recursion is that it's much simpler to write. If you didn't use recursion, this is how you could calculate factorials using an ordinary FOR-NEXT loop:

```
FUNCTION Factorial (N as INTEGER) as REAL
  DIM Total as REAL
  DIM M as INTEGER
  Total = 1
  FOR M = N DOWNTO 1
    Total = Total * M
    Factorial = Total
END FUNCTION
```

Compared to the much smaller and simpler recursive subprogram, this subprogram is harder to understand although it calculates the exact same results.

Naturally, recursion has its disadvantages:

✦ Recursion can gobble up lots of memory. It runs the same subprogram multiple times, so it makes additional copies of itself.

✦ Recursion can crash your computer if it doesn't end. Your subprogram can keep making endless copies of itself until it runs out of memory.

If you couldn't isolate commands in a subprogram, you could never have recursion.

The whole idea behind subprograms is to make programming easier by breaking a large problem into progressively smaller problems. As long as you understand that subprograms are one technique for helping you write larger programs, you can use subprograms as building blocks to create anything you want.

**Book II
Chapter 6**

Breaking a Large Program into Subprograms

Chapter 7: Breaking a Large Program into Objects

In This Chapter

✔ Understanding object-oriented programming

✔ Clarifying encapsulation, polymorphism, and inheritance

✔ Explaining design patterns

✔ Using object-oriented languages

✔ Providing real-life programming examples

*B*reaking a large program into multiple subprograms makes programming easier. Instead of trying to write a single, monolithic chunk of code, you just have to write small subprograms that work as building blocks that you can stack together to create a much larger program.

Unfortunately, computer scientists found that just dividing a large program into multiple subprograms didn't magically solve all the problems of creating software. Some of the most prominent problems of subprograms include

✦ **Interconnectedness:** Rather than act as independent entities, subprograms are often allowed to interfere with other parts of a program. Not only does this cause problems in tracking down problems *(bugs),* but it also prevents subprograms from being reused easily in other projects. Instead of easily sliding a subprogram out of a program like a building block, it's more like ripping a plant out of the ground by its roots.

✦ **Task-orientation:** Subprograms focus on solving one specific task. Unfortunately, trying to understand how this one task fits into the overall design of a large program can be confusing, much like trying to understand how a car works by studying a single gear. As a result, subprograms make large programs hard to understand and modify. Not only do you not know how a subprogram works with the rest of the program, but you also don't know how changing a subprogram might inadvertently affect other parts of the program.

✦ **Reusability:** Theoretically, you can yank out a subprogram and reuse it in another program. However, if you copy and later modify a subprogram, you now have two nearly identical copies of the same subprogram. If you find a problem in the original subprogram, you now have to find and fix that same problem in any copies you made of that subprogram — provided you can find them all in the first place.

To overcome the limitations of subprograms, computer scientists invented object-oriented programming (abbreviated as OOP). Like structured programming, which encourages you to break a large program into subprograms, OOP encourages you to break a large program into smaller parts, or *objects*.

Object-oriented programming has actually been around since 1962 when two Norwegian computer scientists Ole-Johan Dahl and Kristen Nygaard developed a language called SIMULA, which was designed to help simulate real-world events. It took object-oriented programming nearly 40 more years to finally get accepted as a practical tool, so just because an idea is proven to work doesn't mean people will accept it if they can continue being comfortable (and getting paid) to keep doing something that doesn't work.

How Object-Oriented Programming Works

Like subprograms, objects divide a large program into smaller, interchangeable parts. The main difference is that subprograms divide a program into separate tasks whereas objects divide a program into real-world items.

For example, consider a hotel reservation program used by the front desk when a guest checks in. Dividing this problem into tasks might create the following:

+ **Subprogram #1:** `RoomAvailable` (Checks if a hotel room is available)

+ **Subprogram #2:** `RoomBeds` (Checks if the room has 1 or 2 beds)

+ **Subprogram #3:** `RoomType` (Checks if it's a smoking or a nonsmoking room)

+ **Subprogram #4:** `RoomPrice` (Checks the price)

Dividing this problem into objects, you could create the following:

+ **Object #1:** `Guest`

+ **Object #2:** `Front desk clerk`

+ **Object #3:** `Hotel room`

Figure 7-1 shows how a task-oriented solution might break a program into multiple subprograms. The main program works by running each subprogram, one at a time, with each subprogram performing a specific task (such as determining whether a room is smoking or nonsmoking).

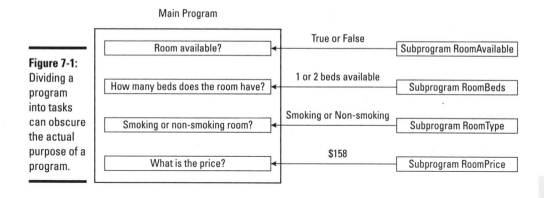

Figure 7-1:
Dividing a
program
into tasks
can obscure
the actual
purpose of a
program.

Figure 7-2 shows an equivalent object-oriented solution to the same program where each object represents a real-world item. Rather than having a single main program controlling multiple subprograms (like one boss controlling a dozen subordinates), OOP divides a program into multiple objects that pass messages to one another (like having a bunch of workers cooperating with one another as equals).

Although both subprograms and objects solve the same problem, they use different solutions. Object-oriented programming is basically a different way of thinking about how to solve problems.

Figure 7-2:
OOP divides
a large
program
into objects
that behave
like their
real-world
counter-
parts.

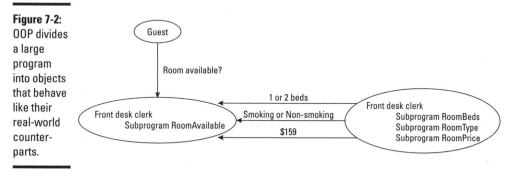

Objects aren't an alternative to subprograms. Subprograms solve a single task. Objects just organize related subprograms together.

There's no single "right" way to divide a large program into objects. Two programmers tackling the same problem will likely divide the same program into different objects. The way you define your objects reflects how you view a particular problem.

Every object consists of two parts, as shown in Figure 7-3:

✦ **Data (also called *properties*)**

✦ **Subprograms (also called *methods*)**

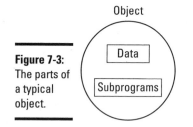

Figure 7-3:
The parts of a typical object.

Objects contain two types of *data:*

✦ **Public data** is accessible by other parts of the program.

✦ **Private data** within the object is hidden from the rest of the program.

Objects contain two types of *subprograms:*

✦ **Public subprograms** allow other parts of a program to control an object.

✦ **Private subprograms** are used by an object to calculate a result needed by its public subprograms *(methods)*.

The difference between public and private data and subprograms is *accessibility:*

✦ **Public** data and subprograms are what the rest of a program can "see" and use in an object:

• Public data typically describes the object in some way. For example, a video game program might create an object that represents a monster. This object may need data, representing X and Y coordinates, to define the monster's location on-screen.

• Public subprograms *(methods)* allow other parts of a program to manipulate an object. For example, an object representing a monster might include a `Move` subprogram that can change the value of the object's X and Y coordinates (to determine where to display the cartoon monster on-screen).

✦ **Private** data and subprograms are what an object uses to do something useful, so the object doesn't need to allow other parts of the program to access this information.

The Monster object might contain a private subprogram that calculates exactly how the Monster object moves. Because other parts of the program don't need to know exactly how the Monster object calculates its movement, this type of information would be private and hidden from the rest of the program.

Ultimately, OOP is another way to make programming easier. Just as high-level languages (like BASIC) simplify programming by using real-life commands (such as `PRINT`), so does OOP simplify organizing programs by modeling real-life items. The three advantages that objects have over ordinary subprograms include

✦ **Encapsulation**

✦ **Inheritance**

✦ **Polymorphism**

Object-oriented programming provides tools for making programming easier, but it's still possible to write horrible software with OOP. Think of OOP like lines painted on the highway. If you follow the lines, you probably arrive safely at your destination, but if you ignore the lines and do whatever you want, you probably crash your car. Like traffic lines painted on the road, OOP guides you into writing software that can be created and modified easily, but you can still mess up things if you're not careful.

Encapsulation Isolates Data and Subprograms

Subprograms have two problems. First, subprograms can work with data from any part of a program. That's what makes subprograms useful, but that's also what makes subprograms harder to modify and fix. If you don't know what data a subprogram might manipulate and when, any changes you make to that subprogram could affect a program in unpredictable ways.

For example, suppose someone writes a weather forecasting program that has a subprogram for predicting tomorrow's temperature measured in Fahrenheit. What happens if another programmer modifies this subprogram to forecast temperatures in Celsius?

Figure 7-4 shows two phases of a program:

The upper phase shows the main program sending the current temperature (32 degrees Fahrenheit) to the forecasting subprogram, which then returns its prediction (as 30 degrees Fahrenheit).

The lower phase shows the same program except now the forecasting subprogram has been modified to return Celsius temperatures. So now when the main program sends the current temperature (in Fahrenheit) to the forecasting subprogram, this subprogram returns its forecast in Celsius. The main program now uses this faulty value.

Figure 7-4:
Changing a subprogram can wreck a perfectly working program.

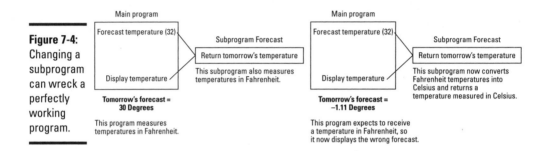

This problem occurs because the forecasting subprogram has no idea how its data is being used by another part of the program. Object-oriented programming can partially solve this problem by organizing data, and all the subprograms that manipulate that data, into a single location, or an *object*. By grouping data and all the subprograms that manipulate that data in one place, it's much easier to understand how that data is being used.

The whole idea behind an object is to isolate and "hide" data and subprograms by using *encapsulation*. Encapsulation acts like a wall, as shown in Figure 7-5, that wraps around data and subprograms to

✦ **Keep other parts of a program from manipulating data inside an object.**

✦ **Keep subprograms inside that object from manipulating data outside that object.**

✦ **Keep programmers from modifying code stored in another object.**

Shielding data inside an object

Think of data as a wallet full of cash. The more people who handle your wallet before giving it back to you, the greater the chance that someone takes money out of that wallet *(manipulating the data)*. Ideally, you want as few people to handle your wallet as possible and if people absolutely must handle your wallet, you want them close enough so you can keep an eye on them.

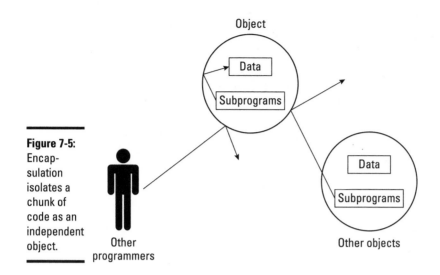

Book II
Chapter 7

Breaking a
Large Program
into Objects

Figure 7-5:
Encap-
sulation
isolates a
chunk of
code as an
independent
object.

That's the same idea behind encapsulating data inside an object. In a program divided into multiple subprograms, data gets passed around like a hot
potato. The more subprograms capable of changing a chunk of data, the
more likely one of those subprograms can accidentally change that data
incorrectly.

By encapsulating data inside of an object, you prevent anything outside that
object from manipulating the data.

Grouping subprograms inside of an object

After you isolate data inside an object, you also need to isolate all the subprograms that manipulate that data inside that same object. By storing all
subprograms that manipulate the same data, objects make it easy to isolate
any problems.

If data inside an object gets messed up, the faulty subprogram can be
located only inside that same object. This makes troubleshooting easier. In
comparison, if data gets messed up in a non-object-oriented program, the
faulty subprogram could be located anywhere. Trying to find a faulty subprogram in an object is like trying to find your lost keys in your apartment.
Trying to find a faulty subprogram in an entire program is like trying to find
your lost keys in a 20-story apartment building.

Protecting code from other programmers

Objects isolate data from other parts of the program, but objects can also isolate subprograms from other programmers.

Without objects, someone might write a useful subprogram that everyone else working on the program can use. One programmer might find that subprogram perfect whereas a second programmer might find that subprogram doesn't quite do what he wants it to do, so he goes into the subprogram and changes the code.

These changes wreck the subprogram for the first programmer, who now has to go back and fix the changes made by the second programmer. These changes make the subprogram work good for the first programmer, but now wreck the subprogram for the second programmer, and so on in an endless cycle.

The problem is that the more people you have working on the same program, the more likely someone might accidentally modify one part of a program without notifying the other programmers. Even one change in a program can affect another part of that same program, so object-oriented programming defines distinct boundaries that keep programmers from modifying code stored in objects created by someone else.

When creating an object-oriented program, every programmer is given control of certain objects and no one is supposed to modify the code in any objects but his own.

Objects let you physically store the source code for your entire object in a separate file, called a *class file* or just a *class.* At this point, a class is no different than storing a group of related subprograms in a separate file and keeping other programmers from modifying that separate file. However, the difference becomes more apparent when you want to reuse code.

Encapsulation serves two purposes:

✦ **Protects data from being changed by other parts of a program**

✦ **Protects subprograms from being changed by other programmers**

Sharing Code with Inheritance

After programmers write some useful subprograms, they often store those subprograms in separate files for other programmers to use. However, no one is supposed to modify these subprograms.

So what happens if someone creates a subprogram that almost does what you need, but not quite? You can't modify the subprogram without the risk of wrecking it for other parts of the program, but you can copy that subprogram and then modify that copy. Now you'll have two separate and nearly identical copies of the same subprograms, as shown in Figure 7-6.

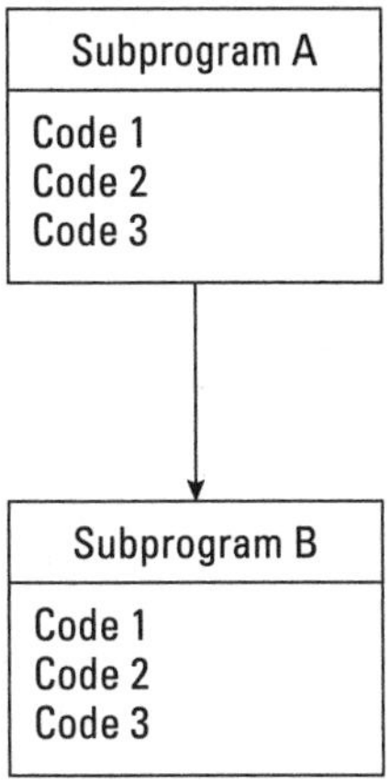

Figure 7-6:
If you modify a subprogram, you need to create a separate copy of that subprogram and modify that copy.

Subprogram A

Code 1
Code 2
Code 3

Subprogram B

Code 1
Code 2
Code 3

What happens if the original subprogram (that you copied) gets modified to make it even more awesome and useful? Now you're stuck with two equally unappealing choices with your modified version of that same subprogram:

✦ **Dump your modified subprogram, copy the new modified subprogram, and re-modify this new version.**

✦ **Modify your subprograms yourself to incorporate the changes made to the subprogram you originally copied.**

Neither solution will be easy because with the first option, you must modify the revised original subprogram all over again. If you made extensive modifications to that subprogram, you'll have to make those same extensive modifications once more. Each time the original subprogram gets modified, you'll have to repeat this step over and over again.

The second option is just as difficult because now you have to study the changes made in the original subprogram and add those changes to your modified subprogram. If you do this incorrectly, your modified version won't work right. Each time the original subprogram gets modified, you'll have to keep up with those changes so you can add them to your modified version of that same subprogram.

Single vs. multiple inheritance

When one object inherits everything from another object, that's *single inheritance.* Some programming languages, such as C++, also can allow objects to inherit from two or more objects, which is *multiple inheritance:*

Good news: Multiple inheritance can use the best parts from two or more objects and smash them together to create a new object.

Without multiple inheritance, you can only inherit code from one object and then you must duplicate code from a second object. Because duplicating code is what object-oriented programming tries to avoid in the first place, multiple inheritance is yet another way to make creating objects easy and fast by reusing existing code from other objects.

Bad news: Multiple inheritance can make programs harder to understand.

By inheriting parts from so many objects, an object can become a hodge-podge collection of parts from everywhere. So a single object that inherits code from multiple objects is not only harder to understand, but also dependent on too many other parts of a program. Such interdependency of code is a problem object-oriented programming tries to eliminate in the first place.

If your programming language offers multiple inheritance, try it to see if its benefits outweigh its drawbacks. If your programming language doesn't offer multiple inheritance, don't feel that you're missing out on anything because most programming languages don't offer multiple inheritance.

Sound like a lot of trouble? It is, which is what makes inheritance so attractive. With *inheritance,* you don't make multiple, physical copies of subprograms. Instead, you first store the subprogram in an object (a *class* file).

Next, you *inherit* that object. Inheritance tells the computer to copy an object (along with all the subprograms stored inside that object) and store all the data and subprograms from that first object into that second object.

Physically, this second object contains no code of its own. Instead, the second object *points* to the code of the original object, as shown in Figure 7-7.

When you run subprograms in this second object, this second object tells the computer, "Hey, those subprograms are really stored in this other object that I inherited them from."

Inheritance offers two advantages:

+ **Because it doesn't make multiple copies of the same subprograms, inheritance saves space.**

+ **Because only one copy of a subprogram physically exists, inheritance makes it easy to update a subprogram.**

Figure 7-7:
Inheritance
lets you
reuse
another
object's
subpro-
grams
without
physically
copying
them.

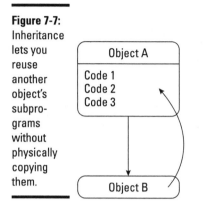

Make a change to the original subprogram, and those changes instantly
appear in any object that inherited that subprogram. The reason for this
instant update is because all those other objects always point to the same
subprogram in the first place.

Inheritance lets you reuse code from another object without physically
copying that code. Now if you can add subprograms to your new object,
your new object contains only your new subprograms, as shown in Figure 7-8.

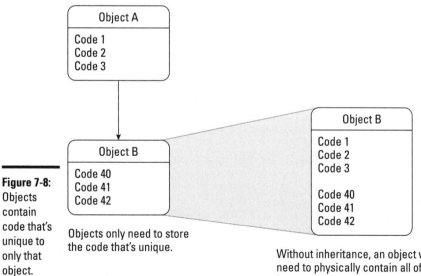

Figure 7-8:
Objects
contain
code that's
unique to
only that
object.

Objects only need to store
the code that's unique.

Without inheritance, an object would
need to physically contain all of its code
in one place.

By keeping the amount of code stored inside each object to a minimum, object-oriented programming makes it easy to understand how each object works. Through inheritance, OOP makes it easy to update one subprogram that's reused in other objects.

As a result, inheritance makes reusing objects (and their subprograms) practical and modifying those objects' subprograms fast, simple, and easy.

Inheritance offers the convenience of reusing code without the inconvenience of updating that code in multiple locations.

Polymorphism: Modifying Code without Changing Its Name

Besides reusing existing subprograms (without modifying them) and adding new subprograms to an object, you can also modify an inherited subprogram through *polymorphism*.

Polymorphism lets you inherit a subprogram from another object and then replace the code in that subprogram with brand new code. So essentially all you're really reusing is the original subprogram's name, as shown in Figure 7-9.

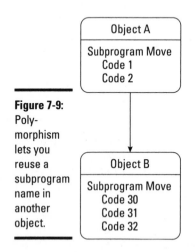

Figure 7-9: Polymorphism lets you reuse a subprogram name in another object.

The purpose of polymorphism is to let multiple objects use the same descriptive subprogram name. Normally, two subprograms can't share the same name. Otherwise, when you call a subprogram by name, the computer doesn't know which subprogram you actually want to use.

However, when you call a subprogram inside an object, you must specify both the object and the subprogram name stored inside that object. So if you wanted to run the `Move` subprogram inside an `Airplane` object, you could call that subprogram by using this command:

```
Airplane.Move
```

This `Airplane.Move` command might tell the computer to move a cartoon airplane in a video game. Now what if this video game needs to display a spaceship on-screen? You could write a new `Spaceship` object from scratch (which takes time) or you could just inherit all the code stored in the `Airplane` object to create a `Spaceship` object.

Of course, a spaceship moves differently than an airplane, so you could inherit the `Move` subprogram from the `Airplane` object, modify that subprogram's code, and you've instantly created a new `Spaceship` object in very little time. Now you can use the same subprogram name (`Move`) to change the position of two different objects, such as

```
Airplane.Move
Spaceship.Move
```

Encapsulation protects data and subprograms from being changed. Polymorphism reuses and modifies code without affecting the original source code. Inheritance reuses code without physically copying it.

Design Patterns

There's no single "right" way to divide a program into objects. When faced with the same problem, two programmers may divide up the program into completely different objects.

However, the more that programmers used object-oriented programming, the more they noticed that some ways of dividing a program into objects worked better than other ways. These specific ways of dividing a program into objects is called a *design pattern.*

A design pattern provides a *blueprint* for the best way to divide specific types of problems into objects. Because these design patterns have been proven already to work, you can use a design pattern to help solve your particular problem.

Without design patterns, you're forced to design objects by yourself and risk choosing a faulty design that you wouldn't know about until you might have already created most of your program.

Three examples of different design patterns (and their unusual names) include

✦ **Interface pattern**

✦ **Flyweight pattern**

✦ **Memento pattern**

An *interface pattern* defines an object that simplifies access to something else. For example, suppose someone has written a library of useful subprograms. Rather than let other programmers access these subprograms directly, an interface pattern defines an object to provide access to these subprograms instead. By doing this, an interface pattern keeps your program focused on using object-oriented features.

So this library might contain subprograms for displaying graphics and calculating mathematical equations. You could use the interface pattern to define one object for accessing the graphics subprograms and a second object for accessing the mathematical equations subprograms, as shown in Figure 7-10.

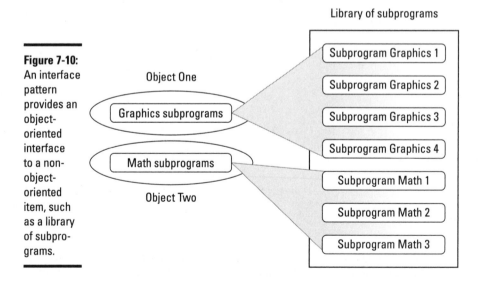

Figure 7-10: An interface pattern provides an object-oriented interface to a non-object-oriented item, such as a library of subprograms.

A *flyweight pattern* is used to create multiple objects. For example, you could create a word processor with every character defined as an object that contains formatting information, such as font, font size, underlining, and so on. However, a typical word processor document would contain thousands of objects *(characters),* and because each object gobbles up memory, creating so many objects would likely swamp the computer's memory.

The flyweight pattern solves this problem by removing repetitive information from multiple objects (such as formatting information) and replacing it with a pointer to another object that contains this information, as shown in Figure 7-11.

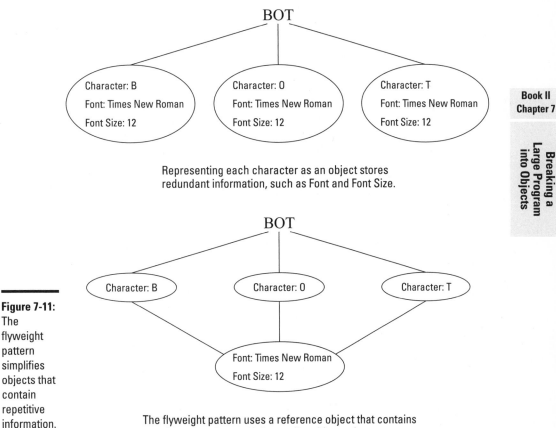

Representing each character as an object stores redundant information, such as Font and Font Size.

The flyweight pattern uses a reference object that contains repetitive data that multiple, smaller objects share.

Figure 7-11:
The flyweight pattern simplifies objects that contain repetitive information.

A *memento pattern* is used to allow an object to restore itself to a previous state. For example, you might use an object to represent a line in a drawing program. If you change that line to make it thicker or a different color, those changes are stored in the line object. If you suddenly decide you want to undo your changes, your program can restore those changes by using the memento object, as shown in Figure 7-12.

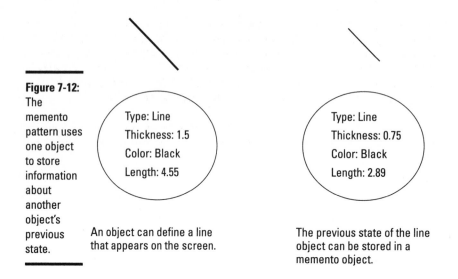

Figure 7-12:
The memento pattern uses one object to store information about another object's previous state.

An object can define a line that appears on the screen.

The previous state of the line object can be stored in a memento object.

These are just a sampling of different design patterns available and how they solve specific problems that occur when using object-oriented programming. Before rushing out to create an OOP, take some time to learn about design patterns. That way you can pick a design pattern that solves your program's specific needs and you don't risk designing a program that doesn't work right because you didn't know anything about design patterns.

Design patterns are guidelines for creating an OOP program, so it's possible to use multiple design patterns in different parts of a program.

Object-Oriented Languages

Two types of object-oriented programming languages exist: Hybrid and pure languages.

Hybrid languages

A *hybrid language* is simply a language originally designed without object-oriented features, but with object-oriented features added on. Some popular examples of hybrid languages include

✦ **BASIC (Visual Basic and REALbasic)**

✦ **C (C++, C#, and Objective-C)**

✦ **Pascal (Delphi)**

✦ **Ada (ObjectAda)**

✦ **COBOL (Object Oriented COBOL)**

Because hybrid languages are based on popular languages, they make it e for current programmers to understand and use. Unlike "pure" object-oriel languages that force you to design a program completely around objects, hybrid languages let you write programs by using the traditional task-oriented, subprogram approach and only using object-oriented features sparingly until you get comfortable with using and designing programs with OOP.

Because hybrid languages are based on languages that have been around for decades, a hybrid language lets you take an existing program and add object-oriented features to it. COBOL programs have been around since the 1960s, so companies are reluctant to rewrite working programs in another language just to gain object-oriented features. Rather than rewrite a perfectly working COBOL program in C++, programmers can just use Object Oriented COBOL instead, which effectively extends the life of ancient COBOL programs.

Hybrid languages do have one major drawback. Because programs written in hybrid languages tend to be a mish-mash collection of traditional and object-oriented programming, they can be hard to understand and even harder to modify.

Pure languages

Although programmers can quickly adapt to the object-oriented language based on a language they already know, most programmers tend to stick with writing programs the way they've always done it, which often means not using object-oriented programming techniques at all or using the object-oriented features poorly.

To get around this problem, computer scientists have developed pure object-oriented languages, which forces programmers to use object-oriented techniques whether they like it or not. Some popular pure OOP languages include

✦ **Java**

✦ **C#**

✦ **Perl**

✦ **Python**

✦ **Smalltalk**

By forcing you to use object-oriented programming techniques, pure object-oriented languages make sure that every program written in that particular language can be easily understood in terms of objects. A program written in a hybrid language can be as sloppy as a native Arabic-speaker writing a letter in both Arabic and English. A program written in a pure object-oriented language may be sloppy and poorly written, but it's like forcing a native

Arabic-speaker to write a letter completely in English, so at least it's easier for English speakers to understand.

So which type of language should you learn and use? If you need to update programs written in older programming languages, like C, BASIC, or Pascal, you have no choice but to update those programs by using a hybrid language.

Ultimately, it's probably best to force yourself to know at least one pure object-oriented language so you fully understand the benefits of OOP and put those benefits into practical use. After you completely understand how to design and use object-oriented techniques, you're more likely to use OOP features in a hybrid language.

The programming language you use is less important than designing a program correctly from the start. Languages are tools to help you achieve a goal, so don't get caught up in the "religious" wars arguing whether one programming language is "better" than another. The "best" programming language is the one that makes you most efficient.

Disadvantages of object-oriented programming

Despite its clear-cut advantages, object-oriented programming isn't perfect and suffers its share of drawbacks:

✦ **OOP is best suited for organizing large programs.** If you need to write a small program to make a printer work with an operating system, organizing your program into objects doesn't likely give you any benefits and may take more time to write.

✦ **OOP requires more memory to run than non-OOP programs.** So if you're writing a small program that needs to be fast and use as little memory as possible, OOP actually makes your program harder to write and slower to run.

Like all programming techniques, such as structured programming, object-oriented programming isn't a magical solution for writing large programs flawlessly. Instead, object-oriented programming is more of a guideline for steering you into using proven techniques for organizing programs and making them easier to modify and update.

The ultimate goal of any programmer is to write software that works, is easy to fix and modify, and gets completed on time. If you can achieve these three goals on a consistent basis, you'll always have plenty of people willing to hire you at whatever salary you want.

Real-Life Programming Examples

To fully understand object-oriented programming, you need to see how to use OOP in a real programming language. Basically, the steps to using OOP involve

+ **Defining an object with a class file**
+ **Creating an object based on a class**
+ **Using subprograms** *(methods)* **in an object**
+ **Inheriting an object**
+ **Using polymorphism to rewrite an inherited subprogram**

Although the following examples use C++, don't worry about the particular syntax of each programming language example. Because every programming language uses different syntax and commands, focus on understanding the principles behind creating and using objects.

Defining an object with a class

To create an object, you must first create a class, stored in a separate file that defines

+ **The data** *(properties)* **the object contains**
+ **The subprograms** *(methods)* **the object uses to manipulate its data**

At the simplest level, a C++ class consists of the `class` keyword along with a descriptive name for your class, such as

```
class ClassName
{
};
```

So if you wanted to name your class `animal`, your class would now look like this:

```
class animal
{
};
```

Next, you need to define the public data *(properties)* and subprograms *(methods)* by using the `public` keyword. Then you must define the private data and subprograms by using the `private` keyword, such as

```
class animal
{
```

```
public:

private:

};
```

Underneath both the `public` and `private` keywords, you must declare your data and subprograms. If you wanted to define an X coordinate and Y coordinate variable as `public` and an X variable as `private`, you'd do this:

```
class animal
{
public:
  int x_coordinate;
  int y_coordinate;

private:
  int x;

};
```

Not all objects have both public and private data and subprograms. Some objects may just have public data and subprograms.

The preceding code creates three integer variables — x_coordinate, y_coordinate, and x. After you define the data your object will use, the next step is to define the subprograms it'll use, such as

```
class animal
{
public:
  int x_coordinate;
  int y_coordinate;

  void initial_position (int, int);
  void move(int, int);

private:
  int x;

};
```

The preceding code defines two subprograms *(methods)* — initial_position and move. The initial_position and move subprograms both accept two integers in their parameter list. After you define the names of the subprograms you want to use, you have to write the actual code to make each subprogram work, such as

```
class animal
```

```
{
public:
  int x_coordinate;
  int y_coordinate;

  void initial_position (int, int);
  void move(int, int);

private:
  int x;

};


void animal::initial_position (int init_x, int init_y);
  {
  x_coordinate = init_x;
  y_coordinate = init_y;
  }

void animal::move (int new_x, int new_y);
  {
  x = 5;
  x_coordinate = x_coordinate + new_x + x;
  y_coordinate = y_coordinate + new_y;
  }
```

The initial_position subprogram defines an initial value for the two public variables x_coordinate and y_coordinate.

The move subprogram adds a new value to the current x_coordinate and y_coordinate values. This subprogram also uses the private variable (x), sets its value to 5, and uses that value to modify the value of the x_coordinate variable.

At this point, you've defined a class. The next step is to use this class in an actual program.

Every class file defines exactly one object. If a program needs a dozen different objects, you need to create a dozen different class files.

Creating an object from a class

Before you can use a class in your program, you need to

✦ **Tell your program which class file to use**

✦ **Define an object based on the class file**

If you stored the `animal` class in an `"animal.h"` file, you'd tell your main C++ program to use this `"animal.h"` file by using the `include` command like this:

```
#include "animal.h"
```

Next, you'd have to define an object name and declare it as an object based on a class. So if you wanted to create a `cow` object with the `animal` class, you'd use this:

```
#include "animal.h"

int main()
    {
    animal cow;
    return 0;
    }
```

The `#include "animal.h"` command tells the program to use the class stored in the `"animal.h"` file. Most C++ also use multiple `#include` commands to make a program work, so the entire C++ program up to this point actually looks like this:

```
#include <stdio.h>
#include <iostream.h>
#include "animal.h"

int main()
    {
    animal cow;
    return 0;
    }
```

Running subprograms stored in an object

After you define an object in your main program, you can run a subprogram stored in that object. So if you wanted to run the `initial_position` subprogram, stored in the `cow` object, you'd identify the object name followed by the object's subprogram to run, such as

```
cow.initial_position (1,1);
```

The `cow.initial_position (1,1)` command tells the computer to use the `cow` object, run the `initial_position` subprogram stored in that `cow` object, and use the values 1 and 1.

If you wanted to run the move subprogram, you'd define the object name (cow) followed by the subprogram name (move) and wind up with a command like this:

```
cow.move (24,9);
```

Putting the whole program together, you might have something like this:

```
#include <stdio.h>
#include <iostream.h>
#include "animal.h"

int main()
  {
  animal cow;
  cow.initial_position (1,1);
  cout << "X-location = " << cow.x_coordinate << "\n";
  cout << "Y-location = " << cow.y_coordinate << "\n";
  cow.move (24,9);
  cout << "New X-location = " << cow.x_coordinate << "\n";
  cout << "New Y-location = " << cow.y_coordinate << "\n";
  cout << "\nPress ENTER to continue..." << endl;
  getchar();
  return 0;
  }
```

If you ran this C++ program, the following would appear on-screen:

```
X-location = 1
Y-location = 1
New X-location = 30
New Y-location = 10

Press ENTER to continue...
```

Inheriting an object

To inherit an object, you must first create another class file. So if you wanted to create a human class and have it inherit from the animal class, you'd do this:

```
class human : public animal
{
};
```

The preceding code tells the computer that the human class inherits from the animal class. At this point, the human class is identical to the animal class.

To use the human class in the main program, you need to use the #include command, such as

```
#include <stdio.h>
#include <iostream.h>
#include "animal.h"
#include "human.h"

int main()
   {
   human cow;
   cow.initial_position (1,1);
   cout << "X-location = " << cow.x_coordinate << "\n";
   cout << "Y-location = " << cow.y_coordinate << "\n";
   cow.move (24,9);
   cout << "New X-location = " << cow.x_coordinate << "\n";
   cout << "New Y-location = " << cow.y_coordinate << "\n";
   cout << "\nPress ENTER to continue..." << endl;
   getchar();
   return 0;
   }
```

In this version of the program, the cow object is declared to be a human class. Because the human class is identical to the animal class, this program runs identically as the preceding version where the cow object was declared as an animal class.

Although the human class behaves identically to the animal class, the human class is actually empty because it inherits all its code from the animal class. Now any code you add to the human class is unique just to that human class, such as

```
class human : public animal
{
public:
   int iq;

   void setiq (int);
   void iqtest (int);
};

void setiq (int startiq)
{
   iq = startiq;
}

void iqtest (int new_iq)
{
   iq = iq + new_iq;
}
```

Because this inherits all the code from the `animal` class, the `human` class is actually equivalent to the following, where the gray shaded code highlights the code unique to the `human` class:

```
class human
{
public:
  int x_coordinate;
  int y_coordinate;

  void initial_position (int, int);
  void move(int, int);

  int iq;

  void setiq (int);
  void iqtest (int);

private:
  int x;

};

void animal::initial_position (int init_x, int init_y);
  {
  x_coordinate = init_x;
  y_coordinate = init_y;
  }

void animal::move (int new_x, int new_y);
  {
  x = 5;
  x_coordinate = x_coordinate + new_x + x;
  y_coordinate = y_coordinate + new_y;
  }
void setiq (int startiq)
{
  iq = startiq;
}

void iqtest (int new_iq)
{
  iq = iq + new_iq;
}
```

As you can see, without inheritance, the code stored inside an object can soon grow out of control, but by using inheritance, each object contains only unique code.

An object that inherits code is treated no differently than an object created entirely from scratch. The following program shows how to use the human class:

```
#include <stdio.h>
#include <iostream.h>
#include "animal.h"
#include "human.h"

int main()
  {
  human cow;
  cow.initial_position (1,1);
  cout << "X-location = " << cow.x_coordinate << "\n";
  cout << "Y-location = " << cow.y_coordinate << "\n";
  cow.move (24,9);
  cout << "New X-location = " << cow.x_coordinate << "\n";
  cout << "New Y-location = " << cow.y_coordinate << "\n";
  cow.setiq (45);
  cout << "The cow's initial IQ is " << cow.iq << "\n";
  cow.iqtest (26);
  cout << "The cow's IQ is now " << cow.iq << "\n";
  cout << "\nPress ENTER to continue..." << endl;
  getchar();
  return 0;
  }
```

Running this program displays the following on-screen:

```
X-location = 1
Y-location = 1
New X-location = 25
New Y-location = 10
The cow's initial IQ is 45
The cow's IQ is now 81

Press ENTER to continue...
```

Using polymorphism to rewrite an inherited subprogram

After you inherit code from another object, you can use polymorphism to rewrite a subprogram. To use polymorphism, you may need to define which subprograms *(methods)* in an object can be changed with polymorphism.

In C++, you define a polymorphic subprogram by using the virtual keyword. So if you wanted to make the Move subprogram polymorphic in the animal class, you'd have to modify the animal class like this:

```
class animal
{
public:
  int x_coordinate;
  int y_coordinate;

  void initial_position (int, int);
  virtual void move(int, int);

private:
  int x;

};
```

After you define that the Move subprogram is polymorphic and can be changed inside an object, the second step is to use the virtual keyword a second time to identify the new version of the subprogram.

So if you want to change the Move subprogram inside the human class, you'd have to use the virtual keyword again like this:

```
class human : public animal
{
public:
  int iq;

  void setiq (int);
  void iqtest (int);
  virtual void move (int, int);
};

void setiq (int startiq)
{
  iq = startiq;
}

void iqtest (int new_iq)
{
  iq = iq + new_iq;
}

void move (int new_x, int new_y)
{
  x_coordinate = new_x * 2;
  y_coordinate = new_y * 2;
}
```

After identifying the polymorphic subprogram with the virtual keyword, you then need to rewrite the Move subprogram. In the preceding example, the new Move subprogram accepts two numbers (new_x and new_y), multiplies them by 2, and uses that result for the `cow` object's new `X` and `Y` coordinates.

Not every object-oriented language requires you to identify polymorphic subprograms. Some languages let you inherit and modify subprograms without identifying them first.

So running the main program would now print the following on-screen:

```
X-location = 1
Y-location = 1
New X-location = 48
New Y-location = 18
The cow's initial IQ is 45
The cow's IQ is now 81
```

Notice that the main program now uses the `Move` subprogram stored in the `human` class, which multiplies each number by 2. So the `cow.move` (24, 9) command sets the cow's `x_coordinate` to 48 (24 * 2) and the `y_coordinate` to 18 (9 * 2).

Although these examples use C++, the basic steps to using objects remain the same:

1. **Create a class that defines the data and subprograms used by an object.**

2. **Create one or more additional classes that inherit code from another class.**

3. **Use polymorphism to rewrite code inherited from another object.**

4. **Declare an object as a specific class type.**

5. **Use an object's subprograms to manipulate that object's data.**

Object-oriented programming can help you design large programs faster, but ultimately, your own skill as a programmer determines the quality of your programs.

Chapter 8: Reading and Saving Files

In This Chapter

✔ Storing data in text files and database files

✔ Storing your fixed size data in random-access files

✔ Storing your varying size data in untyped files

Almost every program needs to save data. Spreadsheets need to save numbers and formulas, word processors need to store text, databases need to store names and addresses, and even video games need to store the top ten highest scores.

To save data, programs store information in a file. After a program stores data in a file, it eventually needs to open that file and retrieve that data again. To save data in files, programs generally use one of four methods:

✦ **Text files**

✦ **Random-access files**

✦ **Untyped files**

✦ **Database files**

Storing Data in Text Files

A *text* file, sometimes called an *ASCII* or *plain text* file, contains nothing but characters, such as letters, numbers, and symbols.

Text files only store actual data, such as names and addresses, but don't contain any formatting information, such as fonts or underlining. Because text files only contain data, they represent a universal file format that any computer, from an ancient Commodore-64 to a Cray super computer, can read and use.

Text files typically store data as one long string of data like this:

```
Joe Smith 123 Main Street New York NY 10012
```

The "other" universal file format

The biggest drawback with text files is that they can't contain any formatting information. So if you need to transfer a word processor document from an ancient Atari ST computer to a modern Macintosh computer, you lose all formatting in that document.

To prevent this problem, computer scientists created a universal file format that can retain both data and formatting. This new file format, *XML (Extensible Markup Language),* contains both data and instructions for how to display the data. For example, the sentence "This is the text you would actually see" looks like this in an XML file:

```
<para>This is the text you
    would actually see</para>
```

Essentially, an XML file is just a text file with formatting instructions or *tags* that define the appearance of data. Because XML files are text files, any computer can read them. To fully read an XML file, a computer needs a special program — an XML parser — which not only reads the data but also translates the XML formatting tags that tell the computer how to display that data.

To create a universal file format for word processor documents, spreadsheets, databases, and presentation files, computer scientists have created a new file format, based on XML — the OpenDocument standard. The main idea behind this OpenDocument standard is to define a universal file format that retains both data and formatting commonly found in word processors, spreadsheets, databases, and presentation program files. Unlike proprietary file formats, which a single company can control, the OpenDocument standard is freely available to anyone.

The OpenDocument file format has even gained the support of many governments, which want to insure that people can still read and edit their files no matter what computer or software they may be using in the future. If you store important files in a proprietary file format, such as Microsoft Word or Microsoft Access, there's a chance that programs in the future won't know how to open those files, which means your data could potentially be lost forever. By using the OpenDocument standard, your data can remain accessible forever (or at least until computer scientists create another "universal" file format).

However, to identify data that should logically be lumped together, programs, such as databases and spreadsheets, offer the option of saving text files as either

+ A **comma-delimited** text file (also known as *CSV* or *Comma Separated Values*) simply divides text into logical chunks, such as

```
Joe Smith, 123 Main Street, New York, NY, 10012
```

+ A **tab-delimited** text file divides text by tabs *(spaces),* like this:

```
Joe Smith    123 Main Street    New York    NY    10012
```

A comma or tab-delimited text file makes it easy for database and spreadsheet programs to read data from a text file and know which data to store in separate *fields* (for databases) or *cells* (for spreadsheets).

Back in 1987, Microsoft tried to define another universal, cross-platform, file format that could retain both data and formatting instructions. This file format, Rich Text Format (RTF), creates *tags* that define the appearance of text. Consider the following text:

✦ This is **bold**.

✦ This is *italicized*.

The RTF file of the preceding text looks like this:

✦ This is \b bold\b0 .\par

✦ This is \i italicized\i0 .\par

So if you ever want to transfer text from one computer or program to another, your safest bet to retain all formatting is to save the file as an RTF file.

Creating a text file

A text file stores data as lines of text. So if you want to store three names in a text file, you could store those names on a single line like this:

```
Joe Smith Mary Evans Donna Dickens
```

Of course, the more names you want to store, the longer this single line of text gets. That's why most text files store data on separate lines where each line of text contains a single chunk of data, such as

```
Joe Smith
Mary Evans
Donna Dickens
```

The end of each line in a text file actually contains two invisible codes:

✦ Carriage Return (CR)

The CR code tells the computer to move to the front of the line.

✦ Line Feed (LF).

The LF code tells the computer to move down to the next line.

So the preceding example of a text file actually looks like this:

```
Joe Smith <CR><LF>
Mary Evans <CR><LF>
Donna Dickens <CR><LF>
```

Creating a text file typically requires three steps:

1. **Name a text file.**

2. **Assign a variable to that text file.**

3. **Store one or more lines of text in the text file.**

The following Python language example creates a text file named `"mytext.txt"` and stores the names `Joe Smith`, `Mary Evans`, and `Donna Dickens` in that file:

```
names = """Joe Smith
Mary Evans
Donna Dickens"""
myfile = open("mytext.txt", "w")
myfile.write(names)
myfile.close()
```

The Python program follows these steps:

1. **This Python program stores the names `Joe Smith`, `Mary Evans`, and `Donna Dickens` in a names variable.**

2. **This program creates *(opens)* a text file named `"mytext.txt"` and assigns this filename to a `"myfile"` variable.**

   The `"w"` symbol tells the program to open the `"mytext.txt"` file so that you can write or add data to that text file.

   The `"w"` symbol tells the computer to erase everything inside the `"mytext.txt"` text file. If you want to add new data to a text file without erasing its entire contents, replace the `"w"` symbol with the `"a"` (append) symbol instead, like this:

   ```
   scraps = open("mytext.txt", "a")
   scraps.write("\nSal Lankins")
   scraps.close()
   ```

   The preceding three lines of code would open the `"mytext.txt"` file, add a new line (the `"\n"` characters), and tack the name `"Sal Lankins"` at the end of the text file.

3. **The `"myfile.write(names)"` command tells the computer to take the data stored in the names variable and store (write) it in the text file assigned to the `"myfile"` variable.**

4. **The `"myfile.close()"` command tells the computer to shut or close the file.**

Reading a text file

After you store data in a text file, you eventually need to retrieve it again by "reading" the text file. *Reading* a text file means retrieving data, starting from the beginning of a text file, line by line, until the computer reaches the end of the file. So if the name Donna Dickens was stored as the third line in a text file, the computer couldn't retrieve Donna Dickens until it first scanned the first and second lines of the text file.

A computer can only retrieve data from a text file starting at the beginning and reading the entire file until it reaches the end. That's why text files are sometimes called *sequential* files because they act like an audio tape that doesn't let you hear the fifth song until you fast forward past the first four songs. Likewise, computers can't retrieve the fifth line in a text file until it scans past the first four lines in that text file.

Reading a text file typically requires three steps:

1. **Identify the name of a text file.**

2. **Assign** *(open)* **the name of the text file to a variable name.**

3. **Read all the lines of data stored in the text file until the end of the text file is reached.**

So if you had a text file named mytext.txt, you could retrieve data out of that file by using the following Python language example:

```
fu = open("mytext.txt", "r")
while 1:
    line = fu.readline()
    if not line:
        break
    print line
fu.close()
```

First, this program identifies the text file to use (mytext.txt) and assigns the text filename to the fu variable. (The "r" symbol tells the computer to read the data from the mytext.txt file.)

Next, a WHILE loop reads the text file, identified by the fu variable, line by line and prints each line. As soon as this loop reaches the end of the file, the WHILE loop stops running.

The fu.close() command closes the text file.

Text files are useful for transferring data between different programs or computers, and for storing small amounts of data. If you need to store and retrieve large amounts of data or if you need to preserve formatting information, you have to use another type of a file besides a text file.

The Portable Document Format (PDF)

Although you can share plain text files among different computers, you always lose the formatting of that data. To avoid this problem, Adobe developed its own "universal" file format — the Portable Document Format (PDF). The idea behind PDF files is to allow people to create and distribute files that display data exactly the same no matter what computer they may use. So if you create a flyer or a newsletter, the appearance of your flyer or newsletter looks the same on a Macintosh computer as it does on a computer running a completely different operating system, such as Windows or Linux.

PDF files have two drawbacks. First, you can't edit them without special software, so PDF files are meant more for displaying information than for letting you actually change that information.

That's why many governments distribute documents and forms as PDF files so people can see the information, such as tax forms, but they can't change it.

Second, you can't view the contents of a PDF file unless you have a special PDF viewing or reader program, which Adobe gives away for free. Unfortunately, if Adobe doesn't make a PDF reader program for your operating system, you can't read PDF files.

Despite these drawbacks, PDF files are popular for sharing information among different computers and operating systems while retaining the original appearance of a file, such as a word processor document. If you just want to share information, PDF files are currently the most popular way to do so.

Many Web sites can store information on your computer in a cookie. A *cookie* is nothing more than a text file that stores your Web site settings, such as your username. That way if you visit that Web site again, the Web site retrieves the cookie off your computer and uses that information to customize the Web page that you see.

For programmers, the most common text file is the source code to any program whether that program is written in C++, Perl, Tcl, or Prolog.

Storing Fixed Size Data in Random-Access Files

One of the biggest problems with text files is that retrieving data requires reading the entire text file from beginning to end. In a large text file, this makes retrieving data clumsy and slow.

Whereas text files act more like audiocassette tapes, random-access files are more like compact discs that allow you to skip right to the data you want to retrieve (which is why they're *random-access* files).

A random-access file organizes data in equal sized chunks called a record. A *record* defines what type of data to store, such as a first and last name, age, and phone number, as shown in Figure 8-1.

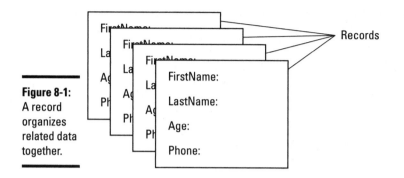

Book II
Chapter 8

Reading and
Saving Files

Figure 8-1:
A record
organizes
related data
together.

Not only do records define what type of data to store, but they also define how much space to allocate for each chunk of data. So if you want to allocate 20 characters for a person's first and last name and 12 characters for a person's phone number, you could define a record in BASIC, as follows:

```
Type PeopleRecord
   LastName as String * 20
   FirstName as String * 20
   Age as Integer
   Phone as String * 12
End Type
```

The preceding code defines the LastName and FirstName variables to hold a maximum of 20 characters, which translates into 20 bytes of storage space. The Age variable is an integer, which requires 2 bytes of storage. The Phone variable can hold a maximum of 10 characters, which translates into 10 bytes of storage space. So the total size of each record is 20 (LastName) + 20 (FirstName) + 2 (Age) + 12 (Phone) for a total of 54 bytes of storage.

A record is a user-defined data type because the user (you) defines the type of information the record can hold. Just as you can't store data directly into other data types (integers, strings, and so on), you can't store data in a record until you first declare a variable to represent your record.

Dividing a random-access file into fixed chunks of space makes it easy to find data later. If you store 26 records in a file and want to retrieve the first record, the computer knows the first record takes up the first 54 bytes of the file. If you want to retrieve the second record, the computer knows this second record is stored in the next 54 bytes of the file (bytes 55–108). By knowing exactly where each record begins and ends, the computer knows how to find each record quickly, as shown in Figure 8-2.

Figure 8-2:
The fixed size of each record makes it easy to identify the physical location of each record in a file.

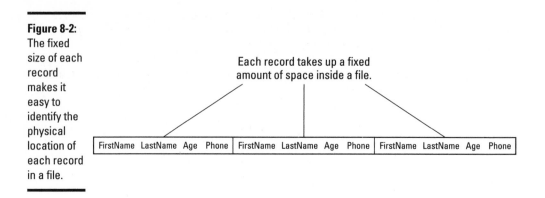

Each record takes up a fixed amount of space inside a file.

| FirstName | LastName | Age | Phone | FirstName | LastName | Age | Phone | FirstName | LastName | Age | Phone |

Writing data

To store *(write)* data to a random-access file, define a variable that represents your records like this:

```
Type PeopleRecord
    LastName as String * 20
    FirstName as String * 20
    Age as Integer
    Phone as String * 12
End Type

Dim Contact as PeopleRecord
```

After you define a variable to represent your record, store data in the Contact variable, such as

```
Contact.LastName = "Smith"
Contact.FirstName = "Joey"
Contact.Age = 28
Contact.Phone = "310-123-1234"
```

The next step is to create a random-access file by defining a filename like this:

```
Open "MyFile.dat" for Random as #1 Len = Len(Contact)
```

This code opens *(creates)* a random-access file named Myfile.dat, identified by the number 1 (#1) and divided into chunks defined by the size or length (Len) of the Contact variable *(record)*.

You can choose any number to represent the random-access file. Using a number, such as #1 or #8, is much easier than typing the entire filename out each time you need to identify which file to use again.

When you open a random-access file to store data, you must correctly define the size of the records. If you define the record size too small, you may lose data. If you define the record size too large, you waste space.

After you create and open a random-access file, you have to store data into that file like this:

```
Put #1, 1, Contact
```

The `Put` command tells the computer to use the file identified as #1 and store the `Contact` data as the first (1) record. To add more data to the random-access file, you'd have to store different data into the `Contact` variable and use additional `Put` commands, such as the following, to store data as the second record in the random-access file:

```
Put #1, 2, Contact
```

When you're done adding records to a random-access file, close the file, which tells the computer that you're done working with that file.

```
Close #1
```

Reading data

After you store one or more records in a random-access file, you can retrieve *(read)* data from that random-access file by identifying the file to use, assigning a number to that file, and defining the size of each record in that file like this:

```
Open "MyFile.dat" For Random As #1 Len = Len(Contact)
```

When you open a random-access file to read data, you must correctly define the size of the records stored in that file. If you incorrectly define the size of the records, the computer can't retrieve the data correctly.

After you open an existing random-access file, you can retrieve data by using the `Get` command like this:

```
Get #1, 2, Contact
```

This command tells the computer to get information out of the file identified as the #1 file, retrieve the second record, and store it back into the `Contact` variable. At this point, you could store the data from the `Contact` variable into another variable and then retrieve another record from the random-access file. When you're done using the random-access file, you have to close it like this:

```
Close #1
```

Random-access files make it easy to store and retrieve data. Because you retrieve only the data you want, random-access files don't waste time reading the entire file.

Storing Varying Size Data in Untyped Files

Random-access files are great for storing chunks of data of equal size. However, what if you want to store data that may vary in size? You could define a record as the largest size data you need to store, but that means you wind up wasting space. As a more efficient alternative, you can store data in untyped files. *Untyped* files still organize data in records, but each record can vary in size, as shown in Figure 8-3.

Figure 8-3:
Untyped files contain records that can vary in size.

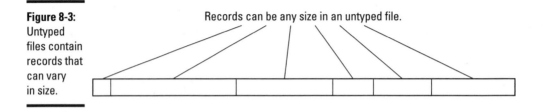

Records can be any size in an untyped file.

Writing data

To store data in an untyped file, you must first name and create an untyped file. In the Delphi programming language, you can create an untyped file by declaring a variable as a `File` type, such as

```
var
  myFile : File;
```

After you create a variable name, you need to assign that variable name to an actual filename, such as

```
AssignFile(myFile, 'MyData.dat');
```

In some languages, such as BASIC, you assign a number to an actual filename. In Delphi and other languages, you assign a name to an actual file. The purpose of assigning a number or a name is so that you can refer to a file without typing the complete filename.

Before you can add any data to an untyped file, use the `ReWrite` command, which defines the filename to use and the number of blocks to add to the file. (Each *block* of data typically corresponds to one byte of data.) So if you want to define a 5-byte block of data, you'd use the following:

```
ReWrite(myFile, 5);
```

After you define the filename (through the `myFile` variable name) and the block size, you can start adding actual data by using the `BlockWrite` command, which specifies the filename to use, the actual data to add, and the number of records to add like this:

```
BlockWrite(myFile, MyData, 1);
```

The preceding command tells the computer to use the file defined by the `myFile` variable and store the data from the `MyData` variable as a single record into the file. After you're done writing data to a file, you need to close the file by using the `CloseFile` command like this:

```
CloseFile(myFile);
```

Reading data

After you store data in an untyped file, you can retrieve it again by first using the `Reset` command that defines the filename to use and the size of the records you want to retrieve.

So if you want to retrieve data from an untyped `MyData.dat` file, you could assign the variable name `myFile` to the `MyData.dat` file, such as

```
AssignFile(myFile, 'MyData.dat');
```

Then you could use the `Reset` command to tell the computer to open the file defined by the `myFile` variable like this:

```
Reset(myFile, 5);
```

The `Reset` command also defines the size of each block of data to retrieve, typically measured in bytes. So the preceding command defines a block of 5 bytes.

Because untyped files contain records of varying sizes, here are two ways to read an untyped file. The first way is to scan the file from beginning to end, like a text file. To do that in Delphi, you can use a `WHILE` loop. Inside the `WHILE` loop, you can put a `BlockRead` command that defines which file to read data from, a variable to store this data, and how many bytes to retrieve at a time like this:

```
while not Eof(myFile) do
  begin
    BlockRead(myFile, Storage, 1);
    ShowMessage(IntToStr(Storage));
  end;
```

The `WHILE` loop tells the computer to keep looping as long as the computer hasn't reached the end of the file *(Eof)* identified by the `myFile` variable.

Inside the WHILE loop is the BlockRead command, which tells the computer to read one (1) block of data at a time (when each block of data is defined in size by the Reset command), as shown in Figure 8-4.

Figure 8-4:
The
computer
can retrieve
data from an
untyped file
in blocks or
chunks.

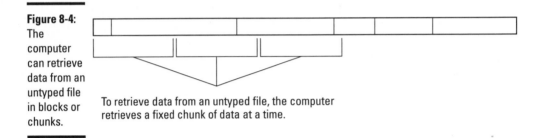

To retrieve data from an untyped file, the computer retrieves a fixed chunk of data at a time.

After the BlockRead command retrieves data from the file identified by the myFile variable, it stores this data in a Storage variable. The ShowMessage command displays the value of the Storage variable on-screen.

Reading an untyped file from start to finish can be as slow and cumbersome as reading an entire text file from start to finish. So as a second way to retrieve data from an untyped file, you can use a pointer to "point" to different data blocks.

For example, suppose you use the Reset command to define a block of 5 bytes:

```
Reset(myFile, 5);
```

This command divides an untyped file into 5-byte blocks.

To access an untyped file, like a random-access file, you can use the Seek command, which defines which untyped file to use and which data chunk to retrieve like this:

```
Seek(myFile, 3);
```

This command tells the computer to use the untyped file identified by the myFile variable and retrieve all the data in the third block of data, as shown in Figure 8-5.

After the computer finishes retrieving data from the file, it needs to close the file by using the CloseFile command:

```
CloseFile(myFile);
```

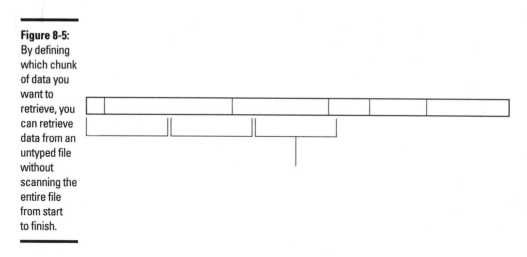

Figure 8-5:
By defining which chunk of data you want to retrieve, you can retrieve data from an untyped file without scanning the entire file from start to finish.

The main idea behind untyped files is that they can hold records of varying sizes. When you retrieve data from an untyped file, you have to read the data in chunks that you define.

In many programming languages, such as C++, an untyped file is considered to be a *stream* of data.

Using Database Files

One problem with random-access and untyped files is that two programs can use untyped files but the structure of one untyped files can differ wildly from the structure of a second untyped file. As a result, transferring or sharing data from one program to another can be difficult.

Proprietary file formats are nothing more than random-access or untyped files that store data in a specific way that only a single company truly understands.

To solve this problem, many programs simply store data in popular file formats used by other programs. Because many programs need to store large amounts of data, they often store data in file formats used by popular database programs to make it easy to share this data.

The most popular databases are Structured Query Language (SQL) databases. Some popular programs used to create and manipulate SQL databases are MySQL and PostgreSQL.

At one time, dBASE was the most popular database file format, so you still see many programs that can create, store, and save data in a dBASE file. Because many companies made dBASE-compatible programs, the dBASE file format is also known by a generic term as xBASE.

Structure of a database

To understand how programs can store information in a database file, you need to understand the basic structure of a database. A database consists of a file, which is what you physically store and save on a disk.

A database file typically consists of one or more tables with each table organizing related data. For example, you might have a database file containing customer information. Then you might divide that database file into three tables with one table containing current customers, a second table containing potential customers, and a third table containing inactive customers, as shown in Figure 8-6.

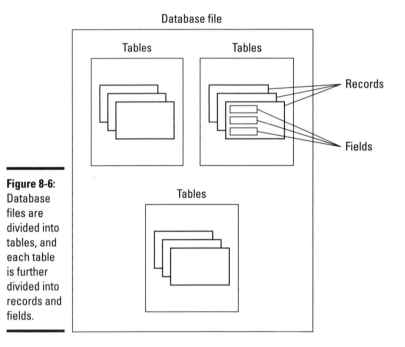

Figure 8-6: Database files are divided into tables, and each table is further divided into records and fields.

Each table is further divided into records with each record containing information about a single item, such as a customer. Each record is further divided into fields with each field storing a single chunk of data, such as a name, a telephone number, or an e-mail address.

Think of a Rolodex file as a database file, the entire collection of business cards as a single table, each business card as a record, and each chunk of information on the business card (name, phone number, address, and so on) as a separate field.

Most database files are *relational* databases because the information stored in each table can be shared to avoid duplication. For example, one table might contain a list of customers, and a second table might contain a list of prospects (potential customers). Sometimes a customer can also be a prospect, so you could store that same person's name twice — once in the customer table and once in the prospect table.

However, you don't want to store duplicate information because if you update that information, you need to make sure you update that same information everywhere. So a simpler solution is to *relate* tables together that essentially share data.

So the prospect table might physically contain the customer information whereas the customer table might only contain unique information, such as the type of product the customer bought and the total sales amount. To retrieve the customer's name and address, the customer table simply points to that information stored in the prospect table, as shown in Figure 8-7.

Connecting to a database

To save information to a database file, a program needs to identify

✦ **The database file to use**

✦ **The table to use**

✦ **The record to use**

✦ **The specific field to view, edit, or store data**

Although it's possible to write your own subprograms to access a database file, retrieve information from a specific table, record, and field, and then save those changes again, this usually takes way too long to write and test. As a faster alternative, most programmers either buy a third-party database toolkit or (if they're lucky) use the built-in database controls that come with their language compiler.

A database toolkit essentially acts like a middleman between your program and a database file, as shown in Figure 8-8. So rather than worry about the physical details of a particular database file, you just have to tell the database toolkit what you want to do and the toolkit figures out how to do it, such as saving new information in a database table.

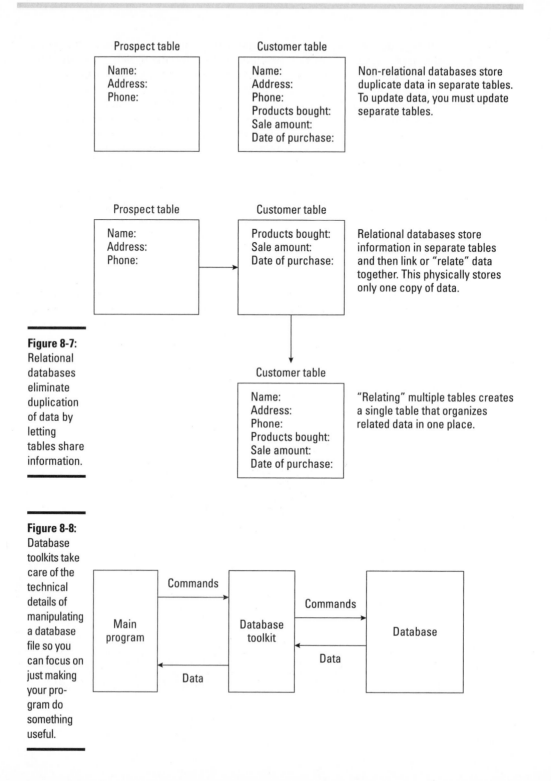

Prospect table

Customer table

Name:
Address:
Phone:

Name:
Address:
Phone:
Products bought:
Sale amount:
Date of purchase:

Non-relational databases store duplicate data in separate tables. To update data, you must update separate tables.

Prospect table

Customer table

Name:
Address:
Phone:

Products bought:
Sale amount:
Date of purchase:

Relational databases store information in separate tables and then link or "relate" data together. This physically stores only one copy of data.

Figure 8-7:
Relational databases eliminate duplication of data by letting tables share information.

Customer table

Name:
Address:
Phone:
Products bought:
Sale amount:
Date of purchase:

"Relating" multiple tables creates a single table that organizes related data in one place.

Figure 8-8:
Database toolkits take care of the technical details of manipulating a database file so you can focus on just making your program do something useful.

Main program

Commands →

Data ←

Database toolkit

Commands →

Data ←

Database

When using any toolkit from a third-party, your program is essentially held "hostage" by that toolkit. If the company making the toolkit goes out of business or doesn't sell a version of its toolkit for a different operating system, you can't do anything about it. So if your program uses a database toolkit that runs only on Windows, you can only write programs that run on Windows but never for Linux or Mac OS X. If a toolkit doesn't offer the features you need or work with your favorite language or compiler, you have to write your own code or find another toolkit — and risk running into the same problems all over again.

Because database access is so common, many RAD (rapid application development) compilers, such as Visual Basic, Delphi, and REALbasic, include database connectivity features. That way you don't have to buy a separate database toolkit or worry about the database toolkit not working with your favorite compiler.

To add database connectivity with a RAD tool, you use database controls, which let you define the database file, table, and field to use. After you define what parts of a database file to use, you also need to use database viewing controls to view and edit data stored in specific fields, as shown in Figure 8-9.

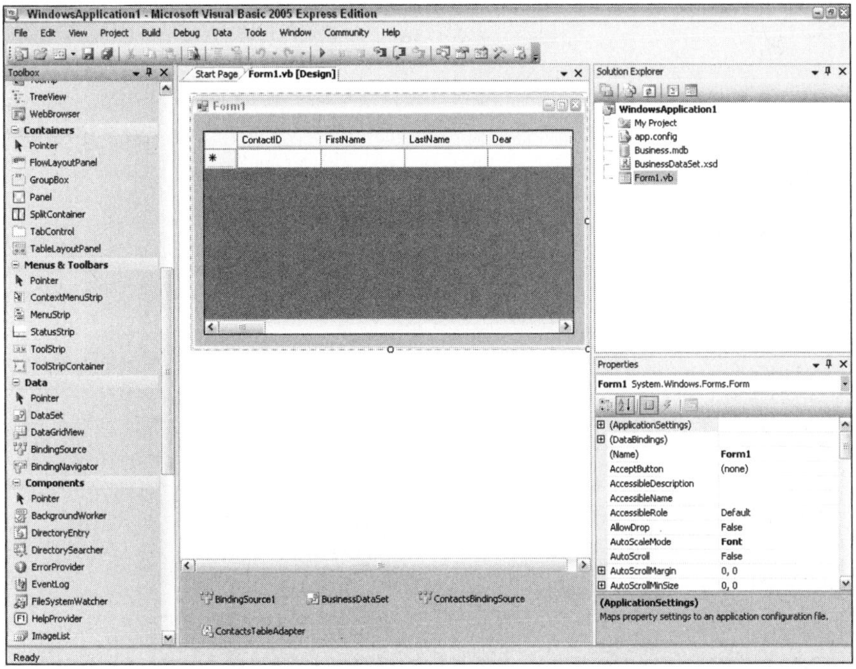

Figure 8-9:
A Visual
Basic
program
uses one
or more
controls to
connect a
program to
a database
file.

Database controls take care of the details of how to connect to a database so you can just focus on using a database file.

When a program connects to a database file, that program often acts as a front-end to that database. A *front-end* basically wraps a friendly user interface around the database file. So rather than force users to figure out arcane commands to retrieve, print, edit, search, or sort through a database file, a front-end provides a simplified interface for manipulating data, as shown in Figure 8-10.

Figure 8-10: Programs often act as a front-end to a database file.

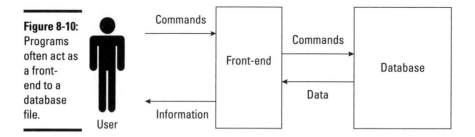

Database files are best for storing large amounts of information that you can share with other people and programs. If sharing data with other programs isn't important, use a random-access or untyped file. The drawback is that both of these files force you to write additional commands to store and retrieve data. For storing small amounts of data, use a text file.

Storing information in a file is a crucial part of most programs, so determine what type of data you need to save and then choose the file format that makes the most sense for your program.

Chapter 9: Documenting Your Program

In This Chapter

- Adding comments to your source code
- Constructing software documentation
- Creating help files

There are two big problems with writing programs. First, you have to worry about getting the program to work. Second, you'll probably need to fix and modify it later. To solve both types of problems, you have to understand how the program works in the first place. To understand how a program works, programmers have to explain

+ **What problem the program is trying to solve**

+ **How the program is designed**

+ **How each part of the program works**

In the early days when programs were small, programmers could figure out all the preceding questions by studying the source code of the program. When programs got bigger and tackled more complicated problems, programmers could no longer understand how a program worked by examining the source code. That's when programmers were forced to start writing additional explanations, or *documentation*. By studying this documentation, other people could understand how a program works without trying to decipher the actual source code of a program.

Adding Comments to Source Code

One of the first attempts at explaining how a program worked was by making the source code more understandable by using high-level languages, like BASIC or Pascal, to create *self-documenting* code. So rather than try to decipher cryptic code like

```
SECTION .data
  msg db "It's alive!!",0xa;
  len equ $ - msg
```

```
SECTION .text
  global main
main:
  mov eax,4;
  write system call
  mov ebx,1
  mov ecx,msg
  mov edx,len
  int 0x80
  mov eax,1 system call
  mov ebx,0
  int 0x80
```

You could replace the preceding assembly language commands with a shorter, more descriptive high-level language command like this:

```
PRINT "It's alive!"
```

Such self-documenting code helps explain what a single line of code does, but doesn't necessarily tell you how the entire program works as a whole or what problem the program even solves.

Rather than rely on "self-explanatory" language commands, programmers started adding explanations directly into the source code itself by using comments.

A *comment* is nothing more than text, embedded in the source code. To keep the compiler from thinking a comment is an actual command, every comment needs a special symbol in front of the comment, such as

```
REM This is a comment in BASIC
' This is another comment in BASIC
// This is a comment in C++ and Java
# This is a comment in Perl and Python
; This is a comment in LISP and assembly language
```

Comments allow you to write short explanations, directly in the source code, that describe what the source code does. Looking at the following code, can you understand what it does?

```
C = SQRT(A * A + B * B)
```

Deciphering this code is straightforward. This command multiplies two variables by themselves, A and B, adds the results together, and finds the square root of the sum, which gets stored in the C variable. However, knowing how the command works doesn't tell you what or why this code is doing this. By adding comments to the source code, you can explain this, as follows:

```
' Calculates the hypotenuse of a triangle (C)
' using the Pythagoras theorem: C² = A² + B²
C = SQRT(A * A + B * B)
```

Even if you don't know (or care) about Pythagoras' theorem, the comments help you understand what the command is calculating.

Some programmers use comments to insert jokes, profanity, or remarks about their co-workers directly in their source code. Just be aware that other people besides you may need to look at your source code. So if you've laced your program with profanity-ridden tirades against your co-workers, don't be surprised if one of your co-workers finds and reads the comments you made about him, which could be humorous or embarrassing.

You can put comments anywhere in a program because the compiler ignores them anyway. The two types of comments are *line comments* and *block comments*.

Line comments

Line comments appear directly on a line that already contains a command like this:

```
C = SQRT(A * A + B * B)   ' Calculates Pythagoras theorem
```

The problem with line comments is that they can make source code somewhat harder to read. That's why some programmers prefer putting comments on separate lines like this:

```
' Calculates Pythagoras theorem
C = SQRT(A * A + B * B)
```

Comments exist purely for other people to read, so it doesn't matter whether you put them on a line with a command or on a separate line.

To make comments easier to read, use plenty of blank lines and spaces. The following example looks crowded:

```
' Calculates the hypotenuse of a triangle (C)
C = SQRT(A * A + B * B) ' Calculates Pythagoras theorem
```

By adding blank lines and extra spaces, you can make each comment easier to find and read:

```
' Calculates the hypotenuse of a triangle (C)

C = SQRT(A * A + B * B)        ' Calculates Pythagoras theorem
```

Block comments

If you need to write several lines of comments, typing the comment character in front of each line can get annoying. As a simpler alternative, many programming languages let you create block comments.

A block comment lets you identify the beginning and end of a comment. So if you wanted to write a comment on two separate lines in C++, you'd have to type the // symbols in front of each line, such as

```
// Calculates the hypotenuse of a triangle (C)
// using the Pythagoras theorem: C² = A² + B²
```

If you created this as a block comment, you could use the /* and */ symbols to mark the start and end of a comment like this:

```
/* Calculates the hypotenuse of a triangle (C)
   using the Pythagoras theorem: C² = A² + B²
*/
```

No matter how many comments you add, you only need to use the /* and */ comment symbols once like this:

```
/* Calculates the hypotenuse of a triangle (C)
   using the Pythagoras theorem: C² = A² + B².
   The length of the hypotenuse is then used to
   move a cartoon figure on the screen.
*/
```

Block comments just make it easier to add multiple lines of comments. Programmers often use both line and block comments in a single program like this:

```
/* Calculates the hypotenuse of a triangle (C)
   using the Pythagoras theorem: C² = A² + B².
   The length of the hypotenuse is then used to
   move a cartoon figure on the screen.
*/
```

```
c = sqrt(a * a + b * b) // Pythagoras theorem
```

The comment symbol in one language may have a completely different meaning in another language, so make sure you don't mix them up.

✦ In the curly bracket languages (such as C++ and Java), the curly brackets are used to define a block of commands like this:

```
int main()
{
    cout << "Hello, world!\n";
}
```

✦ In Pascal, the curly brackets are used to create block comments like this:

```
{  Calculates the hypotenuse of a triangle (C)
   using the Pythagoras theorem: C² = A² + B².
   The length of the hypotenuse is then used to
   move a cartoon figure on the screen.
}
```

To make block comments stand out, many programmers surround comments with additional symbols. So instead of writing a simple block comment like this:

```
/* This code calculates how many megatons will
   be needed to blow up at least 75% of the
   world and throw huge chunks of the planet
   into orbit around the moon.
*/
```

Many programmers emphasize the block comments by inserting extra symbols, such as asterisks, as follows:

```
/***********************************************\
 * This code calculates how many megatons will *
 * be needed to blow up at least 75% of the    *
 * world and throw huge chunks of the planet   *
 * into orbit around the moon.                 *
\***********************************************/
```

The compiler ignores all these extra symbols and just focuses on the /* symbols to identify the beginning of the comments and the */ symbols to identify the end of the comments.

Rather than surround comments with extra symbols, some programmers use extra symbols in the left margin, such as

```
/*
** This code calculates how many megatons will
** be needed to blow up at least 75% of the
** world and throw huge chunks of the planet
** into orbit around the moon.
*/
```

Every programmer eventually develops a preferred style for writing comments, so be consistent and other programmers will have no trouble finding and reading your comments.

Describing code and algorithms

Comments are typically used to explain what one or more lines of code do or how they work. For example, suppose you had the following code:

```
F = P / (1 + (B * exp(-c * t)))
```

Looking at this code, you can tell how the computer calculates a result, but you have no idea what result this code is calculating. So you could add a comment that explains what this code does like this:

```
' This formula calculates the spread of a flu epidemic as a
' a function of time

F = P / (1 + (B * exp(-c * t)))
```

Now that you've identified what the code does, you can use additional comments to explain how it works:

```
' This formula uses the epidemic model to calculate the
' spread of a flu epidemic as a function of time

' F = Function of time
' P = Current population of a city
' t = Time measured in weeks
' c = Number of people in contact with an infected person
' B = A constant value that can be determined by the initial
'       parameters of the flu epidemic

F = P / (1 + (B * exp(-c * t)))
```

Although you may still not understand what the preceding code does, the comments can help you understand what the code does (calculating a flu epidemic) and how it works. Without these comments, the code itself can tell you little about what it does.

There are two schools of thought regarding comments. One school says to use comments liberally to explain both what code does and how it works. The second school believes that if you have to add comments to explain what and how your code works, your code is probably too complicated in the first place. This second school of thought believes that instead of writing comments, programmers should just focus on writing self-explanatory code. Most programmers try to write self-explanatory code and use comments whenever necessary.

Another use for comments is to explain the logic behind your code. For example, if you declared a variable as a `Byte` data type instead of an

Integer data type, you might include a comment explaining why you chose one data type or another like this:

```
' Declared the "Age" variable as a Byte data type since
' Byte data types only accept values from 0 - 255.

Dim Age as Byte
```

Use comments sparingly only when the purpose of code isn't obvious. Redundant comments help no one, as the following example shows:

```
' Calculates interest payments by multiplying the
' principal by the interest rate and the time.

Payments = Principal * Rate * Time
```

If a comment repeats information that anyone could read from the source code, take the comment out. Otherwise, you risk cluttering your source code with useless comments that only make your program harder to read.

Documentation

Comments can explain the purpose of one or more lines of code, but many programmers also use comments to document entire subprograms, such as

✦ **Describing what the subprogram does**

✦ **Listing the original programmer (along with contact information, such as an e-mail address)**

✦ **Defining the original creation date and last date of modification**

The following code shows how to use a block comment to document a subprogram:

```
/************************************************\
 * Description:                                 *
 *                                              *
 * This subprogram calculates the angle needed  *
 * to track and aim a laser for shooting down   *
 * anti-aircraft missiles fired at airplanes    *
 * as they land or take off.                    *
 *                                              *
 * Author: John Smith (Jsmith@dodwaste.com)     *
 *                                              *
 * Creation date: January 21, 2006              *
 *                                              *
 * Last modified: September 5, 2007             *
 \************************************************/
```

By placing such a descriptive comment at the beginning of every subprogram, other people can understand what the subprogram does and who to contact (blame) without having to examine the source code line by line.

Debugging

Comments can temporarily *ignore* lines of code for testing. For example, suppose your program included the following:

```
Y = log(Y) - (500 + sin(Angle))
X = Rate * exp(X) / Y
PRINT "The value of x = ", X
```

If you wanted to see how your program would work if you eliminated the first line of code and replaced it with a new line of code, you could erase the top line and type a new line, such as

```
Y = cos(Angle) * Y
X = Rate * exp(X) / Y
PRINT "The value of x = ", X
```

Now if you wanted to replace the top line with the previously erased line, you'd have to delete the top line and retype the preceding line all over again. A simpler method would be to comment out the top line and type in a new line, such as

```
' Y = log(Y) - (500 + sin(Angle))
Y = cos(Angle) * Y
X = Rate * exp(X) / Y
PRINT "The value of x = ", X
```

This causes the compiler to ignore the top line (treating it as a comment). Now if you want to "insert" the top line back into the program, you can comment out the second line and remove the comment symbol from the first line:

```
Y = log(Y) - (500 + sin(Angle))
' Y = cos(Angle) * Y
X = Rate * exp(X) / Y
PRINT "The value of x = ", X
```

The preceding code is equivalent to the following:

```
Y = log(Y) - (500 + sin(Angle))
X = Rate * exp(X) / Y
PRINT "The value of x = ", X
```

By commenting out code, you can temporarily *ignore* code without *deleting* it. Then you can add the code back into your program by removing the comment symbol rather than retyping the entire line again.

Writing Software Documentation

Most source code makes no sense to non-programmers. Even worse, most source code often makes no sense even to the original programmers after they stop working on it.

Many programmers work on a program and understand all the idiosyncrasies and quirks of that program. Then they work on another program and forget how the first program worked. When they return to the first program, the source code can look as alien as trying to read someone else's handwriting. For that reason, software documentation is crucial.

**Book II
Chapter 9**

Documenting
Your Program

Documentation types

Documentation typically consists of text that's physically separate from the source code. The three types of documentation include

✦ **Design specifications**

✦ **Technical designs**

✦ **User manuals**

Although software documentation is often treated as an afterthought, it can be a crucial step in completing any program. The key to software documentation is to make it easy to create while still being useful. If you can do that, your software documentation will be a success no matter how much (or how little) time you spend putting it together.

Design specifications

Design specifications list the program requirements so the programmers can understand what problem they need to solve. Unfortunately, projects tend to change over time, so it's common to specify one type of program and then halfway through the project, someone suddenly decides to add an entirely new feature.

Trying to design everything beforehand is like trying to describe the perfect apple pie without even knowing what an apple pie looks or tastes like. Design specifications can help give a project focus, but their ultimate goal is to help programmers create a useful, working program.

Video tutorials

Because most people don't read user manuals, many companies are resorting to *video tutorials* that show movies of the program in action. That way users can see exactly how to use the program without having to search for that information buried somewhere inside a thick manual.

Unfortunately, video tutorials are limited. They take time to create, so they usually cover only the more common features of a program. If you need help with a specific command, you need to first find the video file that contains the answer and then you have to skim through the video until you find your answer.

As a result, video tutorials act more as supplements to the user manual than as replacements. Video tutorials work best when they're kept short and focused on common tasks that every user needs to know. After users get familiar with a program with the help of video tutorials, they'll feel more confident using the help files and reading the user manual.

Technical design

Programmers use a technical design document to organize how to write the program. This means specifying how the program will work, what programming language and compiler to use, how to divide the program into parts, and assigning teams of programmers to work on each part.

Technical design documents usually start off being fairly complete and accurate, but trying to design a program is much different than actually writing that same program. Therefore, the design of a program can change as programmers run into obstacles that they didn't foresee ahead of time.

When this happens, the programmers often focus on solving the problem and forget about updating the technical design documents, so the technical design documents eventually become inaccurate and obsolete. Programmers rarely want to update technical design documents because the program may likely change again later anyway.

User manuals

User manuals are meant to teach people how to use the program. Ideally, a program should be so intuitive that users don't need a user manual. Because that rarely happens, most programs include a user manual that explains how to use every feature in a program.

Documentation tools

Unfortunately, most user manuals are notoriously inaccurate, confusing, and incomplete:

✦ **If the programmers write the user manual, they tend to write instructions geared more toward other programmers.**

✦ **If other people write the user manual, they often don't fully understand how the program actually works.**

The problem with all forms of documentation stems from the dual nature of a software project:

✦ **Writing a program is completely different from writing documentation.**

✦ **Writing the best documentation in the world is useless if the program never gets done or works incorrectly.**

Programmers can use a couple of techniques for writing better documentation.

Agile documentation

Many programmers prefer using agile documentation methods. Just as agile programming means being able to adapt to changing conditions, *agile documentation* means updating the documentation just enough to be accurate but without wasting time trying to make it perfect.

Automation

Computer scientists have developed special documentation generators that can examine source code and create simple explanations for how different parts of a large program works.

By using such automated tools, keeping documentation updated is much faster and easier than forcing a reluctant programmer to write and update documentation manually. After documentation has been partially completed with an automated tool, the programmers can edit the documentation to keep it up to date.

Help files

Partially to avoid writing and printing manuals that few people bother to read anyway, programmers are writing help files instead. *Help files* essentially condense the user manual into short explanations that give users three options for finding help by

✦ **Browsing through a table of contents of logically organized topics**

✦ **Searching an index for specific commands or topics organized alphabetically**

✦ **Searching for specific terms or phrases**

Help files can be read like a book, browsed through like a dictionary, or searched like a search engine that returns pages of related information. Like ordinary user manuals, help files often require the aid of programmers to explain and verify that the explanations in the help files are accurate and complete.

To make creating help files easier, many programmers use special help file creation programs, which can turn an ordinary user manual into a help file. By using such tools, programmers don't have to create user manuals and help files separately; they can just create a user manual and then turn that user manual into a help file. Ultimately, any form of documentation is meant to help explain what a program does and how it works. When writing documentation for your program, make it easy on yourself and write as little as possible while trying to be as complete as possible. It's not an easy task, but it's a necessary one.

Chapter 10: Principles of User Interface Design

In This Chapter

✔ Following the evolution of user interfaces

✔ Defining the elements of a user interface

✔ Designing a user interface

You can divide every program into two parts: a user interface and the part of the program that actually does something useful, such as predicting winning lottery numbers or editing video images.

The whole purpose of a user interface is to give a program a way to

✦ **Accept commands from the user.**

✦ **Accept data from the user.**

✦ **Display information back to the user.**

The user interface basically lets you give information to a program and receive useful information back again, as shown in Figure 10-1. Most user interfaces let people control a program, but a user interface can just as well let inanimate objects (like a motion detector) control a program. Without a user interface, you can't control a program or retrieve any useful information from the program.

Figure 10-1:
The user interface lets you control a program, give it commands, and retrieve useful information back.

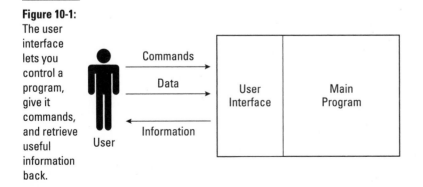

The Evolution of User Interfaces

To better understand user interfaces, you need to know how user interfaces evolved and how current user interface designs are meant to solve the problems of the past.

Command-line interface

In the old days, programmers focused on writing the useful part of their program and then as an afterthought, they created a simple user interface for controlling that program. Because the programmers already know how to control their own program, they often create a bare-bones user interface that looks as confusing as this:

```
A:\>
```

At this point, the user is supposed to know not only all possible valid commands to use, but also how to spell and use each command as well. Such bare-bones user interfaces are *command-line* interfaces because they force users to type in commands one line at a time.

The problem with command-line interfaces is that they're too hard to use:

+ **You have to know all valid commands you can use.**

+ **You have to know what each command does so you know which one to pick.**

+ **You have to type each command in correctly.** Spell a command wrong or leave out a space, and the program rejects that command and makes you type it all over again.

Menus

Command-line interfaces made using programs too difficult for the average person, so user interfaces soon evolved from primitive command-line interfaces to simple menus that listed options for the user to choose, as shown in Figure 10-2.

To choose a command listed in a menu, you had to either press a function key (such as F3) or a unique keystroke combination (such as Ctrl+K+X). The problem with these simple menus was that they gobbled up space on-screen. The more commands a program offered, the bigger the menus got.

The solution to this problem was to organize commands in different menus that would appear only when the user needed them. Such menus typically appeared at the top of the screen and would appear when the user clicked or *pulled down* the menu, like pulling down a window shade, as shown in Figure 10-3.

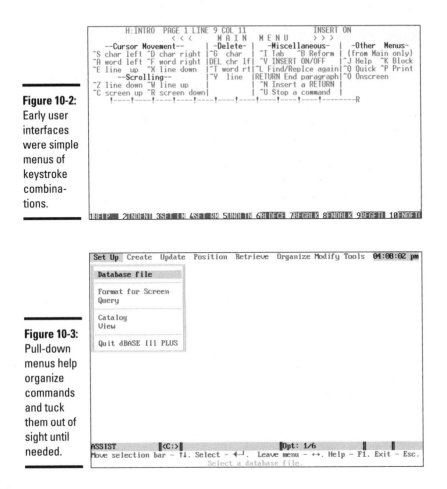

Figure 10-2:
Early user interfaces were simple menus of keystroke combinations.

Figure 10-3:
Pull-down menus help organize commands and tuck them out of sight until needed.

The main advantages of pull-down menus are that they hide program commands until you need them, and you could choose a command from a pull-down menu by clicking it with the mouse as opposed to typing a cryptic keystroke command.

Eventually, more programs started using pull-down menus. To make using different programs even easier, programs started organizing their commands under identical pull-down menu categories.

For example, the File menu typically lists commands that manipulate your data, such as Save, Open, or Print a file. The Edit menu typically lists commands for changing your data, such as Cut, Copy, and Paste. By offering standard pull-down menus, users could figure out one program and then quickly adapt to using another program.

Graphical user interface

The next great leap forward in user interface design occurred with operating systems. In the early days of computers, most operating systems offered only command-line user interfaces, so programs had to create their own pull-down menu user interfaces themselves. Therefore, every program tends to look slightly different even if it used nearly identical pull-down menus.

To create a consistent appearance for all programs and give users the ability to run two or more programs at the same time, operating systems soon abandoned their clunky command-line user interfaces and adapted a graphical user interface (abbreviated as GUI).

The main purpose of a GUI is to give users the chance to point and click the commands they want rather than force them to type in the actual command name.

An operating system's GUI offered three advantages:

✦ **All programs appeared with a consistent look.**

✦ **Each program appeared in its own window.**

✦ **Users could cut, copy, and paste data from one window (program) to another.**

Before GUI operating systems, such as Mac OS X or Microsoft Windows, two programs might both display similar pull-down menus, but one program might display it in black against a white background whereas the other program might display it in red against a blue background. Such visual differences might be functionally trivial, but the jarring visual differences could make figuring out different programs harder for many people.

By forcing all programs to look similar, GUI operating systems made figuring out programs much easier. After you knew how one program worked, you could easily switch to another one.

✦ GUI operating systems can display individual programs in separate windows. Previously, computers could only run a single program at a time, and that program would gobble up the entire screen.

With GUI operating systems, each program could only appear in a separate window. That way you could run multiple programs at a time, arrange them in separate windows, and see and switch between each program just by clicking a different window.

✦ GUI operating systems let you share data between separate windows. So if one window runs a word processor and a second window runs a database, you could copy and paste data from one program into the other. Without a

GUI operating system acting as an intermediary, sharing data between two different programs was difficult to impossible.

The only purpose of a user interface is to make it easy for people to use a program. The best user interface is *transparent* to the user — someone can use the program just by looking at it, rather than being forced to read 300-page manuals first.

Elements of a User Interface

To create a user interface, you have two choices:

Book II
Chapter 10

Principles of User
Interface Design

+ **Write a user interface from scratch.**

+ **Use a RAD (rapid application development) tool.**

Writing a user interface from scratch basically means writing and testing your program and then writing and testing a user interface, essentially doubling your work. Because the code that creates a user interface can be separate from the code that actually makes your program do something useful, many programmers use user interface frameworks that contain libraries of subprograms for creating the standard elements of a user interface, such as pull-down menus and windows.

As an even simpler alternative, programmers also use RAD (rapid application development) tools that let you visually design your user interface. After you design your user interface, write code that attaches this user interface to the rest of your program.

No matter which method you use to create a user interface, every user interface needs to offer ways to do the following:

+ **Give commands to the program.**

+ **Give data to the program.**

+ **Display information for the user to see.**

The user interface has to make sense only to the people who want to use the program. If you design a user interface that looks great to you but confuses the people who use the program, the user interface fails no matter how pretty it may look.

Displaying commands to a user interface

Unlike command-line interfaces that force users to memorize and type commands, GUI user interfaces always display commands on-screen so the user can point and click with the mouse to choose a command.

The simplest way to display a command to the user is through a button. Because buttons can take up so much space on-screen, buttons are most useful for displaying a limited number of commands to the user, such as two or three possible choices, as shown in Figure 10-4.

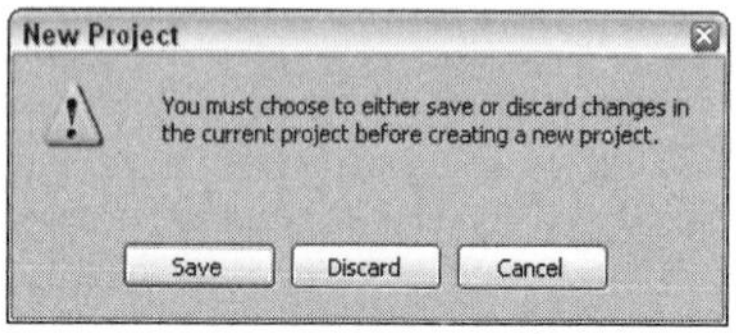

Figure 10-4: Buttons can display the entire command name .

New Project

You must choose to either save or discard changes in the current project before creating a new project.

Save   Discard   Cancel

The problem with buttons is that they take up screen space, so using more than a handful of buttons can crowd the screen and confuse the user. So rather than bombard users with screens full of buttons, programs generally use buttons to offer choices that users need to make immediately.

For example, when quitting a program, the program may ask the user if she wants to save her file before quitting. So the limited number of choices are only: Don't Save, Save, and Cancel.

Buttons are useful for limiting the user's choices to a handful of options. However, buttons are impractical for displaying a large number of commands.

The most popular way for displaying multiple commands to the user is through pull-down menus. Pull-down menus organize commands into categories, such as File, Edit, Window, and Help.

Unfortunately, pull-down menus aren't easy to use when a program has hundreds of possible commands. As a result, commands often get buried within multiple pull-down menus.

To solve this problem, many programs group related commands within submenus, but now you have the problem of trying to find a command buried within a submenu, which is buried in a pull-down menu, as shown in Figure 10-5.

Because pull-down menus can get overloaded with so many commands, user interface designers started displaying commands as icons and grouping icons together in toolbars that usually appear directly underneath pull-down menus, as shown in Figure 10-6.

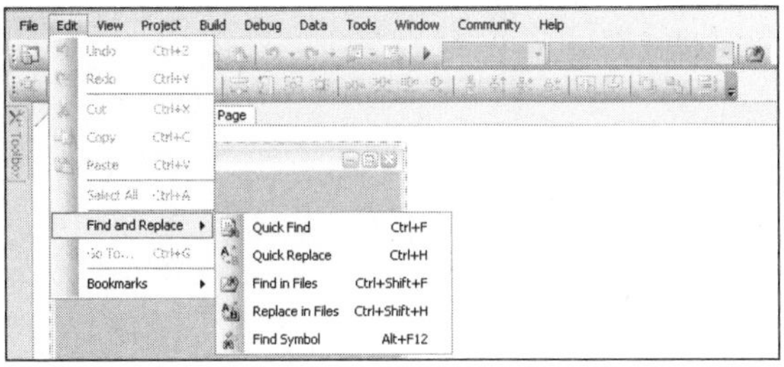

Figure 10-5:
Submenus
reduce the
number of
commands
in a pull-
down menu
but make it
harder to
find a
command.

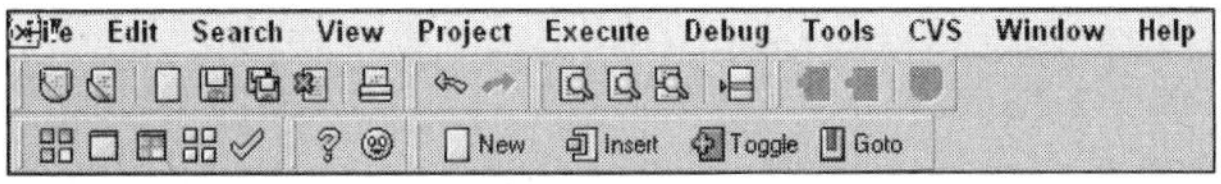

Figure 10-6:
Icons,
organized in
toolbars,
allow
one-click
access .

The advantage of icons is that they take up much less space than buttons
with command names written inside them. The disadvantage of icons is that
users have no idea which icons represent which commands.

As a result, most programs display short descriptions of each icon's purpose
if you move the mouse pointer over that icon. So if you move the mouse
pointer over a disk icon, the program might display the word Save underneath in a little window to let you know that clicking the disk icon represents
the Save command.

Another way to organize icons is in a *toolbox* on the side of the screen, which
is popular for accessing groups of commonly used commands, as shown in
Figure 10-7.

Icons provide one-click access to commonly used commands. However,
users should still be able to choose the same command from a pull-down
menu if they want.

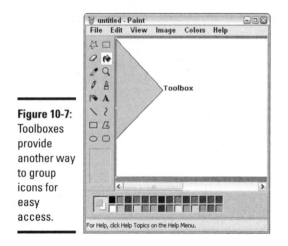

Figure 10-7:
Toolboxes
provide
another way
to group
icons for
easy
access.

Giving data to the user interface

Besides giving a program commands, users also need to give a program data to use for calculating a useful result. At the simplest level, users can just type in data they want to give the program. To accept typed-in data, user interfaces need to display a text box.

A *text box* is nothing more than a box for the user to click and type something in it. Text boxes are commonly used when the program needs data that can't be predicted in advance, such as asking for someone's name, as shown in Figure 10-8.

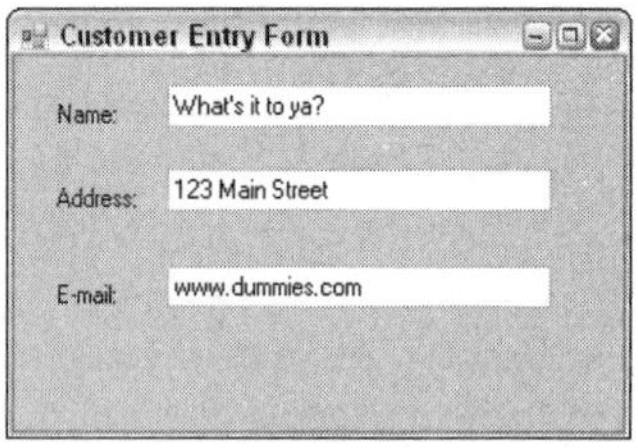

Figure 10-8:
Users can
type any
information
inside a text
box,
including
invalid data.

Text boxes are great for accepting any data, such as names, passwords, or search phrases, but text boxes also allow users to type in invalid data. To weed out invalid data, write extra code to verify that any information typed into a text box is actually valid.

If the type of data the user can give to the program is limited to a fixed range of choices, it's better to use one of the following user interface elements instead:

✦ **Radio buttons**

✦ **Check boxes**

✦ **List boxes**

✦ **Combo boxes**

✦ **Sliders**

Restricting choices to one option with radio buttons

Radio buttons get their name from old car radios that let you assign a favorite radio station to a button. So rather than tune in your favorite radio station manually, you had to press in a radio button, and the radio would jump to a pre-set radio station.

User interface radio buttons work the same way. Each radio button represents one possible choice, and the user can pick only one of them, as shown in Figure 10-9.

Figure 10-9:
Radio buttons display choices, but only let you pick one option.

The main advantage of radio buttons is that they show the user all possible choices, so instead of typing in the data (and risk spelling it wrong), users can just click the radio button that represents the data they want to give a program.

Restricting choices to two or more options with check boxes

Radio buttons are useful for restricting the type of data the user can give to a program. However, if you want to display all possible choices but allow the user to choose two or more of those choices, you can use check boxes instead, as shown in Figure 10-10.

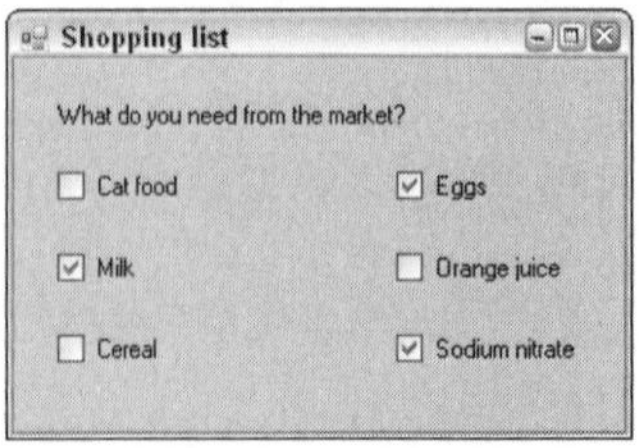

Figure 10-10:
Check
boxes can
display
multiple
choices and
pick more
than one
option.

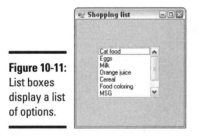

The drawback of both radio buttons and check boxes is that they take up space on-screen. Displaying 4 or 5 radio buttons or check boxes on-screen is reasonable, but displaying 20 or 30 radio buttons or check boxes can get cumbersome.

Displaying multiple choices in a list box or combo box

If you need to display multiple choices, you may find it easier to display all those choices in a list box. A list box can either display all choices or a limited number of choices.

If the list box is large enough, it can display all choices. If the number of options is more than the list box can display at once, the list box displays a scroll bar so users can scroll through the list of all available options, as shown in Figure 10-11.

Figure 10-11:
List boxes
display a list
of options.

Similar to list boxes are *combo boxes,* which combine the features of a text box with a list box. Like a text box, a combo box lets users type data directly into the program. Like a list box, a combo box also displays a list of options that the user can choose, as shown in Figure 10-12.

Figure 10-12:
Combo
boxes let
you either
make a
choice or
type data
directly.

Unlike list boxes, combo boxes always hide all choices until the user clicks
the combo box.

Restricting numeric choices with a slider

If users need to give numeric data to a program, they can type the numeric
values in a text box. However, if you want to restrict the range of valid numbers that the user can type in, you can use a slider.

A *slider* moves along a ruler, with the position of the slider determining a
specific numeric value or setting, as shown in Figure 10-13. Not only can sliders limit the range of a number that users can give a program (such as from
0 to 100), but sliders can also define the increments of numeric data.

Figure 10-13:
A slider
lets users
visually
choose a
numeric
value or
setting by
dragging a
slider along
a ruler.

So if a slider restricted values from 0 to 100 with increments of 0.5, that
means the user could give the program numbers such as 0, 0.5, 1, 1.5,
2, 2.5, and so on.

Showing information back to the user

User interfaces can show information to the user in a variety of ways, such as through text, graphics, or even sound. Typically, a user interface displays data in a window where users can manipulate that data and see their changes directly, as shown in Figure 10-14.

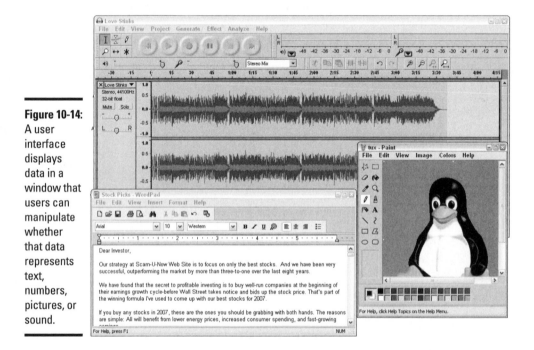

Figure 10-14: A user interface displays data in a window that users can manipulate whether that data represents text, numbers, pictures, or sound.

Using any program is like talking to the computer. You first tell the computer what you want to do (start writing a letter), the computer obeys (loads your word processor) and then waits for you to do something else. You give another command to the computer (to format text you just typed), the computer obeys and then asks what to do next, and so on.

Normally when you give a command to a program, the program responds right away. However, sometimes the program asks the user for more information. For example, if you give the command to print a document, the program may want to know how many pages to print. Whenever a program needs more information to carry out a command, it displays a dialog box, as shown in Figure 10-15.

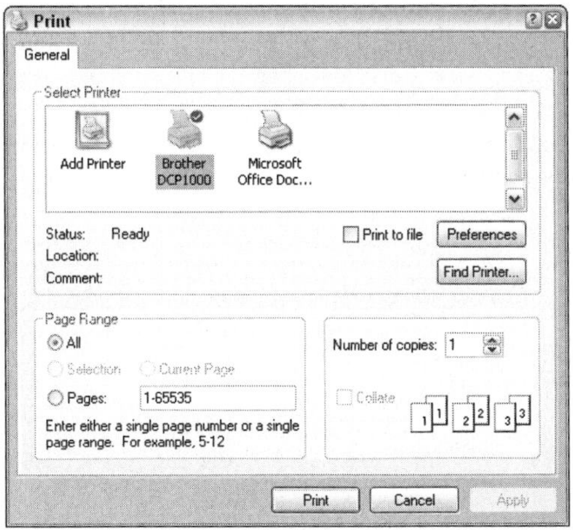

Figure 10-15:
Dialog
boxes ask
the user for
more data
before
carrying out
a command.

A dialog box is the computer's way of saying, "I'm trying to obey your instructions, but I'm not quite sure exactly what you want." Some common dialog boxes are used to

✦ **Open a file.**

✦ **Save a file.**

✦ **Print a file.**

Because dialog boxes are so common in every program, many programming languages provide built-in features for displaying dialog boxes. That way you don't have to create your own dialog boxes from scratch.

The Open dialog box lets you click a filename that you want to open. The Save dialog box lets you click a drive or folder where you want to store a file and then type a name for your file. The Print dialog box lets a program ask the user how many pages and copies to print as well as the page size or orientation.

Dialog boxes provide standard ways for performing common tasks needed by almost every program.

Organizing a user interface

One problem with designing a user interface is fitting everything in a single window. To help organize a user interface, many programs use either boxes or tabs.

Boxes draw lines around items on the user interface, such as multiple radio buttons, and visually separate items, as shown in Figure 10-16.

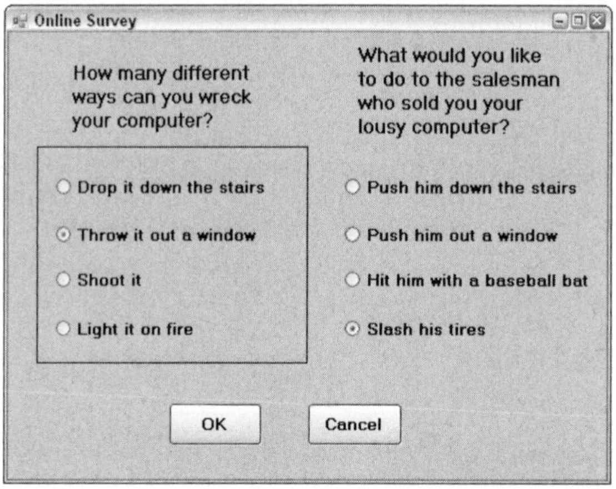

Figure 10-16:
Boxes draw lines to separate and organize different user interface items.

Another way to organize a user interface is to use tabs. Each tab can display entirely different user interface items (buttons, text labels, check boxes, and so on). When you click a different tab, the tab shows you different user interface items, as shown in Figure 10-17.

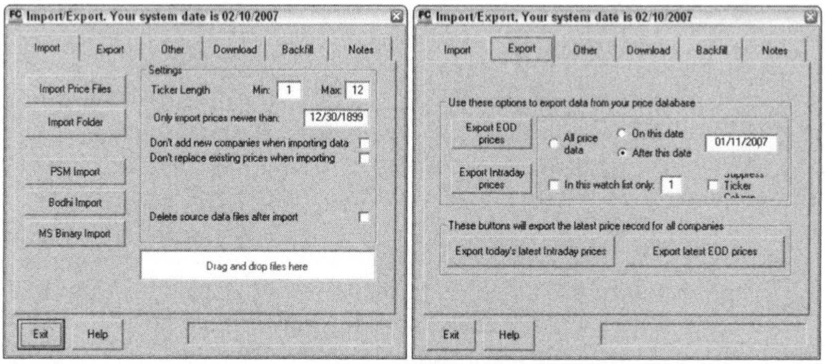

Figure 10-17:
Tabs let you organize and display different user interface items in the same window.

The goal of boxes and tabs is to organize your user interface. As far as users are concerned, the user interface is the only part of your program that they can see, so if you design a cluttered or confusing user interface, people think of your program as cluttered and confusing.

Designing a User Interface

There's a big difference between knowing the elements of a user interface and knowing how to put together an effective user interface. That's like the difference between knowing how to write every letter of the alphabet and knowing how to write a best-selling novel.

That's why designing a user interface is part art and part science. After you design enough user interfaces and use the user interfaces of different programs, you can see what you like and don't like. Then you can apply your own ideas to designing your idea of a perfect user interface.

Although it's difficult to teach the *art* of designing a user interface, it's much easier to teach the *science* behind designing a user interface. By following certain user interface principles, you can increase the chances that your user interface will at least be competent and usable.

**Book II
Chapter 10**

**Principles of User
Interface Design**

 To see drastic differences between user interfaces, compare the user interfaces of commercial programs from Microsoft, Adobe, or Apple and then look at the user interfaces on shareware, freeware, or niche commercial programs (such as astrology charting programs or horse race prediction programs). Big companies spend much time and money testing their user interfaces. In comparison, many individual programmers just slap together a user interface and start selling their program — and the results from their user interface really shows the difference.

Know the user

Most people find computers hard to use because the user interfaces of most programs are too confusing. Usually the problem lies with the fact that the programmers know how their program works, so they automatically assume that everyone else must also know how the program works, too. Essentially, too many programs are written by programmers for other programmers and ignore the ordinary user.

Before you design your user interface, you must determine what your users expect. A program designed for other programmers (such as a compiler or a debugger) can have a drastically different user interface than an educational program designed for 6-year-olds.

No matter who the typical user might be, the user interface's sole purpose is to communicate with the user. Just as you'd talk to a college professor differently than you'd talk to a 6-year-old child, so must you adapt a user interface to the person most likely to use your program. After you know who the user is, you'll know the best ways your user interface can "talk" to that person.

Hide unusable options

At any given time, the users should know what they can do. Unfortunately, poor user interfaces either

✦ **Expect the user to know what to do next.**

✦ **Bombard the user with so much information that the user still doesn't know what to do next.**

The command-line prompt is an example of a poor user interface that expects that the user already knows all valid commands and how to spell them. If you don't know which commands may be valid, the user interface won't help you.

Even worse than sparse user interfaces are user interfaces that show too much information, such as the pull-down menus in Figure 10-18. The program in this figure displays an Attribute submenu within the Text menu title.

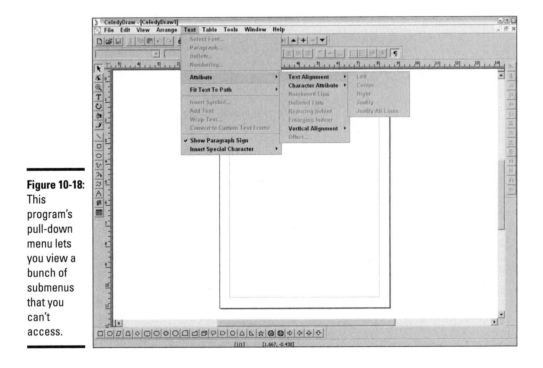

Figure 10-18: This program's pull-down menu lets you view a bunch of submenus that you can't access.

However, every option on the Attribute submenu appears dimmed, which makes the Attribute submenu useless. Why bother showing the users commands that they can't use? Not only does this frustrate the user, but the user never knows when any of the Attribute commands might appear undimmed and available for use.

A well-designed user interface should always show all possible choices and not overwhelm the users with choices they can't pick anyway.

Tolerate mistakes

User interfaces are meant for people to use, and it's no surprise that people make mistakes. Sometimes they type in the wrong data and sometimes they give a command that they didn't really want to give.

If you make a mistake, you should be able to

✦ **Undo or take back that mistake.**

✦ **Give the right command or data.**

Unfortunately, too many user interfaces don't let users undo their mistakes, which can make the user anxious and timid because he's afraid that if he does something wrong, he can't ever reverse his mistake. As a result, anxious and timid users tend not to trust a program or use it to its maximum capabilities.

Even worse is when user interfaces provide cryptic feedback if the user does something wrong. Examining the error message in Figure 10-19, can you tell what you might have done wrong and what you can do in the future to make sure this error message doesn't appear again?

Figure 10-19: A cryptic error message is meaning-less and frustrating because the user never knows how to avoid this problem in the future.

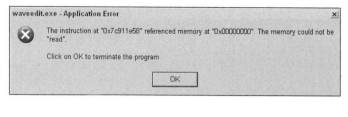

Cryptic messages can make users feel as if the program is scolding them. As a result, users are less likely to enjoy using the program and probably won't take full advantage of all its features either, if they even bother using the program at all.

User interfaces should tolerate and expect that the user will make a mistake and then find a way to recover from these mistakes gracefully. This can be as simple as having the program beep if the user tries to type his name instead of his Social Security number, or having the program display a descriptive error message that not only tells users what they did wrong but also tells them what to do right.

By doing this, a user interface can give the user confidence to experiment with a program and learn its features without reading a 300-page manual. Instead, the user can gradually figure out how to use a program with the program guiding him every step of the way.

Be consistent

One reason why franchise restaurants are so popular is because people know what to expect when they eat there. User interfaces also need to make a great first impression on users and then remain consistent so users generally know what to expect from a program at any given time.

For example, suppose a program displays a toolbox of icons on the left side of the screen. Now what happens if the user chooses a command and suddenly the toolbox of icons either disappears or appears in another part of the screen for no apparent reason at all?

Having the user interface suddenly change its appearance or behavior while the program is running is certain to confuse and annoy users. By staying consistent in appearance and behavior, a user interface can be predictable so the user feels more comfortable using it (just as long as the user interface was designed properly in the first place).

Focus on the task

Ultimately, the user interface must make it easy for the user to achieve a specific result from the program, whether it involves creating greeting cards, editing digital photos, or typing messages into a blog. If the user interface doesn't make the main purpose of the program clear and easy, users don't know or understand what to do.

The program in Figure 10-20 is designed to help people create stories, but rather than display its various tools for story writing, this program forces users to choose a file to open first. At this point, most users will wonder which file to choose, where to find a file, and why they need to open a file if they're using the program for the first time?

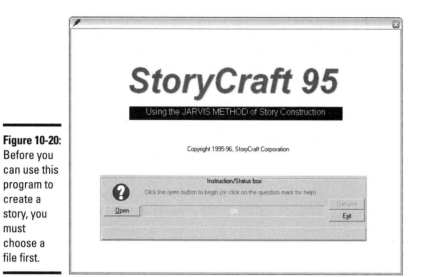

Figure 10-20: Before you can use this program to create a story, you must choose a file first.

Rather than focus on the user's convenience, the program in Figure 10-20 focuses on the program's convenience and forces the user to make things easier for the program instead of the other way around. By not focusing on the main task (creating stories), this program forces users to work harder to use the program than they should.

Make navigation easy

After users start working with a program, they need to switch back and forth between viewing their data in different ways. For example, a Web browser lets users view Web pages (data) and new or previous Web pages easily by either typing in a new Web site address or clicking the Back and Forward buttons. By making it easy for the user to do what she wants, the user interface aids the user without drawing attention to itself.

At any given time, users should always be able to view their data in a previous state (such as seeing the preceding Web page) or view their data in a new way (such as seeing a new Web page or changing the size of text on the current Web page). By making it easy and predictable for users to manipulate data, a good user interface can make even the most complicated program simple to understand and eventually master.

There's no "perfect" user interface because every user interface must cater to different types of users. However, by following user interface design guidelines, you can make sure your program not only looks good but also helps the user get some work done with your program, which is the ultimate goal of any program.

Book III

Data Structures

Contents at a Glance

Chapter 1: Structures and Arrays

In This Chapter

✔ Using structures to store and retrieve data

✔ Creating arrays

✔ Using resizable arrays

✔ Running multi-dimensional arrays

✔ Combining structures with arrays

✔ Detailing the drawbacks of arrays

*A*ll programs need to store data. If a program asks the user to type in her name, the program needs to store that name somewhere so it can find the name again. The most common way programs store data is to dump data in a variable.

Unfortunately, a variable can only hold one chunk of data at a time, such as a single number or a name. If you want to store a person's first and last name along with their age, you have to create three separate variables, such as

```
Dim FirstName as String
Dim LastName as String
Dim Age as Integer
```

Creating separate variables to store related data can be like carrying around three separate wallets with one wallet holding your cash, a second wallet holding your credit cards, and a third wallet holding your driver's license. Just as it's more convenient to store your cash, credit cards, and driver's license in a single wallet, so it's also more convenient to store related data in a single variable. Two ways to store related data in one place are structures and arrays.

Because structures and arrays are two other ways to store data, they're often called *data structures*.

Using Structures

A *structure* (also dubbed a *record* in some programming languages) does nothing more than group separate variables together. So rather than create and try to keep track of three separate variables, a structure lets you store

multiple variables within another variable. So if you had three variables —
FirstName, LastName, and Age — you could store them all within a structure, such as

```
Structure Person
    Dim FirstName as String
    Dim LastName as String
    Dim Age as Integer
End Structure
```

A structure is a *user-defined* data type. You can't use a structure until you
declare a variable to represent that structure like this:

```
Dim Employees as Person
```

The preceding code creates an Employees variable that actually contains
the FirstName, LastName, and Age variables, as shown in Figure 1-1.

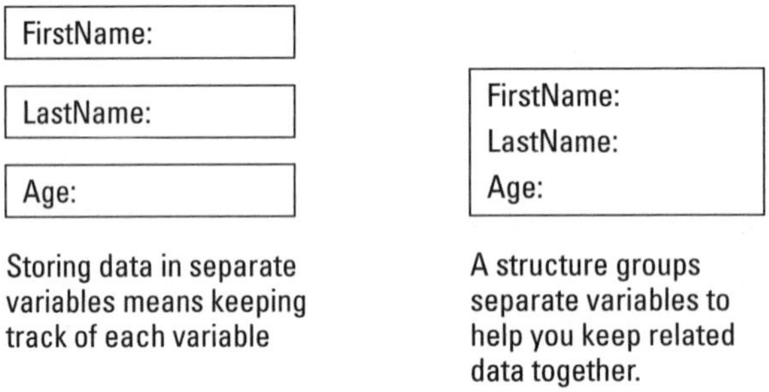

Figure 1-1:
A structure
can contain
multiple
variables.

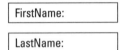

| FirstName: |
| LastName: |
| Age: |

Storing data in separate
variables means keeping
track of each variable

| FirstName:
LastName:
Age: |

A structure groups
separate variables to
help you keep related
data together.

Storing data

To store data in a structure, you must

1. **Identify the variable that represents that structure.**

2. **Identify the specific variable inside the structure to use.**

So if you want to store the name Joe in the FirstName variable inside the
Employee variable, you could do the following:

```
Employee.FirstName = "Joe"
```

If you wanted to store the name Smith in the LastName variable and the number 24 in the Age variable, inside the Employee variable, you could do the following:

```
Employee.FirstName = "Joe"
Employee.Age = "24"
```

Retrieving data

After you store data in a structure, you can always retrieve it again. Just identify

+ **The variable that represents that structure**

+ **The actual variable name that holds the data**

Suppose you defined a structure, as follows:

```
Structure Workers
    Dim Name as String
    Dim ID as Integer
    Dim Salary as Single
End Structure
```

Before you can store any data in a structure, you must first declare a variable to represent that structure like this:

```
Dim Employees as Workers
```

Now you can store and retrieve data from a structure, as follows:

```
' This stores a name in the Employees structure
Employees.Name = "Jessie Balkins"
```

To retrieve data from this structure, identify the variable name that represents that structure and the variable that holds the data like this:

```
Print Employees.Name
```

This would retrieve the data in the Name variable, stored in the Employees variable structure, and print Jessie Balkins on-screen.

Structures are just a way to cram multiple variables into a single variable. A structure can hold only one group of related data. To make structures more useful, programmers typically use structures with another data structure or an *array*.

Using an Array

The problem with a single variable is that it can hold only a single chunk of data. So if you wanted to store a name, you could create a variable, such as

```
Dim Name as String
```

If you wanted to store a second name, you'd have to create a second variable, such as

```
Dim Name as String
Dim Name2 as String
```

The more names you want to store, the more separate variables you need to create. Because creating separate variables to store similar types of information can get tedious, computer scientists have created a "super" variable — an *array*. Unlike an ordinary variable that can hold only one chunk of data, an array can hold multiple chunks of data.

To create an array, you need to define these three items:

✦ **A variable name**

✦ **The number of items you want to store (the *array size*)**

✦ **The type of data to store (such as *integers* or *strings*)**

So if you wanted to store 15 names in a variable, you could create a name array, such as

```
Dim NameArray(15) as String
```

The preceding code tells the computer to create a `NameArray` array, which can hold up to 15 strings, as shown in Figure 1-2.

Figure 1-2:
An array
can hold
multiple
chunks of
data.

| John Doe | Gary Wilkins | Holly Creamer | Bobby Jones |

Defining the size

An array acts like a bunch of buckets (dubbed *elements*) that can hold exactly one item. When you create an array, you must first define the size of the array, which defines how many chunks of data *(elements)* that the array can hold.

Bounds

The size of an array is defined by two numbers:

✦ The **lower bound** defines the number of the *first* array element.

✦ The **upper bound** defines the number of the *last* array element.

Default bounds

The default value of the lower bound depends on the programming language:

✦ Many programming languages, including the curly bracket language family of C and Java, always define the lower bound of an array starting with the number 0 (known as *zero-based arrays*).

✦ Other programming languages always define the lower bound of an array starting with the number 1 (known as *one-based arrays*).

The following BASIC code actually creates a zero-based array that can hold six elements, numbered 0 through 5, as shown in Figure 1-3:

```
Dim LotteryNumbers(5) as Integer
```

Dim LotteryNumbers(5) as Integer

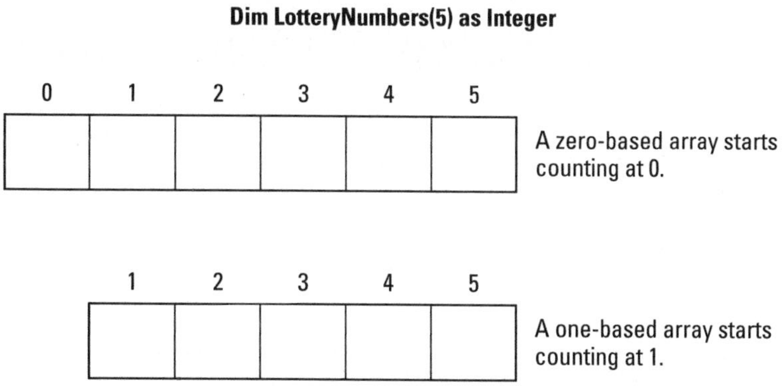

Figure 1-3:
One-based array numbers array elements differently than zero-based arrays.

| 0 | 1 | 2 | 3 | 4 | 5 |

A zero-based array starts counting at 0.

| 1 | 2 | 3 | 4 | 5 |

A one-based array starts counting at 1.

If the programming language created a one-based array, the array would hold only five elements.

Zero-based arrays were made popular in the C language. As a result, any language derived from the C language, such as C++, C#, Java, Python, and Objective-C, will also use zero-based arrays. Because many programmers are familiar with zero-based arrays, many other programming languages also use zero-based arrays, such as Visual Basic and REALbasic. One-based arrays are less common, but found in some versions of BASIC along with less popular languages like Pascal and Smalltalk.

When defining arrays, always make sure you know whether your programming language creates zero-based or one-based arrays. Otherwise, you may try to store data in non-existent array elements.

Definable bounds

To avoid confusion, some programming languages (such as Pascal) let you *define* both the lower and upper bound arrays.

If you wanted to create an array to hold five integers, you could use the following code:

```
Var
   LotteryNumbers[1..5] of Integer;
```

This would number the `LotteryNumbers` array from 1 to 5. However, you could choose *any* number range of five like this:

```
Var
   LotteryNumbers[33..37] of Integer;
```

This would create an array of five elements, numbered from 33 to 37, as shown in Figure 1-4.

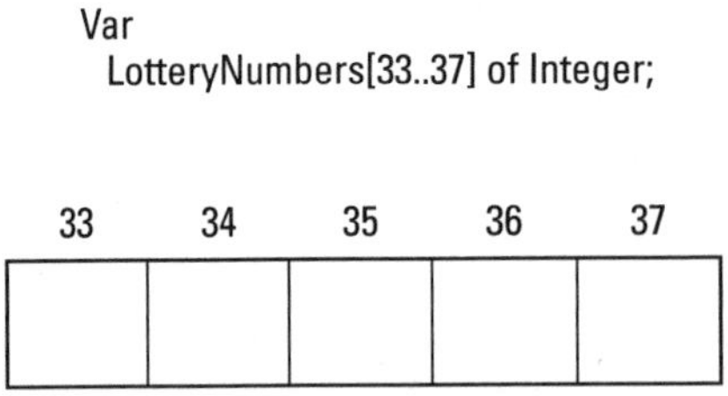

Figure 1-4:
Some programming languages let you define the numbering of an array.

```
Var
   LotteryNumbers[33..37] of Integer;
```

33	34	35	36	37

One advantage of defining the numbering of an array is that you can use meaningful numbers. For example, if you wanted to store the names of employees in an array, you could number the array so each array element is identified by an employee number. So if `Jan Howards` has employee ID number `102`, `Mike Edwards` has employee ID number `103`, and `John`

`Perkins` has employee ID number `104`, you could create a three-element array, as shown in Figure 1-5, like this:

```
Var
  EmployeeList[102..104] of String;
```

Var
EmployeeList[102..104] of String;

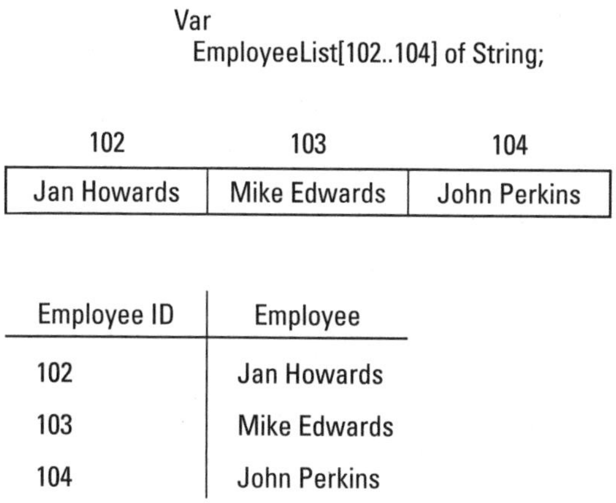

Figure 1-5:
By defining your own numbering for an array, you can make those numbers useful and meaningful.

102	103	104
Jan Howards	Mike Edwards	John Perkins

Employee ID	Employee
102	Jan Howards
103	Mike Edwards
104	John Perkins

**Book III
Chapter 1**

Structures and Arrays

Initializing

When you define an array, it's a good idea to initialize that array. *Initializing* an array means filling it with *initial data,* such as

+ **Zeroes** for storing *numbers* in an array

+ **Spaces** for storing *strings* in an array

If you don't initialize an array, the computer may randomly store data in an array, which could confuse your program later.

Loops

To initialize an array, most programmers use a *loop.* This code uses a FOR-NEXT loop to initialize an array with zeroes:

```
Dim LotteryNumbers(5) as Integer
For I = 1 to 5
  LotteryNumbers(I) = 0
Next I
```

1.1.1.4   @Heading 4:Declarations

Some programming languages let you initialize an array without a loop. Instead, you *declare* an array and its initial data on the same line. This C++ code declares an array that can hold five integers and stores 0 in each array element:

```
int lotterynumbers[] = {0, 0, 0, 0, 0};
```

Storing data

To store data in an array, you need to define two items:

✦ **The array name**

✦ **The array element where you want to store the data**

So if you wanted to store data in the first element of a zero-based array, you could do this:

```
int myarray[5];
myarray[0] = 357;
```

If you wanted to store data in the first element of a one-based array, you could do this:

```
Dim myarray(5) as Integer
myarray(1) = 357
```

You can store data in array elements in any order you want, such as storing the number 47 in the first array element, the number 91 in the fourth array element, and the number 6 in the second array element, such as

```
int myarray[5];
myarray[0] = 47;
myarray[3] = 91;
myarray[1] = 6;
```

Retrieving data

To retrieve data from an array, you need to identify

✦ **The array name**

✦ **The array element number that contains the data you want to retrieve**

Suppose you had the following BASIC code that creates an array that stores three names:

```
Dim Names(3) as String
Names(1) = "Nancy Titan"
Names(2) = "Johnny Orlander"
Names(3) = "Doug Slanders"
```

If you wanted to retrieve and print the data stored in the second element of the Names array, you could use the following:

```
Print Names(2)
```

This would print Johnny Orlander on-screen.

Working with Resizable Arrays

One problem with arrays is that you must define their size before you can use them:

+ **If you define an array too large, you waste memory.**
+ **If you define an array too small, your program can't store all the data it needs to keep.**

To get around these problems, some programming languages let you create *dynamic* or *resizable* arrays. A resizable array lets you change the array's size while your program is running.

Here are reasons *for* and *against* using resizable arrays:

+ **Advantage:** You can make the array *grow* or *shrink* as needed so you don't waste memory creating an array too large or limit your program by creating an array too small.
+ **Drawbacks:** The nuisance of constantly defining the size of an array, and the possibility that some programming languages won't let you preserve the contents of a resizable array each time the array grows or expands.

To create a resizable array, every programming language requires different steps. The following sections provide a couple of examples.

BASIC

In BASIC, you can declare an array, such as

```
Dim BigArray(5) as String
```

Then to change the size of that array, you have to use the ReDim command and define a new upper bound for the array, as shown in Figure 1-6, like this:

```
ReDim BigArray(2)
```

Dim BigArray(5) as String

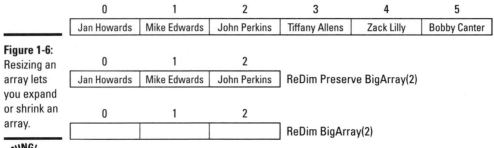

0	1	2	3	4	5
Jan Howards	Mike Edwards	John Perkins	Tiffany Allens	Zack Lilly	Bobby Canter

Figure 1-6:
Resizing an
array lets
you expand
or shrink an
array.

0	1	2
Jan Howards	Mike Edwards	John Perkins

ReDim Preserve BigArray(2)

0	1	2

ReDim BigArray(2)

Resizing an array erases everything currently stored in that array.

If you want to resize an array and save the data in the array, you can use the `Preserve` command like this:

```
ReDim Preserve BigArray(2)
```

Not every programming language lets you resize an array and preserve its contents.

C++

To create a resizable array in C++, you have to go through slightly different steps.

First, you must define a resizable array like this:

```
datatype *arrayname;
```

So if you wanted to create a resizable array of integers, you'd declare your array as follows:

```
int *numberarray;
```

Before you could store any data in this array, you'd have to define its size using the `new` command. So if you wanted to resize the array to hold six elements (numbered 0 to 5), you could use the following:

```
int *numberarray;
numberarray = new int[5];
```

At this point, you could start storing data in your array like this:

```
int *numberarray;
numberarray = new int[5];
numberarray[0] = 23;
numberarray[5] = 907;
```

To resize an array again, you have to use the new command along with a new upper bound, such as

```
int *numberarray;
numberarray = new int[5];
numberarray[0] = 23;
numberarray[5] = 907;
numberarray = new int[2];
numberarray[1] = 48;
```

This C++ code first defines a resizable array and then defines its upper bound as 5 to store the numbers 23 and 907 in the array elements numbered 0 and 5, respectively.

Then the second new command resizes the entire array, erasing all data stored in that array, and defines the array's upper bound as 2. Finally, it stores the number 48 into array element 1, as shown in Figure 1-7.

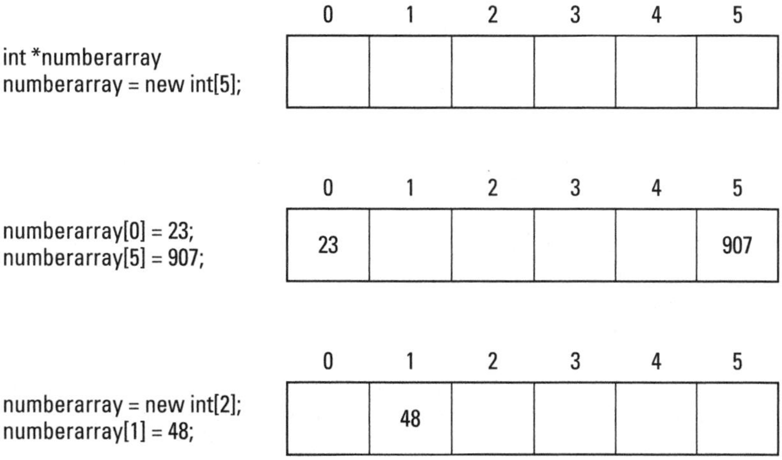

	0	1	2	3	4	5
int *numberarray numberarray = new int[5];						

	0	1	2	3	4	5
numberarray[0] = 23; numberarray[5] = 907;	23					907

Figure 1-7:
Resizing an
array erases
all data in
the array.

	0	1	2	3	4	5
numberarray = new int[2]; numberarray[1] = 48;		48				

Working with Multi-Dimensional Arrays

Most arrays are one-dimensional because you define only the array's length. However, you can create multi-dimensional arrays by defining multiple array sizes.

The most common multi-dimensional array is a two-dimensional array, which looks like a grid, as shown in Figure 1-8.

Dim BigArray (4,2) as String

BigArray(1,1)	BigArray(1,2)
BigArray(2,1)	BigArray(2,2)
BigArray(3,1)	BigArray(3,2)
BigArray(4,1)	BigArray(4,2)

Figure 1-8: A two-dimensional array lets you store data in a grid.

You can create 3-, 4-, or even 19-dimensional arrays. However, after you get past a three-dimensional array, understanding how that array works can be too confusing, so most programmers stick to two-dimensional or three-dimensional arrays.

Creating a multi-dimensional array

To create a multi-dimensional array, you have to define another upper bound for an array. So if you wanted to create a 4 x 2 two-dimensional array, you could use the following BASIC code:

```
Dim BigArray(4,2) as String
```

To create the same two-dimensional array in C++, you could use the following code:

```
string bigarray[4][2];
```

To create three or more dimensional arrays, keep adding on additional bounds, such as

```
Dim BigArray(2,4,3,8) as String
```

The equivalent multi-dimensional array in C++ would look like this:

```
string bigarray[2][4][3][8];
```

Storing and retrieving data

To store data in a multi-dimensional array, you need to specify the specific array location. So if you had a two-dimensional array, you'd have to specify each of the two dimensions, such as

```
Dim BigArray(4,2) as String
BigArray(4,1) = "Ollie Bird"
```

After you store data in a multi-dimensional array, you can retrieve that data again by specifying the array name and the specific array element that contains the data you want. So if you had previously stored the string *Ollie Bird* in a two-dimensional array, you could retrieve the data stored in the 4,1 array element, such as

```
Print BigArray(4,1)
```

This command would print the string *Ollie Bird*.

The more dimensions you add to your array, the more space you create in your array, and the more memory your program needs. Don't be afraid to use a multi-dimensional array; just don't create one unless you really need one.

Two-dimensional arrays can be useful for modeling real-life items, such as checkerboards or tic-tac-toe games, which already look like two-dimensional arrays (grids) anyway.

**Book III
Chapter 1**

**Structures
and Arrays**

Using Structures with Arrays

All arrays can hold only one specific data type, such as integers or strings. So if you create an array that contains five elements, each element must all contain the same data type, such as all integers.

Rather than define an array to contain a data type, like strings or integers, you can also define an array to contain a structure. A structure lets you cram multiple variables into a single variable, but a single structure by itself is fairly useless. After you store data in a single structure, you don't have any room left to store anything else, as shown in Figure 1-9.

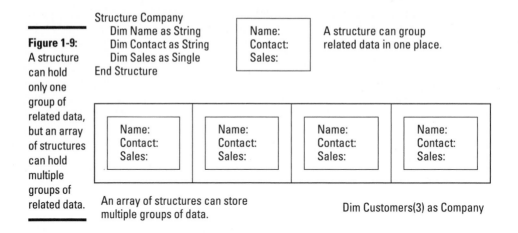

Figure 1-9:
A structure
can hold
only one
group of
related data,
but an array
of structures
can hold
multiple
groups of
related data.

An array of structures can store
multiple groups of data.

Dim Customers(3) as Company

To use a structure with an array, you must first define a structure and the variables you want to store inside that structure. So if you want to store a company name, contact person, and total sales made to the company, you could define a structure like this:

```
Structure Company
   Dim Name as String
   Dim Contact as String
   Dim Sales as Single
End Structure
```

Next, you can define your array, but instead of making your array hold a data type, like strings or integers, you can make your array hold your structure like this:

```
Dim Customers(3) as Company
```

This code creates an array, with elements numbered from 0 to 3, which holds the Company structure that you defined, as shown in Figure 1-10.

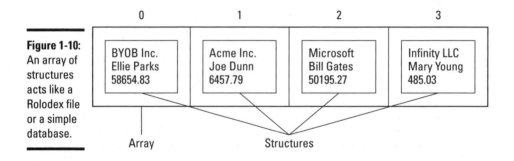

Figure 1-10:
An array of
structures
acts like a
Rolodex file
or a simple
database.

To store data in an array of structures, you need to identify the array element (in this example numbered 0 to 3) and the specific variable inside the structure to store your data. So if you wanted to store data in array element number 2, you could do the following:

```
Customers(2).Name = "Microsoft"
Customers(2).Contact = "Bill Gates"
Customers(2).Sales = 50195.27
```

Retrieving data from an array of structures means identifying the array name, the array element followed by the variable name stored in that structure. So if you wanted to print the name stored in the `Contact` variable of array element number 2, you could do the following:

```
Print Customers(2).Contact
```

This code would print `Bill Gates` on-screen. Storing and retrieving data from an array of structures means identifying the following items:

+ **The array name (such as `Customers`)**
+ **The array element number (such as `2`)**
+ **The variable inside the structure (such as `Contact`)**

Drawbacks of Arrays

Arrays can be handy for storing lists of related data in a single location. However, arrays have several drawbacks:

+ **Large arrays take up space.**
+ **Arrays can hold only one data type at a time.**
+ **Searching and sorting arrays is difficult.**
+ **Inserting and removing data from arrays is clumsy.**

Sizing

The biggest problem with arrays is defining the size of an array ahead of time:

+ If you know you need to store 20 names, it's easy to define an array to hold 20 strings.
+ If you aren't sure if your program needs to store 20 names or 20,000 names, you have to define the largest array you think your program will ever need, so most of the array will be empty and waste memory.

To get around the problem of creating large arrays that aren't needed, you can create *resizable* or *dynamic* arrays that can grow or shrink as you need them (see the earlier section, "Working with Resizable Arrays"). Such resizable arrays can be convenient, but you have to make sure that each time you resize an array, you don't accidentally delete data that you want to keep.

Data types

Another limitation of arrays is that they can hold only one data type at a time. So if you want to store a list of names and numbers, you have to create two separate arrays:

✦ **One array to store the names**

✦ **Another array to store the numbers**

Some programming languages allow you to create a data type called a *variant*. A variant data type can hold any type of data, so if you create an array of variant data types, you can create an array that can hold both strings and numbers.

Searching and sorting

Another problem with arrays is searching and sorting an array. If you create an array to hold 10,000 names, how can you find the name `Bill Gates` stored in that array? To search for data stored in an array, you have to search through the entire array from start to finish. For a small array, this can be acceptable, but searching through an array that contains thousands of names or numbers can get tedious and slow, especially if you need to search through an array on a regular basis.

So if an array contains 10,000 names and the name you want is the last element in that array, you have to search through 10,000 array elements just to find the name you want.

More cumbersome than searching an array is sorting an array. If you store 10,000 names in an array and suddenly decide you want to sort those names in alphabetical order, you have to move and sort the entire list one array element at a time. Doing this once may be acceptable, but doing this on a regular basis can be cumbersome and slow.

Adding and deleting

Rather than dump all your data in an array and try to sort it out later, you might want to sort data while you store it. Adding data to an empty array is easy; dump the data in any array element. The problem comes when you want to add data in between two array elements.

Suppose you have the names `Charles Green` and `Mary Halls` in an array, as shown in Figure 1-11. If you wanted to insert the name `Johnny Grey` in between `Charles Green` and `Mary Halls`, you'd have to copy all array elements starting with `Mary Hall` and move them to the next array element.

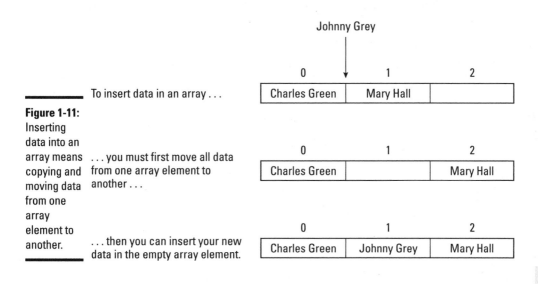

Figure 1-11: Inserting data into an array means copying and moving data from one array element to another.

To insert data in an array . . .

. . . you must first move all data from one array element to another . . .

. . . then you can insert your new data in the empty array element.

For a small array, this isn't a problem, but for a large array of 10,000 names, copying and moving several thousand names consistently is cumbersome and slow.

Even worse, what if you want to delete an array element? It's easy to delete an array element by just setting that array element to a blank value, such as zero or a space. However, the more items you delete from an array, the more empty spaces you have, wasting space.

The time to use arrays depends on both the amount of data you need to store and whether you need to manipulate that data later:

+ **Perfect***:* Store a small, fixed size list of one data type.

+ **Not so good:** Store large amounts of data that can change in quantity, needs to be sorted or searched, or data that contains different types of information, such as numbers and text.

   In this case, arrays can be too restrictive. You may want to look at other data structures, such as *collections* (see Book III, Chapter 3).

The data structure you choose for your program can determine the speed and efficiency of your program:

✦ **Choose the right data structure, and writing your program is easy.**

✦ **Choose the wrong data structure, and you may waste time writing code to overcome the limitations of your chosen data structure, such as writing code to sort an array that contains 10,000 names.**

Chapter 2: Sets and Linked Lists

In This Chapter

✔ **Using sets and linked lists**

✔ **Understanding the drawbacks of sets and linked lists**

An array can be handy for storing data that consists of the same type of information, such as integers. However, arrays can often be too restrictive. You must define the size of an array ahead of time and you can only store one data type. In addition, searching, rearranging, or deleting data from an array can be cumbersome.

To solve the problems of arrays, programming languages have come up with a variety of solutions. The obvious solution involves modifying the way arrays work, such as letting you create resizable *(dynamic)* arrays that can store a special `Variant` data type. Unlike an `Integer` data type (which can only hold whole numbers) or a `String` data type (which can only hold text), a `Variant` data type can hold both numbers and text. (Not all programming languages offer resizable arrays or `Variant` data types.)

Rather than modify the way arrays work, many programming languages allow you to create other types of data structures. Two popular alternatives to arrays are

✦ **Sets**

✦ **Lists**

This chapter shows you how to use sets and lists when arrays are too restrictive and cumbersome.

Using Sets

If someone showed you the days of the week (Monday, Tuesday, Wednesday, Thursday, Friday, Saturday, and Sunday), you'd know that those days are related as a group that defines a week, but how do you tell a computer that? Here's one way:

1. Create an array to hold seven separate variables like this:

```
Dim Day(6) as String
```

2. Assign each variable with a different name like this:

```
Day(0) = "Monday"
Day(1) = "Tuesday"
Day(2) = "Wednesday"
Day(3) = "Thursday"
Day(4) = "Friday"
Day(5) = "Saturday"
Day(6) = "Sunday"
```

This would store all the days of the week inside a single array variable, although it requires multiple lines to store data in each array element.

However, there's a simpler way to lump related data together — use a data structure called a *set*. Like an array, a set groups data in a single variable name, but a set has several advantages:

✦ **You don't have to define a fixed size ahead of time.**

✦ **You don't have to identify each chunk of data with an index number.**

✦ **Sets can store a mixed variety of data types, such as `Integers` and `Strings`.** (An array can only hold a single data type.)

Defining a set *lists* all the data you want to store, as shown in this Python programming language example:

```
from sets import Set
days = Set(['Monday', 'Tuesday', 'Wednesday', 'Thursday',
    'Friday', 'Saturday', 'Sunday'])
```

Certain features aren't always a built-in part of a programming language, such as sets in Python. Rather than create a complicated language with lots of built-in features that not everyone will ever use, many programming languages add additional features through *libraries,* which are separate subprograms. For example, the Pascal language includes sets as a built-in data structure but the Python language does not. To use sets in Python, you must include (or *import*) a separate library that lets you use sets in a program. To use sets in Python, you must use the Python library called (surprise!) Set.

In this Python language example, the variable `days` contains the entire set or group of the days defined by the `Set` command. To print the contents of this set, you can use a `print` command followed by the name of the set like this:

```
print days
```

This command would print:

```
Set(['Monday', 'Tuesday', 'Wednesday', 'Thursday', 'Friday',
    'Saturday', 'Sunday'])
```

Adding (and deleting) data in a set

To add or delete data from a set, use the add and delete commands. In Python, the add command is add, and the delete command is `remove`.

Every programming language uses slightly different names for the same command, so don't worry about the particular command names used just as long as you understand the basic principles.

To add more data to a set in Python, you have to identify the set name followed by the add command and the data you want to add. So if you had a set called clubmembers, you could use these commands:

```
from sets import Set
clubmembers = Set(['Bill Evans', 'John Doe', 'Mary Jacobs'])
```

You could add a new name to that set by using the following command:

```
clubmembers.add('Donna Volks')
```

To remove a name from a set, you have to identify the set name, use the remove command, and specify which data you want to remove, like this:

```
clubmembers.remove('Bill Evans')
```

Figure 2-1 shows how add and remove commands change the contents of a set:

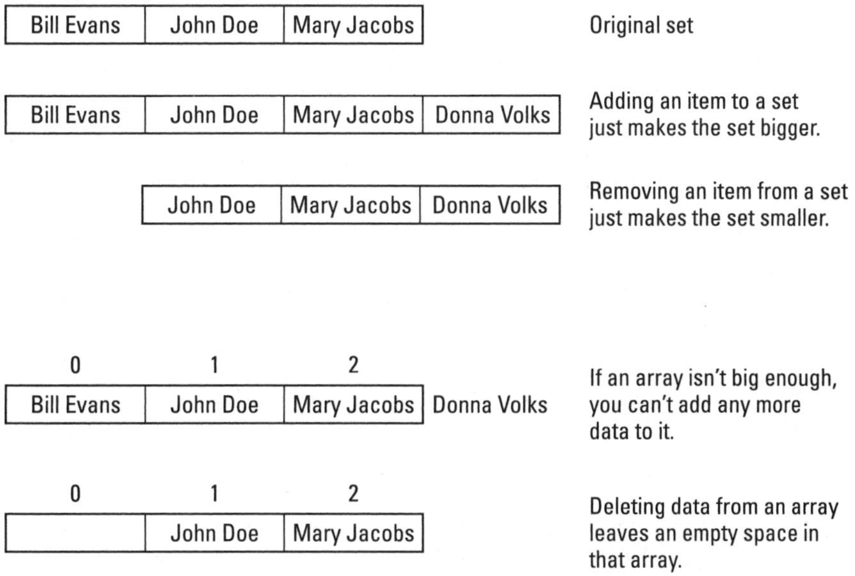

Bill Evans	John Doe	Mary Jacobs

Original set

Bill Evans	John Doe	Mary Jacobs	Donna Volks

Adding an item to a set just makes the set bigger.

John Doe	Mary Jacobs	Donna Volks

Removing an item from a set just makes the set smaller.

Figure 2-1:
Adding and removing data in a set is easier than adding and removing data in an array.

0	1	2	
Bill Evans	John Doe	Mary Jacobs	Donna Volks

If an array isn't big enough, you can't add any more data to it.

0	1	2
	John Doe	Mary Jacobs

Deleting data from an array leaves an empty space in that array.

- ✦ When you delete data from a **set,** the set is just one item smaller.

- ✦ When you delete data from an **array,** you're left with an empty space in the array.

To remove all data in a set, most programming languages include a command that clears out an entire set. In Python, the command is `clear`, such as

```
clubmembers.clear()
```

Checking for membership

If you store a bunch of names in an array, how could you verify whether a specific name is in that array? You'd have to examine each element in the array and compare it with the name you're looking for until you either found a match or reached the end of the array. This typically requires a loop to examine every array element, one by one.

Sets avoid this problem by making it easy to check whether a chunk of data is stored in a set. If you had a list of country club members stored in a set, it might look like this in Python:

```
from sets import Set
clubmembers = Set(['Bill Evans', 'John Doe', 'Mary Jacobs'])
```

To check whether a name is in a set (a member of that set), use a simple `in` command like this:

```
'John Doe' in clubmembers
```

If this command finds the name `John Doe` in the set defined by the `clubmembers` set, this would return a `True` value. If this command can't find the name `John Doe` in the `clubmembers` set, this command would return a `False` value.

From the computer's point of view, it must still exhaustively compare every name in a set to see whether it matches the name you're looking for, but from the programmer's point of view, you can use a simple `in` command rather than write multiple lines of code to examine an array, element by element. The more work you can make the computer do, the less work you have to do.

Another way to check for membership is to use the `not` command with the `in` command like this:

```
'Hugh Lake' not in clubmembers
```

This command asks the computer whether the name Hugh Lake is not in the clubmembers set. In this case, the name Hugh Lake is not in the clubmembers set, so the preceding command would return a True value.

If you used the following command to check whether the name John Doe is not in the clubmembers set, the following command would return a False value because the name John Doe is in the clubmembers set:

```
'John Doe' not in clubmembers
```

Manipulating two sets

A set by itself can be handy for grouping related data together, but if you have two or more sets of data, you can manipulate the data in both sets. For example, suppose you have a set of country club members and a second set of people applying for membership.

You can combine both sets together to create a third set (a *union*) find the common data in both sets (an *intersection*) or take away the common data in both sets (the *difference*).

Combining two sets into a third set with the Union command

Union simply takes data from two sets and smashes them together to create a third set that includes all data from the first two sets, as shown in Figure 2-2.

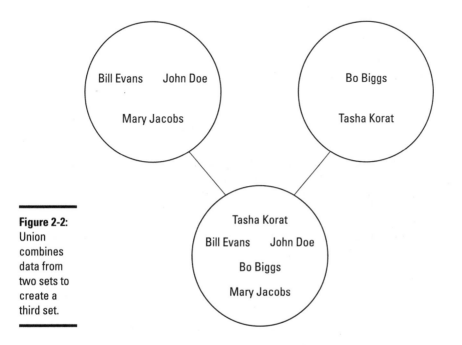

Figure 2-2:
Union combines data from two sets to create a third set.

To use the `union` command in Python, you need to identify the two set names with the `union` command. Suppose you had one set called `clubmembers` and another set called `applicants`, as follows:

```
from sets import Set
clubmembers = Set(['Bill Evans', 'John Doe', 'Mary Jacobs'])
applicants = Set (['Bo Biggs', 'Tasha Korat'])
```

Now if you wanted to combine the data in both sets and store it in a third set called `newmembers`, you could use the `union` command as follows:

```
newmembers = clubmembers.union(applicants)
```

This creates a third set called `newmembers` and stores the data from both sets into the `newmembers` set. The data in the other sets isn't modified in any way.

The order in which you define the two sets is irrelevant:

✦ You can put the `clubmembers` set name first like this:

```
newmembers = clubmembers.union(applicants)
```

✦ You could switch the two set names around like this:

```
newmembers = applicants.union(clubmembers)
```

The end result is identical in creating a third set and dumping data from both sets into this third set. If you combine two sets that happen to contain one or more identical chunks of data, the union (combination of the two sets) is smart enough not to store duplicate data twice.

Combining the common elements of two sets into a third set with the Intersect command

Whereas the `union` commands combines two sets into one, the `intersect` command creates a third set that only includes data stored in both sets, as shown in Figure 2-3.

To use the `intersection` command in Python, you need to identify the two set names with the `intersection` command. Suppose you had one set called `clubmembers` and another set called `politicians`, as follows:

```
from sets import Set
clubmembers = Set(['Bill Evans', 'John Doe', 'Mary Jacobs'])
politicians = Set (['Bo Biggs', 'John Doe'])
```

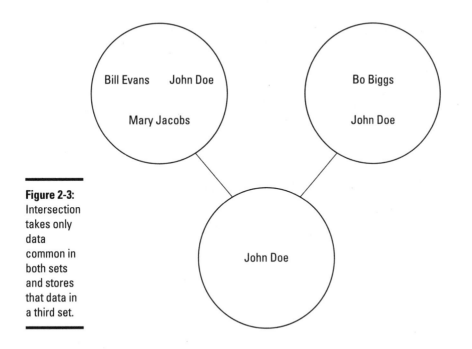

Figure 2-3:
Intersection
takes only
data
common in
both sets
and stores
that data in
a third set.

Now if you wanted to find only that data stored in both sets, you could use
the `intersection` command to store this data in a third set, as follows:

```
newset = clubmembers.intersection(politicians)
```

This creates a third set — `newset` — which contains the name `John Doe`.
The other names are omitted because they aren't in *both* original sets.

Combining the different elements of two sets into a third set with the difference command

If you have two sets, you might want to identify all the data stored in one set
that isn't stored in a second set. To do this, you'd use the `difference` command, as shown in Figure 2-4.

To use the `difference` command in Python, you need to identify the two
set names with the `difference` command. Suppose you had one set called
`clubmembers` and another set called `politicians`, as follows:

```
from sets import Set
clubmembers = Set(['Bill Evans', 'John Doe', 'Mary Jacobs'])
politicians = Set (['Bo Biggs', 'John Doe'])
```

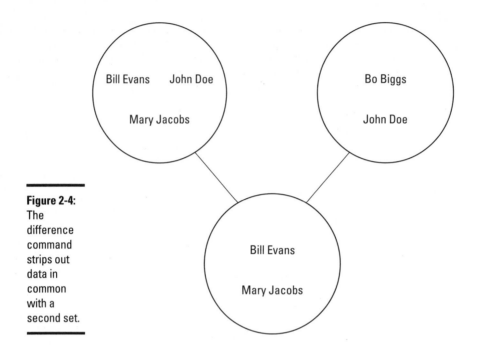

Figure 2-4:
The
difference
command
strips out
data in
common
with a
second set.

Now if you wanted to combine only the different data stored in both sets, you could use the `difference` command to store this data in a third set, as follows:

```
newset = clubmembers.difference(politicians)
```

This creates a third set — `newset` — which contains the names `Bill Evans` and `Mary Jacobs`.

The third set does not contain the name `Bo Biggs`. That's because the order in which you list the sets determines how the `difference` command works. If you list the sets in this order:

```
newset = clubmembers.difference(politicians)
```

You're telling the computer to take all the data from the first set (`clubmembers`), find all the data common in both the `clubmembers` and `politicians` sets, and remove that common data from the first set. Now take what's left and dump this data into the `newest` set (see Figure 2-4).

If you switched the commands around like this, you'd get an entirely different result:

```
newset = politicians.difference(clubmembers)
```

This tells the computer to take the data stored in the `politicians` set, find all the data common in both the `politicians` and `clubmembers` sets, and remove this common data from the `politicians` set. Now store what's left in the `newest` set, as shown in Figure 2-5.

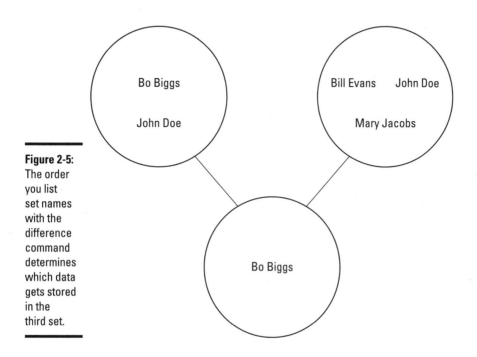

Figure 2-5: The order you list set names with the difference command determines which data gets stored in the third set.

Using Linked Lists

Sets are handy for lumping related data in a group. However, sets aren't organized. So if you want to group related data together and keep this data sorted, you can use another data structure — a *linked list*.

Whereas an array creates a fixed location for storing data (think of an egg carton), a linked list more closely resembles beads tied together by a string. It's impossible to rearrange an array (just as you can't rip an egg carton apart and put it back together again in a different way). However, you can rearrange a linked list easily just as you can rearrange beads on a string.

The basic element of a linked list is a *node,* which is just a *structure* (see Book 3, Chapter 1) that contains two parts:

+ **A pointer**
+ **A variable for storing data**

Figure 2-6 shows how the parts of a linked list work.

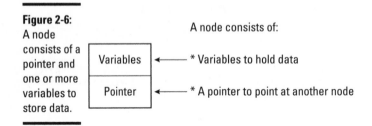

Figure 2-6:
A node consists of a pointer and one or more variables to store data.

Pointers are often used to access specific locations in the computer's memory. If you've stored data in memory and need to share that data, you could make duplicate copies of that data, which would take up space. Or you could use a pointer, which allows different parts of a program to access that same data without creating duplicate copies of that data and wasting space.

Accessing the computer's memory is like probing your brain with a sharp needle. If you know what you're doing, pointers can give you complete control over a computer, but if you make a mistake, pointers can mess up the computer's memory, causing the entire operating system to crash.

Some programming languages (such as BASIC) can't use pointers. If a language can't use pointers, that language won't let you create linked lists.

Creating a linked list

A linked list consists of one or more identical nodes that can hold the same number and types of data, such as a `string` and an `integer`. Each time you create a node, you have to define the following:

✦ **The data to store in the node**

✦ **The node to point at**

Nodes in a linked list must all contain the same data types, much like an array.

A node can store either

✦ **A single data type (such as a `string`)**

✦ **Another data structure (such as a structure or an array)**

Each time you create a node, the node is empty. To make the node useful, you must store data in that node and define which node to point at:

✦ **The first node you create simply points at *nothing*.**

The term NIL is commonly used in programming languages to represent an empty set.

✦ **Any additional nodes you create point to the previous existing nodes, so you create a daisy-chain effect of nodes linked to one another by pointers, as shown in Figure 2-7.**

Figure 2-7:
A linked list stores data in each node that points to another node.

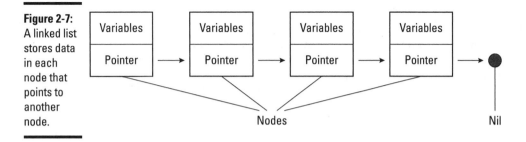

Modifying a linked list

After you create a linked list and store data in it, you can easily modify that linked list by rearranging the pointers, as shown in Figure 2-8.

This linked list organizes names in this order: Abby, Bob, Charlie, and Danny.

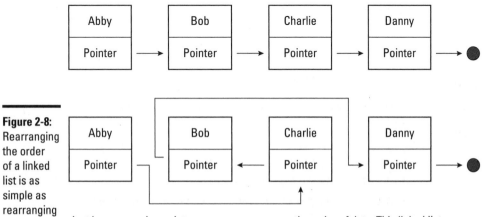

Figure 2-8:
Rearranging the order of a linked list is as simple as rearranging pointers.

Just by rearranging pointers, you can rearrange the order of data. This linked list now organizes names in this order: Abby, Charlie, Bob, and Danny.

To delete data from a linked list, you can delete an entire node. Then you must change the pointers to keep your linked list together, as shown in Figure 2-9. Unlike arrays, linked lists give you the flexibility to rearrange data without physically moving and copying it to a new location.

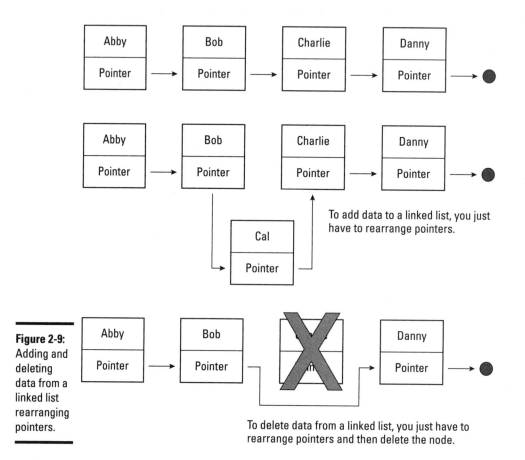

To add data to a linked list, you just have to rearrange pointers.

Figure 2-9: Adding and deleting data from a linked list rearranging pointers.

To delete data from a linked list, you just have to rearrange pointers and then delete the node.

Linked lists also let you add data anywhere just by rearranging the pointers (see Figure 2-9). By using linked lists, you can add, delete, and rearrange data quickly and easily.

Creating a double linked list

An ordinary linked list contains pointers that point in one direction only. That means if you start at the beginning of a linked list, you can always browse the data in the rest of the linked list. However, if you start in the middle of a linked list, you can never browse the previous nodes.

To fix this problem, you can also create *a double linked list,* which essentially creates nodes that contain two pointers:

✦ **One pointer points to the *previous* node in the list.**

✦ **The other pointer points to the *next* node in the list.**

By using double linked lists, you can easily browse a linked list in both directions, as shown in Figure 2-10.

Figure 2-10:
A double linked list lets you traverse a linked list in both directions.

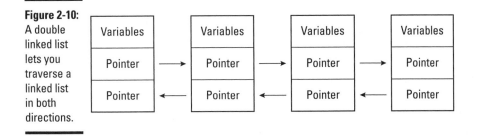

Another type of linked list you can create is a *circular linked list,* as shown in Figure 2-11. Circular linked lists more closely resemble a doughnut with no beginning or ending node. For more flexibility, you can even create a double-linked, circular linked list, which lets you traverse the list both backward and forward.

Book III
Chapter 2

Sets and
Linked Lists

Figure 2-11:
A circular linked list has no beginning or end.

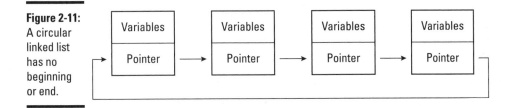

Linked lists are often used to create other types of data structures, such as *graphs, binary trees,* and *queues,* which you can read more about in Chapters 4 and 5 of this mini-book.

Drawbacks of Sets and Linked Lists

Sets make it easy to group and manipulate related data, but unlike arrays, there isn't always an easy way to access and retrieve individual items in a set. Sets are best used for treating data as a group rather than as separate chunks of data.

Linked lists are much more flexible than arrays for adding, deleting, and rearranging data. However, the two biggest drawbacks of linked lists are the complexity needed to create them and the potentially dangerous use of pointers.

Problems with pointers

The most common problem with linked lists occurs when pointers fail to point to either NIL or a valid node of a linked list. If you delete a node from a linked list but forget to rearrange the pointers, you essentially cut your linked list in two, as shown in Figure 2-12.

Figure 2-12:
Pointers must always point to a valid node of a linked list.

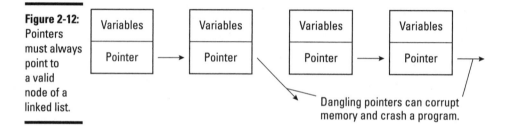

Dangling pointers can corrupt memory and crash a program.

Even worse, you could create a *dangling pointer* — the pointer no longer points to a valid node. Dangling pointers can wind up pointing to any part of the computer's memory, usually with catastrophic consequences that crash the entire computer.

Problems with accessing data

Accessing data in an array is easy. You can access data by its index number or by starting at the beginning of the array and browsing through each element until you reach the end of the array.

If you want to access data stored in a linked list, you have to start at the beginning. If you start in the middle, you can never go backward to the front of the linked list (unless you're using a double linked list). Arrays let you jump straight to specific data by using an index number. Linked lists don't offer that same feature.

For ease in *storing, adding,* and *removing* data, linked lists are more flexible than arrays. For *retrieving* data, arrays are much simpler and faster.

Complexity of creating linked lists and pointers

Creating and managing a linked list with all its pointers is easy in theory, but writing the code to create and manage a linked list can get complicated in a hurry. The more confusing and complicated the code, the more likely errors will creep in and cause your linked list to not work at all or to work in unexpected ways.

To show you how confusing pointers and nodes can be to create, study the following Pascal programming language examples. Pascal is actually designed to be an easy to read language, but even creating linked lists in Pascal can get clumsy. (Don't worry too much about the details of the Pascal code. Just skim through the examples and follow along the best you can. If you get confused, you can see how implementing linked lists in any programming language can get messy.)

To create a linked list, you must first create a node, which is a *structure*. (In Pascal, structures are called *records*.) To define a structure in Pascal, you could do this:

```
Type
  NodePtr = ^Node;
  Node = RECORD
    Data : String;
    Next : NodePtr;
  END;
```

This Pascal code creates a `NodePtr` variable, which represents a pointer to the Node structure (record). The caret symbol (^) defines a pointer, whereas the Node name defines what structure the pointer can point at.

The Node structure declares two variables: `Data` and `Next`. The `Data` variable holds a string (although you can change this to `Integer` or any other data type). The `Next` variable represents a pointer to the Node record. Every node absolutely must have a

pointer because pointers are how the nodes can point, or *link*, together to form a linked list.

If this were a double linked list, you'd have two variables (such as `Previous` and `Next`) declared as node pointers like this:

```
Type
  NodePtr = ^Node;
  Node = RECORD
    Data : String;
    Previous, Next : NodePtr;
  END;
```

After you define a node as a structure, you can't use that node until you declare a variable to represent that node, like this:

```
Var
  MyNode : NodePtr;
```

After you declare a variable to represent a pointer to a node (structure), you must create a new node, stuff data into it, and then set its pointer to point at something, such as NIL or another node:

```
Begin
  New (MyNode);        (* Creates a new
          node *)
  With MyNode^ do      (* Stores data in
        the node *)
    Begin
      Data := "Joe Hall";
      Next := NIL;
    End;
End.
```

To create a linked list in a language like Pascal, you must

1. **Define a node structure.**

2. **Declare a pointer to that node (structure).**

3. **Declare a variable to represent that pointer.**

(continued)

(continued)

Now you can use your node to store data and link with other nodes.

If you mess up on any one of those steps, your linked list won't work, and because linked lists use pointers, your pointers could point anywhere in memory, causing all sorts of random problems. The moral is that linked lists are a powerful and flexible data structure, but they come at a price of added complexity for the programmer. Accidentally create one dangling pointer, and you can bring your entire program crashing to a halt.

Chapter 3: Collections and Dictionaries

An array can be handy when you need to store the same type of information, such as a group of integers. However, if you need to store different information, such as both integers and strings, and you aren't sure how many items you need to store, you probably can't use an array. Instead, you can use a collection or a dictionary.

A *collection* acts like a resizable array that can hold different data types at the same time while identifying each chunk of data with a number. A *dictionary* acts like a collection that identifies each chunk of data with a unique key.

The purpose of both collections and dictionaries is to make it easier to store different types of data and retrieve them again with the size and single data type restrictions of an array.

Using a Collection

A collection acts like a super array that can grow and expand without requiring any special commands. In addition, a collection can store different data types (such as integers or strings) or even other data structures, such as an array.

Not all programming languages offer the collection data structure:

✦ **In some programming languages (like Python and Smalltalk), collections are a built-in feature of the language.**

✦ **In other languages (like C or Pascal), you have to use more primitive data structures (like arrays) to mimic the features of a collection.**

✦ **In many newer languages (like C# and Visual Basic.NET), someone else has already created a collection out of more primitive data structures, so you can use them without knowing how they were created.**

Because a collection is nothing more than a data structure, like an array, the first step to creating a collection is to declare a variable as a collection, such as the following Visual Basic.NET example shows:

```
Dim MyStuff as New Collection
```

This command simply identifies a `MyStuff` variable as a collection data structure. The `New` command tells the computer to create a new collection.

Adding data to a collection

When you first create a collection, it contains zero items. Each time you add a new chunk of data to a collection, it expands automatically so you never have to specify a size beforehand (like an array) or deliberately resize it later (like a dynamic array).

To add data to a collection in Visual Basic.NET, you must use an `Add` command like this:

```
Dim MyStuff as New Collection
MyStuff.Add ("Dirty socks")
```

Each time you add another element to a collection, the computer tacks that new data at the end of the collection. So if you added the string *Dirty socks,* the number *7348,* and the number *4.39,* the collection would look like Figure 3-1.

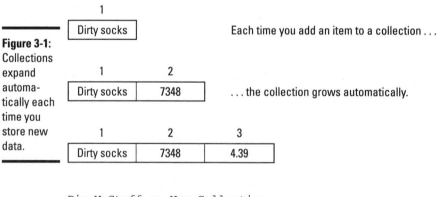

Figure 3-1:
Collections expand automatically each time you store new data.

Each time you add an item to a collection . . .

. . . the collection grows automatically.

```
Dim MyStuff as New Collection
MyStuff.Add ("Dirty socks")
MyStuff.Add (7348)
MyStuff.Add (4.39)
```

Every element in a collection gets numbered with the first element given an index number of 1, the second given an index number of 2, and so on, similar to an array.

Although some programming languages number the first element of an array as 0, they often number the first item in a collection with 1.

For greater flexibility in adding data to a collection, you may be able to insert data before or after existing data, depending on the programming language. (In Visual Basic.NET, you can add data before or after existing data in a collection, but in REALbasic, you can't.)

Suppose you had the following Visual Basic.NET code to create a collection:

```
Dim HitLIst as New Collection
HitList.Add ("Billy Joe")
HitList.Add (99)
HitList.Add ("Johnny McGruffin")
```

If you wanted to add the name `Hal Perkins` to the end of the collection, you could use this command:

```
HitList.Add ("Hal Perkins")
```

Rather than always adding data to the end of a collection, you can also specify that you want to store new data before or after a specific location in the array. The location is specified by the collection's *index number*.

So if you wanted to add the number `3.14` before the second element in a collection, you could use the following:

```
HitList.Add (3.14, ,2)
```

Don't worry about the extra space between the two commas. That extra space is reserved for using collections with *keys* (which you read about later in this chapter).

The preceding command inserts the number 3.14 before the second element of the collection, as shown in Figure 3-2.

If you wanted to add the name `Gini Belkins` after the third element in the collection, you could use the following command:

```
HitList.Add ("Gini Belkins", , , 3)
```

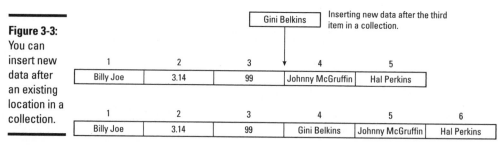

Figure 3-2:
You can insert data before a specific location in an array.

Adding new data in the middle of a collection automatically renumbers the rest of the collection.

This command would insert the name `Gini Belkins` after the third element in the collection, as shown in Figure 3-3.

Figure 3-3:
You can insert new data after an existing location in a collection.

Inserting new data after the third item in a collection.

Don't worry about the extra spaces between the three commas in the preceding command:

✦ **The first extra space is reserved for using collections with *keys* (which you read about later in this chapter).**

✦ **The second extra space is used to store data before a location in a collection.**

Deleting data from a collection

After you store data in a collection, you can always delete data from that collection. To delete data, you must specify the location of that data by defining an index number. So if you want to delete the fourth item in a collection, you'd specify deleting data stored at index 4 like this:

```
HitList.Remove (4)
```

When you delete data from an array, that array now contains empty space, but when you delete data from a collection, the collection automatically renumbers the rest of its data so there isn't any empty space, as shown in Figure 3-4.

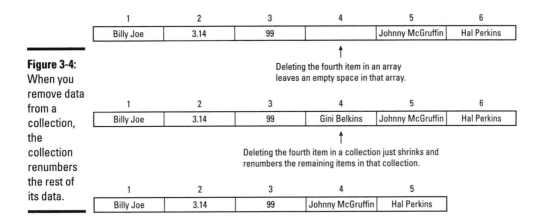

Figure 3-4: When you remove data from a collection, the collection renumbers the rest of its data.

Identifying data with keys

One problem with collections is that they identify data by their position in the collection. If you don't know the location of specific data in a collection, you have to search the entire collection, item by item, to find specific data.

Because trying to find data in a collection by its location can be clumsy and unintuitive, collections give you the option of identifying data with any descriptive string, or a *key*.

For example, if you stored the name of your boss in a collection, you could identify it with the key `boss`. If you stored the name of your friend in a collection, you could identify it with the key `best friend`. And if you stored the name of your ex-boss in a collection, you could identify it with the key `moron`, as shown in Figure 3-5.

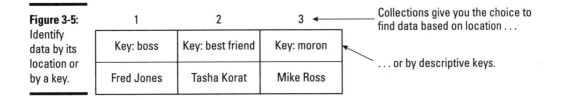

Figure 3-5: Identify data by its location or by a key.

When you add data to a collection, you can optionally also assign a key to that data, which you can later use to search and retrieve that data again. So if you wanted to add the data Mike Ross along with the key moron, you could use the following command:

```
HitList.Add ("Mike Ross", "moron")
```

When adding a key to data in a collection, your key must meet these criteria:

✦ **You must add a key at the same time you add data to a collection.** After you add data to a collection, you can't go back later and add a key to that data.

✦ **Every key must be a string.**

✦ **Every key must be unique; no two items in a collection can share the same key.**

Searching and retrieving data

After you store data in a collection, here are two ways to search and retrieve data from that collection:

✦ **Use the index number of that data.**

✦ **Use the key of that data.**

If you don't store a key with data originally, you can't retrieve that data with a key.

Index numbers

To retrieve data based on its location, you can do something as simple as the following:

```
Dim Junk as New Collection
Junk.Add (3.1415)
Junk.Add (99)
Junk.Add ("Bo")
```

If you wanted to retrieve the name *Bo* from the collection, you'd have to know that *Bo* is stored as the third item (index number 3), so the following would store the string *Bo* in the Good variable:

```
Good = Junk.Item(3)
```

The problem with relying on index numbers alone is that as you add and delete items from a collection, the index numbers may change, as shown in Figure 3-6.

Figure 3-6:
Retrieving data by index numbers is unreliable because they can change.

1	2	3
3.1415	99	Bo

Originally, the "Bo" string is located at index 3.

1	2	3	4
3.1415	99	Ollie Bird	Bo

But if new items are added to the front of the collection, the "Bo" string may get placed in a different location such as at index 4.

Because index numbers don't always stay matched with each item in a collection, a better solution is to assign a unique string, or a *key,* to each item, as described in the following section.

Keys

By assigning a descriptive key to each item, you can use that key to retrieve that item no matter where it might be stored in the collection.

The following code assigns the key "pi" to the first item, the key "secret agent" to the second item, and the key "my cat" to the third item:

```
Dim MoreJunk as New Collection
MoreJunk.Add (3.1415, "pi")
MoreJunk.Add (99, "secret agent")
MoreJunk.Add ("Bo", "my cat")
```

To retrieve items from a collection with a key, you have to remember the key associated with each chunk of data. The following code stores the number 3.1415 into the CircleSecret variable:

```
CircleSecret = MoreJunk.Item ("pi")
```

The preceding code tells the computer to find the chunk of data assigned the "pi" key and then store that data in the CircleSecret variable.

The preceding code retrieves the number 3.1415 no matter where its location may be in a collection.

You can always retrieve data with either its key or its location (index number).

Using Dictionaries

Essentially, a *dictionary* is like a collection but with two additional advantages:

✦ **Searching for that data in a dictionary is much *faster*.**

Dictionaries use a data structure known as a *hash table* (which you read more about later in this chapter). Every item stored in a dictionary must include a unique *key*.

Collections don't require keys because searching for data in a collection is *sequential*. Therefore, the computer must start at the beginning of the collection and examine each item one by one to retrieve a specific item. The more items in a collection, the slower the search process.

If a programming language offers collections, it usually also offers dictionaries. If a programming language doesn't offer collections, it probably doesn't offer dictionaries either.

✦ **In a dictionary, the key can be any value, including strings or numbers, which gives you greater flexibility in assigning keys to data.**

If a collection uses a key to identify data, that key must be a string.

Dictionaries are also called *associative arrays*. When you store data and a key, that's known as a *key-value pair* (refer to Figure 3-5).

Like a collection, a dictionary is a data type, so you must first declare a variable as a dictionary. Then you must create a new dictionary and store data in that dictionary.

To create a dictionary in the Smalltalk programming language, you could use the following:

```
blackbook := Dictionary new.
```

This code declares the blackbook variable as a dictionary data type. The new command simply creates an empty dictionary.

Adding data to a dictionary

After you declare a variable as a dictionary data type, you can start adding data to that dictionary by defining both the data and the key you want to associate with that date. So if you want to add the name Dick Ross to a dictionary and assign it a moron key, you could use the following:

```
blackbook := Dictionary new.
blackbook at: 'moron'       put:  'Dick Ross'.
```

Every time you add data to a dictionary, you must include a corresponding key.

In Smalltalk, the key appears directly after the `at` command, and the data appears after the `put` command, as shown here:

```
blackbook := Dictionary new.
blackbook at: 'moron'      put:  'Dick Ross'.
blackbook at: 'imbecile'   put:  'John Adams'.
blackbook at: 'idiot'      put:  'Sally Parker'.
```

Searching and retrieving data from a dictionary

To access and retrieve data from a dictionary, you need to identify the dictionary variable and the key associated with the data you want to find. So if you wanted to find the data associated with the key `idiot`, you could use the following command:

```
blackbook at: 'idiot'
```

This would return:

```
'Sally Parker'
```

Dictionaries are more efficient at searching and retrieving data because the computer doesn't need to search through the entire dictionary sequentially. Instead, the computer searches through data using a hash table. This is like the difference between looking through the phone book, starting from page one, trying to find the phone number of the Versatile Plumbing company, or just skipping straight to the V section of the phone book and then looking alphabetically from the beginning of that V section to find the phone number of Versatile Plumbing, as shown in Figure 3-7.

Understanding Hash Tables

If you stored data without a key in a collection, searching for a specific chunk of data is difficult because the data isn't sorted. So to ensure you find data in a collection, you must search the entire collection from start to finish. The more data you store, the longer the search takes, just as it takes longer to find a specific playing card in a deck of 52 cards compared to a deck of only 4 cards.

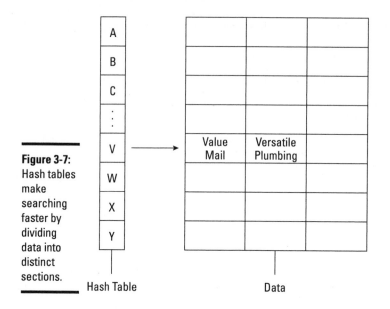

Figure 3-7:
Hash tables make searching faster by dividing data into distinct sections.

When you store data with a unique key (a *key-value pair*), the key is used to help identify and retrieve the data. However, just using a key alone is no better than storing data alone because keys are just another chunk of data. The more data (and keys) you store, the longer it takes the computer to search through its entire list of keys.

Converting keys with a hash function

To speed up searching, dictionaries use hash tables. Basically, a hash table takes the keys used to identify data and then converts that key into a *hash value*. This hash value gets stored into a sorted list (table), as shown in Figure 3-8.

The exact method used to convert a key into a value is a *hash function*. The converted key, or *hash,* now points directly to the stored data. At this point, the computer actually stores just two chunks of data:

✦ **The data itself**

✦ **A hash value calculated from the key**

When you want to retrieve data, you give the computer the key associated with the data that you want. The computer takes the key and uses its hash function to convert the key to a value.

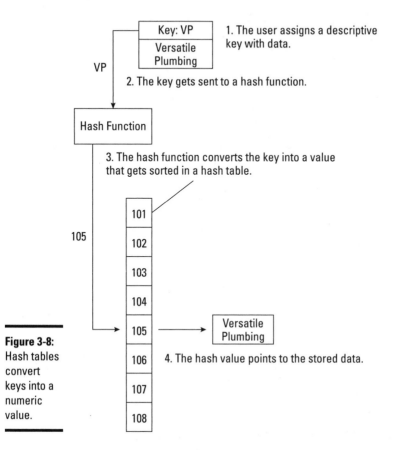

1. The user assigns a descriptive key with data.

2. The key gets sent to a hash function.

3. The hash function converts the key into a value that gets sorted in a hash table.

4. The hash value points to the stored data.

Figure 3-8: Hash tables convert keys into a numeric value.

Now the computer tries to match this calculated value to its list of values stored in the hash table. When it finds a match, it can then find the data associated with that key.

A simple hash function might just add up all the characters in a key and use that total as a value. For example, consider the keys moron and imbecile.

```
blackbook := Dictionary new.
blackbook at: 'moron'      put:  'Dick Ross'.
blackbook at: 'imbecile'   put:  'John Adams'.
```

Such a simple hash function could create a table like this:

Hash table	Data
5	Dick Ross
8	John Adams

If you wanted to find the data associated with the key moron, the computer would first calculate its hash value, which is five.

Next, it'd try to match this value with an existing value stored in the hash table. In this case, it finds that the hash value of 5 matches up to the key moron and the data Dick Ross, which is the data you wanted in the first place.

Basically, a hash table works by searching through a sorted list of data (the hash values calculated from the key) rather than the unsorted list of data.

Hash function collisions

The hash function used to create a hash table can greatly determine the efficiency of that hash table. Ideally, the hash function should create a different hash value for every key. Unfortunately, that's not always possible, which means that sometimes the hash function can create identical hash values from different keys.

In the previous example, the hash function converted a key to a hash value just by counting the number of characters used in the key. So if two different keys have the same number of characters, the hash function will create the same hash value like this:

```
blackbook := Dictionary new.
blackbook at: 'moron'      put:  'Dick Ross'.
blackbook at: 'imbecile'   put:  'John Adams'.
Blackbook at: 'idiot'      put:  'Sally Evans'.
```

Using the simple hash function to count the number of characters in each key would create a table like this:

Hash table	Data
5	Dick Ross
8	John Adams
5	Sally Evans

Hash tables can't have duplicate values because every hash value must match with a single chunk of data. A *collision* occurs when a hash function creates duplicate values from different keys. Here are two ways to prevent collisions:

✦ **Develop a better hash function.**

Unfortunately, no matter how many different hash functions you create, the more data stored, the greater the chance that any hash function will eventually calculate a duplicate value from two different keys.

✦ **Find a way to deal with hash value collisions.**

The following sections provide solutions.

Solving collisions by chaining

The simplest way to deal with collisions (duplicate hash values) is *chaining*.

Normally, each hash value points to a single chunk of data. The idea behind chaining is that each hash value can actually point to a list of data, as shown in Figure 3-9.

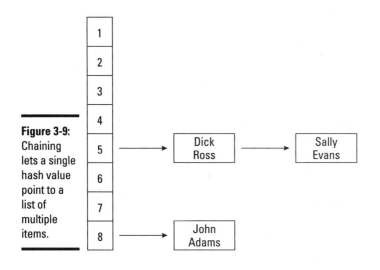

Figure 3-9: Chaining lets a single hash value point to a list of multiple items.

Book III Chapter 3

Collections and Dictionaries

Now if you search for data using a key, the computer

1. **Calculates the hash value of that key, which points to a list of data**

2. **Searches through this list sequentially, one by one**

Chaining works because searching a *shorter list* sequentially is faster than searching the *whole list* sequentially. (It's like finding the Versatile Plumbing company in the phone book by starting with the V section instead of the first page of the book.)

Avoiding collisions with double hashing

Another way to avoid collisions is to use *double hashing:*

1. **The hash function calculates a hash value for each key.**

2. **If a collision occurs, the computer calculates a second hash value.**

    Essentially, you wind up with a hash table within another hash table, as shown in Figure 3-10.

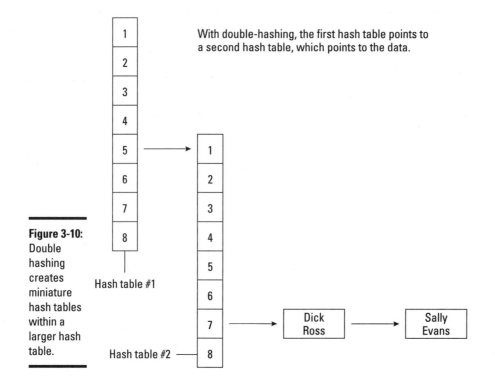

With double-hashing, the first hash table points to a second hash table, which points to the data.

Figure 3-10: Double hashing creates miniature hash tables within a larger hash table.

Hash table #1

Hash table #2

Double hashing can reduce the number of duplicate hash values *(collisions)*, but here are a couple of drawbacks:

✦ **A collision can occur even after the double hashing.**

✦ **Double hashing is a more complicated solution than chaining.**

    The more complex a program, the greater the chances of something going wrong.

In general, the simpler the data structure (such as arrays), the easier they are to implement and the less chance that something goes wrong. Of course, the simpler the data structure, the more restrictive the data structure.

Both collections and dictionaries (using hash tables) give you added flexibility but at the cost of added complexity:

✦ **In many programming languages, such as C, you have to create dictionaries and hash tables from scratch.**

✦ **In other programming languages, such as C# or Python, collections and dictionaries are built-in features of that language, which makes these data structures easy to use and implement.**

Sometimes you may find collections or dictionaries easier to use and sometimes you may find arrays or sets easier to use. By understanding the different types of available data structures and the pros and cons of each, you're more likely to choose the best one that makes it easy to solve your particular problem.

Book III
Chapter 3

**Collections and
Dictionaries**

Chapter 4: Stacks, Queues, and Deques

In This Chapter

✔ **Using a stack**

✔ **Using a queue**

✔ **Using a deque**

Collections and dictionaries are best suited for storing and organizing data, but they aren't as useful for retrieving data in an orderly fashion. Trying to keep track of data stored by index numbers or by keys can get cumbersome. As a simpler alternative, computer scientists have created three other data structures:

✦ **Stacks**

✦ **Queues**

✦ **Deques**

Unlike collections or dictionaries, these three data structures are designed for storing and removing data in a predictable order.

Using a Stack

The stack data structure gets its name because it resembles a stack of clean dishes, typically found in a cafeteria. When you put the first plate on the counter, that plate appears at the bottom of the stack. Each time you add a new plate to the stack, the first plate gets buried farther underneath. Add another plate to the stack, and the newest plate appears on top. To remove a plate, you have to take the top plate off.

That's the same way the stack data structure works, as shown in Figure 4-1. With a stack, you don't keep track of the data's location. Instead, you can keep adding new data to store, and the stack expands automatically.

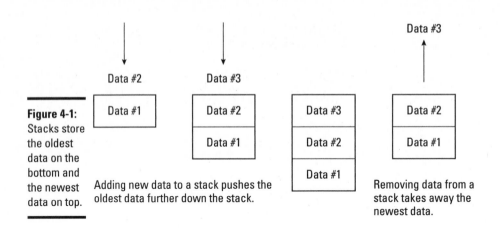

Figure 4-1: Stacks store the oldest data on the bottom and the newest data on top.

Data #2

Data #1

Adding new data to a stack pushes the oldest data further down the stack.

Data #3

Data #2

Data #1

Data #3

Data #2

Data #1

Data #3

Data #2

Data #1

Removing data from a stack takes away the newest data.

The only way to remove data from a stack is from its top. Each time you remove data, the stack shrinks automatically. Because a stack only lets you remove the last item stored on the stack, it's often called a *Last In, First Out* (LIFO) data structure because the last item stored is always the first item you can remove from the stack.

Few programming languages offer the stack data structure as a built-in feature. Instead, you have to create a stack using other data structures, such as an array or a linked list. When you create another data structure out of a built-in data structure, the new data structure created is an *abstract data structure*. To save you the time and trouble of creating a stack data structure, many programming language compilers come with libraries (or *classes* in object-oriented languages) of subprograms that have created the stack data structure for you.

Because a stack is just a data structure, you can declare a variable to represent a stack in Visual Basic.NET by doing the following:

```
Dim BlowMyStack as New Stack
```

This command simply identifies a `BlowMyStack` variable as a stack data structure. The `New` command tells the computer to create a new stack.

Adding data to a stack

When you first create a stack, it contains zero items. Each time you add a new chunk of data to a stack, it expands automatically. Unlike other data structures, such as collections, you can only add new data to the top of the stack; you can never add data in a specific location in a stack.

Like a collection or a dictionary, a stack can typically hold different data, such as both numbers and strings.

The only way you can store or remove data from a stack is through the top of the stack. To add data to a stack, you *push* that data on the stack. In Visual Basic.NET, you specify the Push command along with the stack name like this:

```
Dim BlowMyStack as New Stack
BlowMyStack.Push ("My cat")
```

This command stores the string *"My cat"* on top of the stack. Each time you add another chunk of data to a stack, you have to put that data on the top, which pushes any existing data farther down the stack.

If you added the string *"My cat,"* the number *108.75,* and the string *"Fat dog,"* the stack would look like Figure 4-2.

```
Dim BlowMyStack as New Stack
BlowMyStack.Push ("My cat")
BlowMyStack.Push (108.75)
BlowMyStack.Push ("Fat dog")
```

Book III
Chapter 4

Stacks, Queues, and Deques

Figure 4-2: When you add data to a stack, the oldest data keeps getting pushed farther down the stack.

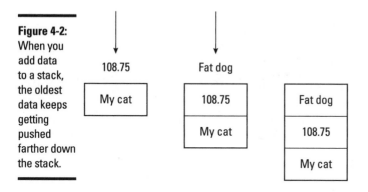

Removing data from a stack

After you store data in a stack, the only way you can remove data from that stack is by removing the top item. Removing data from a stack is known as *popping* the data off the stack. If you just want to retrieve the data from a stack without removing it, you can use a Peek command, which lets you retrieve the top item from a stack.

To use the `Peek` command, you have to assign the value of the `Peek` command to a variable like this:

```
Dim BlowMyStack as New Stack
Dim X as Object
BlowMyStack.Push ("My cat")
BlowMyStack.Push (108.75)
BlowMyStack.Push ("Fat dog")
X = BlowMyStack.Peek
```

The preceding code assigns the value `"Fat dog"` to the X variable, which is declared as an `Object` data type. (In Visual Basic.NET, an `Object` data type can hold any type of data including integers, strings, and decimal numbers, such as (47.748).

The `Peek` command retrieves the data but leaves it on top of the stack.

If you want to remove data, you use the `Pop` command, which retrieves and removes data, as shown in the following Visual Basic.NET example:

```
Dim BlowMyStack as New Stack
Dim X as Object
BlowMyStack.Push ("My cat")
BlowMyStack.Push (108.75)
BlowMyStack.Push ("Fat dog")
X = BlowMyStack.Pop
```

Figure 4-3 shows the difference between the `Peek` and the `Pop` commands.

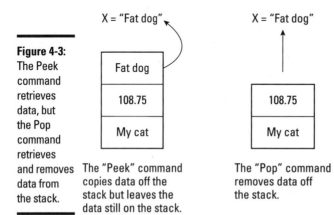

Figure 4-3: The Peek command retrieves data, but the Pop command retrieves and removes data from the stack.

X = "Fat dog"

| Fat dog |
| 108.75 |
| My cat |

The "Peek" command copies data off the stack but leaves the data still on the stack.

X = "Fat dog"

| 108.75 |
| My cat |

The "Pop" command removes data off the stack.

Counting and searching a stack

Because stacks can expand and shrink depending on the amount of data you push on them, many programming languages give you commands to count the total number of items currently stored in a stack.

In Visual Basic.NET, the command to count the number of items currently stored in a stack is Count. Here's an example:

```
Dim BlowMyStack as New Stack
Dim X as Object
BlowMyStack.Push ("My cat")
BlowMyStack.Push (108.75)
BlowMyStack.Push ("Fat dog")
X = BlowMyStack.Count
```

In this example, the Count command stores the number 3 in the X variable.

Visual Basic.NET also provides a Contains command, which tells you whether a chunk of data is stored in a stack (but doesn't tell you the location of that data in the stack). To use the Contains command, you have to specify the data you want to find like this:

```
Dim BlowMyStack as New Stack
Dim X, Y as Object
BlowMyStack.Push ("My cat")
BlowMyStack.Push (108.75)
BlowMyStack.Push ("Fat dog")
X = BlowMyStack.Contains("Good dog")
Y = BlowMyStack.Contains("Fat dog")
```

In this example, the first Contains command looks for the *"Good dog"* string. Because this string isn't stored in the stack, the Contains command returns a False value, which it stored in the X variable.

The second Contains command looks for the *"Fat dog"* string. Because this string is stored in the stack, this Contains command returns a True value, which is stored in the Y variable.

The Contains command tells you whether a chunk of data is in a stack, but it doesn't tell you where in the stack that data might be.

Using Queues

Similar to a stack is another data structure — a *queue*.

A queue gets its name because the data structure resembles a line of waiting people, such as a line at a bank teller. The first person in the line (queue) is also the first person who gets to leave the line. As a result, a queue is often a *First In, First Out* (FIFO) data structure, as shown in Figure 4-4.

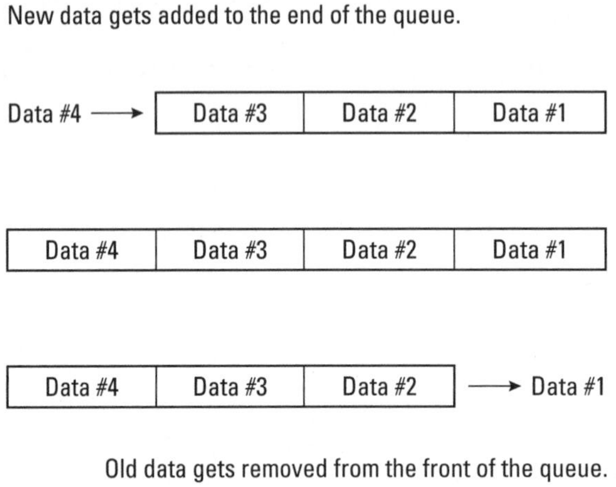

New data gets added to the end of the queue.

Data #4 →	Data #3	Data #2	Data #1

Figure 4-4:
The queue data structure mimics a line of people.

Data #4	Data #3	Data #2	Data #1

Data #4	Data #3	Data #2	→ Data #1

Old data gets removed from the front of the queue.

Like a stack, a queue can expand and shrink automatically, depending on the amount of data you store in it. Unlike a stack that only lets you store and retrieve data from the top, a queue lets you store data on one end but remove that data from the opposite end.

Most programming languages don't offer the queue data structure as a built-in feature. Instead, you have to create a queue with other data structures, such as an array or a linked list, to create an *abstract data structure*. Fortunately, many programming language compilers come with libraries (or *classes* in object-oriented languages) of subprograms that have created the queue data structure for you.

Because a queue is just a data structure, you can declare a variable to represent a queue in Visual Basic.NET by doing the following:

```
Dim LongLine as New Queue
```

This command simply identifies a `LongLine` variable as a queue data structure. The `New` command tells the computer to create a new stack.

Adding data to a queue

New data always gets stored at the end of the queue:

✦ **When you first create a queue, it contains zero items.**

✦ **Each time you add a new chunk of data to a queue, the queue expands automatically.**

✦ **The front of the queue always contains the first or oldest data.**

Like a collection or a dictionary, a queue can hold different data, such as both numbers and strings.

To add data to a queue, Visual Basic.NET uses the Enqueue command along with the queue name like this:

```
Dim LongLine as New Queue
LongLine.Enqueue ("Tasha Korat")
```

This command stores the string *"Tasha Korat"* as the first item in the queue. Each time you add another chunk of data to this queue, the new data gets tacked on to the end, which *pushes* the oldest data to the front of the queue.

If you added the string *"Tasha Korat,"* the number *7.25,* and the string *"Gray,"* the stack would look like Figure 4-5.

```
Dim LongLine as New Queue
LongLine.Enqueue ("Tasha Korat")
LongLine.Enqueue (7.25)
LongLine.Enqueue ("Gray")
```

Figure 4-5:
The oldest data appears at the front while the newest data appears at the end of the queue.

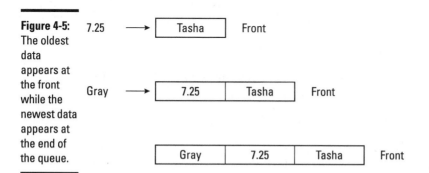

Removing data from a queue

You always remove data from a queue by taking that data off the front of the queue. The front of the queue always contains the data that's been stored in the queue the longest.

In Visual Basic.NET, you can remove and retrieve data off a queue by using the Dequeue command, as shown in the following Visual Basic.NET example:

```
Dim LongLine as New Queue
Dim X as Object
LongLine.Enqueue ("My cat")
LongLine.Enqueue (108.75)
LongLine.Enqueue ("Fat dog")
X = LongLine.Dequeue
```

As an alternative to removing data from a queue, you can retrieve data by using the Peek command. To use the Peek command, you have to assign the value of the Peek command to a variable like this:

```
Dim LongLine as New Queue
Dim X as Object
LongLine.Enqueue ("Tasha Korat")
LongLine.Enqueue (7.25)
LongLine.Enqueue ("Gray")
X = LongLine.Peek
```

The preceding code assigns the value "Tasha Korat" to the X variable, which is declared as an Object data type. (In Visual Basic.NET, an Object data type can hold any type of data including integers, strings, and decimal numbers, such as 57.98).

The Peek command only retrieves the data but leaves it at the front of the queue. Figure 4-6 shows the difference between the Peek and the Dequeue commands.

Counting and searching a queue

Because a queue can keep growing each time you add more data to it, most programming languages provide a way to count the total number of items currently stored in the queue.

Figure 4-6:
The Peek command retrieves data, but the Dequeue command retrieves and removes data.

The "Peek" command retrieves data from a queue without removing data from the queue.

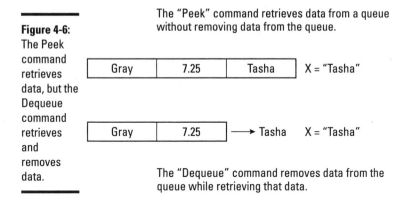

The "Dequeue" command removes data from the queue while retrieving that data.

In Visual Basic.NET, the command to count the number of items currently stored in a stack is Count. Here's an example:

```
Dim LongLine as New Queue
Dim X as Object
LongLine.Enqueue ("Tasha Korat")
LongLine.Enqueue (7.25)
LongLine.Enqueue ("Gray")
X = LongLine.Count
```

In this example, the Count command stores the number 3 in the X variable.

Visual Basic.NET also provides a Contains command, which tells you whether a chunk of data is stored in a queue (but doesn't tell you the location of that data in the queue). To use the Contains command, you have to specify the data you want to find like this:

```
Dim LongLine as New Queue
Dim X, Y as Object
LongLine.Enqueue ("Tasha Korat")
LongLine.Enqueue (7.25)
LongLine.Enqueue ("Gray")
X = LongLine.Contains("Gray")
Y = LongLine.Contains("Orange juice")
```

In this example, the first Contains command looks for the *"Gray"* string. Because this string is stored in the queue, the Contains command returns a True value, which it stored in the X variable.

The second `Contains` command looks for the *"Orange juice"* string. Because this string isn't stored in the stack, this `Contains` command returns a `False` value, which is stored in the `Y` variable.

The `Contains` command just tells you whether a chunk of data is in a queue, but it doesn't tell you where in the queue that data might be.

Using Deques

A queue only lets you add data on one end of the data structure and remove data from the opposite end. A deque (pronounced *deck*) acts like a queue that lets you add or remove data from either end, as shown in Figure 4-7.

A deque allows you to add or remove data
from both ends of the data structure.

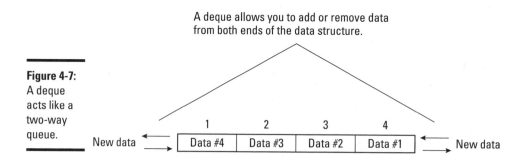

Figure 4-7:
A deque
acts like a
two-way
queue.

Most programming languages don't offer the deque data structure as a built-in feature. Instead, you have to create a queue with other data structures, such as a linked list, and then write code to manage the storage and removal of data from both ends of the deque.

A deque is basically a linked list of nodes that contain data and two pointers:

✦ **One pointer points to the previous node.**

✦ **The second pointer points to the next node, as shown in Figure 4-8.**

Figure 4-8:
Each node
in a deque
contains two
pointers that
point to the
next and pre-
vious node.

A double-linked list consists of nodes that hold data and two
pointers that point to the next and previous nose.

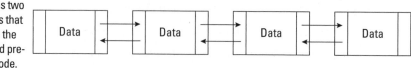

Initially, a deque consists of a single node with both pointers pointing to nothing, which is often defined in most programming languages as a NIL value. When you add (or remove) data, you must specify which end of the deque to put that data, either the front or the back.

Deques can either be implemented as a double-linked list or a circular double-linked list, as shown in Figure 4-9. In both implementations, you need to keep track of which node represents the front and which represents the end.

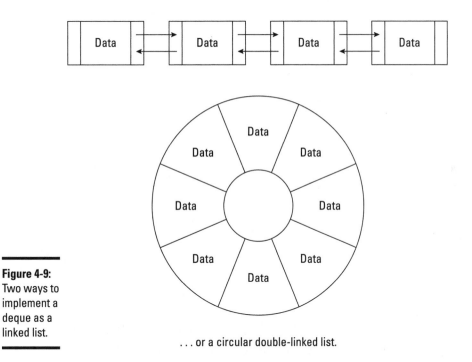

A double-linked list can either be a straight line . . .

. . . or a circular double-linked list.

Book III
Chapter 4

Stacks, Queues, and Deques

Figure 4-9:
Two ways to implement a deque as a linked list.

The common command names used for adding or removing data from a deque include

✦ **Push_front:** Adds data to the front of the deque

✦ **Push_back:** Adds data to the end of the deque

✦ **Pop_front:** Removes data from the front of the deque

✦ **Pop_back:** Removes data from the end of the deque

Because you can add data to both ends of a deque, a deque can grow in both directions, as shown in Figure 4-10.

Data #2	Data #1	← Data #3

Data #4 →

Data #2	Data #1	Data #3

Data #4	Data #2	Data #1	Data #3

Unlike a stack that always removes the newest data or a queue that always removes the oldest data, a deque can never predictably remove either the oldest or newest data. When you add data to both ends of the deque, the oldest data tends to get sandwiched and buried in between the newest data on both ends.

Like stacks and queues, deques only allow you to remove data from a specific part of the data structure. In general, the more complicated the data structures, the more code you have to write to manage that data structure.

A list or an array is much simpler to use, but much less flexible than a queue or a stack. Unfortunately, stacks, queues, and deques add greater complexity to your program in exchange for their added flexibility.

If you need to store and remove data in an orderly fashion, stacks, queues, and deques are better suited than arrays, collections, or dictionaries, which are better suited for long-term storage of data. A queue might be useful for an online reservation system that handles the oldest request first.

Although the idea of removing the last item first might seem counterintuitive, stacks are a commonly used data structure. Most programs offer an Undo command, which lets you undo the last command you gave the computer. If you give five different commands, the program may store each command in a stack.

When you want to undo a command, you want to start with the last command you gave it, which appears on the top of the stack, as shown in Figure 4-11. Each succeeding Undo command removes an additional command until you get to the last command, which is the oldest one that was buried at the bottom of the stack.

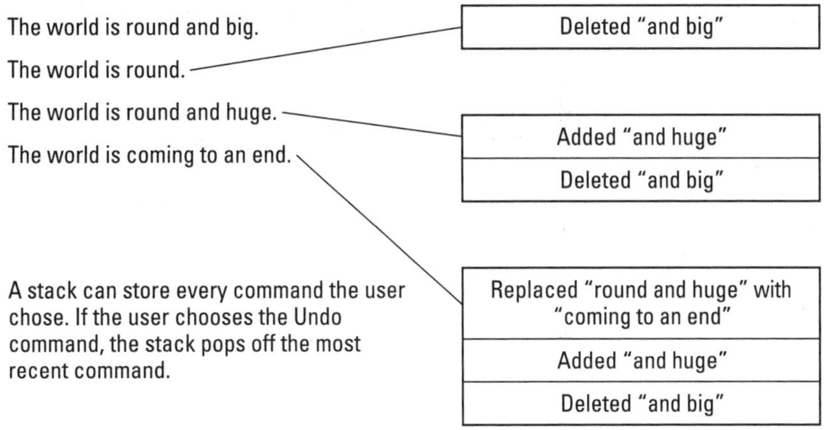

The world is round and big.
The world is round.
The world is round and huge.
The world is coming to an end.
A stack can store every command the user chose. If the user chooses the Undo command, the stack pops off the most recent command.
Deleted "and big"
Added "and huge"
Deleted "and big"
Replaced "round and huge" with "coming to an end"
Added "and huge"
Deleted "and big"

Figure 4-11: The Undo command offered in most programs can be easily implemented in a stack.

A deque might be useful for an antivirus program that needs to examine messages being sent out and coming in to a particular computer. When messages come in, the antivirus program stores each message in the deque. Messages scanned as virus-free are sent through the other end of the deque, whereas messages caught carrying a virus are rejected from the same end of the dequeue, as shown in Figure 4-12.

Antivirus program scanning e-mail
Reject
New e-mail
E-mail
E-mail
E-mail
Read e-mail
Send e-mail
A deque data structure

Figure 4-12: A deque could be used by an antivirus program to scan messages.

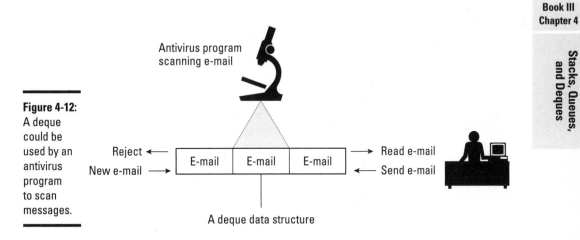

Different data structures can be useful for different purposes. Choose the right data structure, and a program can suddenly be easier to write. Choose the wrong data structure, and your program can suddenly become much tougher to write.

Chapter 5: Graphs and Trees

In This Chapter

✔ **Understanding and using graphs**

✔ **Creating different types of trees**

✔ **Manipulating a tree**

*M*ost data structures (such as arrays, dictionaries, and queues) store data in a linear format with one chunk of data neatly sandwiched in between exactly two other chunks of data. Linear data structures can be fine for just storing data, but what if you want a data structure that can model a real-life problem?

Picking the right data structure to model a real-life problem can greatly simplify programming. One advantage of a queue is that it closely mimics a line of people (or orders on a Web site) that need to be handled one at a time, starting with the oldest item. Using a queue data structure to handle incoming orders from a Web site makes logical sense but using a dictionary or even an array makes less sense because dictionaries require keys assigned to each data (which isn't needed) and arrays need to be resized constantly.

So if you have a problem that doesn't mimic a linear data structure, using a linear data structure can just make programming harder, much like trying to use a screwdriver to pound in a nail when you really need a hammer.

For example, suppose you're creating a chess game. You could use a collection data structure to represent each space on the chessboard, but a more intuitive data structure would just be a two-dimensional array.

Modeling a chessboard with a two-dimensional array works because both a two-dimensional array and a chessboard are a regular shaped grid. Now what if you need to model a real-life problem that doesn't neatly match a uniformly shaped grid?

Suppose you need to keep track of trucks traveling to different cities so you can route them to the shortest distance between two cities, as shown in Figure 5-1.

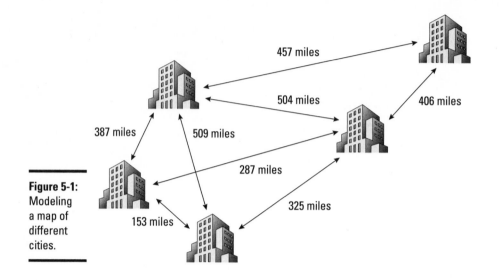

Figure 5-1:
Modeling
a map of
different
cities.

You could model this problem as a two-dimensional array like this:

	Los Angeles	San Diego	Las Vegas	San Francisco	Salt Lake City
Los Angeles	0	153	287	387	X
San Diego	153	0	325	509	X
Las Vegas	287	325	0	504	406
San Francisco	387	X	504	0	457
Salt Lake City	X	X	406	457	0

Although this two-dimensional array accurately models the map of different city distances, it's not easy to understand what this data represents. A better data structure would be a graph.

Understanding Graphs

A graph is typically created by using a linked list that can point to multiple nodes. As a result, a graph doesn't follow a linear structure but a more haphazard appearance, which makes it perfect for modeling non-linear data, such as the map of different cities and distances, as shown in Figure 5-2.

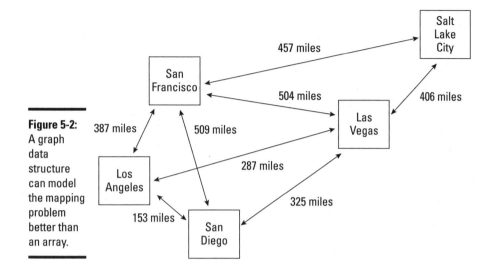

**Book III
Chapter 5**

Graphs and Trees

Figure 5-2: A graph data structure can model the mapping problem better than an array.

The two parts of every graph are

✦ **Nodes (or *vertices*):** Contain the actual data.

✦ **Connections (or *edges*):** Represent some relationship between two or more nodes.

In the map example, nodes represent cities and connections represent distances.

An entire branch of mathematics is dedicated to studying graphs *(graph theory)*.

Graph data structures are used less for storing and retrieving data and more for understanding the relationship between data.

Types of graphs

Three types of graphs are shown in Figure 5-3:

✦ **Undirected graph:** Connects data in different ways to show a relationship, such as modeling all the links connecting the pages of a Web site.

✦ **Directed graph:** Adds arrows to show you the direction of a relationship between data. For example, a directed graph could model the flow of messages passed between computers in a network.

✦ **Weighted graph:** Labels each link with a value or weight; each weight might measure distances, resistance, or cost between nodes. In the example of the graph in Figure 5-3, each weight represents a distance measured in miles. The higher the weight, the farther the distance.

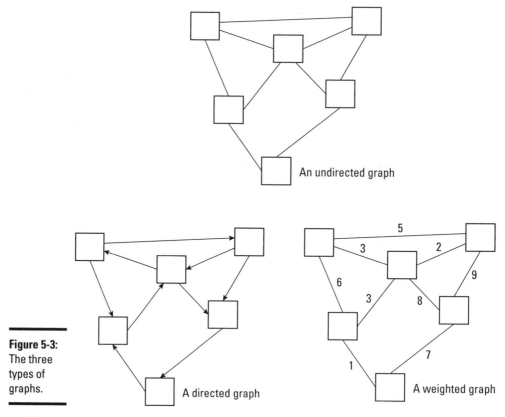

An undirected graph

A directed graph

A weighted graph

Figure 5-3:
The three
types of
graphs.

You can also combine weights with direction and create a *directed, weighted* graph.

Uses for graphs

Graphs are used to model a variety of real-world problems, such as finding the most efficient way to route e-mail through a computer network to finding the shortest way for airplanes to travel to different cities. Molecular biologists even use graphs to model the structure of molecules.

Designing a single path with the Seven Bridges of Königsberg

One of the first uses for graphs appeared in 1736 in a problem known as the Seven Bridges of Königsberg. The question was whether it was possible to walk across all seven bridges of Königsberg exactly once, as shown in Figure 5-4.

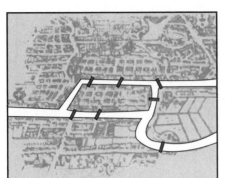

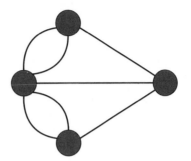

Figure 5-4:
The Seven
Bridges of
Königsberg
represented
as a graph.

The seven bridges of Konigsberg

The seven bridges of Konigsberg
represented as a graph

A mathematician named Leonhard Euler used a graph to prove that this was impossible. In the seven bridges problem, one node has five bridges leading to it (5 degrees) while the other three nodes only have three bridges leading to it (3 degrees). Euler proved that the only way you could cross every bridge exactly once was if a graph had, at the most, two nodes with an odd number of bridges (degrees), and each odd-numbered degree node had to be the starting and ending point.

Although solving a problem of walking across a bridge exactly once might seem trivial, knowing how to solve this problem can help design truck or airplane routes as efficiently as possible.

Finding the shortest path through a graph

After using Euler's proof to design a graph that can be traversed in a single path, graph theory can now help you find the shortest path through that graph.

This problem, dubbed the Chinese Postman problem after the Chinese mathematician Mei-Ko Kuan, involves finding the shortest route a postman can travel to visit every node in a graph.

The answer to this problem can help airlines choose the shortest routes for each airplane route to visit multiple cities. The shorter the route, the less fuel needed and the lower the operating costs. Another use for the Chinese Postman problem is finding the most efficient way to route e-mail from one computer to another. In both cases, one node in the graph is the starting point and a different node is the ending point.

A related problem, dubbed the Traveling Salesman problem, takes this one step further by finding the shortest round-trip route through a graph where the same node is both the starting and ending point. In this case, the shortest route through a graph may not necessarily be the shortest round-trip route to return to the same starting point.

Both the Traveling Salesman and the Chinese Postman problem can get more complicated with a weighted or directed graph. A directed graph may restrict movement in one direction, such as traveling through one-way streets in a city, whereas a weighted graph can make one route longer than two shorter routes combined. Adding in directed and weighted graphs can alter the best solution.

If you ever looked up directions on a map Web site such as MapQuest, you've used a graph to find the most efficient way from one location to another.

Connecting nodes in a graph

Another use for graphs involves *topological graph theory.* This problem is highlighted by the Three Cottage problem with three cottages needing to connect to the gas, water, and electricity companies, but their lines can't cross each other. (It's impossible, by the way.)

Connecting lines in a graph without crossing is a problem that circuit board designers face in the placement of chips. Another example of eliminating intersections involves transportation designs, such as the design of highways or railroad tracks.

Creating Trees

Graphs typically represent a chaotic arrangement of data with little or no structure. To give graphs some form of organization, computer scientists have created special graphs dubbed *trees.* Like a graph, a tree consists of nodes and edges, but unlike a graph, a tree organizes data in a hierarchy, as shown in Figure 5-5.

A tree arranges a graph in a hierarchy with a single node appearing at the top (or the *root node*) and additional nodes appearing connected underneath (or *internal nodes*). If a node has no additional nodes connected underneath, those nodes are *leaf nodes,* as shown in Figure 5-6.

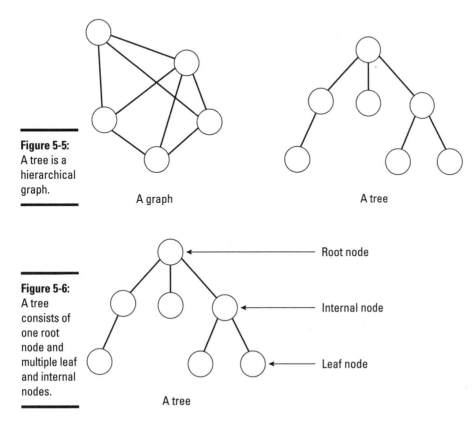

Figure 5-5:
A tree is a hierarchical graph.

A graph   A tree

Figure 5-6:
A tree consists of one root node and multiple leaf and internal nodes.

Root node

Internal node

Leaf node

A tree

Ordered trees

A tree can store information at random in its different nodes, which is dubbed an *unordered tree*. However, the tree is already in the form of a hierarchy, so it only makes sense to take advantage of this built-in structure and create an *ordered tree*.

An ordered tree provides a distinct beginning node (the *root node*) with additional nodes organized in a hierarchy. Such a hierarchy can store and show relationships of a corporate management team or the spread of a flu epidemic through different cities. As a result, ordered trees are a common data structure used to both model and organize data.

One common use for ordered trees involves storing data. Under each root node, you can have 26 internal nodes that each represent a single letter of the alphabet from A to Z. Under each of these letter nodes, you can have multiple nodes that contain the actual data, as shown in Figure 5-7.

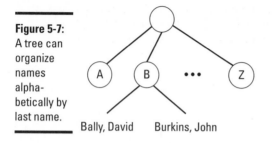

Figure 5-7:
A tree can organize names alpha- betically by last name.

Bally, David   Burkins, John

To save the name *David Bally,* the computer stores the name under the B node. To save the name *John Burkins,* the computer also stores this name under the B node. To determine whether to store this new name before or after any existing data, the computer examines the data and sorts it alpha- betically. In this way, the tree data structure not only stores data, but sorts and organizes it as well.

If you had a long list of names stored in an array or a collection, finding a name would require searching through the entire array or collection. How- ever, if that same list of names is stored in a tree, a name would be much simpler to find because you'd only need to look at the first letter of a person's last name to find where it might be stored.

So if you want to find the name *John Bally,* start at the B node and ignore any data stored under the other nodes. This makes searching and retrieving data much faster than other types of data structures, which is why trees are so commonly used in databases.

Binary trees

A variation of an ordered tree is a *binary tree.* Unlike an ordinary tree, every node in a binary tree has at the most two nodes connected underneath. To sort data, the left node contains values less than its parent node whereas the right node contains values greater than its parent node, as shown in Figure 5-8. By limiting each node to a maximum of two connected nodes, binary trees make searching and sorting data fast and efficient.

Figure 5-8:
Binary trees store and sort data by value.

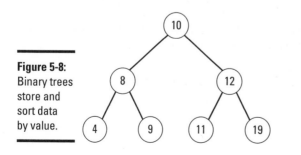

For example, an ordinary tree allows each node to have multiple nodes underneath. As a result, the more data an ordinary tree stores, the more nodes that can appear directly underneath a single node, as shown in Figure 5-9.

Figure 5-9:
An ordinary tree is more difficult to search than a binary tree.

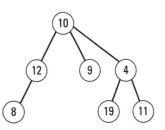

To find the number 11 in a sorted binary tree, you have to search three nodes.

To find the number 11 in an unordered, non-binary tree means having to search every node.

To find the number 11 in an ordered binary tree is simple. Start with the root (top) node and compare the number 11 to the root node value (10). Because the number you want to find is greater than the root node, you'd branch to the right. At this next node (12), the computer repeats the process and determines that 11 is less than 12, so it branches to the left node, which is where it finds the number 11.

Searching through a sorted binary tree is simple, especially when compared to an unordered tree. Because an unordered tree can scatter data anywhere, searching an unordered tree means methodically searching each node, one by one, until you find the data you want. In a large unordered tree, this search time can be slow and inefficient.

Ordered binary trees are one of the most common tree data structures used in many types of programs, such as databases.

B-trees

Another variation of a tree is a *B-tree*. The two main features of a B-tree are

✦ All nodes can only have a fixed number of other nodes underneath it (such as three nodes compared to a binary tree, which has a maximum of two nodes).

✦ All leaf nodes remain at the same level or depth of the tree, as shown in Figure 5-10.

Book III
Chapter 5

Graphs and Trees

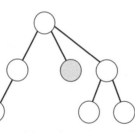

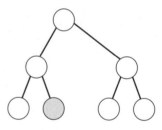

Figure 5-10:
In a B-tree, all leaf nodes appear at the same level.

In an ordinary tree, leaf nodes can appear on different levels.

In a B-tree, all leaf nodes appear on the same level.

When you add or subtract data, the binary tree constantly adjusts to keep all leaf nodes at the same level. Keeping all leaf nodes at the same level ensures that searching for some data (stored farther down a tree) won't take a long time compared to searching for other data (stored closer to the root node of the tree).

A variation of a B-tree is a B+ tree. The main difference is that a B-tree can store data in all its nodes. Because some nodes appear closer to the root node than others, this makes searching for data closer to the root node fast but searching for data farther from the root node slower in comparison.

A B+ tree only stores data in its leaf nodes and connects all leaf nodes together as a linked list. Because all leaf nodes are the same distance from the root node, this makes searching for any type of data equal.

Microsoft Windows and Linux are two operating systems that use B+ trees for keeping track of files on a disk.

Taking Action on Trees

Trees are flexible data structures because they organize data and allow fast retrieval of that data. Some of the different actions you can perform on trees include

✦ **Searching for a specific item**

✦ **Adding a new node or a sub-tree**

✦ **Deleting data or a sub-tree**

Traversing a tree

When you store data in an array or a collection, that data is stored in a line so you can search the entire data structure by starting at one end and examining each data chunk one by one until you get to the end. However, trees are different because they offer multiple branches.

To search a tree, the computer must examine multiple nodes exactly once, which is known as *traversing a tree*. Four popular ways to search a tree, as shown in Figure 5-11, include

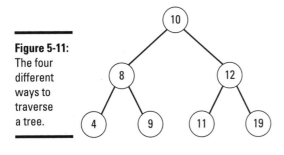

Figure 5-11: The four different ways to traverse a tree.

Preorder: 10, 8, 4, 9, 12, 11, 19

In-order: 4, 8, 9, 10, 11, 12, 19

Postorder: 4, 9, 8, 11, 19, 12, 10

Level order: 10, 8, 12, 4, 9, 11, 19

✦ **Preorder**

✦ **In-order**

✦ **Postorder**

✦ **Level order**

Preorder traversal

Preorder traversal starts at the top of a tree (the *root node*) and then traverses the left nodes. When it reaches a leaf node, it backtracks and goes down the right nodes, as follows:

1. **Visit the root node.**

2. **Traverse the left sub-tree in preorder.**

3. **Traverse the right sub-tree in preorder.**

In-order traversal

When traversing an ordered binary tree, the in-order traversal retrieves data in order by following these steps:

1. **Traverse the left sub-tree using in-order.**

2. **Visit the root node.**

3. **Traverse the right sub-tree by using in-order.**

Postorder traversal

Postorder traversal traverses the left and right sub-trees first and then visits the root node, as follows:

1. **Traverse the left sub-tree in postorder.**

2. **Traverse the right sub-tree in postorder.**

3. **Visit the root node.**

Level order traversal

Level order traversal starts at the top level of a tree and traverses the row of nodes on the same level from left to right. Then it drops to the next lower level and repeats the process all over again.

When writing actual code to traverse a tree, it's often easier to write a recursive subprogram that calls itself and traverses a successively smaller part of the tree (sub-tree) until it finally stops.

Adding new data

Adding data to a linear structure, like a collection or a stack, is straightforward because the data structure simply gets bigger. Adding data to a tree is slightly more complicated because you can add new data at the end of a tree (on one of its leaf nodes) or anywhere in the middle of the tree.

In an unordered tree, you can insert data anywhere, but in an ordered binary tree, inserting new data means sorting the data at the same time, as shown in Figure 5-12.

The order that you store data determines the position of that data in a tree because newly added data gets added based on the existing data's values.

Deleting data

Deleting data from a tree can cause special problems because after deleting data, you may need to rearrange any nodes that were underneath the deleted data, as shown in Figure 5-13.

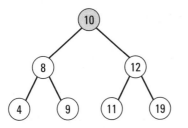

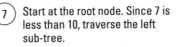

Start at the root node. Since 7 is less than 10, traverse the left sub-tree.

Compare 7 with the first node on the left sub-tree. Since 7 is less than 8, traverse the left sub-tree.

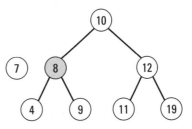

Figure 5-12: Inserting new data in an ordered binary tree.

Compare 7 with the next node on the left sub-tree. Since 7 is greater than 4, add the 7 node to the right of the 4 node.

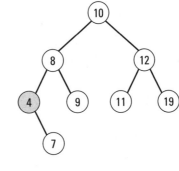

If you delete data and immediately add it back to the tree again, the tree looks different because reinserting the data sorts and organizes it based on the existing data. So if you delete the 12 node and immediately add it back again, it now appears as a left node under the 19 node.

Pruning and grafting sub-trees

A *sub-tree* is a smaller tree, such as part of an existing tree. Rather than delete a single node, it's possible to delete an entire sub-tree, which is known as *pruning a tree,* as shown in Figure 5-14.

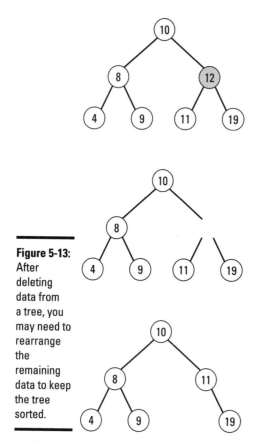

Figure 5-13: After deleting data from a tree, you may need to rearrange the remaining data to keep the tree sorted.

After pruning a sub-tree, there may be more than one way to rearrange the remaining nodes.

Adding or grafting a sub-tree to an existing tree can cause problems if the sub-tree data contains different values than the original tree. In that case, you can't just graft the sub-tree to the existing tree; you have to rearrange the data in both the tree and the grafted sub-tree to sort data once more, as shown in Figure 5-15.

Tree data structures are most useful for storing and sorting data, such as for databases. However, tree data structures are also handy for creating artificial intelligence in games, such as chess.

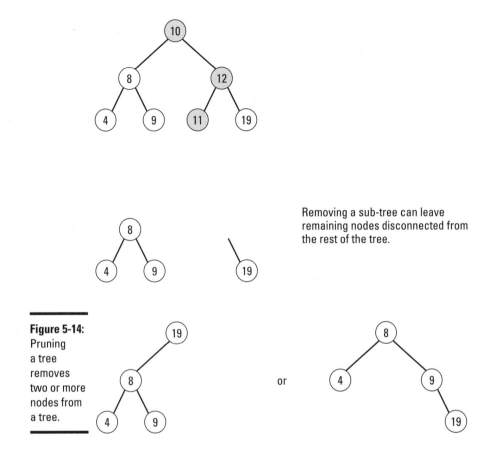

Removing a sub-tree can leave remaining nodes disconnected from the rest of the tree.

Figure 5-14:
Pruning a tree removes two or more nodes from a tree.

or

The computer might use a tree data structure to represent all possible moves when the root node represents one possible move. Then each alternating level in the tree represents the possible human responses and the best possible computer responses, as shown in Figure 5-16.

By organizing possible moves in a tree, a computer can determine the best possible move to make that will give its human opponent the worst possible moves later. This strategy is *min-max* — the computer *minimizes* the human's best possible moves and *maximizes* its own best moves.

Despite having to create trees out of other data structures (such as linked lists) and being more complicated to create and manage than other data structures, trees are one of the most useful and flexible data structures available.

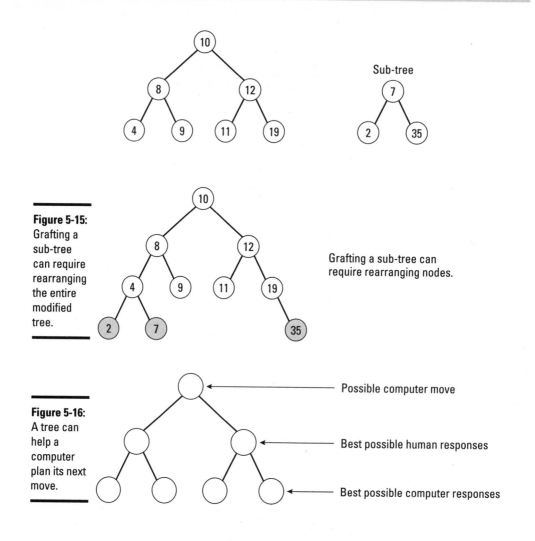

Sub-tree

Figure 5-15:
Grafting a
sub-tree
can require
rearranging
the entire
modified
tree.

Grafting a sub-tree can
require rearranging nodes.

Figure 5-16:
A tree can
help a
computer
plan its next
move.

Possible computer move

Best possible human responses

Best possible computer responses

Book IV

Algorithms

The 5th Wave   By Rich Tennant

"This program's really helped me learn a new language. It's so buggy I'm constantly talking with overseas service reps."

Contents at a Glance

Chapter 1: Sorting Algorithms

In This Chapter

✔ Using bubble, selection, and insertion sorts

✔ Using shell, heap, merge, and quick sorts

✔ Comparing different sorting algorithms

*E*very program handles data (numeric or text). Besides saving data, most programs also need to organize that data in some way, which involves sorting that data in a specific order, such as alphabetically or numerically. A database needs to sort names alphabetically by last name or by sales region whereas a video game needs to sort the top ten highest scores.

Despite the simple idea behind sorting a list of names or numbers, sorting is practically a field of computer science in itself. Computer scientists constantly study different ways to sort through data to find the fastest, most efficient method possible. Each of these different sorting methods is a *sorting algorithm.*

An algorithm is a fancy term for a method of doing something, so a sorting algorithm is a specific method for telling the computer how to sort data. The reason computer scientists keep creating and studying sorting algorithms is because no single sorting algorithm is best for all purposes.

Some sorting algorithms are easy to create but work slowly. Other sorting algorithms are much harder to create but work much faster. Ironically, some sorting algorithms work horribly when sorting a small number of items, such as a dozen numbers, but work quickly when sorting thousands of items.

Four factors for considering sorting algorithms include

✦ **Ease of implementation**

✦ **Speed**

✦ **Memory requirements**

✦ **Stability**

Ease of implementation defines how complicated the sorting algorithm is to implement in any programming language. Some sorting algorithms are easy to write but slow in actual use. Other sorting algorithms are much harder to write but perform much faster.

Speed measures how fast the algorithm can sort data of different sizes. Some sorting algorithms work quickly with small lists but slow down dramatically when dealing with larger lists. Other sorting algorithms work quickly when a list is mostly sorted but slow to a crawl when working with completely unsorted lists.

Memory requirements define how much memory the sorting algorithm needs to run. Some sorting algorithms can accept and sort data while they receive the data, which is an *online algorithm*. (An *offline algorithm* has to wait to receive the complete set of data before it can even start the sorting process.) Sorting algorithms that use recursion (see Book II, Chapter 6) may be easy to implement and fast but can require lots of memory to sort large amounts of data.

Another factor that determines a sorting algorithm's memory requirements is whether the algorithm is an *in-place algorithm*. An in-place algorithm can sort data by using the existing data structure that holds the data. For example, if you have an array of numbers, an in-place algorithm can sort the data in that array without needing a separate data structure to hold the data temporarily.

Stability refers to whether a sorting algorithm preserves the order of identical data. Suppose you had a list of first and last names, such as John Smith and Mary Smith, and the name John Smith appears at the beginning of a list and Mary Smith appears at the end. A stable sorting algorithm sorts both names and keeps John Smith ahead of Mary Smith, but an unstable algorithm moves Mary Smith ahead of John Smith. (Out of all the sorting algorithms presented in this chapter, heap sort is the only unstable algorithm.)

Ultimately, there's no perfect sorting algorithm; however, a trade-off in size, speed, and ease of implementation finds the best sorting algorithm.

Using Bubble Sort

The simplest way to sort any amount of data is to start at the beginning and compare the first two adjacent items. So if you need to sort a list of numbers, you compare the first number with the second number. If the first number is bigger, you swap its place with the second number. If the second number is bigger, you don't do anything at all.

After comparing the first two items, you move down to comparing the second and third items, and so on. Repetitively comparing two adjacent items is the basic idea behind the bubble sort algorithm, as shown in Figure 1-1. The bubble sort algorithm gets its name because small values tend to *bubble up* to the top.

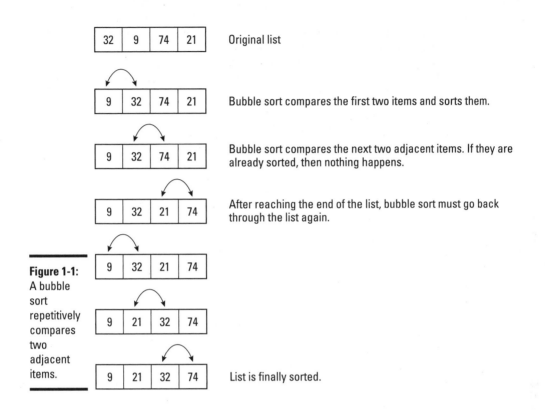

Figure 1-1:
A bubble sort repetitively compares two adjacent items.

32 | 9 | 74 | 21   Original list

9 | 32 | 74 | 21   Bubble sort compares the first two items and sorts them.

9 | 32 | 74 | 21   Bubble sort compares the next two adjacent items. If they are already sorted, then nothing happens.

9 | 32 | 21 | 74   After reaching the end of the list, bubble sort must go back through the list again.

9 | 32 | 21 | 74

9 | 21 | 32 | 74

9 | 21 | 32 | 74   List is finally sorted.

Basically the bubble sort algorithm works like this:

1. **Compare two adjacent items.**
2. **Swap the two items if necessary.**
3. **Repeat Steps 1 and 2 with each pair of adjacent items.**
4. **Repeat Steps 1–3 to examine the entire list again until no swapping occurs and then the list is sorted.**

Although the bubble sort algorithm is easy to implement, it's also the slowest and most inefficient algorithm because it must examine an entire list multiple times. For sorting a small list of pre-sorted data, the bubble sort algorithm works efficiently. For sorting large lists of unsorted data, any other sorting algorithm is much faster than the bubble sort algorithm, as shown in Figure 1-2.

**Book IV
Chapter 1**

Sorting Algorithms

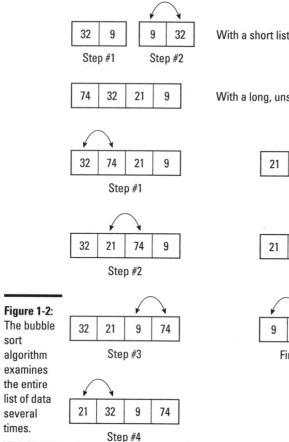

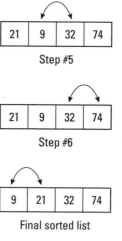

With a short list, bubble sort can work quickly.

With a long, unsorted list, bubble sort takes too much time.

Figure 1-2:
The bubble sort algorithm examines the entire list of data several times.

Using Selection Sort

Another simple way to sort a list is to search the entire list until you find the smallest value. Then move that value to the front of the list. Now repeat the process all over again, skipping the first item. By repetitively searching for the smallest item and moving it to the front of the list, the selection sort algorithm can eventually sort an entire list, as shown in Figure 1-3.

The selection sort algorithm works like this:

1. **Find the smallest item in a list.**

2. **Swap this value with the value currently at the front of the list.**

3. **Repeat Steps 1 and 2 with the current size of the list minus one (list size = list size − 1).**

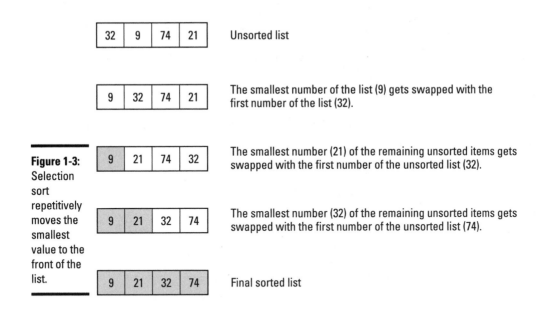

Figure 1-3: Selection sort repetitively moves the smallest value to the front of the list.

| 32 | 9 | 74 | 21 | Unsorted list |

The smallest number of the list (9) gets swapped with the first number of the list (32).

The smallest number (21) of the remaining unsorted items gets swapped with the first number of the unsorted list (32).

The smallest number (32) of the remaining unsorted items gets swapped with the first number of the unsorted list (74).

Final sorted list

For sorting small lists, selection sort is fast, but for sorting large lists, selection sort needs too much time progressively examining smaller sections of a list. Despite this drawback with sorting large lists, selection sort is popular because it's simple to implement.

Using Insertion Sort

The insertion sort algorithm acts like a cross between the bubble sort and the selection sort algorithm. Like bubble sort, insertion sort examines two adjacent values. Like selection sort, insertion sort moves smaller values from their current location to an earlier position near the front of the list.

The insertion sort algorithm works like this:

1. **Start with the second item in the list.**

2. **Compare this second item with the first item. If the second value is smaller, swap places in the list.**

3. **Compare the next item in the list and insert it in the proper place in relation to the previously sorted items.**

4. **Repeat Step 3 until the entire list is sorted.**

The main difference between insertion sort and selection sort is that the selection sort only swaps two adjacent values whereas insertion sort can move a value to a non-adjacent location, as shown in Figure 1-4.

**Book IV
Chapter 1**

Sorting Algorithms

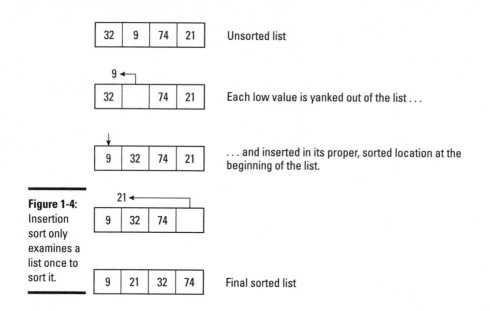

Figure 1-4: Insertion sort only examines a list once to sort it.

Unsorted list

Each low value is yanked out of the list . . .

. . . and inserted in its proper, sorted location at the beginning of the list.

Final sorted list

One major advantage of the insertion sort algorithm is that it only needs to examine an entire list once to sort it. In comparison, bubble sort must repetitively examine the entire list multiple times, and selection sort must repetitively examine progressively smaller lists multiple times. As a result, the insertion sort algorithm is much faster while being easy to implement as well.

Using Shell Sort

To speed up the performance of the insertion sort algorithm, Donald Shell, a computer scientist, created a variation of the insertion sort algorithm dubbed *shell sort.*

One problem with insertion sort is that it must examine one value at a time. In a long list, this can take a long time. Shell sort works by dividing a long list into several smaller ones and then performing an insertion sort on each smaller list. After each smaller list gets sorted, the shell sort algorithm uses an ordinary insertion sort to sort the entire list one last time. By this time, the longer list is nearly sorted so this final insertion sort occurs quickly, as shown in Figure 1-5.

Basically, shell sort works like this:

1. **Divide a long list into multiple smaller lists.**

2. **Arrange each list in a grid or table consisting of rows and columns.**

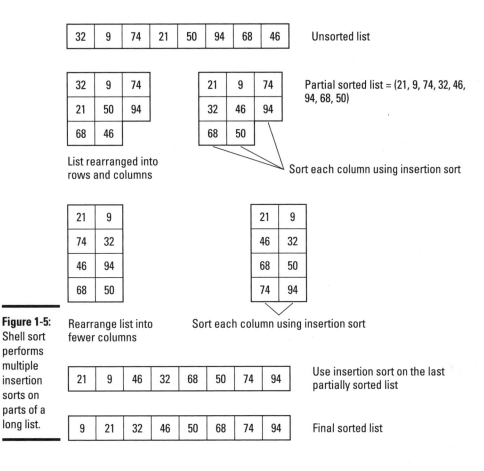

Figure 1-5: Shell sort performs multiple insertion sorts on parts of a long list.

Each row represents the original, unsorted list. Each column holds one item in the list.

3. **Use an insertion sort to sort the columns.**

4. **Repeat Steps 1–3 with progressively smaller lists until only a single list is left to be sorted with the insertion sort algorithm.**

The shell sort algorithm isn't necessarily a different sorting algorithm. Instead, shell sort is a way to use the insertion sort algorithm more efficiently.

Using Heap Sort

The heap sort algorithm works by using a separate data structure — a *heap* (which is a binary tree data structure). The highest value gets stored in the root node while the remaining values get tossed on the heap.

Book IV
Chapter 1

Sorting Algorithms

The two criteria for storing data in a heap are that

✦ **Every parent node must contain a value greater than either of its child nodes.**

✦ **The tree must fill each level before adding nodes to the next lower level.**

If there aren't enough nodes to fill out an entire level, the nodes must fill out as much of the last level as possible, starting from the left.

Figure 1-6 shows a valid heap and two invalid heaps.

The heap sort algorithm works like this:

1. **Store an unsorted list in a heap data structure, which sorts data so the highest values appear near the top of the heap.**

2. **Yank off the highest value stored in the root node and store this value as the end of the sorted list.**

3. **Re-sort the heap so the highest values appear near the top of the heap.**

4. **Repeat Steps 2 and 3 until all values have been removed from the heap and sorted.**

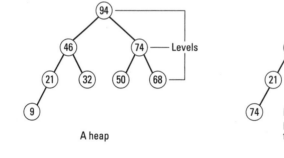

A heap

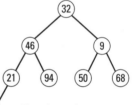

Not a heap since not every parent node value is greater than its child node values.

Figure 1-6:
Valid and invalid heap binary trees.

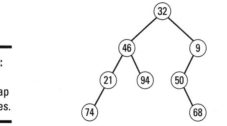

Not a heap since earlier levels are not full.

Heap sort dumps an unsorted list of data into the heap, always making sure the highest value appears in the root node. Then this highest value in the root node gets stored at the end of the list. Now the heap rearranges its values once more, putting the highest remaining value in the root node, repeating the process all over again, as shown in Figure 1-7.

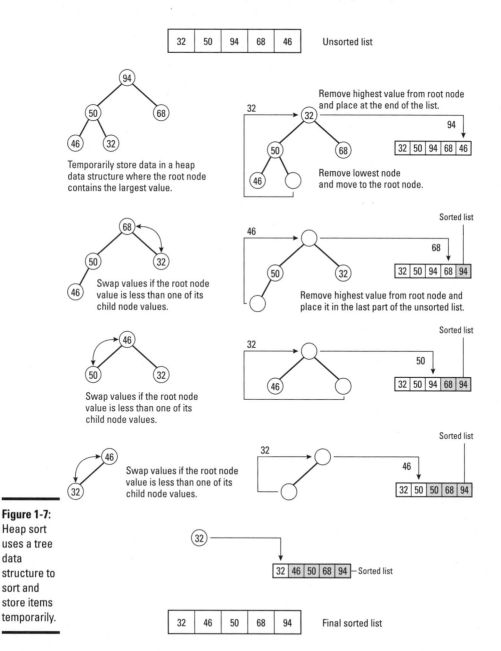

Figure 1-7: Heap sort uses a tree data structure to sort and store items temporarily.

Initially, the heap sort algorithm may seem complicated because you need to create a heap data structure, copy and sort values among nodes, and delete nodes while you remove values and store them back in a sorted list. Although you can create a heap data structure by using a linked list, a much simpler method is to create a heap data structure by using an array, as shown in Figure 1-8.

The first array element represents the root node, the next two elements represent the child nodes of the root, and so on. Rather than manipulate a linked list as a heap, it's much simpler to rearrange values stored in an array, as shown in Figure 1-9. Because arrays are easy to implement in any programming language, the heap sort algorithm is also easy to implement. Although slightly more complicated than bubble sort or selection sort, the heap sort algorithm offers faster performance.

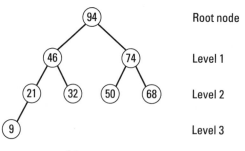

Root node

Level 1

Level 2

Level 3

A heap

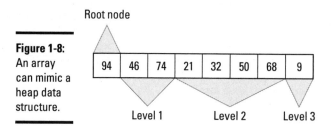

Root node

Figure 1-8:
An array
can mimic a
heap data
structure.

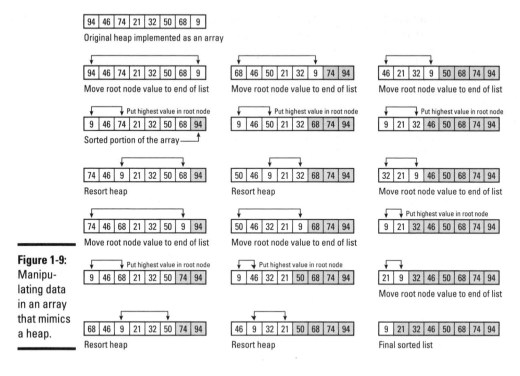

Figure 1-9:
Manipulating data in an array that mimics a heap.

Using Merge Sort

The merge sort algorithm works on the principle that it's easier to sort a small list than a large list. So merge sort breaks a large list of data into two or more smaller lists. Then it sorts each small list and smashes or merges them together. This merged list is still partially unsorted. Because it's easier to sort a partially sorted list than a completely unsorted list, the merge sort algorithm sorts this partially sorted list, which ultimately sorts the entire list quickly.

The merge sort algorithm works like this:

1. **Divide a large list in half.**

2. **Divide each smaller list in half until each small list consists only of one value.**

3. **Sort this single value with a neighboring single value list.**

4. **Merge these smaller, sorted lists into larger lists.**

5. **Sort each merged list.**

6. **Repeat Steps 4 and 5 until the entire list is sorted.**

Figure 1-10 shows how merge sort works.

Because the merge sort algorithm successively divides a list in half, merge sort needs to create temporary data structures (such as arrays) to store data while it divides and merges values. When sorting a small list, creating a temporary data structure is simple, but when sorting a large list, creating a temporary large data structure can gobble up memory.

In Perl 5.8, the default sorting algorithm is merge sort. In earlier versions of Perl, the default sorting algorithm was quick sort.

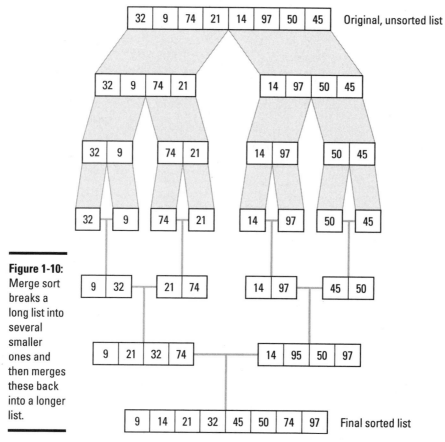

Figure 1-10: Merge sort breaks a long list into several smaller ones and then merges these back into a longer list.

Using Quick Sort

The quick sort algorithm gets its name because it's generally the fastest sorting algorithm in most cases. Like the merge sort algorithm, the quick sort algorithm works on the principle that it's easier and faster to sort a small list than a large list, so quick sort divides a large list into two parts.

To divide a list into two parts, quick sort picks a value (or a *pivot*) from the list:

✦ **Any value less than the pivot goes into one list.**

✦ **Any value greater than the pivot goes into the second list.**

Quick sort repetitively divides each list into two parts until it creates two lists that contain only one value each. Then the algorithm sorts these two values and starts combining the multiple smaller lists to create larger sorted lists until the entire list ultimately gets sorted, as shown in Figure 1-11.

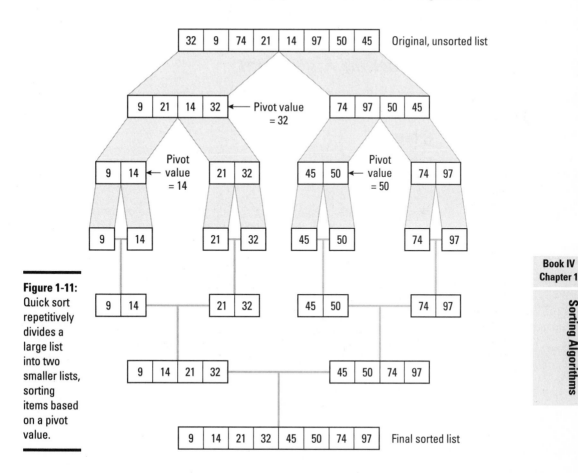

Figure 1-11: Quick sort repetitively divides a large list into two smaller lists, sorting items based on a pivot value.

The quick sort algorithm works nearly identically to merge sort, but quick sort uses a pivot value to pre-sort values into two different lists. Sorting values by this pivot value alone makes quick sort generally faster than merge sort.

Basically, the quick sort algorithm works likes this:

1. **Pick a pivot value from the list.**
2. **Divide the list in two, placing values less than the pivot value in the first list and values greater than the pivot value in the second list.**
3. **Repeat Steps 1 and 2 until the lists contain only one item.**
4. **Combine these smaller lists into a larger, sorted list.**

 The key to speeding up the quick sort algorithm is to choose the proper pivot for dividing each list. The pivot value must be a middle value in a list. Notice that the merge sort algorithm (see Figure 1-10) still sorts values through every step whereas pivot values make the quick sort algorithm (see Figure 1-11) sort the entire list in far fewer steps.

Comparing Sorting Algorithms

To compare the speed of sorting algorithms, computer scientists consider the following scenarios:

✦ **Best-case**

✦ **Worst-case**

✦ **Average-case**

A *best-case scenario* measures the speed of different algorithms sorting a list of values that are already completely sorted. The *worst-case scenario* measures the speed of different algorithms sorting a list that's completely unsorted. The *average-case* scenario measures the speed of different algorithms sorting random values in a list.

To measure the speed and efficiency of an algorithm, computer scientists measure how much time an algorithm needs to run based on different sizes of input, which is designated by the letter (n). A small value of (n) means the input is short whereas a large value of (n) means the input is large.

An algorithm's *efficiency* (how fast it runs) is thus based on its input size (n). In mathematical terms, this is referred to as an order of (n). If an algorithm runs at the same speed no matter how much data it receives, it's said to run at constant time, which can be written in Big-O notation as $O(1)$.

If an algorithm's speed depends directly on the number of items it receives, it's said to run at a linear time, written as O(n). Some common Big-O notations for different algorithms include

✦ **O(logn):** Logarithmic time

✦ **O(n^c):** Polynomial

✦ **O(c^n):** Exponential

✦ **O(n!):** Factorial

Describing algorithm efficiency as its order is known as Big-O notation because the letter O is always capitalized.

Computer scientists have already calculated the Big-O values of different sorting algorithms. Table 1-1 gives different Big-O values for different sorting algorithms for the best-case, worst-case, and average-case scenarios.

To compare the efficiency of different algorithms, plug in different values for (n).

Table 1-1	Comparison of Different Sorting Algorithms		
Algorithm	*Average*	*Best*	*Worst*
Bubble sort	O(n^2)	O(n^2)	O(n^2)
Selection sort	O(n^2)	O(n^2)	O(n^2)
Insertion sort	O(n^2)	O(n)	O(n^2)
Heap sort	O(n*log(n))	O(n*log(n))	O(n*log(n))
Merge sort	O(n*log(n))	O(n*log(n))	O(n*log(n))
Quick sort	O(n*log(n))	O(n*log(n))	O(n^2)

For example, the Big-O notation for the bubble sort algorithm is O(n^2). To sort one item, the bubble sort algorithm's efficiency is O(1^2) or O(1). To sort five items, the bubble sort's efficiency is O(5^2) or O(25). The higher the Big-O value, the slower and less efficient the algorithm is, which means that the more items the bubble sort algorithm needs to sort, the slower it runs.

The quick sort algorithm has a Big-O notation of O(n*log(n)). To see how quick sort compares to bubble sort when sorting five items, plug in a value of 5 for (n), such as O(5*log(5)), O(5*0.70), or O(3.5).

**Book IV
Chapter 1**

Sorting Algorithms

With the bubble sort algorithm, the more items needed to sort (n), the higher its Big-O value. To sort five items, the bubble sort algorithm's Big-O notation is O(25), which is much larger than the quick sort algorithm's similar Big-O notation of O(3.5). The difference in these two values can give you a rough idea how much slower bubble sort works compared to quick sort when sorting the same number of items.

Table 1-1 shows that some algorithms, such as bubble sort, behave the same in best-case, worst-case, and average-case scenarios. That's because the bubble sort algorithm repetitively examines and sorts a list whether or not the values need to be sorted.

The insertion sort algorithm is unique in that it runs the fastest in a best-case (already-sorted) scenario. Although the quick sort algorithm is considered the fastest, notice that in a worst-case scenario, it's actually one of the slowest algorithms. If your data will be completely unsorted, avoid using the quick sort algorithm.

The best sorting algorithm is the one that's the fastest for sorting your type of data. If you need to write a program that regularly needs to sort random data (average-case scenario), you might choose one sorting algorithm whereas if you need to sort completely unsorted data (worst-case scenario), you'd probably choose a different algorithm. The fastest sorting algorithm always depends partially on the sorted (or unsorted) data that the algorithm needs to manipulate.

The three fastest sorting algorithms are *heap sort, merge sort,* and *quick sort.* Although quick sort is considered the fastest of the three algorithms, merge sort is faster in worst-case scenarios.

Chapter 2: Searching Algorithms

In This Chapter

✔ Conducting sequential and binary tree searches

✔ Using an index

✔ Comparing search algorithms

*O*ne of the most common functions of a computer program is searching. A database needs to search through names and addresses, a word processor needs to search through text, and even a computer chess game needs to search through a library of moves to find the best one.

Because searching is such an important part of computer programming, computer scientists have developed a variety of algorithms to search for data. When searching for data, the main limitation is time. Given enough time, any search algorithm can find what you want, but there's a big difference between finding data in five seconds or five hours.

The time a search algorithm takes is always related to the amount of data to search, which is the *search space.* The larger the search space, the slower the search algorithm. If you only need to search a small search space, even a simple and slow search algorithm is fast enough.

The two main categories of search algorithms are

✦ **Uninformed (or *brute-force*)**

✦ **Informed (or *heuristic*)**

Uninformed, or brute-force, search algorithms work by simply examining the entire search space, which is like losing your car keys in your apartment and searching every apartment in the entire building. Eventually, you find your keys, but it may take a long time to do it.

Informed, or heuristic, search algorithms work by selectively examining the most likely parts of the search space. This is like losing your car keys in your apartment but only examining the bedroom where you last saw your car keys. By using knowledge of the search space, informed search algorithms can speed up a search algorithm by eliminating obvious parts of the search space that don't contain the data you want to find.

Uninformed (or brute-force) search algorithms are much simpler and faster to write in any programming language, but the price you pay may be slower searching speed. Informed (or heuristic) search algorithms always take more time to write, but the speed advantage may be worth it especially if your program needs to search data on a regular basis. One problem with informed (or heuristic) search algorithms is that they often require that the data be sorted first or stored in a data structure that requires more complicated traversing through all items, such as a tree data structure.

The perfect search algorithm is *easy* for you to implement in your favorite programming language while also being *fast* enough for your program.

Sequential Search

A *sequential search* is an example of an uninformed search algorithm because it searches data one item at a time starting from the beginning and searching through to the end. In the best-case scenario, a sequential search finds data stored as the first element in a data structure. In the worst-case scenario, a sequential search has to search an entire data structure to find the last item stored, as shown in Figure 2-1.

Figure 2-1: The speed of sequential search depends directly on the size of the data to be searched.

A small list is faster to search than a large list.

To speed up sequential searching, you can add simple heuristics. Some popular ways to speed up sequential searching include

✦ **Backward or forward searching**

✦ **Block searching**

✦ **Binary searching**

✦ **Interpolation searching**

Backward or forward searching

If the data is sorted, you can make the sequential search start looking through a data structure from either the beginning or the end. So if you need to search an array that contains numbers organized in ascending order from 1 to 100, searching for the number 89 will be faster if you start at the end of the array, as shown in Figure 2-2.

Figure 2-2:
Sequential search can be made faster by searching from either the front or end of a data structure.

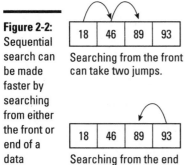

Searching from the front can take two jumps.

Searching from the end can be faster is the data is near the end of the list.

The backward or forward searching algorithm works like this:

1. **Compare the value to find the number of items stored in a sorted data structure.**

2. **If the data to find is in the first half of the data structure, start at the front of the data structure; otherwise, start at the end.**

3. **Search sequentially until the data is found or confirmed not to exist in the data structure.**

Searching either backward or forward also has an advantage when searching through data structures that organize data by age. If data is stored in a queue, the oldest data appears at the end, and the newest data appears at the beginning. So if you can identify the age of the data you want to find, you could speed up the search for knowing whether to start at the beginning of the queue or the end.

**Book IV
Chapter 2**

**Searching
Algorithms**

Block searching

Another technique to speed up sequential searching on sorted data is jump, or block searching. Rather than search one item at a time, this method jumps over a fixed number of items (such as five) and then examines the last item:

+ **If this last item is greater than the value the algorithm is trying to find, the algorithm starts searching backward.**

+ **If this last item is less than the value the algorithm is trying to find, the algorithm jumps another block forward, as shown in Figure 2-3.**

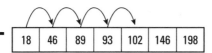

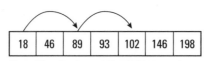

Figure 2-3: Jump, or block, searching can speed up a sequential search on sorted data.

Searching for the number 102 takes four jumps in a normal sequential search.

Searching for the number 102 can only take two jumps in a block search.

The block searching algorithm works like this:

1. **Jump ahead a fixed number of items (a *block*).**

2. **Compare the last value of the block:**

- If this value is less than the data to find, search sequentially within the block.

- Otherwise, jump to the end of a new block and repeat Step 2.

The basic idea behind block searching is to skip ahead through a sorted list of data and then slow down when it gets closer to that data. This is like looking through a telephone book for the name Winston Smith by skipping every ten pages until you reach the S section and then searching sequentially until you find the name Smith and finally the name Winston Smith.

Block searching can work only with sorted data. If data isn't sorted, block searching can't work at all.

Binary searching

A variation of block searching is *binary searching,* which essentially uses a block half the size of the list. After dividing a list in half, the algorithm compares the last value of the first half of the list. If this value is smaller than the value it's trying to find, the algorithm knows to search the second list instead. Otherwise, it searches the first half of the list.

The algorithm repeatedly divides the list in half and searches only the list that contains the range of values it's trying to find. Eventually, the binary search finds the data, as shown in Figure 2-4.

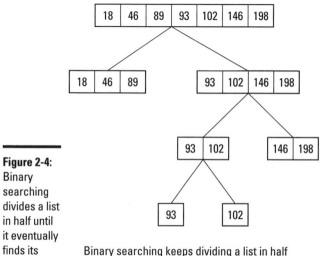

Figure 2-4: Binary searching divides a list in half until it eventually finds its data.

Binary searching keeps dividing a list in half until it eventually finds the data, such as finding the number 102.

The binary search algorithm works like this:

1. **Divide a sorted list in half.**

2. **Compare the last value of the first half of the list.**

   If this last value is less than the desired value, search this half of the list. Otherwise, search the other half of the list.

3. **Repeat Steps 1 and 2 until the desired value is found or confirmed not to exist.**

Interpolation searching

Instead of jumping a fixed number of items, like block searching, or dividing a list in half, like binary searching, *interpolation searching* tries to guess the approximate location of data in a sorted list. After it jumps to the approximate location, the algorithm performs a normal sequential search, as shown in Figure 2-5.

Figure 2-5:
Interpolation searching tries to jump straight to the approximate location of the target data.

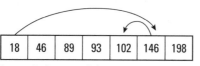

18	46	89	93	102	146	198

Interpolation search jumps as close to the target data as possible, and then searches sequentially.

Interpolation searching mimics the way a person might look up a name in a telephone book. If you're looking for the name Winston Smith, you jump straight to the S section. Then you slow down to look for the Smith name, and slow down even more to look for all Smith names whose first name begins with W until you find Winston Smith.

Although potentially faster than other forms of sequential searching, interpolation searching requires enough knowledge to jump as close to the desired data as possible. Because this might not always occur, interpolation searching isn't always faster than other forms of searching, such as binary searching.

Interpolation searching follows these steps:

1. **Jump to the approximate location of the target data in a sorted list.**

2. **Start searching sequentially until the desired data is found or confirmed not to exist.**

The key to interpolation searching relies on the computer accurately jumping to the position where the data is likely to be stored. One way of guessing the location of data is to use *Fibonacci numbers,* creating the *Fibonacci searching* technique.

Fibonacci numbers are a series of numbers that are calculated by adding the last two numbers in a series to determine the next number in the series. So the first Fibonacci number is 0, the second is 1, the third is 1 (0 + 1), the fourth is 2 (1 + 1), the fifth is 3 (1 + 2), the sixth is 5 (2 + 3), and so on like this:

0, 1, 1, 2, 3, 5, 8, 13, 21, 34, 55, and so on . . . .

Fibonacci numbers tend to occur in nature, such as measuring the branching of trees or the curves of waves. So the idea behind Fibonacci searching is rather than divide a list in half, like binary searching, Fibonacci searching divides a sorted list into progressively smaller lists, based on Fibonacci numbers, until it finally finds the data or confirms that the data doesn't exist. Surprisingly, this method works consistently faster than binary searching.

Fibonacci searching works like this, as shown in Figure 2-6:

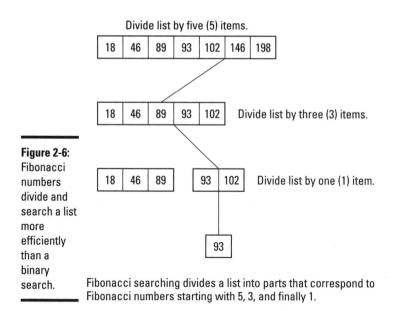

Figure 2-6: Fibonacci numbers divide and search a list more efficiently than a binary search.

Fibonacci searching divides a list into parts that correspond to Fibonacci numbers starting with 5, 3, and finally 1.

1. **Determine the size of the sorted list (dubbed *n*).**

2. **Find the largest Fibonacci number that's less than the size of the sorted list (dubbed *p*).**

3. **Examine the value stored at the pth location of the sorted list.**

If this value is the one you want to find, stop.

4. **If the value at this pth location is less than the data you're searching for, search the list to the right of the pth location. If the value at this pth location is greater than the data you're searching for, search the list to the left of the pth location.**

5. **Repeat Steps 1–4.**

Using Indexes

Imagine yourself trying to find a certain store in a large shopping mall. You could wander up and down the corridors and examine each store, one by one, which is like a sequential search. Even if you use the various sequential search tactics, like block searching, sequential searching can still take a long time.

Instead of searching each store sequentially, here's a faster way: Look at the mall directory, find the store you want, and then walk straight to that store. That's the difference between sequential searching and indexes. An index points you directly toward the item you want to find no matter how many items there may be. Indexes basically act like a shortcut to searching.

Creating an index

Indexes are similar to hash tables (see Book III, Chapter 3). The main difference is that a hash table calculates a unique value based on the total data stored whereas an index typically stores part of the data in a separate table that points to the rest of the data, as shown in Figure 2-7.

Indexes are most often used in databases. If you organize a list of data in rows and columns with each column representing a field (such as Name or Phone Number) and each row representing a record (that contains one person's name and phone number), an index can be as simple as a single column that consists of the data you're most likely to use for searching.

For example, if you have a database of names, addresses, and phone numbers, you probably spend more time looking up someone's phone number by looking up his last name. So you could use the last name field as an index. At the simplest level, an *index* is nothing more than an organized list of existing data, such as a list of last names organized alphabetically (see Figure 2-7).

If you create an index based on last names and you need to search by last name, an index can find your data faster. However, what if you want to search by phone number or city, but your index consists only of last names? In that case, you can create multiple indexes, one for each type of data.

102	→	John Smith	555-1462
148	→	Mary Adams	555-7001
152	→	Nancy Wiggins	555-9604
166	→	Travis Gullins	555-0147
170	→	Sam Perkins	555-8136
193	→	Gail Hall	555-8772

Hash table — A hash table converts data into a numeric value, which is then used to point to the actual data.

Adams	→	Mary	555-7001
Gullins	→	Travis	555-0147
Hall	→	Gail	555-8772
Perkins	→	Sam	555-8136
Smith	→	John	555-1462
Wiggins	→	Nancy	555-9604

Figure 2-7: Comparison of hash tables and indexes.

Index — An index uses part of the data to organize the rest of the data

Clustered and unclustered indexes

Here are two types of indexes — *clustered* and *unclustered*.

A *clustered* index sorts the actual data. If you have a list of names and addresses, a clustered index could sort the data by last name, which physically rearranges the data in order. Because a clustered index physically rearranges data, you can have only one clustered index per file. Sorting data by a single field, such as last name, is an example of a clustered index.

An *unclustered* index doesn't physically rearrange data but creates pointers to that data. Because unclustered indexes don't rearrange the data, you can have as many unclustered indexes as you need. The drawback of unclustered indexes is that they're slower than clustered indexes. A clustered index finds the data right away whereas an unclustered index needs an extra step to search the index and then follow the pointer to the actual data, as shown in Figure 2-8.

Book IV Chapter 2

Searching Algorithms

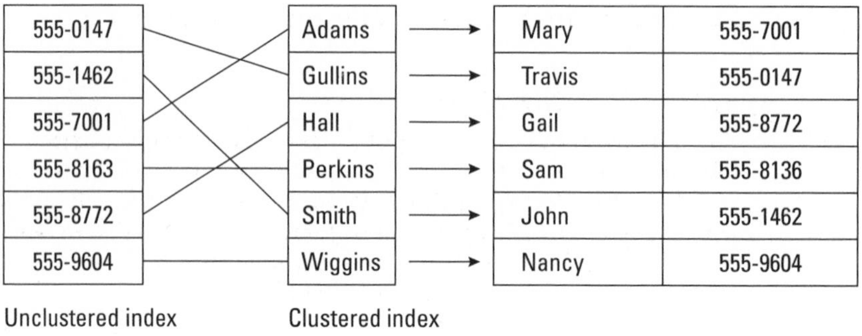

Figure 2-8:
Clustered
indexes
physically
rearrange
data
whereas
unclustered
indexes
point to
data.

| 555-0147 |
| 555-1462 |
| 555-7001 |
| 555-8163 |
| 555-8772 |
| 555-9604 |

| Adams |
| Gullins |
| Hall |
| Perkins |
| Smith |
| Wiggins |

Mary	555-7001
Travis	555-0147
Gail	555-8772
Sam	555-8136
John	555-1462
Nancy	555-9604

Unclustered index   Clustered index

Problems with indexes

A single clustered index makes sense because it rearranges data in a specific way. Multiple, unclustered indexes can help search data in different ways. Although indexes make searching faster, they make inserting and deleting slower because every time you add or delete data, you must update and organize the index at the same time.

If you've created multiple indexes, adding or deleting data means having to update every multiple index. If you have a small amount of data, creating and using an index may be more trouble than it's worth. Only when you have large amounts of data is an index (or multiple indexes) worth using.

Adversarial Search

One of the most popular uses for searching is an *adversarial search.* This type of search is often used to create artificial intelligence in video games.

Essentially, the computer analyzes the current game situation, such as a tic-tac-toe game, and calculates its list of possible moves. For each possible move, the computer creates a tree where the root node represents one of the computer's possible moves and each alternating level represents the human opponent's possible counter-moves, as shown in Figure 2-9.

Each possible move is given a specific value:

+ **A high value signifies a good move.**
+ **A negative value signifies a bad move.**

Assuming the human opponent chooses one possible counter-move, the next level of the tree displays the computer's possible responses and so on.

The more levels (or *plys*) the computer can analyze, the more it can anticipate and plan ahead and the *smarter* the computer can appear.

Depth versus time

Given enough time, the computer can examine every possible move and all possible counter-moves until it finds the best move to make that will lead to its inevitable victory. In simple games, like tic-tac-toe, where the number of choices is finite, this approach of searching all possible moves, called *brute-force,* works. When applied to more complicated games, like chess, such a brute-force approach takes way too long.

To reduce the amount of time needed to search, computer scientists have come up with a variety of solutions. The simplest method is to reduce the number of plys the computer examines for each move.

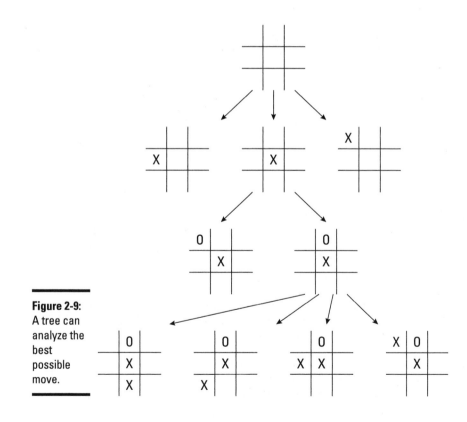

Figure 2-9: A tree can analyze the best possible move.

This is how many games offer beginner, intermediate, and expert modes. The expert mode may search 24 levels in each tree, the intermediate mode may only search 12 levels, and the beginner mode may only search 4 levels. Because the beginner mode searches far fewer levels than the expert mode, it runs faster and doesn't appear as *smart* as the intermediate or expert modes.

When a computer doesn't search beyond a fixed number of levels, it can miss potential problems that it might have discovered if it had just searched a little bit deeper. This event is dubbed the *horizon effect* because the computer doesn't see the consequences beyond a certain move, so the problem appears to lie outside the computer's sight or *beyond the horizon*.

Alpha-beta pruning

Another way to speed up searching is to use *alpha-beta pruning*. The idea behind this tactic is that it's relatively pointless to keep searching a tree if a potential move would represent a horrible choice. For example, in a chess game, two possible moves might be moving the king into a position where it'll get checkmated in two moves or moving a pawn to protect the king.

If a computer always searches every possible move down to 12 levels, it wastes time evaluating the bad move that results in the king getting checkmated in two moves. To save time, alpha-beta pruning immediately stops searching a tree the moment it detects a losing move and makes the computer focus on studying good moves instead. As a result, the computer's time can be spent more profitably examining good moves.

For example, consider the tree in Figure 2-10; the boxes represent possible moves for the computer, and the circles represent possible counter-moves by a human opponent. The higher the value in each box or circle, the better the move. So the human opponent will most likely choose moves with high values. In response, the computer must look at the best possible counter-moves based on what the human opponent is likely to choose.

Figure 2-10: Assigning values to possible moves helps the computer evaluate the best possible move.

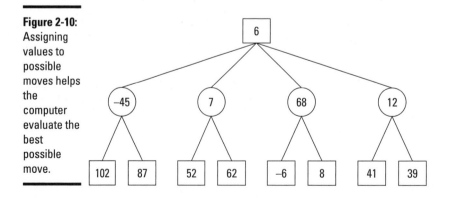

So if the computer considers a move with a value of 6 (the root node), the human opponent might have 4 possible moves with values ranging from –45 to 68. Assuming the human chooses the best move (68), the computer may have a choice of only 2 possible moves (–6 and 8). The goal is to choose the best possible move *(max)* for the computer (max) that leaves the human opponent with a choice of nothing but the worst possible moves *(min),* so arranging moves on a tree and assigning values is known as a *min-max tree.*

Assuming the computer chooses this original move (6) and the human opponent responds with the best possible move of 68, the computer now has a choice of evaluating the –6 or 8 move. Because there's no point in evaluating the –6 move, alpha-beta pruning would stop the computer from further evaluating this move and just focus on the 8 move instead.

Looking up a library of good moves

Alpha-beta pruning relies on examining every tree of possible moves and immediately cutting off the least promising ones. Obviously, some moves aren't worth considering, but the computer has no way of knowing that until it evaluates every move.

However, at the beginning of every game, there's always a list of good and bad moves, so many games include a library of these good moves. Now at the start of the game, the computer doesn't have to waste time searching every move but can just pick from its library of best possible moves and examine those moves in depth.

A way to use this technique in the middle of a game is to analyze all possible moves in two steps. In the first step, the computer only examines every possible move through a small number of levels, such as two. The idea is that most bad moves can be identified immediately, like moving a queen in a chess game so it can be captured by the opponent's pawn in the next move.

After the computer examines all possible moves in such shallow depth, it can eliminate the obviously bad moves and then for the second step, examine the remaining moves in more detail. Although this technique takes slightly more time to examine all possible moves through a shallow depth, it ultimately saves time by preventing the computer from examining both bad and good moves at a much deeper level.

Ultimately, searching always involves examining every item in a list, which means the larger the list, the longer the search time. The only way to speed up searching algorithms is to use different techniques to maximize the chances of finding data as soon as possible.

**Book IV
Chapter 2**

**Searching
Algorithms**

The simplest way to speed up any search algorithm is to sort the data beforehand. After a list has been sorted, the computer can use various techniques, such as block jumping or Fibonacci searching, to speed up the search.

If data isn't sorted, it may be possible to use an index. An index works most effectively when it organizes part of the stored data, such as indexing the last names of a customer list that contains names, addresses, and phone numbers. Although indexes can speed up searching, their need for constant updating makes adding and deleting data slower.

Rather than search through stored data, strategy games, such as chess, must search through continuously changing data based on the position of the game pieces. To search through this ever-changing data, strategy games must rely on techniques to quickly eliminate bad moves so the computer can spend its time focusing only on evaluating the best moves.

Chapter 3: String Searching

In This Chapter

- ✓ **Searching text sequentially**
- ✓ **Searching by using regular expressions**
- ✓ **Searching strings phonetically**

*S*earching for data is one of the most common functions in writing a computer program. Most searching algorithms focus on searching a list of values, such as numbers or names. However, there's another specialized type of searching, which involves searching text.

Searching text poses unique problems. Although you can treat text as one long list of characters, you aren't necessarily searching for a discrete value, like the number 21 or the last name Smith. Instead, you may need to search a long list of text for a specific word or phrase, such as ant or cat food. Not only do you need to find a specific word or phrase, but you also may need to find that same word or phrase multiple times. Because of these differences, computer scientists have created a variety of searching algorithms specifically tailored for searching text.

Computers only recognize and manipulate numbers, so every computer represents characters as a universally recognized numeric code. Two common numeric codes include the American Standard Code for Information Interchange (ASCII) and Unicode. ASCII contains 256 codes that represent mostly Western characters whereas Unicode contains thousands of codes that represent languages as diverse as Arabic, Chinese, and Cyrillic. When searching for text, computers actually search for numeric codes that represent specific text, so text searching is ultimately about number searching.

One of the most popular uses for text searching algorithms involves a field called *bioinformatics,* which combines molecular biology with computer programming. The basic idea is to use long text strings, such as *gcacgtaag,* to represent a DNA structure and then search for a specific string within that DNA structure (such as *cgt*) to look for matches that could indicate how a particular drug could interact with the DNA of a virus to neutralize it.

Sequential Text Search

The simplest text searching algorithm is the brute force sequential search, which simply examines every character. To look for the string *gag* in text, the brute force sequential search examines the text character by character. The moment it finds the letter *g*, it checks to see whether the next letter is *a* and so on. To find anything, this search algorithm must exhaustively examine every character, as shown in Figure 3-1.

In searching for the string GAG, a brute force search starts with the first character and finds a matching *G* character. Next, it checks whether the next two characters are an *A* and a *G*.

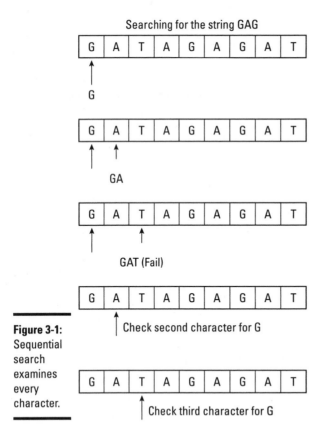

Figure 3-1: Sequential search examines every character.

In this example, the third character *(T)* doesn't match, so the brute force algorithm starts all over again by examining the second character, even though it had previously examined that character. Because the brute force method examines every character individually, this method is the slowest and least efficient method for finding text.

Although the brute force method works, it can take too much time, especially when searching through large amounts of text. To make text searching faster and more efficient, computer scientists have developed a variety of alternative algorithms.

The Boyer-Moore algorithm

To speed up text searching, the computer should skip any previously examined text and jump straight to unexamined text. That's the basis for a text searching algorithm developed by two computer scientists (Bob Boyer and J. Strother Moore) called the Boyer-Moore algorithm.

Like the brute force algorithm, the Boyer-Moore algorithm examines text character by character. After the Boyer-Moore algorithm finds a partial match, it's smart enough to skip over previously examined characters and start searching from the end of all examined characters, speeding up the entire search process, as shown in Figure 3-2.

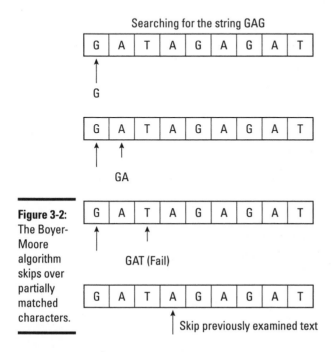

Figure 3-2: The Boyer-Moore algorithm skips over partially matched characters.

The Rabin-Karp algorithm

Although much faster than a brute force search, the Boyer-Moore algorithm still searches one character at a time. If you're searching for a text string, you can speed up the search by examining blocks of text rather than individual characters.

For example, if you're searching for the string *GAG,* you could examine three characters at a time rather than examining a single character three times. To make searching blocks of characters faster, two computer scientists (Michael O. Rabin and Richard M. Karp) created the Rabin-Karp algorithm.

This algorithm uses a hash function to convert a block of characters into a numeric value. Instead of examining individual characters, the Rabin-Karp algorithm uses its hash function to convert the original search string into a numeric value. So a hash function might convert the three-character string to search *(GAG)* into a numeric value of 3957.

After converting the search string into a numeric value, the Rabin-Karp algorithm repetitively searches for blocks of characters that are the same length of the search string (such as three-characters) and uses its hash function to convert those blocks of text into a numeric value. Now instead of searching for matching characters, the Rabin-Karp algorithm searches just for matching hash values, as shown in Figure 3-3.

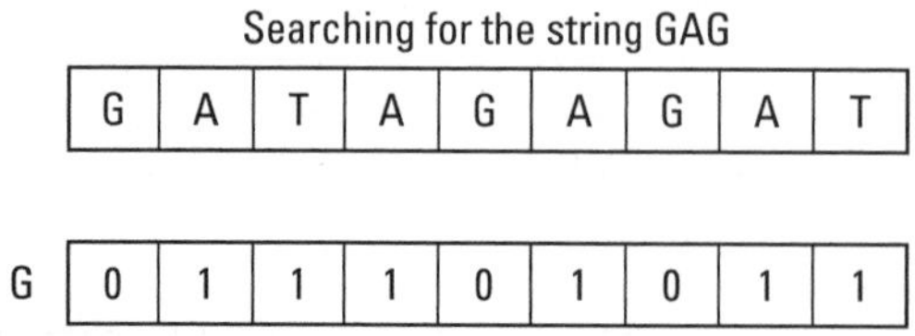

Figure 3-3:
The Rabin-Karp algorithm searches for hash values.

Searching for the string GAG

G	A	T	A	G	A	G	A	T

G

0	1	1	1	0	1	0	1	1

The key to the Rabin-Karp algorithm is the speed and method of its hash function. If the hash function can create values quickly and insure that different strings never create the same hash value, this algorithm can run quickly. If the hash function calculates hash values slower than the computer can examine characters individually, this algorithm may run slower than another algorithm, such as the Boyer-Moore algorithm. Also if the hash function calculates identical hash values for two different strings, this algorithm won't be accurate enough because it finds the wrong data.

The Shift Or algorithm

The Shift Or algorithm takes advantage of the fact that computers are much faster manipulating 1s and 0s than they are in manipulating and comparing characters. First, the algorithm creates an empty array the same length as the text that you want to search. Then, it compares the first character of the target string (what you're trying to find) with each character in the search string. Every time it finds a match, it stores a 0 in the array element. Every time it doesn't find a match, it stores a 1 in the array element, as shown in Figure 3-4.

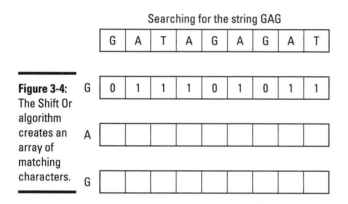

Figure 3-4: The Shift Or algorithm creates an array of matching characters.

After creating an array by comparing the first character with each character in the search string, the algorithm next looks only for a zero (0), which identifies where the first character of the target string was found. Now it compares the character to the right. If a match is found, it stores a 0 in a second array that represents matching the second character of the target string. If a match isn't found, it stores a 1 in this second array.

The algorithm repeats this step for each character in the target string, eventually creating a two-dimensional array of 1s and 0s, as shown in Figure 3-5.

When searching for the first character *(G)*, in Figure 3-5, the algorithm must check every character in the entire string. However, when searching for the second character *(A)*, the algorithm only has to look for the 0s in the previous row of the two-dimensional array, which identifies where the *G* character appears. In Figure 3-5, this means only searching three characters out of the entire string to look for a possible match of the *GA* string.

When searching for the third character *(G)*, the algorithm now only checks for 0s in the second row of the two-dimensional array, which means it only checks three characters out of the entire string.

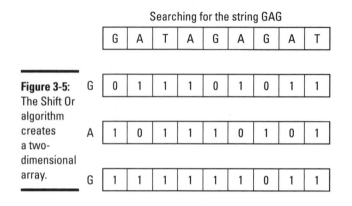

Searching for the string GAG

| G | A | T | A | G | A | G | A | T |

Figure 3-5: G
The Shift Or
algorithm

| 0 | 1 | 1 | 1 | 0 | 1 | 0 | 1 | 1 |

creates A
a two-

| 1 | 0 | 1 | 1 | 1 | 0 | 1 | 0 | 1 |

dimensional
array. G

| 1 | 1 | 1 | 1 | 1 | 1 | 0 | 1 | 1 |

As soon as the algorithm finds three 0s that form a diagonal line in the two-dimensional array, it can identify the exact location of the *GAG* string in the much larger string. The Shift Or algorithm gets its name because the matching string patterns look like binary numbers where the 0 constantly gets shifted one place to the right, like this:

$$G \rightarrow 011$$
$$A \rightarrow 101$$
$$G \rightarrow 110$$

Although the shift or algorithm takes more steps than a simple brute force search, it's much faster. Sometimes the simplest algorithms aren't always the fastest.

The finite automaton string search algorithm

First, the algorithm creates a finite state machine, which is a directed graph (see Book III, Chapter 5) where each node represents a single character in the target string to find. So if you wanted to find the string *GAG*, this algorithm creates a finite state machine consisting of three nodes with one node representing a starting state where the string hasn't been found yet. The first node represents finding the first letter *G;* the second node represents finding the second letter *A;* and the third node represents finding the final letter *G,* as shown in Figure 3-6.

After this algorithm creates a finite state machine for the target string, it next examines each character in the search string. In this example, the search string is *GAAGGAGAA.*

Searching for the string GAG

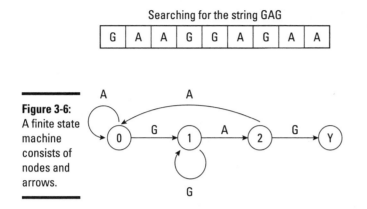

| G | A | A | G | G | A | G | A | A |

Figure 3-6:
A finite state
machine
consists of
nodes and
arrows.

Initially, the algorithm starts at node 0. The first character it finds is the
letter *G,* so it moves to node 1. The second character it finds is the letter *A,*
so it moves to node 2. However, the third character it finds is the letter *A,* so
it starts back at node 0 again.

The fourth character it finds is the letter *G,* so it moves back to node 1. The fifth
character it finds is also the letter *G,* so it stays at node 1. The sixth character that it finds is the letter *A,* so now it moves to node 2. The seventh character
that it finds is the letter *G,* so it moves to the last node that signals a match has
been found.

This algorithm is commonly used in Internet search engines, such as Google
and Yahoo!

Searching with Regular Expressions

The finite automaton string search algorithm is the basis for a special text
searching technique known as regular expressions (sometimes abbreviated
as RegEx). Rather than write your own code to implement a finite automaton
search algorithm, you can use regular expressions that are built-in to many
languages (such as Perl and PHP) or added as libraries (such as Java and
.NET languages like C# and Visual Basic).

The basic idea behind regular expressions is to search not just for specific
strings but also for patterns. This provides greater flexibility because you
may not always know exactly what you want to find. For example, a normal
search algorithm doesn't find a string unless you know the entire string you
want to find, such as the last name of *Smith.* If you only know the first three
or four characters of a last name, you can use regular expressions instead.

Searching for single character patterns

The simplest regular expression pattern searches for a single character. Some single character patterns are shown in Table 3-1.

Table 3-1	Single Pattern Regular Expressions		
Pattern Character	*What It Finds*	*Example*	*Find*
. (period)	Any single character	s.m	sum sam
\w	Any letter or number	\wats	cats 8cats
\W	Any character except a letter or number	213\W	213-213@
\d	Any number from 0–9	\d\d\d-1234	597-1234 409-1234
\D	Any character except a number from 0–9	W\D9-1234	WP9-1234 W$9-1234

Suppose you want to search for a string that begins with the letters *c* or *f*. To specify specific characters, you can define your own set, like this:

    [cf]at

This regular expression finds strings, such as *cat* and *fat* but not *rat*. Sometimes it may be easier to define which characters you don't want rather than the ones you do want. In that case, you can use the ^ character in a set to define which characters you don't want, like this:

    [^rht]oss

This finds any four-character strings that end with *oss* except for *ross, hoss,* and *toss.* The ^rht expression tells the computer to match any characters except for *r, h,* and *t.*

Searching for multiple character patterns

If you want to search for multiple characters, you could use a single character pattern several times. For example, to find a three-number string, you could use this regular expression pattern:

    \d\d\d

However, if you want to find a string consisting of one hundred numbers, typing **\d** one hundred times is impractical. As an alternative, you can specify multiple patterns with either the * or + symbol.

Both symbols appear directly after a single-character pattern, such as \d*
or \d+. The * symbol looks for zero or more instances of the pattern whereas
the + symbol looks for one or more instances of the pattern. So \d*123 finds
the strings *9123, 899123,* and *123* but \d+123 finds only the *9123* and *899123*
strings.

The * and + symbols can also work with single character sets, like this:

```
[rht]*oss
```

This searches for any string that ends with *oss* and contains zero or more of
the *r, h,* or *t* characters, such as *oss, thtrtoss,* and *tthrrhhhhhtoss.*

Searching for alternate patterns

If you want to find the names *John Smith* and *Mary Smith,* you could search
twice. However, a simple solution is to search for both patterns at the same
time with the alternation operator (|), like this:

```
John Smith | Mary Smith
```

This regular expression tells the computer to find either the string *John
Smith* or *Mary Smith.* You can combine the alternation operator with any pattern, like this:

```
[rht]*oss | \d+-1234
```

This regular expression finds strings, such as *rthrross* and *5-1234.*

Searching Phonetically

Regular expressions can make it easy to find strings when you only know
part of the characters to find. However, sometimes you may know the pronun-
ciation of a string you want to find, but you aren't sure of the exact spelling.
Trying to find the word *elephant* with a regular expression of elefa\w* doesn't
work if you don't realize that the *ph* sound in elephant makes an *f* sound. To
search strings phonetically, use a phonetic algorithm, such as the Soundex
algorithm.

The Soundex algorithm was actually patented in 1918 by Margaret O'Dell and
Robert C. Russell. This algorithm is based on dividing spoken speech into six
phonetic classifications based on where you put your lips and tongue to
make sounds.

Basically, the Soundex algorithm converts each string into a numeric code that begins with the first letter of the string. So if you had the name *Harry*, the Soundex algorithm might convert that name into the code H600 by following these steps:

1. **Capitalize all letters in the string.**

2. **Retain the first letter of the word.**

3. **Change all occurrences of the following letters to *0* (zero):**
A, E, I, O, U, H, W, Y

4. **Replace any letters with the following numbers:**

1 = B, F, P, V

2 = C, G, J, K, Q, S, X, Z

3 = D, T

4 = L

5 = M, N

6 = R

5. **Replace all pairs of identical digits with a single digit, such as replacing *66* with just *6*.**

6. **Remove all zeros from the string.**

7. **Pad the string with trailing zeros so the entire Soundex code consists of the following format:**

`<uppercase letter> <digit> <digit> <digit>`

Table 3-2 shows how the Soundex algorithm calculates identical Soundex codes for the strings *Harry* and *Hairy*.

Table 3-2	Calculating a Soundex Code	
Soundex Algorithm Step	*String #1 (Harry)*	*String #2 (Hairy)*
1	HARRY	HAIRY
2	H	H
3	H0RR0	H00R0
4	H0660	H0060
5	H060	H060
6	H6	H6
7	H600	H600

If you had the strings *Harry* stored in a text file, the Soundex algorithm converts that string into the H600 code. Now if you searched for the string *hairy* with the Soundex algorithm, the computer converts *hairy* into the Soundex code H600 and then finds the same H600 code stored at the string *Harry,* thus finding a matching string phonetically.

Phonetic algorithms are used most often in spell checkers. The algorithm calculates a code for each misspelled word and then matches that code to correctly spelled words that have the same phonetic code.

String searching algorithms must examine every character, so the only way to speed up an algorithm is to simplify how it examines a string of text. Paradoxically, string searching algorithms often run faster by organizing text in a specific way and then searching that method of organization rather than the actual text itself, which is how the Shift Or and Soundex algorithms work. As a general rule, the faster the string searching algorithm, the harder and more complicated it is to implement.

Chapter 4: Data Compression Algorithms

In This Chapter

✓ Lossless compression

✓ Lossy compression

✓ Audio and video compression

The main idea behind data compression is to shrink information, which takes up less space. Not only does compressed data take up less storage space, but it also takes less time to transfer.

Here are two types of data compression algorithms — lossless and lossy.

With *lossless compression,* the algorithm can compress the data without losing any information, which is used for archiving and compressing multiple files into a single file, such as a ZIP archive. Think of lossless compression as a way to pack existing data more efficiently, like refolding clothes to make them fit in a suitcase.

With *lossy compression,* the algorithm actually loses some information to compress data. Typically, this lost information isn't noticed anyway. The most common examples of lossy compression involve MP3 audio files and video files. When compressing audio, the MP3 standard throws out the audio parts that the human ear can't distinguish. When compressing video, compression algorithms toss out colors that the human eye doesn't notice. By throwing out information, lossy compression algorithms can save space, much like throwing away clothes to make packing the remaining clothes in a suitcase easier.

Because lossy compression throws out data, it can compress the same data much smaller than lossless compression. However, lossy compression has only limited use. You wouldn't want to use lossy compression when storing documents because you can't afford to lose any data, for example. If you absolutely must preserve data, use lossless compression. If you can afford to lose some data in exchange for tighter compression, use lossy compression.

Lossless Data Compression Algorithms

The basic idea behind lossless data compression is to find a way to pack data in a smaller space more efficiently without losing any of the data in the process. To do this, lossless data compression algorithms are typically optimized for specific data, such as text, audio, or video, although the general principles remain the same no matter what type of data the algorithm is compressing.

Run-length encoding

The simplest lossless data compression algorithm is *run-length encoding* (RLE). Basically, this method looks for redundancy and replaces any redundant data with a much shorter code instead. Suppose you had the following 17-character string:

WWWBBWWWWBBBBWWWW

RLE looks for redundant data and condenses it into a 10-character string, like this:

3W2B4W4B4W

The number in front of each letter identifies how many characters the code replaced, so in this example, the first two characters, 3W represents *WWW,* 2B represents *BB,* 4W represents *WWWW,* and so on.

Run-length encoding is used by fax machines because most images consist of mainly white space with occasional black areas that represent letters or drawings.

The Burrows-Wheeler transform algorithm

One problem with run-length encoding is that it works best when repetitive characters appear grouped together. With a string, like *WBWBWB#*, RLE can't compress anything because no groups of W and B characters are bunched together. (However, a smart version of the RLE algorithm notices the two-character repetitive string *WB* and encodes the string as 3(WB)#, which would tell the computer to repeat the two-character pattern of WB three times.)

When redundant characters appear scattered, run-length encoding can be made more efficient by first transforming the data to group identical characters together and then use run-length encoding to compress the data. That's the idea behind the Burrows-Wheeler transform (BWT) algorithm, developed by Michael Burrows and David Wheeler.

The BWT algorithm must use a character that marks the end of the data, such as the # symbol. Then the BWT algorithm works in three steps. First, it rotates text through all possible combinations, as shown in the Rotate column of Table 4-1. Second, it sorts each line alphabetically, as shown in the Sort column of Table 4-1. Third, it outputs the final column of the sorted list, which groups identical characters together in the Output column of Table 4-1. In this example, the BWT algorithm transforms the string *WBWBWB#* into *WWW#BBB.*

Table 4-1	Rotating and Sorting Data	
Rotate	*Sort*	*Output*
WBWBWB#	BWBWB#W	W
#WBWBWB	BWB#WBW	W
B#WBWBW	B#WBWBW	W
WB#WBWB	WBWBWB#	#
BWB#WBW	WBWB#WB	B
WBWB#WB	WB#WBWB	B
BWBWB#W	#WBWBWB	B

At this point, the BWT algorithm hasn't compressed any data but merely rearranged the data to group identical characters together; the BWT algorithm has rearranged the data to make the run-length encoding algorithm more efficient. Run-length encoding can now convert the *WWW#BBB* string into *3W#3B,* thus compressing the overall data.

After compressing data, you'll eventually need to uncompress that same data. Uncompressing this data *(3W#3B)* creates the original BWT output of *WWW#BBB,* which contains all the characters of the original, uncompressed data but not in the right order. To retrieve the original order of the uncompressed data, the BWT algorithm repetitively goes through two steps, as shown in Figure 4-1.

The BWT algorithm works in reverse by adding the original BWT output *(WWW#BBB)* and then sorting the lines repetitively a number of times equal to the length of the string. So retrieving the original data from a 7-character string takes seven adding and sorting steps.

After the final add and sort step, the BWT algorithm looks for the only line that has the end of data character (#) as the last character, which identifies the original, uncompressed data. The BWT algorithm is both simple to understand and implement, which makes it easy to use for speeding up ordinary run-length encoding.

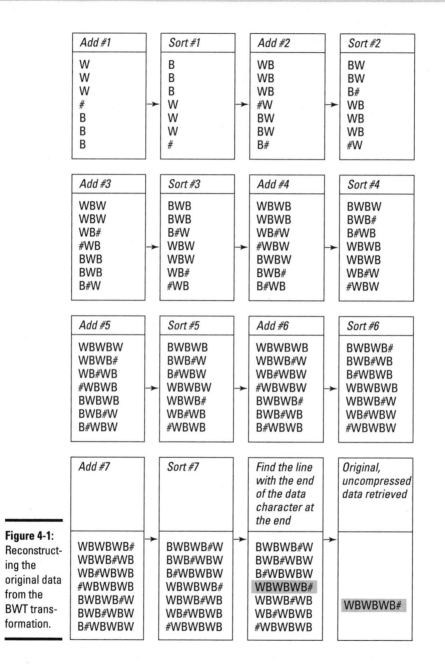

Figure 4-1: Reconstructing the original data from the BWT transformation.

Dictionary encoding

Run-length encoding is a simple algorithm that works well with redundant characters grouped together but doesn't work as well with redundant data scattered throughout. An alternative to RLE is dictionary coding. The basic idea behind *dictionary coding* is to replace large data chunks with much smaller data chunks. Suppose you had the following text:

See Dick. See Jane.

You could replace the redundant text *See* by a simple code, such as 1, and create a new string:

1 Dick. 1 Jane.

Now you could replace *Dick* with 1 code and *Jane* with another code, such as 2 and 3 respectively, to create a compressed version, like this:

1 2. 1 3.

Uncompressing this data means replacing the codes with the actual data, using a dictionary. Each code refers to the actual data, so looking up 1 retrieves the *See* string, 2 retrieves *Dick,* and 3 retrieves *Jane,* as shown in Figure 4-2.

Figure 4-2:
Uncompres-
sing data
requires
using a
dictionary to
replace
codes with
actual data.

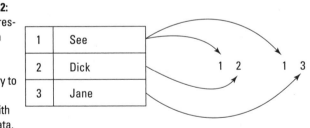

If you know the data you want to compress ahead of time, such as condensing the entire contents of an encyclopedia on a DVD, you can optimize the dictionary to create the smallest codes, which represent the most common data chunks, such as the word *the.* In most cases, you don't know the data to compress ahead of time, so you need an algorithm that can analyze data, create a dictionary on the fly, and then compress data using that dictionary. Three popular dictionary encoding algorithms include LZ77, LZ78, and LZW.

The LZ77 algorithm

The LZ77 algorithm was created by two computer scientists — Abraham Lempel and Jakob Ziv, who first published their algorithm in 1977 (hence the name LZ77). The LZ77 algorithm works by looking for repetitive data. Rather than storing this repetitive data in a separate dictionary, the LZ77 remembers the location of this data in the original file.

When the algorithm finds this same data stored somewhere else, it removes this data (compressing the overall information) and substitutes a pointer to the previously recognized data, as shown in Figure 4-3.

Figure 4-3:
The LZ77 algorithm replaces redundant data with pointers.

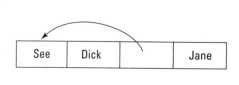

Because pointers take up less space than the actual data, the LZ77 algorithm compresses information. The more redundant data, the more efficient the compression.

The LZ78 algorithm

One problem with the LZ77 algorithm is that it stores redundant data directly in the compressed data itself. To improve compression, the same computer scientists developed a variation of the LZ77 algorithm — the LZ78 algorithm.

The *LZ78 algorithm* removes all redundant data and stores it in a separate dictionary. Then the algorithm substitutes the redundant data with much smaller codes stored in the dictionary. By removing this data, the LZ78 algorithm can compress data even further than the LZ77 algorithm.

To uncompress this data, the computer follows each code to the dictionary to retrieve the appropriate data chunk.

The LZW algorithm

The LZW algorithm gets its name from Terry Welch, who created his own variation of the LZ78 algorithm, dubbed the *LZW algorithm*. The LZW algorithm works by creating a dictionary, just like the LZ78 algorithm. But whereas the

LZ78 algorithm creates a dictionary of codes that consist of the same size, the LZW algorithm creates a dictionary of codes of different sizes.

When compressing text, the LZW algorithm starts out by creating a dictionary of individual letters. Assuming all uppercase letters, *A* would be represented by 1, *B* by 2, and so on. However, substituting a number for a single character isn't likely to save much space, so the LZW algorithm continues examining the text for repetitive multiple-character strings to store as a number, such as *AB, ABC, ABCD,* and so on.

Like most compression algorithms, the LZW algorithm works best on data that contains redundant information, like this:

    IAMSAMSAMIAM#

First, the LZW algorithm creates a dictionary of single characters represented by numbers. *I* gets stored as 9, *A* as 1, *M* as 13, and *S* as 19.

When the LZW algorithm finds the second letter *A,* it doesn't encode the letter *A* all over again because it's done that once already. Instead, the algorithm encodes the next two characters, which happen to be *AM,* and assigns this two-character combination to the next available number, which is 27. (Numbers 1 through 26 are assigned to the individual letters of the alphabet.)

When the algorithm sees the letter *S* again, it encodes the next two-character string, *SA,* as the number 28. Then it finds the letter *M* again, so it encodes the next two-character string, *MI,* as the number 29. Finally, it sees the letter *A* again, so it checks the next two-character string, which is *AM.* Because the algorithms already encoded *AM* before (as the number 27), the algorithm expands to encode the three-character string, *AM#,* as the number 30, as shown in Figure 4-4.

At the beginning of data, the LZW algorithm isn't very efficient because it's slowly creating its dictionary. When the algorithm's dictionary grows with larger amounts of redundant data, it can replace these large chunks of redundant data with small number codes.

The LZW algorithm is used to compress graphic images stored in the Graphic Interchange Format (GIF). Originally, this algorithm was patented in 1985 and the patent holder, Unisys, demanded royalties from software companies that sold programs that could create GIF files. This patent problem caused computer scientists to create and promote an alternate graphics format — Portable Network Graphics (PNG). However, the PNG format never replaced the GIF file format, especially after the LZW patent expired on June 20, 2003.

**Book IV
Chapter 4**

Data Compression Algorithms

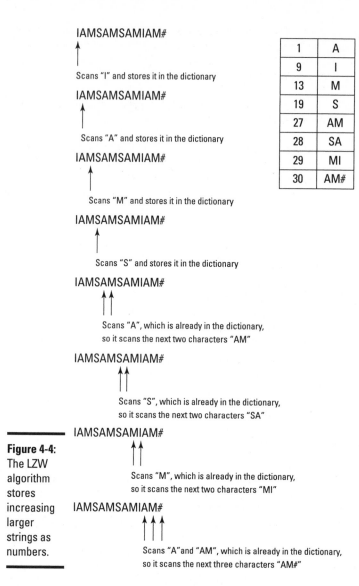

Figure 4-4:
The LZW algorithm stores increasing larger strings as numbers.

Lossy Data Compression

Lossy data compression shrinks data through a combination of packing data more efficiently (like lossless compression) and by throwing out chunks of data that aren't considered crucial. As a result, lossy compression is used less often for text (where losing data is unacceptable because a single missing word or number can alter the entire meaning of the text) and more often for audio, graphics, and video.

Basically, lossy data compression reduces data much greater than lossless compression because lossy data compression can pack data more efficiently, like lossless compression, while also saving additional space by throwing out small chunks of data that aren't missed anyway.

Most lossy compression methods use lossless compression algorithms in addition to throwing out unnecessary data.

For example, the human eye and ear can only distinguish a fixed range of colors and sounds. So lossy compression simply removes colors and audio that most people don't notice. When done selectively, compressed audio, graphic, or video can be indistinguishable from the original, but at a certain point, lossy compression eventually degrades the original to an unacceptable level, as shown in Figure 4-5.

Figure 4-5:
Comparison of compressed graphic images.

A specific method for compression audio or video files is a *codec,* or COmpressor-DECompressor. Some popular audio codecs include MP3, AAC (Advanced Audio Coding), and WMA (Windows Media Audio). Some popular video codecs include RealVideo, WMV (Windows Media Video), and MPEG-4.

The trick behind lossy compression is knowing which data can be removed without degrading quality too far. In an audio file, such as an MP3 file, lossy compression throws out the audio portion that's beyond the human hearing range. In graphics, an image might consist of three shades of blue that are so close as to be nearly indistinguishable. That's when the algorithm strips out the two least-used shades of blue and replaces them with the most frequently used shade of blue. This saves space by reducing the number of colors to store in the file.

Video basically saves successive still images, so lossy compression can save space by looking for identical backgrounds between video frames. Rather than store the same background multiple times, lossy compression stores the background only once and uses that identical image multiple times. Because the same background may appear in several video frames, this technique can shrink the size of a video considerably.

Another way to compress data is to alter the bit depth. *Bit depth* defines how many bits are used to store data, such as 96-bit or 160-bit. The more bits used, the greater the quality but the larger the file size. The fewer bits used, the less storage space required and the less data saved, reducing the file size. That's why a 96-bit MP3 file is smaller than the same file saved as a 160-bit MP3 file. The 96-bit file can't store as much data as the 160-bit file, which means lower audio quality than the 160-bit file.

When compressing a file, lossy compression may use constant bit rate (CBR) or variable bit rate (VBR) compression. CBR reduces the bit rate uniformly throughout the entire file and makes compression faster. Unfortunately, this also means that silent portions of an audio file get compressed at the same rate as noisier parts of the audio file, resulting in less-than-optimum compression.

VBR alters the bit rate, depending on the complexity of the data. This improves quality but at the cost of a slower compression time. For even higher quality, some compression algorithms offer two-pass VBR, which means the program analyzes the file twice to get the maximum quality and the smallest file size possible, but at the expense of much slower compression speed.

All types of compression are always a trade-off. With lossless compression, the trade-off is between size and speed. The smaller you want to compress the file, the longer it takes. With lossy compression, the trade-off is mostly between size and quality. The smaller the file size, the lower the overall quality. Both lossless and lossy compression algorithms are necessary, depending on which type better suits your needs.

Chapter 5: Encryption Algorithms

In This Chapter

✔ **Encryption basics**

✔ **Symmetric and asymmetric encryption**

✔ **Cracking encryption with attacks**

*E*ncryption involves scrambling information, or *plaintext,* and converting it into another format — *ciphertext* — essentially turning ordered data into seemingly random gibberish. By encrypting information, you can keep data information out of the hands of other people, which can be useful for sending coded messages for military use, sending credit card information over the Internet to online shopping Web sites, or just hiding your personal documents from the prying eyes of family members, co-workers, or strangers.

The simplest form of encryption is *substitution cipher,* which basically replaces each letter with a specific symbol, such as another letter. A substitution cipher simply replaces one letter with another letter from the alphabet a fixed distance away, such as replacing the letter A with the letter Z, the letter B with the letter A, the letter C with the letter B, and so on.

In this case, each letter gets replaced by the previous letter in the alphabet, like this:

I AM HOT

Replacing the letter I with the letter H, the letter A with the letter Z, and so on creates the following ciphertext:

H ZL GNS

This information may be scrambled, but after someone discovers that each letter in the ciphertext actually represents the next letter in the alphabet, this simple substitution cipher can be cracked easily. When an encryption method can be broken easily, it's *weak* encryption. If an encryption method can't be broken easily, it's *strong* encryption.

The key to deciphering the substitution cipher is recognizing both the method it's using (replacing one letter with another) and the specific way it implements that method (replacing each letter with the previous letter in the alphabet). A slightly more-complicated substitution cipher might replace each letter with the third letter from the current letter. So the letter A would be replaced by the letter D, the letter B by the letter E, and so on. In this case, the method is the same, but the implementation is slightly different while being only marginally harder to decipher.

Although substitution ciphers are easy to implement, they're also easy to break. After you know to replace a letter in the ciphertext by another letter that's shifted by a specific distance in the alphabet (such as the third letter), you can easily break the code. One way to avoid this problem is to use a *one-time pad,* which consists of a series of random numbers that tell how far to shift the next letter in a message. So a one-time pad might contain three random numbers, like this:

2 7 –3

The first number (2) tells the algorithm to shift the first letter of the text by two letters. So if the first three letters of the message are SAM, the first letter, S, would get replaced by the second letter from S in the alphabet, which is U.

The second number (7) tells the algorithm to shift the second letter by seven letters. So the letter A gets replaced by the seventh letter down, which is H. Finally, the third number (3) tells the algorithm to shift the third letter by the third letter down, so the letter M gets replaced by the letter P. Now the entire message SAM gets encrypted as the ciphertext UHP.

The one-time pad gets its name because the random series of numbers are used only once. Now it's virtually impossible for anyone to discover how the letters are substituted because the replacement letters are picked at random. The only way to decipher this ciphertext is to get a copy of the one-time pad.

Of course, the one-time pad has its drawbacks. To work, both parties need a copy of the same one-time pad. If you could transfer a copy of the one-time pad securely, you might as well transfer the message you're delivering instead. Also, one-time pads can be used only once. If they're used more than once, someone can eventually guess the random pattern of letters.

Even worse is that a one-time pad must specify how far to shift each letter in a message. If you're encrypting a message consisting of 1,000 letters, you need a one-time pad to specify how to shift all 1,000 letters. If you're encrypting a message consisting of 10,000 letters, you need a one-time pad that specifies how to shift all 10,000 letters.

Given these problems, one-time pads are generally impractical for normal use. A slight variation of the one-time pad is the use of a password. A *password* acts like a one-time pad; instead of defining how to alter each individual character in a message, the password determines how to scramble data. Even if you know how data is being scrambled, you won't know how to read the scrambled data without knowing the right password. Passwords are simply smaller and more convenient versions of one-time pads.

The Basics of Encryption

Encryption involves three parts:

+ **The encryption algorithm**
+ **The implementation of the encryption algorithm**
+ **The length of the encryption key**

The encryption algorithm defines the specific method for scrambling data. Some people try to invent their own, obscure encryption algorithms under the theory that if no one knows how the algorithm works, he or she won't know how to break the encryption. This theory is *security through obscurity,* and it usually fails because a single flaw can leave the encryption vulnerable, much like how locking a bank is useless if a single door is left unlocked. Because it's nearly impossible for a single person to spot all possible flaws in an encryption algorithm, most encryption algorithms are published for anyone to see.

The idea behind publishing an encryption algorithm is to let as many people as possible examine an encryption algorithm for flaws. The more people examining an encryption algorithm, the more likely any flaws will be discovered and patched before people start using the algorithm to encrypt critical information.

Two common ways to encrypt data involve substitution and permutation. *Substitution* involves replacing data with another chunk of data. The group of algorithms that substitutes data is typically called a *substitution box* or *S-box.* *Permutation* involves altering bits of data, usually represented as a binary number. The group of algorithms that performs this permutation is typically called a *permutation box* or *P-box.* Most encryption algorithms use a combination of S-boxes and P-boxes to scramble data.

After an encryption algorithm is deemed mathematically sound and secure, the second step is correctly implementing that algorithm in a particular programming language. Because there are virtually millions of different ways to accomplish the same task in any programming language, the encryption algorithm may be secure but the implementation of the encryption algorithm may not be secure.

After you have a valid encryption algorithm that's been implemented properly in a particular programming language, the final step to creating a secure encryption algorithm is the key length used to scramble the data.

In a simple substitution cipher, the key length could be considered as the value 1 because it offers only one way of replacing letters with another letter, such as shifting each letter by a fixed position in the alphabet. To encrypt a 1,000-character message, a one-time pad would need 1,000 different random numbers for shifting each letter in the message, so the key length could be considered as 1,000.

The key length is crucial because the details of an encryption algorithm are often published for anyone to examine. As a result, the security of most encryption algorithms rests solely on the key length used for the password. You don't need to create a long password of 1,000 or more characters; the encryption algorithm needs to use more bits of data to store any password whether the password consists of 1 character or 100.

The length of the password simply makes it harder for other people to guess. A 1-letter password means someone needs only 26 guesses. A 100-letter password forces someone to try all possible combinations of letters, making guessing much more difficult. The key length simply defines the amount of space used to store the password but doesn't specify the physical length of the password.

As a simple analogy, think of encryption key lengths like the physical key to your front door. A physical key consists of rods that drop down to prevent a doorknob from turning. The more rods used, the harder it is to pick the lock. The fewer rods used, the easier it is to pick the lock.

In the same way, encryption keys are used to hold passwords. The shorter the key length (measured in bits), the fewer possibilities exist and the weaker the encryption, making it more vulnerable to being broken. The longer the encryption key length, the less likely the encryption will break.

No encryption is considered unbreakable, but the goal of every encryption algorithm is to make unscrambling data *so difficult* that the time needed to read the encrypted message takes too long. Typically an encrypted message might take the world's fastest computer a million years to break, which effectively makes the encryption "unbreakable."

At one time, a 56-bit key was considered unbreakable, but with today's computers, the smallest secure key length is 128-bits, although many people prefer using 256-bit or 512-bit keys for added security.

Stream ciphers

Encryption algorithms generally fall into two categories — stream and block ciphers. A *stream cipher* encrypts data one item at a time, such as individual characters in a message. A *block cipher* encrypts data in fixed chunks or blocks. So rather than encrypt individual characters, a block cipher might encrypt text in ten-character blocks.

Generally, stream ciphers are used when encrypting data of unknown length, such as voice messages, whereas block ciphers are used to encrypt data of fixed lengths, such as a file.

A stream cipher borrows the features of the one-time pad. Whereas a one-time pad must be as long as the message being encrypted, a stream cipher uses smaller keys of fixed lengths, such as 128-bits. Another major difference is that a one-time pad consists of truly random numbers whereas a stream cipher generates a list of random numbers based on a *key* (password). Computers can't generate truly random numbers, so computer-generated random numbers are often called *pseudorandom numbers.*

A computer uses an algorithm to generate random numbers, but these aren't true random numbers because the algorithm generates the same list of random numbers over and over again. To alter the way computers generate random numbers, give the computer a value, or a *seed.* The computer uses this seed to generate a list of numbers; so by giving the computer different values for its seed, a computer can generate a different list of random numbers. Because this list always changes based on the seed value, any computer-generated random numbers are pseudorandom numbers.

A stream cipher uses a key to generate a list of pseudorandom numbers. Then it uses this generated list of pseudorandom numbers to encrypt each character, as shown in Figure 5-1.

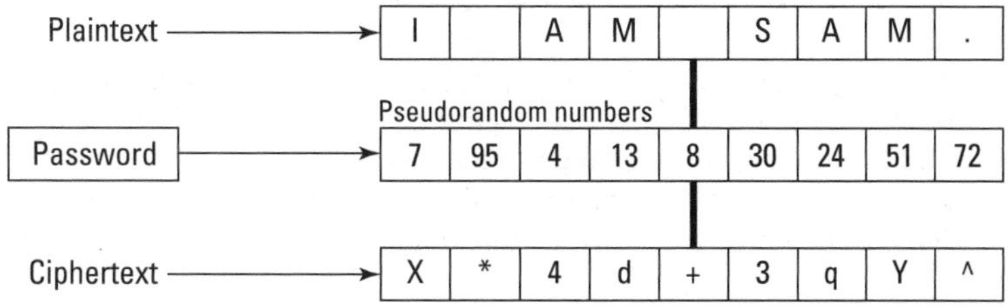

Figure 5-1:
How a stream cipher works.

Plaintext	I		A	M		S	A	M	.

Pseudorandom numbers

Password	7	95	4	13	8	30	24	51	72

Ciphertext	X	*	4	d	+	3	q	Y	^

Hacking a slot machine

The fact that computers can't generate truly random numbers allowed computer hackers to hack the newest computerized slot machines used in many casinos. The slot machine would seed its random number generator with a value and then use this list of pseudorandom numbers to determine payoffs.

Hackers soon discovered that certain slot machines used the same seed value every time, so the generated list of pseudorandom numbers could be predicted. Then they used a handheld computer that generated that same list of pseudorandom numbers as the slot machine. By knowing which pseudorandom number the slot machine would use next, the hackers could determine when the slot machine would hit a jackpot.

So, all the hackers did was watch a certain slot machine and wait for someone else to churn through all the losing pseudorandom numbers and leave. When the slot machine was close to a winning pseudorandom number, the hackers would only have to put a few coins into the slot machine before they'd hit a jackpot. Then they'd leave and wait for someone else to churn through the next batch of losing pseudorandom numbers before playing that same slot machine and hitting another jackpot.

Stream ciphers use two different methods to generate a list of pseudorandom numbers:

+ A **synchronous stream cipher** generates pseudorandom numbers independent of the plaintext data.

+ A **self-synchronizing stream cipher** generates pseudorandom numbers based on part of the plaintext.

   By creating pseudorandom numbers based on the plaintext, a stream cipher can further randomize the encryption process because no two messages are ever encrypted the exact same way.

The most popular stream cipher is *RC4,* named after its creator, Ron Rivest. RC4 is used in the two wireless encryption standards — Wired Equivalent Privacy (WEP) and Wi-Fi Protected Access (WPA), which protects wireless Internet connections.

Block ciphers

Block ciphers encrypt data in chunks, although you can think of a stream cipher as a block cipher with each character representing a single data chunk. A typical block size is 64- or 128-bits. Because most data doesn't fit into neat 64- or 128-bit blocks, a block cipher must pad the last chunk of data with information, such as zeroes.

Electronic codebook (ECB)

After a block cipher divides plaintext into blocks, it has several different ways to encrypt that data. The simplest way to encrypt data is to encrypt each block of data separately with the same key, which is *the electronic codebook method,* as shown in Figure 5-2.

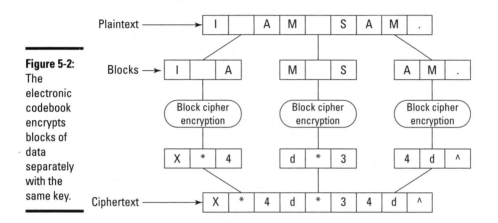

Figure 5-2: The electronic codebook encrypts blocks of data separately with the same key.

Encrypting with the electronic codebook method is simple and fast, but because it uses the same key to encrypt data, it tends to encrypt redundant data in identical chunks. So the message I am Sam. Sam I am might create two blocks of encrypted data that would look nearly identical, such as X*4d*34d^ and 34d*X*4d^. A cursory examination of these two encrypted blocks can reveal that X represents the letter *I,* * represents a *space,* 4d represents *am,* 3 represents *S,* and ^ represents a *period.*

Cipher-block chaining (CBC)

The ideal encryption algorithm takes identical data and scrambles it in two different ways to avoid revealing any redundant data. So the idea behind the cipher-block chaining (CBC) method is to use the encrypted output from one block as input to encrypt a second block. Because the output from one encrypted block directly affects the encryption of another block, identical plaintext data gets converted into completely different ciphertext, as shown in Figure 5-3.

**Book IV
Chapter 5**

Encryption
Algorithms

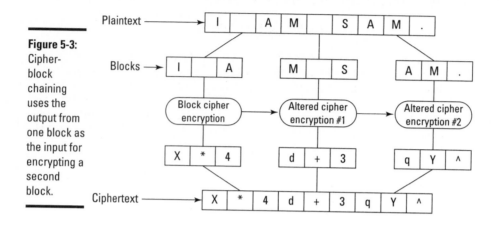

Figure 5-3:
Cipher-
block
chaining
uses the
output from
one block as
the input for
encrypting a
second
block.

Symmetric/Asymmetric Encryption Algorithms

The most common type of encryption algorithm is a *symmetric algorithm,*
which uses the same password to encrypt and decrypt data. Basically, this
means that the password that scrambles the data can also reverse the
process and unscramble the data, as shown in Figure 5-4.

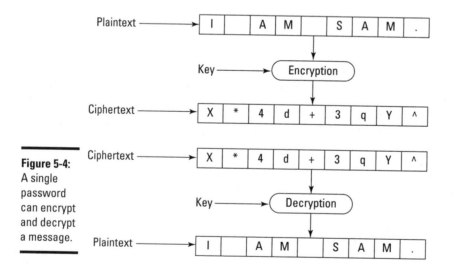

Figure 5-4:
A single
password
can encrypt
and decrypt
a message.

Hash functions

One type of algorithm commonly associated with encryption is a *hash function*. A hash function takes data as input and based on the size and content of that data, the hash function calculates a unique mathematical value. This value isn't used as part of the encryption but as a way to authenticate that certain data hasn't been altered.

Hash functions are often used when downloading files. A Web site might offer a file for download and display its hash value. Now if you download that file and run that file through the hash function, you should get the same hash value. If you get a different value, the file you downloaded is corrupt and missing some information. In encryption, hash functions can verify that an encrypted message hasn't been altered. If a file has been altered, it could mean the file simply got corrupted, or that someone tried to insert or remove data from the encrypted message, which means you shouldn't trust the validity of that message.

The biggest problem with symmetric encryption is that both parties need the same password to encrypt and decrypt data, so if you can't securely transfer the password to someone else, that person can never read the message.

A second problem with symmetric encryption is that the weakest link is the password itself. The encryption algorithm could be the strongest in the world, but if someone steals the password, that's like giving someone the key to unlock the ten-foot-thick steel doors guarding all the gold in the vault of Fort Knox.

Some popular symmetric encryption algorithms include the Data Encryption Standard (DES) and the Advanced Encryption Standard (AES). DES was the original government encryption standard approved in 1976. After computers became fast enough, they could crack DES encryption; so after a five-year contest between cryptographers, the government selected a new encryption standard — AES.

Symmetric encryption is often called *private-key encryption* because both the sender and the receiver need an identical copy of the key to encrypt and decrypt a message. Another type of encryption algorithm is the *asymmetric,* or *public-key encryption.* Unlike symmetric encryption, asymmetric encryption requires two keys for both the sender and the receiver.

These two keys are the *public key* and the *private key.* You can make a million copies of your public key and give them out, but you want only one copy of your private key. If someone wants to send you a message, he needs to encrypt a message with your public key. After someone encrypts a message with your public key, the only way to decrypt that message is to use your private key, as shown in Figure 5-5.

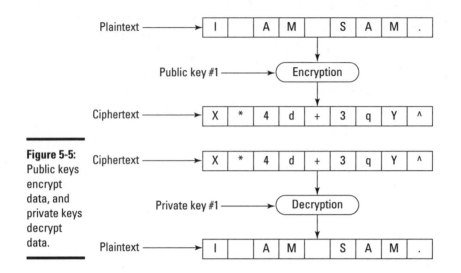

Figure 5-5:
Public keys
encrypt
data, and
private keys
decrypt
data.

Public key encryption is commonly used in digital signatures to verify who actually sent an encrypted message. When you encrypt a message with your private key, that message can be decrypted only with your public key. Because you're the only person with a copy of your private key, the only possible way a message can be decrypted with your public key is if it was originally encrypted with your private key. (Unless, of course, someone steals your private key. In that case, he can mimic you online.)

Public key and private key encryption is commonly used together in programs, such as Pretty Good Privacy (PGP), which are designed for sending encrypted messages. First, you encrypt your message with private key encryption. Then you use public key encryption to send the password (private key) to another person. The receiver unlocks the password using her private key and then uses this password to unlock the actual message, as shown in Figure 5-6.

The reason for using both private key and public key encryption is that public key encryption tends to run much slower than private key encryption. That's because with public key encryption, you need to encrypt data using the combination of the sender's private key with the receiver's public key. With private key encryption, you need only one key to encrypt data.

Public key encryption is used in SSL (Secure Sockets Layer), which is how you can connect to a secure shopping Web site and safely transfer your credit card numbers over the Internet. The shopping Web site basically gives your computer its public key so you can encrypt your credit card number and send it over the Internet. Now the only one who can decrypt your credit card number is the shopping Web site holding the private key.

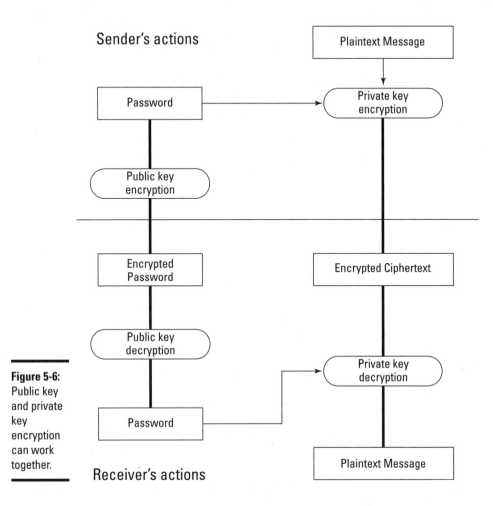

Sender's actions

Plaintext Message

Password

Private key encryption

Public key encryption

Encrypted Password

Encrypted Ciphertext

Public key decryption

Private key decryption

Figure 5-6:
Public key and private key encryption can work together.

Password

Plaintext Message

Receiver's actions

Cracking Encryption

Encryption works by scrambling data, but anything scrambled can always be unscrambled. What makes the difference between strong and weak encryption is how many possible ways exist to unscramble the encrypted data.

If only ten possible ways exist to scramble data, that's much easier to crack than a message that offers ten million different ways to scramble data. To unscramble data that offers ten possible ways of scrambling a message, you can just use a brute force attack.

**Book IV
Chapter 5**

**Encryption
Algorithms**

Hiding in plain sight with steganography

One unusual form of encryption involves hiding data within another chunk of data, such as hiding a text message inside an audio or graphic image. Hiding data within another form of data is *steganography*. The idea is that no one can read your messages if he can't find them in the first place.

Steganography works on the principle that data in audio, video, and graphic files can be removed without noticeably affecting the quality of the original file. After removing chunks of information from such a file, which leaves gaps in the original file, the next step is to insert the plaintext or ciphertext into these open gaps.

If you insert plaintext into an audio, video, or graphic file, anyone can read your message if he knows how to find it. If you encrypt your message and then insert the ciphertext into a file, someone would need to know where to find your message and then know the password to decrypt that message. Steganography isn't necessarily a form of encryption so much as it's a way to keep anyone from knowing you're sending secret messages at all.

Brute force attack

Basically, a *brute force* attack tries every possible combination of ways a message can be scrambled. Think of a combination lock that opens only if you align the right number. If the combination lock offers 36 numbers, you can use a brute force attack and exhaustively try all 36 numbers until you find the one that opens the lock.

Now consider a more complicated combination lock that not only displays 36 numbers but forces you to choose three different numbers in the correct order. You can still exhaustively try every possible number combination, but the time needed to do this is likely more than most people are willing to take, which effectively makes the lock secure.

That's the same idea behind encryption. Every form of encryption can eventually be cracked with a brute force attack, but the time needed to exhaustively try every possibility takes too much time. It's possible to crack even the toughest encryption algorithm with a brute force attack, but you might need a room full of million-dollar supercomputers running 24 hours a day for the next million years to eventually crack the encryption. By making the costs in resources and time too high, encryption algorithms are essentially unbreakable through a brute force attack alone.

A variation of the brute force attack is the *Chinese lottery*. The idea is that if you gave each person in China (with its billion+ population) a computer and assigned each computer a different range of brute force attacks on the same encrypted data, eventually one of them will crack the encryption and hence "win" the lottery.

Instead of performing a brute force attack sequentially, the Chinese lottery attack performs the same brute force attack in parallel, drastically cutting down the time needed to crack the encryption.

A second improvement of the Chinese lottery attack involves reducing the cost of resources necessary to conduct the brute force attack. A typical brute force attack requires a fast computer to exhaustively search all possible combinations. The Chinese lottery attack requires a vast network of much slower and less expensive computers because each computer needs only to exhaustively brute force attack a much smaller range of possibilities.

Although the Chinese lottery attack is mostly theoretical, it's possible for someone to write a computer worm that can spread and infect computers all over the world and conduct a brute force attack on a problem. The worm that finally cracks the problem can then send its *winning ticket* (the cracked message) to the original programmer of the worm.

Dictionary attacks

A brute force attack is the simplest encryption cracking method, but it's never the fastest. Because the strength of any encryption algorithm relies solely on the password used, it's often much simpler just to guess the password instead.

Most people use simple passwords that they can remember, such as PASSWORD, SEX, LOVE, 123, or names, such as their own name or the name of their favorite movie stars. Because passwords can vary in length, a simple brute force attack is impractical because not only do you need to exhaustively check all five-character passwords, but also all six-, seven-, eight-, nine-, and ten-character passwords.

So a dictionary attack simply combines a brute force attack, but rather than try all possible character combinations, it tries the most common passwords. Besides trying the previously mentioned common passwords, like LOVE and 123, a dictionary attack tries common words from *Star Trek,* Shakespeare, sports, and popular culture.

Because many people use a common password along with an additional character, such as PASSWORD5, a dictionary attack combines its dictionary with a brute force attack by picking a common word and trying different variations of that word, such as adding a different character at the beginning or end of the password or spelling the password backward.

Think of a dictionary attack as a smarter and faster version of a brute force attack. The odds of someone choosing a password, like S&$J#, is much less than someone choosing a password of SONYA, which is why dictionary attacks are so often successful.

Plaintext and ciphertext attacks

The easiest way to defeat any form of encryption is to steal the original plaintext message. Although this lets you read a single message, it doesn't help you read any additional messages encrypted with the same password. However, after you have the plaintext version of a message along with the encrypted version of that same message, you can deduce the password used to encrypt that message.

Comparing the plaintext version of a message with its encrypted version is a *plaintext attack*. Because it's rarely possible to retrieve the plaintext of an entire message, a more common code-breaking technique is to examine the ciphertext for patterns with *frequency analysis*.

The idea behind frequency analysis is that certain letters (such as *e*) or words (such as *and*) are more likely to appear in a message. A poor encryption algorithm encrypts the letter *e* and the word *and* with identical characters in different parts of the encrypted message. From this simple clue, it's possible to gradually deduce the encrypted symbols that represent the second-most-frequently used letters and words.

Although no form of encryption is unbreakable, the goal of every encryption algorithm is to resist all known forms of attack so as to make cracking the encryption unfeasible due to the lack of time or resources. As computers get faster and more powerful, today's encryption algorithms will only get weaker and easier to crack. By the time that occurs, mathematicians and computer scientists will have created newer and better encryption algorithms until those age and become easily broken all over again.

Code cracking in the Battle of Midway

Sometimes cracking a code is pointless if you can't understand the message inside. During World War II, American code breakers broke the Japanese encryption, so they could read every message the Japanese military sent. Based on these cracked messages, the United States knew that the Japanese were planning a large-scale attack some time around June 1942, but the big question was where?

According to the Japanese messages, the next target was *AF.* Some military analysts thought that AF represented Hawaii while others feared that AF actually meant the Japanese were going to attack and invade the West Coast itself. However, military analysts soon suspected that

AF really referred to a tiny island in the Pacific called Midway.

To verify their suspicions, the American commanders ordered the military base on Midway to send a plain, unencrypted message claiming that their water station had broken down. Soon afterward, the American code breakers intercepted a Japanese encrypted message stating that "AF was out of water." The Japanese never knew their encryption had been broken and the Americans managed to trick them into revealing their intentions. Based on the knowledge that AF meant Midway, the American Navy was able to surprise and ambush the Japanese task force, effectively turning the tide in the Pacific.

Book V

Web Programming

The 5th Wave By Rich Tennant

©RICHTENNANT

"Yes, I know how to query information from the program, but what if I just want to leak it instead?"

Contents at a Glance

Chapter 1: HyperText Markup Language

In This Chapter

✔ Defining a Web page

✔ Putting in graphics

✔ Defining your background

✔ Creating hyperlinks with anchor points

✔ Making your tables

The language used to create every Web page in the world is HyperText Markup Language (HTML). Although you can create Web pages with specialized Web page editing programs, such as Adobe Dreamweaver or Microsoft FrontPage, it's still nice to know how HTML works so you can modify Web pages manually or create unique effects that may be difficult or impossible to accomplish with a Web page editing program.

Much like a traditional programming language relies on keywords, HTML also relies on keywords, or *tags,* that follow a rigidly defined syntax. Instead of creating a working program like a traditional programming language, HTML creates Web pages that browsers can view.

In a traditional programming language, an error or bug can keep the entire program from running or make it calculate incorrectly. In HTML, an error can keep a Web page from appearing or just make the Web page display incorrectly. If you're interested in understanding the heart of Web page designing, you need to understand the basics of using HTML.

The Structure of an HTML Document

The basic HTML tab defines the entire HTML document like this:

```
<html>

</html>
```

Anything between the <html> and </html> tags will appear on the Web page.

The last tag uses a slash (/) to identify the end of the tag.

Generally, HTML tags work in pairs — the first tag defines something, and the second tag (the one beginning with a slash) marks the end of that definition. If you omit one of the `<html>` or `</html>` tags, your HTML Web page won't appear.

HTML tags are not case sensitive, so you could've defined the tags as `<HTML>` and `</HTML>`.

Creating a title

Most Web pages include a title, which appears in the title bar of a window. To display text in a window's title bar, type text in between the `<title>` and `</title>` tags inside the `<head>` and `</head>` tags like this:

```
<html>
    <head>
        <title>This text appears in the title bar.</title>
    </head>
</html>
```

Creating the body text

The bulk of a Web page falls within the `<body>` and `</body>` tags. To display text, you need to use the paragraph tags `<p>` and `</p>` like this:

```
<html>
    <head>
        <title>This text appears in the title bar.</title>
    </head>

    <body>
        <p>This text appears on the web page.</p>
    </body>
</html>
```

If you want to make sure a line of text breaks at a certain point, you can use the `<br>` tag, such as

```
<html>
    <head>
        <title>This text appears in the title bar.</title>
    </head>

    <body>
        <p>This text appears on the web page.<br>This appears
    on a separate line.</p>
    </body>
</html>
```

The preceding HTML code displays two lines of text like this:

```
This text appears on the web page.
This appears on a separate line.
```

With lots of text appearing on a Web page, you may want to separate text with headings. HTML offers six types of headings that use tags, such as `<h1>` and `</h1>`. The following code produces the results shown in Figure 1-1:

```html
<html>
    <head>
        <title>This text appears in the title bar.</title>
    </head>

    <body>
        <h1>Heading 1</h1>
        <h2>Heading 2</h2>
        <h3>Heading 3</h3>
        <h4>Heading 4</h4>
        <h5>Heading 5</h5>
        <h6>Heading 6</h6>
        <p>This text appears on the web page.</p>
    </body>
</html>
```

Figure 1-1:
HTML can create six different headings.

Aligning text

Text normally appears left-aligned, but you can also right-align or center-align text as well. To align text, you need to insert the following inside the first part of the paragraph or heading tag. The following code produces the results shown in Figure 1-2:

```
<html>
   <head>
      <title>This text appears in the title bar.</title>
   </head>

   <body>
      <h1 align = "center">Heading 1</h1>
      <p align = "right">This text appears on the web
   page.</p>
   </body>
</html>
```

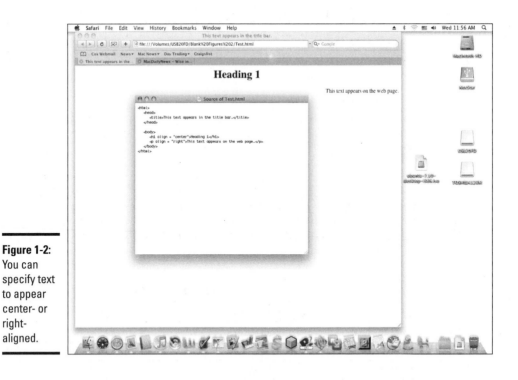

Figure 1-2:
You can specify text to appear center- or right-aligned.

Emphasizing text

To make text stand out, you can emphasize it as bold, italics, or underline by using the following tags:

✦ `<b>` and `</b>` to display text in bold

✦ `<i>` and `</i>` to display text in italic

✦ `<u>` and `</u>` to display text as underline

Just place these tags around the text you want to emphasize, such as

```
<html>
   <head>
      <title>This text appears in the title bar.</title>
   </head>

   <body>
     <p>This text appears <b>bold</b>.</p>
     <p>This text appears <i>italicized</i>.</p>
     <p>This text appears <u>underlined</u>.</p>
   </body>
</html>
```

Adding color

Color can further emphasize the appearance of text. To color text, surround it with the `<font color = #xxyyzz>` and `</font>` tags where `#xxyyzz` represents a color code, as shown in Table 1-1.

Colors are defined in shades of red, blue, and green, represented as hexadecimal values. The `xx` portion defines the amount of red, the `yy` defines the amount of blue, and the `zz` defines the amount of green. The absence of a color is `00` whereas the maximum amount of a color is `FF`. By varying the shades of red, blue, and green as hexadecimal values, you can define your own colors.

Table 1-1	HTML Color Codes
Color	*Color Code*
Red	#FF0000
Turquoise	#00FFFF
Light blue	#0000FF
Dark blue	#0000A0
Light purple	#FF0080
Dark purple	#800080

(continued)

Table 1-1 *(continued)*

Color	Color Code
Yellow	#FFFF00
Pastel green	#00FF00
Pink	#FF00FF
White	#FFFFFF
Light grey	#FFFFCC
Black	#000000
Orange	#FF8040
Brown	#804000
Burgundy	#800000
Forest green	#808000
Grass green	#408080

The following HTML code displays text in red (#FF0000):

```
<html>
   <head>
      <title>This text appears in the title bar.</title>
   </head>

   <body>
      <p>This text appears in <font color =
   #FF0000>red</font> on the web page.</p>
   </body>
</html>
```

Changing the font size

You can also make text appear larger or smaller by defining a size from 1 (smallest) to 7 (largest). The following HTML code makes the text appear large:

```
<html>
   <head>
      <title>This text appears in the title bar.</title>
   </head>

   <body>
      <p>This text appears <font size = 7>large</font> on the
   web page.</p>
   </body>
</html>
```

Adding comments

Because pages filled with HTML code can often be confusing to understand, you can sprinkle comments anywhere on your Web page. Comments always begin with < ! and end with >, so anything you place within those two comment tags are ignored by the computer, such as

```
<html>
   <head>
      <title>This text appears in the title bar.</title>
   </head>

   <! This is a comment in a web page. >

   <body>
      <p>This text appears <font size = 7>large</font> on the
   web page.</p>
   </body>
</html>
```

Adding Graphics

The three types of graphic files you can add on a Web page are JPEG (Joint Photographic Experts Group), GIF (Graphics Interchange Format), and PNG (Portable Network Graphics) files.

To add graphics on a Web page, you need to specify the graphic filename that you want to appear. So if you had a graphic image named duck.jpg, you could add it to a Web page like this:

```
<html>
   <head>
      <title>This text appears in the title bar.</title>
   </head>

   <body>
      <img src = "duck.jpg">
   </body>
</html>
```

Defining the Background

By default, Web pages can look pretty boring with a plain white background. To spice up the appearance of a Web page, you can modify the background to display a color or a graphic image. To define a background color, you have to define the RGB hexadecimal values like this:

```
<body bgcolor = #xxyyzz>
```

To define a background graphic, you need to specify the graphic filename like this:

```
<body background = "filename.ext">
```

You can define both a background color and a background image by combining both HTML commands on a single line like this:

```
<body bgcolor = #xxyyzz background = "filename.ext">
```

Creating Hyperlinks

Web pages typically contain text and graphics, but the heart of Web pages are *hyperlinks* that connect a Web page to another Web page or a different part of the currently displayed Web page. The HTML code to create a hyperlink looks like this:

```
<a href = "address">hyperlink text</a>
```

The `"address"` can be a Web site URL (Uniform Resource Locator), such as www.whitehouse.gov or www.dummies.com, or a Web page filename, such as index.html. The *hyperlink text* is the word or phrase that appears as a link. So if you wanted to turn the phrase White House into a link, you could use the following HTML code:

```
<a href = "www.whitehouse.gov">White House</a>
```

When you click a link to a Web page, the link takes you to the top of that Web page. If you want a link to jump to a specific part of a Web page, such as a paragraph in the middle of the Web page, you have to go through two steps:

1. Define an anchor that represents the specific part of the Web page that you want people to see when they click a link.

2. Define a link to take users to that specific part of the Web page.

Defining an anchor point

When you define an anchor point, you need to create a name for your anchor point and then define the actual text that will act as the anchor point, such as

```
<a name = "#anchorname">Anchor text here</a>
```

The anchor point is defined by the # symbol and can be any descriptive name. The *anchor text* is the text that you want users to see after they click a link.

Linking to an anchor point

After you've created an anchor point, you can create a hyperlink that points to that anchor point. If the hyperlink appears on the same Web page as the anchor point, you can just specify the anchor point name, such as

```
<a href = "#anchor point">Jump to anchor point</a>
```

If the anchor point appears on another Web page, you must specify the Web page filename followed by the anchor point name, such as

```
<a href = "webpage.html#anchor point">Jump to anchor
   point</a>
```

Making Tables

Tables help align text and graphics in rows and columns. For greater flexibility, you can choose to make the table borders appear visible or invisible. When table borders appear invisible, any items stored in the table appear aligned but without the distraction of borders.

When creating a table, you need to define the table appearance, the table headings, and the actual data that appears inside the table.

Defining a table

When you create a table, you have the option to define one or more of the following:

✦ **Alignment:** Defines how data appears within a table

✦ **Border:** Defines the thickness of the lines that define the table

✦ **Cell padding:** Defines the spacing between data and the cell borders

✦ **Cell spacing:** Defines the spacing between adjacent cells

✦ **Width:** Defines the size of the table as a percentage of the window

To define the alignment of data in a table, you can choose between center, left, or right, such as

```
<table align = "center"> </table>
```

To define the border of a table, specify a border value like this:

```
<table border = "2"> </table>
```

To define the cell padding and cell spacing, specify a value like this:

```
<table cellpadding = "2" cellspacing = "3"> </table>
```

To define the width of the table, define a percentage like this:

```
<table width = "75"> </table>
```

If you want to define multiple options, it's probably easier to store them on separate lines like this:

```
<table>
   <align = "center">
   <border = "2">
   <cellpadding = "2">
   <cellspacing = "3">
   <width = "75">
</table>
```

Defining a table heading

You may want to define headings for a table with the <th> and </th> tags. The following code produces the results shown in Figure 1-3:

```
<html>
   <head>
      <title>This text appears in the title bar.</title>
   </head>

   <table border = "1">
      <th>Column 1</th>
      <th>Column 2</th>
   </table>
</html>
```

Each time you use the <th> and </th> tags, you create another column in your table.

Figure 1-3:
The `<th>`
and `</th>`
tags define
the
headings for
the table.

Creating table rows and data

To fill a table with data, you need to use the `<tr>` and `</tr>` tags to define a
row and then fill in that row with the `<td>` and `</td>` tags, which define the
data. The following code produces the results shown in Figure 1-4:

```
<html>
   <head>
      <title>This text appears in the title bar.</title>
   </head>

   <table border = "1">
      <th>Column 1</th>
      <th>Column 2</th>
      <tr>
         <td>Stuff here</td>
         <td>Useful data</td>
      </tr>
      <tr>
         <td>Second row</td>
         <td>More data</td>
      </tr>
   </table>
</html>
```

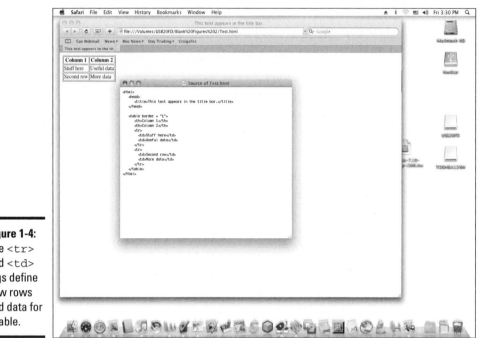

Figure 1-4:
The `<tr>`
and `<td>`
tags define
new rows
and data for
a table.

Displaying a table caption, header, and footer

If you want to create a caption to appear above your table, you can use the `<caption>` and `</caption>` tags. Captions can be useful to name or describe the data stored inside the table.

Tables can also store a header and footer. The header typically appears as the first row of the table whereas the footer typically appears as the last row of the table. To define a table header and footer, you need to use the `<thead>` and `<tfoot>` tags, respectively. The following code produces the results shown in Figure 1-5:

```
<html>
   <head>
      <title>This text appears in the title bar.</title>
   </head>

   <table border = "1">
     <caption>This is a table caption.</caption>
      <thead>
        <tr>
          <td>This is a table header</td>
```

```
      </tr>
    </thead>
    <th>Column 1</th>
    <th>Column 2</th>
    <tr>
      <td>Stuff here</td>
      <td>Useful data</td>
    </tr>
    <tr>
      <td>Second row</td>
      <td>More data</td>
    </tr>
    <tfoot>
      <tr>
        <td>This is a table footer</td>
      </tr>
    </tfoot>
  </table>
</html>
```

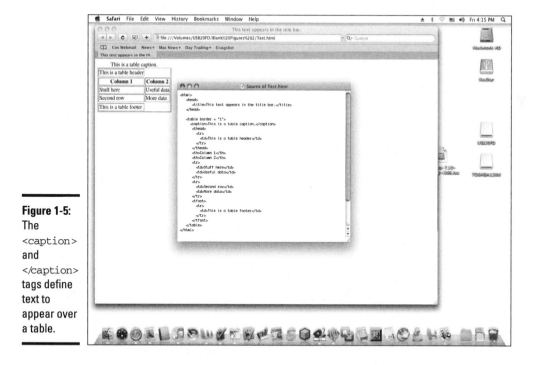

Figure 1-5:
The
`<caption>`
and
`</caption>`
tags define
text to
appear over
a table.

Chapter 2: CSS

Designing Web pages with HTML (HyperText Markup Language) lets you create and display text that can be read through a browser on a variety of devices such as personal computers, mobile phones, and game consoles. However, changing the content on a Web page often means changing the HTML code as well. Ideally, you want to leave the HTML code untouched and just change the text, much like pouring different liquids (such as coffee, juice, or milk) into a bottle so each type of liquid always appears in the shape of that bottle.

That's the idea behind cascading stylesheets (CSS). First, you store different styles in a separate file or in a separate area in the same file, which contain instructions for formatting text. Second, you apply that stylesheet to a text file or text in that same file. The combination of the stylesheet file and the text creates the display of the Web page inside a browser.

Cascading stylesheets get their name because you can apply multiple stylesheets to the same text file. The end result is a combination of styles defined by two or more stylesheets. If one stylesheet defines a certain font but a second stylesheet defines a different font, the text appears with the font defined by the last stylesheet.

By using stylesheets, you can make formatting text on your Web pages easy, fast, and simple.

The Structure of a Stylesheet

Like ordinary HTML, stylesheets use tags to define how to format text. To define a style, you use the `<style>` and `</style>` tags and then define the type of text you want to format such as heading 1 text (defined by the `<h1>` and `</h1>` tags), such as

```
<style>
<!--
  textstylename {
    attribute: value;
  }
-->
</style>
```

So if you wanted to display the color red for all heading 1 text, your style would look like this:

```
<html>
   <head>
      <title>This text appears in the title bar.</title>
   </head>

  <style>
  <!--
    h1 {
      color : #FF0000;
    }
  -->
  </style>

  </head>
  <body>
    <h1>This heading is defined by the style.</h1>
  </body>
</html>
```

You can define multiple styles that define additional attributes, such as

✦ Border

✦ Font-family

✦ Text-align

The following stylesheet defines text in both the `<h1>` heading and the `<p>` paragraph text:

```
<html>
   <head>
      <title>This text appears in the title bar.</title>
   </head>

  <style>
  <!--
    h1 {
```

```
      color : #FF0000;
    }
   p {
      color : #00FF00;
      background-color: $FF0000;
      text-align : center;
    }
  -->
  </style>

  </head>
  <body>
    <h1>This heading is defined by the style.</h1>
    <p>This is text is modified by the paragraph style.</p>
  </body>
</html>
```

Creating Style Classes

Styles can define the formatting for a particular type of text, such as text displayed as a <h2> heading or <p> paragraph. Unfortunately, every time you
display text in those <h2> or <p> tags, your style formats that text.

If you want the flexibility to choose different styles to use for text stored
within identical tags, you can define style classes. A *style class* lets you
define formatting and then you can apply this style class to any type of text
stored within different types of tags. For example, the following style defines
formatting for the <p> paragraph text:

```
<html>
  <head>
    <title>This text appears in the title bar.</title>
  </head>

  <style>
  <!--
    h1 {
      color : #FF0000;
    }
   p {
      color : #00FF00;
      background-color: $FF0000;
      text-align : center;
    }
  -->
  </style>

  </head>
  <body>
    <h1>This heading is defined by the style.</h1>
```

```
    <p>This is paragraph text gets modified by the paragraph
  style.</p>
    <p>This is paragraph text also gets modified.</p>
  </body>
</html>
```

In this example, a single style formats text stored in both <p> tags. To create a style class, define a class name and its formatting attributes like this:

```
<style>
<!--
  .classname {
    attribute: value;
  }
-->
</style>
```

To use a style class, include the class name within a tag, such as

```
<tag class = "classname">Text to be formatted</tag>
```

Style classes let you apply different styles to text stored within identical tags, such as

```
<html>
    <head>
        <title>This text appears in the title bar.</title>
    </head>

  <style>
  <!--
    .firstclass {
      color : #FF0000;
    }
    .secondclass {
      color : #00FF00;
      text-align : center;
    }
  -->
  </style>

    </head>
    <body>
      <h1 class = "firstclass">This heading is defined by the
    firstclass style.</h1>
      <p class = "firstclass">This is paragraph text gets
    modified by the firstclass style.</p>
      <p class = "secondclass">This is paragraph text gets
    modified by the secondclass style.</p>
    </body>
</html>
```

Separating Styles in Files

You can embed styles directly into an HTML page. However, if you want to reuse those styles in another HTML page, you have to copy those styles and store them a second time. To separate styles completely from the HTML Web page they're modifying, store stylesheets in separate files.

When stored as a separate file, the stylesheet simply contains the tag or class names along with the attributes you want to modify, such as

```
h1 {
    color : #FF0000;
    }

.myclass {
    color : #00FF00;
    text-align : center;
    }
```

After you store one or more styles in a separate file saved with the .css file extension, you need to include that stylesheet file in your HTML Web page by adding the <link> tag:

```
<link rel = "stylesheet" jref = "stylesheet.css" type =
    "text/css" media = "screen">
```

The media portion of the <link> tag defines how the Web page will be viewed. Besides "screen", some other media types include

✦ **"braille":** For tactile Braille readers

✦ **"aural":** For speech synthesis software

✦ **"handheld":** For handheld devices such as mobile phones

For example, suppose you stored the following styles in a styleme.css file:

```
.firstclass {
    color : #FF0000;
    }
    .secondclass {
    color : #00FF00;
    text-align : center;
    }
```

Now you can include this stylesheet in any HTML Web page by using the `<link>` tag like this:

```
<html>
  <link rel = "stylesheet" href = "./styleme.css" type =
  "text/css" media = "screen">
  <head>
    <title>This text appears in the title bar.</title>
  </head>

  <body>
    <h1 class = "firstclass">This heading is defined by the
    firstclass style.</h1>
    <p class = "firstclass">This is paragraph text gets
    modified by the firstclass style.</p>
    <p class = "secondclass">This is paragraph text gets
    modified by the secondclass style.</p>
  </body>
</html>
```

Storing stylesheets in separate files makes it easy to modify formatting without having to modify any of your actual HTML Web pages.

Cascading Stylesheets

You can store stylesheets as external files or embedded as part of the HTML code that defines a Web page. If one stylesheet defines how to format text stored inside the `<h1>` and `</h1>` tags and a second stylesheet defines how to format text stored inside the `<p>` and `</p>` tags, both stylesheets act as one *(cascade)* to define the text on a single Web page. By applying the formatting of different stylesheets, you get more flexibility in formatting your Web pages.

If two stylesheets try to format text stored within the same tags, the *internal* stylesheet (the one embedded in the HTML code of the Web page) takes precedence over the *external* stylesheet (the one stored in a separate file).

In this way, you can use external stylesheets to provide the bulk of the formatting for a Web page and then use smaller internal stylesheets within your HTML code to define a particular tag, such as text within the `<h3>` and `</h3>` tags.

If you have two external stylesheets that format the same text, define the order to apply the external stylesheets by using multiple <link> tags like this:

```
<html>
  <link rel = "stylesheet" href = "./file1.css" type =
    "text/css" media = "screen">
  <link rel = "stylesheet" href = "./file2.css" type =
    "text/css" media = "screen">
  <body>
  </body>
</html>
```

In the preceding example, the styles stored in the file2.css stylesheet take precedence over the styles stored in the file1.css. Any styles stored in the HTML code of your Web page takes precedence over any styles stored in either the file2.css or file1.css external files.

The general rule is that text will be formatted according to the stylesheet closest to the text. So an internal stylesheet is closer to text than an external stylesheet, which is why styles stored in an internal stylesheet take precedence over an external stylesheet.

If you want to create a Web page with a unified appearance, you might define the formatting for every tag inside a single external stylesheet. Then modify one or two styles (stored in additional external stylesheets or embedded in the HTML code of a specific Web page) in case you want to format some text differently.

Chapter 3: JavaScript

In This Chapter

🖙 **Understanding the JavaScript structure**

🖙 **Creating comments and declaring variables**

🖙 **Using operators and arrays**

🖙 **Branching and looping statements**

🖙 **Creating functions and designing user interfaces**

*T*he problem with most Web pages is that they're static, much like staring at a page from a book except displayed on a computer screen. Although nothing's wrong with static Web pages for displaying information, you may want to create interactive Web pages that can respond to the user's actions. To create interactive or dynamic Web pages, computer scientists developed various programming languages dubbed *scripting languages.* Although you can choose several languages for creating dynamic Web pages, the most popular scripting language is JavaScript.

JavaScript programs are stored either as part of a Web page file or in a separate file altogether. When you visit a Web site, the computer storing the Web pages (the *server*) sends its Web pages and JavaScript files to your computer (the *client*). Your computer now runs an interpreter to run the JavaScript programs.

Instead of creating standalone applications like a systems programming language can do (such as C++ or BASIC), JavaScript programs are often much shorter and designed to create simpler programs. For example, a JavaScript program may display a text box for you to type a password. Whatever you type, the JavaScript program can verify if the password is valid and then decide whether to let you into the Web site.

Because JavaScript works with most browsers and computers, JavaScript is a simple and easy way to create dynamic Web pages without relying on browser plug-ins that users might not have or want. However, one major disadvantage is that JavaScript programs may run slowly. Even worse, some people turn off JavaScript support to speed up their browser. So if your Web pages rely on JavaScript, anyone who turned off JavaScript won't see your fancy Web pages.

Despite its name, JavaScript is a completely different programming language from Java, although both languages borrow heavily from the C++ syntax that includes the use of curly brackets and semicolons ending each statement.

On the Mac OS X, *Dashboard widgets,* which are tiny programs that pop up on the screen, are made with JavaScript code.

The Structure of a JavaScript Program

At the simplest level, a JavaScript program can consist of one or more commands, such as

```
<html>
  <script language=javascript>
    document.writeln("This is a simple JavaScript program.");
  </script>
  <body>
  </body>
</html>
```

The `<script>` and `</script>` tags define the beginning and ending of a JavaScript program. The first `<script>` tag identifies the scripting language used, which in this case is always JavaScript. Sandwiched in between the two `<script>` tags are the actual JavaScript commands.

However, it's more common to divide a JavaScript program into functions with each function acting like a separate building block. For example, a simple JavaScript program might look like this:

```
<html>
  <script language=javascript>
    <!--
    function hello() {
      window.alert("This is also a simple JavaScript
    program.");
    }
    -->
  </script>
  <body onLoad = "hello()">
  </body>
</html>
```

The `onLoad` command tells your computer when to run a particular function.

As an alternative to storing JavaScript code directly in the HTML code of a Web page, you can store JavaScript programs in separate files. Then you

need to define the name of that JavaScript file to load and run it within your
Web page, such as

```
<html>
  <script language=javascript src="filename.js"></script>
  <body>
  </body>
</html>
```

Creating Comments

To write a comment in JavaScript, use the double slash character so that
anything that appears to the right is a comment, such as

```
<html>
  // The JavaScript code is stored in a file that
  // has the .js file extension.
  <script language=javascript src="filename.js"></script>
  <body>
  </body>
</html>
```

The double slash character is handy for adding a comment to a single line. If
you want to write a comment over multiple lines, you can use the /* and */
characters, such as

```
<html>
  /* The JavaScript code is stored in a file that
    has the .js file extension. */
  <script language=javascript src="filename.js"></script>
  <body>
  </body>
</html>
```

Declaring Variables

JavaScript variables can hold any type of data, such as numeric (integers
and decimals), strings ("like this"), Boolean values (True or False), or
nothing at all (defined as null). JavaScript variables act like temporary con-
tainers that can hold any data. One moment it might hold an integer, the next
a decimal value, and then a string.

To declare a variable in JavaScript, you must use the var keyword followed
by the variable name, such as

```
var VariableName;
```

`VariableName` can be any descriptive name. Because JavaScript is a case-sensitive language, it treats `My2008Tax` as a completely different variable than `my2008tax`. Some programmers use uppercase letters to make variable names easier to find whereas others use all lowercase. To declare multiple variables, just cram them all on a single line, separated by a comma, such as

```
var VariableName1, VariableName2, VariableName3;
```

Using Operators

The three types of operators used are mathematical, relational, and logical. Mathematical operators calculate numeric results such as adding, multiplying, or dividing numbers, as shown in Table 3-1.

Table 3-1	Mathematical Operators	
Mathematical Operator	*Purpose*	*Example*
+	Addition	5 + 3.4
-	Subtraction	203.9 − 9.12
*	Multiplication	39 * 146.7
/	Division	45 / 8.41
%	Modula division (returns the remainder)	35 % 9 = 8

The + operator can also concatenate two strings together, such as `"Hi there," + "good looking."` This would create one string that contains `"Hi there, good looking."`

Relational operators compare two values and return a `True` or `False` value. The six comparison operators available are shown in Table 3-2.

Table 3-2	Relational Operators
Relational Operator	*Purpose*
==	Equal
!=	Not equal
<	Less than
<=	Less than or equal to
>	Greater than
>=	Greater than or equal to

The relational operator in JavaScript is two equal sign symbols (==), whereas the relational operator in other programming languages is just a single equal sign symbol (=). If you use only a single equal sign to compare two values in JavaScript, your program will work but not the way it's supposed to.

Logical operators compare two Boolean values (True or False) and return a single True or False value, as shown in Table 3-3.

Table 3-3	Logical Operators
Logical Operator	*Truth Table*
&&	True && True = True True && False = False False && True = False False && False = False
||	True || True = True True || False = True False || True = True False || False = False
!	!True = False !False = True

Increment and decrement operators

Like C/C++, JavaScript has special increment (++) and decrement (−−) operators, which simply add or subtract 1 to a variable. Typically, adding 1 to a variable looks like this:

```
j = 5;
i = j + 1;
```

The increment operator replaces the + 1 portion with ++, such as

```
j = 5;
i = ++j;
```

In this example, the value of i is j + 1 or 6, and the value of j is also 6.

If you place the increment operator after the variable, such as

```
j = 5;
i = j++;
```

Now the value of i is 5, but the value of j is 6.

The decrement operator works the same way except that it subtracts 1 from a variable, such as

```
j = 5;
i = --j;
```

In this example, the value of i is j - 1 or 4, and the value of j is also 4.

If you place the decrement operator after the variable, such as

```
j = 5;
i = j--;
```

Now the value of i is 5, but the value of j is 4.

Assignment operators

Most programming languages use the equal sign to assign values to variables, such as

```
i = 59;
```

However, JavaScript also includes combination assignment and mathematical operators, as shown in Table 3-4.

Table 3-4	Assignment Operators	
Assignment Operator	*Purpose*	*Example*
+=	Addition assignment	i += 7 (equivalent to i = i + 7)
-=	Subtraction assignment	i -= 4 (equivalent to i = i - 4)
*=	Multiplication assignment	i *= y (equivalent to i = i * y)
/=	Division assignment	i /= 3.5 (equivalent to i = i / 3.5)
%=	Modulo assignment	i %= 2.8 (equivalent to i = i % 2.8)

Branching Statements

The simplest branching statement is an IF statement that only runs one or more commands if a Boolean condition is True, such as

```
if (condition) {
  Command;
  }
```

To make the computer choose between two mutually exclusive sets of commands, you can use an IF-ELSE statement, such as

```
if (condition) {
  Command;
  }
else {
  Command;
  }
```

As an alternative to the IF-ELSE statement, you can also use the SWITCH statement to offer two or more choices, such as

```
switch (expression) {
case value1:
  Command;
  break;
case value2:
  Command;
  break;
default:
  Command;
}
```

The SWITCH statement always needs to include the *break* command to tell the computer when to exit out of the SWITCH statement.

The above SWITCH statement is equivalent to the following IF-ELSE statement:

```
if (expression = value1) {
  Command;
  }
else if (expression = value2) {
  Command;
  }
else {
  Command;
  }
```

To check if a variable matches multiple values, you can stack multiple case statements, such as

```
switch (expression) {
case value1:
case value2:
  Command;
  break;
```

```
case value3:
case value4;
   Command;
   break;
default:
   Command;
}
```

This SWITCH statement is equivalent to the following IF-ELSE statement:

```
if (expression = value1) || (expression = value2) {
   Command;
   }
else if (expression = value3) || (expression = value4) {
   Command;
   }
else {
   Command;
   }
```

Looping Statements

A *looping* statement repeats one or more commands for a fixed number of times or until a certain Boolean condition becomes True. To create a loop that repeats for a fixed number of times, use the FOR loop, which looks like this:

```
for (startvalue; endvalue; increment) {
   Command;
   }
```

If you wanted the FOR loop to run four times, you could set the Start value to 1 and the End value to 4, such as

```
for (i = 1; i <= 4; i++) {
   Command;
   }
```

If you don't know how many times you need to repeat commands, use a WHILE loop, which looks like this:

```
while (condition) {
   Command;
}
```

If the condition is True, the loop runs at least once. If this condition is False, the loop doesn't run.

A variation of the WHILE loop is the DO-WHILE loop, which looks like this:

```
do {
  Command;
} while (condition);
```

The main difference between the two loops is that the WHILE loop may run zero or more times, but the DO-WHILE loop will always run at least once.

Somewhere inside a WHILE and DO-WHILE loop, you must have a command that can change the condition from True to False; otherwise, the loop will never end, and your program will appear to hang or freeze.

Creating Functions

In JavaScript, every subprogram is a function that can return a value. (A function that returns a null value simply acts like a procedure in other programming languages.) The format of a typical function looks like this:

```
function functionname (Parameter list)
  {
  Commands;
  return value;
  }
```

The two parts of a JavaScript function are

+ **Parameter list:** Defines any data and their data types that the function needs to work. If the function doesn't need to accept any values, the parameter list can be empty.

+ **Return:** Defines a value to return.

If a function doesn't return a value or accept any parameters, it might look like this:

```
function myfunction ()
  {
  Command;
  }
```

Using Arrays

JavaScript offers two ways to create an array. First, you can define an array and the elements inside that array by using square brackets like this:

```
var myarray = [data1, data2, data3];
```

JavaScript arrays can store any type of data, such as integers, decimal values, strings, or Boolean values like this:

```
var myarray = [93.42, "Hi there", 3];
```

Another way to create a JavaScript array is to define the array size and then store data in that array like this:

```
var myarray = new Array(x);
```

Here x is the size of the array, such as 4 or 9. After defining an array, you can store items in that array like this:

```
myarray[2] = "This works";
```

JavaScript arrays are zero-based, which means if you define an array like this:

```
 var myarray = new Array(2);
```

The array elements are numbered `myarray[0]`, `myarray[1]`, and `myarray[2]`.

Designing User Interfaces

JavaScript can retrieve data from the user by creating different types of user interface elements, such as dialog boxes and windows. Such user interface items can display information to the user, creating an interactive Web page.

Creating dialog boxes

The three types of dialog boxes JavaScript can create are alert, confirmation, and prompt. An *alert* dialog box displays a message on the screen and gives the user the option of closing the dialog box. A *confirmation* dialog box displays a message and offers the user two or more choices. A *prompt* dialog box gives users a chance to type in data.

To create an alert dialog box, you need to define the text you want displayed, such as

```
alert("Message here");
```

An alert dialog box displays an OK button. As soon as the user clicks this OK button, the alert dialog box goes away.

A confirmation dialog box gives users a choice of OK and Cancel buttons. To create a confirmation dialog box, you must display text and include commands that do something when the user clicks either OK or Cancel:

```
if (confirm("Text message"))
  command;
else
  command;
```

The following JavaScript code creates a confirmation dialog box:

```
<html>
  <script language=javascript>
    <!--
    if (confirm("Do you want to retaliate with nuclear
    weapons?"))
      document.write("Now starting World War III.");
    else
      document.write ("Let's give peace a chance.");
    -->
  </script>
  <body>
  </body>
</html>
```

To create a prompt dialog box, you need to display text to appear in the dialog box and then optional text to appear as a default value, such as

```
prompt("Text to display", optionalvalue);
```

If you wanted to display the text `"How many times do you think you'll be disappointed by your Presidential elections?"` and display a default value of `"Infinity"`, you'd use this JavaScript code:

```
<html>
  <script language=javascript>
    <!--
    prompt ("How many times do you think you'll be
    disappointed by your Presidential elections?",
    "Infinity");
    -->
  </script>
  <body>
  </body>
</html>
```

Creating windows

JavaScript can open windows, which can display additional Web pages inside. (Many browsers may include a feature to block pop-up windows. This feature blocks JavaScript from opening a window because many pop-up ads rely on JavaScript to display annoying ads on your screen.)

To create a window, you need to use the following:

```
variablename = window.open ("address");
```

So if you wanted to open the Dummies Web site, you could use this code:

```
mywindow = window.open ("http://www.dummies.com");
```

Chapter 4: PHP

*I*n the old days, Web pages were used to display information, such as text and graphics. Nowadays, Web pages are dynamic, so they not only need to respond to the user, but they often need to retrieve information off a Web page and store it in a database, such as when you type your credit card number to buy something off a Web site.

HTML can create simple user interfaces, but when you need to transfer data from a Web page to another program, such as a database, you need to use a programming language. Although programmers have used C, Perl, and Java to link Web pages to other programs like databases, one of the most popular programming languages for this task is PHP, which is a recursive name that stands for PHP Hypertext Processor (www.php.net).

Although languages such as C and Perl can be used to create standalone applications, PHP programs are unique in that they can run only on Web pages. Not only is PHP designed for creating programs within Web pages, but PHP is also free and capable of running under many different operating systems. If you're already familiar with C and Perl, you'll find that PHP mimics much of the syntax from both languages. Although you can create dynamic Web sites with other programming languages, you may find PHP easier and simpler to use.

The Structure of a PHP Program

At the simplest level, a PHP program can consist of one or more commands embedded in a Web page's HTML code, such as

```
<html>
  <body>
    <?php
      echo "<h1>Greetings from PHP.</h1>";
```

```
  ?>
 </body>
</html>
```

The `<?php` and `?>` tags define the beginning and ending of a PHP program. PHP programs *(scripts)* are usually stored in a file that ends with the `.php` file extension.

Creating Comments

To write a comment in PHP, you have three choices: `//`, `#`, or `/*` and `*/` symbols. Both the double slash (`//`) and the number (`#`) characters are used to create comments on a single line, such as

```
<html>
 <body>

 // This is the beginning of the PHP program.

   <?php
     echo "<h1>PHP is a unique Web-specific language</h1>";
   ?>

 # This is the end of the PHP program

 </body>
</html>
```

If you want to write a comment over multiple lines, use the `/*` and the `*/` characters, such as

```
<html>
 <body>

 /* This is the beginning of the PHP program.
    If a comment extends over multiple lines,
    It's easier to use these types of comment
    symbols instead. */

   <?php
     echo "<h1>PHP can be fun and profitable</h1>";
   ?>
 </body>
</html>
```

Declaring Variables

PHP variables can hold any type of data, so a variable might hold a string one moment and a number the next. To declare a variable in PHP, you must begin every variable name with the dollar symbol ($), such as

```
$VariableName = value;
```

VariableName can be any descriptive name, but PHP is a case-sensitive language so $MyAge is considered a completely different variable from $myage. Some programmers use uppercase letters to make variable names easier to find, and others use all lowercase.

One unique feature of PHP is its ability to reference the same value. For example, consider the following code:

```
$myage = 35;
$yourage = $myage;
$myage = 109;
```

In this example, the $myage variable is initially set to 35 and the $yourage variable is set to the $myage variable, which means the $yourage variable also contains the value of 35. The third line stores the value 109 into the $myage variable, but the $yourage variable still holds the value of 35.

By referencing variables with the ampersand symbol (&), PHP allows a variable to contain identical data without specifically assigning those values. For example:

```
$myage = 35;
$yourage = &$myage;
$myage = 109;
```

The second line in the preceding PHP code tells the computer that the $yourage variable references the $myage variable, so whatever value the $myage variable contains from now on will automatically get stored in the $yourage variable.

After the third line, the $myage variable now contains the value of 109, so the $yourage variable contains 109 too.

Using Operators

The three types of operators used in PHP are mathematical, relational, and logical operators.

Mathematical operators calculate numeric results such as adding, multiplying, or dividing numbers, as shown in Table 4-1.

Table 4-1	Mathematical Operators	
Mathematical Operator	*Purpose*	*Example*
+	Addition	5 + 3.4
-	Subtraction	203.9 – 9.12
*	Multiplication	39 * 146.7
/	Division	45 / 8.41
%	Modula division (returns the remainder)	35 % 9 = 8

Relational operators compare two values and return a True or False value. The seven comparison operators available are shown in Table 4-2.

Table 4-2	Relational Operators
Relational Operator	*Purpose*
==	Equal
===	Identical
!= or <>	Not equal
<	Less than
<=	Less than or equal to
>	Greater than
>=	Greater than or equal to

PHP uses three equal signs (===) to compare to values and determine if they are of the same data type. For example, PHP treats 14.0 and 14 as identical because both are numbers, but 14.0 and "14.0" wouldn't be considered equal because one is a number and the other is a different data type (a *string*).

Logical operators compare two Boolean values (True or False) and return a single True or False value, as shown in Table 4-3.

Table 4-3	Logical operators
Logical Operator	*Truth Table*
&& (AND)	True && True = True True && False = False False && True = False False && False = False
|| (OR)	True || True = True True || False = True False || True = True False || False = False
XOR	True XOR True = False True XOR False = True False XOR True = True False XOR False = False
!	!True = False !False = True

PHP

Increment and decrement operators

PHP has a special increment (++) and a decrement (--) operator, which simply adds or subtracts 1 to a variable. Typically, adding 1 to a variable looks like this:

```
j = 5;
i = j + 1;
```

The increment operator replaces the + 1 portion with ++, such as

```
j = 5;
i = ++j;
```

In the preceding example, the value of i is j + 1 or 6, and the value of j is also 6.

If you place the increment operator after the variable, such as

```
j = 5;
i = j++;
```

Now the value of i is 5, but the value of j is 6.

The decrement operator works the same way except that it subtracts 1 from a variable, such as

```
j = 5;
i = --j;
```

In the preceding example, the value of i is j - 1 or 4, and the value of j is also 4.

If you place the decrement operator after the variable, such as

```
j = 5;
i = j--;
```

Now the value of i is 5, but the value of j is 4.

Assignment operators

Most programming languages use the equal sign to assign values to variables, such as

```
i = 59;
```

However, PHP also include combination assignment and mathematical operators, as shown in Table 4-4.

Table 4-4	Assignment Operators	
Assignment Operator	*Purpose*	*Example*
+=	Addition assignment	i += 7 (equivalent to i = i + 7)
-=	Subtraction assignment	i -= 4 (equivalent to i = i - 4)
*=	Multiplication assignment	i *= y (equivalent to i = i * y)
/=	Division assignment	i /= 3.5 (equivalent to i = i / 35)
%=	Modulo assignment	i %= 2.8 (equivalent to i = i % 2.8)

Branching Statements

The simplest branching statement is an IF statement that runs only one or more commands if a Boolean condition is True, such as

```
if (condition) {
  Command;
  }
```

To make the computer choose between two mutually exclusive sets of commands, you can use an IF-ELSE statement, such as

```
if (condition) {
  Command;
  }
else {
```

```
Command;
    }
```

Although the `IF-ELSE` statement can only give the computer a choice of two groups of commands to run, the `IF-ELSEIF` statement can offer the computer multiple groups of commands to run, such as

```
if (condition1) {
  Command;
  }
elseif (condition2) {
  Command;
  }
elseif (condition3) {
  Command;
  }
```

As an alternative to the `IF-ELSEIF` statement, you can also use the `SWITCH` statement to offer two or more choices, such as

```
switch (expression) {
case value1:
  Command;
  break;
case value2:
  Command;
  break;
default:
  Command;
}
```

The `SWITCH` statement always needs to include the `break` command to tell the computer when to exit out of the `SWITCH` statement.

The preceding `SWITCH` statement is equivalent to the following `IF-ELSE` statement:

```
if (expression == value1) {
  Command;
  }
elseif (expression == value2) {
  Command;
  }
else {
  Command;
  }
```

To check if a variable matches multiple values, you can stack multiple case statements, such as

```
switch (expression) {
case value1:
case value2:
   Command;
   break;
case value3:
case value4;
   Command;
   break;
default:
   Command;
}
```

The preceding SWITCH statement is equivalent to the following IF-ELSE statement:

```
if (expression == value1) || (expression == value2) {
   Command;
   }
else if (expression == value3) || (expression == value4) {
   Command;
   }
else {
   Command;
   }
```

Looping Statements

A looping statement repeats one or more commands for a fixed number of times or until a certain Boolean condition becomes True. To create a loop that repeats for a fixed number of times, use the FOR loop, which looks like this:

```
for (startvalue; endvalue; increment) {
   Command;
   }
```

If you wanted the FOR loop to run four times, you could set the Start value to 1 and the End value to 4, such as

```
for ($i = 1; $i <= 4; $i++) {
   Command;
   }
```

If you don't know how many times you need to repeat commands, use a WHILE loop, which looks like this:

```
while (condition) {
  Command;
}
```

If the condition is True, the loop runs at least once. If this condition is False, the loop doesn't run.

Somewhere inside a WHILE loop, you must have a command that can change the condition from True to False; otherwise the loop will never end and your program will appear to hang or freeze.

Creating Functions

To break up programming problems, you can create subprograms that solve a specific task. Such subprograms are *functions*. The format of a typical function looks like this:

```
function functionname (Parameter list)
   {
   Commands;
   return $value;
   }
```

The two parts of a PHP function are

> **Parameter list:** Defines any data that the function needs to work. If the function doesn't need to accept any values, the parameter list can be empty.

> **Return:** Defines a value to return.

If a function doesn't return a value or accept any parameters, it might look like this:

```
function myfunction ()
   {
   Command;
   }
```

Using Arrays

PHP creates arrays that can hold any type of data and grow as large as you need them without having to define a size ahead of time. To create an array, define an array name, the data you want to store, and the index number where you want to store that item in the array like this:

```
$arrayname[index] = data;
```

So if you wanted to store the string "Hello" and the number 4.23 in the first and second elements of an array, you could do the following:

```
$myarray[0] = "Hello";
$myarray[1] = 4.23;
```

For greater flexibility in retrieving data, PHP lets you create associative arrays, which let you identify data by a unique string (called a *key*) rather than an arbitrary index number. Instead of assigning data to a specific index number, you assign data to a unique string, such as

```
$arrayname["key"] = data;
```

If you wanted to assign the number 3.14 to the "pi" key, you'd do this:

```
$myarray["pi"] = 3.14;
```

To retrieve data from an associative array, use the key value, such as

```
$variable = $arrayname["key"];
```

So if you wanted to retrieve data stored under the key "pi", you could do the following:

```
$myarray["pi"] = 3.14;
$number2use = $myarray["pi"];
```

The first line stores the value 3.14 into the array and assigns it to the key "pi". The second line yanks out the data, associated with the key "pi", and stores that data into the $number2use variable.

PHP includes a library of built-in array functions for manipulating arrays such as array_pop (which removes the last element from an array), array_push (which adds an element to the end of an array, and sort (which sorts arrays in ascending order).

Creating Objects

PHP supports object-oriented programming. To create an object, you must define a class, which specifies the properties and methods, such as

```
class classname {
  public $propertyname;

  public function methodname() {
    commands;
  }
}
```

To create an object, you must use the following syntax:

```
$objectname = new classname;
```

To assign a value to an object's property, specify the object name and the property you want to use, such as

```
$objectname->propertyname = value;
```

When assigning a value to an object's property, notice that the dollar symbol ($) isn't used to designate the property name.

To tell an object to run a method, specify the object name followed by the method name, such as

```
$objectname->methodname();
```

PHP allows *single inheritance* where an object can inherit from one class (in contrast to *multiple inheritance,* which allows an object to inherit from two or more classes). To inherit from a class, use the `extends` keyword followed by the class name you want to inherit from, such as

```
class classname1 {
  public $propertyname;

  public function methodname() {
    commands;
  }
}

class classname2 extends classname1 {
  public $propertyname;

  public function methodname() {
    commands;
  }
}
```

Chapter 5: Ruby

In This Chapter

✔ **Understanding the structure of a Ruby program**

✔ **Creating comments and declaring variables**

✔ **Using operators and data structures**

✔ **Branching and looping statements**

✔ **Creating functions and objects**

The Ruby programming language was created by Yukihiro "Matz" Matsumoto, a Japanese programmer who named the language after a gemstone in reference to the Perl (pearl) programming language. Although most languages focus on wringing out extra performance from computer hardware, Ruby focuses on a clean language syntax that's easy for programmers to understand and use. Instead of trying to increase machine efficiency, Ruby tries to increase programmer efficiency. The overriding principle of Ruby is to create a language of *least surprise,* meaning that after you're familiar with Ruby, you aren't suddenly surprised that its features can be used in an entirely different way, which often occurs with languages such as C++.

Ruby is an interpreted, object-oriented language for creating interactive Web pages. Although Ruby is similar to Perl and Python, Ruby abandons the C-syntax of Perl and more closely resembles the syntax of programming languages like Smalltalk or Ada. Instead of enclosing blocks of commands in curly brackets like C or Perl, Ruby encloses blocks of commands with keywords like Ada or more modern versions of BASIC.

A programming framework, dubbed *Ruby on Rails,* makes it easy to manipulate databases through Web pages and has attracted the attention of many former Java programmers. Like Ruby itself, Ruby on Rails is free, which has further fueled its growth. Although still a relatively young language (created in 1995), Ruby has attracted a worldwide following and will likely play a major role in future applications developed for the Web.

Mac OS X and many Linux distributions include an interpreter for the Ruby language. To get a copy of the free Ruby interpreter for other operating systems, visit the official Ruby Web site (www.ruby-lang.org).

The Structure of a Ruby Program

A Ruby program can consist of one or more commands:

```
print('What is your name? ' )
myname = gets()
puts( "Welcome to Ruby, #{myname}" )
```

Unlike other programming languages, Ruby programs don't need to define a *main* program, don't enclose blocks of commands with curly brackets, and don't end statements with a semicolon. Type a command, and Ruby obeys without its syntax interfering with your thinking.

The preceding Ruby program simply asks the user to type in a name. Whatever name the user types gets stored in the myname variable. Then the last line prints the string "Welcome to Ruby, " followed by the contents of the myname variable.

Creating Comments

To write a comment in Ruby, use the # symbol. Anything that appears to the right of the # symbol is considered a comment, which the computer ignores.

```
# This is a comment
print('What is your name? ' )
myname = gets()   # This is also a comment
puts( "Welcome to Ruby, #{myname}" )
```

If you want to write a comment over multiple lines, define the start and end of a comment block with =begin and =end, such as

```
=begin This is a block of comments
       that make it easy to comment
       out multiple lines. However,
       Ruby's block commenting is kind
       of ugly so it's rarely used.
=end
print('What is your name? ' )
myname = gets()
puts( "Welcome to Ruby, #{myname}" )
```

Defining comments with the =begin and =end lines is often cumbersome, so it's more common for programmers to use multiple # symbols in front of each line instead like this:

```
# This program was written by John Doe
# on January 24, 2009. It took him a
```

```
# long time to write so maybe he deserves
# a big fat raise or at least some extra
# sick days so he can look for a better job.
print('What is your name? ' )
myname = gets()
puts( "Welcome to Ruby, #{myname}" )
```

Declaring Variables

Ruby uses symbols to identify different types of variables:

✦ **Local:** Begins with a lowercase letter, such as `myage`

✦ **Instance:** Begins with an @ symbol, such as `@house`

✦ **Class:** Begins with two @ symbols, such as `@@mathclass`

✦ **Global:** Begins with a $ symbol, such as `$mymoney`

In Ruby, constants are identified with an initial uppercase letter like `Pi` or `Taxrate`. To avoid confusing constants with local variables, it's best to use all uppercase letters to name constants like `PI` or `TAXRATE`.

Both class and instance variables are used inside classes that define objects.

To store data into a variable, define the variable name and set it equal to a value:

```
variableName = value
```

The name of your variables can be anything, but Ruby is a case-sensitive language so `myAge` is considered a completely different variable than `myage`.

Using Operators

The three types of operators used in Ruby are mathematical, relational, and logical operators. *Mathematical* operators calculate numeric results such as adding, multiplying, or dividing numbers, as shown in Table 5-1.

Table 5-1	**Mathematical Operators**	
Mathematical Operator	*Purpose*	*Example*
+	Addition	5 + 3.4
-	Subtraction	203.9 – 9.12
*	Multiplication	39 * 146.7
/	Division	45 / 8.41
%	Modula division (returns the remainder)	35 % 9 = 8
**	Exponentiation	2**3 = 8

If you divide two integers with the / operator, the answer will be rounded to the nearest integer. If you want to return a decimal value, at least one of the numbers must be written as a decimal value such as 2.0 / 3 or 2 / 3.0. If you just type 2 / 3, the answer will be 0.

Relational operators compare two values and return a True or a False value. The seven comparison operators available are shown in Table 5-2.

Table 5-2	**Relational Operators**
Relational Operator	*Purpose*
==	Equal
===	Identical
!=	Not equal
<	Less than
<=	Less than or equal to
>	Greater than
>=	Greater than or equal to

Ruby uses three equal signs (===) to compare to values and determine if they're of the same data type. For example, Ruby treats 1.0 and 1 as identical because both are numbers, but 1.0 and "1.0" wouldn't be considered equal because one is a number and the other is a different data type (a *string*).

Logical operators compare two Boolean values (True or False) and return a single True or False value, as shown in Table 5-3.

Table 5-3	Logical Operators
Logical Operator	*Truth Table*
&& (AND)	True && True = True True && False = False False && True = False False && False = False
|| (OR)	True || True = True True || False = True False || True = True False || False = False
^ (XOR)	True ^ True = False True ^ False = True False ^ True = True False ^ False = False
! (NOT)	!True = False !False = True

Most programming languages use the equal sign to assign values to variables, such as

```
i = 59
```

However, Ruby also includes combination assignment and mathematical operators, as shown in Table 5-4.

Table 5-4	Assignment Operators	
Assignment Operator	*Purpose*	*Example*
+=	Addition assignment	i += 7 (equivalent to i = i + 7)
-=	Subtraction assignment	i -= 4 (equivalent to i = i - 4)
*=	Multiplication assignment	i *= y (equivalent to i = i * y)
/=	Division assignment	i /= 3.5 (equivalent to i = i / 35)
%=	Modulo assignment	i %= 2.8 (equivalent to i = i % 2.8)

Because Ruby lacks an increment and decrement operator like C++, you must increment variables with the assignment operator. So although C++ lets you use an increment operator like this:

```
++i;
```

The equivalent increment operator in Ruby might look like this:

```
i += 1
```

Branching Statements

The simplest branching statement is an IF statement that runs only one or more commands if a Boolean condition is True, such as

```
if condition
   Command
end
```

If you write the entire IF statement on a single line, you must make sure you include the then keyword, such as

```
if condition then Command end
```

Ruby also includes a negated form of the IF statement called the UNLESS statement that looks like this:

```
unless condition
   Command
end
```

The UNLESS statement runs only if the condition is False.

```
a = 5
unless a < 1
   puts "This will print out."
end
```

Because the condition a < 1 is False, the preceding UNLESS statement runs the command sandwiched between the UNLESS keyword and the END keyword.

Both the IF and UNLESS statements can make the computer choose between two mutually exclusive sets of commands by including an ELSE keyword, such as

```
if condition
   Command1
else
   Command2
end
```

Although the IF-ELSE statement can only give the computer a choice of two groups of commands to run, the IF-ELSIF statement can offer the computer multiple groups of commands to run, such as

```
if condition1
   Command
elseif condition2
```

```
   Command
elseif condition3
   Command
end
```

As an alternative to the IF-ELSIF statement, you can also use the CASE statement to offer two or more choices, such as

```
case variable
when value1
   Command
when value2
   Command
else
   Command;
end
```

Rather than check if a variable equals a specific value, the CASE statement can also check if a variable falls within a range of values by using the . . characters, such as

```
case variable
when value1..value4
   Command
when value5
   Command
else
   Command;
end
```

Looping Statements

A looping statement repeats one or more commands for a fixed number of times or until a certain Boolean condition becomes True. To create a loop that repeats for a fixed number of times, use the FOR loop, which looks like this:

```
for variable in startvalue..endvalue
   Command
end
```

If you wanted the FOR loop to run four times, you could set the Start value to 1 and the End value to 4, such as

```
for i = 1..4
   Command
end
```

If you don't know how many times you need to repeat commands, use a WHILE loop, which looks like this

```
while condition
    Command
end
```

If the condition is True, the loop runs at least once. If this condition is False, then the loop doesn't run.

Ruby also offers a negated form of the WHILE loop called an UNTIL loop, which looks like this:

```
until condition
    Command
end
```

The UNTIL loop keeps running until a condition becomes True.

Somewhere inside a WHILE or an UNTIL loop, you must have a command that can change the condition from True to False; otherwise the loop will never end and your program will appear to hang or freeze.

Creating Functions

To break up programming problems, you can create subprograms that solve a specific task. Such subprograms are *functions* or *methods*. The format of a typical function looks like this:

```
def functionname (Parameter list)
    Commands
    return value
end
```

The two parts of a Ruby function are

✦ Parameter list: **Defines any data that the function needs to work. If the function doesn't need to accept any values, omit the parentheses altogether.**

✦ **Return:** Defines a value to return.

If a function doesn't return a value or accept any parameters, it might look like this:

```
def myfunction
    Command
end
```

Using Data Structures

Ruby offers two built-in data structures: collections and hashes (also known as an associative array).

✦ A **collection** can hold any number of items of different data types, such as strings and numbers. In a collection, each item is identified by an index number, starting with 0.

✦ A **hash** is like a collection, but stores a unique key value with every item. To retrieve a value from a hash, you need to know its key.

To create a collection, define a collection name and list the items to store in the collection inside square brackets like this:

```
collectionname = [data1, data2, data3]
```

So if you wanted to store the string `"Ruby is cool"` and the number `84.3` in the first and second elements of a collection, you could do the following:

```
mystuff = ["Ruby is cool", 84.3]
```

To retrieve data from a collection, specify the collection name and index number. So if you wanted to retrieve the first item in a collection, you could do this:

```
puts mystuff [0]
```

One problem with collections is that to retrieve specific data, you need to know its exact location in the collection. For greater flexibility, Ruby offers hashes so you can assign a unique value (a *key*) to each item. To create a hash and store data along with a key, do this:

```
hashname = {key => value, key => value}
```

Ruby defines a collection with square brackets but defines a hash with curly brackets.

If you wanted to assign the number `3.14` to the `"pi"` key, you could do this:

```
myhash = {"pi" => 3.14}
```

If you need to store multiple keys and values in a hash, you might prefer this alternate way of storing keys and data in a hash:

```
hashname = Hash.new
hashname[key] = value
hashname[key] = value
```

When defining a hash with multiple lines, use square brackets.

To retrieve data from a hash, identify the hash name and a key value, such as

```
puts hashname["key"]
```

So if you wanted to retrieve data stored under the key "pi", you could do the following:

```
hashname = Hash.new
hashname["pi"] = 3.14
puts hashname["pi"]
```

The first line creates a hash data structure. The second line stores the value 3.14 into the hash using the key "pi". The third line prints out the value identified by the "pi" key in the hash data structure.

Creating Objects

Ruby supports object-oriented programming. To create an object, you must define a class, which specifies the properties and methods, such as

```
class Classname
  def propertyname
    @propertyname
  end
  def propertyname=(propertyname)
    @propertyname = propertyname
  end

  def methodname(parameter list)
    commands
  end
end
```

To create an object, you must use the following syntax:

```
objectname = Classname.new
```

To assign a value to an object's property, you need to specify the object name and the property you want to use, such as

```
objectname.propertyname = value
```

To tell an object to run a method, you need to specify the object name followed by the method name, such as

```
objectname.methodname(parameters)
```

Ruby allows *single inheritance,* where an object can inherit from one class (in contrast to *multiple inheritance,* which allows an object to inherit from two or more classes). To inherit from a class, use the < symbol followed by the class name you want to inherit from, such as

```
class Classname
  def propertyname
    @propertyname
  end
  def propertyname=(propertyname)
    @propertyname = propertyname
  end

  def methodname(parameter list)
    commands
  end
end

class Classname2 < Classname1
  # property and method definitions go here
end
```

Book VI

Programming Language Syntax

The 5th Wave
By Rich Tennant

"It's a horse racing software program. It analyzes my betting history and makes suggestions. Right now it's suggesting I try betting on football."

Contents at a Glance

Chapter 1: C and C++

The C language focuses on simplicity. Whereas other programming languages include a large numbers of keywords, the C language consists of a much smaller number of keywords. As a result, creating C compilers is relatively easy compared to creating compilers for other programming languages, which means that C compilers are easy to write for every operating system. This makes it easier to transfer, or *port,* C programs from one computer to another.

Because the C language consists of relatively few keywords, it lacks features commonly found in other programming languages, such as offering a string data type. To compensate for its relative sparseness of features, most C compilers include a variety of library files that contain pre-written C code that adds these useful features to the C language. The main problem with C compilers is that every C compiler tends to offer different library files, so a C program designed to run on Windows may not run correctly with a different C compiler on Linux.

The C++ language builds on the C language by adding object-oriented features while retaining the C language's hardware access, speed, and portability. Most large and complicated programs, such as operating systems, are written in C++.

Because C/C++ gives complete access to all parts of the computer, a mistake in a C/C++ program can wipe out data off a hard disk or crash the entire operating system of the computer. Writing C/C++ programs may be easy, but understanding and fixing C/C++ programs can be difficult.

Despite these problems, C/C++ is heavily used throughout the computer industry. To understand programming, you must become familiar with the C/C++ programming language.

The Structure of a C/C++ Program

A C program is divided into multiple functions where each function acts like a separate building block. To identify the starting point of a C program, one function is always designated as the main function. A simple C program looks like this:

```
main()
{
   printf("This is a simple C program.\n");
}
```

Large C programs consist of multiple functions where each additional function appears defined separate from the main function. In the following example, the separate function is `printme` as follows:

```
main()
{
   printme;
}

printme()
{
   printf("This is a simple C program.\n");
}
```

In many programming languages, you can define a function inside another function. However in C/C++, you can't do this.

Oftentimes a C program needs to use a feature defined in a separate library, so you may see programs that define a library to add, such as

```
#include <stdio.h>
main()
{
   printf("This is a simple C program.\n");
}
```

The structure of a typical C++ program looks similar. The following C++ example includes a C++ library called `iostream` and uses elements defined in a standard C++ library called `std`:

```
#include <iostream>
using namespace std;

int main ()
{
   cout << "This is a simple C++ program.";
   return 0;
}
```

Despite minor differences, C and C++ programs basically consist of a single main function and zero or more additional functions.

Creating Comments

To write a comment in C/C++, you have two choices. First, you can use the double slash character so that anything that appears to the right is a comment, such as

```
#include <iostream>
using namespace std;

// This is a comment at the beginning of the program
int main ()
{
  cout << "This is a simple C++ program.";
  return 0;
}
```

The double slash character is handy for adding a comment to a single line. If you want to write a comment over multiple lines, you can use the /* and */ characters, such as

```
/* This C program was written as a simple example
   to show people how easy C can be to learn. */

#include <stdio.h>
main()
{
  printf("This is a simple C program.\n");
}
```

Declaring Variables

When declaring variables in C/C++, you first declare the data type and then the variable name, such as

```
datatype VariableName;
```

`VariableName` can be any descriptive name. Because C/C++ is a case-sensitive language, it treats `SalesTax` as a completely different variable than `salestax`. Some programmers use uppercase letters to make variable names easier to find whereas others use all lowercase. To declare multiple variables, cram them all on a single line, separated by a comma, such as

```
datatype VariableName1, VariableName2, VariableName3;
```

Declaring string data types

Unlike other programming languages, C/C++ doesn't support a string data type. Instead, C/C++ offers two alternatives — a character data type and a library.

First, C/C++ offers a character data type, which can hold a single character. Instead of using a string data type, you can use an array of character data types, which is clumsier, but workable. To declare a character data type, use the `char` keyword followed by your variable name, such as

```
char variablename;
```

To mimic a string data type, declare an array of characters, such as

```
char arrayname[arraylength];
```

So if you wanted to create an array that can hold 20 characters, you could do this:

```
char firstname[20];
```

A second alternative is to include a library (string) that implements a string data type, such as

```
#include <string>
using namespace std;
string stringvariable;
```

Declaring integer data types

Whole numbers represent integers, such as –59, 692, or 7. A whole number can be positive or negative. The most common type of integer data type is `int` and is used as follows:

```
int variablename;
```

If you need to restrict a variable to a smaller range of values, you can declare a short `int` or a `short` variable as follows:

```
short int smallvariable;
short smallvariable;
```

The `long` integer data type is often identical to the regular `int` data type.

All integer types (int, short, and long) can also be signed or unsigned. *Signed* data types can represent positive or negative numbers whereas *unsigned* data types can represent only positive numbers.

To define positive values for an integer variable, you could do this:

```
unsigned int variablename;
```

The signed declaration isn't necessary because

```
signed long variablename;
```

is identical to

```
long variablename;
```

Table 1-1 shows the range of values common integer data types in C/C++ can hold.

Table 1-1	Typical Storage and Range Limitations of C/C++ Integer Data Types	
Data Type	*Number of Bytes*	*Range*
short	2	Signed: –32,768 to 32,767 Unsigned: 0 to 65,535
int	4	Signed: –2,147,483–3,648 to 2,147,483,647 Unsigned: 0 to 4,294,967,295
long	4 or 8	Signed: –2,147,483,648 to 2,147,483,647 Unsigned: 0 to 4,294,967,295

The exact number of bytes and range of all integer data types depends on the compiler used and the operating system, such as whether you're using a 32-bit or a 64-bit operating system. With many compilers, the range of values is identical between int and long data types.

Declaring floating point data types

Floating point values represent decimal values, such as 3.158 or –9.4106. Just as you can limit the range of integer values a variable can hold, so can you limit the range of floating point values a variable can hold.

The three types of floating data types are float, double, and long double, as shown in Table 1-2.

Table 1-2	Typical Floating Point Data Types	
Data Type	*Number of Bytes*	*Range*
Float	4	−1.4023 E−45 to 3.4028 E38
Double	8	−4.9406 E−324 to 1.7977 E308
Long double	8 or 12	−4.9406 E−324 to 1.7977 E308

Real numbers (float, double, and long double) are always signed data types (positive or negative). With many compilers, the range of values is identical between double and long double data types.

Declaring Boolean values

In the C language, there are no `Boolean` data types. Any nonzero value is considered to represent True, and zero represents False. To mimic a `Boolean` data type, many C programmers define numeric values for True and False, such as

```
#define FALSE 0
#define TRUE 1
int flag = FALSE;
```

Although this is workable, such an approach forces you to create an integer variable to represent a Boolean value. To avoid this problem, C++ offers a special `Boolean` data type (like most programming languages), such as

```
bool variablename;
```

A C++ `Boolean` data type can hold a value of 0 (False) or 1 (True).

Using Operators

The three types of operators used are mathematical, relational, and logical. *Mathematical* operators calculate numeric results such as adding, multiplying, or dividing numbers, as shown in Table 1-3.

Table 1-3	Mathematical Operators	
Mathematical Operator	*Purpose*	*Example*
+	Addition	5 + 3.4
-	Subtraction	203.9 − 9.12
*	Multiplication	39 * 146.7
/	Division	45/ 8.41
%	Modula division (returns the remainder)	35 % 9 = 8

Relational operators compare two values and return a True or False value. The six comparison operators available are shown in Table 1-4.

Table 1-4	Relational Operators
Relational Operator	*Purpose*
==	Equal
!=	Not equal
<	Less than
<=	Less than or equal to
>	Greater than
>=	Greater than or equal to

The relational operator in C/C++ is two equal sign symbols (==) whereas the relational operator in other programming languages is a single equal sign symbol (=). If you use only a single equal sign to compare two values in C/C++, your program will work but not the way it's supposed to.

Logical operators compare two Boolean values (True or False) and return a single True or False value, as shown in Table 1-5.

Table 1-5	Logical Operators
Logical Operator	*Truth Table*
&&	True && True = True True && False = False False && True = False False && False = False
||	True || True = True True || False = True False || True = True False || False = False
!	!True = False !False = True

Increment and decrement operators

Both C/C++ have a special increment (++) and a decrement (--) operator, which simply adds or subtracts 1 to a variable. Typically, adding 1 to a variable looks like this:

```
j = 5;
i = j + 1;
```

The increment operator replaces the + 1 portion with ++, such as

```
j = 5;
i = ++j;
```

In the preceding example, the value of i is j + 1 or 6, and the value of j is also 6.

If you place the increment operator after the variable, such as

```
j = 5;
i = j++;
```

Now the value of i is 5, but the value of j is 6.

The decrement operator works the same way except that it subtracts 1 from a variable, such as

```
j = 5;
i = --j;
```

In the preceding example, the value of i is j - 1 or 4, and the value of j is also 4.

If you place the decrement operator after the variable, such as

```
j = 5;
i = j--;
```

Now the value of i is 5, but the value of j is 4.

Assignment operators

Most programming languages use the equal sign to assign values to variables, such as

```
i = 59;
```

However, C/C++ also includes combination assignment and mathematical operators, as shown in Table 1-6.

Table 1-6	Assignment Operators	
Assignment Operator	*Purpose*	*Example*
+=	Addition assignment	i += 7 (equivalent to i = i + 7)
-=	Subtraction assignment	i -= 4 (equivalent to i = i - 4)
*=	Multiplication assignment	i *= y (equivalent to i = i * y)
/=	Division assignment	i /= 3.5 (equivalent to i = i / 35)
%=	Modulo assignment	i %= 2.8 (equivalent to i = i % 2.8)

Branching Statements

The simplest branching statement is an IF statement that only runs one or more commands if a Boolean condition is True, such as

```
if (condition) {
  Command;
  }
```

To make the computer choose between two mutually exclusive sets of commands, you can use an IF-ELSE statement, such as

```
if (condition) {
  Command;
  }
else {
  Command;
  }
```

Unlike C, C++ includes an IF-ELSEIF statement, which uses two or more Boolean conditions to choose which of two or more groups of commands to run, such as

```
if (condition1) {
  Command;
  }
else if (condition2) {
  Command;
  }
```

Although the IF-ELSE statement can only give the computer a choice of two groups of commands to run, the IF-ELSEIF statement can offer the computer multiple groups of commands to run, such as

```
if (condition1) {
  Command;
  }
else if (condition2) {
  Command;
  }
else if (condition3) {
  Command;
  }
```

As an alternative to the IF-ELSEIF statement, you can also use the SWITCH statement, such as

```
switch (expression) {
case value1:
  Command;
  break;
case value2:
  Command;
  break;
default:
  Command;
}
```

The SWITCH statement always needs to include the break command to tell the computer when to exit the SWITCH statement.

The preceding SWITCH statement is equivalent to the following IF-THEN-ELSEIF statement:

```
if (expression = value1) {
  Command;
  }
else if (expression = value2) {
  Command;
  }
else {
  Command;
  }
```

To check if a variable matches multiple values, you can stack multiple case statements, such as

```
switch (expression) {
case value1:
case value2:
  Command;
  break;
case value3:
case value4;
  Command;
  break;
default:
  Command;
}
```

The preceding SWITCH statement is equivalent to the following IF-ELSEIF statement in C++:

```
if (expression = value1) || (expression = value2) {
  Command;
  }
else if (expression = value3) || (expression = value4) {
  Command;
  }
else {
  Command;
  }
```

Looping Statements

A *looping statement* repeats one or more commands for a fixed number of times or until a certain Boolean condition becomes True. To create a loop that repeats for a fixed number of times, use the FOR loop, which looks like this:

```
for (startvalue; endvalue; increment) {
  Command;
  }
```

If you wanted the FOR loop to run five times, you could set the Start value to 1 and the End value to 5, such as

```
for (i = 1; i <= 5; i++) {
  Command;
  }
```

If you don't know how many times you need to repeat commands, you'll have to use a WHILE loop, which looks like this:

```
while (condition) {
  Command;
}
```

If the condition is True, the loop runs at least once. If this condition is False, the loop does not run.

A variation of the WHILE loop is the DO-WHILE loop, which looks like this:

```
do {
  Command;
} while (condition);
```

The main difference between the two loops is that the WHILE loop may run zero or more times, but the DO-WHILE loop always runs at least once.

Somewhere inside a WHILE and a DO-WHILE loop, you must have a command that can change the condition from True to False; otherwise, the loop will never end, and your program will appear to hang or freeze.

Creating Functions

In C/C++, every subprogram is a function that can return a value. The format of a typical function looks like this:

```
Datatype functionname (Parameter list)
  {
  Commands;
  Return value;
  }
```

The three parts of a C/C++ function are

+ **Data type:** Defines the type of value the function returns, such as an integer (int) or a floating point number (float). If you don't want a function to return a value, declare its data type as void. This makes the function act like a procedure in other programming languages.

+ **Parameter list:** Defines any data and their data types that the function needs to work.

+ **Return:** Defines a value to return. This value must be the same data type specified right before the function name.

If a function doesn't return a value or require any data, it might look like this:

```
void myfunction ()
  {
  Command;
  }
```

If the function needs to return an integer value, it might look like this:

```
int myfunction ()
  {
  Command;
  return value;
  }
```

In the preceding example, `value` represents any integer value.

To accept data, a function needs a parameter list, which simply lists a variable to hold data along with its specific data type, such as an integer or character. To create a function that accepts an integer and a character, you could do something like this:

```
int myfunction (int mynumber, char myletter)
  {
  Command;
  return value;
  }
```

The preceding function accepts two values by value, so the function can change the values of variables in its parameter list, but those changed values won't appear outside that function.

If you want a function to change the values of its parameters, you need to define a parameter list by identifying which variables accept values by reference. To identify values passed by reference, use the `&` sign, such as

```
int myfunction (int& mynumber, char myletter)
  {
  Command;
  return value;
  }
```

Data Structures

Many C/C++ compilers include libraries that offer data structures, such as stacks or collections. However, three built-in data structures of C/C++ are the structure (sometimes called a record in other programming languages), enumerated variables, and the array.

Creating a structure

A *structure* is a variable that typically holds two or more variables. To create a structure, use the `struct` keyword as follows:

```
struct name {
  datatype variable;
};
```

The name of a structure can be any descriptive name, such as `baseball_team` or `sales_dept`. Inside a structure, you must declare one or more variables. A typical structure might look like this:

```
struct MyGrades {
  char grade;
  int class_number;
};
```

After defining a structure, you can declare a variable to represent that structure, such as

```
struct MyGrades chemistry;
```

As a shortcut, you can define a structure and declare a variable to represent that structure as follows:

```
struct MyGrades {
  char grade;
  int class_number;
} chemistry;
```

Creating enumerated variables

Enumerated variables act like a list that lets you name a group of items, such as the days of the week, names of people in a group, and so on. A typical enumerated variable list might look like this:

```
enum name {item1, item2, item3};
```

So if you wanted to define the names of the days in a work week, you could do the following:

```
enum weekend {saturday, sunday};
```

Now you can declare a variable as a weekend data type, such as:

```
enum weekend timeoff;
```

As an alternative, you can define an enumerated list of variables and give them a name at the same time, such as

```
enum {saturday, sunday} timeoff;
```

Creating an array

Arrays in C/C++ are known as zero-based arrays, which means that the first element of the array is located at index number 0, the second element of the array is located at index number 1, and so on.

To create an array, declare its data type and size, such as

```
datatype arrayname[size];
```

The array name can be any descriptive name. The array size defines how many items the array can hold. To create an array that can hold ten integers, you could define an array like this:

```
int mynumbers[10];
```

You can create an array and store values in it at the same time by doing the following:

```
int mynumbers[4] = {23, 8, 94, 102};
```

This is equivalent to

```
int mynumbers[4];
mynumber[0] = 23;
mynumber[1] = 8;
mynumber[2] = 94;
mynumber[3] = 102;
```

Using Objects

Before C++, object-oriented programming was more of an academic exercise that required special programming languages. After C++ appeared, ordinary programmers could use their knowledge of C to use object-oriented programming for practical purposes.

To create an object, you must create a separate class stored in a class file. A typical class looks like this:

```
class className
  {
  public:
    datatype propertyname;

    void methodname();
  };
```

The class lists one or more properties and the type of data that property can hold, such as an integer or floating point number. A class also lists one or more method names, which contains code for manipulating an object in some way. The class defines the method name and its parameter list, but the actual code for that method appears outside the class definition, such as

```
 class className
   {
   public:
     datatype propertyname;

     void methodname();
   };
void classname::methodname()
   {
   Commands;
   }
```

After you define a class, you can create an object from that class by declaring a variable as a new class type, such as

```
className objectname;
```

So if you created an `animal` class, you could create an object (`things_at_the_zoo`) from that class as follows:

```
animal things_at_the_zoo;
```

The C++ language allows both single and multiple inheritance. With single inheritance, you can declare a class name and state the class to inherit from with a colon, such as

```
class className : public classtoinheritfrom
  {
  // Code goes here
  };
```

To inherit from multiple classes, name each class as follows:

```
class className : public class1, public class2
  {
  // Code goes here
  };
```

Understanding inheritance can be confusing enough, but trying to understand multiple inheritance can be even more complicated. As a result, many C++ programmers never use multiple inheritance, so don't feel you're missing out on anything if you ignore multiple inheritance too.

Chapter 2: Java and C#

In This Chapter

✔ Understanding the C#/Java program structure

✔ Declaring variables and using operators

✔ Branching and looping statements

✔ Creating data structures and objects

The Java language was meant to build upon the success of C++, but with added safety features and true cross-platform capabilities. Unlike C++, which gives programmers access to every part of the computer (along with the equal capability of screwing up every part of the computer), Java restricts access to the computer hardware. Although this limits Java's flexibility, it provides greater stability and reliability of Java programs.

The most appealing feature of Java is its cross-platform capabilities. Although porting a C++ program to run on other operating systems is possible, it's rarely easy or painless. Theoretically, Java lets you write a program once and then run it on multiple operating systems, a feature often described as *Write Once, Run Everywhere* (or more whimsically, Write Once, Test Everywhere).

Sun Microsystems developed Java and in response to Java's popularity, Microsoft developed a similar language with equivalent goals — *C#*. Like Java, C# is meant to build upon the C++ language while providing safety features to make it harder to write programs that could crash an entire computer.

To make programming easier, C# relies on the .NET framework. The idea behind .NET is to shield the programmer from the complexities of the operating system. Theoretically, the .NET framework can be ported to other operating systems, so C# could run on any operating system that can run the .NET framework. Realistically, .NET runs only on Windows, although programmers are trying to port the .NET framework for Linux too.

Although C/C++ remains the most popular programming language on the planet, both Java and C# are poised as programming languages of the future. Java is popular because it's platform independent, so Macintosh and Linux users can take advantage of Java. C# is most popular among Windows programmers because Microsoft has positioned C# as the future programming language for Windows.

The Structure of a Java/C# Program

Java forces object-oriented programming on you whether you like it or not. Every Java program consists of a class, such as

```
class programname
{
  public static void main(String args[])
  {
  System.out.println("This is a simple Java program.");
  }
}
```

Because Java relies on object-oriented programming, a Java program looks more complicated than it should. Basically, the main program is considered a class that has a single main function. To print something, the preceding program uses a `println` command, which is accessed through the `System` class. Because Java forces object-oriented thinking on you, Java programs consist of multiple classes.

Like Java, C# also forces object-oriented thinking on every program you write.

```
using System;
class MyClass
{_static void Main()
  {_Console.WriteLine("This is a simple C# program.");
  }
}
```

Creating Comments

To write a comment in Java/C#, you have two choices. First, you can use the double slash character so that anything that appears to the right of the character is a comment, such as

```
using System;_
class MyClass _// This is a C# comment
{_static void Main() _
  {_Console.WriteLine("This is a simple C# program.");_
  }
}
```

The double slash character is handy for adding a comment to a single line. If you want to write a comment over multiple lines, you can use the /* and */ characters, such as

```
/* This is a multiline comment to show people how
   easy Java can be to learn. */

class programname
{
  public static void main(String args[])
  {
  System.out.println("This is a simple Java program.");
  }
}
```

Declaring Variables

Because Java and C# are closely derived from C/C++, they both declare variable data types the same way by first listing the data type and then listing the variable name, such as

```
datatype VariableName;
```

`VariableName` can be any descriptive name. Both Java and C# are case-sensitive, so the variable `TeamMembers` is a completely different variable than `Teammembers`. Some programmers use uppercase letters to make variable names easier to find whereas others use all lowercase. To declare multiple variables, cram them all on a single line, separated by a comma, such as

```
datatype VariableName1, VariableName2, VariableName3;
```

Declaring string data types

Both Java and C# offer a `string` data type (which isn't found in C/C++), which you can declare as this:

```
string variablename;
```

Like all variables, both Java and C# allow you to declare and initialize a variable at the same time, such as

```
string variablename = "text";
```

Declaring integer data types

Whole numbers represent integers, such as –9, 62, or 10. A whole number can be positive or negative. The most common integer data type is `int` and is used as follows:

```
int variablename;
```

Besides integer values, Java also offers a variety of other integer data types that can hold a different range of values, as shown in Table 2-1.

Table 2-1	Typical Storage and Range Limitations of Java Integer Data Types	
Data Type	*Number of Bytes*	*Range*
byte	1	–128 to 127
short	2	–32,768 to 32,767
int	4	–2,147,483,648 to 2,147,483,647
long	8	–9,223,372,036,854,775,808 to 9,223,372,036,854,775,807

C# also offers a variety of different integer data types, which can be signed (positive and negative values) or unsigned (only positive values), as shown in Table 2-2. To declare a signed or unsigned variable, use the `signed` (or `unsigned`) keyword, such as

```
signed int profit;
unsigned short pets_owned;
```

Table 2-2	Typical Storage and Range Limitations of C# Integer Data Types	
Data Type	*Number of Bytes*	*Range*
byte	1	Signed: –128 to 127 Unsigned: 0 to 255
short	2	Signed: –32,768 to 32,767 Unsigned: 0 to 65,535
int	4	Signed: –2,147,483,648 to 2,147,483,647 Unsigned: 0 to 4,294,967,295
long	8	Signed: –9,223,372,036,854,775,808 to 9,223,372,036,854,775,807 Unsigned: 0 to 1.8x1019

Declaring floating point data types

Floating point values represent decimal values, such as 78.52 or –5.629. Just as you can limit the range of integer values a variable can hold, so can you limit the range of floating point values a variable can hold.

The three types of floating data types are float, double, and decimal (C# only), as shown in Table 2-3.

Table 2-3	Typical Floating Point Data Types	
Data Type	*Number of Bytes*	*Range*
float	4	–1.4023 E-45 to 3.4028 E38
double	8	–4.9406 E-324 to 1.7977 E308
decimal (C# only)	16	–1.0 E-28 to 1.0 E28

The ranges of the different data types listed in Table 2-3 are approximate values.

Declaring Boolean variables

To remedy the deficiency of C/C++, both Java and C# offer a `Boolean` data type. In Java, you can declare a Boolean variable like this:

```
boolean variablename;
```

In C#, you can declare a Boolean variable, such as

```
bool variablename;
```

Using Operators

The three types of operators used are mathematical, comparison, and logical. *Mathematical* operators calculate numeric results, such as adding, multiplying, or dividing numbers, as shown in Table 2-4.

Table 2-4	Mathematical Operators	
Mathematical Operator	*Purpose*	*Example*
+	Addition	5 + 3.4
-	Subtraction	203.9 - 9.12
*	Multiplication	39 * 146.7
/	Division	45/ 8.41
%	Modula division (returns the remainder)	35 % 9 = 8

Relational operators compare two values and return a `True` or `False` value. The six relational operators available are shown in Table 2-5.

Table 2-5	Relational Operators
Relational Operator	*Purpose*
==	Equal
!=	Not equal
<	Less than
<=	Less than or equal to
>	Greater than
>=	Greater than or equal to

The relational operator in Java/C# is two equal sign symbols (==) whereas the relational operator in other programming languages is just a single equal sign symbol (=). If you only use a single equal sign to compare two values in Java/C#, your program will work but not the way it's supposed to.

Logical operators compare two Boolean values (`True` or `False`) and return a single `True` or `False` value, as shown in Table 2-6.

Table 2-6	Logical Operators
Logical Operator	*Truth Table*
&&	True && True = True True && False = False False && True = False False && False = False
||	True || True = True True || False = True False || True = True False || False = False
!	!True = False !False = True

Increment and decrement operators

Both Java and C# have a special increment (++) and a decrement (--) operator, which simply adds or subtracts 1 to a variable. Typically, adding 1 to a variable looks like this:

```
j = 5;
i = j + 1;
```

The increment operator replaces the + 1 portion with ++, such as

```
j = 5;
i = ++j;
```

In the preceding example, the value of i is j + 1 or 6, and the value of j is also 6.

If you place the increment operator after the variable, such as

```
j = 5;
i = j++;
```

Now the value of i is 5, but the value of j is 6.

The decrement operator works the same way except that it subtracts 1 from a variable, such as

```
j = 5;
i = --j;
```

In the preceding example, the value of i is j - 1 or 4, and the value of j is also 4.

If you place the decrement operator after the variable, such as

```
j = 5;
i = j--;
```

Now the value of i is 5, but the value of j is 4.

Assignment operators

Most programming languages use the equal sign to assign values to variables, such as

```
i = 59;
```

However, Java/C# also includes a combination assignment and mathematical operators, as shown in Table 2-7.

Table 2-7	Assignment Operators	
Assignment Operator	*Purpose*	*Example*
+=	Addition assignment	i += 7 (equivalent to i = i + 7)
-=	Subtraction assignment	i -= 4 (equivalent to i = i - 4)

(continued)

Table 2-7 *(continued)*

Assignment Operator	Purpose	Example
*=	Multiplication assignment	i *= y (equivalent to i = i * y)
/=	Division assignment	i /= 3.5 (equivalent to i = i / 35)
%=	Modulo assignment	i %= 2.8 (equivalent to i = i % 2.8)

Branching Statements

The simplest branching statement is an `IF` statement that only runs one or more commands if a Boolean condition is `True`, such as

```
if (condition) {
  Command;
  }
```

To make the computer choose between two mutually exclusive sets of commands, you can use an `IF-ELSE` statement, such as

```
if (condition) {
  Command;
  }
else {
  Command;
  }
```

Java and C# also offer an `IF-ELSEIF` statement, which uses two or more Boolean conditions to choose which of two or more groups of commands to run, such as

```
if (condition1) {
  Command;
  }
else if (condition2) {
  Command;
  }
```

Although the `IF-ELSE` statement can only give the computer a choice of two groups of commands to run, the `IF-ELSEIF` statement can offer the computer multiple groups of commands to run, such as

```
if (condition1) {
  Command;
  }
else if (condition2) {
  Command;
  }
else if (condition3) {
  Command;
  }
```

As an alternative to the IF-ELSEIF statement, you can also use the SWITCH statement, such as

```
switch (expression) {
case value1:
  Command;
  break;
case value2:
  Command;
  break;
default:
  Command;
}
```

The SWITCH statement always needs to include the break command to tell the computer when to exit the SWITCH statement.

The preceding SWITCH statement is equivalent to the following IF-ELSEIF statement:

```
if (expression = value1) {
  Command;
  }
else if (expression = value2) {
  Command;
  }
else {
  Command;
  }
```

To check if a variable matches multiple values, you can stack multiple CASE statements, such as

```
switch (expression) {
case value1:
case value2:
  Command;
  break;
case value3:
case value4;
  Command;
  break;
default:
  Command;
}
```

The preceding SWITCH statement is equivalent to the following IF-ELSEIF statement in C++:

```
if (expression = value1) || (expression = value2) {
  Command;
  }
else if (expression = value3) || (expression = value4) {
  Command;
  }
else {
  Command;
  }
```

One main difference between C# and Java is the way each language handles *fall-through,* where multiple CASE statements can run if a break command isn't inserted into each one. Consider the following SWITCH statement in Java, which allows fall-through:

```
switch (age) {
case 17:
case 18:
case 19;
case 20;
  System.out.println("You're too young to drink.");
case 21:
  System.out.println("You're old enough to drink.");
}
```

In this example, the SWITCH statement will print the following if the value of age is 17, 18, 19, or 20:

```
You're too young to drink.
You're old enough to drink.
```

Because no `break` command is right above the `case 21:` statement, the Java program falls-through to the next CASE statement. In C#, you must explicitly define the fall-through (if this is what you want), such as

```
switch (age) {
case 17:
case 18:
case 19;
case 20;
  System.out.println("You're too young to drink.");
  goto case 21;
case 21:
  System.out.println("You're old enough to drink.");
}
```

This C# SWITCH statement explicitly tells the computer to fall-through to the `case 21:` statement. If you omit the `goto case 21` statement, the preceding C# SWITCH statement won't work. By forcing you to explicitly define the fall-through in a SWITCH statement, C# helps prevent mistakes in writing a SWITCH statement incorrectly.

Looping Statements

A *looping* statement repeats one or more commands for a fixed number of times or until a certain Boolean condition becomes True. To create a loop that repeats for a fixed number of times, use the FOR loop, which looks like this:

```
for (startvalue; endvalue; increment) {
  Command;
  }
```

If you wanted the FOR loop to run five times, you could set the Start value to 1 and the End value to 5, such as

```
for (i = 1; i <= 5; i++) {
  Command;
  }
```

If you don't know how many times you need to repeat commands, use a WHILE loop, which looks like this:

```
while (condition) {
  Command;
}
```

If the condition is `True`, the loop runs at least once. If this condition is `False`, the loop doesn't run.

A variation of the `WHILE` loop is the `DO-WHILE` loop, which looks like this:

```
do {
  Command;
} while (condition);
```

The main difference between the two loops is that the `WHILE` loop may run zero or more times, but the `DO-WHILE` loop will always run at least once.

Somewhere inside a `WHILE` and `DO-WHILE` loop, you must have a command that can change the condition from `True` to `False`; otherwise, the loop will never end, and your program will appear to hang or freeze.

Creating Functions

In Java/C#, every subprogram is a function that can return a value. The format of a typical Java function looks like this:

```
Datatype functionname (Parameter list)
  {
  Commands;
  Return value;
  }
```

The three parts of a C/C++ function are

+ **Data type:** Defines the type of value the function returns, such as an integer (`int`) or floating point number (`float`). If you define the data type as void, then the function doesn't return a value.

+ **Parameter list:** Defines any data and their data types that the function needs to work.

+ **Return:** Defines a value to return. This value must be the same data type specified right before the function name.

If a function doesn't return a value or require any data, it might look like this:

```
void myfunction ()
  {
  Command;
  }
```

If the function needs to return an integer value, it might look like this:

```
int myfunction ()
   {
   Command;
   return value;
   }
```

In the preceding example, `value` represents any integer value.

To accept data, a function needs a *parameter list,* which simply lists a variable to hold data along with its specific data type, such as an integer or character. To create a function that accepts an integer and a character, you could do something like this:

```
int myfunction (int mynumber, char myletter)
   {
   Command;
   return value;
   }
```

The preceding function accepts two values by value, so the function can change the values of variables in its parameter list, but those changed values won't appear outside that function.

If you want a function to change the values of its parameters, define a parameter list by identifying which variables accept values by reference. To identify values passed by reference in C#, use the `ref` keyword, such as

```
int myfunction (ref int mynumber, char myletter)
   {
   Command;
   return value;
   }
```

Data Structures

Through built-in libraries, Java and C# offer a variety of data structures beyond most programming languages. In Java, the most common data structures are arrays and linked lists. In C#, the .NET framework provides a variety of data structures including structures, arrays, collections, dictionaries, queues, and stacks.

Creating a C# structure

Unlike Java, C# offers a structure, which acts like a variable that typically holds two or more variables. To create a structure, use the `struct` keyword as follows:

```
struct name {
  public datatype variable;
};
```

The name of a structure can be any descriptive name, such as `people2get` or `my_relatives`. Inside a structure, you must declare one or more variables. A typical structure might look like this:

```
struct MyGrades {
  public char grade;
  public int class_number;
};
```

After defining a structure, you can declare a variable to represent that structure, such as

```
struct geology = MyGrades();
```

After declaring a variable as a structure, you can store data in the individual fields of a structure like this:

```
struct geology = MyGrades();
geology.grade = "A";
geology.class_number = 302;
```

Creating an array

Arrays in Java/C# are known as zero-based arrays, which means that the first element of the array is located at index number 0, the second element of the array is located at index number 1, and so on.

To create an array in Java, declare its data type and size, such as

```
datatype [] arrayname = new datatype[arraysize];
```

The array name can be any descriptive name. The array size defines how many items the array can hold. To create an array that can hold ten integers, you could define an array like this:

```
int [] mynumbers = new int[10];
```

You can create an array and store values in it at the same time by doing the following:

```
int [] mynumbers = new int[4] {25, 81, 4, 712};
```

This is equivalent to

```
int [] mynumbers = new int[4];
mynumber[0] = 25;
mynumber[1] = 81;
mynumber[2] = 4;
mynumber[3] = 712;
```

Creating a Java linked list

Java offers a linked list class, which simplifies managing a linked list. By using a linked list, you can create other data structures, such as stacks and queues. To create a linked list, define a variable, such as

```
LinkedList listname = new LinkedList();
```

You can also define the data type to store in a linked list, such as

```
LinkedList <datatype>listname = new LinkedList<datatype>();
```

To add an item to a linked list, use the add, addFirst, or addLast method with the name of the linked list, such as

```
LinkedList shopping_list = new LinkedList();
shopping_list.add("Eggs");
shopping_list.addFirst("Milk");
shopping_list.addLast("Bacon");
```

The first item stored in the linked list would be "Milk", followed by "Eggs", and "Bacon".

To retrieve data from a linked list, you can use the getFirst, remove, removeFirst, or removeLast method. The getFirst method retrieves data only from the linked list whereas the remove, removeFirst, and removeLast methods physically yank that data out of that linked list:

```
LinkedList shopping_list = new LinkedList();
shopping_list.add("Eggs");
shopping_list.addFirst("Milk");
System.out.println("First = " + shopping_list.removeFirst());
System.out.println("First = " + shopping_list.getFirst());
```

The preceding Java code would print the following:

```
First = "Milk"
First = "Eggs"
```

Creating C## data structures

C# includes queues, stacks, and hashtables, which you can create by using the same syntax, such as

```
Queue queuename = new Queue();
Stack stackname = new Stack();
Hashtable tablename = new Hashtable();
```

Each type of data structure uses different methods for adding and removing data. A queue uses the `Enqueue` and `Dequeue` methods to add and remove data. A stack uses the `Push` and `Pop` methods to add and remove data. A hashtable uses the `Add` and `Remove` methods to add and remove data.

Using Objects

Both Java and C# are true object-oriented programming languages (unlike C++), so you have no choice but to create and use objects in your programs. To create an object, you must define a class stored in its own file. A typical class definition looks like this:

```
class ClassName
  {
  datatype propertyname;

  void methodname()
    {
     Commands;
    }
  };
```

The class lists one or more properties and the type of data that property can hold, such as an integer or a floating point number. A class also lists one or more method names, which contains code for manipulating an object in some way.

After you define a class, you can create an object from that class by declaring a variable as a new class type, such as

```
className objectname = new className();
```

So if you created a `furniture` class, you could create a `table` object from that class as follows:

```
furniture table = new furniture();
```

To use inheritance in Java, use the `extends` keyword, such as

```
class className extends classtoinheritfrom
   {
   // Code goes here
   };
```

To use inheritance in C#, use the colon to identify the class to inherit from, such as

```
class className : classtoinheritfrom
   {
   // Code goes here
   };
```

Chapter 3: Perl and Python

In This Chapter

✔ **Understanding the structure of Perl/Python programs**

✔ **Declaring variables**

✔ **Using mathematical operators**

✔ **Branching and looping statements**

✔ **Creating data structures and objects**

*P*erl and Python languages are both scripting languages meant to help programmers create something easily. The main difference between Perl and Python over traditional programming languages is their intended use.

Systems languages (such as C/C++) are meant to create standalone applications, such as operating systems or word processors, which is why systems languages are almost always compiled.

Scripting languages are meant more for linking different programs together, such as transferring data that someone types into a Web page and storing it in a database. As a result, scripting languages are almost always interpreted, which makes them more portable across different operating systems.

Systems languages are often known as *type-safe* because they force you to declare a specific data type (such as integer or string) for each variable. In contrast, scripting languages often allow a variable to hold anything it wants. One moment it may hold a string, the next an integer, and after that, a decimal number. Such typeless scripting languages give you greater flexibility at the possible expense of causing errors by variables containing unexpected data.

Perl's philosophy is that there's always more than one way to do it, so Perl often offers multiple commands that accomplish the exact same thing. The goal is to let you choose the way you like best.

Python takes the opposite approach and emphasizes a small and simple language that relies less on symbols (like C/C++) and more on readable commands to make programs easier to understand. Although Perl retains much of the syntax familiar to C/C++ programmers, Python abandons curly brackets and semicolons for a cleaner language that's simpler to read and write.

Both Perl and Python are used in Web applications but also for more specialized uses, such as text manipulation. Perl is particularly popular in the field of bioinformatics and finance whereas Python has been adapted as a scripting language for many graphics and animation programs.

Although system programming languages like C/C++ were designed to maximize the efficiency of computer equipment, languages like Perl and Python are designed to maximize the efficiency of programmers, who are now more expensive than computer equipment. When programmers need to write something in a hurry that doesn't involve manipulating the hardware of a computer, they often turn to Perl and Python.

Python is often associated with the British comedy troupe "Monty Python's Flying Circus." It's considered good form among Python programmers to slip in *Monty Python* references in their programs whenever possible.

The Structure of a Perl/Python Program

Because Perl and Python are interpreted languages, you can often type in commands a line at a time or type and save commands in a file. A simple Perl program might look like this:

```
print "This is a simple Perl program.\n";
exit;
```

A Python program is even simpler:

```
print "This is a simple Python program."
```

Perl adapts the syntax of the C language including the use of semicolons at the end of each statement and the use of curly brackets to identify a block of commands. Python omits semicolons, and instead of using curly brackets to identify a block of comments, Python uses indentation. To identify a block of commands in Perl, use curly brackets like this:

```
if $x > 5
   {
   command1;
   command2;
   }
```

In Python, the same program might look like this:

```
if x > 5:
   command1;
   command2;
```

You can write both Perl and Python programs from a command-line prompt (meaning you type in commands one at a time) or saved as a file and then loaded into the interpreter. For testing short programs, typing them in one line at a time is probably faster, but for creating large programs, saving commands in a text file is easier.

Creating Comments

To write a comment in Perl, use the # symbol. Anything that appears to the right of the # symbol is treated as a comment, such as

```
# This is a comment
print "This is a simple Perl program.\n";
exit;   # This is another comment
```

In Python, you can also use the # symbol to create comments on a single line. If you want to create a comment covering multiple lines, use triple quotes to define the start and end of a comment, such as

```
""" This is a multiple line comment.
    The triple quotes highlight the beginning
    and the end of the multiple lines. """
print "This is a simple Python program."
```

Defining Variables

Both Perl and Python allow variables to hold any data types. In Perl, variable names begin with the dollar sign symbol, such as $myVar. Perl and Python are case-sensitive languages, so the Perl variable $myVar is considered completely different from $MYVar while the Python variable DueDate is completely different from the variable duedate.

If you misspell a variable in Perl or Python, both languages will treat the misspelled variable as a completely new and valid variable.

Using Operators

The three types of operators used are mathematical, relational, and logical. *Mathematical* operators calculate numeric results such as adding, multiplying, or dividing numbers, as shown in Table 3-1.

Table 3-1	Mathematical Operators	
Mathematical Operator	*Purpose*	*Example*
+	Addition	5 + 3.4
-	Subtraction	203.9 - 9.12
*	Multiplication	39 * 146.7
/	Division	45/ 8.41
%	Modula division (returns the remainder)	35 % 9 = 8
**	Exponentiation	5**2 = 25
divmod (x,y) (Python only)	Returns both x / y and x % y	divmod (12,8) = (1,4)

When Python uses the division operator (/) to divide two integers, the result will be an integer, such as

9/4 = 2

If at least one number is a decimal, the result will also be a decimal, such as

9.0/4 = 2.25

Or

9/4.0 = 2.25

Relational operators compare two values and return a `True` or `False` value. The six relational operators available are shown in Table 3-2.

Table 3-2	Relational Operators
Relational Operator	*Purpose*
==	Equal
!=	Not equal
<	Less than
<=	Less than or equal to
>	Greater than
>=	Greater than or equal to
< = > (Perl only)	Comparison with signed result

The relational operator in Perl/Python is two equal sign symbols (==) whereas the relational operator in other programming languages is just a single equal sign symbol (=). If you only use a single equal sign to compare two values in Perl/Python, your program will work but not the way it's supposed to.

Perl offers a unique *comparison with signed result* operator (< = >), which compares two values and returns 0 (if the two values are equal), 1 (if the first value is greater than the second), or –1 (if the first value is less than the second), as shown in Table 3-3.

Table 3-3	Using Perl's Comparison with Signed Result Operator
Example	*Result*
5 < = > 5	0
7 < = > 5	1
2 < = > 5	–1

Logical operators compare two Boolean values (True [1] or False [0]) and return a single True or False value, as shown in Table 3-4.

Table 3-4	Logical Operators
Logical Operator	*Truth Table*
&& (Perl) and (Python)	1 and 1 = 1 1 and 0 = 0 0 and 1 = 0 0 and 0 = 0
|| (Perl) or (Python)	1 or 1 = 1 1 or 0 = 1 0 or 1 = 1 0 or 0 = 0
! (Perl) not (Python)	!1 = False (0) !0 = True (1)

Increment and decrement operators

Perl (but not Python) has a special increment (++) and a decrement (--) operator, which simply adds or subtracts 1 to a variable. Typically, adding 1 to a variable looks like this:

```
j = 5;
i = j + 1;
```

The increment operator replaces the + 1 portion with ++, such as

```
j = 5;
i = ++j;
```

In the preceding example, the value of i is j + 1 or 6, and the value of j is also 6.

If you place the increment operator after the variable, such as

```
j = 5;
i = j++;
```

Now the value of i is 5, but the value of j is 6.

The decrement operator works the same way except that it subtracts 1 from a variable, such as

```
j = 5;
i = --j;
```

In the preceding example, the value of i is j - 1 or 4, and the value of j is also 4.

If you place the decrement operator after the variable, such as

```
j = 5;
i = j--;
```

Now the value of i is 5, but the value of j is 4.

Assignment operators

Most programming languages use the equal sign to assign values to variables, such as

```
i = 59;
```

However, Perl/Python also include combination assignment and mathematical operators, as shown in Table 3-5.

Table 3-5	Assignment Operators	
Assignment Operator	*Purpose*	*Example*
+=	Addition assignment	i += 7 (equivalent to i = i + 7)
-=	Subtraction assignment	i -= 4 (equivalent to i = i - 4)

(continued)

Table 3-5 *(continued)*

Assignment Operator	Purpose	Example
*=	Multiplication assignment	i *= y (equivalent to i = i * y)
/=	Division assignment	i /= 3.5 (equivalent to i = i / 35)
%=	Modulo assignment	i %= 2.8 (equivalent to i = i % 2.8)

Branching Statements

The simplest branching statement is an `IF` statement that only runs one or more commands if a Boolean condition is `True`. In Perl, the `IF` statement uses curly brackets to enclose one or more commands:

```
if (condition) {
  Command1;
  Command2;
  }
```

In Python, the `IF` statement uses indentation to enclose one or more commands:

```
if (condition):
  Command1
  Command2
```

To make the computer choose between two mutually exclusive sets of commands, you can use an `IF-ELSE` statement in Perl like this:

```
if (condition) {
  Command;
  Command;
  }
else {
  Command;
  Command;
  }
```

In Python, the `IF-ELSE` statement looks like this:

```
if (condition):
  Command
  Command
else:
  Command
  Command
```

The `IF-ELSE` statement only offers two choices. If you want to offer multiple choices, you can use the `IF-ELSEIF` statement, which uses two or more Boolean conditions to choose which of two or more groups of commands to run. In Perl, use the `ELSIF` keyword, such as

```
if (condition1) {
  Command;
  Command;
  }
elsif (condition2) {
  Command;
  Command;
  }
elsif (condition3) {
  Command;
  Command;
  }
```

In Python, use the `ELIF` keyword, such as

```
if (condition1):
  Command
  Command
elif (condition2):
  Command
  Command
elif (condition3):
  Command
  Command
```

Unlike other programming languages, neither Perl nor Python provides a `SWITCH` statement.

Looping Statements

A *looping* statement repeats one or more commands for a fixed number of times or until a certain Boolean condition becomes `True`. To create a loop that repeats for a fixed number of times, use the `FOR` loop, which looks like this:

```
for (startvalue; endvalue; increment) {
  Command;
  }
```

If you wanted the `FOR` loop to run five times, you could set the Start value to 1 and the End value to 5, such as

```
for (i = 1; i <= 5; i++) {
  Command;
  }
```

In Python, the FOR loop looks dramatically different:

```
for variable in (list):
   Command
   Command
```

To make a Python FOR loop repeat five times, you could do this:

```
for x in (1,2,3,4,5):
   print x
```

The preceding Python FOR loop would print

```
1
2
3
4
5
```

If you want a FOR loop to repeat many times (such as 100 times), it can be tedious to list 100 separate numbers. So Python offers a range() function that eliminates listing multiple numbers. To use the range() function to loop five times, you could do this:

```
for x in range(5):
   print x
```

Because the range() function starts with 0, the preceding Python FOR loop would print

```
0
1
2
3
4
```

Another way to use the range() function is by defining a lower and upper range like this:

```
for x in range(25, 30):
   print x
```

This FOR loop would print the numbers 25, 26, 27, 28, and 29. Rather than increment by one, you can also use the range() function to define your own increment, which can be positive or negative, such as

```
for x in range(25, 30, 2):
   print x
```

This FOR loop would print 25, 27, and 29.

If you don't know how many times you need to repeat commands, use a WHILE loop, which looks like this:

```
while (condition) {
    Command;
    Command;
}
```

If the condition is True, the loop runs at least once. If this condition is False, the loop doesn't run. In Python, the WHILE loop looks like this:

```
while (condition):
    Command
    Command
```

Somewhere inside a WHILE loop, you must have a command that can change the condition from True to False; otherwise, the loop will never end, and your program will appear to hang or freeze.

Creating Functions

In Perl and Python, every subprogram is a function that can return a value. The format of a typical Perl function looks like this:

```
sub functionname {
    Commands;
    return $value;
    }
```

When you pass parameters to a Perl function, that function can access them with the foreach keyword and the @_ array, such as

```
sub functionname {
    foreach $variablename (@_) {
      Commands;
    }
    return $value;
    }
```

The foreach $variablename (@_) line stores a list of parameters in the @_ array. Then the foreach command plucks each item from the @_ array and temporarily stores it in $variablename.

A typical Python function looks like this:

```
def functionname (variablename)
  Commands
  return value
```

If you don't want a function to return a value, omit the return line.

Perl Data Structures

Perl offers three data structures: arrays, hash arrays, and references. An *array* stores multiple items, identified by an index number. A *hash array* stores multiple items, identified by a key, which can be a number or a string.

Creating a Perl array

Like C/C++, Perl arrays are zero-based, so the first element of an array is considered 0, the second is 1, and so on. When you create a Perl array, you must name that array with the @ symbol. You can also define the elements of an array at the time you create the array, such as

```
@arrayname = (element1, element2, element3);
```

If you want to create an array that contains a range of numbers, you can list each number individually like this:

```
@numberarray = (1, 2, 3, 4, 5);
```

You can also use the range operator (..) to define the lower and upper bounds of a range, such as

```
@numberarray = (1..5);
```

To access the individual elements stored in an array, use the dollar sign ($) symbol in front of the array name, such as

```
@numberarray = (1..10);
$thisone = $numberarray[0];
```

The value stored in the $thisone variable is the first element of the @numberarray, which is 1.

One unique feature of Perl arrays is that you can use arrays to mimic a stack data structure with Perl's push and pop commands. To push a new item onto an array, you can use the push command:

```
push(@arrayname, item2add);
```

To pop an item off the array, use the pop command like this:

```
$variablename = pop(@arrayname);
```

Creating a Perl hash array

A hash array stores an item along with a key. Perl offers two ways to store values and keys. The first is like this:

```
%hasharray = (
  key1 => value1,
  key2 => value2,
  key3 => value3,
);
```

Notice that hash arrays are identified by the percentage (%) symbol.

A second way to define a hash array is like this:

```
%hasharray = ("key1", value1, "key2", value2, "key3",
    value3);
```

To retrieve data from a hash array, you need to know the key associated with that value and identify the hash array name by using the $ symbol like this:

```
$variable = $hasharray ("key1");
```

The preceding command would store the value associated with "key1" into the $variable.

Python Data Structures

Python offers tuples, lists, and dictionary data structures. Both tuples and lists contain a series of items, such as numbers and strings. The main difference is that items in a tuple can't be changed whereas items in a list can be changed. A dictionary stores values with keys, allowing you to retrieve values using its distinct key.

Creating a Python tuple

A *tuple* can contain different data, such as numbers and strings. To create a tuple, list all the items within parentheses like this:

```
tuplename = (item1, item2, item3)
```

To retrieve a value from a tuple, you must identify it by its index number, where the first item in the tuple is assigned a 0 index number, the second item is assigned a 1 index number, and so on. To retrieve the second item (index number 1) in a tuple, you could use this:

```
variablename = tuplename[1]
```

Creating a Python list

Unlike a tuple, a Python *list* lets you change, add, or delete items. To create a list, identify all items in the list by using square brackets like this:

```
listname = [item1, item2, item3]
```

To retrieve a value from a list, you must identify it by its index number, where the first item in the list is assigned a 0 index number, the second item is assigned a 1 index number, and so on. To retrieve the first item (index number 0) in a list, you could use this:

```
variablename = listname[0]
```

To add new items to a list, use the append command, such as

```
listname.append(newitem)
```

The append command always adds a new item at the end of a list. If you want to insert an item in a specific location in the list using its index number, use the insert command like this:

```
listname.insert(index, newitem)
```

To remove the first instance of an item in a list, use the remove command, such as

```
listname.remove(existingitem)
```

If a list contains identical items (such as 23), the remove command deletes the item with the lowest index number.

Creating a Python dictionary

A dictionary contains values and keys assigned to each value. To create, use curly brackets like this:

```
dictionaryname = {key1:value1, key2:value2, key3:value3}
```

To retrieve a value using its key, use the `get` command like this:

```
Variable = dictionary.name.get(key)
```

Using Objects

Both Perl and Python are true object-oriented programming languages (unlike C++), so you have no choice but to create and use objects in your programs. To create an object, you must define a class. In Perl, a typical class definition looks like this:

```
package className;
sub new {
  my $objectname = {
  Data;
  Data;
  };
  bless $objectname, $className;
  return $objectname;
sub methodname{
  Commands;
  Commands;
  };
```

In Python, a class looks like this:

```
class ClassName:
  Data
  Data
  def methodname (self):
    Commands
    Commands
    Commands
```

A class lists *properties* (data) along with one or more methods, which contain code for manipulating an object in some way.

After you define a class, you can create an object from that class by declaring a variable as a new class type. In Perl, you create an object by creating a `constructor` method commonly called new, such as

```
my $variablename = classname->new();
```

In Python, create an object like this:

```
objectname = new classname();
```

To use inheritance in Perl, use the `@ISA` variable inside a new class, such as

```
package newobject;
use class2inheritfrom;
@ISA = qw(class2inheritfrom);
```

To use inheritance in Python, identify the class to inherit from when you create a new class, such as

```
class ClassName (class2inheritfrom):
    Data
    Data
    def methodname (self):
        Commands
        Commands
        Commands
```

To inherit from multiple classes in Python, define additional classes, separated by a comma, such as

```
class ClassName (class2inheritfrom, anotherclass):
    Data
    Data
    def methodname (self):
        Commands
        Commands
        Commands
```

Chapter 4: Pascal and Delphi

*P*ascal was originally designed to teach structured programming techniques. However, Pascal soon proved popular and powerful enough that people started using it to create commercial applications. Unlike C/C++, which emphasizes machine efficiency, Pascal emphasizes readability. Pascal programs may not be as fast or as easy to type as C/C++ programs, but Pascal programs are much easier to read and modify. Because the bulk of programming involves updating an existing program, Pascal is ideally suited for maximizing the efficiency of programmers by making programs easier to understand and update.

Like many programming languages, Pascal has evolved into many different dialects, but one of the most popular Pascal dialects is based on Borland Software's old Turbo Pascal language — *Borland Pascal.* At one time, the Borland Pascal dialect dominated programming the MS-DOS operating system. However with the introduction of Microsoft Windows, programmers shifted to the easier Visual Basic or the more powerful C/C++. As a result, Pascal has fallen out of favor in North America but maintains a surprisingly large following in Europe and South America.

To create Windows programs with Pascal, Borland Software (www.codegear.com) introduced *Delphi,* which was similar to Visual Basic except that it uses an object-oriented version of Pascal — *Object Pascal* — although it's more commonly referred to as the Delphi programming language. (You can get a free copy of Delphi by visiting www.turboexplorer.com.)

Because the financial health of Borland Software has gone up and down, a group of programmers have banded together to create the Free Pascal compiler (www.freepascal.org), which allows you to write Pascal programs for Windows, Linux, and Mac OS X. Best of all, Free Pascal closely follows the Borland Pascal language dialect, which makes it possible to take your old Turbo Pascal programs for MS-DOS (or your newer Delphi programs for Windows) and run them on Mac OS X and Linux with minor modifications.

Although it's unlikely that Pascal will ever regain its popularity as a major programming language, Pascal has inspired other programming languages, most notably the Ada programming language, which is used in critical, real-time systems, such as the Boeing 777 avionics system. As a result, Pascal remains an influential programming language to this day.

The Structure of a Pascal Program

The strength (or weakness, depending on your point of view) of Pascal is that it forces you to structure your programs. At the beginning of a Pascal program, you must declare any constants, types, or variables, such as

```
Program name;
Const
   (* Constants here *)
Type
   (* Type definitions here *)
Var
   (* Variable declarations here *)
Begin
   (* Commands here *);
End.
```

A typical Pascal program might look like this:

```
Program TaxRefund;
Const
   TaxRate = 0.35;
Type
   ClassLevel = (Upper, Middle, Lower);
Var
   MyClass : ClassLevel;
   TaxesOwed, Income : integer;
Begin
   Income := 60000;
   TaxesOwed := Income * TaxRate;
   If MyClass = Upper then
      Begin
        Writeln ('Bribe a corrupt politician.');
      End;
End.
```

Pascal ends every statement with a semicolon but uses a period at the end of the entire program.

Creating Comments

Pascal/Delphi allows you to enclose comments with curly brackets { } or a parentheses and an asterisk pair (* *), such as

```
Program name;
(* This is a short Pascal program. *)
Begin
  {The Writeln command is used to display text on the screen,
    much like the Print command in other languages.}
  Writeln ('This is a simple Pascal program.');
End.
```

Declaring Variables

In every Pascal/Delphi program, define a separate section for declaring your variables by using the Var keyword, such as

```
Program namehere;
Var
  Variablename1 : datatype;
  Variablename2 : datatype;
Begin
  (* Commands go here *)
End.
```

Unlike C/C++, Pascal isn't a case-sensitive language, so the variable names TaxRate, taxrate, and Taxrate are all considered the same variable.

Declaring string data types

Strings represent text, such as a single character ('A') or several words ('"This is a string of text'"). To declare a string variable, use the String keyword, such as

```
Var
  Variablename1 : String;
```

In Pascal, strings are enclosed in single quote marks (not double quote marks as in other languages). After you declare a variable to hold a string, you can assign a string to that variable, such as

```
Variablename1 := 'This string gets stored in the variable.';
```

If you only want to store a single character, you can use the Char keyword, such as

```
Var
  Variablename1 : Char;
```

To assign values to a variable in Pascal, use the colon and the equal sign symbols, such as `:=`, instead of just the equal sign (=) like other programming languages.

Declaring integer data types

Whole numbers represent integers such as 349, –152, or 41. A whole number can be positive or negative. The most common type of integer data type is Integer and is used as follows:

```
Var
  Variablename1 : Integer;
```

To accept different ranges of integer values, Pascal offers several integer data types. For example, if a variable needs only to hold a positive value, you can declare it as a Byte data type, such as

```
Var
  Variablename1 : Byte;
```

Besides limiting the range of integer values, different integer data types also require different amounts of memory to store that data. The greater the range of values you need to store, the more memory needed (measured in bytes). The smaller the range of values, the less memory required. Table 4-1 shows different integer data types, the memory needed, and the range of values they can hold.

Table 4-1	Pascal Integer Data Types	
Data Type	*Number of Bytes*	*Range*
Byte	1	0 to 255
ShortInt	1	–128 to 127
Word	2	0 to 65,535
SmallInt	2	–32,768 to 32,767
Integer	4	–2,147,483,648 to 2,147,483,647
LongWord	4	0 to 4,294,967,295
Int64	8	–9,223,372,036,854,775,808 to 9,223,372,036,854,775,807

Declaring decimal data types

Decimal values are numbers such as 1.88 or –91.4. Just as you can limit the range of integer values a variable can hold, so can you limit the range of decimal values a variable can hold. In Visual Basic, the four types of decimal data types are `Single`, `Double`, `Currency`, and `Extended`, as shown in Table 4-2.

Table 4-2	Pascal Decimal Data Types	
Data Type	*Number of Bytes*	*Range*
Single	4	1.5 E–45 to 3.4 E38
Double	8	5.0 E–324 to 1.7 E308
Currency	8	-922,337,203,685,477.5808 to 922,337,203,685,477.5807
Extended	10	3.4 E–4932 to 1.1 E4932

To declare a variable as a decimal data type, use the `Single`, `Double`, `Currency`, or `Extended` keyword, such as

```
Var
   Variablename1 : Single;
```

Declaring Boolean values

Besides storing text and numbers, variables can also hold a Boolean value — `True` or `False`. To declare a variable to hold a Boolean value, use the `Boolean` keyword as follows:

```
Var
   Variablename1 : Boolean;
```

Declaring Constants

Constants always represent a fixed value. In Pascal, you can declare a constant and its specific value as follows:

```
Const
   Constantname1 = value;
```

So if you wanted to assign 3.14 to a `pi` constant, you could do this:

```
Const
  pi = 3.14;
```

Using Operators

The three types of operators used are mathematical, relational, and logical. *Mathematical* operators calculate numeric results such as adding, multiplying, or dividing numbers. Table 4-3 lists the mathematical operators used in Pascal.

Table 4-3	Mathematical Operators	
Mathematical Operator	*Purpose*	*Example*
+	Addition	5 + 3.4
-	Subtraction	203.9 - 9.12
*	Multiplication	39 * 146.7
/	Division	45/ 8.41
Div	Integer division	35 div 9 = 3
Mod	Modula division (Returns the remainder)	35 mod 9 = 8

Relational operators compare two values and return a `True` or `False` value. The six relational operators available in Pascal are shown in Table 4-4.

Table 4-4	Relational Operators
Relational Operator	*Purpose*
=	Equal
<>	Not equal
<	Less than
<=	Less than or equal to
>	Greater than
>=	Greater than or equal to

Logical operators, as shown in Table 4-5, compare two Boolean values (`True` or `False`) and return a single `True` or `False` value.

Table 4-5	Logical Operators
Logical Operator	*Truth Table*
And	True And True = True True And False = False False And True = False False And False = False

(continued)

Table 4-5 *(continued)*

Logical Operator	Truth Table
Or	True Or True = True True Or False = True False Or True = True False Or False = False
Xor	True Xor True = False True Xor False = True False Xor True = True False Xor False = False
Not	Not True = False Not False = True

Branching Statements

The simplest branching statement is an IF-THEN statement that only runs one or more commands if a Boolean condition is True, such as

```
IF condition THEN
BEGIN
    Commands;
END;
```

To make the computer choose between two mutually exclusive sets of commands, you can use an IF-THEN-ELSE statement, such as

```
IF condition THEN
  BEGIN
    Commands;
  END
ELSE
  BEGIN
    Commands;
  END;
END;
```

If a Boolean condition is True, the IF-THEN-ELSE statement runs the first group of commands; but if the Boolean condition is False, the IF-THEN-ELSE statement runs the second group of commands. An IF-THEN-ELSE statement will always run one set of commands or the other.

One problem with the IF-THEN statement is that it only gives you two possible choices. To offer multiple choices, Pascal also uses the CASE statement, such as

```
CASE variable OF
  value1: BEGIN
            Commands;
          END;
  value2: BEGIN
            Commands;
          END;
END;
```

The preceding CASE statement is equivalent to the following IF-THEN-ELSE statement:

```
IF variable = value1 THEN
  BEGIN
    Command
  END;
ELSE
  IF variable = value2 THEN
    BEGIN
      Commands;
    END;
END;
```

To check if a variable matches multiple values, you can separate multiple values with commas or you can match a range of values, such as

```
CASE variable OF
  value1: BEGIN
            Commands;
          END;
  Value2..value4: BEGIN
                    Commands;
                  END;
END;
```

The preceding CASE statement is equivalent to the following IF-THEN-ELSEIF statement:

```
IF variable = value1 THEN
  BEGIN
    Commands;
  END
ELSE IF (variable >= value2) AND (variable <= value4) THEN
  BEGIN
    Commands;
  END;
```

Looping Statements

A *looping* statement repeats one or more commands for a fixed number of times or until a certain Boolean condition becomes True. To create a loop that repeats for a fixed number of times, use the FOR loop, which looks like this:

```
FOR variable := Start TO End DO
   BEGIN
      Commands;
   END;
```

If you wanted the FOR loop to run five times, you'd set the Start value to 1 and the End value to 5, such as

```
FOR variable := 1 TO 5 DO
   BEGIN
      Commands;
   END;
```

Normally the FOR loop counts up, but you can use the DOWNTO keyword to make the FOR loop count backwards, as shown in this example:

```
FOR variable = 30 DOWNTO 1 DO
   BEGIN
      Commands;
   END;
```

If you don't know how many times you need to repeat commands, use a WHILE or a REPEAT loop.

The WHILE loop repeats until a certain condition becomes False and looks like this:

```
WHILE condition DO
   BEGIN
      Commands;
   END;
```

The WHILE loop checks if a condition is True. If not, this loop won't even run at least once. If you want a loop that runs at least once, use the REPEAT-UNTIL loop, which looks like this:

```
REPEAT
   Commands;
UNTIL condition;
```

This loop runs at least once before checking a condition. If the condition is `True`, the loop stops.

The `REPEAT-UNTIL` loop doesn't need enclosing `BEGIN-END` keywords because the `REPEAT` and `UNTIL` keywords serve that function.

Creating Subprograms and Functions

You can create a *subprogram* (or a *procedure*) by using the `PROCEDURE` keyword as follows:

```
PROCEDURE Name (Parameter list)
Const
  (* Constants here *)
Type
  (* Type definitions here *)
Var
  (* Variable declarations here *)
Begin
  (* Commands here *);
End;
```

Every subprogram must have a unique name, which usually describes the purpose of that subprogram (such as `Calculate_Credit_Rating` or `DenyHealthBenefits`). The parameter list declares variables to hold any data the procedure may need from another part of the program. For example, a simple parameter list might look like this:

```
PROCEDURE Name (FirstName : string, Age : integer)
Begin
  (* Commands here *);
End;
```

In the preceding example, a copy of the parameter is passed to the procedure. If the procedure changes the value of that data, the new value of that data appears only in the procedure and not in any other part of the program.

If you want a procedure to change the value of a parameter, declare that variable in the parameter list with the `Var` keyword, such as

```
PROCEDURE Name (FirstName : string, Var Age : integer);
Begin
  (* Commands here *);
End;
```

A *function* is a special version of a subprogram that always returns a single value. To create a function, use the `FUNCTION` keyword, such as

```
FUNCTION FunctionName (Parameter list) : Datatype;
Const
  (* Constants here *)
Type
  (* Type definitions here *)
Var
  (* Variable declarations here *)
Begin
  (* Commands here *);
  FunctionName := value;
End;
```

The two main differences between a function and a procedure are that a function needs to define the function name as a specific data type and the last line in the function must store a value into the function name.

Data Structures

Pascal provides three data structures:

+ **Records** (known as structures in C/C++) – Stores multiple variables inside a single variable.

+ **Arrays** – Stores a list of items that consist of the same data type.

+ **Sets** – Stores an arbitrary list of items.

Creating a record

A *record* is a variable that typically holds two or more variables. To create a record, declare the record under the Type section and use the RECORD keyword as follows:

```
Type
  Recordname = RECORD
    Variables : datatype;
  END;
```

The name of a record can be any descriptive name, such as Customers or Students_1stGrade. Inside a record, you must declare one or more variables like this:

```
Type
  Suckers = RECORD
    Name : string;
    Address : string;
    Age : integer;
  END;
```

Creating an array

To create an array in Pascal, you must create a variable that represents an array under the Var section of a program like this:

```
Var
   Arrayname : ARRAY [LOWER..UPPER] OF datatype;
```

If you wanted to create an array to hold five strings, you could do this:

```
Var
   HitList : ARRAY [1..5] OF string;
```

If you don't want your array elements to be numbered from 1 to 5, you could pick any range of numbers, such as

```
Var
   HitList : ARRAY [25..29] OF string;
```

Defining different lower and upper ranges for the size of your array gives you the flexibility of using meaningful array index numbers (such as employee IDs), but at the risk of making the actual size of the array harder to understand. An array bounded by 1..5 easily identifies five elements in the array, but an identical array bounded by 25..29 also identifies five elements in an array but it's not as obvious.

You can also create a dynamic array that can change in size while your program runs. To create a dynamic array, define the array without specifying its size, such as

```
Var
   Arrayname : ARRAY OF datatype;
```

Before you can store data in a dynamic array, define its size with the SetLength command, such as

```
SetLength (Arrayname, Size);
```

So if you created a HitList dynamic array, you could define its size to hold ten items by using the following:

```
SetLength (HitList, 10);
```

When you define the size of a dynamic array, you define only the size of the array because the first element of the array is always 0. When you want to clear a dynamic array from memory, set the dynamic array's name to `NIL`, such as

```
HitList := NIL;
```

Creating a set

Pascal includes a unique data structure known as a *set*. A set lets you define a group of items, such as characters or a range of numbers:

```
Type
  Name1 = SET OF (Red, Green, Blue);
  Name2 = SET OF 1..10;
```

After you define a set, you can use the `In` operator to determine if a variable contains data that's within a set, such as

```
Program TestMe;
Var
  FixedSet = SET OF 1..10;
  X : integer;
Begin
  X := 5;
  If X in FixedSet then
    Writeln ('The number in X is in the FixedSet range');
End.
```

In the preceding example, the program checks if the number stored in the `X` variable lies within the set of numbers defined by the `FixedSet` variable. Because the `FixedSet` variable contains `1` through `10`, `5` does fall in the set, so the condition `X in FixedSet` is `True`.

Without sets, a program might resort to multiple `IF-THEN` or `CASE` statements to determine if a variable falls within a range of values. However, checking if a variable falls within a range of values is a simple one-line command in Pascal. This makes sets one of the more interesting data structures in Pascal, and they aren't commonly found in other programming languages.

Creating Objects

The object-oriented version of Pascal is often called Object Pascal or the Delphi language because Delphi uses object-oriented programming. To create an object, you must define a class under the `Type` section of a program like this:

```
Type
  Classname = CLASS
  PRIVATE
    Variablename : datatype;
    PROCEDURE name (paramater list);
    FUNCTION name (parameter list) : datatype;
  PUBLIC
    Variablename : datatype;
    PROCEDURE name (paramater list);
    FUNCTION name (parameter list) : datatype;
  END;
```

Any procedure or function declarations defined in a class must be fully defined outside the class.

Anything defined under the PRIVATE section represents methods and properties that only the object can use. Anything defined under the PUBLIC section represents methods and properties that other parts of the program can access within that object.

After you define a class, you can create an object from that class by declaring a variable as a new class type, such as

```
Var
  Objectname : Classname;
```

Object Pascal allows only single inheritance — a new class can inherit features from a single class. To create a new class from an existing class, use the CLASS keyword and include the name of the class to inherit from, such as

```
Type
  Classname = CLASS (classToInheritFrom)
  PRIVATE
    Variablename : datatype;
    PROCEDURE name (paramater list);
    FUNCTION name (parameter list) : datatype;
  PUBLIC
    Variablename : datatype;
    PROCEDURE name (paramater list);
    FUNCTION name (parameter list) : datatype;
  END;
```

Chapter 5: Visual Basic and REALbasic

In This Chapter

✔ Understanding the structure of a BASIC program

✔ Declaring variables

✔ Using mathematical operators

✔ Branching and looping statements

✔ Creating data structures and objects

Since its origins as a teaching language, the BASIC language has evolved dramatically, incorporating structured programming techniques (which was once the strength of languages like Pascal) and object-oriented features (which were once available only in languages like C++). Writing a program in BASIC is usually faster and easier than writing an equivalent program in another programming language, such as C++.

Despite its ease of understanding, BASIC has three drawbacks: speed, hardware access, and portability. BASIC programs typically run much slower than equivalent C++ programs, so if speed is critical, such as creating a real-time program that monitors airplane controls or a patient's heart condition, BASIC may not be the best choice.

BASIC deliberately limits access to the computer's hardware, such as memory, which makes BASIC unsuitable for writing hardware-dependent programs such as disk defragmenters, operating systems, or anti-virus programs.

Because BASIC language has evolved over the years, numerous dialects of BASIC have emerged, so programs written in one type of BASIC dialect often won't run on another computer that uses a different BASIC dialect. This problem is most prominent when programmers use Visual Basic (www.microsoft.com/express/vb), which runs only on Windows computers.

To avoid this problem, another popular version of BASIC, dubbed *REALbasic* (www.realbasic.com), offers cross-platform capabilities so you can write a single REALbasic program that runs on Windows, Linux, and Mac OS X with little or no modification. The REALbasic language is similar to Visual

Basic, which makes it possible to translate or port a Visual Basic program into REALbasic so you can create a Linux or Macintosh version of a Visual Basic program.

Both Visual Basic and REALbasic are the most prominent BASIC dialects that offer structured programming and object-oriented programming. Two simpler BASIC dialects that omit object-oriented features are Liberty BASIC (`www.libertybasic.com`) for Windows and Chipmunk BASIC (`www.nicholson.com/rhn/basic`) for the Macintosh. You can also visit the Run BASIC site (`www.runbasic.com`) to practice writing BASIC programs through any browser.

The Structure of a BASIC Program

In the original BASIC language, a program consisted of one or more commands listed one after another, such as

```
PRINT "This is a simple BASIC program"
END
```

For creating simple programs, BASIC lets you get started right away by focusing only on the commands you need. To create more complicated programs, you can create a single main program and one or more subprograms. The main program always runs first and determines when to run commands stored in different subprograms.

In both Visual Basic (VB) and REALbasic (RB), there's no main program. Instead, a typical VB/RB program consists of a single project file that lists the names of all files that make up that program. The three main types of files used in a project are

+ **Window files**
+ **Module files**
+ **Class files**

Using windows files

A *window* file contains a single window and various controls that appear on that window, such as buttons, pull-down menus, or sliders. Besides containing the user interface, a window file also contains subprograms that tell each control, on that user interface, how to respond to an event.

Such subprograms, or *event* subprograms, tell the computer how to respond when the user does something, such as click the mouse or move the mouse over a control. Unlike a traditional BASIC program where the main program determines when and how many times a subprogram runs, a VB/RB program consists of multiple subprograms that may run in the order determined solely by what the user does.

A Visual Basic or REALbasic program typically consists of at least one window file where you place controls, such as buttons, check boxes, or sliders, as shown in Figure 5-1.

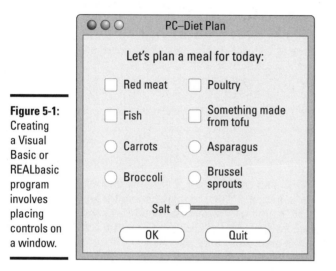

Figure 5-1:
Creating
a Visual
Basic or
REALbasic
program
involves
placing
controls on
a window.

Stored inside each window file are event subprograms that tell the computer how to respond when the user clicks or manipulates that control. To create an event subprogram, double-click a control. This creates a blank event subprogram that you can fill with commands that tell the computer what to do.

Using module files

A *module* file is optional but is often used to store commonly used subprograms. By storing subprograms in separate module files, you can create a library of subprograms that you can copy and plug in to another Visual Basic/REALbasic project. Typically, a VB/RB project consists of zero or more module files.

Using class files

A *class* file contains BASIC code to define one or more classes, which is used in object-oriented programming to create objects. A typical Visual Basic/REALbasic project consists of zero or more class files. Each time you create a new object, create a new class file. As a result, if you use object-oriented features, your project can consist of dozens of separate class files.

Creating Comments

Visual Basic lets you create comment lines with the apostrophe (') or REM keyword, such as

```
' The apostrophe defines a line comment
PRINT "This is a simple BASIC program"
REM The REM (Remark) keyword is another way
REM to create a comment
END    ' This is the end of the program
```

REALbasic uses both the apostrophe and the REM keyword along with the double slash characters (//), such as

```
PRINT "This is a simple BASIC program"
END    // This is the end of the program
```

Declaring Variables

In early versions of BASIC, you could create a variable any time you needed it. However as BASIC adopted structured programming techniques, more modern dialects of BASIC (such as Visual Basic and REALbasic) now force programmers to declare variables by defining the variable name and data type. A typical variable declaration looks like this:

```
Dim VariableName As DataType
```

VariableName can be any descriptive name, such as SalesTax, Players_on_Team, or MoneyEmbezzled. The data type defines the *type* of data the variable can hold and the *amount* of data the variable can hold. You can also declare multiple variables on a single line, such as

```
Dim VariableName1, VariableName2, VariableName3 As DataType
```

Declaring string data types

Strings represent text, such as a single character ("A") or several words ("This is a string of text"). To declare a string variable, use the String keyword, such as

```
Dim FirstName As String
```

In Visual Basic (but not in REALbasic), you can also declare a variable as a Char data type, which can only hold a single character, such as the letter "H." To declare a Char data type, use the Char keyword, such as

```
Dim Grade As Char
```

Declaring integer data types

Whole numbers represent integers, such as 39, −1092, or 4. A whole number can be positive or negative. The most common type of integer data type is `Integer` and is used as follows:

```
Dim TaxRefund As Integer
```

Because the range of integers is infinite, you can declare a variable to accept a range of integer values. For example, if a variable only needs to hold a positive value, you can declare it as a `Byte` data type in Visual Basic, such as

```
Dim Age As Byte
```

In Visual Basic, a `Byte` data type can hold a value from 0 to 255 whereas an `Integer` data type can hold a value as small as −2,147,483,648 or as large as 2,147,483,647.

Besides limiting the range of integer values, different integer data types also require different amounts of memory to store that data. The greater the range of values you need to store, the more memory needed (measured in bytes). The smaller the range of values, the less memory required. Table 5-1 and Table 5-2 show different integer data types, the memory needed, and the range of values they can hold for Visual Basic and REALbasic.

Table 5-1	Visual Basic Integer Data Types	
Data Type	*Number of Bytes*	*Range*
Byte	1	0 to 255
Short	2	−32,768 to 32,767
Integer	4	−2,147,483,648 to 2,147,483,647
Long	8	−9,223,372,036,854,775,808 to 9,223,372,036,854,775,807

Table 5-2	REALbasic Integer Data Types	
Data Type	*Number of Bytes*	*Range*
Int8 or Byte	1	−128 to 127
Int16	2	−32,768 to 32,767
Int32 or Integer	4	−2,147,483,648 to 2,147,483,647
Int64	8	−2^63 to 2^63−1
UInt8	1	0 to 255

(continued)

Table 5-2 (continued)

Data Type	Number of Bytes	Range
Uint16	2	0 to 65535
Uint32	4	0 to 4,294,967,295
Uint64	8	0 to 2^64–1

Declaring decimal data types

Decimal values represent numbers such as 1.28 or –90.4. Just as you can limit the range of integer values a variable can hold, so can you limit the range of decimal values a variable can hold. In Visual Basic, the three types of decimal data types are Single, Double, and Decimal (as shown in Table 5-3). In REALbasic, the only two decimal data types are Single and Double (as shown in Table 5-4).

Table 5-3	Visual Basic Decimal Data Types	
Data Type	Number of Bytes	Range
Single	4	–3.402823 E38 to –1.401298 E-45 (negative values) 1.401298 E–45 to 3.402823 E38 (positive values)
Double	8	–1.79769313486231 E308 to –4.94065645841247 E–324 (negative values) 4.94065645841247 E–324 to 1.79769313486232 E308 (positive values)
Decimal	12	+/–79,228,162,514,264,337,593, 543,950,335 (no decimal point) +/–7.9228162514264337593543950335 (up to 28 decimal places)

Table 5-4	REALbasic Decimal Data Types	
Data Type	Number of Bytes	Range
Single	4	1.175494 E–38 and 3.402823 E+38
Double	8	2.2250738585072013 E–308 and 1.7976931348623157 E+308

To declare a variable as a Decimal data type, use the Single, Double, or Decimal keyword, such as

```
Dim TaxRefund As Single
```

Declaring Boolean values

Besides storing text and numbers, variables can also hold a `True` or `False` value, known as *Boolean* values. To declare a variable to hold a Boolean value, use the `Boolean` keyword as follows:

```
Dim House_Is_Empty As Boolean
```

Declaring generic values

The main reason to declare a variable as a certain data type is to restrict the type of information the data can hold. For example, you don't want someone to store a negative number in a variable meant to store someone's age. However, you may need to create a variable that you want to store different types of values, such as strings, numbers, or Boolean values.

In Visual Basic, an `Object` data type can hold anything, such as

```
Dim Chameleon As Object
Chameleon = "This is a string"
Chameleon = 89.303
```

In REALbasic, a `Variant` data type can hold anything, such as

```
Dim Chameleon As Variant
Chameleon = "This is a string"
Chameleon = 89.303
```

Use `Object` or `Variant` data types sparingly. If you know a variable should contain only a certain range of data, declare it as a specific data type, such as `Integer` or `Single`. This not only reduces the amount of memory to store data, but also speeds up the program and reduces the chance that variables may store incorrect data.

Declaring Constants

Constants always represent a fixed value. In Visual Basic, you can declare a constant, its data type, and its actual value as follows:

```
Const ConstantName As DataType = Value
```

So if you wanted to assign `3.14` to a `pi` constant, you could do this:

```
Const Pi As Single = 3.14
```

In REALbasic, you can declare a constant without the data type declaration, such as

```
Const Pi = 3.14
```

Using Operators

The three types of operators used are mathematical, relational, and logical. *Mathematical* operators calculate numeric results such as adding, multiplying, or dividing numbers. Table 5-5 lists the mathematical operators used in Visual Basic and REALbasic.

Table 5-5	Mathematical Operators	
Mathematical Operator	*Purpose*	*Example*
+	Addition	5 + 3.4
-	Subtraction	203.9 - 9.12
*	Multiplication	39 * 146.7
/	Division	45 / 8.41
\	Integer division	35 \ 9 = 3
Mod	Modula division (returns the remainder)	35 mod 9 = 8
^	Exponentiation	2 ^ 4

Relational operators compare two values and return a `True` or `False` value. The six relational operators available in Visual Basic and REALbasic are shown in Table 5-6.

Table 5-6	Relational Operators
Relational Operator	*Purpose*
=	Equal
<>	Not equal
<	Less than
<=	Less than or equal to
>	Greater than
>=	Greater than or equal to

Logical operators compare two Boolean values (`True` or `False`) and return a single `True` or `False` value. Both Visual Basic and REALbasic use the same logical operators but Visual Basic includes two additional operators — `AndAlso` and `OrElse`, as shown in Table 5-7.

Table 5-7	Logical Operators
Logical Operator	*Truth Table*
And	True And True = True True And False = False False And True = False False And False = False
Or	True Or True = True True Or False = True False Or True = True False Or False = False
Xor	True Xor True = False True Xor False = True False Xor True = True False Xor False = False
Not	Not True = False Not False = True
AndAlso (only in Visual Basic)	True AndAlso True = True True AndAlso False = False False AndAlso (never evaluated) = False False AndAlso (never evaluated) = False
OrElse (only in Visual Basic)	True OrElse (never evaluated) = True True OrElse (never evaluated) = True False OrElse True = True False OrElse False = False

In Visual Basic, the `AndAlso` and `OrElse` operators act as faster versions of the traditional `And` and `Or` operators. The `And` operator must always compare two Boolean values, but if the `AndAlso` operator determines that the first Boolean value is `False`, it doesn't waste time evaluating the second Boolean value because one `False` Boolean value automatically makes the entire `AndAlso` operator evaluate to `False`.

The `OrElse` operator works the same way. If the `OrElse` operator identifies the first Boolean value as `True`, it doesn't waste time evaluating the second Boolean value because it will always evaluate to `True` anyway.

Branching Statements

The simplest branching statement is an `IF-THEN` statement that only runs one or more commands if a Boolean condition is `True`, such as

```
IF condition THEN
  Command
END IF
```

To make the computer choose between two mutually exclusive sets of commands, you can use an IF-THEN-ELSE statement, such as

```
IF condition THEN
   Command
ELSE
   Command
END IF
```

If a Boolean condition is True, the IF-THEN-ELSE statement runs the first group of commands, but if the Boolean condition is False, the IF-THEN-ELSE statement runs the second group of commands. An IF-THEN-ELSE statement will always run one set of commands or the other.

A variation of this is the IF-THEN-ELSEIF statement, which uses two or more Boolean conditions to choose which of two or more groups of commands to run, such as

```
IF condition1 THEN
   Command
ELSEIF condition2 THEN
   Command
END IF
```

Whereas the IF-THEN-ELSE statement can only give the computer a choice of two groups of commands to run, the IF-THEN-ELSEIF statement can offer the computer two or more groups of commands to run, such as

```
IF condition1 THEN
   Command
ELSEIF condition2 THEN
   Command
ELSEIF condition3 THEN
   Command
END IF
```

As an alternative to the IF-THEN-ELSEIF statement, you can also use the SELECT-CASE statement, such as

```
SELECT CASE variable
CASE value1
   Command
CASE value2
   Command
CASE value3
   Command
END SELECT
```

The preceding SELECT-CASE is equivalent to the following IF-THEN-ELSEIF statement:

```
IF variable = value1 THEN
   Command
ELSEIF variable = value2 THEN
   Command
ELSEIF variable = value3 THEN
   Command
END IF
```

To check if a variable matches multiple values, you can separate multiple values with commas or use the TO keyword to match a range of values, such as

```
SELECT CASE variable
CASE value1, value2, value3
   Command
CASE value4 TO value10
   Command
END SELECT
```

The preceding SELECT-CASE is equivalent to the following IF-THEN-ELSEIF statement:

```
IF variable = value1 OR variable = value2 OR variable =
   value3 THEN
   Command
ELSEIF variable >= value4 AND variable <= value10 THEN
   Command
END IF
```

Besides checking for exact values, the SELECT CASE statement can also compare values with the <, <=, >, or >= comparison operators, such as

```
SELECT CASE variable
CASE IS >= value1
   Command
CASE IS < value2
   Command
END SELECT
```

When the SELECT-CASE statement uses comparison operators, it uses the IS keyword.

The preceding SELECT-CASE statement is equivalent to

```
IF variable >= value1 THEN
   Command
ELSEIF variable < value2 THEN
   Command
END IF
```

Looping Statements

A *looping* statement repeats one or more commands for a fixed number of times or until a certain Boolean condition becomes True. To create a loop that repeats for a fixed number of times, use the FOR-NEXT loop, which looks like this:

```
FOR variable = Start TO End
   Command
NEXT
```

If you wanted the FOR-NEXT loop to run five times, you'd set the Start value to 1 and the End value to 5, such as

```
FOR variable = 1 TO 5
   Command
NEXT
```

Normally the FOR-NEXT loop counts by one, but you can use the STEP keyword to make the FOR-NEXT loop count by any value, such as by three, as shown in this example:

```
FOR variable = 1 TO 36 STEP 3
   Command
NEXT
```

Rather than count up, the FOR-NEXT loop can also count down. In Visual Basic, you can count down by using a negative number after the STEP keywords, such as

```
FOR variable = 100 TO 1 STEP -1
   Command
NEXT
```

In REALbasic, you can count down by replacing the TO keyword with the DOWNTO keyword, such as

```
FOR variable = 100 DOWNTO 1
   Command
NEXT
```

If you don't know how many times you need to repeat commands, use a DO loop. The two variations of a DO loop are DO-UNTIL and DO-WHILE (available only in Visual Basic).

The DO-UNTIL loop repeats until a certain condition becomes True. The DO-WHILE loop repeats while a certain condition remains True. The two variations of the DO-UNTIL loop look like this:

```
DO UNTIL condition
   Command
Loop
```

In this version, the DO-UNTIL loop checks if a condition is True. If so, this loop never runs. If not, this loop runs at least once. The second variation of the DO-UNTIL loop looks like this:

```
DO
   Command
Loop UNTIL condition
```

This loop runs at least once before checking a condition. If the condition is True, the loop stops. The DO-WHILE loops work nearly identically. If you want to make a loop that may run zero or more times, you'd use this DO-WHILE loop:

```
DO WHILE condition
   Command
Loop
```

If you want a DO-WHILE loop that runs at least once, you'd use this variation:

```
DO
   Command
Loop WHILE condition
```

Although REALbasic lacks the DO-WHILE loop, it does offer a WHILE-WEND loop, which looks like this:

```
WHILE condition
   Command
WEND
```

Creating Subprograms and Functions

You can create a subprogram (or a *procedure*) by using the SUB keyword as follows:

```
SUB Name (Parameter list)
   Command
END SUB
```

Every subprogram must have a unique name, which usually describes the purpose of that subprogram, such as `Calculate_Velocity` or `Check-Password`. The *parameter list* declares variables to hold any data the subprogram may need from another part of the program. For example, a simple parameter list might look like this:

```
SUB Name (BYVAL Age AS Integer)
   Command
END SUB
```

The `BYVAL` keyword stands for *By Value* and means that the subprogram receives a copy of data sent to it from another part of the program. If the subprogram changes the value of that data, the new value of that data only appears in the subprogram and not in any other part of the program. The `BYVAL` keyword is optional in REALbasic.

Instead of the `BYVAL` keyword, you could also use the `BYREF` keyword, which stands for *By Reference,* such as

```
SUB Name (BYREF Age AS Integer)
   Command
END SUB
```

When accepting data By Reference, a subprogram can change the value of that data, which can affect the rest of the program.

A *function* is a special version of a subprogram that always returns a single value. To create a function, use the `FUNCTION` keyword, such as

```
FUNCTION Name (Parameter list) AS Datatype
   Command
   RETURN value
END SUB
```

The two main differences between a function and a subprogram (procedure) are that a function needs to include the `RETURN` keyword and needs to be defined as a specific data type.

The `RETURN` keyword defines a variable that contains a specific value that the function calculates. This value gets returned back to another part of the program. Because a function represents a single value, you must define the data type of this value, such as an `Integer` or a `String`.

Data Structures

Visual Basic provides three data structures:

✦ **Structures** – Allows storing multiple variables inside a single variable.

✦ **Arrays** – Stores a list of items of the same data type such as all integers.

✦ **Collections** – Stores a list of items of different data types.

REALbasic offers two data structures:

✦ **Arrays** – Stores a list of items of the same data type such as all integers.

✦ **Dictionaries** – Stores a list of items along with a corresponding key value used to retrieve the data.

Creating a structure

A *structure* is a variable that typically holds two or more variables. To create a structure (in Visual Basic only), use the STRUCTURE keyword as follows:

```
STRUCTURE Name
   PUBLIC VariableName AS DataType
END STRUCTURE
```

The name of a structure can be any descriptive name, such as MyTeam or Accounting_Department. Inside a structure, you must declare one or more variables with the PUBLIC keyword. A typical structure might look like this:

```
STRUCTURE MyGirlfriends
   PUBLIC Name AS String
   PUBLIC Age AS Integer
   PUBLIC Phone AS String
END STRUCTURE
```

Creating an array

Arrays in Visual Basic and REALbasic are known as zero-based arrays, which mean that the first element of the array is located at index number 0, the second element of the array is located at index number 1, and so on.

To create an array, declare it with the DIM keyword, specify the number of elements, and define the type of data the array can hold, such as

```
DIM ArrayName (ArraySize) AS DataType
```

The array name can be any descriptive name. The array size defines how many items the array can hold. Because the array is zero-based, an array defined as a size 10 can actually hold 11 items. The data type defines the type of data the array can hold, such as all strings or all integers. To create an array that can hold 11 strings, you could define an array like this:

```
DIM PetNames (10) AS String
```

If you want an array to grow or shrink while your program runs, you can define a dynamic array. To define a dynamic array, omit the array size and then define the array size right before you start storing items into that array, such as

```
DIM ArrayName () AS DataType
REDIM ArrayName (ArraySize)
```

The REDIM keyword tells the program to resize the array.

Creating a collection and a dictionary

Arrays can be too restrictive because they can only hold one data type. For a more flexible alternative, use a *collection* instead. Two big advantages of a collection over an array are that a collection can hold different data types and can grow and shrink without having to define its size. To define a collection, define a collection name as follows:

```
DIM Name AS NEW COLLECTION
```

Unlike arrays where the first item is assigned an index number of 0, a collection assigns the first item an index number of 1.

A variation of a collection is a *dictionary* (available only in REALbasic). The two main advantages of a dictionary are that you can assign descriptive values, or *keys,* to each item stored in a dictionary. This makes it easier and faster to retrieve data.

To retrieve an item from a dictionary, specify the key. To retrieve an item from an array or a collection, you must either know the exact position of the item you want or you must search the entire array or collection to find the data you want. As a result, searching for items in a dictionary is much faster and easier than searching for items in arrays or collections.

Creating Objects

To create an object, you must create a separate class stored in a class file. A typical class in Visual Basic looks like this:

```
PUBLIC CLASS ClassName
  DIM PropertyVariable AS DataType

  PROPERTY PropertyName() AS DataType
    GET
      RETURN PropertyVariable
    END GET

    SET (BYVAL Value AS DataType)
      PropertyVariable = Value
    END SET

    SUB MethodName()
      Commands
    END SUB

END CLASS
```

In REALbasic, you don't even have to type any code. Instead, type the name of your class, properties, and methods and then REALbasic takes care of creating the code to define a class.

After you define a class, you can create an object from that class by declaring a variable as a new class type, such as

```
DIM ObjectName AS NEW ClassName
```

Both Visual Basic and REALbasic allow only single inheritance where a new class can inherit features from a single class. In Visual Basic, you can create a new class from an existing class by using the `Inherits` keyword, such as

```
PUBLIC CLASS ClassName
  INHERITS AnotherClassName
  ' Additional code goes here
END CLASS
```

In REALbasic, you can use a pop-up menu to define a class that you want to inherit from, so you don't need to type any code at all.

Book VII

Applications

The 5th Wave — By Rich Tennant

"Well, here's your problem. You only have half the ram you need."

Contents at a Glance

Chapter 1: Database Management

In This Chapter

✔ **Discovering the basics of databases**

✔ **Figuring out how to manipulate data**

✔ **Understanding database programming**

Database management is all about storing organized information and knowing how to retrieve it again. Although the idea of storing and retrieving data is simple in theory, managing databases can get complicated in a hurry. Not only can data be critical, such as bank records, but data retrieval may be time-sensitive as well. After all, retrieving a person's medical history in a hospital emergency room is useless if that information doesn't arrive fast enough to tell doctors that the patient has an allergic reaction to a specific antibiotic.

Because storing and retrieving information is so important, one of the most common and lucrative fields of computer programming is database management. Database management involves designing and programming ways to store and retrieve data. Because nearly every business from agriculture to banking to engineering requires storing and retrieving information, database management is used throughout the world.

The Basics of Databases

A database acts like a big bucket where you can dump in information. The two most important parts of any database is storing information and yanking it back out again. Ideally, storing information should be just as easy as retrieving it no matter how much data you may need to store or retrieve.

To store and retrieve data, computer scientists have created three types of database designs:

✦ **Free-form**

✦ **Flat-file**

✦ **Relational**

Free-form databases

Free-form databases are designed to make it easy to store and retrieve information. A free-form database acts like a scratch pad of paper where you can scribble any type of data, such as names and addresses, recipes, directions to your favorite restaurant, pictures, or a list of items that you want to do the next day. A free-form database gets its name because it gives you the freedom to store dissimilar information in one place, as shown in Figure 1-1.

Being able to store anything in a database can be convenient, but that convenience is like the freedom to throw anything you want in a closet, such as pants, books, written reports, and photographs. With such a wide variety of stuff dumped in one place, finding what you need can be much more difficult.

Database File

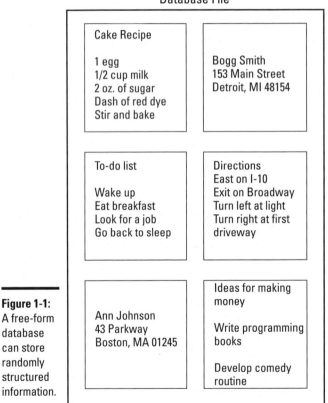

Figure 1-1:
A free-form database can store randomly structured information.

To retrieve data from a free-form database, you need to know at least part of the data you want to find. So if you stored a name and phone number in a free-form database, you could find it again by just typing part of the name you want to find (such as typing **Rob** to find the name *Robert*). If you stored a recipe in a free-form database, you could find it by typing one of the ingredients of that recipe, such as **milk**, **shrimp**, or **carrots**.

Free-form databases have two big disadvantages:

✦ **They're clumsy for retrieving information.** For example, suppose you stored the name *Robert Jones* and his phone number *555-9378*. The only way to retrieve this information is by typing part of this data, such as **Rob**, **555**, or **nes**. If you type **Bob**, the free-form database doesn't find *Robert*. So it's possible to store information in a free-form database and never be able to find it again, much like storing a cherished photo album in an attic and forgetting exactly where it might be.

✦ **They can't sort or filter information.** If you want to see the phone numbers of every person stored in a free-form database, you can't. If you want to see only information in the free-form database that you stored in the past week, you can't do that either.

Because free-form databases are so limited in retrieving information, they're best used for simple tasks, such as jotting down notes or ideas but not for storing massive amounts of critical information. To store data with the ability to sort, search, and filter data to view only specific types of information, you need a flat-file database.

Book VII
Chapter 1

Database
Management

Flat-file databases

The biggest difference between a free-form database and a flat-file database is that a flat-file database imposes *structure*. Whereas a free-form database lets you type random information in any order, flat-file databases force you to add information by first defining the structure of your data and then adding the data itself.

Before you can store data, you must design the structure of the database. This means defining what type of data to store and how much room to allocate for storing it. So you might decide to store someone's first name and last name and allocate up to 20 characters for each name.

Each chunk of data that you want to record, such as a first name, is a *field*. A group of fields is a *record*. If you want to store names and telephone numbers, each name and telephone number is a field, and each name and its accompanying telephone number make up a single record, as shown in Figure 1-2.

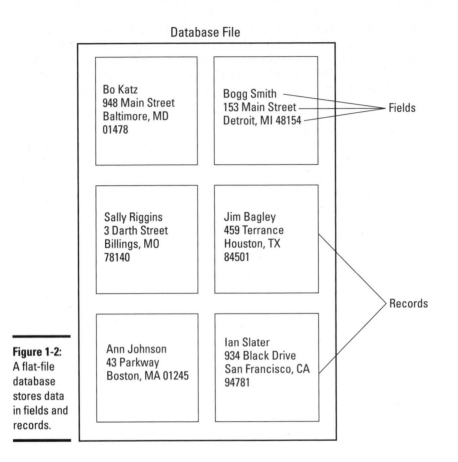

Database File

Bo Katz
948 Main Street
Baltimore, MD
01478

Bogg Smith
153 Main Street
Detroit, MI 48154 — Fields

Sally Riggins
3 Darth Street
Billings, MO
78140

Jim Bagley
459 Terrance
Houston, TX
84501

Records

Ann Johnson
43 Parkway
Boston, MA 01245

Ian Slater
934 Black Drive
San Francisco, CA
94781

Figure 1-2:
A flat-file
database
stores data
in fields and
records.

Flat-file databases impose a structure on the type of information you can store to make retrieving information much easier later. However, you need to design the structure of your database carefully. If you define the database to store only first and last names, you can't store any other information other than first and last names.

Designing the size and types of fields can be crucial in using the database later. If you create a Name field but allocate only ten characters to hold that data, the name *Bob Jones* fits but another name, such as *Daniel Jonathan Perkins,* cuts off.

Another problem is how you define your fields. You could store names in one big field or separate them into three separate fields for holding first, middle, and last names. Using a single field to store a name might initially look simpler, but separating names in different fields is actually more useful because this allows the database to sort by first, middle, or last name.

Although such a rigid structure might seem to make flat-file databases harder to use, it does make flat-file databases easier to search and sort information. Unlike free-form databases that may contain anything, every record in a flat-file database contains the exact same type of information, such as a name, address, and phone number. This makes it possible to search and sort data.

If you want to find the telephone number of *Robert Jones,* you could tell the flat-file database to show you all the records that contain a first name beginning with the letter R. If you want to sort your entire database alphabetically by last name, you can do that, too.

A flat-file database gets its name because it can work only with one file at a time. This makes a flat-file database easy to manage but also limits its usefulness. If you have a flat-file database containing names and addresses and a second flat-file database containing names and telephone numbers, you might have identical names stored in the two separate files. Change the name in one flat-file database and you need to change that same name in the second flat-file database.

Relational databases

For storing simple, structured information, such as names, addresses, and phone numbers (similar to a Rolodex file), flat-file databases are adequate. However, if you need to store large amounts of data, you're better off using a *relational database*, which is what the majority of database programs offer.

Like a flat-file database, you can't store anything in a relational database until you define the number and size of your fields to specify exactly what type of information (such as names, phone numbers, and e-mail addresses) that you want to save.

Unlike flat-file databases, relational databases can further organize data into groups, or *tables.* Whereas a free-form database stores everything in a file and a flat-file database stores everything in file, but organizes it into fields; a relational database stores everything in a file that's divided into tables, which are further divided into fields, as shown in Figure 1-3.

Think of database tables as miniature flat-file databases that can connect with each other.

Just as storing a name in separate First Name and Last Name fields gives you more flexibility in manipulating your data, grouping data in separate tables also give you more flexibility in manipulating and sharing information.

Database File

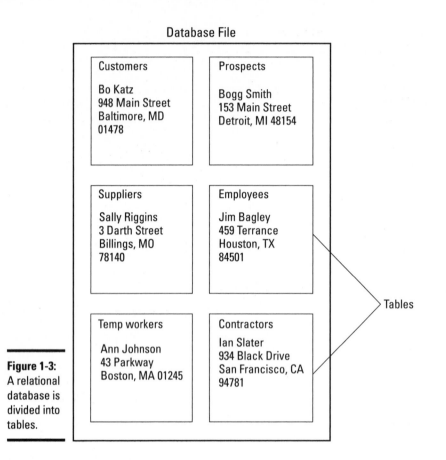

Figure 1-3:
A relational database is divided into tables.

Suppose you have a list of employees that includes names, addresses, and telephone numbers. Now you may want to organize employees according to the department where they work. With a flat-file database, you'd have to create a separate file and store duplicate names in these separate databases, as shown in Figure 1-4.

Every time you add a new employee, you'd have to update both the employee database and the specific department database that defines where he works. If an employee leaves, you'd have to delete his name from two separate databases as well. With identical information scattered between two or more databases, keeping information updated and accurate is difficult.

Relational databases solve this problem by dividing data into tables with a table grouping the minimum amount of data possible. So, one table might contain names and employee ID whereas a second table might contain only employee names and department names, as shown in Figure 1-5.

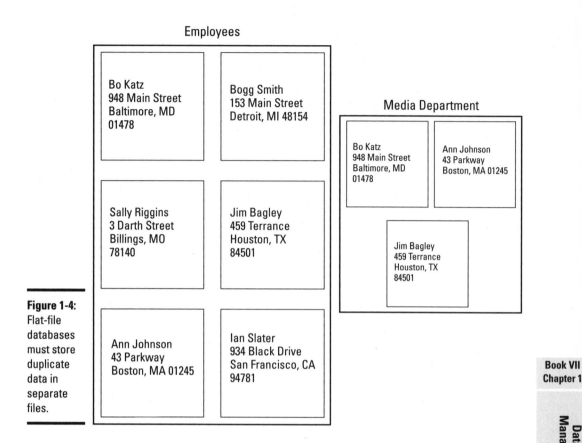

Employees

Bo Katz
948 Main Street
Baltimore, MD
01478

Bogg Smith
153 Main Street
Detroit, MI 48154

Media Department

Bo Katz
948 Main Street
Baltimore, MD
01478

Ann Johnson
43 Parkway
Boston, MA 01245

Sally Riggins
3 Darth Street
Billings, MO
78140

Jim Bagley
459 Terrance
Houston, TX
84501

Jim Bagley
459 Terrance
Houston, TX
84501

Ann Johnson
43 Parkway
Boston, MA 01245

Ian Slater
934 Black Drive
San Francisco, CA
94781

Figure 1-4:
Flat-file
databases
must store
duplicate
data in
separate
files.

Table

Name	Employee ID
Bill Adams	4Y78
Sally Tarkin	8U90
Johnny Brown	4T33
Doug Hall	4A24
Yolanda Lee	9Z49
Sam Collins	1Q55
Randy May	2E03
Al Neander	4M79
Kal Baker	2B27

Table

Name	Department
Bill Adams	Public relations
Sally Tarkin	Human resources
Johnny Brown	Engineering
Doug Hall	Engineering
Yolanda Lee	Human resources
Sam Collins	Engineering
Randy May	Public relations
Al Neander	Public relations
Kal Baker	Human resources

Figure 1-5:
Tables
separate
data into
pieces.

A column in a table represents a single field, often called an *attribute*. A row in a table represents a single record, often called a *tuple*.

What makes tables useful is that you can link them together. So whereas one table may appear to contain names and addresses while a second table might also contain names and departments, the two tables are actually sharing information. Instead of having to type a name twice in both tables, you need to type the name only once, and the link between separate tables automatically keeps that information updated and accurate in all other linked tables.

By linking or relating tables together, you can combine data in different ways. If you have a list of customers stored in one table and a list of sales in another table, you can relate these two tables to show which customers are buying which products, or which products are most popular in specific sales regions. Basically, relating tables together allows you to create *virtual* databases by sharing and combining data from separate database tables. By combining data from separate tables, you can uncover hidden information behind your data, as shown in Figure 1-6.

Table

Name	Employee ID
Bill Adams	4Y78
Sally Tarkin	8U90
Johnny Brown	4T33
Doug Hall	4A24
Yolanda Lee	9Z49
Sam Collins	1Q55
Randy May	2E03
Al Neander	4M79
Kal Baker	2B27

Table

Name	Department
Bill Adams	Public relations
Sally Tarkin	Human resources
Johnny Brown	Engineering
Doug Hall	Engineering
Yolanda Lee	Human resources
Sam Collins	Engineering
Randy May	Public relations
Al Neander	Public relations
Kal Baker	Human resources

Name	Employee ID	Department
Bill Adams	4Y78	Public relations
Sally Tarkin	8U90	Human resources
Johnny Brown	4T33	Engineering
Doug Hall	4A24	Engineering
Yolanda Lee	9Z49	Human resources
Sam Collins	1Q55	Engineering
Randy May	2E03	Public relations
Al Neander	4M79	Public relations
Kal Baker	2B27	Human resources

Figure 1-6:
Relational databases let you combine data from different tables.

Tables divide data into groups, but taken on a larger scale, it's possible to divide an entire database into multiple databases that are physically separate. Such databases are *distributed databases*.

A company might use a distributed database to keep track of all its employees. A branch office in Asia might have a database of employees in Singapore, another branch in Europe might have a database of employees in England, and a third branch in America might have a database of employees in California. Combining these separate databases would create a single database of all the company's employees.

Manipulating Data

After you define the structure of a database by organizing information in tables and fields, the next step is to write commands for modifying and manipulating that information. This can be as simple as adding data to a specific table or as complicated as retrieving data from three different tables, reorganizing this information alphabetically by last name, and displaying this list on the screen with mathematical calculations showing sales results for each person and a total amount for an entire department and company.

The three basic commands for manipulating data are *Select, Project,* and *Join.* The Select command retrieves a single row or tuple from a table. So if you want to retrieve someone's name to find her e-mail address, you could use the Select command, as shown in Figure 1-7.

Name	Employee ID	Department
Bill Adams	4Y78	Public relations
Sally Tarkin	8U90	Human resources
Johnny Brown	4T33	Engineering
Doug Hall	4A24	Engineering
Yolanda Lee	9Z49	Human resources
Sam Collins	1Q55	Engineering
Randy May	2E03	Public relations
Al Neander	4M79	Public relations
Kal Baker	2B27	Human resources

Select →

Name	Employee ID	Department
Sam Collins	1Q55	Engineering

Figure 1-7:
The Select command retrieves a single record or tuple.

Besides retrieving a single record or tuple, the Select command can retrieve multiple tuples, such as a list of all employees who work in a certain department.

The Project command retrieves the entire column or attribute from a database table. This can be useful when you just want to view certain information, such as the names of employees along with the department where they work, as shown in Figure 1-8.

The Project command acts like a filter, hiding data that you don't want to see and displaying only data that you do want to see. Combining the Select and Project commands can find just the names and e-mail addresses of all employees who work in a certain department.

Project

Name	Employee ID	Department
Bill Adams	4Y78	Public relations
Sally Tarkin	8U90	Human resources
Johnny Brown	4T33	Engineering
Doug Hall	4A24	Engineering
Yolanda Lee	9Z49	Human resources
Sam Collins	1Q55	Engineering
Randy May	2E03	Public relations
Al Neander	4M79	Public relations
Kal Baker	2B27	Human resources

Name	Department
Bill Adams	Public relations
Sally Tarkin	Human resources
Johnny Brown	Engineering
Doug Hall	Engineering
Yolanda Lee	Human resources
Sam Collins	Engineering
Randy May	Public relations
Al Neander	Public relations
Kal Baker	Human resources

Figure 1-8:
The Project command retrieves an entire column or attribute.

The Join command combines separate tables together to create a virtual table that can show new information. For example, a Join command might combine a table of products, and a table of customers with a table of sales people can show which sales person is best at selling certain products and which products are most popular with customers, as shown in Figure 1-9.

The Select, Project, and Join commands are generic terms. Every database uses its own terms for performing these exact same actions, so be aware of these terminology differences.

Table

Name	Employee ID
Bill Adams	4Y78
Sally Tarkin	8U90
Johnny Brown	4T33
Doug Hall	4A24
Yolanda Lee	9Z49
Sam Collins	1Q55
Randy May	2E03
Al Neander	4M79
Kal Baker	2B27

Table

Name	Department
Bill Adams	Public relations
Sally Tarkin	Human resources
Johnny Brown	Engineering
Doug Hall	Engineering
Yolanda Lee	Human resources
Sam Collins	Engineering
Randy May	Public relations
Al Neander	Public relations
Kal Baker	Human resources

Join

Name	Employee ID	Department
Bill Adams	4Y78	Public relations
Sally Tarkin	8U90	Human resources
Johnny Brown	4T33	Engineering
Doug Hall	4A24	Engineering
Yolanda Lee	9Z49	Human resources
Sam Collins	1Q55	Engineering
Randy May	2E03	Public relations
Al Neander	4M79	Public relations
Kal Baker	2B27	Human resources

Figure 1-9:
The Join command matches two tables together.

**Book VII
Chapter 1**

**Database
Management**

Writing database commands

Every relational database program includes commands for manipulating data. These commands essentially form a proprietary programming language specific to that database program. Microsoft Access uses a programming language called VBA (Visual Basic for Applications) whereas FileMaker uses a language called FileMaker Script. Most databases actually consist of separate files with one file containing the actual data and a second file containing programs for manipulating that data.

The main difference between a general purpose language, like C++, and a database language is that the database language needs only to define what data to use and how to manipulate it, but the database program (or the *database engine*) takes care of the actual details. Database languages only need to define what to do, not how to do it.

The SQL language

Although every relational database program comes with its own language, the most popular language for manipulating large amounts of data is SQL (Structured Query Language). SQL is used by many different database programs, such as those sold by Oracle, Microsoft, and Sybase. If you're going to work with databases as a programmer, you have to figure out SQL.

SQL commands, like all database programming languages, essentially hide the details of programming so you can focus on the task of manipulating data. To retrieve names from a database table named Employees, you could use this SQL command:

```
SELECT FirstName, LastName FROM Employees
```

To selectively search for certain names, you could use this variation:

```
SELECT FirstName, LastName FROM Employees
WHERE FirstName = 'Richard'
```

To add new information to a table, you could use this command:

```
INSERT INTO Employees
VALUES ('John', 'Smith', '555-1948')
```

To delete information from a table, you could use the delete command, such as:

```
DELETE FROM Employees
WHERE LastName = 'Johnson'
```

To modify a phone number, you could use this command:

```
UPDATE Employees
```

```
SET PhoneNumber = '555-1897'
WHERE LastName = 'Smith'
```

An ordinary user can type simple database commands to retrieve information from a database, but because most users don't want to type a series of commands, it's usually easier for someone else to write commonly used database commands and then store these commands as miniature programs. Then instead of forcing the user to type commands, the user can just choose an option and the database will run its program associated with that option, such as sorting or searching for information.

Data integrity

With small databases, only one person may use the database at a time. However with large databases, it's possible for multiple people to access the database at the same time. The biggest problem with multi-user databases is data integrity.

Data integrity is insuring that data is accurate and updated, which can cause a problem when multiple users are modifying the same data. An airline reservation system might let multiple travel agents book seats on the same airplane, but the database must make sure that two travel agents don't book the same seat at the same time.

To prevent two users from modifying the same data, most database programs protect data by letting only the first user modify the data and locking others out. While the first user is modifying the data, no one else can modify that same data.

Locking can prevent two users from changing data at the same time, but sometimes, changing data may require multiple steps. To change seats on an airline reservation system, you may need to give up one seat (such as seat 14F) and take another one (such as seat 23C). But in the process of giving up one seat, it's possible that another user could take the second seat (23C) before the first user can, which would leave the first user with no seats at all.

To prevent this problem, database programs can lock all data that a user plans to modify, such as preventing anyone from accessing seats 14F and 23C. Another solution to this problem is a *rollback*. If a second user takes seat 23C before the first user can get to it, the database program can rollback its changes and give the first user back the original seat 14F.

Multi-user databases have algorithms for dealing with such problems, but if you're creating a database from scratch, these are some of the many problems you need to solve, which explains why most people find it easier just to use an existing database program rather than write their own database program.

Book VII
Chapter 1

Database
Management

Data mining

Large chunks of data are *data warehouses. Data mining* simply looks at separate databases to find information that's not obvious in either database. For example, one database might contain tax information, such as names, addresses, and Social Security numbers. A second database might contain airline passenger information, such as names, addresses, and flight numbers. A third database might contain telephone calling records that contain names, addresses, and phone numbers called.

By themselves, these separate databases may seem to have no connection, but link the tax database with an airline passenger database and you can tell which passengers traveled to certain countries and reported an income less than $25,000. Just by combining these two databases, you can flag any suspicious travel arrangements. If someone reports income under $25,000, but has made ten different trips to Saudi Arabia, Venezuela, and the Philippines, that could be a signal that something isn't quite right.

Now toss in the telephone calling database and you can find everyone who reported less than $25,000 income, made ten or more overseas trips to other countries, and made long-distance phone calls to those same countries. Retrieving this type of information from multiple databases is what data mining is all about.

Data mining finds hidden information stored in seemingly innocuous databases. As a result, data mining can be used to track criminals (or anti-government activists) and identify people most likely to have a genetic disposition to certain diseases (which can be used for preventative treatment or to deny them health insurance). With so many different uses, data mining can be used for both helpful and harmful purposes.

Database Programming

At the simplest level, a database lets you store data and retrieve it again. For storing a list of people you need to contact regularly, a Rolodex-type database can be created and used with no programming. However, if you want to store large amounts of data and manipulate that information in different ways, you may need to write a program.

The three parts of a database program include the *user interface*, the *database management system* (which contains commands for manipulating data), and the actual *information* stored in a database, as shown in Figure 1-10.

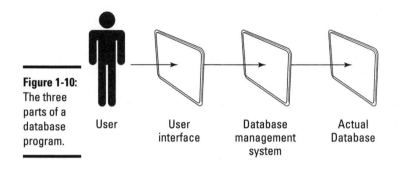

Figure 1-10:
The three
parts of a
database
program.

User   User   Database   Actual
        interface   management   Database
                    system

The user interface lets people use the data without having to know how the data is stored or how to write commands to manipulate the data. The database stores the actual information, such as dividing data into tables and fields. The commands for manipulating that data may include printing, searching, or sorting through that data, such as searching for the names of all customers who recently ordered over $10,000 worth of products in the past month.

Here are three ways to write a database program. The first way is to use an ordinary programming language, such as C++ or BASIC. The problem with using a programming language like C++ is that you have to create all three parts of a database from scratch. Although this gives you complete control over the design of the database, it also takes time.

As a simpler alternative, many programmers buy a database toolkit, written in their favorite programming language, such as C++. This toolkit takes care of storing and manipulating data, so all you need to do is design the database structure (tables and fields) and create the user interface.

A second way to write a database program is to start with an existing relational database program and use its built-in programming language to create a user interface and the commands for manipulating the data. The advantage of this approach is that you don't have to create an entire database management system from scratch, but the disadvantage is that you have to know the proprietary language of that particular database, such as Microsoft Access or FileMaker.

A third way to write a database program involves a combination of existing database programs and general-purpose programming languages, like C++:

1. **Use a database program to design the structure of the data and then you use the database's programming language to write commands for manipulating that data.**

2. Use your favorite programming language, such as C++ or BASIC, to create a user interface for that database.

This approach takes advantage of the database program's strengths (designing database structures and manipulating data) while avoiding its weakness in designing user interfaces. General-purpose languages, like C++ or BASIC, are much better for designing user interfaces, which can make your database program much easier to use.

If you have a lot of time on your hands, create an entire database from scratch with C++ or BASIC. However, if you don't want the hassle of creating an entire database management system yourself, buy a commercial database program and customize it using the database program's own programming language. This second approach is the most common solution for creating database programs.

If you find a database programming language too clumsy or too restrictive for designing user interfaces, write your own user interface in your favorite programming language and slap it on an existing database program. This may involve the hassle of integrating your user interface (written in C++) with the database file and data manipulating commands created by a database program (such as Microsoft Access).

Ultimately, database programming involves making data easy to access and retrieve no matter which method you choose. Because storing information is so crucial in any industry, database programming will always be in demand. If you figure out how to design and program databases, you'll always have plenty of work to choose from.

Chapter 2: Bioinformatics

*B*ioinformatics, or *computational biology,* combines computer science with molecular biology to solve biological problems on a molecular level. This basically means using computers to study proteins and genes to predict protein structures, drug interactions, and gene splicing.

Because bioinformatics embraces both computer science and molecular biology, there are two common paths to working in bioinformatics. The first involves studying computers and then learning about molecular biology so you'll know what your programs are supposed to do. The second involves studying molecular biology and then learning computer programming so you can write programs to aid in your research.

Each way depends on your main interest. Not all computer scientists want to know or study molecular biology and not all molecular biologists want to go through the hassle of learning computer programming. As a result, bioinformatics is a rare combination of diverse skills that will be in high demand in the near future. If the idea of using a computer to study cloning, genetic engineering, and cures for diseases appeals to you, bioinformatics may be the perfect outlet for your talent.

The terms bioinformatics and computation biology are often used interchangeably. Technically, bioinformatics focuses more on creating algorithms and writing programs whereas computational biology focuses more on using computers as tools for biological research.

The Basics of Bioinformatics

To understand bioinformatics, you must first understand its purpose. Before computers, biologists had two ways to study any problem. First, they could perform an experiment in a laboratory under controlled conditions, which is known as *in vitro,* or *in glass.*

A second way to study a problem is to perform an experiment on a living organism, such as a guinea pig or a human volunteer. Because this type of experiment occurred on a living creature, it's called *in vivo,* or *in life.*

Both in vitro and in vivo experiments are expensive and time-consuming. Performing in vitro experiments requires laboratory equipment whereas performing in vivo experiments requires live subjects.

Bioinformatics offers biologists a third way to conduct experiments — *in silico,* or *in silicon.* Instead of using an expensive laboratory, equipment, and living creatures, bioinformatics lets biologists conduct simulated experiments with a computer.

What makes in silico experiments just as valid as in vitro or in vivo experiments is that they all work with molecules. An in vitro experiment studies molecules in a test tube, an in vivo experiment studies molecules in a live animal, and in silico experiments study molecules as nothing more than data inside the computer. Specifically, in silico experiments (bioinformatics) represent molecules as strings that the computer manipulates.

By using knowledge of how different molecules interact, bioinformatics can simulate molecular interactions, such as how a certain drug might interact with cancer cells. This not only makes experimenting faster, but easier and less expensive to conduct as well. After a bioinformatics experiment confirms a certain result, biologists can go to the next step — testing actual drugs and living cells in test tubes *(in vitro)* or on living creatures *(in vivo).*

Representing molecules

Bioinformatics manipulates molecules. Of course, biologists don't care about every molecule in existence, just the ones involved in life, such as proteins. Four important molecules that biologists study are the ones that make up the structure of deoxyribonucleic acid, or *DNA.* These four molecules are identified by a single letter: *Adenine* (A), *cytosine* (C), *guanine* (G), and *thymine* (T).

When these molecules form a DNA strand, they link together in a sequence, such as:

```
ACTGTTG
```

In a computer, such sequences of molecules can be represented as a string, such as

```
$DNA = 'ACTGTTG';
```

Of course, these aren't the only four molecules that biologists study, but the idea is the same. Represent every molecule as a single letter and then re-create the molecular structure as nothing more than a string.

Unfortunately, most molecular structures consist of long strings of redundant one-letter codes. Trying to read these long molecular structures, let alone manipulate them by hand, is nearly impossible. That's where computers and bioinformatics come in.

Computers simplify and automate the tedious process of examining and manipulating molecular structures. Biologists simply have to type the molecular structure correctly and then tell the computer how to manipulate that structure as a series of strings.

Manipulating molecules in a computer

The type of programming language used to manipulate strings of molecules is irrelevant. What's more important is how to manipulate molecular structures. The simplest form of string manipulation is *concatenation,* which joins multiple strings into one.

In the world of biology, concatenation is similar to gene splicing — biologists can experiment with tearing a molecular structure apart and putting it back together again to see what they can create. In Perl, concatenation can be as simple as the following example:

```
$DNA1 = 'ACTGTTG';
$DNA2 = 'TGTACCT';
$DNA3 = "$DNA1$DNA2";
print $DNA3;
```

This simple Perl program would print:

```
ACTGTTGTGTACCT
```

Another way to manipulate strings (molecular structures) is by replacing individual molecules with other ones, which can simulate mutation. A mutation simulation program could pick a molecule at random and replace it with another molecule. So the initial structure might look like this:

```
CCCCCCCCCCC
```

Then each mutation could progressively scramble the structure by a single molecule, such as:

```
CCCCCCCCCCC
CCCCCCCTCCC
CCCCACCTCCC
CCCCACCTCCG
CACCACCTCCG
```

Mutation and concatenation are just two ways to manipulate molecular structures within a computer. If you created half a DNA sequence, you still need to determine the other half. Because DNA consists of two strands bound together in a double helix form, it's easy to determine the second sequence of DNA after you know the first one. That's because each adenine (A) links up with thymine (T) and each cytosine (C) links up with guanine (G).

The two strands of DNA are *complimentary sequences.* To calculate a complimentary sequence by knowing only one of the sequences, you can use a simple program that replaces every A with a T, every C with a G, every T with an A, and every G with a C. A Perl program to do this might look like this:

```
$DNA = 'ACTGTTG';
$compDNA = tr/ACGT/TGCA/;
```

The `tr` command simply tells Perl to translate or swap one character for another. So the above `tr/ACGT/TGCA/;` command tells Perl to translate every A into a T, every C into a G, every G into a C, and every A into a T all at once.

The second step in determining a complimentary sequence is to reverse the order of that sequence. That's because sequences are always written a specific way, starting with the end of the sequence known as 5' phosphoryl (also known as 5 prime or 5') and ending with 3' hydroxyl (known as 3 prime or 3'). So to display the complimentary sequence correctly, you have to reverse it using this Perl command:

```
$DNA = 'ACTGTTG';
$compDNA = tr/ACGT/TGCA/;
$revDNA = reverse $compDNA;
```

It's important to know both sequences that make up a DNA strand so you can use both DNA sequences to search for information. When faced with an unknown structure, there's a good chance someone else has already discovered this identical molecular structure. So all you have to do is match your molecular structure with a database of known structures to determine what you have.

Searching Databases

After biologists discover a specific molecular structure, they store information about that sequence in a database. That way other biologists can study that sequence so everyone benefits from this slowly growing body of knowledge.

Unfortunately, there isn't just one database, but several databases that specialize in storing different types of information:

✦ **GenBank** stores nucleotide sequences.

✦ **Swiss-Prot** stores protein sequences.

✦ **OMIM (Online Mendelian Inheritance in Man)** stores human genes and genetic disorders data.

After you find a particular sequence, you can look up articles about particular sequences in *PubMed,* a database of articles published in biomedical and life science journals.

Although it's possible to search these databases manually, it's usually much faster and easier to write a program that can send a list of sequences to a database, search that database for known sequences that match the ones sent, and then retrieve a list of those known sequences for further study.

Because searching databases is such a common task, biologists have created a variety of tools to standardize and simplify this procedure. One of the more popular tools is *Basic Local Alignment and Search Tool,* otherwise known as *BLAST.*

BLAST can look for exact matches or just sequences that are similar to yours within specified limits, such as a sequence that's no more than ten percent different. This process of matching up sequences is *sequence alignment* or just *alignment.*

By finding an exact match of your sequence in a database, you can identify what you have. By comparing your sequence with similar ones, you can better understand the possible characteristics of your sequence. For example, a cat is more similar to a dog than a rattlesnake, so a cat would likely behave more like a dog than a rattlesnake.

The BLAST algorithm and computer program was written by the U.S. National Center for Biotechnology Information (NCBI) at Pennsylvania State University (www.ncbi.nlm.nih.gov/BLAST).

The basic idea behind BLAST is to compare one sequence (called a *query sequence*) with a database to find exact matches of a certain number of characters, such as four. For example, suppose you had a sequence like this:

ATCACCACCTCCG

With BLAST, you could specify that you only want to find matches of four characters or more, such as:

ATCACCTGGTATC

Although you could type molecular sequences by hand, it's far easier to let the computer do it for you, especially if you want to compare a large number of sequences with BLAST. After BLAST gets through comparing your sequences, it returns a list of matching sequences.

Using BLAST to compare sequences to a database of known sequences is an example of data mining. (See Chapter 1 of this mini-book for more information about data mining.)

You could scan through this list of matching yourself, but once again, that's likely to be tedious, slow, and error-prone. Writing a program that can parse through reports generated by BLAST to look for certain characteristics is much simpler. Essentially, you can use the computer to automate sending data to BLAST and then have the computer filter through the results so you see only the sequences that you care about.

Now you could write another program to skim or parse through the database results to filter out only the results you're looking for. Because every database stores information in slightly different formats, you might need to write another program that converts file formats from one database into another one.

Because every biologist is using different information to look for different results, there's no single bioinformatics program standard in the same way that everyone has flocked to a single word processor standard, like Microsoft Word. As a result, bioinformatics involves writing a lot of little custom programs to work with an ever-growing library of standard programs that biologists need and use every day.

Some biologists can learn programming and do much of this work themselves, but it's far more common for biologists to give their data to an army of bioinformatics technicians who take care of the programming details. That way the biologists can focus on what they do best (studying biology) while the programmers can focus on what they do best (writing custom programs). The only way these two groups can communicate is if biologists understand how programming can help them and the programmers understand what type of data and results the biologists need.

Bioinformatics Programming

Because biologists use a wide variety of computers (UNIX, Windows, Linux, and Macintosh), they need a programming language that's portable across all platforms. In addition, biologists need to work with existing programs, such as online databases. Finally, because most biologists aren't trained as programmers, they need a simple language that gets the job done quickly.

Although a language like C/C++ runs on multiple platforms, porting a program from Windows to Linux often requires rewriting to optimize the program for each particular operating system. While figuring out C/C++ isn't necessarily hard, it's not easy either.

A more appropriate programming language is a *scripting language*. Scripting languages, such as Perl, run on almost every operating system, are easy to learn and use, and include built-in commands for manipulating strings. Best of all, scripting languages are specifically designed to work with existing programs by feeding data to another program and retrieving the results back again.

Although Perl has become the unofficial standard programming language for bioinformatics, biologists also rely on other programming languages because many people feel that Perl is too confusing. Perl's motto is "There's more than one way to do it" — you can perform the exact same action in Perl with entirely different commands.

For example, to concatenate two strings, Perl offers two different methods. The first is to smash two strings together, like this:

```
$DNA3 = "$DNA1$DNA2";
```

The second way to concatenate the same two strings uses the dot operator, like this:

```
$DNA3 = $DNA1 . $DNA2;
```

**Book VII
Chapter 2**

The second most popular language used in bioinformatics is Python. Python offers identical features as Perl but many people feel that Python is a simpler language to understand and use because its motto is, "There should be one — and preferably only one — obvious way to do it." To concatenate strings in Python, you can use this command:

```
$DNA3 = $DNA1 + $DNA2
```

Bioinformatics

Another popular bioinformatics programming language is Java. Not only are more programmers familiar with Java, but Java's cross-platform capability also allows it to create compiled programs for each operating system. In comparison, both Perl and Python are *interpreted languages* — you must load the source code of a Perl or Python program and run it through an interpreter first. Java gives you the convenience of copying and running a compiled program without the nuisance of running source code through an interpreter.

Despite the advantages of other programming languages, Perl is still the language of bioinformatics. If you're going to work in bioinformatics, first learn Perl and then learn Python or Java.

Biologists have written subprograms in various programming languages to make writing bioinformatics programs easier:

+ **Perl:** BioPerl (www.bioperl.org)

+ **Python:** BioPython (http://biopython.org/wiki/Main_Page)

+ **Java:** BioJava (http://biojava.org/wiki/Main_Page)

+ **C++:** BioC++ (http://biocpp.sourceforge.net)

For true hard-core computer users, there's even a *BioLinux* (http://envgen.nox.ac.uk/biolinux.html), which is a version of the Linux operating system that comes loaded with various bioinformatics tools installed and ready to use right away for bioinformatics work.

Because bioinformatics involves performing the same type of tasks, these libraries of bioinformatics subprograms offer code for

+ **Accessing databases**

+ **Transforming database information from one file format to another**

+ **Manipulating sequences**

+ **Searching and comparing sequences**

+ **Displaying results as graphs or 3-D structures**

The field of bioinformatics is still growing and changing — the tools and techniques used today may become obsolete tomorrow. (If you've spent any time in the computer industry, you probably already know that applies to every aspect of computers by now.)

In most other fields of computer science, programmers spend more time maintaining and updating existing programs than writing new ones. In bioinformatics, every biologist has different needs, so you could actually spend more time writing custom programs and less time getting stuck patching up someone else's program.

With its curious mix of computer science and biology, bioinformatics is a unique field that's wide open for anyone interested in life science and computer science. If the idea of working in the growing field of biotechnology appeals to you, bioinformatics might be for you.

Chapter 3: Computer Security

In This Chapter

✔ **Stopping malware and hackers**

✔ **Understanding secure computing**

Computer security is the equivalent of playing cops and robbers with a computer. On one side are the bad guys, trying to destroy, modify, or steal data. On the other side are the good guys, trying to protect that data.

In the early days of computers, the biggest threat to data was losing it through an accident. Then malicious computer hackers emerged. Unlike the original band of computer hackers, responsible for creating operating systems and language compilers, malicious hackers use their programming skills to break into computers and hurt others.

Initially these computer break-ins were more of a nuisance than a danger. Computer hackers might tie up resources, but they rarely wrecked anything except by sheer accident. In fact, many computer administrators grudgingly allowed hackers to stay on their computers as long as they didn't disturb anything, and many hackers returned the favor by warning computer system administrators of flaws in their programs that could allow less honorable hackers to sneak in and destroy files.

As more people picked up hacking skills, inevitably a small percentage of these hackers began using their skills for destructive purposes. At first, there was only the joy of crashing a computer or wrecking data for bragging rights to other hackers, but hackers soon had a new motive for breaking into computers. As more people began shopping online and more computers began storing credit card numbers and other personal information, such as Social Security numbers, hackers were now motivated by money.

Malicious hackers are bad enough, but what makes them an even greater threat is when they have the financial support and legal protection of corporations. Corporations have borrowed hacker tricks for financial purposes ranging from spying and stealing corporate secrets to flooding computers with unwanted advertising. The bad guys are no longer stereotypical computer nerds staying up late at night. Today's threats are well-financed organizations intent on breaking into computers for financial gain.

With so much money at stake, it's no surprise that one of the hottest fields of computer science is now *computer security.* Computer security is more than just locking doors and guarding computer rooms. Today, computer security is stopping threats, repairing damage, and hunting the criminals by using nothing more than programming skills.

Stopping Malware

One of the earliest and most prominent threats to computers is malicious software, often called *malware.* Malware is any program designed specifically to damage another computer, such as by erasing all its files. What makes malware particularly dangerous is that it's so common and capable of spreading without the intervention of the original programmer. The four common types of malware include

✦ **Viruses**

✦ **Worms**

✦ **Trojan horses**

✦ **Spyware**

Viruses

Computer *viruses* are nothing more than programs that attach themselves onto another file, such as a program or a word processor document. The virus spreads when you copy an infected file to another computer.

When a computer virus infects a file, it sometimes damages that file. What's worse is that most viruses also carry a *payload.* This payload can range from the harmless (such as displaying a humorous message on the screen) to the malicious (such as erasing every file stored on a hard disk). The most effective way to stop viruses is to capture one and dissect it to see how it works.

To dissect a virus (or any program), you need to use a *disassembler,* which essentially converts, or reverse engineers, a program into assembly language source code. By studying the assembly language code of a virus, you can understand how it works and, more importantly, how to identify the virus, essentially capturing that virus's digital fingerprint.

Capturing the digital fingerprint of a virus is crucial because that's how most antivirus programs work. Antivirus programs scan all the files on a hard disk for known signs of specific viruses. Because new variations of viruses appear every day, the database of an antivirus program must be updated constantly.

Worms

Similar to viruses are *worms*. Unlike a virus, a worm doesn't need to infect a file to propagate itself. Instead, a worm can duplicate and spread to other computers all by itself. In the early days of computers, when computers were isolated from one another, the only way files could spread from one computer to another was by physically copying a file to a floppy disk and inserting that floppy disk into another computer. That's why viruses were so popular in the early days of computers.

Nowadays, most computers are connected to the Internet, so there's no need to infect any files to spread. Instead, worms can spread on their own by looking for connections to another computer and then copying themselves over that connection, such as through a group of networked computers.

Here are two steps to protecting a computer against a worm. First, security professionals must capture a worm and dissect it like a virus to see how the worm works. After they capture a worm's digital fingerprint, they can store this information in an antivirus program's database so it knows how to recognize and remove that particular worm.

A second way to guard against worms is to block their access to other computers over a network. The way computers connect to one another is through virtual openings, or *ports*. Worms simply look for open ports on an infected computer so they can travel out and infect another computer.

The simplest way to block ports on a computer is to use a special program called a *firewall*. Firewalls can defeat worms in two ways. First, a firewall can block a computer's ports to keep a worm from infecting the computer in the first place. If the worm has already infected the computer, a firewall can also block its ports that could allow the worm to sneak out and infect another computer.

Although you could write your own firewall in your favorite programming language, it's much easier just to use an existing firewall program and configure it properly. Configuring a firewall means defining exactly what the firewall allows and what the firewall blocks.

On the simplest level, you can tell a firewall to allow certain programs to connect over the Internet; on a more complicated level, you can configure a firewall to allow only certain types of data to pass in and out. Allowing certain data to pass through a firewall, rather than just allowing certain programs, can defeat both Trojan horses and spyware.

Trojan horses

Trojan horses are programs that masquerade as something else to entice you to copy and run them. The moment you run them, the Trojan horse unleashes its payload, which can range from attacking your hard disk to installing another program, such as a virus, on your computer. The main reason to sneak a virus or worm on a computer through a Trojan horse is to get the virus or worm past the computer's defenses.

If a firewall allows a browser to access the Internet, that browser can be used to download a Trojan horse, which the firewall will allow. However, if you configure the firewall to allow only certain data (such as Web pages) but block any other data (such as a downloaded file that might contain a Trojan horse), the firewall can protect a computer from Trojan horses.

One common version of a Trojan horse is a *remote access Trojan,* or *RAT.* A RAT sneaks on to a computer and then allows a hacker to control that computer remotely over a network connection. RATs are often used to steal passwords, read e-mail, and even delete files.

The two main defenses against a Trojan horse are a *firewall* and an *antivirus* program. A firewall can block a Trojan horse from getting into a computer and also keep it from communicating with another computer. An antivirus program can search for digital fingerprints of a Trojan horse and remove it.

Spyware

Spyware are special programs that install themselves on a computer and connect to an outside computer over the Internet. Instead of allowing a hacker to remotely control an infected computer, spyware simply sends advertisements on to the infected computer.

Seeing advertisements pop up can be annoying, but the real problem is that most spyware programs display a constant barrage of advertisements that can keep you from actually using your computer. Even worse, a computer with multiple spyware programs can actually crash your computer.

The process of removing spyware is similar to removing other forms of malware. First, you have to get a copy of the spyware to dissect it and figure out how it works. Then, you have to write a program to detect and remove that spyware.

Like viruses that can infect multiple files, spyware often copies and hides itself in multiple locations on a hard disk. The moment you wipe out one copy of the spyware program, the other copies immediately re-infect the computer. Because spyware is motivated by advertising dollars with the support of corporations, spyware is often written by teams of professional programmers, which can make spyware particularly difficult to remove.

Stopping Hackers

Malware is a constant threat to computers that can strike at any time. Besides worrying about malware infection, computer security professionals have to also worry about the source of malware: The hackers who create malware in the first place.

Unlike malware, which can behave predictably, every hacker is different and can attack a computer network from inside or outside that network. As a result, stopping computer hackers involves both programming skills and detective work at the same time.

The basic defense against a hacker is a firewall. Hackers can sneak in only through an open port on a computer, so a firewall shuts the hacker out as effectively as locking the front door. Unfortunately, although firewalls can stop worms from sneaking in, firewalls aren't as effective against hackers. That's because a hacker can always find another way into a computer network that can circumvent any firewalls.

The simplest way to circumvent a firewall is to use a computer that's already located beyond the protective firewall. This is the way insiders can break into a computer network because as employees of a company, they're already authorized to use that computer network anyway. To detect intruders on a computer network, computer security professionals have to rely on special programs known as *intrusion detection systems* (IDS).

Intrusion detection systems

An intrusion detection system acts like a burglar alarm. The moment the program detects suspicious activity, such as someone on the network at 2 a.m., the IDS sounds the alarm to alert a human system administrator. At this point, the system administrator's job is to study the activity on the computer network to determine whether it's a valid or a false threat.

The problem is that seemingly false threats could actually turn out to be real. Seeing an authorized user on a computer network at 2 a.m. may look suspicious, but if that authorized user regularly accesses the computer at that time of night, a system administrator may simply ignore that alert. However, a hacker could have hijacked an authorized user's ID and password to masquerade as an authorized user.

At this point, a system administrator might study the authorized user's actions to determine whether anything looks out of place, such as deleting files or accessing files in other parts of the computer that the authorized user should have no business peeking at (such as an engineer poking around the accounting department's files).

To help identify potential hackers, many system administrators rely on a special program called a *honeypot,* which acts like a trap to snare hackers. A honeypot creates an entirely phony part of a computer network and loads it with tempting, but fake data, such as blueprints for a new weapon, a list of Social Security numbers, or usernames and passwords of nonexistent employees.

No authorized users would ever need to browse though the fake files of a honeypot because authorized users won't know the honeypot even exists. The moment anyone accesses the phony honeypot files, the IDS can positively identify that user as an intruder.

A honeypot isolates an intruder into a fictional part of the computer network where he (or she) can't cause any damage. However, after a hacker has accessed a computer network, system administrators have two problems. One, they have to find a way to keep the intruder out. Two, they need to make sure the intruder can never get back in.

Rootkit detectors

After breaking into a computer network, the hacker's first goal is to plant a rootkit. A *rootkit* provides tools for covering the hacker's tracks to avoid detection along with providing tools for punching holes in the computer network's defenses from the inside. By installing a rootkit on a computer network, hackers insure that if one way into the network gets discovered, they still have half a dozen other ways to get right back into that same network all over again.

Even if a honeypot isolates a hacker from sensitive areas of a network, the mere presence of a hacker means that some part of the network's defenses has been breached. To insure that hackers can't get back into a computer, system administrators need to rely on rootkit removal programs.

Rootkit removal programs simply automate the process a computer expert would follow to look for and remove a rootkit from a network. Unfortunately, hackers develop new rootkits all the time, and one rootkit might hide in a different way than another rootkit. Rather than create a single rootkit removal program, system administrators often have to create custom rootkit removal programs.

An IDS can find a hacker, and a rootkit removal program can detect and wipe out a rootkit from a network. For many companies, those two tasks alone are enough to keep an army of programmers busy. But if a company wants to take legal action against a hacker, they'll need to provide evidence of the hacker's activities, and that evidence falls under the category of forensics.

Forensics

If you've ever accidentally deleted a file and then recovered it again, you've practiced a simple form of forensics. Basically, *forensics* is about finding and restoring deleted data. When hackers break into a computer network, the network often keeps track of all activity on the computer in a special file, or a *log*. To cover their tracks, hackers often modify this log to erase all traces of the hacker's activities on the computer network.

Of course, anything deleted on a computer can always be recovered again, so computer forensics captures and restores this information. Such forensics computer evidence can pinpoint exactly what day and time a hacker entered a computer network, what the hacker did while on the network, and which computer the hacker used to access the network. This pile of evidence can pinpoint the hacker's physical location, which the police can use to find and arrest the hacker.

Computer forensics has another use in supporting criminal cases unrelated to computer hacking. Many Internet predators store e-mail and photographs of their contact with their victims, but if they suspect the police might be watching them, they'll erase this incriminating evidence off their hard disk. To recover this evidence, the police can turn to computer forensics to retrieve these missing e-mails and photographs.

Finally, computer forensics can come in handy if a hacker or malware wipes out an entire hard disk loaded with valuable files. Forensics can simply recover these files as if they were never wiped out at all.

The art of computer forensics involves low-level access to computer hardware, which means forensic practitioners are often skilled in assembly language and C programming. If the idea of combining detective work with mysteries and computer programming sounds appealing, computer forensics and computer security might be a field for you.

Secure Computing

Most computer security revolves around preventing intrusions and fixing any problems that occur because of the intrusion. Such a reactive approach is fine, but for a proactive approach that stops malware and hackers from attacking at all, programmers are learning a new field — *secure computing*.

The idea behind secure computing is to design computer programs with security in mind right from the start. This might seem logical until you realize that nearly all software has been developed without thinking of security at all. If anything, security has always been considered a distant afterthought.

That's one of the reasons why Microsoft Windows XP (and earlier incarnations of Windows) has proven so vulnerable to malware and hackers. Windows was designed under the assumption that only one person would use the computer and no programs (or people) would deliberately try to wreck the computer.

Then along came the first wave of computer viruses, followed by a second wave of computer worms, Trojan horses, and spyware that has cluttered and clogged most Windows computers as effectively as throwing sand and metal shavings inside a Formula One race car engine.

Now the assumption is that malware will try to take down computers and hackers will try to break into them. That's why secure computing tries to build security into a program as part of the design process. So not only must programmers learn the basics of object-oriented programming and algorithm analysis, but they must also learn the practices of secure computing as well.

Patching as an afterthought

Because so many programs were originally designed without security in mind, it's no surprise that much computer security work involves analyzing the security flaws of an existing program and then writing a patch that fixes those problems.

Every program has flaws, so every program needs patching. Armies of programmers love probing programs — especially the major ones, like Windows XP, Linux, Max OS X, and Vista — so they can be the first one to report a possible flaw in a program. Programmers devote their time to uncovering the flaws in other programs to enhance their own reputation (which can translate into better job opportunities), but also for the sheer challenge of looking for weaknesses in other people's programs.

After someone discovers a flaw in a program, other programmers typically verify that the flaw does exist, examine how the flaw could be exploited as a security risk, and then write a software patch that fixes that problem (and hopefully doesn't introduce any new problems).

Microsoft's service packs for Windows are typically one massive patch to fix numerous flaws found in Windows. Of course, people find flaws in Linux and Mac OS X regularly too, but Windows gets the most attention because it's been the dominant operating system for so many years.

Security in coding

Rather than wait for flaws to appear and then waste time patching these flaws that shouldn't have been in the program in the first place, another form of computer security involves making securing programs from the start. The idea is that if programmers focus on security when designing a program, they won't have to waste time patching up their programs later.

The first type of security involves examining the code of a program to remove any flaws. The most common type of flaw involves code that works but can be manipulated to cause an unexpected result. A common example of this type of problem is a *buffer overflow*.

A buffer overflow occurs when a program expects data that fits a certain size, such as accepting up to ten characters for a password. If you feed the computer data that's larger than expected, such as a 12-character password, the program should just ignore these extra 2 characters. However, a computer might accidentally store these extra two characters in its memory.

Normally such excess data would be harmless, but sometimes this excess data gets stored in a part of memory that contains other data that the computer uses, such as a list of tasks the computer will follow next. By flooding the computer with excess data, a hacker can literally change the computer's behavior.

One way to exploit this flaw is to shove excessive data to flood the computer's memory and then tack on an extra set of commands for the computer to follow. This tacked-on command then gets buried in the computer's memory, which causes the computer to follow those instructions. Oftentimes, those instructions tell the computer to weaken its defenses, such as opening a hole in the firewall to let the hacker into the computer.

To prevent problems, such as buffer overflows, programmers need to sift through their code and make sure that their code handles unexpected data correctly rather than just dumping it anywhere in memory. Examining code can be tedious, so programmers often use special testing tools that can spot such problems automatically.

Buffer overflow problems are especially common in programs written in C and C++. That's why more programmers are flocking to newer languages, like C# and Java, because these languages prevent buffer overflows, which can result in more secure and reliable software.

Security by design

Most security patches close common flaws in programs, but just removing these flaws is like locking a screen door to keep out intruders. A more proactive solution is to design security into a program from the beginning, which is like getting rid of a screen door and replacing it with a solid metal door instead.

The idea behind designing security into a program from the start is to antici-pate possible flaws and then design the program so those types of flaws can never even appear. This is like designing banks with only one entrance to limit the number of escape routes, and designing the lobby so anyone in the bank can be seen at all times.

Because operating systems are the most common target for an attack, many operating systems include a variety of defensive mechanisms. The most common defense is to divide access to a computer into separate accounts. This is like limiting bank tellers to just handling a certain amount of money while only the bank president and a few other trusted people have actual access to the bank's vaults.

Such access control limits what people can do from within their specific account on the computer. This reduces the chance of a catastrophic acci-dent wiping out data used by other people while also reducing the threat from hackers at the same time. If a hacker breaks into an ordinary user account, the hacker can't cause too much damage, which is like a burglar breaking into a garage but not being able to access the rest of the house.

Another common defense mechanism is *data execution protection* (DEP), which protects against buffer overflow attacks. Trying to wipe out all possi-ble buffer overflow exploits may be impossible, so DEP simply tells the com-puter never to run any commands found in its memory buffer. Now hackers can flood the computer with all the malicious commands they want, but the computer simply refuses to run any of those commands.

One way that hackers exploit programs is that they know programs behave predictably by storing data in the same areas. So another defense mecha-nism is *address space layout randomization* (ASLR). The idea behind ASLR is to keep changing the address of its memory. If hackers or malware can't reli-ably predict where a program is storing specific data, they can't insert their own commands or programs into the computer to trick the computer into running those commands instead.

Computer security is actually less about protecting the physical parts of a computer and more about protecting the data stored on those computers. As individual hackers have given way to organized criminals, untrustworthy gov-ernment agencies, and self-serving corporations, the field of computer secu-rity is constantly growing and changing. If there's one certainty in society, it's that crime will never go away, which means guaranteed opportunities for anyone interested in protecting computers from the prying eyes of others.

Chapter 4: Artificial Intelligence

In This Chapter

✔ **Solving problems**

✔ **Understanding machine learning**

✔ **Applications of artificial intelligence**

Computers have always been so quick at calculating mathematical problems that people inevitably looked at computers as nothing more than electronic brains. As computers grew in power, a lot of people naturally assumed it'd only be a matter of time before computers could become just as smart as human beings. To study how to make computers smart, computer scientists have created a special field — *artificial intelligence,* or *AI.*

One mathematician, Alan Turing, even proposed a test for measuring when a computer's calculating ability could be considered a form of intelligence. This test, known as the *Turing Test,* consisted of hiding a computer and a human being in a locked room. A second human being, acting as the interrogator, could type questions to both the computer and the human without knowing which was which. If the computer could consistently respond in a way that the human interrogator couldn't tell whether he was chatting with a computer or a human, the Turing Test claimed the computer could be considered intelligent. (No one suggested the Turing Test might really prove that the human interrogator could just be a moron.)

In 1990, Hugh Loebner, Ph.D., proposed a contest to determine the most human-like conversational programs. This contest, known as the Loebner Prize (`www.loebner.net/Prizef/loebner-prize.html`), is held annually, although at the time of this writing, no computer program has successfully passed the Turing Test.

The main goal of artificial intelligence (AI) is to give computers greater reasoning and calculating abilities because most interesting problems don't have a single, correct solution. Calculating mathematical formulas is an easy problem for computers because there's only one right answer. Calculating the best way to translate one foreign language into another language is a hard problem because there are multiple solutions that depend on the context, which is difficult to teach computers to understand.

Strong versus weak AI

The idea that computers can think has divided computer scientists into two camps — *strong* and *weak* AI. The strong AI camp claims that not only can computers eventually learn to think, but they can become conscious of their thinking as well. The weak AI camp claims that computers can never think in the same sense as humans because their thinking process is nothing more than clever algorithms written by a human programmer in the first place.

Strong AI proponents claim that the human brain is nothing more than a set of algorithms, known as *instinct,* that's already embedded in our brains, so putting algorithms in a computer is no different. Weak AI proponents claim that consciousness is something that only living creatures can have, so it's impossible for a computer to ever become aware of itself as a sentient being.

Neither side will likely persuade the other, but this endless debate does prove that just because someone has earned a Ph.D. in computer science from a prestigious university doesn't mean that he or she can't waste time arguing about a topic that no one can ever answer anyway, like politics, religion, or sports.

Basically, AI boils down to two topics — problem-solving and machine learning:

+ **Problem solving:** When faced with a situation with missing information, the computer can calculate an answer anyway.

+ **Machine learning:** The computer can gradually learn from its mistakes so it won't repeat them again (which is something even humans have a hard time mastering in their lifetime).

Problem Solving

Computers are great at solving simple problems that have a clearly defined path to a solution. That's why a computer can calculate the optimum trajectory for launching a rocket to the moon because this problem involves nothing more than solving a lot of math problems one at a time.

Although the idea of calculating the trajectory of a moon rocket may seem daunting, it's a problem that a human programmer can define how to solve ahead of time. Computers don't need to be smart to solve this type of problem. Computers just need to be fast at following directions.

Unfortunately, human programmers can't write algorithms for solving all types of problems, so in many cases, the computer is left with trying to solve a problem without any distinct instructions for what to do next. To teach computers how to solve these types of problems, computer scientists have to create algorithms that teach computers how to gather information and solve indistinct problems by themselves.

Game-playing

Because teaching a computer how to solve a variety of problems is hard, computer scientists decided to limit the scope of the problems a computer might face. By limiting the types of problems a computer might need to solve, computer scientists hoped to figure out the best ways to teach computers how to learn.

Solving any problem involves reaching for a goal, so the first test of artificial intelligence revolved around teaching computers how to play games. Some games, such as tic-tac-toe, have a small set of possible solutions that can be identified in advance. Because there's only a small number of possible solutions to the problem of playing tic-tac-toe, it's easy to write algorithms that specifically tell the computer what to do in any given situation.

The game of chess is an example of a hard problem because the possible number of valid moves is far greater than any human programmer can write into a program. Instead, human programmers have to give the computer guidelines for solving a problem. These guidelines are *heuristics*.

A heuristic is nothing more than a general set of rules to follow when faced with similar problems. Telling a child to look both ways before crossing the street is an example of a heuristic. Telling a child to look left and then look right before crossing the corner of 5th Street and Broadway is an example of a specific direction, which is absolutely useless for solving any problem except that one.

To teach a computer to play chess, programmers typically use a tree data structure (see Book III, Chapter 5) that the computer creates before making a move. The tree represents all possible moves, so the human programmer simply writes algorithms for telling the computer how to solve each problem by gathering information about that problem. Because games have distinct rules, teaching a computer to play a game also taught computer scientists the best way to teach a computer to solve any type of problem.

Of course, the problem with this theory is that teaching a computer to play chess created a great computer that can only play chess. Game-playing taught computer scientists only how to make computers play better games but not be able to solve problems outside a fixed set of rules.

Not surprisingly, the one area that has benefited from game-playing research has been using artificial intelligence techniques to create better computer opponents in video games. The next time you play your favorite video game and the computer seems particularly clever, you can thank all the research in AI for making smarter video games.

The ultimate goal of chess-playing computers is to beat a human chess grand-master. In 2005, a computer specially built for playing chess, dubbed Hydra, defeated grandmaster Michael Adams. In 2006, another dedicated chess-playing computer called Deep Fritz defeated Vladimir Kramnik. Computers have now proven they're capable of defeating chess grandmasters, so this goal of AI has finally been achieved, although the lessons learned by beating chess grandmasters aren't easily transferred to solving other types of problems.

Expert systems

If computers are good at figuring out how to solve problems within a limited domain, computer scientists reasoned that computers could also be useful for helping humans solve problems as well. The type of program designed to help humans solve problems is an *expert system*.

The idea behind an expert system is to capture the knowledge of a real human expert and store it in a program, essentially cloning the human expert's thought process. Instead of consulting a human expert for help, someone can just consult the expert system instead.

One of the first expert systems developed was Mycin, which was developed by Stanford University. The goal of Mycin is to help humans diagnose infectious blood diseases and recommend the proper type and dosage of antibiotics.

Like all expert systems, Mycin worked by asking questions to get information about the problem. By gathering more information about the problem, Mycin could keep narrowing its list of questions until it could identify a possible solu-tion. In tests, Mycin actually proved more accurate than Stanford's own med-ical staff in solving problems. However, Mycin was never used in actual practice for legal reasons. If Mycin makes a mistake, who's responsible — the expert system programmers or the doctor relying on the expert system's advice?

An expert system consists of three parts, as shown in Figure 4-1:

+ **A knowledge base** — stores the information about a particular subject.

+ **An inference engine** — manipulates the information stored in its knowledge base.

+ **A user interface** — lets users interact with the knowledge base and inference engine.

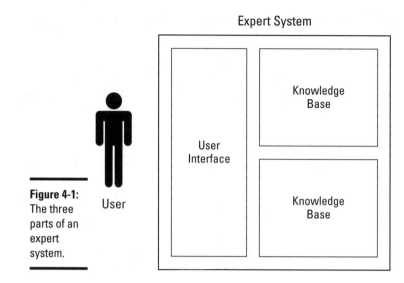

Expert System

Figure 4-1:
The three
parts of an
expert
system.

The *knowledge base* contains the expert's information for solving a specific
type of problem. Typically this knowledge is stored in the form of rules,
which resemble IF-THEN statements, such as:

```
IF white blood cell count < 3,000 THEN
   Antibiotic = penicillin
```

Rules define the thought process of a human expert in tackling a problem. The
inference engine is the part of the expert system that examines the rules in its
knowledge base and asks questions to the user through the user interface. In
the above example, the inference engine would examine the rule and ask the
user, "What is the white blood cell count of the patient?" Based on this answer,
the inference engine would follow the rule and could decide to use penicillin.

Expert systems typically solve problems by using one of two methods —
backward chaining or *forward chaining*. With backward chaining, the expert
system picks the most likely solution and tries to verify that this is indeed
the correct solution. As soon as the expert system determines that its solution isn't the correct one, it picks the next most-likely solution, tries to verify
this might be the correct answer, and so on.

Forward chaining means the expert system starts asking questions, and based
on the user's answers, the expert system tries to determine what might be the
best solution. Neither method is better than the other; they're just two ways
to solve the same type of problem.

Although expert systems have proven to work within a limited domain, such as troubleshooting an aircraft or diagnosing patients for diseases, they haven't proved popular in commercial applications.

One problem is the difficulty in extracting a human expert's knowledge and translating it into a set of rules. After you've translated an expert's knowledge into a set of IF-THEN rules, a second problem is debugging these rules with the help of the human expert to make sure the expert system works just like the human expert. A third problem is that expert systems are clumsy to use.

When someone wants help with a problem, he can tell a human expert what the problem may be and the human expert can start examining the problem directly. Computer expert systems don't have that luxury, so using an expert system is like playing a game of Twenty Questions with the expert systems constantly asking questions, like "What is the white blood cell count?" After the human user responds, the expert system bombards the user with another question to get more information. Using an expert system can be slow, clumsy, and frustrating, which is why they're rarely used despite so many years of research.

Besides the problem of storing a human expert's knowledge into a series of IF-THEN rules, a final problem is updating the expert system's knowledge, which requires interviewing the human expert all over again and then debugging the expert system once more to make sure the update information is accurate. Given these problems, expert systems are more often too much trouble to use than they're worth.

Natural language processing

In science fiction movies, artificially intelligent computers are always able to understand human language, which is known as *natural language processing* (NLP). The goal of NLP is to make computers even easier to use. By accepting spoken or written commands to the computer, NLP frees users from having to learn the arcane and cryptic syntax of ordinary computer commands.

The first problem with understanding any human language is to understand the meaning of each specific word. This problem is rather trivial because it involves nothing more than identifying a word and then looking up its meaning in a dictionary data structure that links the word to its definition.

If human language was logical, this would be all that NLP would have to do. Unfortunately, the meaning of words often depends on their context, which is difficult to program into a computer. For example, the phrases *fat chance* and *slim chance* actually mean the same thing although the adjectives *fat* and *slim* might seem like antonyms.

Humans can understand this difference by virtue of their exposure to different use of words and phrases, but computers need this information programmed into them. With so many words and alternate meanings, programming the context of every possible word is nearly impossible, so computer scientists have to rely more on rules for deducing the meaning of words rather than providing actual definitions for every word.

More confusing than understanding the context of words is understanding misspellings of words. When faced with a misspelled word, a computer must guess at its meaning, based on the meaning of surrounding words.

Perhaps the ultimate test for NLP involves translating from one language to another. Although you could simply translate a sentence, word for word, the syntax of languages may differ. To translate languages accurately, computers would need to know the meaning of words in two different languages along with the context and syntax of each language. Because computers have a hard enough time understanding one human language, trying to teach the computer to translate between languages is an extremely difficult problem.

One NLP translated English to Russian and back again. To test the translation capabilities, a programmer gave the program the English sentence, "The body is willing, but the flesh is weak." The program dutifully translated this English sentence into Russian. Then the programmer fed this Russian translation back to the program to convert it to its English equivalent, which wound up stating, "The vodka is good, but the meat is rotten."

One of the most successful NLP programs was written by Joseph Weizenbaum, Ph.D., and dubbed ELIZA after *Eliza Doolittle,* a working-class character who is taught to speak properly in George Bernard Shaw's play *Pygmalion.*

The ELIZA program mimicked a Rogerian therapist by asking questions and parroting back replies based on the user's answers. A typical conversation with ELIZA might look like this:

> ELIZA: How are you?
>
> PATIENT: I'm feeling sad.
>
> ELIZA: Why are you feeling sad?
>
> PATIENT: My sister is mad at me.
>
> ELIZA: Do you have problems with your family?
>
> PATIENT: They say I spend too much time with my computer.
>
> ELIZA: Do computers frighten you?

ELIZA doesn't actually understand the meaning of words. Instead, ELIZA just knows how to arrange words in their proper position to mimic an intelligent conversation. When ELIZA spots a word, such as *sister, brother,* or *father,* it immediately searches its database for a list of canned replies related to asking the user questions about his or her family.

By combining both canned phrases and parroted replies, ELIZA succeeded in mimicking an ordinary conversation. Although Joseph Weizenbaum originally created ELIZA to research natural language processing, he was astounded at how readily people accepted ELIZA and treated it as an intelligent computer even though they knew how it was programmed. When Weizenbaum found his secretary typing her problems into ELIZA and requested that he leave so she could have privacy, he became an advocate against artificial intelligence.

One common application of natural language processing can be seen in the help system of many programs. If you type **How do I print a document**, the help system for your word processor might display a list of topics for printing files. The computer didn't actually understand the sentence. Instead, the computer, like ELIZA, just scanned the sentence, looking for keywords that it could recognize and then responded based on the keywords that it found.

To poke fun at ELIZA, Kenneth Colby, a psychiatrist at Stanford University, wrote a similar program dubbed PARRY. Whereas ELIZA mimicked a therapist, PARRY mimicked a paranoid, schizophrenic patient. Computer scientists often connect ELIZA with PARRY to see what amusing conversation these two programs could create from each other.

Speech recognition

Similar to natural language processing is speech recognition. Like NLP, speech recognition must identify a word and deduce its meaning. But unlike NLP, speech recognition has the added burden of trying to do all this in real-time. The moment someone says a word, the speech recognition computer must quickly understand that word because the speaker won't likely pause for long before saying the next word.

The simplest form of speech recognition involves choosing from a limited selection of distinctly different sounding words. Many voicemail systems offer this feature by asking a question such as, "Do you want to leave a message?" At this point, the speech recognition computer listens for any sound that resembles either Yes or No. Because the speech recognition computer has such a limited selection to choose from, its accuracy rate can be almost perfect.

A second way to understand speech is to force users to train the computer first by saying a limited selection of words. The computer then stores these spoken sounds in a database so the next time the user talks, the speech recognition matches every spoken word with the closest match in its database.

Such speech recognition systems are extremely accurate, but suffer both from the hassle of forcing users to train the computer for long periods of time and from the fact that after training the computer, it can still understand only a limited vocabulary.

Even worse is that accuracy among speech recognition systems degrades dramatically with background noise or if the user's own voice changes from the time of training to the time of actually using the speech recognition system.

For example, someone with a cold sounds different than normal, which might cause the speech recognition system to be unable to identify his spoken commands. Noise in the background can often affect the speech recognition system's accuracy, which is why most speech recognition systems require the use of a microphone positioned directly in front of the user's mouth.

The ultimate goal of speech recognition systems is to recognize spoken language no matter who's speaking, what background noise there may be, or what he might actually be saying. In other words, speech recognition systems strive for understanding spoken language as easily as people do.

Image recognition

Another form of pattern recognition involves recognizing images, such as faces in a picture or handwritten letters on a piece of paper. Recognizing written characters is known as *optical character recognition* (OCR) and is commonly used in computer scanners.

OCR software studies an image of a character, and based on its knowledge of letters, the OCR program tries to match the written character with its database of known characters. After OCR finds a match, it can decipher the contents of a written phrase letter by letter.

OCR programs have trouble identifying near-identical characters, such as the lowercase letter *l* and the number *1,* or the letter *O* and the number zero, *0.* That's why OCR scanning programs often insert incorrect characters in the middle of scanned text.

Image recognition is a much harder problem, but one that's commonly used in security systems, such as in casinos. Every casino contains a photographic database of known cheaters. If a casino suspects one of these known cheaters has entered its premises, security guards can zoom in on the suspect and use image recognition software to determine whether that person is actually a known cheater in the database.

Such image recognition software examines the shape of a person's face along with the physical position of the nose in relation to the eyebrows, lips, and chin. No matter how many disguises cheaters may wear, they can't hide or change the physical dimensions of their faces, which is how such image recognition programs can spot them.

In the field of robotics, image processing is crucial because it gives robots the ability to sense their environment and avoid or move toward certain objects. Teaching a robot to avoid objects in its path might seem easy until the robot looks through a plate glass window and mistakes the window for an opening that it can roll through to get to the other side.

Although image recognition might help a robot identify the edges of walls or the end of a road, image recognition must also teach a computer to recognize shadows or reflections that can distort images. Primitive image recognition might simply distinguish between patches of light and dark, but more sophisticated image recognition could not only recognize an object in its path but also identify what that object might be, which involves a related category of artificial intelligence known as *image processing*.

In a limited domain of objects, seeing and understanding images can be determined in advance, but in the real world, the number of images a computer might see and need to recognize is nearly infinite. To solve the problem of not only recognizing an image but also understanding what that image might be, computers need to learn independent of their human programmers.

Machine Learning

The preceding examples of problem-solving artificial intelligence programs only mimic intelligence, but all a computer's intelligence is programmed by humans ahead of time. When faced with different situations, these problem-solving programs behave the same way no matter what the circumstances might be.

That's why the second, and more important, focus of artificial intelligence involves teaching computers to learn, otherwise known as *machine learning*. Machine learning can involve training by humans, but it's more commonly associated with self-learning in an unsupervised environment.

One way to mimic machine learning is to insert problem-solving knowledge into a program and then allow the program to modify its database of knowledge. That's the idea behind two popular programming languages — *LISP* and *Prolog* — which are specially designed for artificial intelligence.

With LISP, every command is also considered data that can be manipulated. So a LISP program can literally rewrite its own commands and data while it runs. Prolog works in a similar way. Basically a Prolog program consists of rules and data, so Prolog programs can modify both the rules that they follow and their data.

Both languages make self-modifying programs possible for mimicking machine learning, but using an artificial intelligence language alone doesn't make your program any smarter. Instead, programmers also need specific methods for mimicking intelligence in a computer.

Bayesian probability

One simple example of machine learning is based on *Bayes' theorem,* after Thomas Bayes. This theorem deals with probabilities. Put into practical application, many junk e-mail (spam) filters use Bayesian filtering, which basically examines junk e-mail and compares it to valid e-mail.

Based on this comparison, a spam filter based on Bayes' theorem can gradually assign probabilities that new messages are either junk or valid messages. The more junk and valid e-mail the Bayesian filter can examine, the "smarter" it gets in recognizing and sorting e-mail into their proper categories. Essentially an anti-spam filter's "intelligence" is stored in its growing database of characteristics that identify spam.

Neural networks

One problem with machine learning is organizing information so that the computer can modify its own data. Although languages — like LISP and Prolog — allow self-modifying programs, computer scientists have created a way to model the human brain using ordinary data structures, such as graphs with each node mimicking a neuron in a brain. This entire connection of interlocking nodes, or mimicking neurons, is a *neural network,* as shown in Figure 4-2.

Book VII
Chapter 4

Artificial
Intelligence

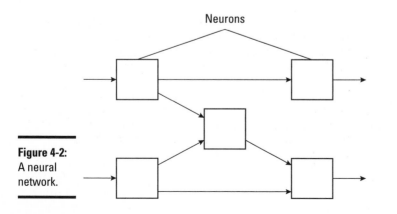

Figure 4-2:
A neural
network.

A neural network models itself on the human brain, which is divided into a network of interlocking neurons. Each neuron acts like a primitive computer that can receive input and produce output, which gets fed into another neuron as input.

Although a single neuron may not be capable of doing much, a network of interconnected neurons acts like a group of tiny computers that can tackle different parts of a problem simultaneously, which is known in computer science as *parallel processing*. Ordinary computers represent a single, fast machine that can tackle a problem in sequential steps. The strength of a computer is that it can perform these multiple steps much faster than a human can, which is what makes computers so powerful.

Human brains can't calculate as fast as a computer, but they can process multiple data simultaneously. That makes human brains better at solving seemingly simple problems, like recognizing a face from a crowd. On the other hand, computers have trouble recognizing faces because computers try to follow a sequential series of steps. As a result, computers are slow at recognizing faces while a human's ability to recognize faces is nearly instantaneous.

In a neural network, each neuron can accept data. The data is weighted by a specific value. This total value is then compared to the neuron's threshold. If this value is less than the threshold, the neuron produces an output of zero (0). If this value is greater than the threshold, the neuron produces an output of one (1), as shown in Figure 4-3.

Figure 4-3:
How a neuron processes and outputs a value.

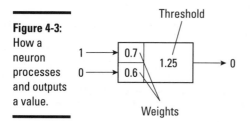

The neuron in Figure 4-3 receives an input of 1 and 0. The 1 value is weighted by 0.7 while the 0 value is weighted by 0.6, such as:

(1)*(0.7) + (0)*(0.6) = 0.7.

Because this value is less than the threshold value of 1.25, the neuron outputs a value of 0.

Robotics and artificial intelligence

Throughout the years, artificial intelligence (AI) has always aimed at a moving target. Initially, opponents boasted that computers could never beat a chess grandmaster, but when a computer finally did it, AI critics claimed that chess computers were nothing more than fast search algorithms that had little to do with actual reasoning. Although natural language programs, like ELIZA, can already claim to have passed the Turing Test, AI critics claim that parroting back phrases to trick a human still doesn't qualify as true intelligence.

Robotics may be the final test of AI because the stereotypical robot combines multiple aspects of AI: Speech recognition, image recognition, machine learning, and expert systems. AI critics will have a hard time dismissing an intelligent robot that can talk, understand spoken commands, and learn while it walks up and down a flight of stairs.

Before robotics can ever achieve this ultimate dream of creating a robot that mimics a human being, robotic engineers must literally first learn to crawl before they can walk. Like early AI research, most robots are designed to excel within an extremely narrow domain. Assembly-line robots know how to weld car frames together but can't answer a simple question. Military-drone robots may know how to recognize targets on the ground but can't understand spoken commands.

Despite these limitations, robotics has a growing future. Essentially, robots are nothing more than computers capable of moving or manipulating their environment. Maybe one day we'll finally have true artificial intelligence at the same time we finally have a true robot that meets the criteria set by science fiction authors so long ago. Until then, however, robotics is likely to remain a fledging offshoot of computer science and artificial intelligence. Don't expect a robot servant capable of understanding spoken commands and able to reason and learn any time soon, but don't be surprised when someone finally invents one either.

A single neuron accepts data and produces a response, much like an ordinary IF-THEN statement used in an expert system. To train a neural network, you can feed it specific data and examine the output of the neural network. Then you can adjust the weights of different neurons to more closely modify the output to a specific result.

Such training can be time-consuming, so another approach is to let the neural network train itself. Based on its output, a neural network can use its own output as input to change the overall neural network's result. Such self-training neural networks effectively mimic the learning process.

Applications in Artificial Intelligence

Initially, artificial intelligence had grand plans that bordered on science fiction. Computer scientists had visions of intelligent computers that could carry on spoken conversations while being fully conscious of their own thoughts. The reality proved much less dramatic. Instead of intelligent computers, we just have faster ones. Instead of thinking machines, we still have computers that are only faster than before, but no closer to consciousness than before.

Although artificial intelligence never lived up to its initial dreams, its applications have seeped into ordinary use. Spam filters are one simple way that machine learning has been put to use along with game-playing techniques for making smarter computer-generated opponents in video games.

Intrusion detection systems use a primitive form of an expert system to determine whether a computer hacker has penetrated a computer network, whereas many financial traders on Wall Street use neural networks to track the movement of stocks and commodities to figure out how to predict future stock prices. Perhaps the ultimate goal of artificial intelligence is to create thinking robots that can not only move on their own but also reason for themselves.

Whether computer scientists can ever create an actual thinking machine is beside the point. The real use for artificial intelligence isn't in re-creating human brains in electronic form, but in finding ways to make computers help us solve numerous tasks on their own. The more problems computers can solve without human supervision, the more time people can spend working on more difficult problems that computers can't solve — at least not yet.

Chapter 5: The Future of Computer Programming

In This Chapter

✔ Picking your programming language

✔ Picking your operating system

✔ Understanding cross-platform programming

✔ Exploring the programming language of the future

The computer industry is changing all the time, which means that the programming tools and techniques of today will likely become obsolete by tomorrow. Just trying to keep up with the computer industry is a full-time occupation, and even computer experts can never agree on what the future may bring.

Although it's impossible to predict the future, it is possible to identify trends in the computer industry, and based on these trends, predict what might occur in the future. In the world of computer programming, the most important lesson is to learn the logic of programming without getting bogged down by the specific syntax of any particular programming language. That's because programming languages rise and fall out of favor. If you learn to program in only one particular language, your programming ability will be restricted by the limitations of that particular language.

Programming is nothing more than problem solving, and problem solving is invaluable no matter which programming language, computer, or operating system may be popular at any given time. If you can solve problems, you'll always have a job.

Picking a Programming Language

Computer scientists eternally debate the merits of one programming language over another, but no matter which programming language may be popular today, the real issue boils down to efficiency and complexity.

Throughout history, the most popular language has always been the one that offers the greatest amount of efficiency for solving the most complicated problems. Initially, programmers used machine language to write entire programs because that was all they had available. However, as soon as assembly language appeared, few people wrote entirely in machine language. Instead, they switched to assembly language because it allows programmers to write more complicated programs.

In the early days of personal computers, nearly every programmer used assembly language. One of the first popular word processors, WordStar, even ran on two different processors — the Zilog Z-80 and the Intel 8088. To run on these two different processors, the company had to write WordStar in two completely different assembly languages.

When programs were fairly simple, that could be possible; but as programs grew in complexity, writing programs entirely in assembly language proved too cumbersome. That's when programmers switched to C.

Most operating systems today are written entirely in C for maximum efficiency; but as programs grow in complexity, C is quickly falling out of favor just as assembly language and machine language have done before. To maintain maximum efficiency to deal with growing complexity, most programmers have now switched to C++.

In the future, the complexity of programs will always make today's popular programming language too cumbersome to use tomorrow. So, it's likely that today's popular C++ language will one day become too clumsy to use for writing programs in the future. If you learn C++ today, plan on adapting and learning a newer programming language to write more complicated programs in the shortest amount of time.

The successor to C++ will have to make writing complicated programs easier than C++ while retaining maximum efficiency. This language of the future will depend heavily on the operating systems of the future.

Picking an Operating System

In the early days of computers, every computer had its own operating system, which made writing programs difficult. Not only did you have to learn a specific programming language, but you also had to learn how to write programs for a specific operating system.

To avoid this problem, computer companies standardized around a single operating system. The first standard operating system is CP/M-80, which later gave way to MS-DOS and finally to Microsoft Windows.

Initially, a single operating system made writing programs easier because you had to write programs for only one operating system instead of a handful of operating systems. By focusing on a single operating system, you could optimize your program for that one operating system. Knowing which operating system to support can define the success (or failure) of an entire software company.

Back in the early days of personal computers, two companies developed a program that everyone called a *killer application* (or *killer app* for short). Both of these programs were greatly improved spreadsheet programs used by businesses, but each company took a different approach. One company wrote its spreadsheet program entirely in assembly language and optimized it to run quickly on a single operating system (MS-DOS). The second company developed its spreadsheet to run on multiple operating systems, but to achieve this feat, the company wrote its program in the UCSD Pascal programming language, which runs slowly on all operating systems.

Although both programs offer similar features, there was no comparison from the user's point of view. The program written in assembly language and optimized for the MS-DOS operating system became *Lotus 1-2-3,* one of the most popular programs ever. The second program, *Context MBA,* ran so slowly on every operating system that nobody had the patience to use it. Context MBA went out of business, and Lotus 1-2-3 dominated the spreadsheet market — until the standard operating system changed from underneath it.

Lotus 1-2-3 had originally been written in assembly language, but as the program grew in complexity, major portions of the program had been rewritten in C. When personal computers switched from MS-DOS to Microsoft Windows, Lotus 1-2-3 wasn't ready. That's when Microsoft Excel, written in C, took over and has dominated the spreadsheet market ever since.

As Microsoft Excel grows in complexity, major portions of the program are now being rewritten in C++. Eventually, it's likely that maintaining Microsoft Excel in C++ will become too difficult, and a new spreadsheet program will emerge, written in an entirely different programming language.

That's because the days of a single operating system standard seem to be fading. Instead of Microsoft Windows being the dominant operating system, rivals — such as Linux and Mac OS X — have grown in popularity to challenge Microsoft Windows' popularity. Unlike the early days when you could write a program for the dominant operating system and capture 90 percent of the market, today if you write a program for a single operating system, you'll capture an ever-shrinking chunk of the market.

If you use a programming language that runs only on a single operating system, you're locking your programs into future obsolescence. With multiple operating systems becoming common, programs need to run on these major operating systems. If they don't, they risk losing market share to rivals that do run on multiple operating systems.

The growing trend these days is to support multiple operating systems, which requires a language that not only makes it easy to write more complicated programs, but also makes it easy to write and develop programs for multiple operating systems. To thrive, the language of the future needs to make writing complicated programs easier than C++, be as efficient as possible, and run on multiple operating systems at the same time.

Cross-Platform Programming

In the old days, writing programs to run on multiple operating systems was a waste of time because most people only used the same operating system. *WordPerfect,* a once popular word processor, wasted millions of dollars and several years devoting itsresources to creating a version of WordPerfect that ran on MS-DOS, Macintosh, Commodore Amiga, and Atari ST computers. Although WordPerfect focused on making its word processor run on multiple operating systems (known *as cross-platform capabilities*), Microsoft focused on making its Microsoft Word program run efficiently on a single operating system (Windows) and nearly wiped WordPerfect off the face of the Earth.

The problem wasn't that WordPerfect spent time writing a cross-platform version of its word processor. The problem was that it wasted time supporting operating systems that hardly anybody used. The number of people who used Atari ST and Commodore Amiga computers was miniscule compared to the number of people who used Macintosh computers, and the number of people who used Macintosh computers was just as tiny compared to the number of people who used MS-DOS and Microsoft Windows.

Cross-platform capabilities make sense only when supporting operating systems of near equal popularity. The most straightforward way to write a cross-platform program is to do what WordStar did — write identical programs with two completely different languages. That's possible for simple programs, but for more complicated programs, that approach takes too much time.

The portability of C

One reason why the C language has proven so popular is because of its portability. The C language is relatively simple, which makes it easy to create C compilers for different operating systems. That also makes compiling C programs to run on different operating systems with minimal changes easy.

Writing programs in C is how companies, like Microsoft and Adobe, can develop and sell programs that run on both Windows and the Macintosh, such as Microsoft Word and Photoshop. The bulk of their programs run identically on both operating systems, so all they need to do is write a small portion of their program to customize it to run on each particular operating system.

Unfortunately, as programs grow more complicated, writing programs in C is getting more difficult. Although most programmers have now switched to C++, eventually a time will come when even C++ will be too hard to use. Computer scientists may come out with a new and improved version of C++, but there's a better chance that a new language will take over instead.

Cross-platform languages

As operating systems grow more complicated, programmers are finding they're spending more time customizing their C/C++ programs for each specific operating system and less time actually updating their program. So another way to write cross-platform programs is to use a cross-platform compiler.

The idea behind a *cross-platform compiler* is that you can write a program in a specific programming language, and the compiler takes care of creating identically working programs for different operating systems, as shown in Figure 5-1.

Figure 5-1:
A cross-platform compiler can turn a single source code into programs for multiple operating systems.

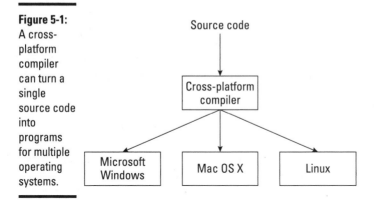

One popular cross-platform compiler is REALbasic, which is based on the BASIC programming language. Not only is BASIC much easier for writing programs, but by taking care of the details of specific operating systems, REALbasic makes it easy to create a program that can run on Windows, Macintosh, and Linux with little modification. Essentially, REALbasic gives you the benefit of C portability with the simpler language of BASIC.

One problem with cross-platform compilers is that they're never perfect. Ideally, you want to write a single program, compile it for multiple operating systems, and have all versions of your program run identically under each different operating system. In reality, every operating system has its quirks, so you often have to write specific code for each operating system. The amount of operating system specific code is much less than rewriting your entire program from scratch for a different operating system, but this process isn't trivial.

Create a program that can run on three different operating systems, and now you have to worry about maintaining and fixing problems with your program on three different operating systems. It's possible for your program to work perfectly under Linux, but crash under Windows and the Macintosh. The more operating systems your program supports, the greater the complexity in getting your program to work right under all these different operating systems.

Virtual machines

The main advantage of cross-platform compilers is that they compile programs directly into machine language for each specific operating system, which makes your programs run as fast as possible. With today's faster computers, speed is rarely as important as in the old days when slow programs could literally take hours to perform a single task.

Because speed isn't as crucial as in the past, computer scientists have created another way to create cross-platform programs known as *virtual machines*. Rather than compile a program for a specific processor, virtual machine programming languages compile programs to a generic format (called *bytecode, pseudocode,* or *p-code*) that can run on a virtual machine. This virtual machine, running on different operating systems, essentially tricks the program into thinking it's running on a single computer, as shown in Figure 5-2.

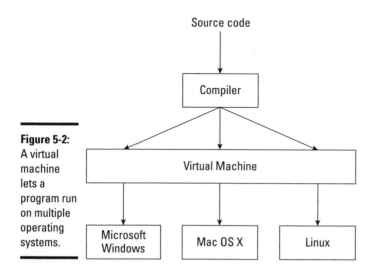

Figure 5-2:
A virtual machine lets a program run on multiple operating systems.

The biggest problem with virtual machine programming languages, such as Java, is their lack of speed. Because virtual machine languages aren't compiled, they run slower than true compiled programs.

Even worse, virtual machine languages can run only on operating systems that have virtual machines written for them. Sun Microsystems, the creator of the Java programming language, has created Java virtual machines for all the major operating systems, including Windows, Macintosh, and Linux. To maintain this ability to run on multiple operating systems, Sun Microsystems must constantly update each virtual machine for each operating system. This added complexity earned Java its initial reputation as a "write once, debug everywhere" language — you had to fix your program on multiple operating systems.

Despite this constant need to create and modify virtual machines for multiple operating systems, Java has proven capable of creating truly cross-platform programs. One company has even created a Microsoft Office clone, *ThinkFree* (www.thinkfree.com), which can run on Windows, Linux, and the Macintosh.

Software as service

As successful as ThinkFree and other virtual machine-based programs have been, the latest trend is toward selling software as a service. The idea is that instead of having a copy of a program stored on your computer, you use the Internet to access a program stored on another computer, or a *server*.

The main advantage of this software as service model is consistency. With programs written in C, cross-platform compilers (like REALbasic), or virtual machine languages (like Java), the end result is always a program stored on each person's computer. Therefore, one person could be using version 1.0 of a program, another could be using version 1.4, and a third could be using version 1.57, which makes supporting all these different versions difficult.

A second advantage of the software as service model is that it's based on Internet Web browsing standards, so if a computer can access the Internet, it can use any software as service program. This gives you a cross-platform program without the hassle of making sure your program runs on each particular operating system.

A third advantage of the software as service model is that it frees up space on your hard disk. Instead of cluttering your computer with dozens of separate programs, you only need to store your actual files on your computer because the software as service programs are stored on another computer.

Unfortunately, the software as service model has two drawbacks. If you aren't connected to the Internet, you can't use any software as service program. So if you use a word processor over the Internet but take your laptop computer on an airplane with no Internet connection, you can't use that word processor.

A second problem with the software as service model is that using it constantly costs money. Most software as service programs charge a monthly fee, which gives you the right to use the program for that month. Although this monthly fee is nominal (such as $5 a month), the cost can add up. Buying a simple word processor might cost you $50. Using a word processor as a software as service model might cost you $5 a month, so after ten months, you could've just bought a word processor instead.

For each succeeding month, the cost continues, so you'll wind up paying several hundred dollars just to use a single program. For large corporations, the software as service model can make sense. For individuals, the software as service model is too expensive.

To eliminate monthly fees, software as service companies are offering their programs for free but earning profits by selling advertising. Seeing advertisements may be a minor annoyance, but it makes software as service available to everyone, although there's still the problem of not being able to use a program without a constant and reliable Internet connection.

Rich Internet applications (RIA)

Rich Internet applications (*RIAs*) overcome the problems of the software as service model by creating a program that's stored on your computer but can update itself over the Internet. RIA programs combine the ideas of virtual machines with software as service.

Like a virtual machine language, RIA programs need a special virtual machine for each operating system. This gives RIA programs the ability to run on multiple operating systems. Because RIA programs are stored directly on your computer, you can use them any time without an Internet connection and you aren't locked into paying a monthly fee to access the software. Like the software as service model, RIAs can connect to the Internet and update themselves to insure that you're always using the latest version.

One popular RIA programming tool is *Adobe AIR,* which combines the languages of Web page designing (HTML and Flash) with scripting languages (JavaScript) to run on multiple operating systems through a virtual machine (like Java).

Another popular RIA programming tool is Microsoft Silverlight, which allows programmers to create RIA programs using any .NET language such as Microsoft's own C#, C++, or Visual Basic languages, or third-party .NET compatible languages including Delphi, IronPython, and IronLisp. Unlike Adobe AIR, which is designed to run on Windows, Mac OS X, and Linux, Microsoft Silverlight runs only on Windows and Mac OS X, and you can only run Silverlight applications on Mac OS X, but not use Mac OS X to develop RIA programs.

As more people gravitate toward other operating systems, RIA programming will likely become the hottest trend for programming. Essentially, RIA programs let you create programs by designing them like Web pages that can run independently of any browser on multiple operating systems.

Robotics programming

If programming a computer sounds like fun, programming a walking, flying, or rolling robot might be even more exciting. Programming a robot is essentially like programming a computer that can move and manipulate its environment.

Since programming a robot from scratch can be tedious, much of robotics programming revolves around developing and using special robotic programming frameworks. The framework provides basic commands for controlling the robot, such as making it move. Such a robotics framework isolates programmers from the tedium of how to make a robot work and just tells the robot what to do. A typical robotic program might look like this:

```
Move arm 34 degrees
Close gripper
Move arm 180 degrees
Open gripper
```

Just as high-level languages like BASIC or FORTRAN isolate you from manipulating the details of a computer, robotics programming frameworks can isolate you from manipulating the specific details of a robot's parts.

Microsoft offers its Robotics Studio development tool, which lets you control a simulated robot on your computer so you can test out your program in the absence of a real robot. After you get your robot program to work, then you can download the program into an actual robot and see your program in action.

Besides Microsoft Robotics Studio, other robotics programmers have used programming languages like Java, C++, and even Python to control a robot, so if you master a popular computer programming language, there's a good chance you'll be able to transfer your skills to program a robot as well.

Book VII Chapter 5

The Future of Computer Programming

For a playful introduction to robotics, buy a copy of Lego's Mindstorms NXT robotic kid, which lets you create a robot out of Legos and use the Lego visual programming language to make your robot move.

Robotics combines mechanical engineering with computer science and artificial intelligence. You can program a robot to learn, recognize spoken commands, navigate around obstacles, and make decisions on its own given incomplete information. While artificial intelligence often remains an academic exercise, robotics lets you put artificial intelligence in a moving robot so you can see how well your programs actually work. (A well-designed robot program might know enough to avoid trying to roll down a staircase. A poorly designed robot program might make the robot cheerfully roll off the top of a staircase and crash at the bottom steps below.)

Robotics is a growing field with no clear-cut robotics language standard yet to emerge. Who knows? With a little bit of creativity, you might be responsible for creating the next standard in robotics programming.

The Programming Language of the Future

Although there will always be dominant programming languages, there will never be a single perfect programming language because everyone's needs and preferences are different. Some people prefer C for its raw power and control, whereas others prefer BASIC and other high-level languages for making programming easier by hiding the technical details of manipulating the computer. If you're planning to learn programming, the only certainty is that the language you learn today will likely not be the language you'll be using tomorrow.

Low-level languages

The three most popular low-level languages are machine language, assembly language, and C. Machine and assembly language are best for creating small, fast programs. Machine language programs are often embedded in chips, such as the ones inside your computer that help your computer boot up. Assembly language is also used to create small, fast programs embedded in chips. The main difference is that assembly language is easier to write, so it allows programmers the ability to write more complicated programs than if they use machine language. The C language is used most often to create much larger programs, such as drivers for running printers, scanners, or Web cams.

Learn these three low-level languages if you need speed or absolute control over the computer. If these aren't your priority, you can safely ignore these languages, although knowing them will definitely help you better understand how a computer works.

The next generation: C++, Objective-C, C#, and Java

Most large programs are no longer written in C but in C++ for its object-oriented features. If you want to write programs professionally, learn C++ because that can get you a job practically anywhere.

Another object-oriented version of C++ is *Objective-C,* which also offers object-oriented features. The most popular use for Objective-C is for programming the Macintosh, so if you want to use the fastest, most powerful programming language to develop Macintosh programs, learn Objective-C. If you want to develop programs for other operating systems, such as Windows or Linux, learn C++.

The latest variant of the C language is C#, which has been embraced as the programming language for Windows. Because C# programs run only on Windows, you can't port your C# programs to run on other operating systems, such as the Macintosh, although there's currently limited support for running C# programs on Linux.

If portability is important, stick with C++. If you want to write programs only for Windows, learn C#. If you want to write programs for the Macintosh, learn Objective-C. All three languages are similar enough that you can switch among writing C++, C#, and Objective-C programs with few problems; but for now, learning C# locks you into a specific operating system, which ultimately will limit the market for your programs.

Java is fast becoming the new standard programming language. If you need true compilation on multiple operating systems, stick with C++. If you want the power of C with the ability to manage large software projects, like C++, learn Java. Because Java is so closely related to the C family of languages, learning Java can indirectly teach you the basics of C, C++, C#, and Objective-C.

REALbasic and Visual Basic

BASIC is one of the easiest programming languages to learn, so it's only natural that so many programmers continue using BASIC. Currently the two most popular versions of BASIC are REALbasic and Visual Basic.

At one time, Visual Basic was one of the most popular programming languages in the world. Then Microsoft introduced a new version that wasn't compatible with previous versions of Visual Basic. Therefore, older Visual Basic programs wouldn't run on newer versions of Visual Basic.

In addition, Microsoft added object-oriented features to Visual Basic that essentially turned Visual Basic into a simplified version of C#. As a result of these changes, Visual Basic users were faced with the choice of learning the new version of Visual Basic or switching to a different programming language altogether. In general, most Visual Basic programmers have switched to C#.

However, some Visual Basic programmers have switched to REALbasic, which not only can run older versions of Visual Basic programs but can also compile them to run on multiple operating systems, such as Windows, Macintosh, and Linux.

All this means that the latest version of Visual Basic has lost much of its appeal to programmers. Think of the current version of Visual Basic as an easier version of C#. If you don't want to learn C#, learn Visual Basic. If you already know older versions of Visual Basic, learn REALbasic.

The scripting languages

Traditional programming languages, like C and BASIC, are known as *systems languages* because they're used to create programs, like word processors and spreadsheets. As a programmer, learn at least one systems language, such as C++, but make sure you also learn a second language so the syntax of one particular programming language doesn't restrict your ability to think about programming in general. Some people learn a second systems programming language, like BASIC, but others prefer learning a scripting language instead.

Scripting languages, such as Perl, Tcl, JavaScript, and Python, are often used to connect, or *glue,* various components together, such as a Web page interface with a database. As a result, scripting languages are designed to solve problems that traditional languages aren't very good at. With more companies needing Web applications, there will be more opportunities for work.

More important, figuring out scripting languages to build Web pages also translates into creating rich Internet applications. The odds are greater that you'll need to use a scripting language more than you'll ever need to use C++, so learning any scripting language is crucial for your future as a programmer.

The best programming language

Finding the best programming language to learn is like finding the perfect car; everyone's needs are different. At the very least, learn one systems programming language (such as C++), one scripting language (such as JavaScript), and one database language (such as SQL). Because you'll likely have more opportunities for writing rich Internet applications than systems programs, like operating systems or word processors, rich Internet application programming is likely the wave of the future, so be sure you understand different Web page languages such as HTML and Flash.

As long as you arm yourself with programming knowledge of a variety of languages, such as C++, JavaScript, and SQL, you can get a job practically anywhere and your skills can be transferred easily to other languages that may become popular in the near future.

Just remember that the programming language you use is less important than your ability to solve problems and create useful programs. What you do with your programming skills will always transcend the specific knowledge of knowing a particular programming language. Ultimately, the most important part of programming is you.

Index

BUSINESS, CAREERS & PERSONAL FINANCE

Fundraising For Dummies
0-7645-9847-3

Investing For Dummies
0-7645-2431-3

Also available:
- Business Plans Kit For Dummies
  0-7645-9794-9
- Economics For Dummies
  0-7645-5726-2
- Grant Writing For Dummies
  0-7645-8416-2
- Home Buying For Dummies
  0-7645-5331-3
- Managing For Dummies
  0-7645-1771-6
- Marketing For Dummies
  0-7645-5600-2

- Personal Finance For Dummies
  0-7645-2590-5*
- Resumes For Dummies
  0-7645-5471-9
- Selling For Dummies
  0-7645-5363-1
- Six Sigma For Dummies
  0-7645-6798-5
- Small Business Kit For Dummies
  0-7645-5984-2
- Starting an eBay Business For Dummies
  0-7645-6924-4
- Your Dream Career For Dummies
  0-7645-9795-7

HOME & BUSINESS COMPUTER BASICS

Laptops For Dummies
0-470-05432-8

Windows Vista For Dummies
0-471-75421-8

Also available:
- Cleaning Windows Vista For Dummies
  0-471-78293-9
- Excel 2007 For Dummies
  0-470-03737-7
- Mac OS X Tiger For Dummies
  0-7645-7675-5
- MacBook For Dummies
  0-470-04859-X
- Macs For Dummies
  0-470-04849-2
- Office 2007 For Dummies
  0-470-00923-3

- Outlook 2007 For Dummies
  0-470-03830-6
- PCs For Dummies
  0-7645-8958-X
- Salesforce.com For Dummies
  0-470-04893-X
- Upgrading & Fixing Laptops For Dummies
  0-7645-8959-8
- Word 2007 For Dummies
  0-470-03658-3
- Quicken 2007 For Dummies
  0-470-04600-7

FOOD, HOME, GARDEN, HOBBIES, MUSIC & PETS

Chess For Dummies
0-7645-8404-9

Guitar For Dummies
0-7645-9904-6

Also available:
- Candy Making For Dummies
  0-7645-9734-5
- Card Games For Dummies
  0-7645-9910-0
- Crocheting For Dummies
  0-7645-4151-X
- Dog Training For Dummies
  0-7645-8418-9
- Healthy Carb Cookbook For Dummies
  0-7645-8476-6
- Home Maintenance For Dummies
  0-7645-5215-5

- Horses For Dummies
  0-7645-9797-3
- Jewelry Making & Beading For Dummies
  0-7645-2571-9
- Orchids For Dummies
  0-7645-6759-4
- Puppies For Dummies
  0-7645-5255-4
- Rock Guitar For Dummies
  0-7645-5356-9
- Sewing For Dummies
  0-7645-6847-7
- Singing For Dummies
  0-7645-2475-5

INTERNET & DIGITAL MEDIA

eBay For Dummies
0-470-04529-9

iPod & iTunes For Dummies
0-470-04894-8

Also available:
- Blogging For Dummies
  0-471-77084-1
- Digital Photography For Dummies
  0-7645-9802-3
- Digital Photography All-in-One Desk Reference For Dummies
  0-470-03743-1
- Digital SLR Cameras and Photography For Dummies
  0-7645-9803-1
- eBay Business All-in-One Desk Reference For Dummies
  0-7645-8438-3
- HDTV For Dummies
  0-470-09673-X

- Home Entertainment PCs For Dummies
  0-470-05523-5
- MySpace For Dummies
  0-470-09529-6
- Search Engine Optimization For Dummies
  0-471-97998-8
- Skype For Dummies
  0-470-04891-3
- The Internet For Dummies
  0-7645-8996-2
- Wiring Your Digital Home For Dummies
  0-471-91830-X

* Separate Canadian edition also available
† Separate U.K. edition also available

Available wherever books are sold. For more information or to order direct: U.S. customers visit www.dummies.com or call 1-877-762-2974.
U.K. customers visit www.wileyeurope.com or call 0800 243407. Canadian customers visit www.wiley.ca or call 1-800-567-4797.

SPORTS, FITNESS, PARENTING, RELIGION & SPIRITUA

0-471-76871-5   0-7645-7841-3

Also availa

📖 Catholicism For Dummies
0-7645-5391-7

📖 Exercise Balls For Dummies
0-7645-5623-1

📖 Fitness For Dummies
0-7645-7851-0

📖 Football For Dummies
0-7645-3936-1

📖 Judaism For Dummies
0-7645-5299-6

📖 Potty Training For Dummies
0-7645-5417-4

📖 Buddhism For Dummies
0-7645-5359-3

📖 Ten Minute Tone-Ups For Dummies
0-7645-7207-5

📖 NASCAR For Dummies
0-7645-7681-X

📖 Religion For Dummies
0-7645-5264-3

📖 Soccer For Dummies
0-7645-5229-5

📖 Women in the Bible For Dummies
0-7645-8475-8

TRAVEL

0-7645-7749-2   0-7645-6945-7

Also available:

📖 Alaska For Dummies
0-7645-7746-8

📖 Cruise Vacations For Dummies
0-7645-6941-4

📖 England For Dummies
0-7645-4276-1

📖 Europe For Dummies
0-7645-7529-5

📖 Germany For Dummies
0-7645-7823-5

📖 Hawaii For Dummies
0-7645-7402-7

📖 Italy For Dummies
0-7645-7386-1

📖 Las Vegas For Dummies
0-7645-7382-9

📖 London For Dummies
0-7645-4277-X

📖 Paris For Dummies
0-7645-7630-5

📖 RV Vacations For Dummies
0-7645-4442-X

📖 Walt Disney World & Orlando
For Dummies
0-7645-9660-8

GRAPHICS, DESIGN & WEB DEVELOPMENT

0-7645-8815-X   0-7645-9571-7

Also available:

📖 3D Game Animation For Dummies
0-7645-8789-7

📖 AutoCAD 2006 For Dummies
0-7645-8925-3

📖 Building a Web Site For Dummies
0-7645-7144-3

📖 Creating Web Pages For Dummies
0-470-08030-2

📖 Creating Web Pages All-in-One Desk
Reference For Dummies
0-7645-4345-8

📖 Dreamweaver 8 For Dummies
0-7645-9649-7

📖 InDesign CS2 For Dummies
0-7645-9572-5

📖 Macromedia Flash 8 For Dummies
0-7645-9691-8

📖 Photoshop CS2 and Digital
Photography For Dummies
0-7645-9580-6

📖 Photoshop Elements 4 For Dummies
0-471-77483-9

📖 Syndicating Web Sites with RSS Feeds
For Dummies
0-7645-8848-6

📖 Yahoo! SiteBuilder For Dummies
0-7645-9800-7

NETWORKING, SECURITY, PROGRAMMING & DATABASES

0-7645-7728-X   0-471-74940-0

Also available:

📖 Access 2007 For Dummies
0-470-04612-0

📖 ASP.NET 2 For Dummies
0-7645-7907-X

📖 C# 2005 For Dummies
0-7645-9704-3

📖 Hacking For Dummies
0-470-05235-X

📖 Hacking Wireless Networks
For Dummies
0-7645-9730-2

📖 Java For Dummies
0-470-08716-1

📖 Microsoft SQL Server 2005 For Dummies
0-7645-7755-7

📖 Networking All-in-One Desk Reference
For Dummies
0-7645-9939-9

📖 Preventing Identity Theft For Dummies
0-7645-7336-5

📖 Telecom For Dummies
0-471-77085-X

📖 Visual Studio 2005 All-in-One Desk
Reference For Dummies
0-7645-9775-2

📖 XML For Dummies
0-7645-8845-1